EUROPEAN HUMAN RIGHTS LAW

EUROPEAN HUMAN RIGHTS LAW

TEXT AND MATERIALS

Second Edition

MARK W. JANIS

William F. Starr Professor of Law
University of Connecticut

Formerly Reader in Law and Fellow of Exeter College
University of Oxford

RICHARD S. KAY

George and Helen England Professor of Law
University of Connecticut

ANTHONY W. BRADLEY

Of the Inner Temple, Barrister

Emeritus Professor of Constitutional Law
University of Edinburgh

OXFORD
UNIVERSITY PRESS

OXFORD
UNIVERSITY PRESS

Great Clarendon Street, Oxford OX2 6DP

Oxford University Press is a department of the University of Oxford.
It furthers the University's objective of excellence in research, scholarship,
and education by publishing worldwide in

Oxford New York

Athens Auckland Bangkok Bogotá Buenos Aires Calcutta
Cape Town Chennai Dar es Salaam Delhi Florence Hong Kong Istanbul
Karachi Kuala Lumpur Madrid Melbourne Mexico City Mumbai
Nairobi Paris São Paulo Shanghai Singapore Taipei Tokyo Toronto Warsaw

with associated companies in Berlin Ibadan

Oxford is a registered trade mark of Oxford University Press
in the UK and in certain other countries

Published in the United States
by Oxford University Press Inc., New York

© Text, Introductory Material, Selection, and Notes
Mark W. Janis, Richard S. Kay, and Anthony W. Bradley 2000

The moral rights of the author have been asserted

Database right Oxford University Press (maker)

First published 1995
This edition 2000

British Library Cataloguing in Publication Data

Data available

Library of Congress Cataloging in Publication Data

Data available

ISBN 0–19–876569–X

3 5 7 9 10 8 6 4

Typeset in Adobe Minion
by RefineCatch Limited, Bungay, Suffolk
Printed in Great Britain by
T.J. International Ltd., Padstow, Cornwall

PREFACE

This book introduces European Human Rights Law. It explores the legal process and the substantive law developed over the last 50 years pursuant to the Council of Europe's Convention for the Protection of Human Rights and Fundamental Freedoms. Ours is a subject of enormous importance that has been heretofore all too often neglected. European Human Rights Law is a great success story too little told.

Nowadays, the European Court of Human Rights in Strasbourg regularly finds nations in breach of their obligations under the international human rights law of the European Human Rights Convention. Remarkably, sovereign states have generally respected the adverse judgments of the Court. As of January 2000, there were 41 member states to the Convention. These states have, in response to the judgments of the Strasbourg Court, reformed police procedures, penal institutions, child welfare practices, administrative agencies, judicial processes, labour relations, morals legislation, and many other important public matters. Moreover, these states have compensated individuals for their injuries. The willingness with which the decisions of the European Court of Human Rights have been accepted demonstrates the emergence of a crucial new fact in the Western legal tradition: an effective system of international law regulating some of the most sensitive areas of what had previously been thought to be within the exclusive domain of national sovereignty.

Obviously, European Human Rights Law is of critical importance to nationals of member states of the Council of Europe. Furthermore, there are at least three ways in which a study of European Human Rights Law ought to be helpful to judges, lawyers and law students outside Europe. First, the emergence of this law is an event of significance in its own right. No one should pretend to even a superficial knowledge of world legal systems without being acquainted with European Human Rights Law. Second, European Human Rights Law sheds light on the legal protection of the rights of individuals in general. It is a particular failing of North Americans, for example, too often to be reluctant to take notice of parallel experiences elsewhere. The Strasbourg Court and the European Human Rights Convention protect many of the same rights that have been interpreted and applied by the United States Supreme Court under the United States Constitution and, more recently, by the Supreme Court of Canada under the Canadian Charter of Rights and Freedoms. The way in which human rights law has been interpreted by the Strasbourg Court, insofar as it differs from courts in the United States and Canada or as it mirrors them, is sure to illuminate both the nature of these rights and the general process of constitutional adjudication. Finally, the development of European Human Rights Law engages some of the most basic issues of jurisprudence. Here in only 50 years has been the creation of a developed system of law. Analysis of this experience is bound to tell us something about what makes law and what law is. Incorporation of European Human Rights Law into the law of the United Kingdom with effect from

October 2000 will enable that jurisprudence to engage directly with the historic traditions of the common law.

The materials that follow can be put to a number of different pedagogic uses. There is sufficient scope and depth here to support an independent course in a law school or in other undergraduate or graduate study. We have used the book in this way. Paired with materials on European Community Law, the book can help constitute a course in European Law. Similarly, the book can be used with other materials in a course on International or Comparative Human Rights Law. The book also may provide supplementary materials for courses in Public International Law, Comparative Law, and Constitutional Law.

The first three chapters (principally prepared by Janis) focus on institutions and procedures. In describing and analysing the structure and process of European Human Rights Law, we have attempted to put them in the context of the development of international law and international dispute settlement generally. The next five chapters (Chapters 4, 5, 6, and 8, principally prepared by Kay, and Chapter 7, principally prepared by Bradley) cover selected substantive areas of adjudication. The technique here is both descriptive and comparative. In particular, we attempt to present parallel law on issues as they have arisen in the United States, Canada and the United Kingdom. The ninth chapter (principally prepared by Bradley) looks at the ways in which European Human Rights Law is applied in domestic law, particularly in the United Kingdom. All the chapters highlight recurring themes in the adjudication of international human rights law.

This book is not intended to provide a comprehensive treatment of European Human Rights Law. It is merely an introduction. The range of topics and the specific illustrations are meant to furnish a solid foundation for understanding the major problems and features of the system. Certain important subjects have, as a concession to time and space, been omitted. In particular, some important questions of procedure and remedy (Article 41) are, regrettably, not discussed. Furthermore, we might point out that generally, except in Chapter 2, we have relied upon the judgments of the European Court of Human Rights rather than upon the extensive reports of the former European Commission of Human Rights. Those reports are a rich and intelligent source, but under the old Convention parties bound themselves only to conform to the final judgments of the Court and the decisions of the Committee of Ministers.

A book of this kind always poses difficult choices both about the items presented and about their editing. While many of the selections have been rather drastically reduced in size, our preference has been to leave enough of the original language intact so that readers will be able to get a sense of the whole dispute and the character of the Court's approach. In our textual discussions, we more freely draw on more limited quotations from court judgments to illustrate certain points. Readers should note that we have generally (although not invariably) omitted citations to other judgments and internal references to other parts of the same judgment. For practical reasons materials appearing after 1 October 1999, have not been included.

No uniform method of citation seems to have emerged for cases of the European

Court of Human Rights. We have in each case given the date of judgment, a citation to the official reports of the Court and one to the European Human Rights Reports published by Sweet and Maxwell. The reference to the official reports for cases decided to 4 December 1995 is the number in Series A of the Court's publications—e.g. No. 313A. For later cases the reference is to the year, volume and page number of the Court's Reports of Judgments and Decisions—e.g. Reports, 1996–VI 2382. The full text of all of the Court's judgments and a useful search engine may be consulted at http://www.echr.coe.int/eng/Judgments.htm.

The initial edition of this book (written by Janis and Kay) was published in 1990 by the University of Connecticut Law School Foundation Press. It was, at that time, something of a risky project. The decision by the Foundation to take that risk made the appearance of the subsequent editions possible.

Though this volume's faults are ours alone, its virtues are largely due to the help and insights of many friends and colleagues. Our thanks are especially due to the judges, commissioners, and staff of the European Human Rights Law system, and especially to: Andràs Baka, Rudolf Bernhardt, Nicolas Bratza, John Hedigan, Karel Jungwiert, Gunnar Lagergren, Egils Levits, Ronald St. John Macdonald, Rolv Ryssdal, Viera Strážnická, Wilhelmina Thomasson, Riza Türmen, Nina Vajić, Brian Walsh, Gérard Wiarda, Jochen Frowein, Henry Schermers, Hans Christian Krüger, Maud Buquicchio, Andrew Drzemczewski and Michael O'Boyle. Warm thanks are owed, too, to our academic and professional colleagues: John Bridge, Ian Brownlie, Thomas Buergenthal, Sally Evans, Christine Gray, Jane Hanna, Hugh Macgill, George Schatzki, David Seymour, Louis Sohn, Dennis Stone and Carol Weisbrod. We have benefited from the careful research assistance of Daniel Bender, Celia Byler, Alice Carey, Sarah Cox, Jerrie Chiu, Jennifer Collins, Sanja Djajic, John Flynn, Jennifer Glaudemans, Michael Hammond, Charles Hickey, Philip Janis, Brent Houston, Rachel Kay, Hilary Kreitner, Peter Morgan, Marianne Reiner-Caputo, Kimberly Troland, Marc Ubaldi, Solange Wallace, Richard Wilde, and Shelby Wilson. In particular, Alice Carey, Sarah Cox and Hilary Kreitner undertook most of the research and drafting of the note on prompt adjudication in Chapter 8. Sarah Karwan provided extraordinary assistance in the preparation of the manuscript for the second edition. We are grateful, too, to Julia Dunlop, Mary Kate Cox and Bobette Reed Kahn of the University of Connecticut Law School Foundation, to Matthew Cotton and Michaela Coulthald of Oxford University Press and also to Kristin Clayton, John Whelan, and Richard Hart, formerly of Oxford University Press, and to our secretaries: Judy Bigelow, Janet Jendrzejewski, Sandy Michalik, Joan Wood and especially to Delia M. Roy, our manuscript coordinator.

Hartford	Mark W. Janis
London	Richard S. Kay
January 2000	Anthony W. Bradley

TABLE OF CONTENTS

TABLE OF CASES BEFORE THE EUROPEAN COMMISSION OF HUMAN RIGHTS AND/OR THE COMMITTEE OF MINISTERS OF THE COUNCIL OF EUROPE

TABLE OF CASES BEFORE THE
EUROPEAN COURT OF HUMAN RIGHTS

TABLE OF CASES FROM THE
UNITED STATES

TABLE OF CASES FROM CANADA

TABLE OF CASES FROM THE
UNITED KINGDOM

TABLE OF OTHER CASES

TABLE OF STATUTES

TABLE OF INTERNATIONAL INSTRUMENTS

PART I

STRUCTURE AND PROCESS

1

THE EUROPEAN CONVENTION ON HUMAN RIGHTS

The European Convention for the Protection of Human Rights and Fundamental Freedoms[1] establishes not only the world's most successful system of international law for the protection of human rights, but one of the most advanced forms of any kind of international legal process. The European Human Rights Convention was drafted in the Council of Europe during 1949 and 1950 in the aftermath of World War II. The Convention was signed on 4 November 1950, and came into force on 3 September 1953, after its ratification by eight countries: Denmark, the Federal Republic of Germany, Iceland, Ireland, Luxembourg, Norway, Sweden, and the United Kingdom. The number of members of the Convention has grown. As of January 2000, 41 states were bound by its terms: Albania, Andorra, Austria, Belgium, Bulgaria, Croatia, Cyprus, the Czech Republic, Denmark, Estonia, Finland, France, Georgia, Germany, Greece, Hungary, Iceland, Ireland, Italy, Latvia, Liechtenstein, Lithuania, Luxembourg, Malta, Moldova, the Netherlands, Norway, Poland, Portugal, Romania, Russia, San Marino, the Slovak Republic, Slovenia, Spain, Sweden, Switzerland, the former Yugoslav Republic of Macedonia, Turkey, Ukraine, and the United Kingdom.[2]

[1] 213 U.N.T.S. 221, E.T.S. 5, U.K.T.S. 71 (1953), signed at Rome 4 Nov. 1950; entered into force 3 Sept. 1953, Council of Europe, www.coe.fr (29 October 1999) (hereinafter cited as 'Convention'). The Convention is set forth in Appendix A.

[2] Council of Europe, *Chart of Signatures and Ratifications of the Convention for the Protection of Human Rights and Fundamental Freedoms*, conventions.coe.int/treaty/EN/cadreintro.htm (accessed 6 July 2000) (hereinafter cited as 'Chart of Signatures and Ratifications').

A. THE CONVENTION AND THE EFFICACY OF INTERNATIONAL LAW

Quand je vais dans un pays, je n'examine pas s'il y a des bonnes lois, mais si on exécute celles qui y sont, car il y a des bonnes lois partout.[3]

When I go to a country, I do not look to see whether there are good laws, but whether those there are enforced, for good laws are everywhere.

Any difficulty in making good international law pales beside the problem of making good international law effective. The history of the international legal discipline is replete with examples of carefully crafted norms disregarded in practice. One need only mention the Kellogg-Briand Pact of 1928 and the Charter of the United Nations and their vain attempts to abolish war to evoke the commonplace that international law does not 'work'.

Yet, international law plainly does 'work' in its most frequent usage, the application of international law by national legal systems. When a treaty provision or a customary international law or any other international law norm is used as a rule of decision by a municipal court or administrative agency, international law has all the efficacy that a municipal legal system can muster.[4] For most international lawyers, this efficacy is enough because most international lawyers, especially those practising some sort of international economic law, such as international commercial, corporate, tax or trade law, rely upon national legal systems, not upon any international legal system, to get their job done. 'Piggy-backing' on national law-applying and law-enforcing institutions is quite an ordinary way in which international law is made effective. Indeed, one of the most helpful contributions which international law makes to international relations is to provide common rules which are applicable and effective simultaneously in two or more municipal legal systems.

When we think of the problem of international law being ineffective, we are not contemplating international law as it comes to be incorporated and enforced in municipal law. Rather, the particular ineffectiveness of international law arises in its application within whatever we have for an international legal system. It is not the body of rules of international law, so much as the process of international law, which is really at issue. The better question might be formulated: how are the rules of international law effective in international legal process?

A focus on the efficacy of international law in international legal process is reflected in the usual critiques of international law as not being real 'law'. In the nineteenth century, the leading English legal positivist, John Austin, concerned especially about

---

[3] Montesquieu, 'Notes sur l'Angleterre', in *Œuvres Complètes* 331, 332 (Editions du Seuil 1964).

[4] In the U.S., for example, Art. VI(2) of the Constitution makes 'all Treaties made, or which shall be made, under the Authority of the United States ... the Supreme Law of the Land'. U.S. Const. Art. VI, cl. 2. Moreover, the Supreme Court has held that customary international law is part of the common law of the U.S. *The Paquete Habana*, 175 U.S. 677, 700 (1900). *See* M. W. Janis, *An Introduction to International Law* 85–109 (3rd edn. 1999) (hereinafter cited as 'Janis').

the link between rules and rule-enforcement, argued that real 'law' required a sovereign to enforce it and that, therefore, with no international sovereign, international law was by definition not 'law' but a form of morality.[5] In 1961, H. L. A. Hart, in his modern construction of positivism, while accepting that, linguistically and because of usage it was right to call international law 'law', wrote that international law, as he then observed it, resembled not a municipal legal system but a primitive legal system where there are primary rules of obligation but no secondary rules efficiently to make, recognize or enforce primary rules.[6]

Whatever their differences, however, neither Austin's nor Hart's nor most other general jurisprudential characterizations of international law pay particular attention to the diversity of international legal process. That is, most discussions of the problem of the efficacy or the law-like quality of international law assume that there is *a* system—ineffective though it may be—of international law and suppose that there is something like a single, general, integrated, if not hierarchical, international legal process. Reality is otherwise. Although there is some international law and process which may purport to be universal, such as the United Nations and its law or some customary international law or perhaps natural law or *jus cogens*, most international law and process is pertinent only to a number of consenting states. This is true even for widely popular treaty frameworks, such as the General Agreement on Tariffs and Trade and the International Monetary Fund. It is no more accurate to say that there is *a* system of international law than to say that there is a system of municipal law. As there are many systems of municipal law, so there are many systems of international law.

Given the diversity of international legal process, the efficacy question might again be reformulated, and its answer tell us more, if we ask: what forms of international legal process are effective? The reformulated question assumes properly that there are different systems of international law and hints that some systems will be more effective than others. In analyzing the relationship between law and society, Max Weber, at the turn of the twentieth century, defined 'law' as 'an order system endowed with certain specific guarantees of the probability of its empirical validity'.[7] Weber's necessary 'guarantees' for law were more sophisticated than Austin's necessary 'sovereigns' for law. Weber wrote of a 'coercive apparatus, i.e., that there are one or more persons whose special task it is to hold themselves ready to apply specially provided means of coercion (legal coercion) for the purpose of norm enforcement'. The 'coercive apparatus' may use psychological as well as physical means of coercion and may operate directly or indirectly against the participants in the system.[8]

Somewhat surprisingly, given the problem of efficacy in international law, there is relatively little academic attention paid to it. Most international legal studies are

---

[5] J. Austin, *The Province of Jurisprudence Determined* 208 (1st edn. 1832).

[6] H. L. A. Hart, *The Concept of Law* 209, 226 (1961) (hereinafter cited as 'Hart').

[7] M. Weber, *Law in Economy and Society* 13 (Rheinstein & Shils trans. 1954).

[8] *Id.* at 13. Hart describes the same kind of characteristics in his discussion of the 'internal' point of view essential to any mature legal system. *See* Hart, *supra* n. 6, at 111–14.

concerned with rules rather than process. Some of the scholarly reluctance is due probably to the division between international lawyers and political scientists; the lawyers feeling comfortable with rules but uncomfortable with international relations, and the political scientists vice versa.

The best known international legal tribunal, the International Court of Justice at the Hague, has been all too often part of a relatively ineffective international legal system, that of the United Nations. This does not make the United Nations system unimportant; politically it is very important indeed. It is only to say that the International Court and United Nations law might at present be relatively uninteresting to legal theorists because they usually are such ineffective legal instruments.

Much more interesting in theory (and perhaps as a harbinger) is the international legal system fashioned by the European Convention on Human Rights where formal legal structures, i.e., the European Court of Human Rights and, until its merger into the Court in 1999, the European Commission of Human Rights at Strasbourg, have exercised actual authority. Their demonstrated effectiveness has been unrivalled on the international plane, save perhaps by those other European international legal institutions, the European Union's Court of Justice and Court of First Instance at Luxembourg.

The discussion and materials below can, to some degree, illuminate the potential for the efficacy of international legal process. European human rights law provides, therefore, not only the most important body of case law about the substance of international human rights law, but one of the most refreshing and interesting examples of an effective international legal process. Of course, the European human rights law system is neither 'sovereign' in Europe nor are its institutions part of any sort of supranational sovereign authority system satisfying a narrow, Austinian positivist definition of 'law'. In some ways, this makes European human rights law a good model. Generally speaking, there are no Austinian supranational authorities operating in the world today, nor are there likely to be any soon emerging. It could be said that international institutions such as those involved in European human rights law evidence the existence of what Hart would call secondary rules. If so, these schemes would seem less like a primitive legal system and more like a familiar municipal legal system. In Weber's terms, an international legal system like European human rights law can, as we shall see, very aptly be described as a structure for legal coercion, using psychological as well as physical means and operating indirectly as well as directly on the participants, specifically states, in the system.

At first blush it may seem surprising that such a phenomenon should emerge in a field like human rights. The kinds of politically sensitive problems with which such a system must deal may appear particularly poor candidates for engendering a supranational psychological consensus. Perhaps the explanation lies in an essential dichotomy between, on the one hand, agreement on the general character of the proposed rules of law and mechanisms for enforcement and, on the other, the actual application of the rules and operation of those mechanisms. That distinction is striking in the materials that follow. It was relatively easy in the wake of the brutal experience of the war against fascism for the European survivors to agree both on the importance of protecting human rights and on the inadequacy of relying solely on national enforcement systems. Moreover, while the debates which accompanied the drafting of the European Convention on Human Rights and Fundamental Freedoms reveal many disparate viewpoints and significant contention, these divisive forces were limited by the fact that the object of the enterprise was, all along, the production of highly general standards of public conduct. The more or less unprecedented machinery for enforcement was made more palatable by providing for phased options for national participation.

The real wonder has been the ever increasing acceptance of the system even after the appearance of highly controversial judgments of the European Court of Human Rights, many of which are reproduced in these materials. As will be seen, the nations adhering to the Convention have submitted to these decisions with a willingness that can only be called startling. The reasons are, no doubt, multiple and complex, but one feature is surely relevant to this discussion. That is the mystique of the forms of law. We cannot know for sure, but it is at least doubtful, that a national state would abandon its sodomy laws or reform its welfare procedures merely on the directive of some nonjudicial board composed almost completely of foreigners. But these same orders, when cast in the form of a judgment of law, have been harder to resist. Resistance would evince not merely a (justifiable) disagreement on matters of policy but a defiance of the commitment to human dignity and the rule of law made by the state when it adhered to the European human rights system in the first place. Such defiance in modern Europe has not usually seemed a politically viable alternative.

Of course, such a view of things is only logical if the Strasbourg Court's judgments are, in fact, nothing more than translations of the general standards of conduct which were agreed upon in the European Convention from its very beginning. Indeed, the Court's form of legal judgment seems to depend on that assumption. A general rule of law is cited and the Court engages in what appears to be a neutral process of reasoning from that rule to a challenged action. The invariable reality of such a direct causal connection has long ago been debunked in adjudication generally.[9] The gap between the promulgation of abstract standards and the controvertible application of those standards to particular cases is a persistent theme in constitutional adjudication. It was clearly foreseen in the deliberations accompanying the drafting of the Convention. One delegate from the United Kingdom cited the fluid construction of the due process clauses of the United States Constitution as a warning. He urged his colleagues to 'define clearly, and in such terms that there be no reasonable latitude for misrepresentation, the purpose we have in mind'. Another British delegate argued against terms with 'a thousand and one interpretations'.[10]

---

[9] A well-known example focusing on American constitutional law is T. R. Powell, 'The Logic and Rhetoric of Constitutional Law', 15 *Journal of Philosophy* 645 (1918).

[10] *Travaux Préparatoires*, vol. 1, 80, 148 (remarks of Mr. Ungoed-Thomas and Mr. Nally). See also *id.* at 88 (remarks of M. Fayet of Belgium).

As the judgments reproduced below make plain, these warnings were both prophetic and unavailing. The language in which the rights were defined was usually broad and unspecific. The Strasbourg Court has exploited that breadth to create novel and, no doubt, little anticipated results. The Court has been explicit in embracing such creative interpretation as a proper part of its judicial duty. Its job, it has noted, is to 'develop the rules instituted by the Convention,' which must be regarded as a living instrument.[11]

We have thus come upon a paradox, but one present in every successful system of law. The existence of a legal system depends on a widely shared psychological attitude towards the rule-making and rule-applying institutions, but that attitude may, itself, be the product of an assumption that such institutions are themselves creatures of pre-existing law. This is a problem of chicken and egg; it is equally pointless here to seek to find which assumption takes priority. We can only say that sometimes a happy (or unhappy) confluence of political decisions, social attitudes, and individual actors and actions makes possible the kind of breakthrough that converts ad hoc decision-making bodies into legal tribunals and turns acquiescence into legal obligation. It is that extraordinary phenomenon which we may now be observing in the European human rights system.

If so, it is a curious kind of legal system, one which crosses the boundaries of national jurisdictions and which lacks plenary authority over its subjects.[12] But, for the reasons suggested, that does not seem an adequate reason to deny it the title of 'law'. Whether European human rights law will maintain that position in the long term remains to be seen. There may be a critical moment in the development of any system of law when each exercise of authority ceases to be a risk but instead comes to reinforce the essential perception that the institutions involved are merely the executors of a pre-existing and binding law. When we consider the varied character of the decisions of the European Court of Human Rights, their controversial content, and even the flaws and weaknesses in the Court's arguments, together with the almost uniform respect and obedience rendered to the judgments, we may conclude that such a critical moment may well have been passed.

B. HUMAN RIGHTS LAW

The principle that law should protect the human rights of individuals against the abuses of governments can at least be dated back to John Locke's *Two Treatises of Government* published in 1690. Locke believed that human rights, not governments, came first in the natural order of things:

---

[11] *Ireland v. United Kingdom*, 18 Jan. 1978 (No. 25), 2 E.H.R.R. 25, para. 154; *Tyrer Case*, 25 Apr. 1978 (No. 26), 2 E.H.R.R. 1, para. 31.

[12] Perhaps not all that curious. Much the same can be said of the 'central' legal systems of federal states.

If Man in the State of Nature be so free, as has been said; If he be absolute Lord of his own Person and Possessions, equal to the greatest, and subject to no Body, why will he part with his Freedom? Why will he give up this Empire, and subject himself to the Dominion and Controul of any other Power? To which 'tis obvious to Answer, that though in the state of Nature he hath such a right, yet the Enjoyment of it is very uncertain, and constantly exposed to the Invasion of others. For all being Kings as much as he, every Man his Equal, and the greater part no strict Observers of Equity and Justice, the enjoyment of the property he has in this state is very unsafe, very unsecure. This makes him willing to quit a Condition, which however free, is full of fears and continual dangers: And 'tis not without reason, that he seeks out, and is willing to join in Society with others who are already united, or have a mind to unite for the mutual *Preservation* of their Lives, Liberties and Estates, which I call by the general name, *Property*.[13]

Locke's prose celebrated the rights of the English under the limited government won by the Glorious Revolution of 1688. The particular advantages of England's unwritten constitution, especially the separation and balance of powers among the executive, legislative and judicial branches of government, were elaborated and popularized by the French political philosopher, Montesquieu, in the *Spirit of the Laws* in 1748.[14] In 1762, the revolutionary potential of human rights—'Man is born free; and everywhere he is in chains'—was proclaimed by Jean Jacques Rousseau.[15] Democratic revolutions were soon to follow in America and throughout Europe.

On 4 July 1776, the American Declaration of Independence issued from Philadelphia. The intellectual influences of Locke, Montesquieu and Rousseau on Thomas Jefferson's document were plain to see. In a ringing affirmation of human rights and the duty of governments to protect them, the delegates of the thirteen United States of America proclaimed:

We hold these truths to be self-evident, that all men are created equal, that they are endowed by their Creator with certain unalienable Rights, that among these are Life, Liberty and the pursuit of Happiness. That to secure these rights, Governments are instituted among Men, deriving their just powers from the consent of the governed. That whenever any Form of Government becomes destructive of these ends, it is the Right of the People to alter or to abolish it, and to institute new Government, laying its foundation on such principles and organizing its powers in such form, as to them shall seem most likely to effect their Safety and Happiness.

Politically, the last decades of the eighteenth century were a good time for affirmations of human rights. As the constitutions of the newly independent American states were drafted in 1776, bills of rights enumerating specific rights were directly incorporated therein, even, as for Virginia, making up its first part.[16] The fashion of bills of rights spread to Europe. Jefferson wrote to James Madison from Paris on 12 January 1789: 'Everybody here is trying their hands at forming declarations of rights'[17] Jefferson

---

[13] J. Locke, *Two Treatises of Government* 368 (3rd edn. 1698) (Laslett 2nd edn. 1970).

[14] Montesquieu, 'L'esprit des lois', *Œuvres Complètes* 527 (Editions du Seuil 1964).

[15] J. J. Rousseau, *The Social Contract* 3 (Cole ed. 1950).

[16] S.E. Morison, H.S. Commager & W.E. Leuchtenburg, 1 *The Growth of the American Republic* 210 (6th edn. 1969).

[17] T. Jefferson, Letter of 12 Jan. 1789, 14 *The Papers of Thomas Jefferson* 436, 437 (Boyd ed. 1958).

continued to play his part, reading and critiquing Lafayette's draft of what, on 27 August 1789, a few weeks after the fall of the Bastille, would become the French National Assembly's Declaration of the Rights of Man and Citizen.[18] Its indebtedness to Rousseau's philosophy and Philadelphia's practice was widely acknowledged.[19]

The French Declaration recognized and proclaimed 'in the presence and under the auspices of the Supreme Being, the following rights of man and citizen':

1. Men are born and remain free and equal in rights; social distinctions may be based only upon general usefulness.

2. The aim of every political association is the preservation of the natural and inalienable rights of man; these rights are liberty, property, security, and resistance to oppression.

3. The source of all sovereignty resides essentially in the nation; no group, no individual may exercise authority not emanating expressly therefrom.

4. Liberty consists of the power to do whatever is not injurious to others; thus the enjoyment of the natural rights of every man has for its limits only those that assure other members of society the enjoyment of those same rights; such limits may be determined only by law.

5. The law has the right to forbid only actions which are injurious to society. Whatever is not forbidden by law may not be prevented, and no one may be constrained to do what it does not prescribe.

6. Law is the expression of the general will; all citizens have the right to concur personally, or through their representatives, in its formation; it must be the same for all, whether it protects or punishes. All citizens, being equal before it, are equally admissible to all public offices, positions, and employments, according to their capacity, and without other distinction than that of virtues and talents.

7. No man may be accused, arrested, or detained except in the cases determined by law, and according to the forms prescribed thereby. Whoever solicits, expedites, or executes arbitrary orders, or has them executed, must be punished; but every citizen summoned or apprehended in pursuance of the law must obey immediately; he renders himself culpable by resistance.

8. The law is to establish only penalties that are absolutely and obviously necessary; and no one may be punished except by virtue of a law established and promulgated prior to the offence and legally applied.

9. Since every man is presumed innocent until declared guilty, if arrest be deemed indispensable, all unnecessary severity for securing the person of the accused must be severely repressed by law.

10. No one is to be disquieted because of his opinions, even religious, provided their manifestation does not disturb the public order established by law.

11. Free communication of ideas and opinions is one of the most precious of the rights of man. Consequently, every citizen may speak, write, and print freely, subject to responsibility for the abuse of such liberty in the cases determined by law.

[18] T. Jefferson, Letter of 3 June 1789, to Rabaut de St. Etienne, 15 *The Papers of Thomas Jefferson* 166 (Boyd ed. 1958). One of Jefferson's biographers has commented that his influence on Lafayette's declaration of rights 'was probably greater than appears in any formal record'. D. Malone, *Jefferson and the Rights of Man* 223 (1951).

[19] L. Madelin, *La Révolution* 84–6 (1911).

12. The guarantee of the rights of man and citizen necessitates a public force; such a force, therefore, is instituted for the advantage of all and not for the particular benefit of those to whom it is entrusted.

13. For the maintenance of the public force and for the expenses of administration a common tax is indispensable; it must be assessed equally on all citizens in proportion to their means.

14. Citizens have the right to ascertain, by themselves or through their representatives, the necessity of the public tax, to consent to it freely, to supervise its use, and to determine its quota, assessment, payment, and duration.

15. Society has the right to require of every public agent an accounting of his administration.

16. Every society in which the guarantee of rights is not assured or the separation of powers not determined has no constitution at all.

17. Since property is a sacred and inviolable right, no one may be deprived thereof unless a legally established public necessity obviously requires it, and upon condition of a just and previous indemnity.

On 25 September 1789, less than a month after the promulgation of the French Declaration, the first Congress of the new Federal Government of the United States of America proposed the first ten amendments to the United States Constitution.[20] Coming into force following the tenth state ratification (Virginia's) on 15 December 1791, they make up the United States Bill of Rights:

1. Congress shall make no law respecting an establishment of religion, or prohibiting the free exercise thereof; or abridging the freedom of speech, or of the press; or the right of the people peaceably to assemble, and to petition the Government for a redress of grievances.

2. A well regulated Militia, being necessary to the security of a free State, the right of the people to keep and bear Arms, shall not be infringed.

3. No Soldier shall, in time of peace be quartered in any house, without the consent of the Owner, nor in time of war, but in a manner to be prescribed by law.

4. The right of the people to be secure in their persons, houses, papers, and effects, against unreasonable searches and seizures, shall not be violated, and no Warrants shall issue, but upon probable cause, supported by Oath or affirmation, and particularly describing the place to be searched, and the persons or things to be seized.

5. No person shall be held to answer for a capital, or otherwise infamous crime, unless on a presentment or indictment of a Grand Jury, except in cases arising in the land or naval forces, or in the Militia, when in actual service in time of War or public danger; nor shall any person be subject for the same offence to be twice put in jeopardy of life or limb, nor shall be compelled in any criminal case to be a witness against himself, nor be deprived of life, liberty, or property, without due process of law; nor shall private property be taken for public use, without just compensation.

6. In all criminal prosecutions, the accused shall enjoy the right to a speedy and public trial, by an impartial jury of the State and district wherein the crime shall have been committed, which district shall have been previously ascertained by law, and to be informed of the nature and cause of the accusation; to be confronted with the witnesses against him; to have compulsory process for obtaining Witnesses in his favor, and to have the Assistance of Counsel for his defence.

[20] For the background to the drafting of the amendments, *see* B. Schwartz, *The Bill of Rights: A Documentary History* (1971).

7. In Suits at common law, where the value in controversy shall exceed twenty dollars, the right of trial by jury shall be preserved, and no fact tried by a jury, shall be otherwise re-examined in any Court of the United States, than according to the rules of the common law.

8. Excessive bail shall not be required, nor excessive fines imposed, nor cruel and unusual punishments inflicted.

9. The enumeration in the Constitution, of certain rights, shall not be construed to deny or disparage others retained by the people.

10. The powers not delegated to the United States by the Constitution, nor prohibited by it to the States, are reserved to the States respectively, or to the people.

Close in kinship and in substance, the American Declaration of Independence, the French Declaration of the Rights of Man and Citizen, and the United States Bill of Rights make up the eighteenth century intellectual and documentary foundation on which two centuries of legal protection of human rights have come to be built. Constitutional guarantees of human rights are now widespread. One study showed that 82 per cent of the national constitutions drafted between 1788 and 1948, and 93 per cent of the constitutions drafted between 1949 and 1975, provided some sort of human rights and fundamental freedoms. Nowadays, more than 100 national constitutions explicitly protect human rights.[21]

However, as Montesquieu observed, the record of observing these guarantees has varied from country to country and from time to time. One possible factor involved in this variety of efficacy has been the reliance or not upon judicial review of executive and legislative action. In the United States, the tradition developed beginning in 1803, in *Marbury v. Madison*,[22] that the courts could and did check the activities of the political branches of government when they violated constitutional standards. In England, France, and generally on the Continent notions of legislative supremacy dictated that the popularly elected parts of government were not to be restrained by appointed judges. It was not until 1920 that a European State, Austria, established a constitutional court that could invalidate acts of the legislature. After the Second World War, more European constitutional courts followed, e.g., in the Federal Republic of Germany in 1951, in Italy in 1953, in France in 1958 and in Spain in 1980.[23]

However, until relatively recently, there were no guarantees of human rights, much less methods of judicial review, at the level of international law, comparable to those sometimes available at municipal law. The prevalent philosophy of international law

---

[21] H. van Maarseveen & G. van der Tang, *Written Constitutions: A Computerized Comparative Study* 191–5 (1978). Some specific rights were more often guaranteed than others. For example, in constitutions drafted between 1949 and 1975, the right to a fair trial was protected in 91 per cent, the right to freedom of expression in 87 per cent, the right to liberty of person in 65 per cent, the right against torture or against cruel, inhuman or degrading treatment or punishment in 53 per cent, and the right to equal access to public service in 30 per cent. *Id.* at 195–8. *Constitutions of the Countries of the World* (Blaustein & Flanz eds. 20 vols. looseleaf). D. Weissbrodt, 'Globalization of Constitutional Law and Civil Rights' 43 *Journal of Legal Education* 261 (1993).

[22] 1 Cranch (5 U.S.) 137 (1803).

[23] Kavass, 'The Emergence of Constitutional Courts in Europe: An Introduction', *Supranational and Constitutional Courts in Europe: Functions and Sources* 6–7 (I. Kavass ed. 1992).

in the nineteenth and early twentieth century, legal positivism, maintained that international law was a law for states alone. Hence, it was thought to be antithetical for there to be international legal rights which individuals could assert against states.[24] The traditional positivist doctrine appeared as late as Lauterpacht's 1955 edition of Oppenheim's classic international law treatise:

Since the Law of Nations is primarily a law between States, States are, to that extent, the only subjects of the Law of Nations. . . . But what is the normal position of individuals in International Law, if they are not regularly subjects thereof? The answer can only be that, generally speaking, they are *objects* of the Law of Nations.[25]

The link of nationality did, according to traditional positivist doctrine, give a state the right to protect its nationals against abuses by other states. So, states might protest and remedy, for example, the uncompensated deprivation of a national's property by a foreign state. The Permanent Court of International Justice held in 1924 that '[i]t is an elementary principle of international law that a State is entitled to protect its subjects, when injured by acts contrary to international law committed by another State'; in so doing, a state was 'in reality asserting its own rights . . . [For] in the eyes of [an international tribunal] the State is sole claimant'.[26]

Nonetheless, the traditional positivist doctrine limited dramatically the access of private persons to international legal process. Whether or not an injury to an individual was to become the subject of an international claim depended ordinarily entirely on the discretionary decision of the individual's protecting state. Importantly, if the individual's own state inflicted an injury, no other state, usually, could protect the individual at international law. Moreover, states alone were given standing to bring contentious cases to the International Court at The Hague.[27]

This traditional nineteenth and early twentieth century positivist philosophy of international law foundered on the shoals of international practice in the 1940s when the Allies repudiated the human rights violations of the Axis powers. In their Moscow Declaration of German Atrocities of 30 October 1943, the United States, the United Kingdom, France, and the Soviet Union declared that individual Germans would be held responsible for their violations of international law.[28] And in the 8 August 1945 Charter of the International Military Tribunal, the same four Allies established the Nuremberg Tribunal where individuals, not states, would be tried for:

[24] *See* Janis, *supra* n. 4, at 235–248.

[25] L. Oppenheim, 1 *International Law* 636, 639 (Lauterpacht 8th ed. 1955). It is important to note that in the classical law of nations of the eighteenth century there was no such insistence that states were the only subjects of the discipline. Janis, 'Individuals as Subjects of International Law', 17 *Cornell International Law Journal* 61 (1984).

[26] *Mavrommatis Palestine Concessions Case*, 1924 P.C.I.J. Reports, ser. A, no. 2, at 12.

[27] 'Only States may be parties in cases before the Court', Statute of the International Court of Justice, Art. 34(1), 59 Stat. 1055, T.S. No. 993, 3 Bevans 1153 (signed at San Francisco 26 June 1945; entered into force 24 Oct. 1945). The P.C.I.J. Statute of 1920–1945 read the same. The International Court may render advisory opinions at the request of some international organizations (but not states).

[28] U.N. Doc. A/CN. 4/5 (3 March 1949), at 87–8.

(a) Crimes against peace: namely, planning, preparation, initiation or waging of a war of aggression, or a war in violation of international treaties, agreements or assurances, or participation in a common plan or conspiracy for the accomplishment of any of the foregoing;

(b) War crimes: namely, violations of the laws or customs of war. Such violations shall include, but not be limited to, murder, ill-treatment or deportation to slave labour or for any other purpose of civilian population of or in occupied territory, murder or ill-treatment of prisoners of war or persons on the seas, killing of hostages, plunder of public or private property, wanton destruction of cities, towns or villages, or devastation not justified by military necessity;

(c) Crimes against humanity: namely, murder, extermination, enslavement, deportation, and other inhumane acts committed against any civilian population, before or during the war, or persecutions on political, racial or religious grounds in execution of or in connexion with any crime within the jurisdiction of the Tribunal, whether or not in violation of the domestic law of the country where perpetrated.

Leaders, organizers, instigators and accomplices participating in the formulation or execution of a common plan or conspiracy to commit any of the foregoing crimes are responsible for all acts performed by any persons in execution of such plan.

The official position of defendants, whether as Heads of State or responsible officials in government departments, shall not be considered as freeing them from responsibility or mitigating punishment.

The fact that the defendant acted pursuant to order of his Government or of a superior shall not free him from responsibility, but may be considered in mitigation of punishment if the Tribunal determines that justice so requires.

The Tribunal shall have the right to impose upon a defendant, on conviction, death or such other punishment as shall be determined by it to be just.[29]

The 1946 judgment of the Nuremberg Tribunal confirmed the non-positivist norm that individuals, as well as states, were appropriate subjects of international law:

It was submitted that international law is concerned with the actions of sovereign states, and provides no punishment for individuals; and further, that where the act in question is an act of state, those who carry it out are not personally responsible, but are protected by the doctrine of the sovereignty of the State. In the opinion of the Tribunal, both these submissions must be rejected. That international law imposes duties and liabilities upon individuals as well as upon states has long been recognized. In the recent case of *Ex Parte Quirin* (1942, 317 U.S. 1, 63 S.Ct. 2, 87 L.Ed. 3), before the Supreme Court of the United States, persons were charged during the war with landing in the United States for purposes of spying and sabotage. The late Chief Justice Stone, speaking for the Court, said:

'From the very beginning of its history this Court has applied the law of war as including that part of the law of nations which prescribes for the conduct of war, the status, rights and duties of enemy nations as well as enemy individuals'.

He went on to give a list of cases tried by the Courts, where individual offenders were charged with offenses against the laws of nations, and particularly the laws of war. Many other authorities could be cited, but enough has been said to show that individuals can be punished for violations of

---

[29] Agreement for the Prosecution and Punishment of the Major War Criminals, arts. 6, 7, 8, 27, 59 Stat. 1544, 1547.

international law. Crimes against international law are committed by men, not by abstract entities, and only by punishing individuals who commit such crimes can be provisions of international law be enforced.[30]

The Nuremberg judgment has come to stand not only for the moral and political imperative that individuals be made legally responsible for violations of international law but also as evidence for the customary international legal rule that individual human rights ought to be protected at the level of international law. These moral, political and legal propositions are also to be found in the Preamble of the 1945 Charter of the United Nations. There the People of the United Nations reaffirm their 'faith in fundamental human rights'. Charter Article 55 calls on the organization to promote 'universal respect for, and observance of, human rights and fundamental freedoms for all without distinction as to race, sex, language, or religion'.[31]

The transformation of the substantive norms of human rights law from national to international law was made complete in 1948 in the promulgation of the Universal Declaration of Human Rights, where the United Nations General Assembly followed in the footsteps of Jefferson, Lafayette, and Madison.[32] The path in the United Nations had been laid by extensive debate in the Third Committee where there was a conscious sentiment among the delegates, for example, Réné Cassin of France, that the Declaration ought to reflect the great eighteenth century declarations of natural rights.[33] The large part of the Universal Declaration enumerated traditional human rights norms at the level of international law.

The emergence of international human rights law in the Nuremberg Judgment and the Universal Declaration of Human Rights has been described as the most 'radical development in the whole history of international law' since it so rapidly established individuals as well as states as subjects of international law.[34] However, the Universal Declaration provided no legal machinery to enforce rules against recalcitrant states. Albeit subject to the norms of international human rights law, states in the United Nations system were left to their own devices in terms of fulfilling their obligations. Given the political disputes then and now dividing the United Nations, it has been slow work developing effective international human rights legal process on a universal basis.[35] So it made sense, especially in Europe, for there to be regional international human rights machinery which might provide realistic enforcement mechanisms.

---

[30] The Nuremberg Trial 1946, 6 F.R.D. 69, 110 (1946).

[31] 59 Stat. 1031, T.S. No. 993, 3 Bevans 1153, signed at San Francisco 26 June 1945; entered into force 24 Oct. 1945.

[32] U.N.G.A. Resolution 217A (III), U.N. Doc. A/810, at 71 (1948). *See Humphrey*, 'The Universal Declaration of Human Rights: Its History, Impact and Juridicial Character', in *Human Rights: Thirty Years After the Universal Declaration* 21 (Ramcharan ed. 1979).

[33] J. Morsink, 'The Philosophy of the Universal Declaration', 6 *Human Rights Quarterly* 309 (1984).

[34] Humphrey, 'The Revolution in the International Law of Human Rights' 4 *Human Rights Law Journal* 205, 208–9 (1974–5).

[35] *See* F. Newman & D. Weissbrodt, *International Human Rights* 61–190 (1990); A. H. Robertson & J. G. Merrills, *Human Rights in the World* 23–101 (3rd ed. 1992).

C. THE NEGOTIATION OF THE CONVENTION

The proceedings at Nuremberg and the United Nations had special meaning for those who had witnessed the awful abuses of human rights in Nazi-occupied Europe. For the Europeans pressing for political union, human rights became an important priority. In May 1948, many of the organizations promoting European integration met at the Hague at the Conference of the International Committee of the Movements for European Unity.[36] There the delegates proclaimed:

We desire a Charter of Human Rights guaranteeing liberty of thought, assembly and expression as well as the right to form a political opposition; we desire a Court of Justice with adequate sanctions for the implementation of this Charter.[37]

Alongside the private pro-union movements, the European governments were preparing a treaty to establish a Council of Europe, with its own Assembly and Committee of Ministers, as a formal institutional step towards European unity. On 5 May 1949, the act creating the Council was signed by ten nations in London. It was widely expected that one of the early tasks of the Council would be to craft and implement a human rights convention for Europe.[38] Indeed, Article 3 of the Statute of the Council provided that: 'Every Member of the Council of Europe must accept the principles of the rule of law and of the enjoyment by all persons within its jurisdiction of human rights and fundamental freedoms'.[39]

On 12 July 1949, a draft European Convention on Human Rights and a draft Statute for a European Court were prepared by Pierre-Henri Teitgen, Sir David Maxwell-Fyfe and Professor Fernand Dehousse and submitted to the Council's Committee of Ministers.[40] Nonetheless, at the first session of the Committee of Ministers on 9 August 1949, a seven to four vote with one abstention decided to eliminate the '[d]efinition, safeguarding and development of human rights and of fundamental liberties' as an agenda item for the forthcoming first meeting of the Council's Consultative Assembly. Delegates from Norway, France and Sweden opposed the human rights agenda item because the matter 'had already been extensively discussed' at the United Nations in the debates leading up to the Universal Declaration of Human Rights.[41]

Despite the decision of the Committee of Ministers, many of the delegates at the Consultative Assembly proved keen to draft a special human rights convention for Europe. Rasmussen, a representative from Denmark, on 13 August 1949, rejected the

---

[36] R. Beddard, 1 *Human Rights and Europe* 19 (3rd edn. 1993).

[37] I Council of Europe, 1 *Collected Edition of the Travaux Préparatoires* xxii (1975) (hereinafter cited as 'Travaux Préparatoires').

[38] A. H. Robertson, *The Council of Europe* 1–83 (1956).

[39] 1 *Travaux Préparatoires, supra* n. 37, at xxiv.

[40] *Id.* at xxiv; the full texts of the drafts are set forth in *id.* at 296–320.

[41] *Id.* at 10–12.

notion that work on human rights in Europe would merely duplicate the United Nations's efforts:

[A]lthough the question of human rights had been discussed at length by the United Nations, it had not yet been possible to draft a text which held good in International Law. The universal declaration lacked precision. It could not be otherwise in view of the differences in civilization and forms of Government existing in different Member States of the United Nations. It would be a very different matter if the question was reconsidered on a purely Western European basis, in which case a text might be elaborated which would be binding in the legal sense.[42]

In response to such criticism, the Committee of Ministers finally agreed, on 13 August 1949, to return human rights to the Consultative Assembly's agenda.[43] A new item read:

Measures for the fulfillment of the declared aim of the Council of Europe in accordance with Article I of the Statute in regard to the maintenance and further realisation of human rights and fundamental freedoms.[44]

On 19 August 1949, a motion was put to the Assembly by Teitgen of France, Maxwell-Fyfe of the United Kingdom and 45 others which read in part:

The Assembly recommends that the Member States of the Council of Europe should, in pursu-ance of the aim enunciated in Article I of the Statute, accept the principle of collective responsibility for the maintenance of human rights and fundamental freedoms, and for this purpose should immediately conclude a convention by which each Member State would undertake:

a) to maintain intact the human rights and fundamental freedoms assured by the constitution, laws and administrative practice actually existing in their respective countries at the date of the signature of the convention; and

b) to set up a European Commission of Human Rights and a European Court of Human Rights for the purpose of assuring the observance of the above mentioned convention.[45]

In support of the motion, Teitgen linked the development of the new legal system to the human rights abuses of Nazi Europe:

Mr. President, while I was in the Gestapo prisons, while one of my brothers was at Dachau and one of my brothers-in-law was dying at Mauthausen, my father who was also a member of our French Parliament, was interned at Buchenwald. He told me that on the monumental gate of the camp was this outrageous inscription: 'Just or unjust, the Fatherland'.

I think that from our First Session we can unanimously proclaim that in Europe there will henceforth only be *just* fatherlands.

I think we can now unanimously confront 'reasons of State' with the only sovereignty worth dying for, worthy in all circumstances of being defended, respected and safeguarded—the sovereignty of justice and of law.[46]

---

[42] *Id.* at 24.
[43] *Id.* at 26.
[44] *Id.* at 28.
[45] *Id.* at 36.
[46] *Id.* at 48–50.

Edberg of Sweden stressed the need to turn human rights theory into international legal practice:

Mankind to-day has had more than enough of high-sounding principles and beautiful declarations. Willingness and ability to make something real out of those declarations has too often been lacking. How many international organizations have undermined their authority by compromising their fundamental ideals, because it seemed for a moment to be the easiest way! When I cast my vote for concrete measures, to secure for the men and women of the European countries their human rights and fundamental freedoms, I shall do it with a fervent desire, first, that the definition of those fundamental freedoms will be so clearly formulated as to leave no room for doubts about their meaning, and secondly, that the Charter of Human Rights, which we are going to adopt, will be regarded as supreme and binding upon all Governments who adopt it. Only if we adhere strictly to those principles will this Council achieve the position in European life for which we all hope.[47]

The general debate on the motion closed on the day it had begun with a proposal for a European human rights convention being forwarded to the Consultative Assembly's Committee on Legal and Administrative Questions. Looking back decades later, Pierre-Henri Teitgen selected that day, 19 August 1949, as 'the date when the European Convention on Human Rights emerged into positive law'.[48] The Legal Committee met between 22 August and 5 September 1949; it decided at its first sitting, by eleven votes to five: '[t]hat it would be useful and opportune to recommend the Member States to organize a collective guarantee within the Council of Europe of all or some of the rights and liberties of man and of citizens'.[49] Unanimously, on 27 August 1949, the Legal Committee resolved that 'although each State is entitled to establish the rules by which human rights are protected within its territory, the object of the collective guarantee should be to ensure that such rules and their application are in accordance with the general principles of law recognized by civilized nations (Article 38 of the Statute of the Permanent Court of International Justice)'.[50]

On 5 September 1949, the Legal Committee reported to the Consultative Assembly.[51] The Legal Committee supported:

the establishment of a collective guarantee of essential freedoms and fundamental rights . . . [T]his guarantee would demonstrate clearly the common desire of the Member States to build a European Union in accordance with the principles of natural law, of humanism and of democracy; it would contribute to the development of their solidarity and would fulfill the longing for security among their peoples.[52]

'The Committee unanimously agreed that for the moment, only those essential rights and fundamental freedoms could be guaranteed which are, to-day, defined and

---

[47] Id. at 78.

[48] Teitgen, 'Introduction to the European Convention on Human Rights', *The European System for the Protection of Human Rights* 3, 9 (Macdonald, Matscher & Petzold eds. 1993).

[49] 1 *Travaux Préparatoires, supra* n. 37, at 154.

[50] Id. at 166.

[51] Id. at 216–34.

[52] Id. at 216.

accepted after long usage, by the democratic regimes.'[53] The rights were to be based 'as far as possible' on the rights enumerated in the Universal Declaration of Human Rights.[54] The Legal Committee's proposed draft convention listed twelve substantive rights, each explicitly referenced to articles of the Universal Declaration, called for the establishment of a European Court and Commission of Human Rights, and gave individuals as well as states the right of petition to the Commission; the Commission and states could refer cases to the Court.[55] Respecting the establishment of a Commission and a Court, the Legal Committee reported:

After a long debate, the Committee rejected as completely insufficient a proposal granting the victim of a violation of the Convention a simple right of petition, whether to the Committee of Ministers or to a Commission of Enquiry. It is in fact well known that any authority which, in such circumstances, receives a petition, may quite likely decide to ignore it.

After this the Committee decided that the guarantee should include a judicial ruling preceded by a preliminary investigation of the complaint, followed, if necessary, by an enquiry, and then an attempt at conciliation, to be carried out by a special Commission.

All persons or corporate bodies who are victims of a violation of the Convention, may petition the Commission, but the latter need not immediately refer it to the Court; the complaint will, if the Commission so decides, only be submitted to the Court for a judicial decision after a preliminary investigation of the case and after an attempt at conciliation has been made.[56]

The proposals for a Commission and a Court were not welcomed by all. Rolin of France and Ungoed-Thomas of the United Kingdom proposed on 6 September 1949 that the Legal Committee's recommendation of a Court be rejected.[57] Among other things, Rolin and Ungoed-Thomas opposed letting private individuals 'bring one of the States to trial even after examination and with the authority of a "sorting organization"'.[58] Rejecting such arguments that supported the sanctity of state sovereignty and pleading in favour of the proposed Court, Teitgen of France returned to the theme of human rights abuses in World War II with a speech on 7 September 1949:

Democracies do not become Nazi countries in one day. Evil progresses cunningly, with a minority operating, as it were, to remove the levers of control. One by one freedoms are suppressed, in one sphere after another. Public opinion and the entire national conscience are asphyxiated. And then, when everything is in order, the 'Führer' is installed and the evolution continues even to the oven of the crematorium.

It is necessary to intervene before it is too late. A conscience must exist somewhere which will sound the alarm to the minds of a nation menaced by this progressive corruption, to warn them of the peril and to show them that they are progressing down a long road which leads far, sometimes even to Buchenwald or Dachau.

An international Court, within the Council of Europe, and a system of supervision and

---

[53] *Id.* at 218.
[54] *Id.* at 218.
[55] *Id.* at 228–34.
[56] *Id.* at 224.
[57] *Id.* at 242.
[58] *Id.* at 244.

guarantees, could be the conscience of which we all have need, and of which other countries have perhaps a special need.[59]

Dominedo of Italy was equally plain in his support of a new European regional international court. He explained on 8 September 1949, why the International Court of Justice at The Hague would not do:

I must observe that The Hague Court of International Justice is not a European court; it does not fulfill the fundamental aim we have in mind, that is to say, the establishment of a European legal organ. Appeal to a Court whose competence is extra-European does not contribute to the progressive formation of European unity.

But that is not good enough. Indeed, according to the Statute of the United Nations, the International Court of Justice at the Hague only admits a complaint made by a State.

We must tackle a delicate but very interesting question. We must decide whether we wish to study the possibility of individual victims who claim that their fundamental human rights have been violated, being able to submit a complaint or an appeal.[60]

Finally, after two full days of debate, on 8 September 1949, the proposed amendment of Rolin and Ungoed-Thomas rejecting a European Court of Human Rights was itself rejected; the idea of establishing a new Court would go ahead.[61]

Ungoed-Thomas then proposed that individuals not be allowed to petition the Commission.[62]

[P]ersonally I object to this right of individuals going to the Commission for this reason. I foresee shoals of applications being made by individuals who imagine that they have a complaint of one kind or another against the country . . . In my opinion the objection to the Commission is as great as the objection to the Court.[63]

Sundt of Norway also opposed the right of individual petition:

I believe that the Commission will be of greater practical importance than the Court, because it is the Commission and its investigations which will form the basis for both public opinion, the decisions the Committee of Ministers will take, and likewise for the case which will eventually be carried to the Court. On the other hand, I also consider that the work of the Commission will be made practically impossible if thousands and thousands of individuals in the different Member States have the opportunity to send in their complaints.[64]

In rebutting such arguments, Maxwell-Fyfe said quite simply: '[W]e have to give the personal opportunity to the individual to establish the dignity of the individual human spirit and to prevent injustice.'[65] Ungoed-Thomas's proposal to delete the right of individuals to petition the Commission was rejected.[66]

---

[59] *Id.* at 292.
[60] 2 *Travaux Préparatoires, supra* n. 37, at 156–8.
[61] *Id.* at 184.
[62] *Id.* at 188.
[63] *Id.* at 188–90.
[64] *Id.* at 190.
[65] *Id.* at 200.
[66] *Id.* at 202.

On 8 September 1949, the Report of the Legal Committee with a few amendments but still recommending a Court, a Commission and the right of individual petition, was adopted by the Consultative Assembly with 64 votes in favor, one against, and 21 abstentions.[67] The Assembly's draft Convention then passed to the Committee of Ministers, which on 5 November 1949 invited the governments of the Member States of the Council of Europe to appoint experts to a committee to draw up its own draft convention paying '[d]ue attention . . . to the progress which has been achieved in this matter by the competent organs of the United Nations'.[68] The Consultative Assembly, through its Standing Committee on 7–9 November 1949, expressed itself none too happy with the action of the Committee of Ministers:

The Standing Committee regrets that the Committee of Ministers did not think it desirable to give its approval in principle to the draft Convention for a collective guarantee of human rights, which the Assembly has adopted. It sees no objection to this question being remitted to a committee of lawyers for study, but it would like to point out that it would be regrettable if this committee was to be given a mandate to undertake the study of the question *ab initio*; the more so since the Assembly's draft was in fact based on work done by the United Nations. The Committee feared that to defer the matter until a decision is taken by the United Nations would mean that the proposal would merely be pigeon-holed.[69]

The Committee of Experts, composed of government lawyers, legislators, judges and law professors from the twelve nations then members of the Council of Europe, met between 2 February and 10 March 1950, at Strasbourg.[70] They had before them not only the draft Convention and Report prepared by Teitgen and the Consultative Assembly, but also Working Papers readied by the Secretariat of the Council of Europe.[71] And, despite or because of the worries of the Assembly, the Committee of Experts did not begin their work *ab initio*, but rather, from their very first sitting, used the Assembly's draft as their working document.[72]

The Committee of Experts reported to the Committee of Ministers on 16 March 1950.[73] The Committee included their own 'preliminary draft convention' which they noted was 'drawn up on the basis of the Consultative Assembly's draft'.[74] The Committee, however, pronounced itself unwilling to finally decide on the detail in which enumerated rights should be drawn or whether a Court should be included since these were fundamentally political decisions; it instead submitted alternative texts in both respects.[75] On receiving the Committee of Experts' Report, the Committee of Ministers decided on 1 April 1950 to convene a Conference of Senior Officials of the

---

[67] *Id.* at 274–86.

[68] *Id.* at 290.

[69] *Id.* at 302.

[70] 3 *Travaux Préparatoires, supra* n. 37, at 180–335.

[71] *Id.* at 2–178.

[72] *Id.* at 182–4. *See* the detailed discussion of proposed changes to the Assembly's draft, *id.* at 258–78.

[73] 4 *Travaux Préparatoires, supra* note 37, at 2–82.

[74] *Id.* at 14.

[75] *Id.* at 16.

governments of the Member States 'to prepare the ground for the political decisions to be taken by the Committee of Ministers'.[76]

The Conference of Senior Officials met between 8–17 June 1950.[77] In their Report to the Committee of Ministers,[78] the Conference noted that four countries (France, Ireland, Italy and Turkey) favoured simply enumerating rights as the Consultative Assembly had proposed and four countries (Greece, Norway, the Netherlands, and the United Kingdom) favoured defining the rights in detail.[79] The Conference's proposed text was a compromise of the two positions ultimately acceptable to a majority of the Conference.[80]

With respect to a Court, seven countries (Denmark, Greece, Norway, the Netherlands, the United Kingdom, Sweden and Turkey) were opposed to its creation, while four (Belgium, France, Ireland and Italy) were in favour.[81] Sweden proposed the creation of an optional Court, a compromise supported by eight countries (Belgium, France, Greece, Ireland, Italy, Luxembourg, Sweden and Turkey), opposed by two (the Netherlands and the United Kingdom), and supported by two (Denmark and Norway) if supported by a majority of the governments.[82] Nine countries (Belgium, Denmark, France, Ireland, Italy, Luxembourg, Norway, Sweden and Turkey) supported the right of individual petition to the Commission, while three (Greece, the Netherlands, and the United Kingdom), 'fearing that the right of petition might easily lead to abuse, particularly in the interests of subversive propaganda,' reserved their position.[83]

With the enumerated rights agreed but disputes still raging about the role of the Court and the right of individual petition, the draft Convention returned to the hands of the Committee of Ministers. In August 1950, the Committee of Ministers decided to make both the jurisdiction of the Court and the right of individual petition optional.[84] This text then was substantially the same as that signed by the governments on 4 November 1950.[85] The European Convention for the Protection of Human Rights and Fundamental Freedoms came into force on 3 September 1953.[86]

---

[76] *Id.* at 84.
[77] *Id.* at 100–240.
[78] *Id.* at 242–96.
[79] *Id.* at 246–8.
[80] *Id.* at 248.
[81] *Id.* at 248–50.
[82] *Id.* at 250–2.
[83] *Id.* at 252.
[84] 1 *Travaux Préparatoires, supra* n. 37, at xxvi–xxviii.
[85] *Id.* at xxviii.
[86] Convention, *supra* n. 1; it is set forth in full in Appendix A.

D. THE PROGRESS OF THE CONVENTION

Merely as a European bill of rights, the Convention as drafted and adopted offered little that was exceptional on the international scene. What is extraordinary about the Convention is Strasbourg's enforcement machinery. The heart of the enforcement machinery was for nearly 50 years provided by what were, until November 1998, two crucial 'optional' clauses: old Article 25 (now mandatory by new Article 34) giving individuals as well as states the right to petition the European Commission of Human Rights for relief and old Article 46 (now mandatory by new Article 32) that gave the European Court of Human Rights judicial jurisdiction to hear and try cases already reported upon by the Commission (the Commission's functions were merged into the Court in 1999).

What was crucial in the early days of the Convention was whether or not the European states would agree to accept individual petition and judicial jurisdiction. Historically, the Europeans were familiar with bills of rights but, unlike the Americans, they were generally unfamiliar with judicial enforcement of those rights. Domestically, they trusted the legislative and executive branches of government rather than the judicial branch to protect fundamental freedoms.[87] In the 1950s the question was whether Europeans would be willing to empower an international commission and a court to safeguard human rights.

At first, the European governments were reluctant to accept the optional clauses. Look, for example, at some of the Parliamentary debates in Great Britain in 1958, several years before the government agreed to accept the two optional provisions:

Mr. Brockway asked the Secretary of State for Foreign Affairs whether Her Majesty's Government have accepted the compulsory jurisdiction of the European Court of Human Rights which is now being set up in accordance with the terms of the European Convention on Human Rights.

The Minister of State for Foreign Affairs (Mr. Ormsby-Gore): No, Sir. As my right Hon. and Learned Friend said on 29th July last year: 'The position which Her Majesty's Government have continuously taken up is that they do not recognize the right of individual petition, because they take the view that States are the proper subject of international law and if individuals are given rights under international treaties, effect should be given to those rights through the national law of the States concerned. The reason why we do not accept the idea of compulsory jurisdiction of a European court is because it would mean that British codes of common and statute law would be subject to review by an international court. For many years it has been the position of successive British Governments that we should not accept this status'. (Official Report, 29th July, 1957; vol. 574, c. 867–8).

Mr. Brockway: May I ask the right Hon. Gentleman what in the world is the good of ratifying a Convention theoretically if one does not accept the application of that Convention? Is it not the case that human rights involve personal individual rights and if we do not recognize that we are giving way to totalitarian conception?

---

[87] J. Frowein, 'European Integration Through Fundamental Rights' 18 *Journal of Law Reform* 5–7 (1984).

Mr. Ormsby-Gore: As I understand it, if one subscribes to a Convention one then sees that the laws of one's country are in conformity with the convention, and the individual cases are then tried under the laws of one's own country.

Mr. S. Silverman: Would the Hon. Gentleman explain how he reconciles that view with the action the British Government—and in the opinion of most of us rightly—took in regard to the Nuremberg trials? Can one really maintain a view of international law, international rights, on the basis that a man may be individually subject to penalties for infractions of it, but not able to claim any rights under the same conception?

Mr. Ormsby-Gore: I quite agree that the procedure in the Nuremberg courts was entirely exceptional and was due to the actions that took place in the war. I agree that it does not square with all the other cases which we have in mind.

Mr. Brockway: In view of that unsatisfactory reply, I wish to ask your permission, Mr. Speaker, to raise the matter at the first opportunity on the Adjournment.[88]

Other sorts of governmental objections were raised elsewhere in Europe, for example in 1959, in the Netherlands, against recognizing the right of individual petition:

It was thought that such recognition was not necessary because there existed in this country effective guarantees in the municipal law; abuse was feared; it was feared that the European Commission, which would deal with the complaints, would have a political structure; it was thought that the procedure for individual petition was cumbersome and costly and, finally, it was pointed out that the right of individual petition would have far-reaching repercussions upon our legal system.[89]

However, over time and one-by-one the members of the Council of Europe consented to what were, until November 1998, the two optional clauses. What had been originally conceived as real as well as legal options became perceived in Europe as politically non-optional. Indeed, by 1995, all 30 states then party to the Convention had accepted both Article 25's right of individual petition and Article 46's jurisdiction of the Court.[90]

---

[88] House of Commons, *Weekly Hansard*, No. 438, 26 Nov. 1958, col. 333–4, quoted in 2 *Yearbook of the European Convention on Human Rights* 546–8 (1958–1959). The relationship between the United Kingdom and the Strasbourg system has long been complex and controversial. See A. Lester, 'Fundamental Rights: The United Kingdom Isolated?' [1984] *Public Law* 46; A. Lester, 'U.K. Acceptance of the Strasbourg Jurisdiction: What Really went on in Whitehall in 1965' [1998] *Public Law* 237; and, for the most recent developments involving the incorporation of the Convention in British law, Chapter 9 *infra*.

[89] Second Chamber of the States General, Session 1959, *Preliminary Report of the Budget Committee for Foreign Affairs*, Document No. 5359, quoted in 2 *Yearbook for the European Convention on Human Rights* 560, 562 (1958–1959).

[90] As of 28 July 1994, the record showed that 21 countries chose to accept simultaneously Art. 25 and Art. 46: Ireland on 25 Feb. 1953; Denmark on 13 April 1953; Belgium on 5 July 1955; the Federal Republic of Germany on 5 July 1955; Luxembourg on 28 April 1958; Austria on 3 Sept. 1958; the United Kingdom on 14 Jan. 1966; Italy on 1 Aug. 1973; Switzerland on 28 Nov. 1974; Portugal on 9 Nov. 1978; Liechtenstein on 8 Sept. 1982; Malta on 1 May 1987; San Marino on 22 March 1989; Finland on 10 May 1990; the Czech Republic on 18 March 1992; the Slovak Republic on 18 March 1992; Hungary on 11 May 1992; Bulgaria on 7 Sept. 1992; Poland on 1 May 1993; Romania on 20 June 1994; and Slovenia on 28 June 1994; four nations first accepted Art. 25 individual petition and subsequently accepted Art. 46 jurisdiction of the Court: Sweden Art. 25 on 4 Feb. 1952 and Art. 46 on 13 May 1966; Iceland Art. 25 on 29 March 1955 and Art. 46 on 3 Sept. 1958; Norway Art. 25 on 10 Dec. 1955 and Art. 46 on 30 June 1964; and Turkey Art. 25 on 28 Jan. 1987, and Art. 46

Looking at the progressive adoption of the optional clauses and the increasing case loads of the Commission and the Court, one sees distinctive tales for each of the five decades of the European Convention on Human Rights.

The 1950s spoke of institutional development but had little actual case law about which to boast. The Convention was signed in 1950 and, ratified by eight states, came into force in 1953. In 1955 the Commission was granted the right to hear individual petitions against consenting states. The Court was constituted in 1958. Only on 2 June 1956 was an application declared admissible by the Commission (by Greece against the United Kingdom respecting Cyprus).[91] Altogether only five applications (two government, three individual) were deemed admissible in the 1950s. No case was heard by the Court.[92]

The 1960s saw both modest triumph and disquieting disobedience. There were some 54 applications admitted by the Commission (five government, 49 individual). The Court rendered its first ten judgments.[93] However, in 1969, following adverse reports by the Commission, Greece withdrew from the Council of Europe and denounced the European Convention on Human Rights.[94] This reduced the total membership in the system from 16 to 15 at the end of the decade. The number of states accepting the right of individual petition had grown to eleven. The same eleven states also accepted the jurisdiction of the Court.[95]

The 1970s showed a solid maturation of the system. Greece rejoined the Convention in 1974. By the end of the decade some 20 countries belonged, 14 accepting individual petition and 17 consenting to the jurisdiction of the Court.[96] 168 applications (five government, 163 individual) were deemed admissible by the Commission.[97] The Court began to develop a meaningful jurisprudence, as it delivered 26 judgments in the decade.[98]

The 1980s witnessed an explosion of activity under the Convention. By the end of the decade, 22 of the 23 nations in the Council of Europe (all except Finland) were parties to the Convention. All 22 ratifying states had also by the end of the decade accepted the right of individual petition and had consented to the jurisdiction of the

---

on 22 Jan. 1990; five countries accepted Art. 46 first: the Netherlands Art. 46 on 31 Aug. 1954 and Art. 25 on 28 June 1960; France Art. 46 on 3 May 1974 and Art. 25 on 2 Oct. 1981; Greece Art. 46 on 30 Jan. 1979 and Art. 25 on 20 Nov. 1985; Spain Art. 46 on 15 Oct. 1979 and Art. 25 on 1 July 1981; and Cyprus, Art. 46 on 24 Jan. 1980 and Art. 25 on 1 Jan. 1989. The acceptances up to 2 Sept. 1993 are shown in Council of Europe, *Chart of Signatures and Ratifications of European Treaties: Updating as at 2 September 1993* (hereinafter cited as 'Ratifications') and updated by conversation with the Secretariat of the Commission 10 Mar. 1995.

[91] 1 *Yearbook of the European Convention on Human Rights* 128–30 (1955–1956–1957).

[92] 2 *Yearbook of the European Convention on Human Rights* (1958–1959).

[93] 'Alphabetical list of the 469 judgments delivered by the Eur Court HR (as of 23 June 1994),' 15 *Human Rights Law Journal* 116 (1994) ('hereinafter cited as 'List of Judgments').

[94] 12 *Yearbook of the European Convention on Human Rights* 78–84 (1969).

[95] *Id.* at 88–9.

[96] 22 *Yearbook of the European Convention on Human Rights* 39–44 (1979).

[97] European Commission of Human Rights, *Stock-Taking on the European Convention on Human Rights: Supplement 1986* 105–7 (1988).

[98] List of Judgments, *supra* n. 93, at 116.

Court.[99] In the 1980s some 455 applications were deemed admissible by the Commission.[100] And, most dramatically, 169 judgments were delivered by the Court, more than six times as many cases as had been decided by the Court in the previous decade.[101]

The 1990s exhibited the price of success. The system of European human rights law burst at the seams in terms of both its membership and its caseload. Finland, freed by the end of the Cold War from a rigidly 'neutral' foreign policy, adhered to the Convention in 1990, the twenty-third member state, newly non-Communist Central and East European states joined soon thereafter: Czechoslovakia (later the Czech Republic and the Slovak Republic), Hungary and Bulgaria in 1992, Poland in 1993, Romania and Slovenia in 1994, Lithuania in 1995, Estonia and Albania along with Andorra in 1996, the former Yugoslav Republic of Macedonia, Ukraine, Latvia, Moldova and Croatia in 1997, Russia in 1998, and Georgia in 1999.[102] From 'only' 22 states parties in 1989, state participation almost doubled in a decade: 41 states were parties to the European Human Rights Convention in 1999. Looking at the caseload in the 1990s, admitted applications before the Commission in the eight years between 1990 and 1997 totalled 3,491, about ten times as great as the 1980s.[103] In nine years of the decade, 1990–8, the Court delivered 818 judgments, roughly eighty times as many as in the 1960s, 30 times the 1970s, and five times the 1980s.[104] The combined pressure of new members and burgeoning caseload persuaded the Council of Europe to reform Strasbourg's legal machinery, leading to the drafting and adoption of Protocol No. 11, resulting in the merger of the Commission and the Court in November 1998.

Debate about the reform of Strasbourg's legal machinery stretched from 1982 to 1998. Documentation and discussion about the then-ongoing debate occupied a chapter of the 1995 edition of this book.[105] The results of the reform figure significantly in the text in Chapters 2 and 3 below. Whether in the long (or indeed short) run the reforms instituted by Protocol No. 11 will prove adequate in meeting the increased membership and workload in Strasbourg is still open to question. The pressures generated by Strasbourg's success continue unabated.[106]

[99] Ratifications, *supra* n. 90.

[100] Council of Europe, European Commission of Human Rights, *Survey of Activities and Statistics 1992* 18 (1993).

[101] List of Judgments, *supra* n. 93, at 116.

[102] Chart of Signatures and Ratifications, *supra* n. 2.

[103] *1997 Yearbook of the European Convention on Human Rights* 77 (1998).

[104] Council of Europe, European Court of Human Rights, *List of Judgments and Decisions 1990–1995*, www.dhcour.coe.fr (16 Dec. 1997); Council of Europe, European Court of Human Rights, *List of Judgments and Decisions 1996–1998*, www.dhcour.coe.fr (24 Feb. 1999).

[105] M. W. Janis, R. S. Kay & A. W. Bradley, 'Reform of the Commission and the Court', Chapter 4, *European Human Rights Law: Text and Materials* 88–118 (1st ed. 1995).

[106] Commentary is to be found, *inter alia*, in A. Drzemczewski, 'Protocole no. 11 à la CEDH: préparation à l'entrée en vigueur', 8 *European Journal of International Law* 59 (1997); M. W. Janis, 'Russia and the "Legality" of Strasbourg Law', 8 *European Journal of International Law* 93 (1997); P. Leuprecht, 'Innovations in the European System of Human Rights Protection: Is Englargement Compatible with Reinforcement?' 8 *Transnational Law & Contemporary Problems* 313 (1998).

2

STRASBOURG'S LEGAL MACHINERY

A. THE EUROPEAN COMMISSION OF HUMAN RIGHTS: 1953–1999

As we have seen, during the negotiation of the Convention in the Council of Europe in 1949–50, delegates expressed the opinion that it would be advisable to establish not only a European Court but also a European Commission of Human Rights. The Commission's role was originally foreseen as being protective of the judicial function. A 'commission could form a kind of barrier—a practical necessity well known to all jurists—which would weed out frivolous or mischievous petitions'.[1] It was also intended that the Commission facilitate suits against states by private parties, perceived as a vital element in the system's efficacy:

If the Court is to carry out its work effectively in every case of a violation of human rights or fundamental freedoms, access to the Court must be available not only to the States, but also, after an opinion has been rendered by a Committee of the Council, to individuals and corporate bodies, thereby differing from the timid provisions of the Statute of The Hague Court.[2]

So, from its very beginnings, the Commission was blessed and cursed with an intermediate position in the system of European human rights law. On the one side, the Commission was meant to shield the Court from a possible deluge of individual complaints, a function that also protected the traditional sovereignty of the member states. On the other side, the Commission was meant to serve as an international institution directly accessible to individuals, a radical departure from traditional state-centered international legal process. Fashioned and acting in compromise, the Commission stood as an intermediary both between individuals and governments, and between individuals and the Strasbourg Court.

What was Article 19 of the European Convention on Human Rights set up the European Commission of Human Rights alongside the European Court of Human Rights, both explicitly required to 'ensure the observance of the engagements

---

[1] Council of Europe, *Collected Edition of the Travaux Préparatoires*, at 48 (1975); speech by Teitgen to the Consultative Assembly, 19 Aug. 1949.
[2] *Id.* at 74; speech by Dominedo to the Consultative Assembly, 19 Aug. 1949.

undertaken by the High Contracting Parties in the present Convention'.[3] The members of the Commission, equal in number to the number of parties to the Convention, were elected by the Council of Europe's Committee of Ministers from slates drawn up by the Consultative Assembly to serve six year renewable terms. The Commission met in Strasbourg ordinarily for periodic two-week sessions. For example, in 1992, with the press of considerable business, the Commission held eight sessions, meeting altogether for 16 weeks.[4] Though meant to be part-time, the Commission usually took up half or more of the time of an individual's employment. Many of the Commissioners were law professors whose universities released them for their work in Strasbourg (for which they were only partly compensated);[5] others were already retired from government, judicial or university employment. The Commission was assisted by a full-time and fully salaried Secretariat in Strasbourg, numbering in 1993, about 95 persons of whom about 40 were lawyers.[6]

Complaints about violations of the human rights protected by the Convention were sent first to the Commission. Pursuant to old Article 24 of the Convention, states could refer to the Commission 'any alleged breach of the provisions of the Convention by another High Contracting Party'.[7] The Commission, which became competent to entertain Article 24 inter-state cases in 1953, heard its first such cases in 1955. These involved suits, brought by Greece against the United Kingdom, complaining about British administration of Cyprus, which were eventually settled in 1959.[8]

It should be noted that old Article 24 of the Convention was more generous to state suitors than is the comparable provision of the Statute of the International Court of Justice. Article 24 permitted any contracting state to complain about the conduct of any other contracting state, regardless of the nationality of the injured individual. Hence, there was no requirement, as imposed by the International Court that a private party only be protected by that person's own national state.[9] So, as proved important in practice, individuals were protected by foreign states even against their own government.

Furthermore and radically dissimilar from Article 34 of the ICJ Statute, which provides that '[o]nly States may be parties in cases before the Court', the European Convention provided that a state might agree to permit private parties themselves to

---

[3] European Convention for the Protection of Human Rights and Fundamental Freedoms, 213 U. N. T. S. 221, E.T.S. 5, U. K. T. S. 71 (1953) signed at Rome 4 Nov. 1950; entered into force 3 Sept. 1953, Council of Europe print of Jan. 1994 (hereinafter cited as 'Old Convention'), art. 19.

[4] European Commission of Human Rights, *Survey of Activities and Statistics: 1992* 1.

[5] S. Trechsel, 'Towards the Merger of the Supervisory Organs: Seeking a Way Out of the Deadlock', 8 *Human Rights Law Journal* 11, 16–17 (1987).

[6] P. van Dijk & G. J. H. van Hoof, *Theory and Practice of the European Convention on Human Rights* 23 (2nd edn. 1990); numbers up-dated in conversations with the Commission Secretariat, April 1993.

[7] Old Convention, *supra* n. 3.

[8] 1 *Yearbook of the European Convention on Human Rights* 128–30 (1955–57); 2 *Yearbook of the European Convention on Human Rights* 178–86 (1958–59).

[9] The ICJ has so held both for individuals and for corporations. *See* the *Nottebohm Case*, 1955 I.C.J. Reports 4, 26, and the *Barcelona Traction Case*, 1970 I.C.J. Reports 4, 46.

petition the Commission for relief. This vital aspect of European human rights law was first to be found in old Article 25:

The Commission may receive petitions addressed to the Secretary General of the Council of Europe from any person, non-governmental organization or group of individuals claiming to be the victim of a violation by one of the High Contracting Parties of the rights set forth in this Convention, provided that the High Contracting Party against which the complaint has been lodged has declared that it recognizes the competence of the Commission to receive such petitions. Those of the High Contracting Parties who have made such a declaration undertake not to hinder in any way the effective exercise of this right.[10]

The Commission became legally competent to receive individual petitions pursuant to Article 25 in 1955.[11] By 28 July 1994, all 30 of the states then party to the Convention had agreed to recognize the admissibility of private petitions, ordinarily called 'applications' in the practice of the Commission.[12] The Commission's three principal functions—filtering complaints through admissibility proceedings, mediating disputes through the process called friendly settlement, and fact-finding and reporting on admitted but unsettled disputes—have all been absorbed since 1999 by the reformed European Court of Human Rights.

Until the recent merger of the Commission and the Court, a case already heard and reported upon by the Commission was referred by the Commission or a concerned state for the consideration of the European Court of Human Rights, which had and has the power to issue a binding legal decision; if a case was not referred to the Court within three months of referral of the Commission's report to the Committee of Ministers of the Council of Europe, then the Committee of Ministers had been entitled by a two-thirds vote, to decide that there was a violation of the Convention.[13] If no such majority was forthcoming, the Committee of Ministers simply decided to take no action. Before the Court became particularly active, the Commission left important cases, such as the *Greek Case* discussed below, to the Committee of Ministers. Thereafter, the Commission usually only turned to the Committee of Ministers, a political body made up of the foreign ministers of the member states represented by permanent delegates in Strasbourg, when the majority of the Commission felt there had been no breach of the Convention or when it felt that the case needed the special political influence of the Committee of Ministers.[14]

---

[10] Old Convention, *supra* n. 3, art. 25(1).

[11] European Commission of Human Rights, *Stock-Taking on the European Convention on Human Rights: The First Thirty Years: 1954 until 1984* 1 (1984) (hereinafter cited as 'Stock-Taking').

[12] 'European Convention on Human Rights and Additional Protocols: Chart of Signatures and Ratifications as of 28 July 1994'. 15 *Human Rights Law Journal* 114–15 (1994); J. E. S. Fawcett, *The Application of the European Convention on Human Rights* 346 (2nd edn. 1987).

[13] Old Convention, *supra* n. 3, arts. 32(1), 48, 52, 53.

[14] Beddard, *Human Rights and Europe* 57–9 (3rd edn. 1993); A. H. Robertson & J. G. Merrills, *Human Rights in Europe: A Study of the European Convention on Human Rights* 301 (3rd edn. 1993).

B. STRASBOURG'S PRE-JUDGMENT
FUNCTIONS

Strasbourg's legal machinery serves four rather discrete functions. First, it filters out complaints; most submissions are deemed not admissible. Secondly, it mediates disputes, striving to reach friendly settlements between complainants and governments. Thirdly, it conducts fact-finding. Fourthly, if a complaint has been admitted, if the dispute can not be compromised, and once all necessary facts have been found, the European Court of Human Rights adjudicates the case, rendering a binding legal judgment. The first three Strasbourg functions—admissibility, friendly settlement, and fact-finding—are addressed here in Chapter 2. The fourth function— adjudication—is explored procedurally and in terms of efficacy in Chapter 3, and substantively in Chapters 4, 5, 6, 7, and 8.

1. STRASBOURG AS FILTER

A. ADMISSIBILITY

In 1960, noting that 710 of the first 713 individual applications submitted to the Commission had been declared inadmissible, one commentator remarked that cases 'denying the individual further hearing before an international tribunal, form by far the most significant part of the jurisprudence of the Commission'.[15] Moreover, many petitions never reached the members of the Commission for a formal decision on admissibility, but were screened out prior to registration by the lawyers in the Commission's Secretariat in Strasbourg.

Hans Christian Krüger, formerly the Secretary to the European Commission of Human Rights, has described the formal structure of the Secretariat's pre-Commission screening-out process:

[R]egistration may be refused, on the instructions of the President where the claim is wholly and totally outside the competence of the Commission, or where the applicant himself refuses to provide the information which is necessary for the adjudication of the matter under the Convention and which he is clearly able to provide.[16]

Professor Michael Reisman has observed:

Nor should we be formalistic in identifying the role players. One cannot ignore, in bureaucracies such as those of the European rights system, the critical role of permanent clerks and administra-

---

[15] Weil, 'Decisions on Inadmissible Applications by the European Commission of Human Rights' 54 *American Journal of International Law* 874 (1960).

[16] H. C. Krüger, 'The European Commission of Human Rights' 1 *Human Rights Law Journal* 66, 72 (1980).

tive officials, those faceless bureaucrats who may sometimes play determinative roles by their characterization of claims, formulation of issues, and advice.[17]

The importance of the bureaucracy of the European human rights system is well illustrated by some statistics. In 1983, though the Commission opened some 3,150 provisional files, it formally registered only 499 applications, dismissed 407 applications and finally declared merely 29 applications admissible.[18] By 1989, the number of provisional files had grown to 4,900, while the number of registered applications reached 1,445; the cases declared inadmissible or struck off the list were 1,243 and those declared admissible were in total 95.[19] Between 1973 and 1985, about 80 per cent of all complaints were handled by the Secretariat without going to the Commission.[20]

In its first 43 years from 1955 to 1997, the Commission registered some 39,047 applications,[21] of which only 13 came from states,[22] the balance being submitted by individuals, and declared some 4,161 applications admissible.[23] In 1997, among the 4,750 applications registered that year more than half were against five states: 833 against Italy, 558 against France, 451 against the United Kingdom, 383 against Germany, and 365 against Turkey.[24]

Since the implementation of Protocol No. 11 and the institution of the new European Court of Human Rights on 1 November 1998, admissibility proceedings have become the province of the Court itself.[25] Complaints are now sent in the first instance, not to the Commission, but directly to the Court. For inter-state cases, new Article 33 of the Convention replaces old Article 24 and reads: '[a]ny High Contracting Party may refer to the Court any alleged breach of the provisions of the Convention and the protocols thereto by another High Contracting Party'.[26] For individual applications, besides newly providing for direct reference to the Court, new Article 34 also makes jurisdiction over private suits, what was the province of old Article 25, mandatory for all states parties to the Convention: '[t]he Court may receive applications, from any person, non-governmental organisation or group of individuals claiming to be the victim of a violation by one of the High Contracting Parties of the rights set forth in the Convention or the Protocols thereto. The High Contracting Parties undertake not to hinder in any way the effective exercise of this right.'[27]

---

[17] M. Reisman, 'Book Review' 77 *American Journal of International Law* 345, 346 (1983).

[18] Stock-Taking, *supra* n. 11, at 312.

[19] 1989 *Yearbook of the European Convention on Human Rights* 19 (1993).

[20] Fribergh, 'The Commission Secretariat's Handling of Provisional Files', *Protecting Human Rights: The European Dimension* 181 (eds. Matscher & Petzold 2nd edn. 1990).

[21] 1997 *Yearbook of the European Convention on Human Rights* 76 (1998).

[22] *Id.* at 79.

[23] *Id.* at 77.

[24] *Id.* at 78.

[25] Council of Europe, Convention for Protection of Human Rights and Fundamental Freedoms (ETS No. 5), signed at Rome, 4 Nov. 1950, entered into force 3 Sept. 1953, as amended by Protocol No. 11 (ETS no. 155), signed at Strasbourg, 11 May 1994, entered into force 1 Nov. 1998, www.coe.fr (2 Feb. 1999) (hereinafter cited as 'Convention').

[26] *Id.* Art. 33.

[27] *Id.* Art. 34.

Respecting individual applications, Article 28 of the new Convention provides that a committee of three members of the Court[28] may, by a unanimous vote declare inadmissible an application or strike out of its list of cases an application submitted under Article 34 where such a decision can be taken without further examination. The decision shall be final.'[29] If no decision is made by a Committee that a private claim is inadmissible, for example, if a three-judge Committee either favours admission of an individual application or if there is a dissent on a vote of inadmissibility, then the decision on admissibility is made by a chamber of seven judges; this chamber may also decide on the merits of the individual claim, ordinarily in a subsequent decision.[30] Seven-judge chambers, not three-judge Committees, always decide on the admissibilty of state versus state cases.[31]

New Article 35 of the Convention deals with admissibility criteria in much the same language as old Article 27. The first admissibility criterion applies to both inter-state and individual applications: '[t]he Court may only deal with the matter after all domestic remedies have been exhausted, according to the generally recognised rules of international law, and within a period of six months from the date on which the final decision was taken'.[32] Non-exhaustion of domestic remedies is the theme of the first case, *Spencer v. United Kingdom*, explored below. Several other criteria apply only to individual applications: the claim must not be anonymous[33] nor can it be 'substantially the same as a matter that has already been examined by the Court or has already been submitted to another procedure of international investigation or settlement and contains no relevant new information'.[34] Moreover, the Court has the power to 'declare inadmissible any individual application submitted under Article 34 which it considers incompatible with the provisions of the Convention or the protocols thereto, manifestly ill-founded, or an abuse of the right of application'.[35] The second case below, *X v. Iceland*, is an example of an inadmissibility decision based on the grounds that the application was 'manifestly ill-founded'.

B. EARL SPENCER'S CASE

Spencer v. United Kingdom
Applications Nos. 28851/95 and 28852/95
Decision of the Commission of 16 January 1998
92–A Decisions and Reports of the European
Commission of Human Rights 56–75 (March 1998)

---

[28] *Id.* Art. 27.
[29] *Id.* Art. 28.
[30] *Id.* Art. 29(1),(3).
[31] *Id.* Art. 29(2).
[32] *Id.* Art. 35(1).
[33] *Id.* Art. 35(2)(a).
[34] *Id.* Art. 35(2)(b).
[35] *Id.* Art. 35(3).

The facts

The application was introduced by the ninth Earl of Spencer (who is the brother of the late Diana Spencer, former Princess of Wales) and by his wife. The first applicant is a British citizen, born in 1964, and he has a permanent address in Northampton. The second applicant is a British citizen, was born in 1965 and has an address in South Africa. The applicants are represented before the Commission by Mr Simon Ekins, a solicitor practising in London.

A. Particular circumstances of the case

The facts of the case, as submitted by the parties, may be summarised as follows.

On 2 April 1995 the *News of the World*, a mass circulation newspaper, published an article entitled 'Di's sister-in-law in booze and bulimia clinic'. This article extended from the front page to the following two pages of that newspaper and reported the second applicant's admittance to a private clinic for treatment for an eating disorder and for alcoholism. It went into considerable detail on the applicants' personal and family problems and incidents (including the applicants' relationship, the second applicant's unhappiness about living on the large family estate inherited by the first applicant and the first applicant's alleged affair shortly after their marriage). Close friends of the applicants were referred to as sources. The article was accompanied by a photograph of the second applicant taken with a telephoto lens while she walked in the grounds of the private clinic, which photograph was captioned 'So thin: Victoria walks in the clinic grounds this week'.

On 2 April 1995 *The People*, also a mass circulation newspaper, published an article about the applicants in two parts. The first part was entitled 'Di's sister in therapy clinic . . . exclusive' and also referred to the second applicant's admission to a private clinic for treatment for an eating disorder. The second part covered two pages, was entitled 'Dorm for Di's sister-in-law as she fights slimming disease' and detailed the state of the second applicant's health and the treatment regime at the clinic, and made reference to the amount of telephone calls made by the first applicant to the second applicant at the beginning of her stay at the clinic.

On the same day the *Sunday Mirror* (also a mass circulation newspaper) published an article entitled 'Althorp wife in clinic — Di's sister-in-law in addiction clinic'. This article announced that the 'long suffering' second applicant was being treated at a private clinic for a slimming disease and referred to the effect of the illness on the applicants' marriage and noted that it was also believed that the second applicant was receiving treatment for a drink problem.

Later on 2 April 1995 the first applicant issued a statement confirming the second applicant's admission to the clinic. He condemned the intrusion into the second applicant's personal affairs, asserted that the second applicant was a private individual and stated that he could see no justification for the publication of the story. He argued that if anybody needed privacy and freedom from harassment it was a person suffering from psychological disorders.

A response by the associate editor of the *News of the World* to that statement of the first applicant was reported in that newspaper on 14 May 1995. That editor argued that the first applicant was a public figure by birth, was no stranger to publicity, and had on many occasions encouraged media interest in his home and family in return for fees. As regards the second applicant's health, the associate editor referred to a report dated August 1993 in a magazine on the second applicant's attendance as a guest of honour at a charity evening in aid of the Eating Disorders Association where she had allegedly confirmed to the magazine journalist that she had suffered from such a disorder for many years. He also referred to an interview with the first applicant published in the *Daily Mail* on 5 August 1993 about the family estate, where the first applicant had revealed that the second applicant worked as a volunteer part-time at a hospital for young girls suffering from anorexia, which illness had plagued the second applicant's teenage years.

On 3 April 1995 the *Daily Mirror*, also a mass circulation newspaper, published a number of articles entitled 'Vicky's bravest battle'. The articles referred, *inter alia*, to the second applicant's admission to the clinic, to her illnesses, to the usual causes and symptoms of such illnesses, and to the alleged rift between the applicants which dated back, according to the article, to the first applicant's alleged affair shortly after their marriage. The applicants' friends were referred to as sources. A photograph of the second applicant, similar to that published by the *News of the World*, accompanied this article and was captioned 'Courageous Victoria strolls in the grounds of the clinic where she is trying to battle her way back to health'.

All of the articles were published and the photographs of the second applicant in the clinic were taken and published without the applicants' prior knowledge or consent.

On 3 April 1995 the first applicant complained about the *News of the World*, *The People* and the *Daily Mirror* to the Press Complaints Committee (PCC), claiming breaches of certain provisions of the Code of Practice relating to privacy (clause 4 of the Code of Practice), activities of journalists in hospitals and other similar institutions (clause 6) and harassment (clause 8).

Further to this complaint to the PCC, the *News of the World* printed an article entitled 'hypocrisy of the arrogant Earl Spencer' on 9 April 1995. The article alleged that the first applicant had seized every opportunity to put himself in the public eye. It claimed that the first applicant had received £250,000 in October 1992 from a magazine for an interview with the applicants at the family estate which resulted in a nineteen-page article. The article also stated that approximately two years later the same magazine was invited to a maternity hospital on the occasion of the birth of the applicants' fourth child. The article went on to point out that the first applicant had admitted having had an affair in interviews with journalists. The article contested the claim made by the first applicant before the PCC and stated that the relevant photograph was published after careful consideration, as the paper knew that it could be in breach of the Code of Practice.

The paper went on as follows:

'If it caused offence or distress to Lady Spencer, we apologise to her. But one reason we carried it was to prove our story was true. For Earl Spencer has a rather disturbing tendency to lie through the back of his teeth when the press he so loves to manipulate uncover less than complimentary stories against him.'

The PCC concluded that the *News of the World* had breached the Code of Practice. In the absence of a public interest justification, the PCC did not accept that the publication of a photograph 'taken with a telephoto lens of a indisputably unwell person walking in the private secluded grounds of an addiction clinic' could be anything other than a breach of the Code. The PCC considered that, while the first applicant's past relationship with the press may have affected the extent to which he was entitled to privacy in relation to particular aspects of his own life, this did not leave the press free to comment on any matter concerning the second applicant. The PCC did not accept that the second applicant had opened her illness to public scrutiny.

The *Daily Mirror* agreed to publish an apology prior to the determination of the PCC and therefore the PCC ruled that the complaint against that newspaper had been resolved. The apology of the *Daily Mirror* was published on 11 April 1995, was addressed to both applicants, and related to the publication of the photograph of the second applicant.

As regards the article in *The People*, the PCC considered that matters of health fell within the ambit of an individual's private life and that the intrusion into the second applicant's private life was not justified. The PCC considered that while the first applicant's past relationship with the press may have affected the extent to which he was entitled to privacy in relation to particular aspects of his won life, this did not leave the press free to report on any matter concerning the second applicant, particularly on the second applicant's health and psychological well-being. The PCC did not accept that the second applicant had opened her illness to public scrutiny and concluded that *The People* newspaper had breached the Code of Practice.

On 14 May 1995 the *News of the World* published the adjudication of the PCC against that newspaper together with an apology. That apology was addressed to the second applicant and related to both the article and the relevant photograph. *The People* newspaper also published the adjudication and an apology, which apology was addressed to both applicants.

On 17 May 1995 the applicants' solicitors wrote two separate letters to two former friends of the applicants, threatening breach of confidence proceedings for an injunction and the pursuit of a 'financial claim' and requesting an undertaking regarding further disclosures in order to avoid an injunction hearing. The applicants' solicitors noted that the 'grossest example' of their breach of confidence had resulted in the *News of the World* article of 2 April 1995—one of the friends had passed on a private letter from the second applicant to the press, which letter contained information about the state of her health, and both friends had also leaked related information.

. . .

[The applicants sued their former friends. This case was settled on 4 June 1995, the applicants obtaining an injunction restraining their former friends from disclosing information about the applicants' private life to the media.]

B. Relevant domestic law and practice

1. Relevant case-law

There is no law of privacy, as such, in England and Wales (*Kaye v. Robertson* [1991] FSR 62, Glidewell LJ at p. 66).

A remedy of breach of confidence exists. It is made up of three essential elements: the information itself must have 'the necessary quality of confidence about it,' the information 'must have been imparted in circumstances importing an obligation of confidence' and there must have been an 'unauthorised use of that information to the detriment of the party communicating it' (*Coco v. A.N. Clark Engineers Ltd.* [1969] RPC 41, at 47).

. . .

[The relevant case law was reviewed by the Commission.]

2. The Press Complaints Committee (PCC)

This is a non-statutory body which was set up by the newspaper industry for the purposes of self-regulation. It commenced functioning in 1991. It is charged with the enforcement of a Code of Practice which was drafted by the newspaper industry's Committee and approved by the PCC in June 1993. The Code of Practice states that members of the press have a duty to maintain the highest professional and ethical standards and that in doing so they should have regard to the provisions of the Code of Practice. The Code of Practice includes provisions in relation to privacy (clause 4), activities of journalists at hospitals or similar institutions (clause 6), harassment and intimidation of subjects (clause 8) and in relation to certain public interest exceptions (clause 18).

If a newspaper has been found to be in breach of the Code of Practice, the newspaper is bound by the Code to print the adjudication by the PCC in full and with due prominence. However, the PCC has no legal power to prevent publication of material, to enforce its rulings, or to grant any legal remedy against the newspaper in favour of the victim.

Complaints

The first applicant submits that the United Kingdom has failed to comply with its obligations under the Convention to protect his right to respect for his private life in that it has failed to prohibit the publication and dissemination of information relating to his private affairs and to provide a legal remedy whereby he could have prevented such action or claimed damages thereafter for the loss and distress caused.

The second applicant refers to the taking of photographs with a telephoto lens without her knowledge or consent while she was on the private grounds of a clinic where she was obtaining treatment. She also argues that the United Kingdom has failed to effectively protect her private life in that it has failed to prohibit the taking, sale, publication and further publication of such photographs and to provide a legal remedy whereby she could have prevented such action or claimed damages thereafter for the loss and distress caused.

The applicants invoke Articles 8 and 13 of the Convention.

Proceedings before the commission

The applications were introduced on 28 September 1995 and were registered on 5 October 1995.

On 2 September 1996 the Commission decided to join the applications and to communicate the applications to the respondent Government and invite them to submit written observations on the admissibility and merits of the cases.

The Government's observations were received on 23 December 1996 after one extension of the time-limit fixed for that purpose. The applicants' observations were received on 7 April 1997 after two extensions of the time-limit fixed for that purpose.

On 20 October 1997 the Commission decided to hold a hearing on the admissibility and merits of the applications and requested further observations on certain matters. The Government's further observations were received on 23 December 1997 and those of the applicants were received on 6 January 1998.

The hearing was held on 16 January 1998. The Government were represented by Mr Iain Christie, Agent, Foreign and Commonwealth Office and Mr James Eadie, Counsel, together with Mr Paul Jenkins and Mr Philip Stevens as advisers. The applicants were represented by Mr Michael Briggs Q.C., Counsel, Mr Jason Coppel, Counsel, and by Mr Simon Ekins, Solicitor.

The law

The applicants complain about a failure by the United Kingdom to fulfil its obligations under the Convention to protect their right to respect for their private lives in that it has failed to prohibit the publication and re-publication of information (photographs in the case of the second applicant) relating to their private affairs or to provide a legal remedy whereby they could have prevented such publication or claimed damages thereafter for the distress caused. They invoke Articles 8 and 13 of the Convention.

1. Article 8 of the Convention, in so far as relevant, reads as follows:

> '1. Everyone has the right to respect for his private life.
> 2. There shall be no interference by a public authority with the exercise of this right except such as is in accordance with the law and is necessary in a democratic society for the protection of the rights and freedoms of others.'

. . .

The applicants essentially submit that the Government are under a positive obligation to provide effective protection for the rights guaranteed by the Convention. Given the terms of Article 10 of the Convention, the absence of an effective domestic remedy as regards invasions of privacy by the press constitutes a failure effectively to respect their right to respect for their private lives as guaranteed by Article 8 of the Convention.

The Government argue that the domestic system as a whole (including remedies in breach of confidence and against trespass, nuisance, harassment and malicious falsehood, together with the Press Complaints Commission) provides adequate protection to individuals and an appropriate balance between the often competing rights guaranteed by Articles 8 and 10 of the Convention.

The Commission recalls that the obligation to secure the effective exercise of Convention rights imposed by Article 1 of the Convention may involve positive obligations on a State and that these obligations may involve the adoption of measures even in the sphere of relations between individuals (Eur. Court HR, *Plattform 'Ärzte für das Leben' v. Austria* judgment of 21 June 1988, Series A no. 139, p. 12, para. 32).

On the facts as presented by the parties, the Commission would not exclude that the absence of an actionable remedy in relation to the publications of which the applicants complain could show a lack of respect for their private lives. It has regard in this respect to the duties and responsibilities that are carried with the right of freedom of expression guaranteed by Article 10 of the Convention and to Contracting States' obligation to provide a measure of protection to the right of privacy of an individual affected by others' exercise of their freedom of expression (see, *mutatis mutandis*, No. 10871/84, Dec. 10.7.86, D.R. 48, p. 154, and No. 31477/96, Dec. 15.1.97, unpublished).

However, the Government's principal argument is that the failure of the applicants to pursue a breach of confidence action against, *inter alia*, the relevant newspapers amounts to non-exhaustion of domestic remedies within the meaning of Article 26 of the Convention. It is not disputed that the three essential elements of a breach of confidence action are those outlined by Megarry J in *Coco v. Clark Engineers* (*loc. cit.*).

. . .

The applicants submit that the breach of confidence action is in law and practice an ineffective remedy for the invasion of an individual's private life by the media.

. . .

The Commission recalls that Article 26 of the Convention reflects the position that States are dispensed from answering before an international body for their acts before they have had an opportunity to put matters right through their own legal system. In this regard, the provisions of Article 26 represent an important aspect of the principle that the machinery of protection established by the Convention is subsidiary to the national systems safeguarding human rights (Eur. Court HR, *Akdivar v. Turkey* judgment of 16 September 1996, Reports of Judgments and Decisions 1996–IV, p. 15, para. 65).

As to the requirements of Article 26 of the Convention, the Commission recalls that the applicants are only required to exhaust such remedies which relate to the breaches of the Convention alleged and which provide effective and sufficient redress. The applicants do not need to exercise a remedy which, although theoretically of a nature to constitute a remedy, does not in reality offer any chance of redressing the alleged breach (No. 9248/81, Dec. 10.10.83, D.R. 34, p. 78). Accordingly, the Government must establish that the remedy in question was accessible, was one capable of providing redress in respect of the applicants' complaints and offered reasonable prospects of success. Once this burden has been discharged, it falls to the applicants to establish that the remedy advanced by the Government was, *inter alia*, for some reason inadequate and ineffective or that there were special circumstances absolving them from the requirement of exhaustion of domestic remedies (Eur. Court HR, *Akdivar v. Turkey* judgment, loc. cit., p. 16, para. 68). It has not been argued and the Commission does not consider that the applications give rise to any special circumstances which would absolve the applicants from exhausting domestic remedies.

Moreover, where there is doubt as to the prospects of success in a particular case it should be submitted to the domestic courts for resolution. This is particularly so in a common law system since, where the courts extend and develop principles through case-law, it is generally incumbent on an aggrieved individual to allow the domestic courts the opportunity to develop existing rights by way of interpretation (No. 20357/92, Dec. 7.3.94, D.R. 76-A, pp. 80, 88).

. . .

The second main area of dispute between the parties relates to the remedies available on establishing a breach of confidence. The Commission accepts that the applicants have raised some doubt as to the availability of damages for breach of confidence where an injunction could not have been granted. Pursuant to Lord Cairns' Act 1858, it appears that damages are confined to a case where an injunction could have been granted but, for some reason, was not and that where publication has already taken place an injunction could not have been granted.

However, the Commission notes the judgment of Lord Goff in the Spycatcher case (a House of Lords judgment handed down more than ten years after the *Malone* case in the High Court). It considers that, at the very least, the extract quoted above (from p. 286 of that judgment) shows the developing state of the law relating to the award of damages. In any event, it is not disputed that an account of profits arises irrespective of the grant of an injunction. As regards the award of an account of profits where the publication has already taken place, the Commission notes that an account of profits was ordered against *The Sunday Times* in the Spycatcher case in relation to publications which had already taken place. Moreover, in light of Mr Justice Jacob's comments (albeit in the context of breach of copyright) in the Barrymore case (loc. cit.), the award of an account of profits in the Spycatcher case where the relevant articles were published along with numerous others and in view of the extensive nature of the coverage in the relevant newspapers on 2 April 1995, the Commission does not find the applicants' submissions as regards the difficulties in calculating the relevant profits sufficient to warrant a conclusion as to the ineffective nature in Convention terms of an order of an account of profits.

. . .

Finally, the Commission recalls the view expressed in the *Winer* case (No. 10871/84, Dec. 10.7.86, D.R. 48, pp. 154, 170) that the failure to take a breach of confidence action did not constitute a failure to exhaust domestic remedies in view of the uncertainty as to the precise scope and extent of that remedy. The Commission notes that, contrary to the position in the Winer case, the majority of the submissions in the present cases, both written and oral, focused on the scope and extent of that remedy. Based for the most part on judicial authorities dated after the Winer case (the more relevant of which are cited above and which include an important House of Lords judgment of 1990), the parties in the present cases were in a position to describe in detail the essential elements and application in practice of the breach of confidence remedy. Indeed, the Commission considers the extensive and detailed nature of the submissions, of itself, indicates that there has been significant clarification of the scope and extent of a breach of confidence action.

The Commission therefore considers that the parties' submissions in the present cases do not demonstrate the same level of uncertainty as to the remedy of breach of confidence which prevailed at the time of the Winer decision of the Commission, the domestic courts having extended and developed certain relevant principles through their case-law by interpretation (No. 20357/92, Dec. 7.3.94, loc. cit.).

Accordingly, the Commission considers that the parties' submissions indicate that the remedy of breach of confidence (against the newspapers and their sources) was available to the applicants and that the applicants have not demonstrated that it was insufficient or ineffective in the circumstances of their cases. It considers that, in so far as relevant doubts remain concerning the financial awards to be made following a finding of a breach of confidence, they are not such as to warrant a conclusion that the breach of confidence action is ineffective or insufficient but rather a conclusion that the matter should be put to the domestic courts for consideration in order to allow those courts, through the common law system in the United Kingdom, the opportunity to develop existing rights by way of interpretation.

In such circumstances, the Commission considers that the applicants' complaints under Article 8 of the Convention are inadmissible under Article 27 para. 3 of the Convention on the basis that the applicants have not exhausted domestic remedies within the meaning of Article 26 of the Convention.

2. Article 13 of the Convention provides as follows:

'Everyone whose rights and freedoms as set forth in this Convention are violated shall have an effective remedy before a national authority notwithstanding that the violation has been committed by persons acting in an official capacity.'

The Commission notes that it has rejected the applicants' substantive complaints under Article 8 of the Convention on the basis that they have failed to comply with the exhaustion of domestic remedies requirement under Article 26 of the Convention. In such circumstances, the Commission finds their complaints under Article 13 of the Convention must be rejected as manifestly ill-founded within the meaning of Article 27 para. 2 of the Convention.

For these reasons, the Commission, by a majority,

DECLARES THE APPLICATIONS INADMISSIBLE.

C. EXHAUSTION OF DOMESTIC REMEDIES

Article 35(1) of the new Convention requires that '[t]he Court may only deal with the matter after all domestic remedies have been exhausted, according to the generally recognized rules of international law, and within a period of six months from the date on which the final decision was taken',[36] wording identical to that of Article 26 of the old Convention, except that there the Commission rather than the Court is mentioned.[37] This 'generally recognized rule of international law' is stated in many places; the 1992 Jennings and Watts ninth edition of Oppenheim's classic international law text, for example, reads: '[i]t is a recognized rule that, where a state has treated an alien in its territory inconsistently with its international obligations but could nevertheless by subsequent action still secure for the alien the treatment (or its equivalent) required by its obligations, an international tribunal will not entertain a claim put forward on behalf of that person unless he has exhausted the legal remedies available to him in the state concerned'.[38] The exhaustion of local remedies rule respects state sovereignty in that it gives a state itself an opportunity to redress an international wrong done to an individual before allowing the intervention of another state or of an international tribunal.[39]

Traditional international legal rules of exhaustion of local remedies, largely to be found in customary international law, focus on the rights of states to protect their nationals *vis-à-vis* foreign states. The exhaustion of local remedies rule in European human rights law differs, of course, from traditional rules in that it is set black-letter in a treaty. Moreover, the European human rights rule looks to individuals, as well as to states, as subjects of international law. As one commentator has noted: '[t]he individual is under the Convention protected *qua* individual, not as a national of any State but as a human being'.[40] Furthermore, the European rule has been subject to careful and continuous elaboration by the Strasbourg Commission and Court, yielding a complex and technical context in which to evaluate whether local remedies have

---

[36] Convention, *supra* n. 25, Art. 35 (1).

[37] Old Convention, *supra* n. 3, Art. 26.

[38] 1 *Oppenheim's International Law,* 522–523 (Jennings & Watts (eds.), 9th ed. 1992).

[39] G. Schwarzenberger, 1 *International Law,* 602–604 (3rd ed. 1957).

[40] A. Trindade, *The Application of the Rule of Exhaustion of Local Remedies in International Law: Its Rationale in the International Protection of Individual Rights* 15 (1983).

been exhausted or not. Key to the Strasbourg jurisprudence is answering the question whether in any given case it is the individual applicant or the respondent state that has the burden of proof respecting the exhaustion of local remedies.[41] In *Earl Spencer's Case* is it the applicant or the state who is assigned this burden or is the burden really shared, the Court indulging, at the end of the day, with something of a weighing of the possibility of success for the applicant in the English legal system?

Earl Spencer's Case, like the *Sunday Times Case* that we explore in Chapter 3, had the advantage of broadly publicizing the Strasbourg human rights system. *Sunday Times* involved a judgment of the Court, but *Earl Spencer's Case* was 'merely' an admissibility decision by the Commission. Even so, the admissibility decision and an explanation of how the Strasbourg system works was widely reported in the United Kingdom, e.g., by *The Daily Telegraph*,[42] *The Guardian*,[43] *The Independent*,[44] *The Scotsman*,[45] and *The Times*.[46] As we discuss in Chapters 1 and 3, it is just this kind of publicity that helps cement the Strasbourg system into place as a 'legitimate' form of law and legal process.

It may be that Earl Spencer's complaint will be addressed by the incorporation of the European Human Rights Convention into the law of the United Kingdom. Some have suggested that incorporation of the Convention will introduce a right of privacy into British law by the 'back door'.[47]

D. THE ICELANDIC ELECTORAL SYSTEM CASE

X v. Iceland
Application No. 8941/80
Decision of the Commission of 8 December 1981
27 Decisions and Reports of the European
Commission of Human Rights 145–151 (Sept. 1982)

This application concerns the present Icelandic Electoral System . . .

Pursuant to this system the country is divided into 8 constituencies different in size and population, electing a total of 60 deputies to the Icelandic National Assembly (Althingi).

Forty nine of these deputies are chosen by direct elections in the 8 constituencies for proportional representation. The remaining 11 are allotted to the political parties which have seats in Parliament, in an endeavour to even out between the parties the number of deputies as compared to the total votes cast for each party . . .

---

[41] C. Amersinghe, *Local Remedies in International Law* 291–296 (1990).

[42] 17 Jan. 1998, at 2.

[43] 17 Jan. 1998, at 2.

[44] 17 Jan. 1998, at 7.

[45] 17 Jan. 1998, at 2.

[46] 17 Jan. 1998, Home News.

[47] C. P. Carnegie, 'Privacy and the Press: The Impact of Incorporating the European Convention on Human Rights in the United Kingdom,' 9 *Duke Journal of Comparative & International Law* 311 (1998). See Appendix C *infra* for the Human Rights Act itself.

[The Commission describes the Icelandic electoral system, making clear that the system favors the rural districts. This part of the Report concludes:]

If, however, the 60 deputies had been apportioned to the various constituencies on the basis of ordinary mathematical equality, the results would have been as follows:

	Votes	Deputies now	Deputies there ought to be
Reykjavik	56,402	15	24
Reykjanes	29,510	7	12
Vesturland	8,679	6	4
Vestfirdir	6,150	6	3
Nordurland West	6,560	6	3
Nordurland East	15,324	7	6
Austurland	7,683	6	3
Sudurland	11,765	7	5
	142,073	60	60

The applicant believes majority rule to be the cornerstone of democracy and the principle of equal votes, one man/one vote, to be a condition without which the principle of majority rule would be meaningless.

But to rectify this injustice in the Icelandic Electoral System, it would be necessary to make yet another amendment to the constitution.

The machinery set up in the Constitution of 1944 for bringing about amendments calls for a majority vote in favour of an amendment by the Assembly in session, its subsequent dissolution and new election (held under the existing electoral laws), and then a majority vote in the new Assembly in favour of the amendments proposed in the old Assembly.

The applicant submits that it is thus evident that the injustices against which redress is sought tend to be self-perpetuating. The political party or parties who have in the past gained by the unequal votes are reluctant to propose and vote for the relative disenfranchisement of the voters who voted them into power.

In this context the applicant draws attention to the paradoxical fact that all the political parties have for many years had correction of this injustice in their platform, but nothing has been done.

Further, the applicant points out that the Constitutional Committee appointed as far back as 18 May 1972, appears to be able to do nothing. This is why he seeks the help of the Commission and believes that a modicum of outside and authoritative pressure and persuasion might be all it would take.

The applicant maintains that the only domestic remedy he could think of would be in the form of legal action against the Icelandic National Assembly—claiming that it change the constitution of the land—an action which he maintains the courts would be sure to dismiss.

The applicant submits that the Icelandic Electoral System, as described above—where each voter in the fourth constituency (Vestfirdir) is given 4.8 votes against the one vote given to each voter in the second constituency (Reykjanes)—is in breach of the basic assumptions of the Convention for the Protection of Human Rights and Fundamental Freedoms, cf. the reaffirmation in Clause 4 of the Preamble, that the Fundamental Freedoms 'are best maintained on the one hand by an effective political democracy . . . ', and the assumption in Clause 5 of the Preamble, that the High Contracting Parties consists of 'Governments of European countries which are like minded and have a common heritage of political traditions . . . ', cf. also numerous references in the articles of the Convention to 'democratic societies'.

The applicant furthermore submits that Article 3 of the First Additional Protocol would not make any sense except on the basis of an unconditional adherence by the High Contracting Parties to the principle of majority rule and equal votes: one man/one vote.

The applicant alleges that the Icelandic Government is in breach of Article 3 of Protocol No. 1 to the Convention, as they do not ensure the free expression of the opinion of the people in the choice of the legislature because of the great disparity of votes (as much as 1:4.8) behind each candidate in the different constituencies in Iceland.

It is true that Article 3 of Protocol No. 1 obliges the Government to hold free elections at reasonable intervals by secret ballots under conditions which ensure the free expression of the opinion of the people in the choice of the legislature.

It is not in dispute that elections to the Icelandic National Assembly (Althingi) are held at reasonable intervals by secret ballot. The examination of the application therefore relates to the words 'the free expression of the opinion of the people in the choice of the legislature'.

The applicant in effect contends that to ensure conformity with Article 3 of Protocol No. 1, there must be equal weight behind each vote in every constituency in Iceland, i.e. one man/one vote, as opposed to the present system which creates such disparity as 1 against 4.8.

The Commission considers that the words 'free expression of the opinion of the people' primarily signify that the elections cannot be made under any form of pressure in the choice of one or more candidates, and that in this choice the elector should not be unduly induced to vote for one party or another.

Furthermore, the word 'choice' signifies that the different political parties must be ensured a reasonable opportunity to present their candidates at elections.

However, there is here no contention that the present system of electing deputies to the Icelandic National Assembly fails to abide by the above conditions.

When applying Article 3 of the First Protocol, the Commission cannot disregard the wording and the background of the provisions concerned. Article 3 of the First Protocol gives an individual right to vote in the election provided for by this article. This is not the same as a protection of equal voting influence for all voters. The question whether or not equality exists in this respect is due to the electoral system being applied. Article 3 of the First Protocol is careful not to bind the States as to the electoral system and does not add any requirement of 'equality' to the 'secret ballot'.

The disparity of votes behind Members of Parliament from different constituencies has its origin in the migration that has taken place from the scarcely populated areas in Iceland to the densely populated areas. In spite of this fact, it is also clear that the Icelandic electoral system aims to guarantee the inhabitants in the scarcely populated areas a certain representation in Parliament at the expense of the weight of votes in the densely populated areas.

This cannot be considered to be in contravention of Article 3 of the First Protocol, which does not stipulate that the weight of votes behind each Member of Parliament shall be equal.

Full equality in the weight of votes would, as far as Iceland is concerned have the result that the majority of the Members of Parliament would be elected from a comparatively small part of the country, i.e. where it is densely populated (Reykjanes and Reykjavik constituencies). During this century changes have been made on the Icelandic electoral system and on the Icelandic constitution with the purpose of diminishing the difference between the weight of votes in the different constituencies in Iceland.

It is to be noted that the discrepancy between the weight of votes between different constituencies may have the side-effect that discrepancies also occur between political parties as to the number of votes behind Members of Parliament from different parties. Article 3 of the First Protocol to the Convention does not, however, oblige a Member State to establish an electoral system which secures that the number of deputies of each political party be proportionate to the votes cast for the parties.

The discrepancies created by the electoral system cannot be considered to be of such a degree as to be arbitrary or abusive. Furthermore, the system does not favour any particular political party at the expense of another, nor does it give any individual candidate an advantage in elections at the expense of another candidate . . .

The Icelandic electoral system is a proportional representation system. It should further be noted that the Icelandic Constitution does contain provisions which aim specifically at avoiding the occurrence of discrepancies between political parties as to the number of deputies each party gets elected compared to the votes cast for it.

These provisions have in fact fairly well reached their aim, so that there is not a big difference in the number of votes behind each deputy from the different parties.

Consequently, on the basis of the above reasoning, the Commission cannot find that the Icelandic electoral system violates the provisions of Article 3 of the Convention's First Protocol.

It follows that the application is manifestly ill-founded within the meaning of Article 27, paragraph 2 of the Convention.

For these reasons, the Commission Declares this Application Inadmissible.

E. THE DISCRETION OF STRASBOURG

The *Icelandic Electoral System Case* is an example of the broad discretionary power that the Commission often exercised in deciding on the admissibility of individual petitions. A similar kind of admissibility discretion now rests, after the implementation of Protocol No. 11 in November 1998, with the three-judge Committees of the Court. A unanimous Committee decision declaring an individual application inadmissible or striking it out of its list of cases is final and without appeal.[48] State complaints, relatively rare, always, however, require an admissibility decision by a seven-judge chamber of the Court.[49]

A great many applications have been deemed 'manifestly ill-founded' and declared inadmissible by the Commission on the grounds that they did not appear to have any realistic chance of being able to succeed on their merits. This procedure has allowed Strasbourg, at its discretion, to focus on what it decides at early stages of the

---

[48] Convention, *supra* n. 25, art. 28.   [49] *Id.* Art. 29(2).

proceedings to be the more important cases.[50] Will Strasbourg's discretion about inadmissibility only be exercised in cases clearly without merit?

Note in the *Icelandic Electoral System Case* that there is little in the Decision actually explaining why the dispute is inadmissible or even why the application is so without merit. Rather, the Commission rejects X's claim only after seriously, if in a preliminary way, weighing and evaluating Iceland's 'democratic' process: e.g., '[t]he discrepancies created by the electoral system cannot be considered to be of such a degree as to be arbitrary or abusive. Furthermore, the system does not favour any particular party at the expense of another, nor does it give any individual candidate an advantage in elections at the expense of another candidate'. These conclusions, it seems, could well be more fully and better tested after further evidence is provided both by X and by the government of Iceland. Why not admit the application, investigate the claim further, and then make a determination explicitly on the merits? Such a full hearing would also permit the case to be sent to the Court for its legally binding judgment.

Of course, there might have been very good, if unarticulated, political reasons for not admitting X's petition, investigating the claim, deciding on the merits, and sending it along to the Court for judgment. If Strasbourg were to choose to evaluate the legality under the Convention of the electoral system of Iceland, then why not test the legality of electoral schemes in more influential countries—the United Kingdom, France, Germany, or Italy? Such evaluations of the merits of electoral systems of its member states by the Strasbourg legal machinery could be politically explosive. Enforcement of judgments about electoral reform might well be beyond the political capacity of the Council of Europe. In practice, the Commission has shielded the Court from having to settle a politically sensitive dispute. If that was the real reason for the Commission's decision in the *Icelandic Electoral System Case*, why not be more forthright and elaborate a 'political question' doctrine and say frankly that this is the kind of question that should be addressed politically and not judicially?

2. STRASBOURG AS MEDIATOR

A. FRIENDLY SETTLEMENT

Once a case has been deemed admissible, it is still always possible for Strasbourg to decide to strike the case off its list if, as Article 37 of the new Convention provides, the Court determines that '(a) the applicant does not intend to pursue his application; or (b) the matter has been resolved; or (c) for any other reason established by the Court, it is no longer justified to continue the examination of the application'.[51] However, if the case has been deemed admissible and so long it has not been struck off, Article 38

---

[50] T. Zwart, *The Admissibility of Human Rights Petitions: The Case Law of the European Commission of Human Rights and the Human Rights Committee* 146–154 (1994).

[51] Convention, *supra* n. 25, Art. 37(1).

of the Convention obliges the Court to 'pursue the examination of the case, together with the representatives of the parties, and if need be, undertake an investigation, for the effective conduct of which the States concerned shall furnish all necessary facilities'.[52] We explore the fact-finding function of the Court a little later.

While fact-finding is proceeding, Article 38 also obliges the Court to 'place itself at the disposal of the parties concerned with a view to securing a friendly settlement of the matter on the basis of the respect for human rights as defined in the Convention and the protocols thereto.'[53] Friendly settlement proceedings are confidential.[54] Article 39 provides that '[i]f a friendly settlement is effected, the Court shall strike the case out of its list by means of a decision which shall be confined to a brief statement of the facts and the solution reached'.[55] Similar provision was made for friendly settlement by the Commission until it was merged into the Court in 1999.[56]

Although a friendly settlement in law and in fact terminates a Strasbourg legal proceeding, a friendly settlement is not the same as a judgment. For one thing, friendly settlement involves 'neither a winner nor a loser'.[57] A friendly settlement is fundamentally a compromise not an adjudication and, as such, may be in many circumstances 'the most satisfactory termination of a legal dispute'.[58] A friendly settlement can result simply from bilateral negotiations between the parties, but oftentimes a friendly settlement emerges only after considerable mediation by the Strasbourg legal machinery, traditionally the Commission, nowadays the Court. The *Giama Case* that follows illustrates Strasbourg's friendly settlement process, showing not only a compromise agreed to by the parties but the active role played by the Strasbourg machinery.

B. GIAMA V. BELGIUM

Application No. 7612/76
Report of the Commission of 17 July 1980
21 Decisions and Reports of the European
Commission of Human Rights 73, 84–94 (March 1981)
1980 Yearbook of the European Convention on
Human Rights 428

PART I

. . .

4. At its session on 17 July 1980, the Commission noted that the parties had arrived at a

---

[52] *Id.* Art. 38(1)(a).

[53] *Id.* Art. 38(1)(b).

[54] *Id.* Art. 38(2).

[55] *Id.* Art. 39.

[56] Old Convention, *supra* n. 3, Art. 28.

[57] H. C. Krüger & C. A. Norgaard, 'Reflections Concerning Friendly Settlement under the European Convention on Human Rights', *Protecting Human Rights: The European Dimension: Studies in Honour of Gerard J. Wiarda* 329 (eds. F. Matscher & H. Petzold, 2nd edn. 1990) (hereinafter cited as Krüger & Norgaard).

[58] *Id.*

friendly settlement, and adopted this report which, in accordance with Article 30 of the Convention, is confined to a brief statement of the facts and of the solution reached . . .

6. The applicant, who is of African origin and who, at the time when his application was submitted, possessed no papers indicating his identity or nationality, is represented by Maitre R. Cassiers, barrister at Antwerp.

7. The applicant was questioned by the police for the first time in Belgium on 5 July 1975, when a check was carried out in a café at Antwerp. He possessed no identity papers or money. He stated that his name was Manitu Giama, that he had been born in Durban (South Africa) on 26 November 1947 and that he was of South African nationality. He further stated that he was a sailor on the ship, 'White River', which had arrived at Amsterdam three days before, and that he had come to Antwerp by train on 4 July 1975 to visit friends.

8. On 5 July 1975, he was ordered to leave the country within 48 hours, on the grounds that he possessed neither means of subsistence nor identity papers.

9. On 15 July 1975, the Aliens Police found him in Antwerp once again without a passport. He was apprehended and a warrant issued for his arrest on 16 July 1975 for being unlawfully resident and for assaulting a representative of the forces of law and order. For these offenses, the Antwerp police court sentenced him; on 24 October 1975 to six months' imprisonment, including two months suspended for five years, and to a fine of 100 francs or one month in prison, suspended for five years.

10. The applicant's request for refugee status under Sections 2 (B) and 3 (2) of the Aliens Police Act was rejected on the grounds that the time limit had expired. In particular, his entry into Belgium on 4 July 1975 was considered irregular. The fact that the request had been made on 24 August 1975, more than a month after his arrival in the country, was also taken into consideration.

11. In response to a request for information lodged by the Belgian authorities on 10 September 1975, the Netherlands authorities stated that the 'White River' had not docked in Amsterdam since 1 January 1973. They added that the ship had arrived in Rotterdam on 17 July 1975 and left the following day, and that the applicant had not been a member of the crew.

12. In a telegram dated 26 September 1975, Interpol Pretoria (South Africa) stated that the applicant was not a South African citizen. Having visited the applicant on 2 October 1975, the representative in Belgium of the United Nations High Commissioner for Refugees confirmed that, in view of the applicant's refusal to co-operate, he could not recognize him as a refugee.

13. Since the applicant had claimed that he could persuade the Zambian diplomatic authorities to admit him to Zambia, the United Nations representative had referred the matter to the Zambian Ambassador. A letter dated 18 November 1975 showed, however, that immigration to Zambia was out of the question. This being so, the applicant was not released when his sentence expired on 12 November 1975, but was kept in custody at the disposal of the Aliens Police, since he lacked the travel documents and identity papers needed for lawful admission to another country or continued residence in Belgium.

14. Following a conversation with an official of the Aliens Police in the course of which the applicant stated that he did not wish to return to South Africa, the latter was released on 28 November 1975 and ordered to leave the country by midnight on 30 November 1975.

15. In December 1975, the Belgium authorities proceeded to make enquiries in a number of African countries, including Ghana, Niger, Nigeria, Uganda, Zaire and Zambia. On 13 January

1976, Interpol Lusaka (Zambia) replied that the applicant had no criminal record in Zambia. On 3 February 1976, Interpol Lagos (Nigeria) similarly replied that its records contained no mention of the applicant.

[The record continued: Giama was questioned in Antwerp on 1 February 1976, ordered to leave Belgium by 6 February, arrested on 9 February, released and ordered again to leave on 5 September, arrested again in Antwerp on 10 October, sentenced to jail on 4 January 1977, released again and crossed to the Netherlands on 18 October 1977, arrested again in Belgium on 6 October 1978, released again on 13 November 1978 and again ordered to leave the country.] . . .

26. In his application to the Commission, submitted on 26 November 1975, the applicant essentially argued:

a) that he had been obliged to leave South Africa for political reasons and had thus been unable to furnish fuller information for fear of compromising his comrades;

b) that, despite the ministerial orders, his lack of travel documents had prevented him from leaving Belgium;

c) that his periods of detention had left this situation unchanged, since he still lacked identity papers. In this connection, he referred to Article 5 (1) of the Convention;

d) that he had no possibility whatsoever to challenge his detention before a court and considered himself the victim of discrimination, insofar as the authorities had refused to take into account his social position and the special circumstances of his case. In this connection, he referred to Articles 5 (4) and 14 of the Convention.

Proceedings before the commission

27. In accordance with Rule 42, para. 2 (b) of the Commission's Rules of Procedure, the respondent Government was given notice of the application on 8 October 1976 . . .

35. In accordance with Rule 28 (2) of the Commission's Rules of Procedure, the President of the Commission decided, on 22 August 1978, to postpone the hearing scheduled for 6 October 1978 *sine die*, and instructed the Secretary to the Commission to inform the parties that the Commission would consider the procedure to be followed at its next session, beginning on 2 October 1978. By letter dated 25 August 1978, the Secretary to the Commission informed the parties of the President's decision. In accordance with Rule 49(2) of the Commission's Rules of Procedure, the Belgian Government was also invited to indicate its position in respect of the procedure provided for in Rule 49, with a view to striking the case off the list, since the applicant could not be found.

36. On 9 September 1978, the Government indicated that it had no objections on this score.

37. On 4 October 1978, the Commission decided to strike the application off its list of cases in accordance with Rules 44, para. 1. (b) and 49 of its Rules of Procedure.

38. Shortly afterwards, by letter dated 10 October 1978, the applicant's counsel informed the Commission that the applicant had returned to Belgium to discuss the proceedings before the Commission with him and had been rearrested on 6 October 1978. He asked whether the Commission could not continue to consider the merits of the case in the applicant's presence.

39. On 12 October 1978, the Commission decided to restore the application to its list of cases. It also decided to hold a hearing of the parties.

40. By order of the President of the Commission, issued on 28 November 1978, in accordance with Rules 28(2) and 32 of the Rules of Procedure, the applicant was invited to appear before the Commission in person on 11 December 1978, in order to be heard, in the presence of the parties' representatives, on the merits of the case.

41. For this purpose, on 1 December 1978, the Deputy Secretary General of the Council of Europe wrote to the Permanent Representative of France to the Council of Europe, asking him to approach the competent French authorities, in order that they provide all the assistance necessary to ensure that the applicant, who still lacked travel documents, could attend the hearing.

42. The hearing was held on 11 December 1978. The parties were represented as follows:

For the applicant:
— Maitre Cassiers   Barrister at Antwerp

For the Government:
— Mr. J. C. Godfroid   Legal Adviser to the Aliens Office — Agent
— Professor J. De Meyer   Counsel
— Mr. A. Coppue   Assistant Legal Adviser to the Aliens Office.

The applicant attended the hearing, having been temporarily admitted to France for this purpose by the French authorities. Moreover, the applicant had received authorisation from the legal department of the Belgian Ministry of Justice to return to Belgium after the hearing . . .

Finally, a friendly settlement was reached, as described in Part II of this report.

Part II

Solution reached

43. After the hearing on 11 December 1978, the Commission decided, in accordance with Article 28(b) of the Convention, to place itself at the parties' disposal for the purpose of reaching a friendly settlement. Its Secretary was instructed to resume contact with the parties at once and to ascertain any proposals which they might have.

On 12 December 1978, the respondent Government's counsel met the President and the Vice-President of the Commission. At this meeting, the Belgian authorities were asked to postpone expulsion of the applicant until the Commission's next session, which was due to begin on 26 February 1979. The applicant's counsel was immediately informed of this meeting and undertook to do everything possible to regularise the applicant's situation and facilitate his return to Africa. The respondent Government indicated that it would do everything in its power to assist the efforts made by the applicant's counsel.

By letter dated 20 December 1978, the respondent Government informed the Secretary to the Commission that, following the meeting of 12 December 1978, the applicant had been given a safe-conduct, valid until the end of February.

44. At its session in March 1979, the Commission noted that counsel's attempts to arrange for the applicant's departure to another African state had proved unsuccessful and that his position thus remained unchanged. It decided that these efforts should be continued, with a view to solving the problems raised by the application. For this purpose, the Commission, again acting in

accordance with Article 28(b) of the Convention, asked the respondent Government to allow the applicant to remain on its territory until a solution had been found.

The President of the Commission also asked the applicant's counsel to contact various organizations and, in particular, the Organization of African Unity (OAU) and to ask their assistance in finding a country prepared to admit the applicant. The Secretary to the Commission was instructed to give counsel every possible assistance in this matter, provided that such assistance was compatible with the functions of the Commission, as laid down in the Convention and particularly Article 28(b).

In this connection, the Secretary informed counsel that the member-states of the OAU had adopted a convention on specific aspects of the problems of refugees in Africa in September 1969. He also suggested that counsel should approach religious organizations which might be prepared to help in finding a country to receive the applicant.

45. On 21 March 1979, counsel contacted OAU and requested its assistance referring in particular to the above convention. He sent copies of his letter to two religious organizations, asking them to support his request for help in finding a country to admit the applicant.

46. At its session in May 1979, the Commission decided to inform the respondent Government of all the action taken so far by the applicant's counsel.

47. By letter dated 6 June 1979, OAU informed the applicant's counsel, who had repeated his request of 21 March 1979 on 14 May 1979, that a reply had already been despatched on 9 April 1979. This letter, which counsel seemed never to have received, had stated that the applicant's lack of papers made it impossible to deal with his case.

48. On 10 July 1979, the Commission resumed its examination of the case in the light of the information supplied by counsel. It decided to fix the proceedings to be followed and, at the same time, to remain at the parties' disposal for the purpose of reaching a friendly settlement.

49. By letter dated 19 September 1979, the applicant's counsel submitted a new proposal to the Belgian authorities for the purpose of reaching a friendly settlement. He pointed out that, for the applicant to go to an African country, it was sufficient that he should be allowed to leave Belgium in a lawful and proper fashion. He further pointed out that the applicant's lack of papers had prevented OAU from dealing with his case. He referred to the Belgian authorities' view that the applicant should be regarded as being of indeterminate identity, and stressed that aliens in this category could be issued with the documents by the authorities and be authorised by the provincial Government to leave the country. He accordingly requested the authorities to issue the documents to the applicant.

Replying to this request, the Minister of Justice informed counsel that his department was prepared to issue the applicant—as a person lacking diplomatic protection—with a travel document for aliens who were not political refugees, on condition that a receiving country could be found with the help of OAU. Counsel was asked to indicate the States to which the applicant intended to go and his probable dates of departure. The Minister explained that this travel document would be issued merely for the purpose of arriving at a friendly settlement of the case, as envisaged by the Commission, and would in no way prejudice proceedings before the Council of State. The Minister argued that the applicant should still be regarded, provisionally, as being of indeterminate nationality and not as being stateless 'de jure' under Article 1 of the Convention relating to the status of stateless persons, signed in New York on 28 September 1954 and approved by the Act of 12 May 1960.

50. At its session in October 1979, the Commission examined the applicant's situation in the light of these new developments.

The Commission informed the applicant's counsel that this travel document had been issued to meet the conditions laid down by OAU, which had stipulated that the case could only be dealt with if the applicant possessed papers. The applicant was accordingly asked to contact OAU again when he had received the document in question.

51. By letter dated 20 November 1979, the respondent Government's Agent informed the Secretary to the Commission that the Minister for Justice had authorised the issuing of a 'travel document for aliens who are not political refugees' to the applicant. This document would entitle the holder to go abroad and return to Belgium as long as the visa attached to it remained valid.

In the meantime, the applicant's counsel approached OAU. In his letter, he spoke of the applicant's wish to settle in Zaire or Tanzania. OAU's chief legal adviser replied that the applicant who, like other South Africans, had fled the agonies of 'apartheid', would be welcome in any other independent African State. He suggested that the applicant should apply to the authorities of the African state in which he had decided to reside as a refugee for an entry permit, enclosing his passport and a written account of his position.

In response to this communication, the applicant's counsel wrote to the embassy of the Republic of Zaire in Brussels on 22 January 1980. He repeated his request on 3 March 1980.

52. At its session in March 1980, the Commission examined the case in the light of these developments. It considered that the fact of the respondent Government's having issued the applicant with the said travel document for the purpose of reaching a friendly settlement might well be considered as constituting such a settlement. It thus declared its willingness to obtain the parties' agreement to such a settlement and to prepare a report in accordance with Article 30 of the Convention.

53. By letter dated 26 March 1980, the applicant's counsel informed the Secretary to the Commission that the applicant had approached various African embassies with photocopies of the travel document and that the Senegalese authorities had agreed to admit him, making vaccination the only condition.

By letter dated 17 April 1980, the applicant's counsel stated:

'Further to my letter of 26 March, I can only tell you that the applicant left Belgium for Senegal on Saturday, 12 April.

His travel expenses were paid by the Belgian Government.

In my view, this means that a final friendly settlement of the case has been arrived at.'

54. At its session on 17 July 1980, the Commission noted that the measure adopted by the Belgian Government and the declaration made by the applicant's counsel indicated that agreement had been reached between the parties on settlement of the case.

55. In view of this friendly settlement, based on respect for human rights within the meaning of Article 28(b) of the Convention, the Commission has adopted the present report.

56. With regard to its assessment of the general interest, to which it has regard according to its constant practice when a friendly settlement is reached, the Commission has the following observations to make:

It is true that, in principle, the authorities of a State cannot be held responsible for the fact that an alien who has not been authorised to reside in the country is unable to leave the country lawfully. In the present case the applicant was confronted with such a difficulty, which had serious repercussions on his personal situation.

The Commission also points out that Applications No. 7752/76 (*X v. Belgium*, struck off the list of cases on 15 December 1977) and No. 8108 (*X v. the Federal Republic of Germany*, declared inadmissible on 6 October 1978) were concerned with similar situations. Though particularly acute, the problems raised by the present application are thus neither exceptional nor restricted to Belgium.

In the light of these considerations, the Commission believes that the problems call for carefull study by the High Contracting Parties who in a 'particularly liberal and humanitarian spirit'—the terms used in Resolution (67)14 on 'Asylum to persons in danger of persecution', adopted by the Ministers' Deputies on 29 June 1967—might consider it appropriate in arriving at a common solution to situations of this kind.

C. NEGOTIATIONS AT STRASBOURG

The decision whether or not to reach a negotiated settlement of an admitted dispute is in the first place a matter at the discretion of the two parties. The decision to negotiate may be influenced, *inter alia*, by the anticipated length or cost of Strasbourg legal proceedings or by an intimation of the likely Strasbourg determination of the merits of the dispute.[59] However, once the decision to negotiate a settlement is reached, the Strasbourg machinery may, at the choice of the parties, be engaged.[60]

Giama is an excellent example of just how much work Strasbourg may do to reach a friendly settlement. Note how much networking the Commission did in the case. It reached out to at least the following: Belgium, The Netherlands, Interpol (South Africa), the United Nations High Commissioner for Refugees, Zambia, Ghana, Niger, Nigeria, Uganda, Zaire, Interpol (Zambia), the European Commission on Human Rights, the Council of Europe, France, the Organization of African Unity, and Senegal. It is doubtful that Giama or his lawyer could involve so many national and international organizations without the assistance of the Commission. Plainly, the Commission could not devote such time and energy to every refugee. It may well be that the Commission saw *Giama* as a useful precedent for other like cases or as an incentive for the fashioning of a more regular bureaucratic machinery for handling problems of stateless persons.[61]

Friendly settlements, as in *Giama*, though relatively common in cases brought by private parties, are unusual in inter-state cases. The first friendly settlement in an inter-state case came in 1985. The case involved five applications brought by France,

---

[59] Krüger & Norgaard, *supra* note 57, at 330.

[60] *Id.* at 331.

[61] For a consideration of *Giama* in political and legal context, see H. Schermers, 'The Second Generation of Immigrants', 82 *Michigan Law Review* 1415, 1418–19 (1984). The problem of illegal immigration to Europe has only become more difficult over time; there is now a vast literature on the problems of immigration policy within Europe, including the response of European states to requests for political asylum, *see* G. Goodwin-Gill, *The Refugee in International Law* (2nd ed, 1996); S. Juss, 'Sovereignty, Culture, and Community: Refugee Policy and Human Rights in Europe', 3 *UCLA Journal of International Law & Foreign Affairs* 463 (1998–9).

Norway, Denmark, Sweden and the Netherlands in 1982, complaining that Turkey had violated six Articles of the Convention in its 1982 imposition of martial law.[62] In its Report of 7 December 1985, the Commission noted that the friendly settlement recognized the legislative changes and amendments made by Turkey to comply with its obligations under the Convention and imposed upon Turkey a periodic reporting requirement.[63] An 'indirect result' of the friendly settlement was Turkey's initial acceptance of the right of individual petition under Article 25, though the acceptance was limited by a number of controversial reservations.[64] The five applications against Turkey were 'apparently only the second set of inter-State cases which [were] not motivated by the applicants' self-interest, or political, religious or ethnic links with the population of the State against which the application [was] lodged',[65] the other set being the *Greek Case* below.

3. STRASBOURG AS FACT-FINDER

A. THE GREEK CASE

12 Yearbook of the European Convention on Human Rights: The Greek Case 196 (1969)

. . .

40. The applicant Governments of Denmark, Norway and Sweden, in their written applications of 20th September, 1967, and the applicant Government of the Netherlands, in its written application of 27th September, 1967, alleged that the respondent Government had, by a number of legislative and administrative measures, violated Articles 5, 6, 8, 9, 10, 11, 13 and 14 of the Convention. These allegations were further developed at the oral hearing before the Commission on 23rd and 24th January, 1968. In particular, the applicant Governments stated that:

— a state of siege had been declared and Articles 5, 6, 8, 10, 11, 12, 14, 20, 95 and 97 of the Greek Constitution of 1st January, 1952, had been suspended by Royal Decree No. 280 of 21st April, 1967;

— political parties and ordinary political activities had been prohibited and parliamentary elections scheduled for 28th May, 1967, had been cancelled;

— extraordinary courts martial had been established by Royal Decrees Nos. 280 and 281 of 21st April, 1967;

---

[62] Applications No. 9940–44/82 of 1 July 1982.

[63] European Commission of Human Rights, 'Report on the Applications of Denmark, France, Netherlands, Norway and Sweden against Turkey and the Conclusion of a Friendly Settlement', 25, *International Legal Materials* 308, 310, 314–16 (1986).

[64] Cameron, 'Turkey and Article 25 of the European Convention on Human Rights', 37 *International and Comparative Law Quarterly* 887 (1988).

[65] Drzemczewski, 'The European Convention on Human Rights', 2 *Yearbook of European Law* 327, 330 (1982).

— thousands of persons had been imprisoned for a long period without being brought before a 'competent legal authority';

— the right to freedom of expression had been suppressed as was illustrated by an order of the Army Chief of Staff of 14th June, 1967;

— censorship had been applied to the press and private communications;

— many persons had been sentenced by extraordinary courts martial for their political opinions;

— the right to assemble freely or to associate freely with others had been abolished as was demonstrated by criminal charges and resultant harsh sentences in certain cases.

1. Article 3 of the Convention provides that: 'No one shall be subjected to torture or to inhuman or degrading treatment or punishment'.

. . .

9. At five hearings before the Sub-Commission or its delegates—from 25th to 28th November, in Strasbourg, from 18th to 20th December, 1968, in Strasbourg, from 10th to 20th March, 1969, in Athens, from 16th to 17th June, 1969, in Strasbourg, on 26th July, 1969, in Strasbourg—a total of 58 witnesses gave evidence with regard to Article 3 of the Convention.

Among these were:

16 alleged victims of physical ill-treatment or torture;

7 persons who had been detained together with those alleged victims;

25 police officers and other Greek officials;

2 political prisoners with regard to whom no torture allegations were made but who had been proposed by the respondent Government (Zervoulakos and Tambakis);

8 other persons who had made observations concerning the treatment of political prisoners in Greece. . . .

10. 49 further witnesses whom the Sub-Commission decided to hear with regard to Article 3 were not heard for various reasons, among them 21 persons detained in Greece whom the respondent Government did not make available to the Sub-Commission for a hearing. . . .

13. The Sub-Commission also called medical experts who examined 8 alleged victims with their consent:

(a) Prof. J. Bernheim, Director of the Institute of Forensic Medicine at the University of Geneva, assisted by Dr. A. Rohner, Dr. P. Boggio and Dr. J. F. Moody, examined, and submitted opinions in the cases of the witnesses:

(i) Papagiannakis, Lendakis and Karaosman after having exchanged views in Athens with Prof. D. Ekonomos, Dr. J. Matsiotas and Dr. G. Adjutantis;

(ii) Vardikos, Korovessis, Meletis and Vlassis after having received the results of specialist or supplementary examinations from Dr. F. Borer, Geneva; Prof. Dr. M. Adloff, University of Strasbourg; Dr. R. Raber, Strasbourg; Prof. F. E. Camps, London Hospital Medical College; Prof. J. Lundevall, University of Oslo; Dr. R. Weyde, University of Oslo.

(b) Prof. J. Mehl and Prof. Dr. B. Keller of the University of Strasbourg examined the witness Mrs. Tsirka and submitted an opinion in her case.

14. During its investigation the Sub-Commission has received from the parties and from witnesses a great number of documents relating to Article 3, including statements from alleged victims of torture or ill-treatment, in particular also from witnesses whom the Sub-Commission decided to hear but who were prevented by the respondent Government from giving oral evidence.

The Sub-Commission had also requested the respondent Government to submit certain further medical records, reports of the International Committee of the Red Cross, and information on the results of certain administrative enquiries but the respondent Government did not comply with these requests.

15. The Sub-Commission has inspected the Security Police Headquarters of Athens and Piraeus, but was refused access to Averoff prison and the detention camps on the Island of Leros. The Sub-Commission had also envisaged inspecting the Dionysos military camp but, having regard to the refusal by the respondent Government to allow the hearing of the four witnesses allegedly tortured in this camp (Panagoulis, Maria Kallerghi, Petropoulos and Kiaos), did not carry out the visit to the camp. . . .

Case of Vardikos

1. The applicant Governments proposed N. Vardikos as a witness in their letter of 7th February, 1969. In this letter they state that Vardikos, while detained as a political prisoner, had been severely tortured. The applicant Governments submitted an affidavit made by Vardikos in Liverpool on 16th November, 1968, in which he describes the torture in some detail.

2. The respondent Government has made no specific comments on the case of Vardikos and has not proposed any witnesses with regard to this case.

3. Nicolas Vardikos, foreman, aged 30, married, was heard by the Sub-Commission in Strasbourg on 16th June, 1969. He indicated that before 21st April, 1967, he had been Secretary General of a Trade Union, and that he had also been an active member of the Greek Democratic Youth and of the Centre Union Party. Since his escape from Greece and after having been granted political asylum in Great Britain, he works as a waiter in Liverpool. His wife and children are still living in Greece.

4. He stated that he was arrested by three plain clothes police officers on 23rd April, 1967, at 2 o'clock in the morning in his house in Lavrion while he was sleeping. He was not allowed to dress, and was handcuffed. He was taken to the Lavrion police station in an army car. After an hour a captain of the Military Police took him to the Athens Security Headquarters in Bouboulinas Street, where he was locked up in a cell in the basement. Being handcuffed, he hit his head on the stone wall when thrown into the cell. As a result of this he sustained a deep bleeding wound in his head.

5. After some hours two policemen led him to Mr. Lambrou's office on the second floor. Lambrou then started interrogating him:

'When I entered he asked me: "Are you Vardikos?" "Yes, I am Vardikos". "We have a few things to ask you about, and if you love your children and your wife and your relations, it is better to answer us, and you will be set free. Tell us first of all who opened the Greek Democratic Youth offices and if it was you who opened them, what have you done with the documents?" My answer: "I opened the offices, I took the Greek Democratic Youth documents and burnt them". "Why did you burn them?" "They contained nothing against the State. I burnt them only because they contained names of members." "Tell us, at the time of the Valpex Company strike, why did you communicate personally with the Interior Minister,

Tsirimokos, and ask for the withdrawal of the eight police cars which had come for the protection of the Valpex Company?" I answered to this that all this was past. Why did they ask me? Lambrou answered me: "You will answer what I am asking you"'.

6. Lambrou then asked him to sign a declaration in favour of the Government. He refused. Lambrou had him taken to another room where there was a wooden bench. As he still refused to make the declaration, the policemen knocked him against the bench and he lost two teeth. Police Inspector Georgiou struck him with a wire rope on his left arm and as a result he has a permanent scar. He was beaten all over his body, especially on his belly and on his genitals. The witness described the ill-treatment as follows:

'He (Inspector Georgiou) struck me lower down on my arm where my veins opened and I have got the stitches. After that they put me on the bench and they kept on beating me in the belly and the testicles. I lost my senses and after that I couldn't tell either the day or the hour of the day. I was moved to a camp, in a Deutz car. I thought it was a camp because I heard some orders being given. There in the camp they threw me in a cell, pulling off my pyjamas, so that I was left almost naked. After a lapse of two hours they called me in the office where they beat me again very badly. They did not offer me any medical help. The only thing that they offered me was a red medicine for my wounds which were in a terrible condition. All in blisters. How they moved me there I don't know, I was in a coma'.

7. When he recovered his senses, he found himself locked up alone in a wooden hut on the island of Yaros. As he continued to refuse to sign the declaration of loyalty, he was kept in detention.

8. Three months and two days later, on 27th July, 1967, he was released in Athens. He remained in Lavrion under police supervision and was re-arrested on 13th December, 1967, after the King's counter-coup. He was kept in isolation at the Lavrion police station for 17 days without food and drink 'at least from the official police'. As a result he lost a considerable amount of weight.

9. In order to leave Greece, he took up work as a sailor on a Greek merchant ship. But on instructions from the government he was locked in a cabin during the journey from Spain to England and only due to a British Customs check was he able to leave the ship at Liverpool and apply for political asylum.

10. In his detailed affidavit, mentioned above and dated 26th November, 1968, Vardikos mentions also having been tortured with an iron clamp that was placed on his head and screwed into both sides of his temples in a military camp in the presence of police officer Georgiou. He had already noticed in the office, where he was taken after his first interrogation by Lambrou, that there was a 'metal clamp-like instrument with a wooden screw'.

Except for this detail, his written statement coincides essentially with his testimony before the Sub-Commission.

11. As regards the localities described, Lambrou's office is actually on the second floor of the Asphalia building in Bouboulinas Street (office numbered 39 on the plan).

12. The examination carried out by the Sub-Commission's medical experts gave the following results:

'The patient has on the front of his head, near the edge of his scalp in the left paramedian region, an old linear scar probably resulting from an injury sustained when he was flung against a wall at the time of his arrest on 23rd April, 1967. This causal relation cannot, however, be established with certainty.

On his left shoulder, in the deltoid region, there is a broad scar, the size of the palm of one's hand with irregular contours, which is discoloured, particularly round the edge, and may also be a few years old at most.

In the fold of his left elbow is a linear transverse and slightly discoloured scar probably dating from the same period. These two scars were probably left by wounds which were caused by whipping with a metallic cable and subsequently turned septic.

An examination of the mouth shows that the two top left premolars are intact, but these may well be artificial teeth. This might bear out the patient's allegation that two of his teeth were broken when his head was seized by the hair and banged against the edge of a table.

There is no trace of any further injury.

Mr. Vardikos alleges that his skull was squeezed by a kind of metal crown which was placed around his head at the level of his temples and could be tightened by screws. There is at present no mark bearing evidence of such treatment.

The patient tells us that he suffered from severe headaches for a long time afterwards. It is not possible to express a medical opinion on the possible causal relation between the compression of the skull and the headaches from which the patient subsequently suffered. Such consequences can neither be confirmed nor ruled out medically.

We do not consider specialised hospital examinations to be necessary in Mr. Vardikos's case. It would, however, be helpful if we could study the medical reports of the doctors who treated Mr. Vardikos for his dental lesions, his shoulder and elbow wounds and his persistent headaches. The patient preferred, however, not to divulge the names of his doctors'.

13. The applicant Governments submitted that Vardikos's statements contain conclusive evidence as to the fact that he had been subjected to torture.

Analysis of evidence

14. With regard to the allegations of torture made by Vardikos, the respondent Government has submitted no observations, proposed no witnesses, filed no documents in relation to this case.

15. As regards possible motives for the witness to tell a false story:

(i) it is possible to suppose that Vardikos fabricated these allegations of ill-treatment for anti-Government purposes. Though he strongly denied being a Communist and followed the Centre Union party and its leader, G. Papandreou, he made a public statement about his treatment in an interview with the *Sunday Times* newspaper; and it appears that, as a consequence, his wife was called by the police to sign certain declarations and that difficulties of making contact with his family arose;

(ii) another possible motive for Vardikos to give a false story might be to cover up the fact that he had betrayed his friends during an interrogation by the police. He was never tried or summoned as a witness in a trial, and his case ended in deportation to the island of Yaros. No reason appears why he should have to justify himself by fabricating stories of ill-treatment. But, according to his statements, he had burnt documents containing names of his associates and he refused to sign a declaration of loyalty. Further, there is no evidence that he revealed information under interrogation.

16. A possible motive for the police to put Vardikos under pressure might have been to obtain information about the Greek Democratic Youth and its members, as indicated by himself. The police officers might well have doubted his affirmation that he had burnt the archives of the organization and they would naturally have been interested in finding these archives if they still existed.

Further, according to his own statement, Vardikos was a trade union official and had already interfered against the police in strike situations (like the Valpex incident, reported by him). Thus he was known to the police inspectors of the Security Service and it would be understandable that in view of this past a certain animosity existed towards him.

17. From the medical examination of the witness it results that:

— he bears scars on his forehead, left shoulder and left elbow which could correspond to blows received in 1967;

— his two upper teeth which are in perfect condition are possibly replacements. His account cannot be medically excluded;

— his descriptions of the application of an iron clamp screwed on his head can medically not be excluded or confirmed.

18. The Sub-Commission has no evidence before it from the respondent Government or other sources, contradicting the statements of Vardikos. As regards the possibility of fabrication referred to in paragraph 15(i) above, the Sub-Commission notes that his account of his ill-treatment is comparatively limited: for example, it is confined to one occasion and no suggestion is made of the familiar falanga, and the statement about food and drink at Lavrion is limited to its lack of provision by the prison authorities. Such restraint would not, in the view of the Sub-Commission, characterise a story invented for propaganda purposes. Further, the fact that allegations are repeated for propaganda purposes does not in itself make them untrue.

Certain positive evidence in the medical report of scars tends to confirm his statements. The Sub-Commission then accepts his account of his ill-treatment as substantially true.

[About 300 pages of additional evidence respecting other victims follows.]

Opinion of the commission

. . .

17. The Sub-Commission has investigated 30 cases to a substantial degree and expressed some conclusion with regard to 28 of them. With regard to these cases the Commission finds it established that:

(i)   torture or ill-treatment has been inflicted in 11 individual cases, namely:

— Vardikos, Vlassis, Leloudas, Miss Arseni, Mrs. Tsirka, Lendakis, Korovessis (by the Athens Security Police)

— Veryvakis (at the headquarters of the Athens Suburban Gendarmerie in Patissia)

— Meletis, Miss Pangopoulou (by the Security Police of Salonica)

— Livanos (at the 521 Marines Brigade camp near Aghia Paraskevi);

(ii)   there has since April 1967 been a practice of torture and ill-treatment by the Athens Security Police, Bouboulinas Street, of persons arrested for political reasons, and that:

(a) this torture and ill-treatment has most often consisted in the application of 'falanga' or severe beatings of all parts of the body;

(b) its purpose has been the extraction of information including confessions concerning the political activities and associations of the victims and other persons considered to be subversive;

(iii) the evidence before the Commission of torture or ill-treatment having been inflicted on 17 other individuals demands further investigation, since it ranges from indications:

— Ambaticlos (by the Piraeus Security Police)

— Karaosman (at the Interrogation Centre of the Central Intelligence Service in Aghia Paraskevi)

and the establishment of *prima facie* cases:

— Miss Kallerghi, Petropoulos, Kiaos, Tsiloglou, Dakos (by the Athens Security Police)

— Notaras (by the Athens Security Police and on board the ship 'Elli')

to strong indications:

— Xintavelonis, Mrs. Papanicola (at the Athens Security Police)

— Panagoulis (at the 505 Marine Brigade camp near Dionysos)

— Papagiannakis and Yotopoulos (by the Piraeus Security Police)

— Nestor, Sipitanos and Pyrzas (in a military camp near the Sedes airfield in Salonica— Central Intelligence Service).

The Sub-Commission was in effect prevented, directly or indirectly, by the respondent Government from completing its investigation of these cases;

(iv) the competent Greek authorities, confronted with numerous and substantial complaints and allegations of torture and ill-treatment, having failed to take any effective steps to investigate them or to ensure remedies for any such complaints or allegations found to be true.[66]

18. The Commission also finds that:

(i) the conditions of detention in the cells in the basement of the Security Police building in Bouboulinas Street, in which persons arrested for political reasons have been held, are contrary to Article 3;

(ii) the combination of conditions described in Part VI above, in which political offenders are held in the Averoff Prison, and the extreme manner of the separation of detainees from their families and the conditions of gross overcrowding in the camps on Leros, also constitute breaches of Article 3.[67]

Resolution of the Committee of Ministers
of the Council of Europe

Resolution DH (70) 1
(Adopted by the Committee of Ministers on 15 April 1970)
The Greek Case
Applications No. 3321/67, Denmark v. Greece;
No. 3322/67, Norway v. Greece; No. 3323/67, Sweden v. Greece;
No. 3344/67, Netherlands v. Greece

---

[66] Sub-sections (i) and (ii) were adopted by a majority of 12 members. Sub-sections (iii)—except the findings on 4 cases—and (iv) were adopted by a majority of 13 members. The findings on the cases of Ambaticlos, Karaosman, Papagiannakis and Yotopoulos were adopted by a majority of 10 members.

[67] Sub-section (i) was adopted by a majority of 13 members. Sub-section (ii) was adopted by a majority of 11 members.

The Committee of Ministers,

1. Having regard to Article 32 of the European Convention for the Protection of Human Rights and Fundamental Freedoms (hereinafter called 'the Convention');

2. Having regard to the report drawn up by the European Commission of Human Rights (hereinafter called 'the Commission') in accordance with Article 31 of the Convention and relating to the Applications lodged on 20 September 1967 by the Governments of Denmark, Norway and Sweden against the Government of Greece (Nos. 3321/67, 3322/67, 3323/67) and on 27 September 1967 by the Government of the Netherlands against the Government of Greece (No. 3344/67); . . .

8. Considering that the Government of Greece has denounced on 12 December 1969, the European Convention on Human Rights and the First Protocol and that, in accordance with Article 65, paragraph 1 of the Convention, this denunciation will become effective on 13 June 1970;

9. Considering paragraph 2 of Article 65 of the Convention which provides that the denunciation 'shall not have the effect of releasing the High Contracting Party concerned from its obligations under this Convention in respect of any act which, being capable of constituting a violation of such obligations, may have been performed by it before the date at which the denunciation became effective';

10. Voting in accordance with the provisions of Article 32, paragraph 1 of the Convention;

11. Agreeing with the opinion of the Commission;

12. Decides:

(a) that the Government of Greece has violated Articles 3, 5, 6, 8, 9, 10, 11, 13 and 14 of the Convention and Article 3 of the First Protocol;

(b) that the Government of Greece has not violated Article 7 of the Convention and Article 1 of the First Protocol;

13. Having regard to the denunciation of the Statute of the Council of Europe by the Government of Greece on 12 December 1969;

14. Having regard to the denunciation on the same date by the same Government of the European Convention on Human Rights and of its First Protocol, mentioned above;

15. Having regard to Resolution (69) 51 of 12 December 1969;

16. Having considered the proposals made by the Commission in accordance with paragraph 3 of Article 31 of the Convention;

17. Considering that the Greek Government has declared on 7 December 1969 that it considers the report of the Commission as 'null and void' and that it 'does not consider itself legally bound by the conclusions of the said report';

18. Considering that the Greek Government was given an opportunity to take part in the discussions of the Committee of Ministers when it was examining the report of the Commission, but in a letter of 19 February 1970 the Government stated that it had no intention whatsoever of doing so and that such a participation would be 'inconsistent with Greece's formal denunciation of both the Commission's report and the European Convention';

19. Considering that these circumstances and communications clearly established that the Greek Government is not prepared to comply with its continuing obligations under the Convention

and thus with the system of collective protection of human rights established thereby, and that accordingly the Committee of Ministers is called upon to deal with the case in conditions which are not precisely those envisaged in the Convention;

20. Concludes that in the present case there is no basis for further action under paragraph 2 of Article 32 of the Convention;

21. Concludes that it must take a decision, in accordance with paragraph 3 of Article 32 of the Convention, about the publication of the report of the Commission;

22. Decides to make public forthwith the report drawn up by the Commission on the above-mentioned Applications;

23. Urges the Government of Greece to restore, without delay, human rights and fundamental freedoms in Greece, in accordance with the Convention and the First Protocol, taking into account, *inter alia,* the proposals made by the Commission which are attached hereto;

24. Also urges the Government of Greece, in particular, to abolish immediately torture and other ill-treatment of prisoners and to release immediately persons detained under administrative order;

25. And accordingly resolves to follow developments in Greece in this respect.

B. FACT-FINDING AND SHAME AT STRASBOURG

The *Greek Case* is the only example in a half century of a state being shamed by Strasbourg's fact-finding to a degree that it chose to leave the Council of Europe, albeit just before it was excluded by the other members of the institution. Expulsion is the only forcible sanction available to the Council when a state ignores findings of human rights violations. Is it enough? Was it enough in the *Greek Case*? Ultimately the military regime in Greece did collapse. Were the actions at Strasbourg in any way a contribution to the military regime's downfall? Let us look at the *Greek Case* in its political context.

The Greek military's coup d'état on 21 April 1967, was quickly followed on 24 April 1967, by a debate in the Consultative Assembly of the Council of Europe protesting infringements by the new Greek government of the European Human Rights Convention.[68] The four state complaints leading to the proceedings against Greece were lodged in response to a resolution of the Standing Committee of the Consultative Assembly of the Council of Europe on 23 June 1967:

[T]he Governments of the Contracting Parties to the European Convention on Human Rights [should] refer the Greek case, either separately or jointly, to the European Commission of Human Rights in accordance with Article 24 of the Convention.[69]

Before then, states bringing suit against other states before the Commission had had some sort of ethnic or religious link with the injured individuals, i.e., Greece with

---

[68] Coleman, 'Greece and the Council of Europe: the International Legal Protection of Human Rights by the Political Process', 2 *Israel Yearbook on Human Rights* 121–4 (1992).

[69] Buergenthal, 'Proceedings Against Greece Under the European Convention of Human Rights', 62 *American Journal of International Law* 441 (1968) (hereinafter cited as 'Buergenthal').

Greek Cypriots against the United Kingdom, Austria with ethnic Germans against Italy, and Ireland with Roman Catholics in Northern Ireland against the United Kingdom. Denmark, Norway, Sweden and the Netherlands had no such ethnic or religious ties to the Greek population. Rather, it seems that the four countries complained to the Commission because they felt they had a moral duty to do so. There was a sentiment, especially in the legal departments of the four Foreign Ministries, that if European human rights law was not employed against the Greek Colonels' military regime, the whole Strasbourg system would be endangered and the experiment in international human rights machinery defeated.[70]

Besides excluding Greece, the Council of Europe had little power to enforce an adverse decision of the Committee of Ministers. That exclusion was the Council's chief 'punishment' has been viewed by a disappointed Greek commentator as evidence of 'a total lack of effectiveness of the Convention, whether direct or indirect'.[71] However, Thomas Buergenthal, later President of the Inter-American Court of Human Rights, was more positive:

Had they [the four states] not referred this case ... [it] would have [been] unmistakably demonstrated that even as advanced a system for the international protection of human rights as the European Convention on Human Rights is doomed to fail whenever it must depend for its enforcement on disinterested governments.[72]

As the situation developed, were the Strasbourg human rights proceedings at all efficacious? Though Greece denounced the Convention on 12 December 1969, another commentator believed that the Commission's fact-finding, its Report and the Council's Resolution nonetheless constituted a significant restraint on the behaviour of the Greek authorities. Though it is difficult to demonstrate, it is most probable that fewer Greeks were tortured than otherwise might have been. The negotiations over a friendly settlement pushed the government to sign an agreement with the International Red Cross that imposed further restraints. Because of the Commission and international pressure the Greek government did not carry out serious reprisals against witnesses who testified before the Commission in Greece, and because these people testified, the truth was known abroad. The *Greek Case* cannot be considered a success in terms of protecting the human rights of Greeks, but it probably had something of a positive effect.[73]

A similar conclusion was reached by another observer:

Although invocation of the inter-state complaint procedure against it may have prompted Greece's decision to denounce the Council of Europe and the ECHR, the implementation of the complaint procedure arguably did more good than harm. The political motives so commonly

---

[70] Becket, 'The Greek Case Before the European Human Rights Commission', 1 *Human Rights Law Journal* 91, 94–6 (1970) (hereinafter cited as 'Becket').

[71] Bechlivanou, 'Greece', *The European Convention for the Protection of Human Rights: International Protection Versus National Restrictions* 151, 156 (Delmas-Marty ed. Chodkiewicz trans. 1992).

[72] Buergenthal, *supra* n. 69, at 450.

[73] Becket, *supra* n. 70, at 112–13.

associated with inter-state complaints were largely absent in the Greek cases. Greece returned to democracy several years later and the human rights situation improved drastically. While invocation of the inter-state complaint procedure was probably not the only cause of the eventual change in the Greek government, the in-depth and public consideration of the situation of human rights in Greece was a necessary adjunct to redemocratization, which might not have occurred as quickly without it. However, the political pressure exercised by the Consultative Assembly's Recommendation probably contributed to some degree to the resolution of the situation.[74]

It may well be that the increasing diplomatic isolation of Greece to which the *Greek Case* contributed made it difficult for the Colonels' regime to govern effectively. When Turkey invaded Cyprus in July 1974, the Greek military government was unable to respond meaningfully. The Colonels' regime then collapsed precipitously.[75]

[74] Leckie, 'The Inter-State Complaint Procedure in International Human Rights Law: Hopeful Prospects or Wishful Thinking?' 10 *Human Rights Quarterly* 249, 292 (1988).

[75] *See* R. Clogg, *A Short History of Modern Greece* 192–9 (1979).

3

THE EUROPEAN COURT OF HUMAN RIGHTS

The idea of using a regional international court to help protect human rights in Europe surfaced in the earliest debates leading to the European Human Rights Convention. Speaking as a representative of the United Kingdom, Winston Churchill declared at the first session of the Consultative Assembly of the Council of Europe on 17 August 1949:

[O]nce the foundation of human rights is agreed on the lines of the decisions of the United Nations at Geneva [the 1948 Universal Declaration of Human Rights]—but I trust in much shorter form—we hope that a European Court might be set up, before which cases of the violation of these rights in our own body of 12 nations might be brought to the judgment of the civilised world. Such a Court, of course, would have no sanctions and would depend for the enforcement of their judgment on the individual decisions of the States now banded together in this Council of Europe. But these States would have subscribed beforehand to the process, and I have no doubt that the great body of public opinion in all these countries would press for action in accordance with the freely given decision.[1]

Its jurisdiction made optional for many years by Article 46 of the European Human Rights Convention, the European Court of Human Rights was not constituted until 1958. Rarely used until the 1970s, the Court's caseload increased dramatically in the 1980s and 1990s. Nowadays, the European Court of Human Rights in Strasbourg ranks alongside the International Court of Justice in The Hague and the European Court of Justice in Luxembourg as one of the three premier courts of international adjudication.

A. THE CONSTITUTION OF THE COURT

As with any public international institution, the European Court of Human Rights is created and defined by an international agreement. In this case, the European Convention on Human Rights serves as the constitution of the Court. Until 1999, the

---

[1] I Council of Europe, *Collected Edition of the Travaux Préparatoires* at 34 (1975) (hereinafter cited as 'Travaux Préparatoires').

Court existed alongside the Commission both set up by Article 19 of the old Convention, to 'ensure the observation of the engagements undertaken by the High Contracting Parties in the present Convention'[2]

Pursuant to old Article 46, '[a]ny of the High Contracting Parties may at any time declare that it recognises as compulsory *ipso facto* and without special agreement the jurisdiction of the Court in all matter concerning the interpretation and application of the present Convention.[3] Eight state ratifications were needed to create the Court and in 1950 'it was generally doubted that this would ever happen'.[4] However, by 1958, eight states had consented to the jurisdiction of the Court which became officially competent to hear cases on 3 September of that year.[5] As of 7 September 1994, all 30 states then party to the Convention had submitted to Article 46's compulsory jurisdiction.[6]

Since November 1998, the Court has been significantly refashioned under the terms of Protocol No. 11. As we have already seen, Protocol No. 11 merged, as of November 1999, the Commission into the Court and otherwise transformed the enforcement machinery of the Convention.[7] Section II of the new Convention is devoted to the new European Court of Human Rights.[8] New Article 19 constitutes the Court: '[t]o ensure the observance of the engagements undertaken by the High Contracting Parties in the Convention and the Protocols thereto, there shall be set up a European Court of Human Rights, hereinafter referred to as "the Court". It shall function on a permanent basis'.[9]

The number of judges is set at the number of High Contracting Parties,[10] presently 41; judges are to be of 'high moral character' and 'either possess the qualifications required for appointment to high judicial office or be jurisconsults of recognised competence'.[11] The judges 'sit on the Court in their individual capacity',[12] i.e., not as a representative of a state. Judges are elected by the Council of Europe's Parliamentary Assembly for renewable six-year terms, but they must retire at age 70.[13] The Court has a registry and 'shall be assisted by legal secretaries',[14] i.e., court clerks.

[2] European Convention for the Protection of Human Rights and Fundamental Freedoms, 213 U.N.T.S. 221, E.T.S. 5, U.K.T.S. 71 (1953), signed at Rome 4 Nov. 1950; entered into force 3 Sept. 1953, Council of Europe print of Jan. 1994 (hereinafter cited as 'Old Convention').

[3] *Id.* Art. 46(1).

[4] Sohn, 'Book Review' 57 *American Journal of International Law* 168, 169 (1963).

[5] European Commission of Human Rights, *Stock-Taking on the European Convention on Human Rights: The First Thirty Years: 1954 until 1984* 1.

[6] Council of Europe, *Chart of Signatures and Ratifications, as of 9 Sept. 1994.*

[7] Council of Europe, Convention for Protection of Human Rights and Fundamental Freedoms (ETS No. 5), signed at Rome 4 Nov 1950, entered into force 3 Sept 1953, as amended by Protocol No. 11 (ETS no. 155), signed at Strasbourg, 11 May 1994, entered into force 1 Nov 1998, www.coe.fr (2 February 1999) (hereinafter cited as 'Convention').

[8] *Id.* Arts. 19–51.

[9] *Id.* Art. 19.

[10] *Id.* Art. 20.

[11] *Id.* Art. 21(1).

[12] *Id.* Art. 21(2).

[13] *Id.* Arts. 22, 23.

[14] *Id.* Art. 25.

The Court as a whole is referred to as the 'Plenary Court', which elects its own President, two Vice-Presidents, Registrar, and one or more Deputy Registrars.[15] As we have already examined in Chapter 2, the Court sits in three-judge Committees to determine the admissibility of applications submitted by individuals.[16] It also sits in seven-judge chambers, the ordinary judicial panel, and in 17-judge Grand Chambers, special judicial panels for more important cases.[17] Article 30 provides that a chamber is to relinquish jurisdiction to a Grand Chamber when a pending case 'raises a serious question affecting the interpretation of the Convention or the protocols thereto, or where the resolution of a question before the Chamber might have a result inconsistent with a judgment previously delivered by the Court'.[18]

In Chapter 2, we have already reviewed the pre-judgment functions of the Court.[19] If a case is deemed admissible and is not terminated by a friendly settlement and after fact-finding, the Court proceeds to a public hearing which is ordinarily open to the public.[20] 'If the Court finds that there has been a violation of the Convention or the protocols thereto, and if the internal law of the High Contracting Party concerned allows only partial reparation to be made, the Court shall, if necessary, afford just satisfaction to the injured party'.[21] Judgments of chambers of the Court are final unless a case has been referred and accepted by a Grand Chamber, a decision made by a five-judge panel of a Grand Chamber; judgments of a Grand Chamber are final.[22] Final judgments of the Court are binding on states who are parties to a case.[23] 'The final judgment of the Court shall be transmitted to the Committee of Ministers, which shall supervise its execution'.[24]

Until October 1994, only the states party to the Convention and the Commission had standing to bring cases to the Court.[25] Most cases, however, were brought to the Court by the Commission. Though cases not referred to the Court were, by old Article 32, put within the 'adjudicatory' jurisdiction of the Council of Europe's Committee of Ministers, the Commission normally prefered to rely on the Court rather than the Committee of Ministers when the Commission sought a legally binding judgment either to enforce its opinion against a recalcitrant government or when the Commission itself was closely divided.[26]

Although individuals did not for 40 years have standing to bring cases to the Court, private parties were almost always the initiators of the suits before the Commission

---

[15] *Id.* Art. 26.

[16] *Id.* Arts. 27–28.

[17] *Id.* Arts. 27, 30–31.

[18] *Id.* Art. 30.

[19] *Id.* Arts. 28, 29, 32–39.

[20] *Id.* Art. 40.

[21] *Id.* Art. 41.

[22] *Id.* Arts. 42–44.

[23] *Id.* Art. 46(1).

[24] *Id.* Art. 46(2).

[25] Convention, *supra* n. 2, Art. 44.

[26] Nowak, Rosenmayr & Schwaighofer, 'Sixth International Colloquy about the European Convention on Human Rights' 7 *Human Rights Law Journal* 117, 120–1 (1986).

which eventually reached the Court. It was long been recognized that in practice and in principle it was the individual, not the Commission, who was the true 'party' before the Court. As Sir Humphrey Waldock argued in 1960, appearing for the Commission before the Court in its first case, *Lawless*:

[T]he Commission, although not a Party to the case, participates in the proceedings and stands in a position intermediate between the Government and the individual. Moreover, if the Commission considers the rights of the individual to have been violated, it is the Commission's duty to say so in its report, and to present that opinion to the Court. . . . The function of the Commission before the Court, as we understand it, is not litigious: it is ministerial. It is not our function to defend before the Court, either the case of the individual as such or our own opinion simply as such. Our function, we believe, is to place before you all the elements of the case relevant for the determination of the case by the Court.[27]

Such a principle was fitting. One of the reasons the Strasbourg Court was fashioned in the first place was that the International Court of Justice at The Hague was and is still permitted to hear only complaints brought by states.[28] In *Lawless*, the Court rejected Ireland's arguments that the precedent of the International Court be followed and lawyers representing individuals be not allowed to argue before it:

[T]he Court must bear in mind its duty to safeguard the interests of the individual, who may not be a Party to any court proceedings [but] nevertheless the whole of the proceedings in the Court, as laid down by the Convention and the Rules of Court, are upon issues which concern the Applicant [and] accordingly, it is in the interests of the proper administration of justice that the Court should have knowledge of and, if need be, take into consideration, the Applicant's point of view.[29]

Originally, lawyers for individual petitioners could only appear before the Court at the discretion of the Commission and in the guise of rendering 'assistance' to the delegates of the Commission. With the adoption of new Rules of Court on 24 November 1982, effective January 1983, the initiation of proceedings before the Court were transmitted to the applicant who was also invited to be individually represented. 'These provisions should avoid a recurrence of what happened in the *Golder Case*, when the applicant was apparently unaware of the fact that his case had come before the Court until he read newspaper reports about the proceedings.[30]

On 1 October 1994, the standing of individuals before the Court improved dramatically as Protocol No. 9 to the Convention came into force for 13 then consenting states.[31] Protocol No. 9, which was prepared and ready for signature in 1990, amended four articles of the old Convention, most importantly Articles 44 and 48, to include

---

[27] Mahoney, 'Developments in the Procedure of the European Court of Human Rights: The Revised Rules of Court' (1983) 3 *Yearbook of European Law* 127, 128.

[28] *See 1 Travaux Preparatoires, supra* n. 1, at 226.

[29] 14 Nov. 1960 (No. 1), 1 E.H.R.R. 1, para. 15.

[30] Drzemczewski, 'The European Convention on Human Rights' 2 *Yearbook of European Law* 327, 328 (1982).

[31] Austria, the Czech Republic, Finland, Hungary, Ireland, Italy, Luxembourg, the Netherlands, Norway, Romania, Slovakia and Slovenia, Council of Europe. *Human Rights Information Sheet No. 34: January–June 1994* 2 (1995).

persons, non-governmental organizations and groups of individuals who have complained to the Commission among those who can refer a case to the Court. As we have already seen in Chapter 2, since 1 November 1998, persons, non-governmental organizations, and groups of individuals are now entitled by the reforms wrought by Protocol No. 11 to bring cases against states party to the Convention to the Court, albeit in the first instance to three-judge admissibility committees.[32] Individuals are now, formally as well as practically, the real complaintants before the Court.

The Court may not only decide whether the Convention has been violated; it may also award damages, the Convention's term being 'just satisfaction'. Article 50 of the old Convention provided that:

If the Court finds that a decision or a measure taken by a legal authority or any other authority of a High Contracting Party is completely or partially in conflict with the obligations arising from the present Convention, and if the internal law of the said Party allows only partial reparation to be made for the consequences of this decision or measure, the decision of the Court shall, if necessary, afford just satisfaction to the injured party.[33]

Though it could be that the drafters of Article 50 meant it to be a last resort to be employed only when a national legal system failed to provide redress for a Court-decided violation of the Convention, in practice the Court has interpreted the just satisfaction article in a more activist fashion.[34] Looking to Article 52, 'the judgment of the Court shall be final',[35] Court in *Ringeisen* in 1972 rejected Austria's assertion that applicants had to bring a new case after a judgment finding a violation of the Convention if applicants were to seek Article 50 redress:

[Article 52's] sole object is to make the Court's judgment not subject to any appeal to another authority. It would be a formalistic attitude alien to international law to maintain that the Court may not apply Article 50 save on condition that it either rules on the matter by the same judgment which found a violation or that this judgment has expressly kept the case open.[36]

The Court's Article 50 judgments in *Ringeisen* and subsequent decisions 'removed a number of potential obstacles to victims of violations, thereby creating a possibility of both redress and development of the substantive law.[37]

After making its judgment on the merits, the Court has sometimes postpone ruling on just satisfaction, permitting the state involved to settle on compensation or other redress with a private claimant. At other times, no such out-of-court settlement is possible and the parties have returned to the Court for an Article 50 ruling. In general,

---

[32] Convention, *supra* n. 7, Art. 34.

[33] Old Convention, *supra* n. 2, Art. 50.

[34] Gray, 'Remedies for Individuals Under the European Convention on Human Rights'. 6 *Human Rights Law Review* 153, 156 (1986) (hereinafter cited as 'Gray').

[35] Convention, *supra* n. 2, art. 52.

[36] 22 June 1972 (Article 50) (No. 15), 1 E.H.R.R. 504, para. 17–18.

[37] J. G. Merrills, *The Development of International Law by the European Court of Human Rights* 63–6 (1993) (hereinafter cited as 'Merrills').

'the Court has shown itself committed to the provision of swift reparation for individuals injured by violation of the Convention'[38]

Article 50 has been replaced by the more succinct language of Article 41 of the new Convention, but with the same import:

> If the Court finds that there has been a violation of the Convention or the Protocols thereto, and if the internal law of the High Contracting Party concerned allows only partial reparation to be made, the Court shall, if necessary, afford just satisfaction to the injured party.[39]

The 'High Contracting Parties undertake to abide by the final judgment of the Court in any case to which they are parties'; execution of the Court's decisions is entrusted to the supervision of the Committee of Ministers.[40] States have, generally, voluntarily complied with the Court's judgments.[41] Such compliance may involve payments to the injured party, as well as amendment of national law. Between 1959 and 1989 for example, the Court awarded 'just satisfaction' in 85 instances. These ranged from 100 Dutch guilders in *Engel* (about $40) to 1,150,000 Swedish Crowns (about $160,000) in *Spörrong* and *Lonuroth v. Sweden*.[42A] We return to questions of actual compliance in section C(1) below, 'The Efficacy of Strasbourg'.[42]

B. THE NATURE OF THE COURT

1. THE ROLE OF THE COURT

The European Court of Human Rights did not become an effective legal instrument easily or rapidly. Although the European Convention on Human Rights was signed in 1950 and entered into force in 1953, for 20 years it was, in the words of Jochen Frowein, a Vice President of the Commission, 'a sleeping beauty, frequently referred to but without much impact'.[43] It seems that the right of access of private suitors has been crucial to bringing the system of European human rights law alive. Between 1955 and 1997, there were only 13 state petitions filed with the Commission, but there were 39,034 private claims.[44]

Comparing the business of the European Court of Human Rights to that of the International Court of Justice, one is struck by how much it is the access of private

---

[38] Gray, *supra* n. 34, at 171.

[39] Convention, *supra* n. 7, Art. 41.

[40] Convention, *supra* n. 7, Art. 46.

[41] *See* Ganshof van der Meersch, 'European Court of Human Rights', 8 *Encyclopedia of Public International Law* 192, 205 (1985); Merrills, *supra* n. 37, at 2.

[42A] 23 Sept. 1982 (no. 52), 5 E.H.R.R. 35.

[42] Council of Europe, European Court of Human Rights, *Survey of Activities: 1959–1989* 3 (24 Jan. 1990).

[43] Frowein, 'European Integration Through Fundamental Rights' 18 *Journal of Law Reform* 5, 8 (1984).

[44] 1997 *Yearbook of the European Convention on Human Rights* 76–79 (1998).

claimants to the European human rights system that explains the difference in case-load. Unlike the work of the International Court which has remained more or less static for almost 80 years,[45] the activity of the European Court of Human Rights has been rapidly growing. While there were only ten judgments delivered by the European Court in the 1960s, there were 26 judgments in the 1970s, 169 in the 1980s, and, in the first nine years of the 1990s, already 818, an annual average about 30 times that of the ICJ.

If the Court finds that the internal law of a state violates the Convention, then the state is obliged at international law to alter that law. The Court, however, neither has the authority to alter municipal law nor will it instruct the state on how a change in municipal law ought to be made. As the Court ruled in *Marckx* in 1979: 'It is for the respondent State, and the respondent State alone, to take the measures it considers appropriate to assure that its domestic law is coherent and consistent'.[46] This latitude may mean that there will be lingering doubts about whether the measures taken by the respondent government bring the state fully into compliance with the Convention and the Court's judgment.[47]

The Court has been increasingly willing to find states in violation of the Convention. In its early decisions, the Court seemed anxious to reassure its member states that it would be sensitive to their concerns and traditions. For example, in 1961, in its first substantive decision, *Lawless*, the Court decided that although Ireland would have otherwise violated Articles 5 and 6 of the Convention by detaining an IRA suspect for five months without trial, the state was permitted to deviate from the strict rules of the Convention because it was justified under the Convention's Article 15 in declaring a 'public emergency threatening the life of the nation' and taking extraordinary measures.[48] While decisions such as *Lawless* might have reassured states, they did little to encourage individual petitions. It was only in 1968, 18 years after the signing of the European Convention on Human Rights and almost 10 years after the Court became competent to hear cases, that a decision, *Neumeister*, was rendered against a member state, the Court holding that Austria's detention without trial for 26 months of a businessman accused of tax fraud violated Article 5's guarantees to a trial within a reasonable time or to a release pending trial.[49] Even more encouraging to private litigants have been more recent judgments of the Court. Since the late 1970s, many of

---

[45] Between 1921 and 1945, the Permanent Court of International Justice issued roughly three or four decisions a year; the record of the International Court of Justice between 1946 and 1990 has been about three decisions annually. M. W. Janis. *An Introduction to International Law* 126 (3rd ed. 1999).

[46] 13 June 1979 (No. 31), 2 E.H.R.R. 330, para. 20.

[47] *See*, e.g., Van Dijk, 'The Benthem Case and Its Aftermath in the Netherlands' 34 *Netherlands International Law Review* 5, 9–24 (1987). Article 52 of the Convention obliges member states upon request by the Secretary General of the Council of Europe to 'furnish an explanation of the manner in which its internal law ensures the effective implementation of any of the provisions of the Convention' (and see chapter 9 below).

[48] 1 July 1961 (No. 3), 1 E.H.R.R. 15, para. 54–63 (and see *infra*).

[49] 27 June 1968 (No. 8), 1 E.H.R.R. 91; *see* Beddard, *Human Rights and Europe* 11 (1980) (hereinafter cited as 'Beddard').

the Strasbourg judges seem readier now than ever before to upset member states with decisions that stretch the language of the Convention.[50]

However, this readiness to upset states was a risky business. States did not need to accept either the jurisdiction of the Court or the right of individual petition. Both were optional clauses, part of the compromise reached in the process of drafting the Convention.[51] If the Court was perceived by a state as going 'too far', then that state could have decided not to renew its acceptance of the optional clauses. Just such a perception might have arisen as a result of the *Sunday Times Case*. Why it did not may tell us something important not only about the development of the Court but also about its efficacy.

2. THE *SUNDAY TIMES CASE*

Judgment of 26 April 1979
(No. 30), 2 E.H.R.R. 245

. . .

8. Between 1958 and 1961 Distillers Company (Biochemicals) Limited ('Distillers') manufactured and marketed under license in the United Kingdom drugs containing an ingredient initially developed in the Federal Republic of Germany and known as thalidomide. The drugs were prescribed as sedatives for, in particular, expectant mothers. In 1961 a number of women who had taken the drugs during pregnancy gave birth to children suffering from severe deformities; in the course of time there were some 250 such births in all. Distillers withdrew all drugs containing thalidomide from the British market in November of the same year. . . .

10. . . . [B]y 1971, three hundred and eighty-nine claims in all were pending against Distillers. Apart from a statement of claim in one case and a defense delivered in 1969, no further steps were taken in those actions where writs had been issued. Distillers had announced in February 1968 that they would provide a substantial sum for the benefit of the remaining three hundred and eighty-nine claimants and both sides were anxious to arrive at a settlement out of court. The case in fact raised legal issues of considerable difficulty under English law. Had any of the actions come on for trial, they would have been heard by a professional judge sitting without a jury.

In 1971 negotiations began on a proposal by Distillers to establish a charitable trust fund for all the deformed children other than those covered by the 1968 settlement. The proposal was made subject to the condition that all the parents accepted but five refused, one, at least, because payments out of the fund would have been based on need. An application, on behalf of the parents who would have accepted, to replace those five by the Official Solicitor as next friend was refused by the Court of Appeal in April 1972. During subsequent negotiations, the original condition was replaced by a requirement that 'a substantial majority' of the parents consented. By September 1972 a settlement involving the setting-up of a £3,250,000 trust fund had been worked out and was expected to be submitted in October to the court for approval.

11. Reports concerning the deformed children had appeared regularly in *The Sunday Times* since 1967 and in 1968 it had ventured some criticism of the settlement concluded in that year.

---

[50] C. C. Morrisson, *The Dynamics of Development in the European Human Rights System* 19 (1981).
[51] *See* the legislative history in Chapter 1, i.e., 'The Negotiation of the Convention'.

There had also been comment on the children's circumstances in other newspapers and on television. In particular, in December 1971, the *Daily Mail* published an article which prompted complaints from parents that it might jeopardise the settlement negotiations in hand; the *Daily Mail* was 'warned off' by the Attorney-General in a formal letter threatening sanctions under the law of contempt of court but contempt proceedings were not actually instituted. On 24 September 1972, *The Sunday Times* carried an article entitled 'Our Thalidomide Children: A Cause for National Shame': this examined the settlement proposals then under consideration, describing them as 'grotesquely out of proportion to the injuries suffered', criticised various aspects of English law on the recovery and assessment of damages in personal injury cases, complained of the delay that had elapsed since the births and appealed to Distillers to make a more generous offer. The article contained the following passage:

> '. . . the thalidomide children shame Distillers . . . there are times when to insist on the letter of the law is as exposed to criticism as infringement of another's legal rights. The figure in the proposed settlement is to be £3.25 million spread over 10 years. This does not shine as a beacon against pre-tax profits last year of £64.8 million and company assets worth £421 million. Without in any way surrendering on negligence, Distillers could and should think again'.

A footnote in the article announced that 'in a future article *The Sunday Times* [would] trace how the tragedy occurred'. On 17 November 1972, the Divisional Court of the Queen's Bench Division granted the Attorney-General's application for an injunction restraining publication of this future article on the ground that it would constitute contempt of court . . .

17. The unpublished article which was the subject of the injunction opened with a suggestion that the manner of marketing thalidomide in Britain left a lot to be desired. It stated that Distillers:

'— relied heavily on the German tests and had not completed full trials of its own *before* marketing the drug;

— failed to uncover in its research into medical and scientific literature the fact that a drug related to thalidomide could cause monster births;

— before marketing the drug did no animal tests to determine the drug's effect on the foetus;

— accelerated the marketing of the drug for commercial reasons. Were not deflected by a warning from one of its own staff that thalidomide was far more dangerous than had been supposed;

— were not deflected by the discovery that thalidomide could damage the nervous system, in itself a hint that it might damage the foetus;

— continued to advertise the drug as safe for pregnant women up to a month from when it was withdrawn'.

The body of the article described how, after their apparently disappointing initial ventures into pharmaceutics, Distillers learned in 1956 that the German firm of *Chemie Gruenenthal* had developed a sedative considered harmless and unique—thalidomide. The very large market existing at the time for sedatives was becoming overcrowded and Distillers thought it necessary to act quickly. Their decision to market the drug was taken before they had seen technical information, other than the transcript of a German symposium, and before carrying out independent tests. Indeed, they seemed to believe that thalidomide would not need elaborate tests. Distillers put in hand a search of scientific literature but failed to discover the results of research in 1950 by a Dr.

Thiersch showing that a chemical related to thalidomide could cause monster births; opinions differed as to whether his work should have been found.

Sales of thalidomide began in Germany in October 1957 and Distillers were committed under their licensing agreement to commence marketing in April 1958. They put the programme for the drug's launch in hand even though clinical trials were behind. Results of the first British trials were published in January 1958: it had been found that thalidomide suppressed the work of the thyroid gland and that its method of action was unknown; the researcher warned that more tests were needed. Distillers did not rely on this advice, basing their decision on 'flimsy' evidence, namely other trials in the United Kingdom and assurances concerning the results of research in Germany. The warning about anti-thyroid effects was particularly relevant since it was known that drugs affecting the thyroid could affect unborn children; it was reasonable to argue that Distillers should have delayed launching the drug pending further tests.

On 14 April 1958, continued the article, thalidomide went on sale in Britain, advertised as 'completely safe'. At the end of 1959, Distillers' pharmacologist discovered that thalidomide in liquid form was highly poisonous and that an overdose might be lethal, but his report was never published and the liquid product went on sale in July 1961. In December 1960, it was reported that patients who had taken thalidomide in the tablet form in which it had firstly been on sale showed symptoms of peripheral neuritis; this news had the result of holding up an application to market thalidomide in the United States of America where it was, in fact, never sold. Further cases of peripheral neuritis were reported in 1961 but Distillers' advertising continued to stress the drug's safety.

Early in 1961 children were born in the United Kingdom with deformities but there was at the time nothing to connect them with thalidomide. However, between May and October, a doctor in Australia discovered that the common factor in a number of monster births was that the mothers had taken thalidomide during pregnancy. This was reported to *Chemie Gruenenthal* on 24 November who withdrew the drug two days later following newspaper disclosures. Distillers ended the public sale of thalidomide immediately afterwards. Tests on animals, published in April 1962, confirmed that thalidomide caused deformities but sales to hospitals were not ended until December 1962.

The draft article concluded as follows:

'So the burden of making certain that thalidomide was safe fell squarely on [Distillers]. How did the company measure up to this heavy responsibility? It can be argued that:

1. [Distillers] should have found all the scientific literature about drugs related to thalidomide. It did not.

2. It should have read Thiersch's work on the effects on the nervous system of drugs related to thalidomide, have suspected the possible action on unborn babies and therefore have done tests on animals for teratogenic effect. It did not.

3. It should have done further tests when it discovered that the drug had antithyroid activity and unsuspected toxicity. It did not.

4. It should have had proof before advertising the drug as safe for pregnant women that this was in fact so. It did not.

For [Distillers] it could be argued that it sincerely believed that thalidomide was free from any toxicity at the time it was first put on the market in Britain; that peripheral neuritis did not emerge as a side effect until the drug had been on sale in Britain for two years; that testing for teratogenic effects was not general in 1958; that if tests had been done on the usual laboratory animals nothing would have shown because it is only in the New Zealand white rabbit that thalidomide produces the same effects as in human beings; and, finally, that in the one clinical report of thalidomide being given to pregnant women no serious results followed (because thalidomide is dangerous only during the first 12 weeks of pregnancy) . . .

There appears to be no neat set of answers . . .'.

21. Distillers made a formal complaint to the Attorney-General that *The Sunday Times* article of 24 September 1972 constituted contempt of court in view of the litigation still outstanding and, on 27 September, the Solicitor-General, in the absence of the Attorney-General, wrote to the editor of *The Sunday Times* to ask him for his observations. The editor, in his reply, justified that article and also submitted the draft of the proposed future article for which he claimed complete factual accuracy. The Solicitor-General enquired whether the draft had been seen by any of the parties to the litigation, as a consequence of which a copy of the draft was sent by *The Sunday Times* to Distillers on 10 October. On the previous day, *The Sunday Times* had been advised that the Attorney-General had decided to take no action in respect of the matter already published in September and October; Distillers also took no action. On 11 October, the Attorney-General's Office informed *The Sunday Times* that, following representations by Distillers, the Attorney-General had decided to apply to the High Court in order to obtain a judicial decision on the legality of the publication of the proposed article. On the following day, he issued a writ against Times Newspapers Ltd. in which he claimed an injunction 'to restrain the defendants . . . by themselves, their servants or agents or otherwise, from publishing or causing or authorising to be published or printed an article in draft dealing, *inter alia*, with the development, distribution and use of the drug thalidomide, a copy of which article had been supplied to the Attorney-General by the defendants'.

22. The Attorney-General's application was heard by three judges of the Queen's Bench Division from 7 to 9 November 1972; on 17 November the court granted the injunction.

In its judgment the court remarked:

'the article does not purport to express any views as to the legal responsibility of Distillers . . . but . . . is in many respects critical of Distillers and charges them with neglect in regard to their own failure to test the product, or their failure to react sufficiently sharply to warning signs obtained from the tests by others. No one reading the article could . . . fail to gain the impression that the case against Distillers on the footing of negligence was a substantial one'.

The editor of *The Sunday Times* had indicated that any libel proceedings following publication would be defended by a plea that the contents of the article were true and the court approached the article on the footing that it was factually accurate.

23. The reasoning in the court's judgment may be summarised as follows. The objection to unilateral comment, prior to conclusion of the court hearing, was that it might prevent the due and impartial administration of justice by affecting and prejudicing the mind of the tribunal itself, by affecting witnesses who were to be called or by prejudicing the free choice and conduct of a party to the litigation. It was the third form of prejudice that was relevant to the present case . . .

24. An appeal by Times Newspapers Ltd. against the Divisional Court's decision was heard by the Court of Appeal from 30 January to 2 February 1973. The court had before it an affidavit by the editor of *The Sunday Times* setting out developments in the intervening period both in the case itself and in public discussion thereof. With the leave of the court, counsel for Distillers made

submissions on the contents of the proposed article, pointing to errors he said it contained. On 16 February, the Court of Appeal discharged the injunction. . . .

25. Lord Denning said that the proposed article:

'. . . contains a detailed analysis of the evidence against Distillers. It marshals forcibly the arguments for saying that Distillers did not measure up to their responsibility. Though, to be fair, it does summarise the arguments which could be made for Distillers'. . . .

'Trial by newspaper', continued Lord Denning, must not be allowed. However, the public interest in a matter of national concern had to be balanced against the interest of the parties in a fair trial or settlement; in the present case the public interest in discussion outweighed the potential prejudice to a party. The law did not prevent comment when litigation was dormant and not being actively pursued. . . .

28. Following the Court of Appeal's decision, *The Sunday Times* refrained from publishing the proposed article so as to enable the Attorney-General to appeal. The Court of Appeal refused him leave to appeal but this was granted by the House of Lords on 1 March 1973. The hearing before the House of Lords was held in May 1973. On 18 July 1973, the House gave judgment unanimously allowing the appeal and subsequently directed the Divisional Court to grant an injunction in the terms set out in paragraph 34 below. . . .

29. Lord Reid said that the House must try to remove the uncertainty which was the main objection to the present law. The law of contempt had to be founded entirely on public policy; it was not there to protect the rights of parties to a litigation but to prevent interference with the administration of justice and should be limited to what was reasonably necessary for the purpose. Freedom of speech should not be limited more than was necessary but it could not be allowed where there would be real prejudice to the administration of justice. . . .

The Court of Appeal had wrongly described the actions as 'dormant' since settlement negotiations were in hand and improper pressure on a litigant to settle could constitute contempt. As for the Court of Appeal's balancing of competing interests, Lord Reid said:

'. . . contempt of court has nothing to do with the private interests of litigants. I have already indicated the way in which I think that a balance must be struck between the public interest in freedom of speech and the public interest in protecting the administration of justice from interference. I do not see why there should be any difference in principle between a case which is thought to have news value and one which is not. Protection of the administration of justice is equally important whether or not the case involves important general issues'.

Lord Reid concluded that publication of the article should be postponed for the time being in the light of the circumstances then prevailing; however, if things dragged on indefinitely, there would have to be a reassessment of the public interest in a unique situation.

[Summary of the concurring opinion of Lord Morris of Borth-y-Gest in the House of Lords omitted.] . . .

31. Lord Diplock said that contempt of court was punishable because it undermined the confidence of the parties and of the public in the due administration of justice. The due administration of justice required that all citizens should have unhindered access to the courts; that they should be able to rely on an unbiased decision based only on facts proved in accordance with the rules of evidence; that, once a case was submitted to a court, they should be able to rely upon there being no usurpation by any other person, for example in the form of 'trial by newspaper', of the

function of the court. Conduct calculated to prejudice any of these requirements or to undermine public confidence that they would be observed was contempt of court . . .

[Summaries of concurring opinions of Lord Simon of Glaisdale and Lord Cross of Chelsea in the House of Lords omitted.] . . .

34. On 25 July 1973, the House of Lords ordered that the cause be remitted to the Divisional Court with a direction to grant the following injunction:

'That . . . Times Newspapers Ltd., by themselves, their servants, agents or otherwise, be restrained from publishing, or causing or authorizing or procuring to be published or printed, any article or matter which prejudges the issues of negligence, breach of contract or breach of duty, or deals with the evidence relating to any of the said issues arising in any actions pending or imminent against Distillers . . . in respect of the development, distribution or use of the drug ''thalidomide'' '.

The defendants were granted liberty to apply to the Divisional Court for discharge of the injunction.

The Divisional Court implemented the above direction on 24 August 1973.

35. On 23 June 1976, the Divisional Court heard an application by the Attorney-General for the discharge of the injunction. It was said on behalf of the Attorney-General that the need for the injunction no longer arose; most of the claims against Distillers had been settled and there were only four extant actions which could by then have been brought before the courts if they had been pursued diligently. As there was a conflicting public interest in *The Sunday Times* being allowed to publish 'at the earliest possible date', the Attorney-General submitted the matter to the court as one where the public interest no longer required the restraint. The court, considering that the possibility of pressure on Distillers had completely evaporated, granted the application . . .

[A discussion of the Phillimore Report on the Law of Contempt issued in December 1974 omitted.] . . .

38. In their application, lodged with the Commission on 19 January 1974, the applicants claimed that the injunction, issued by the High Court and upheld by the House of Lords, to restrain them from publishing an article in *The Sunday Times* dealing with thalidomide children and the settlement of their compensation claims in the United Kingdom constituted a breach of Article 10 of the Convention. They further alleged that the principles upon which the decision of the House of Lords was founded amounted to a violation of Article 10 and asked the Commission to direct or, alternatively, to request the Government to introduce legislation overruling the decision of the House of Lords and bringing the law of contempt of court into line with the Convention.

39. In its decision of 21 March 1975, the Commission, after describing the question before it as 'whether the rules of contempt of court as applied in the decision of the House of Lords granting the injunction are a ground justifying the restriction under Article 10 §2', declared admissible and accepted the application . . .

[Additional allegations were made by the applicant under Articles 14 and 18 of the Convention; though considered by the Commission and by the Court, neither additional allegation was held by either body to have demonstrated a violation of the Convention.] . . .

41. In its report of 18 May 1977, the Commission . . . expressed the opinion:

— by eight votes to five, that the restriction imposed on the applicant's right to freedom of expression was in breach of Article 10 of the Convention; . . .

42. The applicants claim to be the victims of a violation of Article 10 of the Convention which provides:

'1. Everyone has the right to freedom of expression. This right shall include freedom to hold opinions and to receive and impart information and ideas without interference by public authority and regardless of frontiers. This Article shall not prevent States from requiring the licensing of broadcasting, television or cinema enterprises.

2. The exercise of these freedoms, since it carries with it duties and responsibilities, may be subject to such formalities, conditions, restrictions or penalties as are prescribed by law and are necessary in a democratic society, in the interests of national security, territorial integrity or public safety, for the prevention of disorder or crime, for the protection of health or morals, for the protection of the reputation or rights of others, for preventing the disclosure of information received in confidence, or for maintaining the authority and impartiality of the judiciary'. . . .

45. It is clear that there was an 'interference by public authority' in the exercise of the applicants' freedom of expression which is guaranteed by paragraph 1 of Article 10. Such an interference entails a 'violation' of Article 10 if it does not fall within one of the exceptions provided for in paragraph 2 . . . The Court therefore has to examine in turn whether the interference in the present case was 'prescribed by law', whether it had an aim or aims that is or are legitimate under Article 10 §2 and whether it was 'necessary in a democratic society' for the aforesaid aim or aims.

. . .

[In parts of the Court's opinion omitted here it was held that there had been an 'interference with the applicants' freedom of expression' but that 'the interference with the applicants' freedom of expression had an aim that is legitimate under Article 10 §2'. The crucial part of the judgment then followed: 'Was the interference "necessary in a democratic society" for maintaining the authority of the judiciary?']

65. As the Court remarked in its *Handyside* judgment, freedom of expression constitutes one of the essential foundations of a democratic society; subject to paragraph 2 of Article 10, it is applicable not only to information or ideas that are favourably received or regarded as inoffensive or as a matter of indifference, but also to those that offend, shock or disturb the State or any sector of the population.

These principles are of particular importance as far as the press is concerned. They are equally applicable to the field of the administration of justice, which serves the interests of the community at large and requires the co-operation of an enlightened public. There is general recognition of the fact that the courts cannot operate in a vacuum. Whilst they are the forum for the settlement of disputes, this does not mean that there can be no prior discussion of disputes elsewhere, be it in specialised journals, in the general press or amongst the public at large. Furthermore, whilst the mass media must not overstep the bounds imposed in the interests of the proper administration of justice, it is incumbent on them to impart information and ideas concerning matters that come before the courts just as in other areas of public interest. Not only do the media have the task of imparting such information and ideas: the public also has a right to receive them.

To assess whether the interference complained of was based on 'sufficient' reasons which rendered it 'necessary in a democratic society', account must thus be taken of any public interest aspect of the case. The Court observes in this connection that, following a balancing of the conflicting interests involved, an absolute rule was formulated by certain of the Law Lords to the effect that it was not permissible to prejudge issues in pending cases: it was considered that the law would be too uncertain if the balance were to be struck anew in each case. Whilst emphasizing that it is not its function to pronounce itself on an interpretation of English law adopted in the House of Lords, the Court points out that it has to take a different approach. The Court is faced not with a choice between two conflicting principles but with a principle of freedom of expression that is subject to a number of exceptions which must be narrowly interpreted. In the second place, the Court's supervision under Article 10 covers not only the basic legislation but also the decision applying it. It is not sufficient that the interference involved belongs to that class of the exceptions listed in Article 10 §2 which has been invoked; neither is it sufficient that the interference was imposed because its subject-matter fell within a particular category or was caught by a legal rule formulated in general or absolute terms: the Court has to be satisfied that the interference was necessary having regard to the facts and circumstances prevailing in the specific case before it.

66. The thalidomide disaster was a matter of undisputed public concern. It posed the question whether the powerful company which had marketed the drug bore legal or moral responsibility towards hundreds of individuals experiencing an appalling personal tragedy or whether the victims could demand or hope for indemnification only from the community as a whole; fundamental issues concerning protection against and compensation for injuries resulting from scientific developments were raised and many facets of the existing law on these subjects were called in question.

As the Court has already observed, Article 10 guarantees not only the freedom of the press to inform the public but also the right of the public to be properly informed.

In the present case, the families of numerous victims of the tragedy, who were unaware of the legal difficulties involved, had a vital interest in knowing all the underlying facts and the various possible solutions. They could be deprived of this information, which was crucially important for them, only if it appeared absolutely certain that its diffusion would have presented a threat to the 'authority of the judiciary'.

Being called upon to weigh the interests involved and assess their respective force, the Court makes the following observations:

In September 1972, the case had, in the words of the applicants, been in a 'legal cocoon' for several years and it was, at the very least, far from certain that the parents' actions would have come on for trial. There had also been no public enquiry.

The Government and the minority of the Commission point out that there was no prohibition on discussion of the 'wider issues', such as the principles of the English law of negligence, and indeed it is true that there had been extensive discussion in various circles especially after, but also before, the Divisional Court's initial decision. However, the Court considers it rather artificial to attempt to divide the 'wider issues' and the negligence issue. The question of where responsibility for a tragedy of this kind actually lies is also a matter of public interest.

It is true that, if the *Sunday Times* article had appeared at the intended time, Distillers might have felt obliged to develop in public, and in advance of any trial, their arguments on the facts of the case; however, those facts did not cease to be a matter of public interest merely because they formed the background to pending litigation. By bringing to light certain facts, the article might have served as a brake on speculative and unenlightened discussion.

67. Having regard to all the circumstances of the case on the basis of the approach described in paragraph 65 above, the Court concludes that the interference complained of did not correspond to a social need sufficiently pressing to outweigh the public interest in freedom of expression within the meaning of the Convention. The Court therefore finds the reasons for the restraint

imposed on the applicants not to be sufficient under Article 10 §2. That restraint proves not to be proportionate to the legitimate aim pursued; it was not necessary in a democratic society for maintaining the authority of the judiciary.

68. There has accordingly been a violation of Article 10 . . .

[The European Court then rejected applicants' arguments that the United Kingdom had violated Articles 14 and 18 of the Convention protecting against discrimination and against the use of restrictions in the Convention for improper purposes.] . . .

For These Reasons, The Court

1. *holds* by eleven votes to nine that there has been a breach of Article 10 of the Convention;

2. *holds* unanimously that there has been no breach of Article 14 taken together with Article 10;

3. *holds* unanimously that it is not necessary to examine the question of a breach of Article 18;

4. *holds* unanimously that the question of the application of Article 50 is not ready for decision.

NOTE ON THE *SUNDAY TIMES* CASE

For more background on the thalidomide drug, see H. Sjostrom & R. Nilsson, *Thalidomide and the Power of the Drug Companies* (1972); M. L. Kellmer Pringle & D. O. Fiddes, *The Challenge of Thalidomide* (1970). In the United States, Dr. Francis Kelley of the Food and Drug Administration resisted considerable pressure and prevented thalidomide from being sold. She was awarded the Distinguished Federal Civilian Service Award in 1962 by President Kennedy. R. A. Fine, *The Great Drug Deception* 167–81 (1972).

The Sunday Times was not just being critical of Distillers. It had a complaint about English law, i.e., that it was unclear as a matter of law that Distillers would actually be liable, as well as a grievance against the English legal system, i.e., that the lawyers and the courts were taking too long getting reasonable compensation to the thalidomide children. Several years after the English litigation was concluded, but before the judgment of the Strasbourg Court, the editor of *The Sunday Times*, Harold Evans, wrote about the motivation of the newspaper in pursuing the matter:

When the thalidomide children were born, many without arms and legs, around 1960, they were left to seek remedy through private litigation. No government inquiry was set up. No government settlement was offered. Some 60 parents in Britain issued writs against the Distillers Company. . . . From that moment on the press had to be silent . . .

[When] the *Sunday Times* became aware that the children were being offered sums so grossly inadequate to their real needs on any proper actuarial basis . . . it was decided to mount a campaign. The dilemma was that the very first article of the campaign would have provided a citation for contempt and made it stillborn . . . Thanks to the ingenious advice of James Evans, a lawyer with the *Sunday Times,* we found a way forward. We began a campaign on the moral issue of the low compensation, deliberately saying that the legal issue of negligence was outside our area and that the company denied negligence. But we also announced that in a future issue of the paper we would publish some documentary evidence on the manufacture of the drug.

Evans, 'British Law of Contempt Thwarts Speech and Justice', *Florida Bar Journal*, vol. 52, no. 6 (June 1978), at 462, 464–6. In a case like *Sunday Times* where a municipal legal system is itself under attack, there is an especially good reason to seek adjudication in an international court.

Just satisfaction was decreed by the Court in its Judgment of 6 November 1980 (No. 38), 3 E.H.R.R. 317. There, by a thirteen to three vote, the Court decided to award the *Sunday Times* the costs and expenses of its legal proceedings in Strasbourg before the Commission and the Court, a total of £22, 626.78.

3. ACCEPTANCE OF THE COURT

Decisions such as the *Sunday Times Case* certainly had the potential for discouraging governments from accepting or maintaining the then optional provisions of the European Human Rights Convention. In the *Sunday Times Case*, there was no doubt that the legal issue—balancing the public's right to know and the *Sunday Times*' right to freedom of expression against Distiller's right to a trial by the courts, not by the media, and the interest of the British government in the integrity of the judicial process—was a very close one. Eight British judges (three at the trial level and five in the House of Lords), five European Human Rights Commissioners, and nine European Human Rights Judges felt that the scales tilted towards granting an injunction against *The Sunday Times*. Three British judges (in the Court of Appeal), eight European Human Rights Commissioners, and 11 European Human Rights Judges felt that the balance went for permitting *The Sunday Times* to publish the thalidomide article. Of 44 judges and commissioners who considered the case, half went one way and half the other. Reasonable men and women could and did differ.

Should the Strasbourg Court have been permitted to rule as it did? A distinguished British international lawyer, F.A. Mann, for one, felt that the European Court of Human Rights had gone too far:

However uncertain its definition and scope may be in some respects, contempt of court is undoubtedly one of the great contributions the common law has made to the civilised behaviour of a large part of the world beyond the continent of Europe where the institution is unknown. . . . Yet it is that very branch of the law which the European Court of Human Rights has seriously undermined by, in effect, overturning the unanimous decision of the House of Lords in the *Sunday Times Case*—a unique event in the history of English law. In fact, it is probably no exaggeration to say that the gravest blow to the fabric of English law has been dealt by the majority of 11 judges coming from Cyprus, Denmark, Eire, France, Germany, Italy, Portugal, Spain, Sweden and Turkey, who over the dissent of nine judges from Austria, Belgium, Holland, Iceland, Luxembourg, Malta, Norway, Switzerland and the United Kingdom, decided in favour of the *Sunday Times* . . . The reader will have to make up his or her own mind . . . whether the Strasbourg Court arrogated to itself powers of factual appreciation which it cannot possibly exercise convincingly . . . and ask whether according to the standards and traditions of English law and English public life it is the decision of the House of Lords or that of the European Court of Human Rights which more correctly assesses the 'social need' and 'the legitimate aim' of a civilized society . . . and whether the level of judicial reasoning is higher in London or Strasbourg?[52]

One can understand Mann's discomfort with the 'overturning' of the House of Lords by the Strasbourg Court, but did the *Sunday Times Case* really raise the question of which court's 'judicial reasoning' was 'higher'? As another observer remarked about another judgment against the United Kingdom, the *Golder* case:[53]

Membership of a European institution, and submission to the jurisdiction of its organs, means the acceptance of a European way of thinking. The European Commission and Court of Human Rights are likely to construe texts in the 'continental', not the common law manner.[54]

In any event, the United Kingdom was and is not obliged to forever accept 'a European way of thinking'. For his part Mann strongly suggested that the proper reaction to the *Sunday Times Case* was for Britain to withdraw its acceptance of the optional clauses:

In a potentially wide variety of cases the European Court may assume a revising function and impose continental standards or, perhaps one should say, abuses upon this country which, in the name of freedom of the press and discussion, are likely to lower English usages by the substitution of trial by media for trial by courts. It is a matter for legislative concern whether this country is prepared to assume the risk to which it is now exposed. If the answer is in the negative a change of English law so as to comply with the standards of the Strasbourg judgment, yet to avoid trial by newspaper is unlikely to prove workable. Rather there will be no alternative but to do what the majority of countries have done, which have supplied the judges of the European Court of Human Rights, that is to say, to refuse to make or confirm the declaration under Article 25 of the Convention submitting this country to *individual* applications and thus to the jurisdiction of the European Court. It would be a regrettable and sad course to take, but it may be a necessary one, particularly if it is remembered how poor some of the other judgments of the Court have been [criticizing specifically the Court's decisions in *Northern Ireland* and *Tyrer*].[55]

Mann's view of the seriousness of the challenge posed to the United Kingdom by the *Sunday Times Case* was not shared by all English commentators. Christine Gray, for example, writing in the same year as Mann, felt that:

The European Court [in *Sunday Times*] did not in fact give much general guidance as to the appropriate future development of the law of contempt of court in England, for it is careful (perhaps over-careful if uniform standards are to be established in States Parties to the European Convention on Human Rights) not to substitute its own assessment of what might be the best policy in restricting the exercise of rights under the Convention for the assessment of the national authorities.[56]

[52] Mann, 'Contempt of Court in the House of Lords and the European Court of Human Rights' 95 *Law Quarterly Review* 348, 348–9, 352 (1979) (hereinafter cited as 'Mann').

[53] 21 Feb. 1975 (No. 18), 1 E.H.R.R. 524.

[54] Dale, 'Human Rights in the United Kingdom—International Standards' 25 *International and Comparative Law Quarterly* (1976) 292, 302.

[55] Mann, *supra* n. 52, at 352–3.

[56] Gray, 'European Convention on Human Rights—Freedom of Expression and the Thalidomide Case' [1979] *Cambridge Law Journal* 242.

Gray felt the more important lesson of the *Sunday Times Case* was for the English judge: 'Perhaps this case will remind English courts of the potentially embarrassing consequences of ignoring the existence of the European Convention on Human Rights and encourage in them a more constructive approach to its application'.[57] We return to this lesson in Chapter 9.

As it turned out, Mann was right at least about the general significance of the case. The *Sunday Times Case* did have an impact both on the development of English law respecting contempt of court[58] and on the development of European human rights law respecting the margin of appreciation allowed governments in restricting freedom of expression.[59] Ronald St. John Macdonald, then a judge on the European Court, wrote that the *Sunday Times Case*, was a 'landmark case in the development of the margin of appreciation', which showed the Court ready to reach its own objective evaluation of the balance of interests rather than test merely whether the state had balanced rights and derogations reasonably and in good faith.[60]

However, whatever his foresight in predicting the importance of the *Sunday Times Case*, Mann proved quite wrong about the effect of the case on the readiness of governments to subscribe to the optional provisions of the European Convention. Mann, as we saw, suggested that Britain might have 'no alternative but to do what the majority of countries have done, which have supplied the judges of the European Court of Human Rights, that is to say, to refuse to make or confirm the declaration under Article 25 of the Convention submitting this country to individual applications and thus to the jurisdiction of the European Court',[61] an observation riddled with errors. First of all, Mann's argument mistakenly intertwined the two optional clauses: Article 25 provided for private petitions and Article 46 provided for the Court's jurisdiction. Countries did, over time, opt for one and not the other. Second, Mann was also quite mistaken about the position of the majority of states in 1979. At the time of the *Sunday Times Case*, 14 of the 21 Council of Europe states had already accepted Article 25 individual petition and 16 had consented to Article 46 jurisdiction of the Court.[62] Third and most important, Mann's 'no alternative but' did not prove true. Not only did the United Kingdom continue did to renew its pledges to both Article 25 and Article 46, but so did the other then-consenting states. By 1995, 16

---

[57] *Id.* at 245.

[58] *See* Boyle, 'The Contempt of Court Act 1981', 6 *Human Rights Review* 148 (1981); Lowe, 'Contempt of Court Act of 1981' [1982] *Public Law* 20; Bailey, 'The Contempt of Court Act 1981', 45 *Modern Law Review* 301 (1982); Wong, 'The Sunday Times Case: Freedom of Expression Versus English Contempt-of-Court Law in the European Court of Human Rights', *Journal of International Law and Politics* 35, 67–75 (1984).

[59] *See infra* Chapter 5; *see also* Nathanson. 'The Sunday Times Case: Freedom of the Press and Contempt of Court Under English Law and the European Human Rights Convention', 68 *Kentucky Law Journal* 971, 1015–25 (1979–80); Wagner, 'Human Rights: Government Interference with the Press—The Sunday Times Case,' 21 *Harvard International Law Journal* 260, 265–8 (1980); Duffy, 'The Sunday Times Case: Freedom of Expression, Contempt of Court and the European Convention on Human Rights', 5 *Human Rights Review* 17 (1980).

[60] Macdonald, 'The Margin of Appreciation in the Jurisprudence of the European Court of Human Rights', *International Law at the Time of Its Codification: Essays in Honour of Roberto Ago* 187, 197 (1987).

[61] Mann, *supra* n. 52, at 352–3.

[62] Chart of Signatures and Ratifications, *supra* n. 6.

more states acceded to Article 25 and 14 more to Article 46.[63] Far from discouraging governments, the *Sunday Times* judgment and case like it did not slow the accession of states to the legal machinery of European human rights law. Indeed, as we have seen, since 1998, the Convention has been amended to make these vital aspects of that machinery mandatory for all states and no longer optional.

How far can the Court and the Commission go without upsetting the applecart of state consent? Writing just after *Sunday Times*, Ralph Beddard remarked on the caution exercised by the system's institutions up to that time:

> It is, and always has been, obvious that winning the confidence of the parties and the public was a first step in any attempt to establish judicial determination of the protection of human rights. The last 27 years have not been free of difficulties, however, and the confidence of the parties was won, particularly in the early days, by very careful treading on the part of the Commission. There are cases which, if presented to the Commission today, would probably make greater progress than they did at the time of application. However, a Commission leaning heavily in favor of governments would have lost the confidence of the public.[64]

Such caution apparently paid off. Even in 1980, Sir Humphrey Waldock, then President of the International Court of Justice but previously President of both the European Commission and later the European Court of Human Rights, could conclude that 'whether the system set up by the European Convention on Human Rights is, in general, effective is not, I believe, today open to serious question'.[65] We test this proposition below.

C. THE FUTURE OF THE COURT

The future of the Court depends, of course, on developments in Europe generally. Insofar as there continues to be a political and popular interest in European integration, European human rights law will probably tend to prosper as part of that general trend. If European unity becomes less viable over time, it will be more difficult for the Strasbourg system to survive even in its present form. Nonetheless, the European Court of Human Rights is at least partly master of its fate and will play its own role in the forthcoming story of European integration. Two crucial aspects to the Court's role, albeit neither easy to evaluate, are explored below. First, is the Court an efficacious institution? Will it be? Secondly, has the Court been perceived as a legitimate body? Will it be? If the Court has or will become an efficacious legitimate judiciary, then its achievement is a rarity among international institutions.

---

[63] *Id.*

[64] Beddard, *supra* n. 49, at 4.

[65] Waldock, 'The Effectiveness of the System Set Up by the European Convention on Human Rights' 1 *Human Rights Law Journal* 1 (1980).

1. THE EFFICACY OF STRASBOURG[66]

What do we really know and what might it be useful to know about the efficacy of Strasbourg? How does one define 'efficacy'? Although one might search out a definition that would distinguish 'efficacy' from other terms like 'compliance' and 'obedience', it makes little sense to do so. It seems that virtually all studies about how Strasbourg law 'works' do not bother to do so. Discussion about Strasbourg law 'working' or not, of it being 'efficacious', 'effective', or 'successful' or not, of there being 'compliance' with its norms or judgments or not, of its rules being 'respected' or 'put into practice' or not, makes all these terms more or less interchangeable.[67] Though one could also analyse Strasbourg law using a break-down of levels of compliance,[68] it appears more fruitful to break up the Strasbourg efficacy studies into three categories depending upon the kind of 'law' they explore: (1) judgments (and decisions), (2) legal rules, and (3) the legal system itself. This yields some interesting comparisons.[69]

Studies of the efficacy of Strasbourg judgments and decisons are the most numerous. There are a great many reports and examinations of the effects of individual judgments of the European Court of Human Rights, and the decisions of the European Commission of Human Rights and the Committee of Ministers of the Council of Europe.[70] Almost all of these reports or commentaries are interesting and informative. However, by their very nature, they fail to provide a general picture. The individual case studies must be read together and compared to yield some sort of overall conclusion about compliance or not with Strasbourg judgments and decisions.

It is just this sort of general study that is most lacking. Some of the work asserts to

---

[66] This section is based on M. Janis, 'The Efficacy of Strasbourg Law', 15 *Connecticut Journal of International Law* 39 (2000).

[67] There is no harm in this. Much excellent discussion of compliance questions in international law proceeds similarly. See, for example, H. Koh, 'Why Do Nations Obey International Law?' 106 *Yale Law Journal* 2599 (1997).

[68] Harold Koh helpfully distinguishes coincidence, conformity, compliance, and obedience between norms and practice. *Id.* at 2600–2601, n. 3. Looking at the motivation of those who appear to obey judgments, we can distinguish behavioral explanations based on 'prudential calculation' from those grounded on 'law following'. Kay, The European Human Rights System as a System of Law' 6 *Columbia Journal of European Law* 55 (2000) (hereinafter cited as 'Kay').

[69] Benedict Kingsbury has provided a persuasive account of how definitions of compliance with international law vary depending on the theory of law that one adopts. Kingsbury, 'The Concept of Compliance as a Function of Competing Conceptions of International Law' 19 *Michigan Journal of International Law* 345 (1998).

[70] There are both official and unofficial reports and commentary. For example, the Council of Europe has a website, reporting, usually in a sentence or two, responses of states to judgments of the Strasbourg Court. Http://www.dhcour.coe.fr/eng/effects.htm. In an entry on *Jersild v. Denmark*, 23 Sept. 1994 (No. 298), 19 E.H.R.R. 1, the Council of Europe's website reports: 'On 24 January 1995 the Special Court of Review gave leave for the case against Mr Jersild and Others to be reopened'. *Id.* at 5.

be comprehensive, but is frankly disappointing, being largely uninformative.[71] Other work provides more evidence,[72] but is still rather impressionistic.[73] The most impressive study of compliance with Strasbourg judgments and decisions covers only the compliance record of one country, the United Kingdom,[74] although the 29 cases reviewed do constitute about 31 per cent of all violations decided in the period.[75] This nuanced study of the U.K. shows how difficult it can be to really tell if Strasbourg judgments and decisions have in practice been properly executed.[76] Moreover, the study concludes that though in many cases it seems that the United Kingdom has complied with adverse judgments and decisions,[77] in other cases there

[71] For example, in 1993, Peter Leuprecht, then the Director of Human Rights of the Council of Europe, promised a book chapter the purpose of which was 'to show that judgments of the European Court of Human Rights and decisions of the Committee of Ministers under Article 32 of the European Convention on Human Rights are not only legally binding, but actually executed'. Leuprecht, 'The Execution of Judgments and Decisions', *The European System for the Protection of Human Rights* 791 (Macdonald, Matscher & Petzold eds. 1993). However, the chapter refers in substance only to the formal language of the Convention itself and in no way substantiates the conclusion that '[o]n the whole, the record of execution of judgments of the Court and decisions of the Committee of Ministers is remarkably good'. *Id.* at 800. Probably, the real goal of the chapter is hortatory; Leuprecht concludes: 'It is to be hoped that the States concerned will continue to take *bona fide* all the measures necessary to execute the Court's judgments and the Committee of Ministers' decisions, and that the Committee itself will confirm and develop its now well-established practice to use its powers fully and responsibly, without being impeded by considerations of political expediency'. *Id.*

[72] For example, in 1996, the then President of the Strasbourg Court, Rolv Ryssdal, reviewed the compliance record of the Court, giving about 10 examples of cases either where he noted good compliance, e.g., Germany changing its rules about the cost of translators in criminal proceedings as a result of *Luedicke, Belkacem & Koc v. Germany*, 28 Nov. 1978, (No. 29), or where compliance was long-delayed, e.g., Belgium taking 8 years to implement the amendments to its family law called for by *Marckx v. Belgium*, 13 June 1979 (No. 31). Ryssdal, 'The Enforcement System Set Up Under the European Convention on Human Rights' in *Compliance with Judgments of International Courts* 49, 54 (Bulterman & Kuijer ed. 1996).

[73] Ryssdal concludes that 'to date judgments of the European Court of Human Rights have, I would say, not only generally but always been complied with by the Contracting States concerned'. *Id.* at 67. However, in the same volume, another Strasbourg Court judge, S. K. Martens, in a commentary on Judge Ryssdal's contribution, reaches a slightly more pessimistic conclusion: 'For my part, I also have the impression that as a rule respondent States, after a judgment finding a violation, do modify their legislation sooner or later. There are, however, exceptions'. Martens, Commentary in *Compliance with Judgments of International Courts* 71, 73 (Bulterman & Kuijer eds. 1996). Martens cited three examples of probable non-compliance including the absence of adequate remedial legislation by Ireland in *Norris v. Ireland*, 26 Oct. 1988 (No. 142), 13 E.H.R.R. 186 and by the Netherlands in *Benthem v. Netherlands*, 23 Oct. 1985 (No. 97), 6 E.H.R.R. 283. *Id.*

[74] Churchill & Young, 'Compliance with Judgments of the European Court of Human Rights and Decisions of the Committee of Ministers: The Experience of the United Kingdom, 1975–1987', 62 *British Yearbook of International Law* 283 (1991) (hereinafter cited as 'Churchill & Young').

[75] *Id.* at 284.

[76] 'This paper also demonstrates some of the problems involved in carrying out a study of compliance with judgments of the Court and decisions of the Committee of Ministers . . . The relevant law is not always very accessible (e.g. in relation to prisoners), nor is it always easy to ascertain how the law applies in practice (e.g. in relation to the treatment of detainees in Northern Ireland).' *Id.* at 346.

[77] These cases include *Campbell & Cosans v. United Kingdom*, 25 Feb. 1982 (No. 82), 4 E.H.R.R. 293, concerning corporal punishment, *Gillow v. United Kingdom*, 24 Nov. 1986 (No. 109), 11 E.H.R.R. 335 concerning housing laws in Guernsey; and *Young, James & Webster v. United Kingdom*, 13 Aug. 1981 (No. 44), 4 E.H.R.R. 38, concerning labour unions and the closed shop.

had been doubtful compliance[78] or by some assessments even non-compliance.[79] It may well be that the record of executing Strasbourg judgments is no worse than the record of many domestic courts,[80] but one must be careful not to go too far in asserting a nearly perfect record for compliance with Strasbourg judgments and decisions.[81]

The second category of efficacy, compliance with Strasbourg's legal rules, ought in a way to be even more important than the first. After all, given the large number of alleged violations of European human rights law and the small number of cases that ultimately reach the Strasbourg Court, most meaningful enforcement of Strasbourg's substantive law must take place before national courts. There are a number of studies that discuss the ways in which the substantive legal rules of the Strasbourg Convention figure or not as rules of decision in the domestic legal systems of the member states.[82] There is also work available that discusses the effect of Strasbourg institutional case law on municipal judicial proceedings.[83] What is missing are general studies about how Strasbourg legal rules, whether in the form of the Convention's substantive provisions or in the precedent-like norms created by the Strasbourg institutions, have or have not influenced the actual practice of states or governments.[84]

---

[78] Churchill & Young conclude that as a result of *Sunday Times v. United Kingdom*, 26 Apr. 1979 (No. 30), 2 E.H.R.R. 245 there was no sign of any attempt to review the reform of the law of contempt against the touchstone of the European Convention, with the result that the extent of compliance remains uncertain'. Churchill & Young, *supra* n. 74, at 346.

[79] There was no reform of the law authorizing corporal punishment in the Isle of Man after *Tyrer v. United Kingdom*, 25 Apr. 1978 (No. 26), 2 E.H.R.R. 1, although the authors could find no example of corporal punishment being imposed in subsequent practice. *Id.* at 286–7.

[80] One need go no further than the difficulties of enforcing school desegregation following the U.S. Supreme Court's landmark decision in *Brown v. Board of Education*, 347 U.S. 483 (1954), to see how much the practice of domestic law can vary from its judgments. That we tend to worry rather more about the efficacy of international law than about the efficacy of domestic law is probably due to the lingering doubt many share about international law being 'law' at all, a doubt that goes back to the very origins of the discipline. See M. Janis, 'Jeremy Bentham and the Fashioning of "International Law"', 78 *American Journal of International Law* 405 (1984).

[81] For example, '[t]he [European] Convention's reputation as a bulwark against arbitrary government interference stems at least in part from the fact that the decisions of its judicial enforcement organs, the European Court of Human Rights ("Court") and the European Commission of Human Rights ("Commission"), are almost universally respected and implemented by the twenty-four European nations ("Contracting States") that have ratified the Convention.' L. R. Helfer, 'Consensus, Coherence and the European Convention on Human Rights', 26 *Cornell International Law Journal* 133–4 (1993).

[82] One of the most comprehensive, though now somewhat dated, general surveys is A. Drzemczewski, *The European Human Rights Convention in Domestic Law* (1983). Reviews of individual countries can more easily be kept up-to-date: see for example, U. Bernitz, 'The Incorporation of the European Human Rights Convention into Swedish Law—A Half Measure,' 38 *German Yearbook of International Law* 178 (1995); I. Cameron, 'The Swedish Experience of the European Convention on Human Rights Since Incorporation', 48 *International and Comparative Law Quarterly* 20 (1999); M. Hunt, *Using Human Rights in English Courts* (1997).

[83] J. Polakiewicz & V. Jacob-Foltzer, 'The European Human Rights Convention in Domestic Law: The Impact of Strasbourg Case-Law in States where Direct Effect is Given to the Convention,' 12 *Human Rights Law Journal* 65, 121 (1991).

[84] There is some anecdotal evidence, though, available both in some of the records of the enforcement or not of individual Strasbourg judgments, e.g., Churchill & Young, *supra* n. 74, and in some of the reviews of the respect paid to Strasbourg legal rules.

The third category of efficacy, the efficacy of the legal system of Strasbourg itself, is both the most difficult to gauge and, probably, the most important. International law is sometimes accused of being irrelevant, but increasingly it seems that even ordinary critics of the function of law in international relations have come to acknowledge that international law and international legal institutions are playing increasingly important roles in international society.[85] How, though, to determine the real impact of international law on international society? In particular, are the many assertions about the overall efficacy of the Strasbourg legal system at the end of the day merely impressionistic?[86]

Understanding how deeply a legal system permeates and regulates a society, especially an international society like Europe, may always be more a study in theory than of practice. This is not to say that the theoretical aspects of the question of the deep-rootedness or not of an international legal system will not be illuminating. For example, when explaining to others the nature and efficacy of the Strasbourg legal system, it may be useful to employ some of the ideas from the theoretical paradigm for legal systems in general devised by H.L.A. Hart.[87] Hart grounds much of his theory of a legal system upon a distinction between primary and secondary rules: primary rules being rules of obligation and secondary rules being rules that have to do with the functioning of the system, including rules about making and changing primary rules, as well as a rule of recognition that calls upon actors within the system to agree upon what is and what is not a legitimate legal rule.[88]

It is convenient to describe the Strasbourg system this way: there are primary rules, especially the substantive human rights norms in the European Convention, and secondary rules, including those in the Convention establishing the international enforcement machinery of the Strasbourg Court and Commission, which are tasked with the application, interpretation, and adjudication of the primary rules *vis-à-vis* the member states. What makes the Strasbourg legal system a more thorough-going international legal system than, say, United Nations human rights law, is that Strasbourg displays a much more settled and accepted system of secondary rules and institutions. Moreover, the actors within the system, both governments and individual

---

[85] For the mutual respect between international political scientists and international lawyers inspires this volume. See R.O. Keohane, 'International Relations and International Law: Two Optics,' 38 *Harvard International Law Journal* 487 (1997); and A. M. Slaughter Burley, 'International Law and International Relations Theory: A Dual Agenda', 87 *American Journal of International Law* 205 (1993).

[86] One of the authors is as guilty as anyone in making grand claims about the efficacy of the Strasbourg legal system: 'What makes European human rights law special is not only its increasing case load, but also its effectiveness': M. Janis, *An Introduction to International Law* 267 (3rd edn. 1999) (hereinafter cited as Janis, *An Introduction*).

[87] H. L. A. Hart, *The Concept of Law* (2nd edn. 1994) (hereinafter Hart). See Kay, *supra* n. 69, at 59–71.

[88] Although Hart's theory can be illuminating for understanding the role of international law in international society, Hart's own treatment of international law is disappointing. *Id.* at 213–37. This is probably due to his uncharacteristic reliance on rather simplistic positivist notions of the nature of international law, notions criticized elsewhere. M. Janis, 'Individuals as Subjects of International Law', 17 *Cornell International Law Journal* 61 (1984).

litigants, as well as their lawyers, recognize the Strasbourg rules *and* the Strasbourg institutions as legitimate.

This last aspect, recognition of legitimacy,[89] may be the most crucial 'practical' test for the third sort of efficacy analysis, i.e., the efficacy of the Strasbourg legal system. Yet, testing recognition of the legitimacy of the Strasbourg system is very difficult and largely untried. It is much more usual to simply make positive assertions about the efficacy of the Strasbourg legal system.[90] Are there more quantifiable ways of testing the system's efficacy?

There are at least four possible tests: (1) case load in the European Commission and Court of Human Rights, (2) acceptance of what were before November 1998 the two optional clauses of the European Convention, (3) growth in the number of states joining the Council of Europe and ratifying the Convention, and (4) an increasing recognition of the legitimacy of the system. The first three tests are easily quantifiable and satisfied impressively. To some extent, of course, the fourth test, recognition of the legitimacy of Strasbourg law, can be gleaned from the other three tests. The burgeoning case load of the Commission and the Court, the now universal acceptance of the optional clauses, and the doubled membership of European states in the Strasbourg legal system all point to individuals, governments, and lawyers in Europe taking the system more seriously, and perhaps to the conclusion that the players increasingly recognize the system's legitimacy.

Yet, 'increasing' recognition of Strasbourg's legitimacy is only relative: there is 'increased' legitimacy at least compared to what went before. Does that make it 'enough recognition' to say the system is properly 'legitimate'? This second question is also relative: 'enough recognition' calls for a comparison of the levels of recognition between the Strasbourg system and other legal systems, e.g., *vis-à-vis* both domestic legal systems where legitimacies will vary from country to country, say from an older Western democracy to a newer democratic entrant such as Russia,[91] and other international legal systems where legitimacies will vary too, say from international economic law to the international law regulating the use of force.[92] There are no such comparisons of legitimacy in the literature. This may be because tests of recognition

---

[89] Legitimacy in international law has been most persuasively explored by Thomas Franck. T. Franck, *The Power of Legitimacy Among Nations* (1990).

[90] Such assertions are legion. As early as 1980, when the Strasbourg Court had rendered only about 40 judgments, the then president of the Court, Sir Humphrey Waldock, wrote that whether 'the system set up by the European Convention on Human Rights is, in general, effective is not, I believe, today open to serious question'. H. Waldock, 'The Effectiveness of the System Set Up by the European Convention on Human Rights' 1 *Human Rights Law Journal 1* (1980). Hundreds of judgments later, Strasbourg Judge Juan Antonio Carrillo Salcedo remarked similarly: 'The European Convention constitutes, therefore, the first effective regional enforcement mechanism for human rights'. Salcedo, 'The Place of the European Convention in International Law', *The European System for the Protection of Human Rights* 15, 17 (Macdonald, Matscher & Petzold eds. 1993).

[91] See *infra* (c)(2).

[92] Different international legal systems may be said to vary along a 'structural spectrum', some forms of international law being more 'law'-like than others. Janis, 'Do "Laws" Regulate Nuclear Weapons'? *Nuclear Weapons and International Law* 53, 60–1 (Pogany ed. 1987).

of legitimacy do not easily form part of either legal or, even, political analysis. Gauging recognition of legitimacy of legal systems may be more psychological, rather than legal or political, exercises and in any case difficult to ascertain in any sort of definite way.[93] This may well be true for most any legal system, domestic or international.

2. THE LEGITIMACY OF STRASBOURG

As we have explored above, there can be little doubt that the efficacy of the European Court of Human Rights depends in good measure on its perception as a 'legitimate' institution, accepted as a rule enforcer across Europe. However, it seems in practice that perceptions of the legitimacy of the Court vary from member state to member state, that the Court's judgments are more efficacious in one place than another. Turkey, for example, announced on 4 June 1999 that it would refuse to comply with the judgment of the European Court of Human Rights in the *Loizidou Case*.[94] Such a blunt rejection of the Court is unprecedented in Strasbourg annals. Even the Greek Colonels in 1969, did not reject a judgment of the Court.[95] Moreover, Turkey has had some recent unsettling judgments against it concerning its treatment of its Kurdish population.[96] Turkey's record respecting European Human Rights has had negative implications for its attempts to become a full partner in European integration.[97]

Another test for the legitimacy of the Court is the accession of the newly democratic states of central and Eastern Europe. The excerpt below goes to the question of whether or not there can be a two-tier Strasbourg system with lower expectations of efficacy and legitimacy *vis-à-vis* some states than others.

[93] It may be that antecdotal evidence from the media speaks of psychological acceptance rather well. For example, it seems meaningful when cartoons are printed assuming something of a knowledge of the Strasbourg system, for example, the one showing a student preparing himself to be caned in class with the caption, 'Your complete ignorance on every other subject is only matched by your detailed knowledge of each provision on corporal punishment by the European Court of Human Rights'. *Punch*, 10 Mar. 1982. Or when the main headline of a daily paper reads: '£40,000 Present for IRA Families: Britain Pays Terrorist Court Costs Early', *Daily Mail*, 27 Dec. 1995, at 1.

[94] M2 Communications Ltd, M2 Presswire, 4 June 1999: *Loizidou v. Turkey*, 23 Mar. 1995 (No. 310), 20 E.H.R.R. 99. For more on Turkey and Cyprus, *see* D. Wippman, 'International Law and Ethnic Conflict on Cyprus', 31 *Texas International Law Journal* 141 (1996).

[95] Albeit Greece had not accepted the Court's jurisdiction and was ultimately forced to withdraw from the Council of Europe altogether, *see supra* Chapter 2.

[96] *See infra* Chapter 4.

[97] M. Muftuler-Bac, 'The Never-Ending Story: Turkey and the European Union', 34 *Middle East Studies* 240 (1998); 'Turkey can be part of Europe', *The Economist*, 1 Apr. 1995, at 13.

MARK JANIS, 'RUSSIA AND THE "LEGALITY" OF STRASBOURG LAW'
8 *EUROPEAN JOURNAL OF INTERNATIONAL LAW* 93 (1997)

I

On 28 February 1996, Russia acceded to the Statute of the Council of Europe, becoming the Council's thirty-ninth member.[98] Russia has been allotted eighteen seats in Strasbourg's Parliamentary Assembly, giving it, alongside France, Germany, Italy and the United Kingdom, one of the five largest national delegations.[99] Russia's accession followed an extensive debate within the Council of Europe about the suitability of the applicant for membership, and occurred despite an unfavourable Eminent Lawyers Report prepared at the request of the Bureau of the Parliamentary Assembly.[100] The Report concluded 'that the legal order of the Russian Federation does not, at the present moment, meet the Council of Europe standards as enshrined in the statute of the Council and developed by the organs of the European Convention on Human Rights'.[101] As a condition of joining the Council of Europe, Russia has promised to ratify the European Convention for the Protection of Human Rights and Fundamental Freedoms[102] within one year of its accession to the Statute of the Council.[103]

. . .

IV

The accession of Russia and of the other Central and Eastern European states to the Council of Europe and the European Convention on Human Rights may also be seen as a price of success. The promotion of human rights in the Soviet bloc via the 'Helsinki Process' was long a foreign policy goal of both the United States and Western Europe. At least as early as April 1991, a political decision had been made that there was a political and moral requirement to open up the Council of Europe to the new post-Communist governments in the East.[104] In October 1993, the Summit of the Council of Europe reiterated its commitment to pluralist and parliamentary democracy, the indivisibility and universality of human rights, the rule of law and a common heritage enriched by diversity'.[105] Moreover, the Summit proclaimed that it would welcome new Council members from 'the democracies of Europe freed from communist oppression', so long as an applicant had 'brought its institutions and legal system into line with the basic principles of

---

[98] 'The 39 Member States of the Council of Europe (CoE) according to their date of membership (as at 31 July 1996)', 17 *Human Rights Law Journal* 234 (1996).

[99] *Id.*

[100] Council of Europe, Parliamentary Assembly, Bureau of the Assembly, *Report on the Conformity of the Legal Order of the Russian Federation with Council of Europe Standards Prepared by Rudolf Bernhardt, Stefan Trechsel, Albert Weitzel, and Felix Ermacora*, 7 Oct. 1994, AS/Bur/Russia (1994) 7.

[101] *Id.* at 85.

[102] 213 UNTS 221, ETS 5, UKTS 71 (1953), signed at Rome 4 Nov. 1950, entered into force 3 Sept. 1953, Council of Europe, Human Rights Information Centre (ed. 1995).

[103] Reuters News Service, 'Yeltsin Approves Russia Entry to Council of Europe', *Reuter Textline*, 23 Feb. 1996.

[104] Council of Europe, Committee of Ministers, 88th Session, 25 Apr. 1991, 12 *Human Rights Law Journal* 216 (1991).

[105] Council of Europe, Vienna Declaration of 8/9 Oct. 1993, 14 *Human Rights Law Journal* 373 (1993).

democracy, the rule of law and respect for human rights'.[106] To test whether an applicant's legal system meets these standards, the Council of European commissioned Eminent Lawyers Reports, such as that which Russia failed.[107] The decision in February 1996 to admit Russia to the Council of Europe is commonly viewed as a result of giving greater weight to political factors than to legal criteria, a realistic judgment given the importance of integrating post-Communist Russia into the more democratic liberal realm of Western Europe.[108]

V

No matter how politically rational the decision to admit Russia to the Council of Europe, it must be recognized that Russia's accession will result in two important and probably negative consequences for the 'legality' of the Strasbourg human rights law system. First, the participation of Russia increases the possibility that European human rights law will both be disobeyed and be seen to be flouted. This has, of course, occurred before, notably by the Colonels' regime in Greece between 1967 and 1974. That situation led to the condemnation of Greece by the European Commission of Human Rights and the Committee of Ministers of the Council of Europe, as well as to the denunciation of the Convention by Greece in December 1969. Moreover, doubt has been expressed about the actual efficacy of the system, even with regard to the traditional liberal democracies.

However, three aspects of Russia's accession are particularly troubling for the future of compliance with Strasbourg law. First, at the present time, as the Eminent Lawyers Report makes clear, Russia falls short of the usual European standard of the rule of law and the protection of human rights. Second, given Russia's lack of experience in protecting human rights at the level of municipal law, it is likely that a great many violations of European human rights law will be committed there, and that they will not be remedied domestically. Third, the same political importance of Russia that has prompted the Council of Europe to accept its admittance will make it especially difficult for Strasbourg to force the Russian government to comply with adverse findings.

The other significant consequence for the system of European human rights law posed by Russia's accession is likely to be a new challenge to what, along with Hart, we can call Strasbourg's 'internal point-of-view'. Given the difficulties of Russia effectively complying with European human rights law in its municipal legal order and of Strasbourg imposing its decisions upon the Russian government, there will be a strong temptation for the Strasbourg institutions to fashion a two-tier legal order, which would allow lower than normal expectations for Russia. This will have the likely benefit of enabling Russia's continued participation in the system, but it will threaten the perception of Hart's 'officials, lawyers or private persons' that Strasbourg law 'in one situation after another [is a guide] to the conduct of social life, as the basis for claims, demands,

---

[106] *Id.* at 374.

[107] Council of Europe, *Report on the Conformity of the Legal Order of the Russian Federation with Council of Europe Standards* (1994). Other Eminent Lawyers Reports have been reprinted in the *Human Rights Law Journal*, including those on Slovenia, 14 *Human Rights Law Journal* 437 (1993); the Czech Republic, 14 *Human Rights Law Journal* 442 (1993); and Albania, 15 *Human Rights Law Journal* 242 (1995).

[108] Reuter News Service, 'Russia: Council Vote Pleases Yeltsin, Shocks Rights Monitors', 26 Jan. 1996; Reuter News Service, 'Czech Republic: Havel Gives Qualified Welcome to Russia in Council', 26 Jan. 1996; Reuter News Service, 'Russia: Human Rights Commission Says "Political Expediency" Prevailing Over Human Rights', 7 Feb. 1996; Gazzini, 'Considerations on the Conflict in Chechnya' 17 *Human Rights Law Journal* 93 (1996).

admissions, criticism or punishment, viz., in all the familiar transactions of life according to rules'.[109]

These probable challenges resulting from Russia's accession come at an awkward moment for Strasbourg. Not only is the ambit of European human rights law being widened to reach out to the former Soviet bloc, but the potency of Strasbourg law is being deepened by ever bolder Court judgments against national governments. This deepening, a welcome advance on international legal control, is proceeding just when the basic tenets of European unity are under increasing assault by nationalistic sentiments across Europe. This is true not least in the United Kingdom where both European human rights law and European economic law are perceived more and more, not as solutions to European-wide problems, but as foreign threats to national political and economic objectives. Hence, there is a danger that the failure of Russia to comply with European human rights law domestically and to obey the decisions of the Strasbourg institutions and the creation of a two-tier human rights system to accommodate Russia will give the governments of the existing member states all the more latitude in weakening their own commitment to the Strasbourg system. This all serves as a reminder that the 'breakthrough' of Strasbourg law to genuine legal obligation may not be forever.

[109] H.L.A. Hart, *The Concept of Law* 90 (2nd ed. 1994).

PART II

SUBSTANTIVE ADJUDICATION IN THE COURT

4

TORTURE; INHUMAN OR DEGRADING TREATMENT OR PUNISHMENT

ARTICLE 3

No one shall be subjected to torture or to inhuman or degrading treatment or punishment.

The idea that government can abuse its power by the unwarranted infliction of pain is, naturally, an ancient one. A statement that 'excessive bail ought not to be required nor excessive fines imposed nor cruel and unusual punishments inflicted' was included in Article 10 of the English Bill of Rights of 1689. As part of a more general concern with a perceived corrupt judiciary in the reigns of the later Stuarts, the English Parliament was anxious to limit the imposition of arbitrary and excessive punishments. They may have had one celebrated case particularly in mind. That was the punishment given the cleric, Titus Oates, in 1686 for his part in concocting the 'Popish Plot'. Oates was sentenced to a fine, whipping, defrocking, life imprisonment and pillorying four times a year for the rest of his life.[1]

Practically identical language to that of the English Bill of Rights was included in many of the early state constitutions in the United States, and a similar provision was attached to the United States Constitution as the Eighth Amendment when the Bill of Rights, proposed in 1789, was ratified in 1791. In the first Congress, one opponent of that clause complained about its potential scope, arguing that 'it is sometimes necessary to hang a man, villains often deserve whipping, and perhaps having their ears cut off; but are we in future to be prevented from inflicting those punishments because they are cruel?'[2] In Canada's 1960 statutory Bill of Rights a right to be free of 'cruel and unusual treatment and punishment' was expressed. Identical language was adopted in the constitutional Canadian Charter of Rights and Freedoms of 1982.

The drafters of Article 3 of the European Convention in 1949–50 had before them a number of models besides the British and American Bills of Rights. Most notable was Article 5 of the recently adopted Universal Declaration of Human Rights which

---

[1] *See* L. Schwoerer, *The Declaration of Rights, 1689*, pp. 92–4, 202 (Baltimore, 1981) Johns Hopkins Press.
[2] Quoted in *Furman v. Georgia*, 408 U.S. 238, 244 (1972) (Douglas J., concurring).

forbade 'torture or . . . cruel, inhuman or degrading treatment or punishment'. Initial drafts of the Convention merely declared an all-purpose right to 'security of person in accordance with Articles 3, 5 and 8 of the Declaration of the United Nations'.[3]

When the drafters adopted their own language for Article 3 they reproduced the words of the Universal Declaration of Rights but, for reasons that are unclear, omitted the adjective, 'cruel'. At one stage in the drafting process a Committee of Experts had prepared two drafts. Draft A set forth broad, general standards of human rights, while Draft B attempted to set out more precise guidelines. With respect to the prohibition in question, however, there was little difference in the degree of generality between the two drafts. Draft A copied the Universal Declaration verbatim, referring to torture, and cruel, inhuman and degrading treatment or punishment, while Draft B listed only torture and inhuman treatment of punishment. The language finally adopted first appeared in a draft compiled by a Conference of Senior Officials in June 1950.[4] No reasons for the precise selection of terms is evident in the history of the drafting process.

Certainly the central idea that the drafters had in mind was suggested by the atrocities of the Nazi regime. In an early debate in the Consultative Assembly a British delegate, Seymour Cocks, referred to 'the terrible wave of barbarism and bestialism which was broken over our world during the last 30 years' and described in detail some of the horrors of that period.[5] Later, however, in the debate on a resolution condemning these practices, some of the difficulties inherent in a broad condemnation became apparent. The last sentence of that resolution would have expressed the Assembly's 'abhorrence of the subjection of any person to any form of mutilation, sterilization or beating'. On the request of a Danish delegate the reference to sterilization was withdrawn in light of legislation in Scandinavian countries calling for the sterilization of some sex offenders. Then an English delegate suggested the deletion of the reference to 'beating' since, in England, corporal punishment was still thought an acceptable punishment for robbery and violence. At this point, on the suggestion of the President, the resolution was recommitted for redrafting.[6]

This minor debate illustrates the difficulties masked by the general language of Article 3. It is obvious that in order to maintain social order governments must, and usually ought to be, in the business of inflicting unwanted treatment on their citizens. While it may be readily agreed that the use of 'torture, inhuman and degrading treatment or punishment' for this purpose is unacceptable, once a particular practice is at issue, especially in light of its use in connection with a particular social problem, serious differences are bound to emerge. Like many domestic courts with similar constitutional provisions, the European Court of Human Rights has struggled to define the boundary between tolerable and intolerable punishment and treatment. As the materials in this Chapter illustrate, the Court's efforts have focused, notwithstand-

---

[3] 1 *Travaux Préparatoires* 206.
[4] 4 *Travaux Préparatoires* 52, 58; 4 *Travaux Préparatoires* 274.
[5] 2 *Travaux Préparatoires* 38.
[6] 2 *Travaux Préparatoires* 238–44.

ing their unexplained selection, on each of the three different categories specified in the language of Article 3.

A. DEFINING THE TERMS

1. *IRELAND V. UNITED KINGDOM*

Judgment of 18 January 1978
(No. 25), 2 E.H.R.R. 25

11. The tragic and lasting crisis in Northern Ireland lies at the root of the present case. In order to combat what the respondent Government describe as 'the longest and most violent terrorist campaign witnessed in either part of the island of Ireland', the authorities in Northern Ireland exercised from August 1971 until December 1975 a series of extrajudicial powers of arrest, detention and internment. The proceedings in this case concern the scope and the operation in practice of those measures as well as the alleged ill-treatment of persons thereby deprived of their liberty.

12. Up to March 1975, on the figures cited before the Commission by the respondent Government, over 1,100 people had been killed, over 11,150 injured and more than £140,000,000 worth of property destroyed during the recent troubles in Northern Ireland. This violence found its expression in part in civil disorders, in part in terrorism, that is organized violence for political ends . . .

36. . . . The authorities therefore came to the conclusion that it was necessary to introduce a policy of detention and internment of persons suspected of serious terrorist activities but against whom sufficient evidence could not be laid in court. This policy was regarded as a temporary measure primarily aimed at breaking the influence of the I.R.A. It was intended that a respite would be provided so as to enable the political and social reforms already undertaken to achieve their full effects. [The policy of internment was introduced in August, 1971. In December, the Government of Ireland lodged its application with the Commission.] . . .

93. . . . The procedure followed for the purposes of ascertaining the facts (Article 28, sub-paragraph (a), of the Convention) was one decided upon by the Commission and accepted by the Parties. The Commission examined in detail with medical reports and oral evidence 16 'illustrative' cases selected at its request by the applicant Government. The Commission considered a further 41 cases (the so-called '41 cases') on which it had received medical reports and invited written comments: . . .

96. Twelve persons arrested on 9 August 1971 and two persons arrested in October 1971 were singled out and taken to one or more unidentified centres. There, between 11 to 17 August and 11 to 18 October respectively, they were submitted to a form of 'interrogation in depth' which involved the combined application of five particular techniques.

These methods, sometimes termed 'disorientation' or 'sensory deprivation' techniques, were not used in any cases other than the fourteen so indicated above. It emerges from the Commission's establishment of the facts that the techniques consisted of:

(a) *wall-standing*: forcing the detainees to remain for periods of some hours in a 'stress position', described by those who underwent it as being 'spreadeagled against the wall, with their fingers put high above the head against the wall, the legs spread apart and the feet back, causing them to stand on their toes with the weight of the body mainly on the fingers';

(b) *hooding*: putting a black or navy coloured bag over the detainees' heads and, at least initially, keeping it there all the time except during interrogation;

(c) *subjection to noise*: pending their interrogations, holding the detainees in a room where there was a continuous loud and hissing noise;

(d) *deprivation of sleep*: pending their interrogations, depriving the detainees of sleep;

(e) *deprivation of food and drink*: subjecting the detainees to a reduced diet during their stay at the centre and pending interrogations. . . .

98. The two operations of interrogation in depth by means of the five techniques led to the obtaining of a considerable quantity of intelligence information, including the identification of 700 members of both IRA factions and the discovery of individual responsibility for about 85 previously unexplained criminal incidents. . . .

[On 2 March 1972 (after the initial application before the Commission had been lodged, but before it had been declared admissible) the United Kingdom Prime Minister had announced that the Government was discontinuing use of the five techniques. The United Kingdom Attorney-General, at a hearing before the European Court of Human Rights on 8 February 1977, gave the Court an 'unqualified undertaking, that the "five techniques" will not in any circumstances be reintroduced as an aid to interrogation'.] . . .

The Commission found no physical injury to have resulted from the application of the five techniques as such, but loss of weight by the two case-witnesses and acute psychiatric symptoms developed by them during interrogation were recorded in the medical and other evidence. The Commission, on the material before it, was unable to establish the exact degree of any psychiatric after-effects produced . . . but on the general level it was satisfied that some psychiatric after-effects in certain of the fourteen persons subjected to the techniques could not be excluded . . .

[The Court reviewed numerous other allegations of ill-treatment including claimed assaults and beatings.] . . .

152. The United Kingdom Government contest neither the breaches of Article 3 as found by the Commission, nor—a point moreover that is beyond doubt—the Court's jurisdiction to examine such breaches. However, relying *inter alia* on the case-law of the International Court of Justice they argue that the European Court has power to decline to exercise its jurisdiction where the objective of an application has been accomplished or where adjudication on the merits would be devoid of purpose. Such, they claim, is the situation here. They maintain that the findings in question not only are not contested but also have been widely publicized and that they do not give rise to problems of interpretation or application of the Convention sufficiently important to require a decision by the Court. Furthermore, for them the subject-matter of those findings now belongs to past history in view of the abandonment of the five techniques (1972), the solemn and unqualified undertaking not to reintroduce these techniques (8 February 1977) and the other measures taken by the United Kingdom to remedy, impose punishment for, and prevent the recurrence of, the various violations found by the Commission . . .

154. Nevertheless, the Court considers that the responsibilities assigned to it within the

framework of the system under the Convention extended to pronouncing on the noncontested allegations of violation of Article 3. The Court's judgments in fact serve not only to decide those cases brought before the Court but, more generally, to elucidate, safeguard and develop the rules instituted by the Convention, thereby contributing to the observance by the States of the engagements undertaken by them as Contracting Parties. . . .

162. As was emphasized by the Commission, ill-treatment must attain a minimum level of severity if it is to fall within the scope of Article 3. The assessment of this minimum is, in the nature of things, relative; it depends on all the circumstances of the case, such as the duration of the treatment, its physical or mental effects and, in some cases, the sex, age and state of health of the victim, etc.

163. The Convention prohibits in absolute terms torture and inhuman or degrading treatment or punishment, irrespective of the victim's conduct. Unlike most of the substantive clauses of the Convention and of Protocols Nos. 1 and 4, Article 3 makes no provision for exceptions and, under Article 15 (2), there can be no derogation therefrom even in the event of a public emergency threatening the life of the nation.

164. In the instant case, the only relevant concepts are 'torture' and 'inhuman or degrading treatment', to the exclusion of 'inhuman or degrading punishment'. . . .

167. The five techniques were applied in combination, with premeditation and for hours at a stretch; they caused, if not actual bodily injury, at least intense physical and mental suffering to the persons subjected thereto and also led to acute psychiatric disturbances during interrogation. They accordingly fell into the category of inhuman treatment within the meaning of Article 3. The techniques were also degrading since they were such as to arouse in their victims feelings of fear, anguish and inferiority capable of humiliating and debasing them and possibly breaking their physical or moral resistance.

On these two points, the Court is of the same view as the Commission.

In order to determine whether the five techniques should also be qualified as torture, the Court must have regard to the distinction, embodied in Article 3, between this notion and that of inhuman or degrading treatment.

In the Court's view, this distinction derives principally from a difference in the intensity of the suffering inflicted.

The Court considers in fact that, whilst there exists on the one hand violence which is to be condemned both on moral grounds and also in most cases under the domestic law of the Contracting States but which does not fall within Article 3 of the Convention, it appears on the other hand that it was the intention that the Convention, with its distinction between 'torture' and 'inhuman or degrading treatment', should by the first of these terms attach a special stigma to deliberate inhuman treatment causing very serious and cruel suffering.

Moreover, this seems to be the thinking lying behind Article 1 *in fine* of Resolution 3452 (XXX) adopted by the General Assembly of the United Nations on 9 December 1975, which declares:

'Torture constitutes an *aggravated* and deliberate form of cruel, inhuman or degrading treatment or punishment'.

Although the five techniques, as applied in combination, undoubtedly amounted to inhuman and degrading treatment, although their object was the extraction of confessions, the naming of others and/or information and although they were used systematically, they did not occasion suffering of the particular intensity and cruelty implied by the word torture as so understood.

[The Court held by 16 votes to one that the use of the five techniques constituted inhuman and degrading treatment, in violation of Article 3. It held by 13 votes to four that the use of the five techniques did not constitute torture within the meaning of Article 3.]

[The Court also considered the other alleged violations of Article 3 and found some uncontested and others not supported by adequate proof.

The Court's discussion of claimed violations of Articles 5 and 6 is omitted.]

Separate opinion of Judge Zekia

. . . It seems to me permissible, in ascertaining whether torture or inhuman treatment has been committed or not, to apply not only the objective test but also the subjective test.

As an example I can refer to the case of an elderly sick man who is exposed to a harsh treatment—after being given several blows and beaten to the floor, he is dragged and kicked on the floor for several hours. I would say without hesitation that the poor man has been tortured. If such treatment is applied on a wrestler or even a young athlete, I would hesitate a lot to describe it as inhuman treatment and I might regard it as a mere rough handling. Another example: if a mother, for interrogation, is separated from her suckling baby by keeping them apart in adjoining rooms and the baby, on account of hunger, starts yelling for hours within the hearing of the mother and she is not allowed to attend her baby, again I should say both the mother and the baby have been subjected to inhuman treatment, the mother by being agonized and the baby by being deprived of the urgent attention of the mother. Neither the mother nor the child has been assaulted. . . .

I do not share the view that extreme intensity of physical or mental suffering is a requisite for a case of ill-treatment to amount to 'torture' within the purport and object of Article 3 of the Convention. The nature of torture admits gradation in its intensity, in its severity and in the methods adopted. It is, therefore, primarily the duty and responsibility of the authority conducting the enquiries from close quarters, after taking into account all the surrounding circumstances, evidence and material available, to say whether in a particular case inhuman ill-treatment reached the degree of torture. In other words, this is a finding of fact for the competent authority dealing with the case in the first instance and which, for reasons we give hereunder, we should not interfere with.

Separate opinion of Judge O'Donoghue

. . . One is not bound to regard torture as only present in a mediaeval dungeon where the appliances of rack and thumbscrew or similar devices were employed. Indeed in the present-day world there can be little doubt that torture may be inflicted in the mental sphere. Torture is, of course, a more severe type of inhuman treatment. No amount of careful consideration can alter my opinion that the approach of the Commission . . . was the correct one. Accordingly, I conclude that the combined use of the five techniques constituted a practice of inhuman treatment and torture in breach of Article 3.

Separate opinion of Judge Fitzmaurice

13. . . . [It cannot be said that] everyone knows what torture is, what inhuman treatment is, and what is degrading,—since the present case seems to show conclusively that ideas on these questions can differ very greatly, not only with reference to particular acts, but as to the very factors on which an assessment should be based. Yet it can certainly be said that some kinds of treatment *recognisably* amount to torture or inhuman or degrading treatment; whereas other, though censorable, do not. . . .

22. According to my idea of the correct handling of languages and concepts, to call the treatment involved by the use of the five techniques 'inhuman' is excessive and distorting, unless the term is being employed loosely and merely figuratively (see examples below[7]),—and it is clearly not in any such lax or light-hearted sense that Article 3 intends it. Subjection to the five techniques was certainly harsh treatment, ill-treatment, maltreatment, and other descriptions could be found; but the 'inhuman' involves a totally different order or category of concept to which, in my opinion, the five techniques, even used in combination, do not properly belong. To regard them as doing so is to debase the currency of normal speech, because there is then no way left in which to differentiate or distinguish, or to describe instances of truly inhuman treatment. If anything that causes an appreciable amount of aching, strain, discomfort, distress, etc., or of deprivation of sleep or sustenance, is to be regarded an 'inhuman', what words shall be found to characterize the much graver treatment that could without serious question be considered inhuman? To give concrete examples, if standing someone against a wall in a strained position over a considerable period, or keeping him with a hood over his head for a certain time, amounts to 'inhuman' treatment, what language should be used to describe kicking a man in the groin, or placing him in a blacked-out cell in the company of a bevy of starving rats? That would also be merely inhuman treatment presumably?—and I say 'merely' because, although the latter instances would clearly constitute inhuman treatment, they would apparently be rated no differently from, and as no worse than, the former relatively minor ones, if these also are to be characterized as 'inhuman'. If the extreme term is to be used for any infliction of physical or mental harm or stress, no way of marking out or attaching the necessary weight to the genuine case remains,—for to employ such locutions as 'very inhuman' or 'severely inhuman' would obviously be ridiculous. . . .

25. . . . The essential phrase [in the Court's finding of inhuman treatment]—reads as follows:

> 'they caused, if not actual bodily injury [which means that they did not do so], at least intense physical and mental suffering to the persons subjected thereto and also led to acute psychiatric disturbances during interrogation'.

Most people feel 'disturbed' during an interrogation that must necessarily be of a rigorous, searching and quasi-hostile character, and it is not surprising that there was medical evidence of it in certain particular cases. But what is the basis of the term 'intense', qualifying 'suffering', physical and mental? Such language is surely excessive and disproportionate and not justified by the evidence. To many people, several of the techniques would not cause 'suffering' properly so called at all, and certainly not 'intense' suffering. Even the wall-standing would give rise to something more in the nature of strain, aches and pains, fatigue, and the like. To speak of 'intense physical . . . suffering' comes very near to speaking of torture, and the Judgment rejects torture. The sort of epithets that would in my view be justified to describe the treatment involved (treatment that did not cause bodily injury) would be 'unpleasant, harsh, tough, severe' and others of that order, but to call it 'barbarous', 'savage', 'brutal' or 'cruel', which is the least that is necessary if the notion of the inhuman is to be attained, constitutes an abuse of language and, as I have said earlier, amounts to a devaluing of what should be kept for much worse things. It is hardly a convincing exercise . . .

[7] To give examples of figurative use within most people's experience:—One hears it said 'I call that inhuman', the reference being to the fact that there is no dining-car on the train. 'It's degrading for the poor man', one hears with reference to an employee who is being given all the unpleasant jobs. 'It's absolute torture to me'.—and what the speaker means is having to sit through a boring lecture or sermon. There is a lesson to be learnt here on the potential dangers of hyperbole (footnote by Judge Fitzmaurice).

26. . . . For my part, I consider that the concept of 'inhuman' treatment should be confined to the kind of treatment that (taking some account of the circumstances) no member of the human species ought to inflict on another, or could so inflict without doing grave violence to the human, as opposed to the animal, element is his or her make-up. This I believe is the sense in which the notion of 'inhuman' treatment was intended to be understood in Article 3,—as something amounting to an atrocity, or at least a barbarity. Hence it should not be employed as a mere figure of speech to denote what is bad treatment, ill treatment, maltreatment, rather than, properly speaking, inhuman treatment. . . .

27. . . . ['Degrading treatment' should] denote something seriously humiliating, lowering as to human dignity, or disparaging, like having one's head shaved, being tarred and feathered, smeared with filth, pelted with muck, paraded naked in front of strangers, forced to eat excreta, deface the portrait of one's sovereign or head of State, or dress up in a way calculated to provoke ridicule or contempt,—although here one may pause to wonder whether Christ was really degraded by being made to don a purple robe and crown of thorns and to carry His own cross. Be that as it may, the examples I have given justify asking where exactly the degradation lies in being deprived of sleep and nourishment for limited periods, in being placed for a time in a room where a continuous noise is going on, or even in being 'hooded'—(after all, it has never been suggested that a man is degraded by being blindfolded before being executed although, admittedly, this is supposed to be for his benefit). . . .

28. . . . [The Court states:]

'The techniques were also degrading since they were such as to arouse in their victims feelings of fear, anguish and inferiority capable of humiliating and debasing them and possibly breaking their physical or moral resistance.' . . .

(a) Feelings of 'fear, anguish and inferiority' are the common lot of mankind constantly experienced by everyone in the course of ordinary everyday life: that is '*la condition humaine*'. Yet no one would consider himself, or regard others, as humiliated and debased because of experiencing such feelings, even though some experience them very easily and others only for greater cause. Thus it is not the subjective feelings aroused in the individual that humiliate or debase but the objective character of the act or treatment that gives rise to those feelings—if it does—and even if it does not,—for it is possible for fanatics at one end of the scale, and saints, martyrs and heroes at the other to undergo the most degrading treatment and feel neither humiliated nor debased, but even uplifted. Yet the treatment itself remains none the less degrading. . . .

(b) Nor does 'possibly breaking their physical or moral resistance' furnish any more satisfactory test. Again it is the character of the treatment that counts, not its results. It is easy to think of ways in which physical and moral resistance can be broken without any resort to ill-treatment, the use of force, or acts of degradation. Alcohol will do it, and often does. More generally, simple persuasion, or consideration and indulgence will do it. As has been well said, 'There is no defence against kindness'. The degradation lies not in what the treatment produces, but in how it does it: it might produce no result at all, but still be degrading because of its intrinsic character. . . .

35. Although I agree with the Court's pronouncements [on the absence of 'torture' in this case], and they are correct as far as they go, and propound the essential test that has to be applied, they nevertheless fail to bring out the real point latent in them, which is that not only must a certain intensity of suffering be caused before the process can be called torture, but also that torture involves a wholly different *order* of suffering from what falls short of it. It amounts not to

a mere difference of degree but to a difference of kind. If the five techniques are to be regarded as involving torture, how does one characterize e.g. having one's finger-nails torn out, being slowly impaled on a stake through the rectum, or roasted over an electric grid? That is just torture too, is it? Or might it perhaps amount to 'severe' torture?! Or what words do you find to make the difference between treatment of that kind and the mere aches, pains, strains, stresses and discomforts of the five techniques, which pale into insignificance in comparison with the searing, unimaginable, agony of the other? These are not in the same category at all, and cannot be spoken of in the same breath. Nor is the point academic, as it might be if torture of the order I have mentioned were a thing of the past. But it is not; and in Europe itself there are countries in which such practices have been prevalent in quite recent periods. So what does the European Commission do when, as it easily might, it finds itself faced with a case of real torture? Just pronounce it to constitute treatment contrary to Article 3 of the Convention? Fortunately for the Court, it, at least, has avoided digging this pit for itself.

36. May I conclude this part of the case by registering my emphatic opining that if a commendable zeal for the observance and implementation of the Convention is allowed to drive out common-sense, the whole system will end by becoming discredited. There can be no surer way of doing this than to water down and adulterate the terms of the Convention by enlarging them so as to include concepts and notions that lie outside their just and normal scope. . . .

Separate opinion of Judge Evrigenis

(i) . . . The Court's interpretation in this case seems also to be directed to a conception of torture based on methods of inflicting suffering which have already been overtaken by the ingenuity of modern techniques of oppression. Torture no longer presupposes violence, a notion to which the judgment refers expressly and generically. Torture can be practised—and indeed is practised—by using subtle techniques developed in multidisciplinary laboratories which claim to be scientific. By means of new forms of suffering that have little in common with the physical pain caused by conventional torture it aims to bring about, even if only temporarily, the disintegration of an individual's personality, the shattering of his mental and psychological equilibrium and the crushing of his will. I should very much regret it if the definition of torture which emerges from the judgment could not cover these various forms of technologically sophisticated torture. Such an interpretation would overlook the current situation and the historical prospects in which the European Convention on Human Rights should be implemented.

(ii) I take a stronger position than the majority of the Court as regards the assessment of the combined use of the five techniques from the factual point of view. I am sure that the use of these carefully chosen and measured techniques must have caused those who underwent them extremely intense physical, mental and psychological suffering, inevitably covered by even the strictest definition of torture. . . .

Separate opinion of Judge Matscher

. . . There is no doubt that one can speak of torture within the meaning of Article 3 only when the treatment inflicted on a person is such as to cause him physical or psychological suffering of a certain severity. However, I consider the element of intensity as complementary to the systematic element: the more sophisticated and refined the method, the less acute will be the pain (in the first place physical pain) which it has to cause to achieve its purpose. The modern methods of torture which in their outward aspects differ markedly from the primitive, brutal methods employed in former times are well known. In this sense torture is in no way a higher degree of inhuman treatment. On the contrary, one can envisage forms of brutality which cause much more acute bodily suffering but are not necessarily on that account comprised within the notion of torture.

. . . 'The five techniques were applied in combination, with premeditation and for hours at a stretch; they caused, if not actual bodily injury, at least intense physical and mental suffering to the persons subjected thereto and also led to acute psychiatric disturbances during interrogation' (paragraph 167 of the judgment). They thus constitute a typical example of torture within the meaning of Article 3 of the Convention.

2. JUDICIAL DISTINCTIONS

The *Irish Case* illustrates the tendency to assume that Article 3 prohibits three distinct categories of conduct—(1) torture, (2) inhuman treatment and (3) degrading treatment. The Court's discussion associates inhuman treatment with the following factors: premeditation; long duration; intense physical and mental suffering; acute psychiatric distress. The Court's description of degrading treatment uses these terms: feelings of fear, anguish and inferiority; humiliating and debasing; breaking physical or moral resistance. While one might focus more on physical pain in considering a punishment's inhuman character, and on emotional or dignitary injury when determining whether it is degrading, the three categories still clearly show considerable overlap. Torture, indeed, appears to lack any independent content. In the Court's language, torture is simply 'inhuman and degrading treatment which is more intense with respect to the suffering inflicted'. Torture must cause 'very serious and cruel suffering'. In a later case the Court again found unusually harsh conditions of detention to be inhuman treatment. In that case, although the applicant had alleged much more extreme treatment, the Court based its holding on a factual finding by the Commission that the applicant had been kept in a cold and dark cell, 'blindfolded and treated in a way which left wounds and bruises on his body' in connection with his interrogation.[8] When, however, an applicant claimed that confinement with few interruptions in an overcrowded cell violated Article 3, the Court insisted on specific affirmative evidence of the conditions. Failing such evidence, and in light of a medical report at the time stating he was in good health, the Court refused to find a violation.[9] In another case the applicant was held in the psychiatric wing of a prison. The applicant, who suffered from a mental illness, argued that because he had not received any regular medical or psychiatric attention in prison, the conditions of detention had caused a deterioration in his health. Agreeing that the situation was 'unsatisfactory and not conducive to effective treatment' the Court decided that since no deterioration of the applicant's condition had been established no violation of the Convention had been made out.[10] In dissent Judge Pekkanen, joined by Judge Jambrek, noted

---

[8]   *Tekin v. Turkey*, 9 June 1998, Reports 1998–IV 1504, paras. 9, 53.

[9]   *Assenov and Others v. Bulgaria*, 28 Oct. 1998, Reports 1998–VIII 3264, 28 E.H.R.R. 652, paras. 135–36.

[10] *Aerts v. Belgium*, 30 July 1998, Reports 1998–V 1939, 29 E.H.R.R. 50, paras. 161–7.

that, at the relevant time, the applicant 'urgently needed appropriate psychiatric treatment'. He found the applicant had undergone 'suffering sufficiently great to be considered "inhuman"'.[11]

The Court found no torture in the application of the 'five techniques'. It is of some interest that among the specifications of prohibited punishment suggested, but not acted on in the Consultative Assembly, was a clause stating that no person should 'be subjected to imprisonment with such an excess of light, darkness, noise or silence as to cause mental suffering'[12] The Court found no challenged conduct to be torture until 1996. In *Aksoy v. Turkey*[13] the applicant had been detained on suspicion of participation in terrorist activities on behalf of the PKK, a Kurdish nationalist group.

He was interrogated about whether he knew Metin (the man who had identified him). He claimed to have been told, 'If you don't know him now, you will know him under torture'.

According to the applicant, on the second day of his detention he was stripped naked, his hands were tied behind his back and he was strung up by his arms in the form of torture known as 'Palestinian hanging'. While he was hanging, the police connected electrodes to his genitals and threw water over him while they electrocuted him. He was kept blindfolded during this torture, which continued for approximately 35 minutes.

During the next two days, he was allegedly beaten repeatedly at intervals of two hours or half an hour, without being suspended. The torture continued for four days, the first two being very intensive.

He claimed that, as a result of the torture, he lost the movement of his arms and hands. His interrogators ordered him to make movements to restore the control of his hands. He asked to see a doctor, but was refused permission.[14]

Accepting this account, the Court declared it 'of such a serious and cruel nature that it can only be described as torture.'[15] In subsequent cases the Court has found torture present when a seventeen year old applicant was held by Turkish security forces for three days during which time she was raped and beaten[16] and when an applicant arrested by French police was repeatedly beaten and, on one occasion urinated on as well as threatened and verbally abused.[17]

The notion that violations of Article 3 are determined by an examination of the seriousness of the suffering inflicted is consistent with the Court's summary treatment of the issue in *Marckx v. Belgium*.[18] In that case, the applicants complained of Belgian laws which put illegitimate children at a disadvantage with respect to legal family relations and, particularly, inheritance rights. The Court found violations of Article 8 and of Article 14 in conjunction with Article 8. The applicants' claim that the

[11] *Id.* partly dissenting opinion of Judge Pekkanen joined by Judge Jambrek, paras. 3–6.
[12] 1 *Travaux Préparatoires* 252.
[13] 18 Dec. 1996, Reports, 1996–IV 2260, 23 E.H.R.R. 553.
[14] *Id.* paras. 13–15.
[15] *Id.* para. 64.
[16] *Aydin v. Turkey*, 25 Sept. 1997, Reports, 1997–VI 1866, 25 E.H.R.R. 251.
[17] *Selmouni v. France*, 28 July 1999 (not yet reported).
[18] 13 June 1979 (No. 31), 2 E.H.R.R. 330.

laws created 'degrading treatment' in violation of Article 3 was, however, unanimously rejected. The components of 'degrading treatment' will be separately treated below but, as with inhuman treatment, the Court has insisted on some minimum level of severity. The Court's reasoning in *Marckx* consisted of one sentence: '[W]hile the legal rules at issue probably present aspects which the applicants feel to be humiliating, they do not constitute degrading treatment coming within the ambit of Article 3'.[19] In his separate opinion, Judge Fitzmaurice stated: '[I]n my view [the Court] should have gone much further and held that such a provision as Article 3 [of the Convention] was concerned with a wholly different class of subject matter and had no sort of applicability at all to such circumstances as those of the applicants'.[20]

The court further developed the attributes of 'inhuman and degrading' treatment in *Raninen v. Finland*.[21] In that case the applicant had been handcuffed while being transported by military police after one of a series of arrests for refusing military service. The judgment stated that 'handcuffing does not normally give rise to an issue under Article 3 . . . where the measure does not entail use of force or public exposure exceeding what is reasonably considered necessary in the circumstances'. It was agreed in this case that no action of the applicant made the handcuffs necessary. But the Court found no violation of Article 3. There was no showing that the handcuffs had been intended to debase or humiliate. Public exposure had been minimal. Moreover, there was no convincing evidence that the handcuffing had caused subsequent physical or psychological problems. In these circumstances it was not established 'that the treatment in issue attained the minimum level of severity required by Article 3'.[22]

The Court has held that some treatment may cause such suffering and distress as to be 'inhuman or degrading' even though it involves no physical contact. When Turkish security forces burned down the home of the applicants in their presence the Court observed that

Mrs. Selcuk and Mr. Asker were respectively 54 and 60 at the time and had lived in the village of Islamköy all their lives. Their homes and most of their property were destroyed by the security forces, depriving the applicants of their livelihoods and forcing them to leave their village. It would appear that the exercise was pre-meditated and carried out contemptuously and without respect for the feelings of the applicants. They were taken unprepared; they had to stand by and watch the burning of the homes; inadequate precautions were taken to secure the safety of Mr. and Mrs. Asker; Mrs. Selcuk's protests were ignored and no assistance provided to them afterwards.

Bearing in mind, in particular, the manner in which the applicants' homes were destroyed and their personal circumstances, it is clear that they must have caused suffering of sufficient severity for

---

[19] *Id.* para. 5, fn. 2 (dissenting opinion of Judge Fitzmaurice).

[20] *Id.* para. 66.

[21] 16 Dec. 1997, Reports, 1997–VIII, 1866, 25 E.H.R.R. 563.

[22] *Id.* paras. 56–9. See also *Lopez Ostra v. Spain*, 9 Dec. 1994 (No. 303C), 20 E.H.R.R. 277, paras. 55–60, where the Court summarily dismissed a claim that the suffering, including illness and dislocation, caused by placement of a sewage treatment plant near the applicant's home rose to the level of 'inhuman or degrading treatment'.

the acts of the security forces to be categorized as inhuman treatment with the meaning of Article 3.[23]

Similarly in *Kurt v. Turkey*[24] the Court held the applicant had been subjected to inhuman and degrading treatment caused by the arrest and unexplained disappearance of her son. 'She had witnessed his detention in the village with her own eyes and his non-appearance since that last sighting made her fear for his safety . . . As a result she had been left with the anguish of knowing that her son had been detained and that there is a complete absence of official information as to his subsequent fate. This anguish has endured over a prolonged period of time.'[25] On the other hand in *Çakici v. Turkey*[26] the Court refused to find a violation based on the distress suffered by the disappearance of the applicant's brother. Unlike in *Kurt* the Court held that there were

no special factors which give [] the suffering of the applicant a dimension and character distinct from the emotional distress which may be regarded as inevitably caused to relatives of a victim of a serious human rights violation. Relevant elements will include the proximity of the family tie — in that context, a certain weight will attach to the parent-child bond—,the particular circumstances of the relationship, the extent to which the family member witnessed the events in question, the involvement of the family member in the attempts to obtain information about the disappeared person and the way in which the authorities responded to those inquiries. The Court would further emphasize that the essence of such a violation does not so much lie in the fact of the 'disappearance' of the family member but rather concerns the authorities' reactions and attitudes to the situation when it is brought to their attention. It is especially in respect of the latter that a relative may claim directly to be a victim of the authorities conduct.[27]

In this case the applicant, a brother, had a less intimate bond with the disappeared person and had not, as in *Kurt*, actually seen him detained. The 'brunt' of the work of seeking information, moreover, had not been borne by the applicant but by his father.[28] Judge Thommasen joined by Judges Jungwiert and Fischbach dissented on this point. Noting the deep suffering which a brother can feel at the 'uncertainty of the fate of a sibling' and the applicant's involvement in petitions and inquiries about the disappearance, she concluded that the state had 'left the applicant in uncertainty, doubt and apprehension about his brother for more than five and a half years. In doing so they demonstrated a cruel disregard for his feelings and his efforts to find out about his brother's fate.'[29]

---

[23] *Selcuk and Asker v. Turkey*, 24 Apr. 1998, Reports, 1998–II 891, 26 E.H.R.R. 477.

[24] 25 May 1998, Reports, 1998–III, 1152 27 E.H.R.R. 373.

[25] *Id.* para. 133.

[26] 7 July 1999 (not yet reported).

[27] *Id.* at para. 98.

[28] *Id.* at para. 99.

[29] *Id.* (partly dissenting opinion of Judge Thommasen joined by Judges Jungwiert and Fischbach).

3. FACT FINDING

Allegations that a state has violated Article 3, and especially claims that a state has committed acts of torture, are often contested not on legal but on factual grounds. Therefore, the Court's procedure for determining contested issues of fact is particularly significant in these cases. The Court's jurisdiction over 'all cases concerning the interpretation and application' of the Convention[30] reserves to it the final resolution of such questions. As a practical matter the Court, before November 1998, almost always relied on the factual investigations of the Commission. The Commission, not infrequently, took evidence from witnesses and, when necessary, dispatched delegations to the sites of relevant events to hear such testimony.[31] The Court expressed a policy of deferring to the factual findings of the Commission while retaining the right, in exceptional cases, to draw different conclusions. When reviewing disputed questions of fact the Court has almost uniformly acted on the basis of written submissions developed in the Commission or in domestic judicial proceedings, or presented by the parties.[32]

With the elimination of the Commission the new Court has provided substitute procedures for fact-finding. The new Court's rules give a chamber sweeping authority to require evidence in various forms from a wide assortment of sources: '[t]he Chamber may, inter alia, request the parties to produce documentary evidence and decide to hear as a witness or expert or in any other capacity any person whose evidence or statement seems likely to assist it in the carrying out of its tasks'. It may also 'ask any person or institution of its choice to obtain information for taking evidence'. It may also designate one or more judges to 'conduct an inquiry, carry out an investigation on the spot or take evidence in some other manner.' It may appoint independent external experts to assist such a delegation.[33]

In *Ireland v. United Kingdom*, reproduced above, the Court held that the proper standard of proof for showing a violation was 'beyond a reasonable doubt' but added that 'such proof may follow from the coexistence of sufficiently strong, clear, and concordant inferences or of similar unrebutted presumptions of fact'.[34] In practice, this standard has been applied inconsistently and it certainly has not been used with the rigour generally associated with the 'reasonable doubt' standard in Anglo-American criminal law jurisprudence. In *Gündem v. Turkey*, in which the Court considered allegations that security forces had burned down the applicants' homes, the Court deferred to a Commission determination that the events described by the applicants had not been established beyond a reasonable doubt. The only eyewitness who testified before the Commission's delegates had been unclear about the reasons for the security forces' actions. The applicant himself had not appeared and other

---

[30] Art. 45 (old); Art. 32 (new).
[31] Art. 28 (1) (g) (old). See chapter 2(B)(3), *supra*.
[32] See, e.g., *Ribitsch v. Austria*, 4 Dec. 1995 (No. 336), 21 E.H.R.R. 573, paras. 30–34.
[33] Rules of Court, s. 42 (4 Nov. 1998).
[34] 18 Jan. 1978 (No. 25), 2 E.H.R.R. 25, para. 161.

witnesses had contradicted his account.[35] On the other hand, the Court has often upheld Commission findings of violations even when based on inconsistent and divided evidence. In one such case a dissenting judge described the manner in which the Commission established the facts as 'so superficial and insufficient and the analysis of these facts so clearly unsatisfactory that, in my view, neither provides a sufficiently sound basis for finding a violation'.[36]

While a record of inconclusive and divided evidence may deter the Court from finding a violation based on alleged acts, it may support finding a violation based on a state's failure to carry out an investigation of a plausible claim. In *Assenov and Others v. Bulgaria*[37] the applicant claimed he had been mistreated while in police custody. Given the inconclusive character of the evidence the Court did not take the alleged misconduct to have been established. That evidence, however, was enough to raise 'a reasonable suspicion' of such treatment. The Court decided that in such a case Article 3 'requires by implication that there should be an effective official investigation' which 'should be capable of leading to the identification and punishment of those responsible . . . If this were not the case the general legal prohibition of torture and inhuman and degrading treatment and punishment, despite its fundamental importance would be ineffective in practice and it would be possible in some cases for agents of the state to abuse the rights of those within its control with virtual impunity.'[38] The Court concluded that the state's response to the allegation in this case did not constitute an effective investigation and that, therefore, there had been a violation of Article 3.[39]

Notwithstanding the formal requirement of proof beyond a reasonable doubt, the Court has established a presumption for one situation which not infrequently arises in cases brought under Article 3. Where a person can show that he or she suffered injuries while in official custody, the state bears the burden of explaining why it should not be deemed responsible for the infliction of those injuries. In the case of *Tomasi v. France*[40] the applicant complained of beatings and other mistreatment during 40 hours of police interrogation. The police denied any misconduct and the French courts held that Tomasi had not shown a *prima facie* case justifying proceedings against the police. The European Court noted that medical examinations of the applicant after his interrogation had revealed the presence of injuries which could not have been suffered prior to his arrest and that he had promptly called the investigating

---

[35] 25 May 1998, Reports, 1998–III 1109, paras. 27–9, 66. See also *Ergi v. Turkey*, 28 July 1998, Reports, 1998–IV 1751; *Tanrikulu v. Turkey*, 8 July 1999 (not yet reported).

[36] *Kurt v. Turkey*, 25 May 1998, Reports, 1998–III, 1152, 27 E.H.R.R. 373 (partly dissenting opinion of Judge Matscher). See also *Mentes and Others v. Turkey*, 28 Nov. 1997, Reports, 1997–VIII 2689, 26 E.H.R.R. 595, paras. 62–9 and Joint Partly Dissenting Opinion of Judges Gölcüklü and Matscher. In *Çakici v. Turkey*, 7 July 1999, paras. 91–2, the Court adopted the Commission's finding that the brother of the applicant who had disappeared had been tortured while in custody by beatings and electric shock. The evidentiary basis for this finding was the testimony of a witness who had seen the physical condition of the brother while in detention and the witness's hearsay report of what the brother told him had been done to him.

[37] 28 Oct. 1998, Reports, 1998–VIII 3264, 28 E.H.R.R. 652.

[38] *Id.* at paras. 101–2.

[39] *Id.* at paras. 103–6; See also *Tanrikulu v. Turkey*, *supra* n. 35, paras. 101–11.

[40] 27 Aug. 1992 (No. 241A), 15 E.H.R.R. 1.

judge's attention to marks on his body which he attributed to beatings. This showing was sufficient to justify a conclusion that serious injury had been inflicted by the police and that, therefore, there had been a violation of Article 3.

In contrast, when the facts alleged included a significant period when the applicant was not in custody, during which time the relevant injuries might have been suffered, this presumption has much less force and the Court has refused to find a violation[41] Similarly, a finding of no violation has resulted where the state has offered an alternative explanation. For example, in *Klaas v. Germany*[42] it was conceded that the applicant had received injuries in the course of her arrest. The applicant insisted they were caused by gratuitous violence on the part of the police, while the state (and the domestic courts) had accepted the police version of events, according to which the injuries were the incidental result of the struggle that ensued when the applicant had forcefully resisted the police. The Strasbourg Court emphasized that 'as a general rule, it is for [the domestic] courts to assess the evidence before them'. In this case it noted that the German Regional Court, which had the benefit of seeing the various witnesses . . . , and of evaluating their credibility', had accepted the police officers' version of the facts. On that basis, it found no violation of Article 3.[43] It distinguished *Tomasi* 'where certain inferences could be made from the fact that Mr Tomasi had sustained unexplained injuries during forty-eight hours spent in police custody'.[44]

Three judges dissented, each citing *Tomasi*. Judge Walsh summed up what he took to be the principle established by that case:

Once it has been established that physical injury has been sustained by [a] person, while in police custody, the burden falls on the police or their state to show that such injuries were not caused or brought about by the actions of the police or their want of care.[45]

Since no specific evidence of how the injuries had occurred had been offered by the police and the German Court had merely relied on a presumption in their favour, the dissent asserted that a finding of a violation was proper.

In *Ribitsch v. Austria*, however, the Court sustained a Commission finding of a violation arising from injuries suffered in custody even though the state had argued an alternative but unconvincing explanation. In *Ribitsch* the applicant's claims had been accepted by a District Court in the criminal prosecution of the police officer charged with the relevant actions. But its holding was rejected by the Vienna Regional Criminal Court based on the high standard of proof necessary to support a criminal conviction.[46] Three judges on the European Court dissented, insisting that it was 'not the Court's task to substitute its assessment of the facts for that conducted by the national courts unless there have been improprieties. . . .'[47]

---

[41] *Erdagöz v. Turkey*, 22 Oct. 1997, Reports, 1997–VI 2300, paras. 41–42.
[42] 22 Sept. 1993 (No. 269), 18 E.H.R.R. 305.
[43] *Id.* paras. 29–30.
[44] *Id.* para. 30.
[45] *Id.* dissenting opinion of Judge Walsh. See also the dissenting opinions of Judges Pettiti and Spielmann.
[46] 4 Dec. 1995 (No. 336), 21 E.H.R.R. 573, paras. 32–8.
[47] *Id.* (joint dissenting opinion of Judges Rysdal, Matscher, and Jambrek).

4. COMPARISONS

The sparse case law of the European Court of Human Rights on the meaning of Article 3 makes particularly useful an examination of the interpretation of similar provisions in national constitutions. We have already noted the 'cruel and unusual' punishments provisions of the English Bill of Rights, the Eighth Amendment to the United States Constitution and Section 12 of the Canadian Charter of Rights and Freedoms. The English Bill of Rights, having no constitutional status, is ineffective to control Acts of Parliament which might infringe on the rights enumerated. Nevertheless, Article 10 prohibiting the infliction of 'cruel and unusual punishments' may serve as a legal restriction on executive acts of the government, including the treatment of detained persons dealt with in the principal case.[48] The English Court of Appeal has held that a prisoner may seek judicial review to determine whether his treatment amounted to 'cruel and unusual punishment' in violation of the Bill of Rights. As an example, the Court noted that:

it is generally held to be unacceptable that persons supposedly of normal mentality should be detained in psychiatric institutions as is said to occur in certain parts of the world. Coming close to the alleged facts of this case, if it were to be established that the applicant as a sane person was, for purely administrative purposes, being subjected in the psychiatric wing to the stress of being exposed to the disturbance caused by the behaviour of mentally ill and disturbed prisoners, this might well be considered as a 'cruel and unusual punishment' and one which was not deserved.[49]

One important difference between the European Convention and the American and British (but not the Canadian) guarantees is the inclusion in the former of both punishment and treatment. The distinction, would, for example, have made a difference in the *Irish Case* had the same facts been considered in relation to the Eighth Amendment. The applicants were not being detained for the purpose of *punishment*. The United States Supreme Court has held that persons being detained pending a criminal trial who were unable to post bail did not state an Eighth Amendment case when they challenged the conditions in the facility where they were being held. The Supreme Court held that these issues should be resolved under the due process clause of the Fifth (or Fourteenth) Amendment. The Eighth Amendment was only applicable after an adjudication of guilt and the commencement of punishment.[50] The due process analysis employed turned on whether the conditions complained of amounted to 'punishment' (which could not be inflicted before conviction) or were, instead aspects of the reasonable regulation necessary for maintaining the facility. The Court found that the particular conditions involved in that case were permissible under that test.

Notwithstanding the addition of the word 'treatment' in Section 12 of the Charter

---

[48] A parallel provision was enacted for Scotland in the Claim of Right of 1689, A.P.S. IX, 38.

[49] *R. v. Secretary of State for the Home Department, ex parte Herbage* [1987] 1 All E.R. 324 C.A.

[50] *Bell v. Wolfish*, 441 U.S. 520 (1979). *See also Revere v. Massachusetts General Hospital*, 463 U.S. 239 (1983) (Eighth Amendment inapplicable to alleged maltreatment of an arrested persons).

of Rights and Freedoms, the Canadian Supreme Court had held that not all adverse effects of public action may be examined under that provision. In *Rodriguez v. British Columbia (Attorney-General)* the Court considered a claim that the criminal prohibition on assisted suicide constituted cruel and unusual treatment of the plaintiff, a terminally ill patient. The Court conceded that the 'degree to which "treatment" . . . may apply outside the context of penalties to ensure the application and enforcement of the law has not been definitely determined by this Court'. Assuming, however, that non-penal treatment was governed by Section 12, a majority held that 'a mere prohibition by the state on certain action, without more, cannot constitute "treatment"'.

The fact that, because of the personal situation in which [plaintiff] finds herself, a particular prohibition impacts on her in a manner which causes her suffering does not subject her to 'treatment' at the hands of the state. The starving person who is prohibited by threat of criminal sanction from 'stealing a mouthful of bread' is likewise not subjected to 'treatment' within the meaning of s.12 by reason of the theft provisions of the Code . . .[51]

Despite the difference in terminology, the American jurisprudence on cruel and unusual punishment has sometimes emphasized some of the same factors that appear to have influenced the European Court's adjudication under Article 3. One prominent theme has been the maintenance of human dignity, even for those convicted of serious offences. This theme was elaborated in *Trop v. Dulles* in which a soldier was deprived of his United States citizenship by virtue of his wartime desertion. The Court acknowledged that death would be a proper penalty for desertion, but still found denationalization 'cruel and unusual':

The basic concept underlying the Eighth Amendment is nothing less than the dignity of man. While the state has the power to punish, the Amendment stands to assure that this power be exercised within the limits of civilized standards. Fines, imprisonment and even execution may be imposed depending upon the enormity of the crime but any technique outside the bounds of these traditional penalties is constitutionally suspect . . . [In denationalization] there may be involved no physical mistreatment, no primitive torture. There is instead the total destruction of the individual's status in organized society. It is a form of punishment more primitive than torture, for it destroys for the individual the political existence that was centuries in development . . . In short, the expatriate has lost the right to have rights . . . The punishment is offensive to cardinal principles for which the Constitution stands. It subjects the individual to a fate of ever-increasing fear and distress. He knows not what proscription may be directed against him, and when and for what cause his existence in his native land may be terminated. He may be subject to banishment, a fate universally decried by civilized people. He is stateless, a condition deplored in the international community of democracies.[52]

The idea that the effects of a punishment on the psychological well-being of the subject—'a fate of ever-increasing fear and distress'—and the idea that some punishments are offensive not so much for the physical pain they cause as for their inconsistency with 'human dignity' have their counterparts in the cases reproduced here

---

[51] [1993] 3 S.C.R. 519, 611.
[52] 356 U.S. 86, 100–02 (1958).

under the Convention. The application of this notion, of course, is a matter of great imprecision. In his dissenting opinion in *Trop* Justice Frankfurter asked: 'Is constitutional dialectic so empty of reason that it can be seriously argued that loss of citizenship is a fate worse than death?'[53]

One critical and controversial issue that has pervaded American and Canadian cases on the limits of permissible punishment is that of proportionality—the idea that the punishment should fit the crime. In *Weems v. United States*[54] decided in 1910, one of the earliest Eighth Amendment cases, the Supreme Court found a violation in the imposition by the Philippine territorial government of the 'cadena' for the offence of embezzlement of 616 pesos. The 'cadena', a remnant of the Spanish colonial government, was described by the Court as follows:

Its minimum degree is confinement in a penal institution for twelve years and one day, a chain at the ankle and wrist of the offender, hard and painful labor, no assistance from friend or relative, no marital authority or parental rights or rights of property, no participation even in the family council. These parts of his penalty endure for the term of imprisonment. From other parts there is no intermission. His prison bars and chains are removed, it is true, after twelve years, but he goes from them to a perpetual limitation of his liberty. He is forever kept under the shadow of his crime, forever kept within voice and view of the criminal magistrate, not being able to change his domicil without giving notice to the 'authority immediately in charge of his surveillance', and without permission in writing. He may not seek, even in other scenes and among other people, to retrieve his fall from rectitude. Even that hope is taken from him and he is subject to tormenting regulations that, if not so tangible as iron bars and stone walls, oppress as much by their continuity, and deprive of essential liberty. No circumstance of degradation is omitted. It may be that even the cruelty of pain is not omitted. He must bear a chain night and day. He is condemned to painful as well as hard labor. What painful labor may mean we have no exact measure. It must be something more than hard labor. It may be hard labor pressed to the point of pain. Such penalties for such offenses amaze those who have formed their conception of the relation of a state to even its offending citizens from the practice of the American commonwealths, and believe that it is a precept of justice that punishment for crime should be graduated and proportioned to offense.

The Court found that other more serious crimes were given less severe punishments and that the excesses of the 'cadena' served no useful state functions.

An interesting application of the proportionality analysis was *Robinson v. California*[55] decided in 1962, in which a 90-day sentence was at issue. While the sentence was hardly repugnant in itself, the Court found it disproportionate to the offence of being 'addicted to the use of narcotics', a status which was presumably beyond the capacity of the defendant to avoid. Under this approach there is nothing inherent in any punishment which makes it 'cruel and unusual'. 'Even one day in prison would be cruel and unusual punishment for the "crime" of having a common cold'.[56]

The Court used the same kind of analysis in finding unconstitutional two death

---

[53] *Id.* at 125.
[54] 217 U.S. 349 (1910).
[55] 370 U.S. 660 (1962).
[56] 370 U.S. at 669.

penalty statutes. In one, a death sentence for felony murder in which the defendant had no active part in the taking of life was reversed.[57] In another, the same result obtained with respect to a death penalty for rape.[58] The Court has also examined the constitutionality of long prison sentences when challenged as excessive in relation to the crime involved. In *Solem v. Helm*[59] it struck down a life sentence imposed under the South Dakota recidivist statute. The defendant had been convicted of passing a bad check for $100 after having been previously convicted in the previous ten years of third degree burglary three times, obtaining money under false pretenses, grand larceny and driving while intoxicated. But in *Harmelin v. Michigan*[60] the Court refused to hold unconstitutional a life sentence for possession of more than 650 grams of cocaine. Three judges in the 5–4 majority held that the apportionment of penalty was appropriately within the discretion of the legislature and that the Eighth Amendment forbids 'only extreme sentences that are grossly disproportionate to the crime'. Only on finding such an apparent gross disproportion would it be proper to compare the sentence with those for the same crime in other jurisdictions. The other two judges in the majority went even farther, arguing that it was improper to consider the disproportionality of penalty to offence.[61]

A similar approach has been used by the Supreme Court of Canada in deciding whether or not certain mandatory prison sentences violated Section 12 of the Canadian Charter of Rights and Freedoms. The proper test according to the Court is whether the punishment is 'grossly disproportionate' considering the 'nature of the offense, the circumstances in which it was committed, the character of the offender as well as deterrence and other penological objectives that go beyond the case of an individual offender'.[62] Applying that criterion, it held invalid a minimum sentence of seven years for importation of narcotics into the country in any amount.[63] On the other hand, imposition of an indeterminate sentence was upheld under a statute prescribing it for specified 'serious personal injury offenses' all of which involved conduct tending to cause 'severe physical danger or severe psychological injury'. Before imposing such a sentence, the sentencing court had to be convinced that defendant's action was part of a pattern of behaviour involving violence or a failure to control sexual impulses and that that pattern was very likely to continue, being 'substantially or pathologically intractable'. Even after these conditions were proved, a judge had discretion not to impose the indeterminate sentence. In his reasons for judgment, joined by four other justices, LaForest, J. said the statute involved a 'diligent

---

[57] *Edmund v. Florida*, 458 U.S. 782 (1982).

[58] *Coker v. Georgia*, 433 U.S. 584 (1997).

[59] 463 U.S. 277 (1983).

[60] 501 U.S. 957 (1991).

[61] Proportionality has naturally also been a central concern in the interpretation of that part of the Eighth Amendment proscribing 'excessive fines'. In a recent exposition the Supreme Court has held that this provision only reaches exactions that are 'grossly disporportional to the gravity of the defendant's offense'. *United States v. Bajakajian*, 524 U. S. 321, 331 (1998).

[62] *Smith v. R.* [1987] 1 S.C.R. 1045.

[63] *Id.*

attempt . . . to carefully define a very small group of offenders whose personal characteristics and particular circumstances militate strenuously in favor of preventive incarceration' and that 'it would be difficult to imagine a better tailored set of criteria'.[64]

The Canadian Court has recently gone beyond an examination of the statutory penalties for certain kinds of offences and has examined the circumstances of the particular conduct involved in an individual case. Thus, in holding that a seven-day minimum sentence for 'driving while prohibited' was not cruel and unusual, the majority called for an examination of, among other things, the gravity of the offence and the personal characteristics of the offender. If, in light of these factors, the penalty would 'outrage decency', a *prima facie* violation of the Charter would be present. Even if a violation did not appear on this basis, however, the validity of the challenged provision would be impugned if the offender could show it would be grossly disproportionate in some reasonable hypothetical circumstances.[65] Conversely, the Court has held that an indeterminate sentence with periodic review for 'criminal sexual psychopaths' was not unconstitutional on its face, but, when the reviewing agency misapplied or disregarded the proper statutory criteria for release, a violation of Section 12 was shown.[66]

The Judicial Committee of the Privy Council flatly rejected the idea of portionality in construing the Constitution of the former Southern Rhodesia insofar as it prohibited 'inhuman or degrading punishment or other treatment'. The Committee rejected a challenge to the constitutionality of an act providing a mandatory death sentence for assisting in an attempt to set fire to a house. Expressly rejecting, in this context, the holding of *Weems v. United States*[67] it asserted that an evaluation of the proportionality of the punishment would be an unjustified intrusion into the domain of the legislature:

It can hardly be for the courts, unless clearly so empowered or directed to rule as to the necessity or propriety of particular legislation. The provision contained in . . . the Constitution enables the court to adjudicate as to whether some form or type or description of punishment, . . . is inhuman or degrading, but it does not enable the Court to declare an enactment imposing a punishment to be *ultra vires* on the ground that the court considers that the punishment laid down by the enactment is inappropriate or excessive for the particular offence.[68]

No European Court of Human Rights judgment has applied this kind of proportionality analysis to find a violation of Article 3. Perhaps this is because, unlike many other guarantees of the Convention, Article 3 is drafted in absolute terms. It may not be infringed in the interest of public safety, welfare or morality (compare Articles 6, 8, 9, 10, and 11). Moreover, under Article 15, the proscriptions of Article 3, unlike those in most of the other articles, are effective even 'in time of war or other public emergency,

---

[64] *Lyons v. R.* [1987] 2 S.C.R. 309.

[65] *R. v. Goltz* [1991] 3 S.C.R. 485.

[66] *Steele v. Mountain Institution* [1990] 2 S.C.R. 1385.

[67] See *supra* p. 111.

[68] *Runyowa v. R.* [1967] A.C.26 P.C.

threatening the life of the nation'. Nonetheless, the Court may, on occasion, find it impossible to determine whether some treatment is inhuman or degrading without taking into account the reasons for which it was imposed. When an applicant complained that he was subjected to inhuman and degrading treatment when he was handcuffed while under arrest, the Court responded that

handcuffing does not normally give rise to an issue under Article 3 of the Convention where the measure has been imposed in connection with a lawful arrest or detention and does not entail the use of force, or public exposure, exceeding what is reasonably considered necessary in the circumstances. In this regard, it is of importance, for instance, whether there is reason to believe that the person concerned would resist arrest or abscond, cause injury or suppress evidence.[69]

In another case, the applicant was a prisoner with a history of psychiatric difficulties. When he engaged in a hunger strike, the authorities committed him to a hospital where he was force fed, involuntarily sedated, handcuffed and sometimes strapped to his bed for long periods. The Court held that there was no violation of Article 3, stating that 'as a general rule, a measure which is a therapeutic necessity cannot be regarded as inhuman or degrading'. Moreover, in the case under consideration, the evidence was 'not sufficient to disprove the Government's argument that, according to the psychiatric principles generally accepted at the time, medical necessity justified the treatment in issue'.[70]

5. THE UNITED NATIONS CONVENTION

The special qualities that make some state action torture or inhuman or degrading has been given a somewhat more extended consideration in the definitions provided in the United Nations Convention Against Torture and Other Cruel Inhuman or Degrading Treatment or Punishment.[71]

Article 1

1. For the purposes of this Convention, torture means any act by which severe pain or suffering, whether physical or mental, is intentionally inflicted on a person for such purposes as obtaining from him or a third person information or a confession, punishing him for an act he or a third person committed or is suspected of having committed, or intimidating or coercing him or a third person, or for any reason based on discrimination of any kind, when such pain or suffering is inflicted by or at the instigation of or with the consent or acquiescence of a public official or other person acting in an official capacity. It does not include pain or suffering arising from, inherent in or incidental to lawful sanctions.

---

[69] *Raninen v. Finland*, 16 Dec. 1997, Reports, 1997–VIII 2804, 26 E.H.R.R. 563.

[70] *Herczegfalvy v. Austria*, 24 Sept. 1992 (No. 242B), 15 E.H.R.R. 437. See also the discussion of the relevance of national interests to Art. 3 determinations in connection with expulsions or extraditions. *Infra*, section (C)(1).

[71] Adopted Dec. 1984. Entered into force 26 June 1987. On the operation of the Convention see generally T. Buergenthal, *International Human Rights* 72–6 (2nd ed. 1998).

2. This Article is without prejudice to any international instrument or national legislation which does or may contain provisions of wider application. . . .

Article 3

1. Each State Party shall take effective legislative, administrative, judicial or other measures to prevent acts of torture in any territory under its jurisdiction.

2. No exceptional circumstances whatsoever, whether a state of war or a threat of war, internal political instability or any other public emergency, may be invoked as a justification of torture.

3. An order from a superior officer or a public authority may not be invoked as a justification of torture. . . .

Article 16

1. Each State Party shall undertake to prevent in any territory under its jurisdiction other acts of cruel, inhuman or degrading treatment or punishment which do not amount to torture as defined in Article 1, when such acts are committed by or at the instigation of or with the consent or acquiescence of a public official or other person acting in an official capacity. In particular, the obligations contained in Articles 10, 11, 12 and 13 shall apply with the substitution for references to torture of references to other forms of cruel, inhuman or degrading treatment or punishment.

2. The provisions of this Convention are without prejudice to the provisions of any other international instrument or national law which prohibits cruel, inhuman or degrading treatment or punishment or which relate to extradition or expulsion. . . .

*   *   *

Note particularly the requirement in the United Nations Convention's definition (Article 1) that torture be 'intentionally inflicted'. This element has also been held to be essential to a finding of torture under Article 3 of the European Convention. In *Aksoy v. Turkey*,[72] in which the Court concluded that the applicant had suffered torture by being suspended from his arms and subjected to electric shocks and beatings, the Court stated that 'to allow the special stigma of "torture" requires a showing of "deliberate inhuman treatment causing very serious and cruel suffering"'.[73] In that case the applicant's treatment 'could only have been deliberately inflicted; indeed a certain amount of preparation and exertion would have been required to carry it out. It would appear to have been administered with the aim of obtaining admissions or information from the applicant.'[74]

The United Nations Convention's mention of 'such purpose as obtaining from him or a third person information or a confession' has also resonated in European cases finding torture. In one case the Court noted that the applicant's detention appeared designed to elicit information.[75] In another it concluded that the 'pain and suffering

[72] 18 Dec. 1996, Reports, 1996–VI 2260, 23 E.H.R.R. 553.

[73] *Id.* para. 63 (citing *Ireland v. United Kingdom*, 18 Jan. 1978 (No. 25), 2 E.H.R.R. 25 reproduced in part at section 1, *supra*).

[74] *Id.* para. 64.

[75] *Aydin v. Turkey*, 25 Sept. 1997, Reports, 1997–VI, 1866 25 E.H.R.R. 251, para. 85.

were inflicted on the applicant intentionally for the purpose of, *inter alia*, making him confess to the offense which he was suspected of having committed'.[76] In no case, however, has the Court stated that maltreatment must be motivated by any particular purpose in order to be torture.

B. CORPORAL PUNISHMENT

1. TYRER V. UNITED KINGDOM

Judgment of 25 April 1978
(No. 26), 2 E.H.R.R. 1

. . .

9. Mr. Anthony M. Tyrer, a citizen of the United Kingdom born on 21 September 1956, is a resident in Castletown, Isle of Man. On 7 March 1972, being then aged 15 and of previous good character, he pleaded guilty before the local juvenile court to unlawful assault occasioning actual bodily harm to a senior pupil at his school. The assault, committed by the applicant in company with three other boys, was apparently motivated by the fact that the victim had reported the boys for taking beer into the school, as a result of which they had been caned. The applicant was sentenced on the same day to three strokes of the birch in accordance with the relevant legislation.

10. After waiting in a police station for a considerable time for a doctor to arrive, Mr. Tyrer was birched late in the afternoon of the same day. His father and a doctor were present. The applicant was made to take down his trousers and underpants and bend over a table; he was held by two policemen whilst a third administered the punishment, pieces of the birch breaking at the first stroke. The applicant's father lost his self-control and after the third stroke 'went for' one of the policemen and had to be restrained.

The birching raised, but did not cut, the applicant's skin and he was sore for about a week and a half afterwards.

[The punishment was inflicted under a Manx Statute prescribing caning for males 11 to 16 years old found guilty of assault or beating. The Statute described the cane or rod to be used and the number of strokes. It also called for the caning to take place in private and in the presence of a parent or guardian. Regulations required a medical report prior to imposing the punishment and the presence of a doctor at the caning] . . .

14. Judicial corporal punishment of adults and juveniles was abolished in England, Wales and Scotland in 1948 and in Northern Ireland in 1968.

15. The punishment remained in existence in the Isle of Man. When Tynwald [the local Parliament] examined the question in 1963 and 1965, it decided to retain judicial corporal punishment, which was considered a deterrent to hooligans visiting the Island as tourists and, more generally, a means of preserving law and order . . .

---

[76] *Selmouni v. France*, 28 July 1999 (not yet reported).

29. The Court shares the Commission's view that Mr. Tyrer's punishment did not amount to 'torture' within the meaning of Article 3. The Court does not consider that the facts of this particular case reveal that the applicant underwent suffering of the level inherent in this notion as it was interpreted and applied by the Court in its judgment of 18 January 1978 (*Ireland v. the United Kingdom*).

[Nor does the Court] consider on the facts of the case that that level was attained and it therefore concurs with the Commission that the penalty imposed on Mr. Tyrer was not 'inhuman punishment' within the meaning of Article 3. Accordingly, the only question for decision is whether he was subjected to a 'degrading punishment' contrary to that Article.

30. The Court notes first of all that a person may be humiliated by the mere fact of being criminally convicted. However, what is relevant for the purposes of Article 3 is that he should be humiliated not simply by his conviction but by the execution of the punishment which is imposed on him. In fact, in most if not all cases this may be one of the effects of judicial punishment, involving as it does unwilling subjection to the demands of the penal system.

However, as the Court pointed out in its judgment of 18 January 1978 in the case of *Ireland v. the United Kingdom*, the prohibition contained in Article 3 of the Convention is absolute: no provision is made for exceptions and, under Article 15 Section 2, there can be no derogation from Article 3. It would be absurd to hold that judicial punishment generally, by reason of its usual and perhaps almost inevitable element of humiliation, is 'degrading' within the meaning of Article 3. Some further criterion must be read into the text. Indeed, Article 3, by expressly prohibiting 'inhuman' and 'degrading' punishment, implies that there is a distinction between such punishment and punishment in general.

In the Court's view, in order for a punishment to be 'degrading' and in breach of Article 3, the humiliation or debasement involved must attain a particular level and must in any event be other than that usual element of humiliation referred to in the preceding subparagraph. The assessment is, in the nature of things, relative: it depends on all the circumstances of the case and, in particular, on the nature and context of the punishment itself and the manner and method of its execution.

31. The Attorney-General for the Isle of Man argued that the judicial corporal punishment at issue in this case was not in breach of the Convention since it did not outrage public opinion on the Island. However, even assuming that local public opinion can have an incidence on the interpretation of the concept of 'degrading punishment' appearing in Article 3, the Court does not regard it as established that judicial corporal punishment is not considered degrading by those members of the Manx population who favour its retention: it might well be that one of the reasons why they view the penalty as an effective deterrent is precisely the element of degradation which it involves. As regards their belief that judicial corporal punishment deters criminals, it must be pointed out that a punishment does not lose its degrading character just because it is believed to be, or actually is, an effective deterrent or aid to crime control. Above all, as the Court must emphasise, it is never permissible to have recourse to punishments which are contrary to Article 3, whatever their deterrent effect may be.

The Court must also recall that the Convention is a living instrument which, as the Commission rightly stressed, must be interpreted in the light of presentday conditions. In the case now before it the Court cannot but be influenced by the developments and commonly accepted standards in the penal policy of the member States of the Council of Europe in this field. Indeed, the Attorney-General for the Isle of Man mentioned that, for many years, the provisions of Manx legislation concerning judicial corporal punishment had been under review.

32. As regards the manner and method of execution of the birching inflicted on Mr. Tyrer, the Attorney-General for the Isle of Man drew particular attention to the fact that the punishment was carried out in private and without publication of the name of the offender.

Publicity may be a relevant factor in assessing whether a punishment is 'degrading' within the meaning of Article 3, but the Court does not consider that absence of publicity will necessarily prevent a given punishment from falling into that category: it may well suffice that the victim is humiliated in his own eyes, even if not in the eyes of others.

The Court notes that the relevant Isle of Man legislation, as well as giving the offender a right of appeal against sentence, provides for certain safeguards. Thus, there is a prior medical examination; the number of strokes and dimensions of the birch are regulated in detail; a doctor is present and may order the punishment to be stopped; in the case of a child or young person, the parent may attend if he so desires; the birching is carried out by a police constable in the presence of a more senior colleague.

33. Nevertheless, the Court must consider whether the other circumstances of the applicant's punishment were such as to make it 'degrading' within the meaning of Article 3.

The very nature of judicial corporal punishment is that it involves one human being inflicting physical violence on another human being. Furthermore, it is institutionalised violence, that is in the present case violence permitted by the law, ordered by the judicial authorities of the State and carried out by the police authorities of the State. Thus, although the applicant did not suffer any severe or long-lasting physical effects, his punishment—whereby he was treated as an object in the power of the authorities—constituted an assault on precisely that which it is one of the main purposes of Article 3 to protect, namely a person's dignity and physical integrity. Neither can it be excluded that the punishment may have had adverse psychological effects.

The institutionalised character of this violence is further compounded by the whole aura of official procedure attending the punishment and by the fact that those inflicting it were total strangers to the offender.

Admittedly, the relevant legislation provides that in any event birching shall not take place later than six months after the passing of sentence. However, this does not alter the fact that there had been an interval of several weeks since the applicant's conviction by the juvenile court and a considerable delay in the police station where the punishment was carried out. Accordingly, in addition to the physical pain he experienced, Mr. Tyrer was subjected to the mental anguish of anticipating the violence he was to have inflicted on him.

34. In the present case, the Court does not consider it relevant that the sentence of judicial corporal punishment was imposed on the applicant for an offence of violence. Neither does it consider it relevant that, for Mr. Tyrer, birching was an alternative to a period of detention: the fact that one penalty may be preferable to, or have less adverse effects or be less serious than, another penalty does not of itself mean that the first penalty is not 'degrading' within the meaning of Article 3.

35. Accordingly, viewing these circumstances as a whole, the Court finds that the applicant was subjected to a punishment in which the element of humiliation attained the level inherent in the notion of 'degrading punishment' as explained at paragraph 30 above. The indignity of having the punishment administered over the bare posterior aggravated to some extent the degrading character of the applicant's punishment but it was not the only or determining factor.

The Court therefore concludes that the judicial corporal punishment inflicted on the applicant amounted to degrading punishment within the meaning of Article 3 of the Convention.

[The Court held by six votes to one that the judicial corporal punishment inflicted on the applicant was degrading punishment in breach of Article 3.]

Separate opinion of Judge Fitzmaurice

... 11. Modern opinion has come to regard corporal punishment as an *undesirable* form of punishment; and this, whatever the age of the offender. But the fact that a certain form of punishment is an undesirable form of punishment does not automatically turn it into a degrading one. A punishment may well have an undesirable character without being in the least degrading — or at any rate not more so than punishment in general is. And hitherto, whatever may have been felt about corporal punishment from such standpoints as whether it really deters, whether it may not have a brutalizing effect, whether it harms the psyche of those who carry it out, etc., it has not been generally regarded as degrading *when applied to juveniles and young offenders*, in the same way as it is considered so to be in the case of adults. In that respect, the two things have never been regarded as being quite of the same order[77] or as being on the same plane. This last is the real point, — for to put it in terms of the criterion adopted by the Court, and assuming that corporal punishment does involve some degree of degradation, it has never been seen as doing so for a juvenile to anything approaching the same manner or extent for an adult. Put in terms of the Convention and of the Court's criterion, therefore, such punishment does not, in the case of a juvenile, attain the level of degradation needed to constitute it a breach of Article 3, unless of course seriously aggravating circumstances are present over and above the simple fact of the corporal character of the punishment. This is why I could have understood it if the Court had regarded the infliction of the blows on the bare posterior as bringing matters up to the required level of degradation. I would not necessarily have agreed with that view, but it would have been tenable. However, the Court held that this was not a determining element: the punishment was in any event degrading. ...

12. I have to admit that my own view may be coloured by the fact I was brought up and educated under a system according to which the corporal punishment of schoolboys (sometimes at the hands of the senior ones — prefects or monitors — sometimes by masters) was regarded as the normal sanction for serious misbehaviour, and even sometimes for what was much less serious. Generally speaking, and subject to circumstances, it was often considered by the boy himself as preferable to probably alternative punishments such as being kept in on a fine summer's evening to copy out 500 lines or learn several pages of Shakespeare or Virgil by heart, or be denied leave of absence on a holiday occasion. Moreover, these beatings were carried out without any of the safeguards attendant on Mr. Tyrer's: no parents, nurses or doctors were ever present. They also not infrequently took place under conditions of far greater intrinsic humiliation than in his case. Yet I cannot remember that any boy felt degraded or debased. Such an idea would have been thought rather ridiculous. The system was the same for all until they attained a certain seniority. If a boy minded, and resolved not to repeat the offence that had resulted in a beating, this was simply because it had hurt, not because he felt degraded by it or was so regarded by his fellows: indeed, such is the natural perversity of the young of the human species that these occasions were often seen as matters of pride and congratulation, — not unlike the way in which members of the student corps in the old German universities regarded their duelling scars as honourable — (though of course that was, in other respects, quite a different case). ...

---

[77] It is really not too much to say that throughout the ages and under all skies, corporal methods have been seen as the obvious and natural way of dealing with juvenile misbehaviour (footnote by Judge Fitzmaurice).

14. Finally, I would like to advert to the remarks I made in paragraphs 15 and 16 of my Separate Opinion in the *Irish Case* which, *mutatis mutandis*, are equally applicable to the question of degrading treatment or punishment. The fact that a certain practice is felt to be distasteful, undesirable, or morally wrong and such as ought not to be allowed to continue, is not a sufficient ground in itself for holding it to be contrary to Article 3. Still less is the fact that the Article fails to provide against types of treatment or punishment which, though they may legitimately be disapproved of, cannot, considered objectively and in relation to all the circumstances involved, reasonably be regarded without exaggeration as amounting, *in the particular case*, to any of the specific forms of treatment or punishment which the Article does provide against. Any other view would mean using the Article as a vehicle of indirect penal reform, for which it was not intended.

2. DEGRADING TREATMENT

Note the factors which the Court in *Tyrer* found do *not* save a punishment from violating Article 3. A punishment may be 'degrading' even though (1) it does not outrage public opinion; (2) it is an effective deterrent; (3) it is administered in private; (4) it inflicts no lasting injury; and (5) it is imposed for crimes of violence. The critical language of the judgment seems to be this:

[h]is punishment—whereby he was treated as an object in the power of the authorities— constituted an assault on precisely that which it is one of the main purposes of Article 3 to protect, namely a person's dignity and physical integrity.

Presumably, imprisonment does not violate this test. Why not?[78]

In 1982 in *Campbell and Cosans v. United Kingdom*[79] the Court considered the use of the 'tawse', a leather strap applied to the palm of the hand to discipline students in Scottish schools. In each case the applicants were the parents of students, neither of whom had actually been punished (although in one case the student had been suspended by reason of his and his parents' refusal to accept corporal punishment).

The Court agreed that 'provided it is sufficiently real and immediate, a mere threat of conduct prohibited in Article 3 might be in conflict with that provision'. But in these cases, given the fact that 'corporal chastisement is traditional in Scottish schools and, indeed, appears to be favoured by a large majority of parents:

. . . it is not established that pupils at a school where such punishment is used are, solely by reason of the risk of being subjected thereto, humiliated or debased in the eyes of others to the requisite degree or at all.

30. As to whether the applicants' sons were humiliated or debased in their own eyes, the Court observes first that a threat directed to an exceptionally insensitive person may have no significant

---

[78] Although, as has been noted, infringement of Article 3 rights may not be justified by a public interest, the European Court has held that the intentions with which an action is undertaken may be relevant to the presence or absence of a violation. In holding that the routine handcuffing of an arrested person was not incompatible with Article 3 the Court considered significant to fact that the action was not 'aimed at humiliating or debasing him'. *Raninen v. Finland*, 16 Dec. 1997, Reports, 1997–VIII 2804, 26 E.H.R.R. 563.

[79] 25 Feb. 1982 (No. 48), 4 E.H.R.R. 293.

effect on him but nevertheless be incontrovertibly degrading; and conversely, an exceptionally sensitive person might be deeply affected by a threat that could be described as degrading only by a distortion of the ordinary and usual meaning of the word. In any event, in the case of these two children, the Court, like the Commission, notes that it has not been shown by means of medical certificates or otherwise that they suffered any adverse psychological or other effects.[80]

In *Costello-Roberts v. United Kingdom*[81] the applicant was a seven year old student at an independent boarding school. As a punishment for a series of petty disciplinary breaches, he was subjected to 'three "whacks" on the bottom through his shorts with a rubber-soled gym shoe'. The United Kingdom conceded that it was liable under the Convention, if the violation of a person's rights were the result of a failure of the state to secure them against the actions of the third parties, such as the school.[82] The Court held, however, that on the facts of this case there was no violation. It distinguished *Tyrer*,

Mr. Costello-Roberts was a young boy punished in accordance with the disciplinary rules in force within the school in which he was a boarder. This amounted to being slippered three times on his buttocks through his shorts with a rubbersoled gym shoe by the headmaster in private. Mr. Tyrer, on the other hand, was a young man sentenced in the local juvenile court to three strokes of the birch on the bare posterior. His punishment was administered three weeks later in a police station where he was held by two policemen whilst a third administered the punishment, pieces of the birch breaking at the first stroke . . . While the Court has certain misgivings about the automatic nature of the punishment and the three-day wait before its imposition, it considers [the] minimum level of severity not to have been attained in this case.[83]

Four judges dissented, findings that, where the headmaster "whacked" a lonely and insecure 7-year-old-boy' not spontaneously, but in a formal and official manner, after a three-day wait, this punishment was degrading. (In 1998 corporal punishment in all British Schools, independent as well as state, was prohibited by law.)[84]

The reach of Article 3's prohibitions was held to be even broader in *A. v. United Kingdom*.[85A] The applicant was a 9-year-old boy who was beaten by his stepfather with a garden cane. The stepfather was acquitted on a charge of assault causing bodily harm after the jury was instructed that the crime did not include 'reasonable'

---

[80] The Court did, however, hold that the practice of corporal punishment was inconsistent with Article 2 of Protocol 1 which guarantees respect for parents' religious and philosophical convictions in the education of their children.

The *Tyrer* and *Campbell and Cosans* cases present good illustrations of the distinction between 'punishment' and 'treatment'. In *Tyrer* a punishment for a past act was inflicted. The use of the 'tawse' in *Campbell and Cosans* would have been punishment, but it was never administered to the applicants. The apprehensions generated by its potential use was considered 'treatment'.

[81] 25 Mar. 1993 (No. 247C), 19 E.H.R.R. 112.

[82] *Id.* paras. 26–8: The relation of Convention obligations and the action of private persons is discussed in Chapter 6.

[83] *Costello-Roberts v. United Kingdom, supra* n. 81, at paras. 31–2.

[84] *Id.* Joint dissenting opinion of Judges Ryssdal, Thor Vilhjálmson, Matscher and Wildhaber.

[85] School Standards and Framework Act 1998, chap. 31, s. 131.

[85A] 23 Sept. 1998, Reports 1998–V2692, 27 E.H.R.R. 611.

correction by a parent. Although the government conceded the existence of a violation, the Court briefly discussed the issue. It concluded that the treatment of the child applicant—repeated beating with a garden cane applied with 'considerable force', 'reached the level of severity prohibited by Article 3'. It went on to hold that, although the immediate agent of the treatment was a private person, the Convention 'require[d] states to take measures to ensure that individuals within their jurisdiction are not subject to degrading treatment or punishment including such ill-treatment administered by private individuals'.[86]

In *Ingraham v. Wright*[87] the United States Supreme Court considered the constitutionality of corporal punishment of students for disciplinary infractions in the schools of Dade County, Florida. In discussing the claim that this practice violated the Eighth Amendment the majority opinion included the following:

[T]he prevalent rule in this county today privileges such force as a teacher or administrator 'reasonably believes to be necessary for [the child's] proper control, training, or education'. Restatement (Second) of Torts §147(2); see *id.*, §153(2). To the extent that the force is excessive or unreasonable, the educator in virtually all States is subject to possible civil and criminal liability . . .

Of the 23 States that have addressed the problem through legislation, 21 have authorized the moderate use of corporal punishment in public schools. Of these States only a few have elaborated on the common law test of reasonableness, typically providing for approval or notification of the child's parents, or for infliction of punishment only by the principal or in the presence of an adult witness. Only two States, Massachusetts and New Jersey, have prohibited all corporal punishment in their public schools. Where the legislatures have not acted, the state courts have uniformly preserved the common law rule permitting teachers to use reasonable force in disciplining children in their charge . . .

Petitioners acknowledge that the original design of the Cruel and Unusual Punishments Clause was to limit criminal punishments, but urge nonetheless that the prohibition should be extended to ban the paddling of school children. Observing that the Framers of the Eighth Amendment could not have envisioned our present system of public and compulsory education, with its opportunities for noncriminal punishments, petitioners contend that extension of the prohibition against cruel punishments is necessary lest we afford greater protection to criminals than to schoolchildren. It would be anomalous, they say, if school-children could be beaten without constitutional redress, while hardened criminals suffering the same beatings at the hands of their jailors might have a valid claim under the Eighth Amendment. [citations omitted] Whatever force this logic may have in other settings, we find it an inadequate basis for wrenching the Eighth Amendment from its historical context and extending it to traditional disciplinary practices in the public schools.

The prisoner and the schoolchild stand in wholly different circumstances, separated by the harsh facts of criminal conviction and incarceration . . . The schoolchild has little need for the protection of the Eighth Amendment. Though attendance may not always be voluntary, the public school remains an open institution. Except perhaps when very young, the child is not physically restrained from leaving school during school hours; and at the end of the school day, the child is

---

[86] *Id.* paras. 21–22.
[87] 430 U.S. 651 (1977).

invariably free to return home. Even while at school, the child brings with him the support of family and friends and is rarely apart from teachers and other pupils who may witness and protest any instances of mistreatment.

The openness of the public school and its supervision by the community afford significant safeguards against the kinds of abuses from which the Eighth Amendment protects the prisoner. In virtually every community where corporal punishment is permitted in the schools, these safeguards are reinforced by the legal constraints of the common law. Public school teachers and administrators are privileged at common law to inflict only such corporal punishment as is reasonably necessary for the proper education and discipline of the child; any punishment going beyond the privilege may result in both civil and criminal liability.

We conclude that when public school teachers or administrators impose disciplinary corporal punishment, the Eighth Amendment is inapplicable. The pertinent constitutional question is whether the imposition is consonant with the requirements of due process . . .

The Court also concluded that the imposition of corporal punishment was consistent with the due process requirements of the Fourteenth Amendment.

3. PUBLIC OPINION

In *Tyrer* the Court asserts that the absence of public outrage does not immunize a punishment from violating Article 3. But, in the same judgment, it states that it 'cannot but be influenced by the developments and commonly accepted standards in the penal policy of the member states of the Council of Europe'. Judge Fitzmaurice also observed that, in the context of juvenile offenders, infliction of blows has never been regarded as degrading. Similarly, in *Campbell and Cosans*, the wide acceptance of corporal punishment in the schools was cited by the Court in support of its conclusion that the mere risk of its infliction could not be thought to be sufficiently degrading as to violate the Convention.

General attitudes toward, and practices generally used in, punishment of crime have played a role in constitutional decisions interpreting the Eighth Amendment's prohibition of cruel and unusual punishments. In *Solem v. Helm*[88] in which the Supreme Court found imposition of a life sentence to violate the amendment when imposed for the crime of issuing a bad cheque under South Dakota's recidivist statute, the Court employed, as part of its analysis, an investigation of 'the sentences imposed for commission of the same crime in other jurisdictions'. In declaring that the death penalty may be validly imposed under some circumstances, notwithstanding its apparently contrary opinion in *Furman v. Georgia*[89] the plurality in *Gregg v. Georgia*[90] relied, in part, on the fact that, in the years after the *Furman* decision, numerous state legislatures had re-enacted death penalty statutes:

The petitioners in the capital cases before the Court today renew the 'standards of decency'

[88]   463 U.S. 277 (1983).
[89]   408 U.S. 238 (1972).
[90]   428 U.S. 153 (1976).

argument, but developments during the four years since *Furman* have undercut substantially the assumptions upon which their argument rested. Despite the continuing debate, dating back to the 19th century, over the morality and utility of capital punishment, it is now evident that a large proportion of American society continues to regard it as an appropriate and necessary criminal sanction.

The most marked indication of society's endorsement of the death penalty for murder is the legislative response to *Furman*. The legislatures of at least 35 states have enacted new statutes that provide for the death penalty for at least some crimes that result in the death of another person. And the Congress of the United States, in 1974, enacted a statute providing the death penalty for aircraft piracy that results in death . . .

In the only statewide referendum occurring since *Furman* and brought to our attention, the people of California adopted a constitutional amendment that authorized capital punishment, in effect negating a prior ruling by the Supreme Court of California . . .

In a dissenting opinion, Justice Marshall commented on the relevance of public opinion to the constitutionality of the death penalty:

Since the decision in *Furman*, the legislatures of 35 States have enacted new statutes authorizing the imposition of the death sentence for certain crimes, and Congress has enacted a law providing the death penalty for air piracy resulting in death. I would be less than candid if I did not acknowledge that these developments have a significant bearing on a realistic assessment of the moral acceptability of the death penalty to the American people. But if the constitutionality of the death penalty turns, as I have urged, on the opinion of an *informed* citizenry, then even the enactment of new death statutes cannot be viewed as conclusive. In *Furman*, I observed that the American people are largely unaware of the information critical to a judgment on the morality of the death penalty, and concluded that if they were better informed they would consider it shocking, unjust, and unacceptable. A recent, study, conducted after the enactment of the post-*Furman* statutes, has confirmed that the American people know little about the death penalty and that the opinions of an informed public would differ significantly from those of a public unaware of the consequences and effects of the death penalty.

The relevance of public opinion in determining the reach of constitutional bars on cruel, inhuman or degrading treatment or punishment has been doubted by some courts. Consider, for example, the reasons of the Constitutional Court of South Africa:

If public opinion were to be decisive there would be no need for constitutional adjudication. The protection of rights could then be left to Parliament, which has a mandate from the public and is answerable to the public for the way its mandate is exercised. But this would be a return to parliamentary sovereignty and a retreat from the new legal order established by the 1993 Constitution. By the same token, the issue of the constitutionality of capital punishment cannot be referred to a referendum in which a majority view would prevail over the wishes of any minority. The very reason for establishing the new legal order, and for vesting the power of judicial review of all legislation, in the courts, was to protect the rights of minorities and others who cannot protect their rights adequately through the democratic process . . . This Court cannot allow itself to be diverted from its duty to act as an independent arbiter of the Constitution by making choices on the basis that they will find favour with the public.[91]

Notwithstanding the judgment in *Tyrer*, subsequent attempts to repeal the Manx statute authorizing birching have failed. In 1993 a government proposal to that effect was withdrawn in the face of strong public opposition, even though no actual birchings have been carried out since 1975. One Manx member of parliament who opposed repeal was quoted as saying: 'By keeping birching on the statute book we are sending out a clear message to the world that we believe in law and order. It is true that it cannot actually be implemented. But I think it still has a psychological importance.'[92]

C. EXTRADITION, EXPULSION OR DEPORTATION

1. THE RESPONSIBILITY OF THE DEPORTING STATE

An increasingly important and difficult question for the European human rights system concerns attempts by a contracting state to deport an applicant to a *non-contracting* state where, the applicant claims, he or she will be subject to torture, or inhuman or degrading treatment. The Court first considered this issue in *Soering v. United Kingdom*[93] in which the United Kingdom sought, pursuant to treaty, to extradite Soering to Virginia in the United States to stand trial for murder. The Virginia authorities planned to seek the death penalty. Soering claimed that the circumstances surrounding the administration of death sentences in Virginia, particularly the typical delay of six to eight years between imposition and execution of a death sentence, constituted inhuman treatment or punishment. Therefore, he argued, the action of the United Kingdom in exposing him to the risk of such treatment violated Article 3. The United Kingdom, on the other hand, argued that an extraditing state should not be held responsible, under the Convention, for inhuman or degrading treatment or punishment that might be inflicted outside that state's jurisdiction.

The Court held that the extraditing state did have some responsibility under the Convention for the potential subsequent maltreatment of extradited individuals. For a state 'knowingly to surrender a fugitive to another state where there were substantial grounds for believing that he would be in danger of being subjected to torture [or inhuman or degrading treatment] however heinous the crime', would 'plainly be contrary to the spirit and intendment of [Article 3'].

---

[91] *S. v. Makwanyane*, 1995 (3) S.A. 391 (C.C.) paras. 88–9.
[92] 'Outcry Halts Isle of Man Proposal to Scrap Birch', *The Daily Telegraph* (London), 24 April 1993, 4.
[93] 7 July 1989 (No. 161), 11 E.H.R.R. 439.

89. What amounts to 'inhuman or degrading treatment or punishment' depends on all the circumstances of the case. Furthermore, inherent in the whole of the Convention is a search for a fair balance between the demands of the general interest of the community and the requirements of the protection of the individual's fundamental rights. As movement about the world becomes easier and crime takes on a larger international dimension, it is increasingly in the interest of all nations that suspected offenders who flee abroad should be brought to justice. Conversely, the establishment of safe havens for fugitives would not only result in danger for the State obliged to harbour the protected person but also tend to undermine the foundations of extradition. These considerations must also be included among the factors to be taken into account in the interpretation and application of the notions of inhuman and degrading treatment or punishment in extradition cases.

90. It is not normally for the Convention institutions to pronounce on the existence or otherwise of potential violations of the Convention. However, where an applicant claims that a decision to extradite him would, if implemented, be contrary to Article 3 by reason of its foreseeable consequences in the requesting country, a departure from this principle is necessary, in view of the serious and irreparable nature of the alleged suffering risked, in order to ensure the effectiveness of the safeguard provided by that Article.

91. In sum, the decision by a Contracting State to extradite a fugitive may give rise to an issue under Article 3, and hence engage the responsibility of that State under the Convention, where substantial grounds have been shown for believing that the person concerned, if extradited, faces in a real risk of being subjected to torture or to inhuman or degrading treatment or punishment in the requesting country. The establishment of such responsibility inevitably involves an assessment of conditions in the requesting country against the standards of Article 3 of the Convention. Nonetheless, there is no question of adjudicating on or establishing the responsibility of the receiving country, whether under general international law, under the Convention or otherwise. In so far as any liability under the Convention is or may be incurred, it is liability incurred by the extraditing Contracting State by reason of its having taken action which has as a direct consequence the exposure of an individual to proscribed ill-treatment.

In the case at hand, the court found Soering ran a 'real risk' of being convicted, sentenced to death, and being subjected to a long pre-execution delay. Since the Court also found that such delay would itself violate Article 3, the extradition, would, in these circumstances, also be a violation.

This approach may be contrasted with that adopted by the Supreme Court of Canada in *Kindler v. Canada (Minister of Justice)*[94] A convicted murderer argued that extradition to the United States would violate section 12 of the Canadian Charter of Rights and Freedoms prohibiting 'cruel and unusual punishment or treatment', because he would be subject to the death penalty, which, he argued, would be unconstitutional in Canada under the same section. Speaking for a majority of the Court, Justice McLachlin disagreed, ruling that the Charter is 'confined to legislative and executive acts of Canadian governments'. In an extradition 'the effect of any Canadian law or governmental act is too remote from the imposition of the penalty complained of to attract the attention of Section 12', since 'any punishment which is

---

[94] [1991] 2 S.C.R. 779.

imposed will be the result of laws and actions in [the receiving] jurisdiction'. Never-theless, the extradition (and the potential penalty in the receiving state) was subject to scrutiny under Section 7 of the Charter, which states that 'no person should be deprived of life, liberty or security of the person except in accordance with funda-mental principles of justice'.[95] In light of the fact that extradition 'involves interests and complexities with which judges may not be well equipped to deal', the test for whether an extradition offends Section 7 was whether 'the imposition of the penalty by the foreign state "sufficiently shocks" the Canadian conscience' . . . The fugitive must establish that he or she faces 'a situation that is simply unacceptable'. The Court found that extradition to Pennsylvania in a capital case did not violate this standard. A dissenting opinion argued that section 12 should apply to extradition decisions, citing in support the *Soering* case. To hold that the Canadian action was not responsible for the subsequent punishment was, the opinion argued, 'an indefensible abdication of moral responsibility in the manner of Pontius Pilate'.

The European Court of Human Rights applied the principles of *Soering* in *Cruz Varas v. Sweden*[96] where the applicant and his family challenged Sweden's deportation of them to Chile claiming that in Chile they faced the possibility of political persecu-tion, torture or even death because of Cruz Varas' political activities in opposition to the Chilean military regime. The Court held that the standards set out in *Soering* applied to expulsion as well as to extradition but concluded that 'substantial grounds . . . for believing the existence of a real risk of treatment contrary to Article 3' had not been shown. It found that the evidence presented to support Cruz Varas' claim of having previously been tortured in Chile was not convincing and that his credibility had been undermined by his delay in expressing these claims to the Swedish author-ities. It also was influenced by the fact that a considerably more liberal political atmosphere had begun to develop in Chile.

The character of the 'substantial grounds' analysis was further clarified in *Vilvara-jah v. United Kingdom*[97] involving five Tamils who entered the United Kingdom illegally and were expelled to Sri Lanka despite their claims that they would be subject to maltreatment there. After their removal to Sri Lanka, a British administrative adjudicator upheld their appeals, finding that each applicant 'had a well-founded fear of persecution'. In the case of three applicants, moreover, it was shown before the Commission and Court that they had, indeed, been beaten and tortured after their return to Sri Lanka. In deciding there was no violation of Article 3, the Court emphasized that 'since the nature of the Contracting States' responsibility . . . lies in the act of exposing an individual to the risk of ill-treatment, the existence of the risk must be assessed primarily with reference to those facts which were known or ought

---

[95] Similarly, the Court has held that the Charter cannot apply to interrogations by non-Canadian law enforcement officials conducted outside Canada. The use of statements made in such interrogations in Canadian trials, however, was held to be governed by the Charter's guarantee of a fair trial and against deprivation of liberty not in accordance with 'principles of fundamental justice.' *R. v. Harrer* [1995] 3 S.C.R. 562.

[96] 20 Mar. 1991 (No. 201), 14 E.H.R.R. 1.

[97] 30 Oct. 1991 (No. 215), 14 E.H.R.R. 248 (and 441 below).

to have been known to the Contracting State at the time of the expulsion'. Subsequent facts coming to light may be useful however, in confirming or refuting the state's judgments or the applicant's claims. In this case this obliged the Court to concentrate on 'the foreseeable consequences of the removal of the applicant to Sri Lanka in light of the general situation there in February 1988'. The Court decided that, given the improvement in the political and military situation in Sri Lanka at the time of the United Kingdom's decision, the voluntary repatriation of Tamil refugees going on at that time, and the particular circumstances of the applicants, there had been no breach of the Convention. Even with respect to those applicants who ultimately had been abused on their return, 'there existed no special distinguishing feature in their cases that could or ought to have enabled the Secretary of State to foresee that they would be treated in this way'.

The time at which the compatibility with the Convention of a state's decision to deport should be assessed was raised again in *Chahal v. United Kingdom*.[98] In that case the government sought to expel to India a Sikh political activist on the grounds that his activities constituted a threat to national security. Unlike the applicants in *Vilvarajah*, however, Chahal had been allowed to remain in Britain while the case was adjudicated in Strasbourg. It was argued that between the time of the decision to deport and the decision of the European Court the danger to the applicant had diminished. The Court accepted the government's argument that the later time could be controlling:

[T]he crucial question is whether it has been substantiated that there is a real risk that Mr. Chahal, if expelled, would be subjected to treatment prohibited by that Article [3]. Since he has not yet been deported, the material point in time must be that of the [European] Court's consideration of the case. It follows that, although, the historical position is of interest in so far as it may shed light on the current situation and its likely evolution, it is the present conditions which are decisive.[99]

The Court in *Chahal* also considered another question important to the application of Article 3 to cases of extradition and deportation. The United Kingdom argued that the Court was obliged to consider the state's interest in expelling the applicant. In the instant case this interest, the protection of national security, was presumptively weighty. The Court, noting the fact that, unlike most Convention rights, those in Article 3 were not subject to limitation in order to serve important public interests, and, indeed, were not even defeasible in time of war and public emergency[100] rejected this approach. '[T]he activities of the individual in question, however undesirable or dangerous, cannot be a material consideration.[101]

---

[98]   15 Nov. 1996, Reports, 1996–V 1831, 23 E.H.R.R. 413.
[99]   *Id.* para. 80.
[100]   See section (A)(4) 98 *supra*.
[101]   *Chahal, supra* n. 98, para 80. See also *Ahmed v. Austria*, 17 Dec. 1996, Reports, 1996–VI 2195, 24 E.H.R.R. 278.

2. D. V. UNITED KINGDOM

Judgment of 2 May 1997
Reports, 1997–III 778, 24 E.H.R.R. 423,

[The applicant a native of St. Kitts moved to the United States. In 1991 he was convicted of possession of cocaine. After serving one year of a prison sentence he was deported to St. Kitts. Shortly thereafter he traveled to the United Kingdom. On his arrival at Gatwick Airport in January 1993, he was discovered to be in possession of cocaine valued at about £120,000. He was refused permission to enter the country. Before being deported, however, he was convicted of importing controlled drugs and sentenced, in May 1993, to a prison term of six years. In August 1994, while serving his prison sentence, the applicant was diagnosed as suffering from AIDS. In January 1996, he was released on license at which time steps were taken to deport him. Various requests to British authorities to allow the applicant to remain on compassionate grounds were refused.]

13. Since August 1995, the applicant's CD4 cell count has been below 10. He has been in the advanced stages of the illness, suffering from recurrent anaemia, bacterial chest infections, malaise, skin rashes, weight loss and periods of extreme fatigue.

14. By letter dated 15 January 1996, Dr Evans, a consultant doctor, stated:

'His current treatment is AZT 250 mgs. b.d. and monthly nebulised pentamidine, he occasionally takes my statin pastilles and skin emollients.

In view of the fact that [the applicant] has now had AIDS for over 18 months and because this is a relentlessly progressive disease his prognosis is extremely poor.

In my professional opinion [the applicant's] life expectancy would be substantially shortened if he were to return to St. Kitts where there is no medication; it is important that he receives pentamidine treatment against PCP and that he receives prompt anti-microbial therapy for any further infections which he is likely to develop. . . .

15. In a medical report provided on 13 June 1996, Professor Pinching, a professor of immunology at a London hospital, stated that the applicant had suffered severe and irreparable damage to his immune system and was extremely vulnerable to a wide range of specific infections and to the development of tumours. The applicant was reaching the end of the average durability of effectiveness of the drug therapy which he was receiving. It was stated that the applicant's prognosis was very poor and limited to 8–12 months on present therapy. It was estimated that withdrawal of the proven effective therapies and of proper medical care would reduce that prognosis to less than half of what would be otherwise expected.

16. By letter dated 20 April 1995, the High Commission for the Eastern Caribbean States informed the doctor treating the applicant in prison that the medical facilities in St. Kitts did not have the capacity to provide the medical treatment that he would require. This was in response to a faxed enquiry of the same date by Dr Hewitt, the managing medical officer of H.M. Prison Wayland. By letter of 24 October 1995, Dr Hewitt informed the Home Office of the contents of the letter from the High Commission, which had also been sent to the Parole Unit on 1 May 1995. He stated that the necessary treatment was not available in St. Kitts but was widely and freely available in the United Kingdom and requested due consideration be given to lifting the deportation order in respect of the applicant. By letter dated 1 August 1996, the High Commission for the Eastern Caribbean States confirmed that the position in St. Kitts had not changed: . . .

19. When granted bail on 31 October 1996 . . . the applicant was released to reside in special sheltered accommodation for AIDS patients provided by a charitable organisation working with homeless persons. Accommodation, food and services are provided free of charge to the applicant. He also has the emotional support and assistance of a trained volunteer provided by the Terrence Higgins Trust, the leading Charity in the United Kingdom providing practical support, help, counselling and legal and other advice for persons concerned about or having AIDS or HIV infection.

20. In a medical report dated 9 December 1996 Dr J.M. Parkin, a consultant in clinical immunology treating the applicant at a London Hospital, noted that he was at an advanced stage of HIV infection and was severely immunosuppressed. His prognosis was poor. The applicant was being given antiretroviral therapy with D4T and 3TC to reduce the risk of opportunistic infection and was continuing to be prescribed Pentamidine nebulisers to prevent a recurrence of PCP. Preventative treatment for other opportunistic infections was also foreseen. Dr Parkin noted that the lack of treatment with anti-HIV therapy and preventative measures for opportunistic disease would hasten his death if he were to be returned to St. Kitts.

21. The applicant was transferred to an AIDS hospice around the middle of January 1997 for a period of respite care. At the beginning of February there was a sudden deterioration in his condition and he had to be admitted to a hospital on 7 February for examination. At the hearing before the Court on 20 February 1997, it was stated that the applicant's condition was causing concern and that the prognosis was uncertain. According to his counsel, it would appear that the applicant's life was drawing to a close much as the experts had predicted . . .

40. The applicant maintained that his removal to St. Kitts would condemn him to spend his remaining days in pain and suffering in conditions of isolation, squalor and destitution. He had no close relatives or friends in St. Kitts to attend to him as he approached death. He had no accommodation, no financial resources and no access to any means of social support. It was an established fact that the withdrawal of his current medical treatment would hasten his death on account of the unavailability of similar treatment in St. Kitts. His already weakened immune system would not be able to resist the many opportunistic infections to which he would be exposed on account of his homelessness, lack of proper diet and the poor sanitation on the island. The hospital facilities were extremely limited and certainly not capable of arresting the development of infections provoked by the harsh physical environment in which he would be obliged to fend for himself. His death would thus not only be further accelerated, it would also come about in conditions which would be inhuman and degrading.

41. In June 1996, his life expectancy was stated to be in the region of eight to twelve months even if he continued to receive treatment in the United Kingdom. His health had declined since then. As he was now clearly weak and close to death, his removal by the respondent State at this late stage would certainly exacerbate his fate.

42. The Government requested the Court to find that the applicant had no valid claim under Article 3 in the circumstances of the case since he would not be exposed in the receiving country to any form of treatment which breached the standards of Article 3. His hardship and reduced life expectancy would stem from his terminal and incurable illness coupled with the deficiencies in the health and social welfare system of a poor, developing country. He would find himself in the same situation as other AIDS victims in St. Kitts. In fact he would have been returned in January 1993 to St. Kitts, where he had spent most of his life, had it not been for his prosecution and conviction.

43. The Government also disputed the applicant's claim that he would be left alone and without access to treatment for his condition. They maintained that he had at least one cousin

living in St. Kitts and that there were hospitals caring for AIDS patients, including those suffering from opportunistic infections (see paragraph 17 above). Even if the treatment and medication fell short of that currently administered to the applicant in the United Kingdom, this in itself did not amount to a breach of Article 3 standards.

44. Before the Court the Government observed that it was their policy not to remove a person who was unfit to travel. They gave an undertaking to the Court not to remove the applicant unless, in the light of an assessment of his medical condition after the Court gives judgment, he is fit to travel. . . .

46. The Court recalls at the outset that Contracting States have the right, as a matter of well-established international law and subject to their treaty obligations including the Convention, to control the entry, residence and expulsion of aliens. It also notes the gravity of the offence which was committed by the applicant and is acutely aware of the problems confronting Contracting States in their efforts to combat the harm caused to their societies through the supply of drugs from abroad. The administration of severe sanctions to persons involved in drug trafficking, including expulsion of alien drug couriers like the applicant, is a justified response to this scourge.

47. However in exercising their right to expel such aliens Contracting States must have regard to Article 3 of the Convention which enshrines one of the fundamental values of democratic societies. It is precisely for this reason that the Court has repeatedly stressed in its line of authorities involving extradition, expulsion or deportation of individuals to third countries that Article 3 prohibits in absolute terms torture or inhuman or degrading treatment or punishment and that its guarantees apply irrespective of the reprehensible nature of the conduct of the person in question. . . .

48. The Court observes that the above principle is applicable to the applicant's removal under the Immigration Act 1971. Regardless of whether or not he ever entered the United Kingdom in the technical sense it is to be noted that he has been physically present there and thus within the jurisdiction of the respondent State within the meaning of Article 1 of the Convention since 21 January 1993. It is for the respondent State therefore to secure to the applicant the rights guaranteed under Article 3 irrespective of the gravity of the offence which he committed.

49. It is true that this principle has so far been applied by the Court in contexts in which the risk to the individual of being subjected to any of the proscribed forms of treatment emanates from intentionally inflicted acts of the public authorities in the receiving country or from those of non-State bodies in that country when the authorities there are unable to afford him appropriate protection.

Aside from these situations and given the fundamental importance of Article 3 in the Convention system, the Court must reserve to itself sufficient flexibility to address the application of that Article in other contexts which might arise. It is not therefore prevented from scrutinizing an applicant's claim under Article 3 where the source of the risk of proscribed treatment in the receiving country stems from factors which cannot engage either directly or indirectly the responsibility of the public authorities of that country, or which, taken alone, do not in themselves infringe the standards of that Article. To limit the application of Article 3 in this manner would be to undermine the absolute character of its protection. In any such contexts, however, the Court must subject all the circumstances surrounding the case to a rigorous scrutiny, especially the applicant's personal situation in the expelling State. . . .

51. The Court notes that the applicant is in the advanced stages of a terminal and incurable illness. At the date of the hearing, it was observed that there had been a marked decline in his

condition and he had to be transferred to a hospital. His condition was giving rise to concern (see paragraph 21 above). The limited quality of life he now enjoys results from the availability of sophisticated treatment and medication in the United Kingdom and the care and kindness administered by a charitable organization. He has been counselled on how to approach death and has formed bonds with his carers.

52. The abrupt withdrawal of these facilities will entail the most dramatic consequences for him. It is not disputed that his removal will hasten his death. There is a serious danger that the conditions of adversity which await him in St. Kitts will further reduce his already limited life expectancy and subject him to acute mental and physical suffering. Any medical treatment which he might hope to receive there could not contend with the infections which he may possibly contract on account of his lack of shelter and of a proper diet as well as exposure to the health and sanitation problems which beset the population of St. Kitts. While he may have a cousin in St. Kitts no evidence has been adduced to show whether this person would be willing to or capable of attending to the needs of a terminally ill man. There is no evidence of any other form of moral or social support. Nor has it been shown whether the applicant would be guaranteed a bed in either of the hospitals on the island which, according to the Government, care for AIDS patients.

53. In view of these exceptional circumstances and bearing in mind the critical stage now reached in the applicant's fatal illness, the implementation of the decision to remove him to St. Kitts would amount to inhuman treatment by the respondent State in violation of Article 3.

The Court also notes in this respect that the respondent State has assumed responsibility for treating the applicant's condition since August 1994. He has become reliant on the medical and palliative care which he is at present receiving and is no doubt psychologically prepared for death in an environment which is both familiar and compassionate. Although it cannot be said that the conditions which would confront him in the receiving country are themselves a breach of the standards of Article 3, his removal would expose him to a real risk of dying under most distressing circumstances and would thus amount to inhuman treatment.

Without calling into question the good faith of the undertaking given to the Court by the Government, it is to be noted that the above considerations must be seen as wider in scope than the question whether or not the applicant is fit to travel back to St. Kitts.

54. Against this background the Court emphasises that aliens who have served their prison sentences and are subject to expulsion cannot in principle claim any entitlement to remain on the territory of a Contracting State in order to continue to benefit from medical, social or other forms of assistance provided by the expelling State during their stay in prison.

However, in the very exceptional circumstances of this case and given the compelling humanitarian considerations at stake, it must be concluded that the implementation of the decision to remove the applicant would be a violation of Article 3.

[The court held unanimously that there had been a violation of Article 3]

* * * *

D. v. United Kingdom holds that a violation of Article 3 may result in connection with an expulsion even when the danger to the applicant arises from a source other than the public authority of the receiving state. This conclusion makes more sense when we recall that the only violation of human rights over which the Court has jurisdiction is the act of the state party in effecting the deportation. The question must be whether that action amounts to subjecting the applicant to 'torture or to inhuman or degrading treatment or punishment'. This inquiry raises familiar legal questions of foreseeability and causation.

The holding in *D* was foreshadowed in the *Chahal* case mentioned above. In that case the applicant had expressed fear of ill-treatment by the state police of Punjab. The British government responded that Chahal could be deported to other parts of India. The European Court held that such a possibility did not sufficiently reduce the risk to the applicant since the Punjab police had a record of reprisals against Sikh nationalists in other Indian states, and that such police misconduct had not been brought under control by the concededly good faith efforts of the Indian government.[102] Given the lawless character of the incidents under consideration, this holding effectively included unofficial as well as official mistreatment among the threats that had to be considered by the expelling state. Similarly in *Ahmed v. Austria*[103] an expulsion to Somalia was held to entail a violation of Article 3. The applicant faced a serious risk of torture or inhuman or degrading treatment inflicted by factions in the continuing civil war in that country. That risk was sufficient to support a holding that expulsion would involve a violation of the Convention, despite, indeed largely because of, 'the current lack of state authority in Somalia'.[104] This understanding was made explicit in *H. L. R. v. France*.[105] There the applicant was being deported to Colombia because of his involvement in drug trafficking. He claimed he was at risk of retaliation from criminal organizations because he had co-operated with the French police. Although the majority of the Court held there was insufficient evidence of danger to support finding a violation it stated:

Owing to the absolute character of the right guaranteed, the Court does not rule out the possibility that Article 3 of the Convention may also apply where the danger does not emanate from persons or groups of persons who are not public officials. However, it must be shown that the risk is real and that the authorities of the receiving state are not able to obviate the risk by providing appropriate protection.[106]

3. THE U.N. REFUGEE CONVENTION

Many of the cases concerning deportation or expulsion dealt with under Article 3 also raise questions under the 1951 Geneva Convention and 1967 Protocol Relating to the Status of Refugees.[107] That Convention defines refugees as those who have left their country because of a 'well-founded fear of persecution'. Article 33 prohibits a state

---

[102] *Chahal, supra* n. *98*, paras. 103–5.

[103] 17 Dec. 1996, Reports, 1996–VI 2195, 24 E.H.R.R. 278.

[104] *Id.* paras. 44–7.

[105] 29 Apr. 1997, Reports, 1997–III 745, 26, E.H.R.R. 29.

[106] *Id.* para. 40.

[107] 189 U.N.T.S. 2545; 606 U.N.T.S. 8791. The Convention and Protocol are extensively discussed in J. C. Hathaway, *The Law of Refugee Status* (1991).

from expelling refugees if it would entail a return to their country of origin where their 'life or freedom would be threatened' on account of their 'race, religion, nationality, membership of a particular social group or political opinion'. These requirements plainly overlap with a European state's obligations under Article 3 of the European Convention, as interpreted by the European Court. The Convention, however, may be somewhat narrower in its protection. A reasonable threat of execution or imprisonment on prohibited grounds, triggers a right of asylum under the Geneva Convention and Protocol. But neither imprisonment nor capital punishment alone have been held to constitute 'torture, inhuman or degrading' treatment or punishment under Article 3. Therefore, a person who had a proper claim under the Convention on Refugees might not be able to pursue that claim through the Strasbourg institutions. Of course, the threat of imprisonment for the specified reasons might give rise to a claim of violation of Article 14 on the right to equal treatment, in conjunction with Article 3.

On the other hand, in such circumstances, a claim may be cognizable under Article 3 which would fail under the Convention on Refugees. Article 33(2) of that Convention denies its benefits to a 'refugee whom there are reasonable grounds for regarding as a danger to the security of the country in which he is, or who, having been convicted by a final judgment of a particularly serious crime, constitutes a danger to the community of that country'. As noted, the protection of Article 3 being absolute, it has been held to attach without regard to the public safety interests of the deporting state. Violations have been found even where a state has asserted risks to national security[108] and where the applicant has been convicted of serious crimes[109]

D. THE DEATH PENALTY

Could an argument be made that the infliction of the death penalty, at least in some circumstances, violates Article 3? For most parties to the Convention the question is largely academic in light of Protocol No. 6. That protocol, agreed to in 1983 and in force since 1988, abolishes the death penalty except 'in time of war or imminent threat of war'. As at April 1998 the only parties which had not ratified Protocol No. 6 were Belgium, Bulgaria, Cyprus, Greece, Latvia, Lithuania, Poland, Russia, Turkey, Ukraine and the United Kingdom.[110] The addition of this Protocol is itself some evidence that Article 3 alone does not include capital punishment as, *per se*, an instance of 'inhuman or degrading treatment or punishment'.

The same inference seems clear from Article 2 which declares that 'everyone's right to life should be protected by law'. That article specifies that deaths resulting from the

---

[108] *Chahal, supra* n. 98, para. 80.
[109] *Ahmed, supra* n. 103, para. 41.
[110] Council of Europe, European Treaties, Chart of Signatures and Ratifications, 21 Apr. 1998.

use of force in certain cases, in the interests of public safety, do not contravene the Convention where the use of such force 'is no more than absolutely necessary'.[111] More to the point it also explicitly limits the right to cases other than 'save in the execution of a sentence of court following his conviction of a crime for which this penalty is provided by law'.

The same reasoning might be applied to the interpretation of the Eighth Amendment to the United States Constitution, in light of the Fifth Amendment's prohibition of a deprivation of life only when effected 'without due process of law.[112] The Supreme Court has, in fact, held invalid numerous death penalty statutes as cruel and unusual. Some of these decisions are applications of the requirement of proportionality of punishment to offence.[113] The Court has also held that death sentences which are imposed arbitrarily, as well as those which are mandatory, are unconstitutional.[114] While numerous divisions among the justices make generalization difficult, it appears that current constitutional jurisprudence requires procedures for the imposition of capital punishment which guide, but do not eliminate, discretion in making the decision in each case. Any scheme must satisfy the 'twin objectives' of 'measured consistent application and fairness to the accused'.[115]

In contrast, the Judicial Committee of the Privy Council has held that the mandatory imposition of the death penalty for certain drug offences does not contradict sections of the Singapore Constitution requiring that death sentences only be imposed 'in accordance with law' and requiring equality before the law. Admitting that such a provision inflicts the same penalty on individuals who show 'considerable variation in moral blameworthiness', the Committee concluded that 'the Constitution is not concerned with equal punitive treatment for equal moral blameworthiness; it is concerned with equal punitive treatment for similar legal guilt'[116]

The death penalty was abolished for almost all offences in Canada in 1976, but in the *Kindler* case[117] discussed in the previous section, a majority of the Supreme Court of Canada held that it could not be said that the imposition of such a penalty would, in all cases, 'shock the Canadian conscience' so that an extradition to a country where execution was a possibility would violate Section 7 of the Charter. While the majority did not address the compatibility of the death penalty with Section 12's prohibition of 'cruel and unusual punishment', three dissenting judges asserted that capital punishment was always 'cruel and unusual' as the 'ultimate desecration of human dignity'.

---

[111] See *McCann and Others v. United Kingdom*, 27 Sept. 1995 (No. 324), 21 E.H.R.R. 97; *Kaya v. Turkey*, 19 Feb. 1998, Reports, 1998–I 297, 28 E.H.R.R. 1; *Yasa v. Turkey*, 2 Sept. 1998, Reports, 1998–VI, 2411, 28 E.H.R.R. 408.

[112] Compare *S. v. Makwanyane*, 1995 (3) S.A. 391 (c.c.) in which the Constitutional Court of South Africa held the imposition of the death penalty violated Art. 11(2) of the Transitional Constitution. The Court noted that, unlike the United States Constitution and the European Convention, the South African Constitution did not explicitly or implicitly acknowledge the validity of capital punishment. See *id.*, paras. 40, 68.

[113] *See* Section (A)(4) *supra*.

[114] Compare *Furman v. Georgia*, 408 U.S. 238 (1972) with *Woodson v. North Carolina*, 428 U.S. 280 (1976).

[115] *Eddings v. Oklahoma*, 455 U.S. 104, 110–11 (1982).

[116] *Ong Ah Chuan v. Public Prosecutor* [1981] A.C. 648, 674 P.C.

[117] *Kindler v. Canada (Minister of Justice)* [1991] 2 S.C.R. 779.

In *Soering v. United Kingdom*[118] also discussed above, Soering did not argue that the death penalty itself violated the Convention. Rather he claimed—and the Court agreed—that a violation was caused by the conditions of Virginia prisons in connection with the 'death-row phenomenon'. This was the extended period of time involved in appeals and collateral proceedings between imposition and execution of sentence during which time the condemned person would suffer severe and ever increasing stress and anguish. In Virginia, the Court concluded, this period averaged six to eight years. The Court did not specifically consider the fact that the waiting period was largely the result of deliberate choices by the condemned person.

That issue was addressed extensively in a 1993 judgment of the Judicial Committee of the Privy Council. The appellants in *Pratt v. Attorney-General for Jamaica*[119] had endured a delay of 12 years after the pronouncing of a sentence of death. The Privy Council, citing the *Soering* case, held this amounted to the infliction of 'inhuman or degrading punishment or other treatment' in contravention of Section 17 of the Jamaican Constitution. The Committee noted the 'instinctive revulsion' against hanging a person after such a long period. It agreed that, to the extent the extended time was due 'entirely to the fault of the accused, such as an escape from custody or frivolous and time wasting resort to legal procedures which amount to an abuse of process, the accused cannot be allowed to take advantage of the delay[120] But the same was not true where the accused merely exploited legitimate procedures for review of his conviction and sentence. In such a case:

> a state that wishes to retain capital punishment must accept the responsibility of ensuring that execution follows as swiftly as practicable after sentence, allowing a reasonable time for appeal and consideration of reprieve. It is part of the human condition that a condemned man will take every opportunity to save his life through the use of the appellate procedure. If the appellate procedure enables the prisoner to prolong the appellate hearings over a period of years, the fault is to be attributed to the appellate system that permits such delay and not to the prisoner who takes advantages of it.[121]

The Judicial Committee noted that, given the normal time for appellate review of death sentences, any delay beyond five years might be presumed to be inordinate.[122] In a later case, the Committee held that the relevant period ought not to include time spent in custody before trial 'since the state of mind of the person in question during

---

[118] 7 July 1989 (No. 161), 11 E.H.R.R. 439.

[119] [1993] 4 All E.R. 769. P.C.

[120] *Id.* at 783.

[121] *Id.* at 786.

[122] In a subsequent case arising in the Bahamas (which has an identical constitutional provision) the Privy Council held that this period should be only three and one half years since no account had to be taken of a possible resort to the United Nations Human Rights Committee, the Bahamas not being party to the International Convention on Civil and Political Rights, *Henfield v. Attorney-General* [1997] A.C. 413, 428. When, later, it was pointed out that a parallel petition to the Inter-American Commission on Human Rights was available in the Bahamas, the Board reinstituted the 5-year presumption. *Fisher v. Minister of Public Safety* [1998] A.C. 673.

this earlier period is not the agony of a man facing execution'.[123] This conclusion was disputed by Lord Steyn in dissenting for reasons relying extensively on the Article 3 jurisprudence of the European Court of Human Rights:

> It is true that in contrast [to the condemned person] the man still awaiting trial on a charge of murder is assailed by other uncertainties; he hopes to be acquitted. For him the spectre of the macabre meting with the hangman is somewhat more distant. . . . But from the time of his arrest and charge, or at least from the time of his judicial committal for trial on a charge of murder, he is in real jeopardy of being sentenced to death and hanged. And in cases like the present he will be held in prison conditions where he will be exposed to the terror of execution from time to time. Like a distinguished author in this field who argues that presentence delay is relevant, I too would say that 'it is here that the horror of contemplating the sentence would normally begin'.[124]

Claims that delay in the execution of death sentences constitutes 'cruel and unusual punishment' in violation of the Eighth Amendment have been consistently rejected by courts in the United States. The typical judicial reaction to this claim is captured in the opinion of a Federal Court of Appeals that a defendant who has 'benefitted from this careful and meticulous process [of appellate and collateral review] . . . cannot now complain that the expensive and laborous process . . . which exists to protect him has violated other of his rights'.[125] Although the Supreme Court has not ruled on this question, two justices have indicated that they regard the constitutionality of executions after extended periods of delay as a matter of serious doubt.[126]

The United States has ratified the International Covenant on Civil and Political Rights which prohibits 'torture or . . . cruel, inhuman or degrading treatment or punishment.'[127] It has, however, entered a reservation to the effect that it understands the provision only to prevent actions amounting to ' "cruel and unusual punishment" prohibited by the Fifth, Eighth and/or Fourteenth Amendment to the Constitution of the United States.'[128] A U.S. Senate report on the Covenant recommending the reservation explicitly referred to interpretations of the European Court of Human Rights and United Nations Human Rights Committee to the effect that 'prolonged judicial proceedings in cases involving capital punishment could in certain circumstances constitute such treatment'.[129]

---

[123] For commentary on these cases see S. C. R. McIntosh, 'Cruel Inhuman and Degrading Punishment: A Re-reading of Pratt and Morgan', 8 *Carib. L. Rev.* 1 (1998); Sir Louis Blom-Cooper & C. Gelber, 'The Privy Council and the Death Penalty in the Caribbean' [1998] *Europ. Hum. Rts. L. Rev.* 386.

[124] [1998] A.C. 673, 691.

[125] *White v. Johnson*, 79 F. 3d 432, 439 (5th Cir. 1996). See also *Ceja v. Stewart*, 134 F. 3d 1368 (9th Cir. 1998). In the *Ceja* case, in which the petitioner had been on death row for 23 years, Judge Fletcher entered a dissent relying in part on the *Soering* case.

[126] See *Lackey v. Texas*, 514 U.S. 1045 (1995) of Stevens, J. joined in part by Breyer, J.); *Gomez v. Ruiz*, 519 U.S. 919 (1996) (Stevens, J. joined by Breyer, J., dissenting).

[127] 1057 U.N.T.S. 407, Art. 7.

[128] 138 Cong. Rec. S4781–01, S4783 (daily ed. 12 Apr. 1992).

[129] S. Exec. Rpt. No. 102–23 at 12 (1992).

5

FREEDOM OF EXPRESSION

ARTICLE 10

1. Everyone has the right to freedom of expression. This right shall include freedom to hold opinions and to receive and impart information and ideas without interference by public authority and regardless of frontiers. This article shall not prevent States from requiring the licensing of broadcasting, television or cinema enterprises.

2. The exercise of these freedoms, since it carries with it duties and responsibilities, may be subject to such formalities, conditions, restrictions or penalties as are prescribed by law and are necessary in a democratic society, in the interests of national security, territorial integrity or public safety, for the prevention of disorder or crime, for the protection of health or morals, for the protection of the reputation or rights of others, for preventing the disclosure of information received in confidence, or for maintaining the authority and impartiality of the judiciary.

A. INTRODUCTION

The freedom to express one's opinion is probably the most universally recognized 'human right'. A 1978 survey of 142 world constitutions found that 124, or 87.3 per cent, contained a free expression guarantee. (In contrast, only 66, or 46.5 per cent, prohibited torture or cruel, inhuman or degrading treatment.)[1] Versions of this right were found in the earliest modern constitutions including a number of the eighteenth-century constitutions of the American states, Article 11 of the French Declaration of the Rights of Man and Citizen, and the First Amendment to the United States Constitution.[2] Article 10 of the European Convention for the Protection of Human Rights

---

[1] H. van Maarseveen & Ger van der Tang. *Written Constitutions: a Computerized Comparative Study* 105, 110 (1978). About the same number of constitutions protected some combination of the related freedoms of assembly, association, opinion, thought, conscience or religion. *Id.* at 109–11.

[2] *See* Chapter 1(B), *supra*.

took as a model Article 19 of the Universal Declaration of Human Rights[3] from which it departs in only minor respects.

Article 10 protects 'expression' generally, a term which may have been thought broad enough to justify the omission of the reference to 'any media' that is included in the Universal Declaration. Similarly, it may make unnecessary the kind of separate reference to the 'press' found in the American First Amendment. The parallel provision in the 1982 Canadian Charter of Rights and Freedoms, on the other hand, protects 'freedom of thought, belief, opinion and expression, including freedom of the press and other media of communication'.

The justifications for special protection of expression have sometimes been placed in two categories. In the first, speech is recognized as valuable, because public debate is a useful instrument for achieving other social objectives. In the second category, personal expression is seen as a human good in itself.

In so far as freedom of speech is valued instrumentally, it has been associated with two related objectives. Most broadly, it has been justified as the best way of assuring the discovery of truth. The uninhibited clash and consequent testing of opinions and ideas is claimed to comprise the best way to increase knowledge. This belief is well summarized in a much quoted passage from Milton's *Aeropagitica*, itself a banned work:

[T]hough all the winds of doctrine were let loose to play upon the earth, so truth be in the field, we do injuriously, by licensing and prohibiting, to misdoubt her strength. Let her and falsehood grapple; whoever knew truth put to the worse in a free and open encounter?[4]

Much the same idea was elaborated by John Stuart Mill in the nineteenth century[5] and captured by Justice Oliver Wendell Holmes' metaphor of the 'marketplace of ideas'.[6]

A narrower version of the instrumental view of free expression focuses on its utility in the functioning of a representative democracy. The framers of the First Amendment, said Justice Brandeis, believed 'in the power of reason as applied through public discussion [so] they eschewed silence coerced by law'.[7] Democratic self-government depends upon the ability of electors to choose representatives who best reflect their own convictions and interests and on the ability of the representatives to understand the concerns of their constituents. Neither the character of the issues at stake nor the effectiveness of representation is possible without a thorough airing of facts and arguments.[8]

The second category of justification for free expression turns on the idea that the free communications of feelings, opinions and ideas is essential to the full

---

[3] *Id.*

[4] John Milton, *Aeropagitica: a Speech for the Liberty of Unlicensed Printing to the Parliament of England* (1644).

[5] John Stuart Mill, *On Liberty* (1859).

[6] *Abrams v. United States*, 250 U.S. 616, 630 (1919) (Holmes, J. dissenting).

[7] *Whitney v. California*, 274 U.S. 357, 375–6 (1927) (concurring opinion).

[8] *See* Alexander Meiklejohn, *Free Speech and Its Relation to Self-Government* (1948).

development of human personality in society. The human desires to persuade, to impress, to assert or to inspire have always been a powerful presence in every social situation, and their suppression has often been thought to stunt some of the most admirable aspects of human nature. Likewise, the ability to be challenged, provoked or encouraged by the ideas of others may be critical to the formation of those personal beliefs which are at the core of our capacity for self-definition.[9]

These two kinds of justifications for freedom of expression, which might be called the instrumental and the intrinsic, are evidenced in judicial opinions applying the relevant constitutional guarantees. Thus, Justice Brandeis, in his separate opinion in the United States Supreme Court judgment in *Whitney v. California*[10] spoke of the American founders' appreciation of 'liberty both as an end and as a means'.[11] An early judgment of the German Constitutional Court referred to free expression as 'the most immediate manifestation of the human personality' as well as indispensable for 'the contest of opinions that forms the lifeblood of [a democratic] order'.[12] The Supreme Court of Canada summarized the values underlying the protection of free expression in Section 2 of the Canadian Charter of Rights and Freedoms in the following way:

(1) seeking and attaining the truth is an inherently good activity; (2) participation in social and political decision-making is to be fostered and encouraged; and (3) the diversity in forms of individual self-fulfillment and human flourishing ought to be cultivated in an essentially tolerant, indeed welcoming, environment not only for the sake of those who convey a meaning, but also for the sake of those to whom it is conveyed.[13]

A similar appreciation of the double character of this right has been expressed by the European Court of Human Rights, which has insisted that freedom of expression 'constitutes one of the essential foundations of a democratic society and one of the basic conditions for its progress and for each individual's self-fulfillment'.[14]

B. JUSTIFYING LIMITS ON EXPRESSION

The nature of the 'expression' protected by Article 10 is not always self-evident. In particular, problems may be expected to arise in distinguishing expression from action (intentionally symbolic or otherwise), which is associated with communication

---

[9] *See* T. Scanlon, 'A Theory of Freedom of Expression' 1 *Phil. & Pub. Aff.* 204 (1972); M. Redish, 'The Value of Free Speech' 130 U. Pa. L. Rev. 591 (1982).

[10] 274 U.S. 357 (1927).

[11] *Id.* at 375.

[12] *Lüth* Judgment 7 BverfGe 198, 208 (1958) quoted in and translated by D. Currie, *The Constitution of the Federal Republic of Germany* 175 (1999).

[13] *Irwin Toy Ltd. v. Attorney-General (Quebec)* [1989] 1 S.C.R. 927, 976.

[14] *Lingens v. Austria,* 8 July 1986 (No. 103), 8 E.H.R.R. 103.

of a viewpoint.[15] For the most part, however, the European Court's interpretation of Article 10 has not focused on questions of definition, as has been the case with Article 3's prohibition of inhuman or degrading treatment,[16] and, to a significant degree, with Article 8's protection of 'private and family life'.[17] Rather, as the materials in this chapter illustrate, the Court has more intensively engaged the question of when an admitted public interference with expression may be permissible under Article 10. We have already seen one example of this kind of analysis in *Sunday Times v. United Kingdom*[18] in which the Court rejected a claim that a finding of contempt of court against a newspaper for publishing material related to pending litigation was necessary for 'maintaining the authority and impartiality of the judiciary'.

This question presupposes that expression cannot be protected absolutely. It is uncontestable that the utterance of some kinds of language in some situations may impose grave social harms that the state ought to be able to prevent. Thus, to take an example from American constitutional law, no one would question the right of a government to prohibit 'the publication of the sailing dates of transports or the number and location of troops'.[19] More controversial cases are presented by judgments of the Canadian Supreme Court upholding legislation criminalizing speech promoting the hatred and denigration of ethnic or racial groups[20] or pornography that depicts violent sexual activity or that dehumanizes or degrades women.[21] The Convention explicitly provides that limitations on the right of free expression do not violate the Convention, if they are for one of the purposes and meet the other criteria listed in Article 10(2). In very large measure, the law of free expression under the Convention is the law of Article 10(2).

1. HANDYSIDE V. UNITED KINGDOM

Judgment of 7 December, 1976 (No. 24),
1 E.H.R.R. 737

. . .

9. The applicant, Mr. Richard Handyside, is proprietor of the publishing firm 'Stage I' in London which he opened in 1968. He has published, among other books, *The Little Red Schoolbook* (hereinafter called 'the Schoolbook'), the original edition of which was the subject of the present case and a revised edition of which appeared on 15 November 1971.

---

[15] This has been a persistent issue in American constitutional cases. *See e.g. United States v. O'Brien*, 391 U.S. 367 (1968) (draft card burning not protected); John H. Ely. *Flag Desecration: A Case Study in the Roles of Categorization and Balancing in First Amendment Analysis*, 88 Harv. L. Rev. 1482 (1975).

[16] *See* Chapter 4, *supra.*

[17] *See* Chapter 6, *infra.*

[18] 26 Apr. 1979 (No. 30), 2 E.H.R.R. 245 reproduced in part in Chapter 3 *supra.*

[19] *Near v. Minnesota*, 236 U.S. 697, 716 (1931) (dicta).

[20] *R. v. Keegstra* [1990] 3 S.C.R. 697.

[21] *R. v. Butler* [1992] 1 S.C.R. 452.

11. . . . The book had first been published in Denmark in 1969 and subsequently, after translation and with certain adaptations, in Belgium, Finland, France, the Federal Republic of Germany, Greece, Iceland, Italy, the Netherlands, Norway, Sweden and Switzerland as well as several non-European countries. Furthermore it circulated freely in Austria and Luxembourg.

12. After having arranged for the translation of the book into English the applicant prepared an edition for the United Kingdom with the help of a group of children and teachers. He had previously consulted a variety of people about the value of the book and intended publication in the United Kingdom on 1 April 1971 . . .

[The applicant was convicted of violating the Obscene Publication Act. He was fined and the books in his possession were ordered destroyed.] . . .

20. The original English language edition of the book, priced at thirty pence a copy, had altogether 208 pages. It contained an introduction headed 'All grown-ups are paper tigers', an 'Introduction to the British edition', and chapters on the following subjects: Education, Learning, Teachers, Pupils and The System. The chapter on Pupils contained a twenty-six page section concerning 'Sex' which included the following sub-sections: Masturbation, Orgasm, Intercourse and petting, Contraceptives, Wet dreams, Menstruation, Child-molesters or 'dirty old men', Pornography, Impotence, Homosexuality, Normal and abnormal, Find out more, Venereal diseases, Abortion, Legal and illegal abortion, Remember, Methods of abortion, Addresses for help and advice on sexual matters. The Introduction stated: 'This book is meant to be a reference book. The idea is not to read it straight through, but to use the list of contents to find and read about the things you're interested in or want to know more about. Even if you're at a particularly progressive school you should find a lot of ideas in the book for improving things'.

21. The applicant had planned the distribution of the book through the ordinary book-selling channels although it was said at the appeal hearing to have been accepted that the work was intended for, and intended to be made available to, school-children of the age of twelve and upwards . . .

[The Obscene Publications Acts (the '1959/1964 Acts') defined an item as obscene if its effect,

'if taken as a whole, [was] such as to tend to deprave and corrupt persons who are likely, having regard to all relevant circumstances, to read, see or hear the matter contained or embodied in it'.

A conviction could be avoided if the work involved was

'justified as being for the public good on the ground that it is in the interests of science, literature, art or learning, or of other objects of general concern'.

The defence could be proven by evidence of the opinion of 'artistic, literary or scientific' experts.] . . .

30. Concerning the Schoolbook itself, the [British] court first stressed that it was intended for children passing through a highly critical stage of their development. At such a time a very high degree of responsibility ought to be exercised by the courts. In the present case, they had before them, as something said to be a perfectly responsible adult opinion, a work of an extreme kind, unrelieved by any indication that there were any alternative views; this was something which detracted from the opportunity for children to form a balanced view on some of the very strong advice given therein.

31. The court then briefly examined the background. For example, looking at the book as a

whole, marriage was very largely ignored. Mixing a very one-sided opinion with fact and purporting to be a book of reference, it would tend to undermine, for a very considerable portion of children, many of the influences, such as those of parents, the Churches and youth organisations, which might otherwise provide the restraint and sense of responsibility for one-self which found inadequate expression in the book. . . .

32. Passing to the tendency to deprave and corrupt, the court considered the atmosphere of the book looked at as a whole, noting that the sense of some responsibility for the community as well as to oneself, if not wholly absent, was completely subordinated to the development of the expression of itself by the child. As indications of what it considered to result in a tendency to deprave and corrupt, the court quoted or referred to the following:

A. The passage headed 'Be yourself':

'Maybe you smoke pot or go to bed with your boyfriend or girlfriend—and don't tell your parents or teachers, either because you don't dare to or just because you want to keep it secret.

Don't feel ashamed or guilty about doing things you really want to do and think are right just because your parents or teachers might disapprove. A lot of these things will be more important to you later in life than the things that are "approved of".'

The objectionable point was that there was no reference there to the illegality of smoking pot which was only to be found many pages further on in an entirely different part of the book. Similarly there was no specific mention at all in the book of the illegality of sexual intercourse by a boy who has attained the age of fourteen and a girl who has not yet attained sixteen. It had to be remembered that the Schoolbook was indicated as a work of reference and that one looked up the part which one wanted rather than read it as a whole book. . . .

33. The court concluded 'in the light of the whole of the book, that this book or this article on sex or this section or chapter on pupils, whichever one chooses as an article, looked at as a whole does tend to deprave and corrupt a significant number, significant proportion, of the children likely to read it'. Such children would, it was satisfied, include a very substantial number aged under sixteen. . . .

The court asked itself whether, granted the degree of indecency which it found, the good likely to result from the Schoolbook was such that it ought, nevertheless, to be published in the public interest; it regretfully came to the conclusion that the burden on the appellant to show that 'publication of the article in question is justified as being for the public good' had not been discharged. . . .

43. The various measures challenged—the applicant's criminal conviction, the seizure and subsequent forfeiture and destruction of the matrix and of hundreds of copies of the schoolbook—were without any doubt, and the Government did not deny it, 'interferences by public authority' in the exercise of his freedom of expression which is guaranteed by paragraph 1 of the text cited above. Such interferences entail a 'violation' of Article 10 if they do not fall within one of the exceptions provided for in paragraph 2, which is accordingly of decisive importance in this case . . .

45. . . . According to the Government and the majority of the Commission, the interferences were 'necessary in a democratic society', 'for the protection of . . . morals'.

46. Sharing the view of the Government and the unanimous opinion of the Commission, the Court first finds that the 1959/1964 Acts have an aim that is legitimate under Article 10 § 2, namely, the protection of morals in a democratic society. Only this latter purpose is relevant in this

case since the object of the said Acts—to wage war on 'obscene' publications, defined by their tendency to 'deprave and corrupt'—is linked far more closely to the protection of morals than to any of the further purposes permitted by Article 10 § 2 . . .

47. . . . The Commission's report and the subsequent hearings before the Court in June 1976 brought to light clear-cut differences of opinion on a crucial problem, namely, how to determine whether the actual 'restrictions' and 'penalties' complained of by the applicant were 'necessary in a democratic society' 'for the protection of morals'. According to the Government and the major-ity of the Commission, the Court has only to ensure that the English courts acted reasonably, in good faith and within the limits of the margin of appreciation left to the Contracting States by Article 10 § 2. On the other hand, the minority of the Commission sees the Court's task as being not to review the Inner London Quarter Sessions judgment but to examine the Schoolbook directly in the light of the Convention and of nothing but the Convention.

48. The Court points out that the machinery of protection established by the Convention is subsidiary to the national systems safeguarding human rights (Judgment of 23 July 1968 on the merits of the *'Belgian Linguistic' Case)*. The Convention leaves to each Contracting State, in the first place, the task of securing the rights and freedoms it enshrines. The institutions created by it make their own contribution to this task but they become involved only through contentious proceedings and once all domestic remedies have been exhausted (Article 26).

These observations apply, notably, to Article 10 § 2. In particular, it is not possible to find in the domestic law of the various Contracting States a uniform European conception of morals. The view taken by their respective laws of the requirements of morals varies from time to time and from place to place, especially in our era which is characterized by a rapid and far-reaching evolution of opinions on the subject. By reason of their direct and continuous contact with the vital forces of their countries, State authorities are in principle in a better position than the inter-national judge to give an opinion on the exact content of these requirements as well as on the 'necessity' of a 'restriction' or 'penalty' intended to meet them. The Court notes at this juncture that, whilst the adjective 'necessary', within the meaning of Article 10 § 2, is not synonymous with 'indispensable' (cf., in Article 2 § 2 and 6 § 1, the words 'absolutely necessary' and 'strictly necessary' and, in Article 15 § 1, the phrase 'to the extent strictly required by the exigencies of the situation'), neither has it the flexibility of such expressions as 'admissible', 'ordinary' (cf. Article 4 § 3), 'useful' (cf. the French text of the first paragraph of Article 1 of Protocol No. 1), 'reason-able' (cf. Articles 5 § 3 and 6 § 1) or 'desirable'. Nevertheless, it is for the national authorities to make the initial assessment of the reality of the pressing social need implied by the notion of 'necessity' in this context.

Consequently, Article 10 § 2 leaves to the Contracting States a margin of appreciation. This margin is given both to the domestic legislator ('prescribed by law') and to the bodies, judicial amongst others, that are called upon to interpret and apply the laws in force.

49. Nevertheless, Article 10 § 2 does not give the Contracting States an unlimited power of appreciation. The Court, which, with the Commission, is responsible for ensuring the observance of those States' engagements (Article 19), is empowered to give the final ruling on whether a 'restriction' or 'penalty' is reconcilable with freedom of expression as protected by Article 10. The domestic margin of appreciation thus goes hand in hand with a European supervision. Such supervision concerns both the aim of the measure challenged and its 'necessity'; it covers not only the basic legislation but also the decision applying it, even one given by an independent court. . . .

The Court's supervisory functions oblige it to pay the utmost attention to the principles characterising a 'democratic society'. Freedom of expression constitutes one of the essential foundations of such a society, one of the basic conditions for its progress and for the development of every man. Subject to paragraph 2 of Article 10, it is applicable not only to 'information' or 'ideas' that are favourably received or regarded as inoffensive or as a matter of indifference, but also to those that offend, shock or disturb the State or any sector of the population. Such are the demands of that pluralism, tolerance and broadmindedness without which there is no 'democratic society'. This means, amongst other things, that every 'formality', 'condition', 'restriction' or 'penalty' imposed in this sphere must be proportionate to the legitimate aim pursued.

From another standpoint, whoever exercises his freedom of expression undertakes 'duties and responsibilities' the scope of which depends on his situation and the technical means he uses. The Court cannot overlook such a person's 'duties' and 'responsibilities' when it enquiries, as in this case, whether 'restrictions' or 'penalties' were conducive to the 'protection of morals' which made them 'necessary' in a 'democratic society'.

50. It follows from this that it is in no way the Court's task to take the place of the competent national courts but rather to review under Article 10 the decisions they delivered in the exercise of their power of appreciation. . . .

52. The Court attaches particular importance to a factor to which the judgment of 29 October 1971 did not fail to draw attention, that is, the intended readership of the Schoolbook. It was aimed above all at children and adolescents aged from twelve to eighteen. Being direct, factual and reduced to essentials in style, it was easily within the comprehension of even the youngest of such readers. The applicant had made it clear that he planned a wide-spread circulation. He had sent the book, with a press release, to numerous daily papers and periodicals for review or for advertising purposes. What is more, he had set a modest sale price (thirty pence), arranged for a reprint of 50,000 copies shortly after the first impression of 20,000 and chosen a [title] suggesting that the work was some kind of handbook for use in schools.

Basically the book contained purely factual information that was generally correct and often useful, as the Quarter Sessions recognised. However, it also included, . . . sentences or paragraphs that young people at a critical stage of their development could have interpreted as an encouragement to indulge in precocious activities harmful for them or even to commit certain criminal offences. In these circumstances, despite the variety and the constant evolution in the United Kingdom of views on ethics and education, the competent English judges were entitled, in the exercise of their discretion, to think at the relevant time that the Schoolbook would have pernicious effects on the morals of many of the children and adolescents who would read it. . . .

56. The treatment meted out to the Schoolbook and its publisher in 1971 was, according to the applicant and the minority of the Commission, all the less 'necessary' in that a host of publications dedicated to hard core pornography and devoid of intellectual or artistic merit allegedly profit by an extreme degree of tolerance in the United Kingdom. They are exposed to the gaze of passers-by and especially of young people and are said generally to enjoy complete impunity, the rare criminal prosecutions launched against them proving, it was asserted, more often than not abortive due to the great liberalism shown by juries. The same was claimed to apply to sex shops and much public entertainment. . . .

In principle it is not the Court's function to compare different decisions taken, even in apparently similar circumstances, by prosecuting authorities and courts; and it must, just like the respondent Government, respect the independence of the courts. Furthermore and above all, the Court is not faced with really analogous situations: as the Government pointed out, the documents in the file do not show that the publications and entertainment in question were aimed, to the same extent as the Schoolbook (paragraph 52 above), at children and adolescents having ready access thereto.

57. The applicant and the minority of the Commission laid stress on the further point that, in addition to the original Danish edition, translations of the 'Little Book' appeared and circulated freely in the majority of the member states of the Council of Europe.

Here again, the national margin of appreciation and the optional nature of the 'restrictions' and 'penalties' referred to in Article 10 § 2 prevent the Court from accepting the argument. The Contracting States have each fashioned their approach in the light of the situation obtaining in their respective territories; they have had regard, *inter alia*, to the different views prevailing there about the demands of the protection of morals in a democratic society. The fact that most of them decided to allow the work to be distributed does not mean that the contrary decision of the Inner London Quarter Sessions was a breach of Article 10. Besides, some of the editions published outside the United Kingdom do not include the passages, or at least not all the passages, cited in the judgment of 29 October 1971 as striking examples of a tendency to 'deprave and corrupt' . . .

59. On the strength of the data before it, the Court thus reaches the conclusion that no breach of the requirements of Article 10 has been established in the circumstances of the present case. . . .

[The Court held 13 to 1 that there had been no violation of Article 10.]

[The separate opinions of Judges Mosler and Zekia are omitted.]

2. THE JUSTIFICATION OF INTERFERENCES WITH CONVENTION RIGHTS

A. THE MARGIN OF APPRECIATION

Central to the Court's judgment in the *Handyside Case* is the concept of the margin of appreciation' used to decide whether or not a state's interference with a protected right is 'necessary in a democratic society' to achieve certain interests. The possibility of such justification is provided in connection with several of the rights specified in the Convention. (See Articles 8(2), 9(2), 11(2), Protocol No. 4, Article 2(3)). The way in which the Court determines the presence or absence of such 'necessity' will play a major role in defining the extent of the protection actually required.

Underlying the doctrine of the margin of appreciation are two assumptions: First, what is necessary to achieve the stated interests may vary from state to state even in 'democratic societies'; and second, a government's estimate of that necessity is entitled to some deference by an international court, presumably less familiar with relevant local circumstances. At the extreme, however, such deference could lead to automatic and blanket approval of every state interference with the relevant rights.

One apparent limit on such total deference is the Convention's use of the word 'necessary', itself. Note the Court's discussion in paragraph 48 of *Handyside*, comparing its use in Article 10(2) with other expressions in the Convention such as Article

2(2).[22] This provision declares that no violation of the right to life occurs when a death results from the use of such force as is 'absolutely necessary for specified purposes'. The Court has interpreted this phrase as denoting 'a stricter and more compelling test of necessity than that normally applicable when determing whether state action is 'necessary in a democratic society' under paragraphs 2 of Articles 8 to 11.[23] Also telling is the comparison with the terms of Protocol No. 1, Article 1 which protects an individual against deprivation of his 'possessions', but which also recognizes 'the right of a state to enforce such laws as it *deems necessary* to control the use of property in accordance with the general interest'.

In 1988, relying on a number of its precedents, the European Court summarized the test for necessity in a democratic society as follows:

According to the Court's established case-law, the notion of necessity implies that the interference corresponds to a pressing social need and, in particular, that it is proportionate to the legitimate aim pursued; in determining whether an interference is 'necessary in a democratic society', the Court will take into account that a margin of appreciation is left to the Contracting States. . . .

. . . In the first place, [the Court's] review is not limited to ascertaining whether a respondent State exercised its discretion reasonably, carefully and in good faith . . . In the second place, in exercising its supervisory jurisdiction, the Court cannot confine itself to considering the impugned decisions in isolation, but must look at them in the light of the case as a whole; it must determine whether the reasons adduced to justify the interferences at issue are 'relevant and sufficient'. . . .[24]

A factor related to the margin of appreciation is the requirement that any interference be 'proportional' to the interest served. This is not a requirement that the infringement not be excessive in light of what is necessary to protect the relevant interest.[25] Rather it seems to involve an examination of the severity of the interference with Convention rights in comparison with the public injury which might follow from *not completely protecting* the interest cited.[26] This calls for some kind of weighing of the relative injuries to the individual and the state which would follow one or another decision.

Note the Court's discussion in paragraph 57 of the practice of other European states in dealing with this publication. Such comparison has become a staple of the Court's margin of appreciation jurisprudence. In this case the Court was not impressed with the more tolerant attitude exhibited elsewhere in light of the necessary variation in moral attitudes in different societies. Generally, however, the showing of a consistent policy of regulation or abstention from regulation in other European states will influence the Court's determination of the breadth of the margin of appreciation.[27] Such attention is reasonable when it is recalled that the underlying question is

---

[22] Note, however, that the term 'strictly required' in Article 15, dealing with derogations in time of national emergency, has been construed with reference to a state's margin of appreciation. *See Ireland v. United Kingdom*, 18 Jan. 1978 (No. 25), 2 E.H.R.R. 25, paras. 207, 243.

[23] *McCann & Others v. United Kingdom*, 27 Sept. 1995 (No. 324), 21 E.H.R.R. 97, para. 149.

[24] *Olsson v. Sweden*, 24 Mar. 1988 (No. 130), 11 E.H.R.R. 259.

[25] *See* the excerpts from the American and Canadian cases *infra*.

[26] *See Dudgeon v. United Kingdom*, 22 Oct. 1981 (No. 45), 4 E.H.R.R. 149, para. 60.

[27] *See, e.g. Dudgeon v. United Kingdom*, 22 Oct. 1981 (No. 45), 4 E.H.R.R. 149; D.J. Harris, M. O'Boyle and C. Warbrick, *Law of the European Convention on Human Rights* 9–11 (1995).

whether or not certain restrictions are 'necessary in a democratic society'. The general resort to such restrictions among members of the Council of Europe is some indication that it is necessary. Its absence is some evidence that it is not necessary.[28]

B. THE SPYCATCHER CASE

The distinctions drawn by the Court between measures which are and are not necessary to serve the interests listed in Article 10(2) are illustrated by its judgment in *Observer and Guardian v. United Kingdom*.[29] That case arose from the efforts of the United Kingdom government to stop the publication, in various forms, of the memoirs of Peter Wright, a former officer of the British Security Service (MI–5). Wright alleged in his book, *Spycatcher*, that MI-5 had engaged in numerous illegal activities.

After information from the book was published in the applicants' newspapers, the Attorney General instituted judicial proceedings for a permanent injunction against further publication. His claim was based on the newspapers' knowledge that the material arose from a breach of a confidential relationship between the author and the Security Service. Pending trial, the government successfully obtained interlocutory orders against further publication. These orders were the subject of the European Court's judgment. They were granted by the domestic courts under governing law, based on an assessment of the 'balance of convenience'. The English courts considered this question in a series of appeals culminating in a judgment in the House of Lords, maintaining the prohibitions.[30] The Law Lords held by three to two that the Attorney-General had an arguable case and that the government's interest both in maintaining national security and the efficient operation of the security service would be destroyed were the information to become public before a final determination could be made. On the other hand, the orders caused the newspapers only a temporary delay, and, as the information at issue concerned events which were already somewhat dated, the burden on the newspapers was not oppressive. The dissenting Lords, on the other hand, insisted that, in light of the widespread dissemination of the material through foreign publication, the interest of the government in continuing the restriction did not outweigh the very serious harm to the value of free speech. Lord Bridge lamented the failure of the judges to maintain 'the capacity of the common law to safeguard the fundamental freedoms essential to a free society'. He also predicted that if the government were to persist in its attempt at suppression it would 'face inevitable condemnation and humiliation by the European Court of Human Rights in Strasbourg'.[31]

---

[28] For critical discussion of the Court's use of comparative material see; *ibid*; H.C. Yourow, *The Margin of Appreciation Doctrine in the Dynamics of European Human Rights Jurisprudence* 193–6 (1996); P.G. Carozza, 'Uses and Misuses of Comparative Law in International Human Rights: Some Reflection on the Jurisprudence of the European Court of Human Rights' (1998) 73 *Notre Dame L. Rev.* 1217.

[29] 26 Nov. 1991 (No. 216), 14 E.H.R.R. 153.

[30] *Attorney-General v. Guardian Newspapers Ltd.* [1987] 3 All E.R. 316.

[31] Id. at 347.

At the time the action was begun some of the information at issue was already public, having appeared in other books or television broadcasts. During the pendency of the action, while the interlocutory orders were in force, much more of it came to light. Excerpts and summaries were published in British newspapers as well as newspapers in Australia and the United States, and the entire book was published in the United States. Numerous copies were brought into the United Kingdom by individuals who had visited the United States or by mail orders from American book sellers. These events preceded the judgment of the House of Lords upholding the orders against publication.

The judgment of the European Court of Human Rights examined the necessity of the admitted limitation on freedom of expression in the interests of national security and for maintaining the authority and impartiality of the judiciary. The Court found that the interlocutory restriction was justified, but only until 30 July 1987. Further extensive excerpts from the book had been published in another newspaper on 12 July and it had been published in full in the United States on 14 July. The English courts did not dissolve the restriction until the conclusion of appeals from the trial on the merits in October 1988:

[T]he contents of the book ceased to be a matter of speculation and their confidentiality was destroyed. Furthermore, Mr. Wright's memoirs were obtainable from abroad by residents of the United Kingdom, the Government having made no attempt to impose a ban on importation.

* * *

. . . It is also true that there is some difference between the casual importation of copies of *Spycatcher* into the United Kingdom and mass publication of its contents in the press. On the other hand, even if the Attorney General had succeeded in obtaining permanent injunctions at the substantive trial, they would have borne on material the confidentiality of which had been destroyed in any event—and irrespective of whether any further disclosures were made by [the applicants]—as a result of the publication in the United States. Seen in terms of the protection of the Attorney General's rights as a litigant, the interest in maintaining the confidentiality of that material had, for the purposes of the Convention, ceased to exist by 30 July 1987.

* * *

. . . [The] injunctions were sought at the outset, inter alia, to preserve the secret character of information that ought to be kept secret. By 30 July 1987, however, the information had lost that character and, as was observed by Lord Brandon of Oakbrook [in the House of Lords], the major part of the potential damage . . . had already been done. By then, the purpose of the injunctions had thus become confined to the promotion of the efficiency and reputation of the Security Service, notably by: preserving confidence in that Service on the part of third parties; making it clear that the unauthorised publication of memoirs by its former members would not be countenanced; and deterring others who might be tempted to follow in Mr. Wright's footsteps.

The Court does not regard these objectives as sufficient to justify the continuation of the interference complained of. It is, in the first place, open to question whether the actions against [the applicant] could have served to advance the attainment of these objectives any further than had already been achieved by the steps taken against Mr. Wright himself. Again, bearing in mind the availability of an action for an account of profits[32] the Court shares the doubts of Lord Oliver of Aylmerton as to whether it was legitimate, for the purpose of punishing Mr. Wright and providing an example to others, to use the injunctive remedy against persons, such as [the applicants] who had not been concerned with the publication of *Spycatcher*. Above all, continuation of the restrictions after July 1987 prevented newspapers from exercising their right and duty to purvey information, already available, on a matter of legitimate public concern.[33]

Having regard to the foregoing the Court concludes that the interference complained of was no longer necessary in a democratic society after 30 July 1987.

However, the Court held (14 votes to 10) that the orders were appropriate in the period before July 30:

. . . At that time [of the initial order], the applicants had only published two short articles which, in their submission, constituted fair reports concerning the issues in the forthcoming hearing in Australia; contained information that was of legitimate public concern, that is to say allegations of impropriety on the part of officers of the British Security Service; and repeated material which, with little or no action on the part of the Government to prevent this, had for the most part already been made public.

[But the applicant also] wished to be free to publish further information deriving directly or indirectly from Mr. Wright and disclosing alleged unlawful activity on the part of the Security Service, whether or not it had been previously published . . . [I]n July 1986 *Spycatcher* existed only in manuscript form. It was not then known precisely what the book would contain and, even if the previously-published material furnished some clues in this respect, it might have been expected that the author would seek to say something new. And it was not unreasonable to suppose that where a former senior employee of a security service—an 'insider', such as Mr. Wright—proposed to publish, without authorisation, his memoirs, there was a least a risk that they would compromise material the disclosure of which might be detrimental to that service; it has to be borne in mind that in such a context damaging information may be gleaned from an accumulation of what appear at first sight to be unimportant details. What is more, it was improbable in any event that all the contents of the book would raise questions of public concern outweighing the interests of national security.

. . . [T]o refuse interlocutory injunctions would mean that [the applicant] would be free to publish that material immediately and before the substantive trial; this would effectively deprive the Attorney General, if successful on the merits, of his right to be granted a permanent injunction, thereby irrevocably destroying the substance of his actions and, with it, the claim to protect national security. . . .

---

[32] Compare *Snepp v. United States*, 444 U.S. 507 (1979) in which the United States Supreme Court held that it was proper for a court to impose a constructive trust on the profits from the publication of a former agent's book about the Central Intelligence Agency. This remedy was approved *in addition* to an injunction against further publication (footnote by editors).

[33] Paras. 67–9. See also *Weber v. Switzerland*, 22 May 1990 (No. 177), 12 E.H.R.R. 508 holding that a penalty on a litigant for disclosing information about a pending case was not necessary for 'maintaining the authority of the judiciary' since the information disclosed had already been made public at the time of the public statement (footnote by editors).

* * *

In forming its own opinion, the Court has borne in mind its observations concerning the nature and contents of *Spycatcher* and the interests of national security involved; it has also had regard to the potential prejudice to the Attorney General's breach of confidence actions, this being a point that has to be seen in the context of the central position occupied by Article 6 of the Convention and its guarantee of the right to a fair trial. Particularly in the light of these factors, the Court takes the view that, having regard to their margin of appreciation, the English Courts were entitled to consider the grant of injunctive relief to be necessary and that their reasons for so concluding were 'sufficient' for the purposes of paragraph 2 of Article 10.

64. It has nevertheless to be examined whether the actual restraints imposed were 'proportionate' to the legitimate aims pursued.

In this connection, it is to be noted that the injunctions did not erect a blanket prohibition. Whilst they forbade the publication of information derived from or attributed to Mr. Wright in his capacity as a member of the Security Service, they did not prevent [the applicants] from pursuing their campaign for an independent inquiry into the operation of that service. Moreover, they contained provisos excluding certain material from their scope, notably that which had been previously published . . . Again, it was open to [applicants] at any time to seek—as they in fact did—variation or discharge of the orders.

It is true that although the injunctions were intended to be no more than temporary measures, they in fact remained in force—as far as the period now under consideration is concerned—for slightly more than a year. And this is a long time where the perishable commodity of news is concerned. As against this, it may be pointed out that the Court of Appeal certified the case as fit for a speedy trial—which [applicants] apparently did not seek—and that the news in question, relating as it did to events that had occurred several years previously, could not really be classified as urgent . . .[34]

65. Having regard to the foregoing the Court concludes that, as regards the period from 11 July 1986 to 30 July 1987, the national authorities were entitled to think that the interference complained of was 'necessary in a democratic society'.

Some of the dissenting opinions doubted whether there was a significant difference between the two periods distinguished by the majority. Partly, this was based on an estimate of the information that had already become known when the orders were issued, and on the likelihood that the applicants would have access to new and different information. (See, for example, the separate opinion of Judge Walsh.) In addition, some of the dissenting judges emphasized the inevitability, apparent even in the

---

[34] Paras. 61–4. See also *Vereniging Weekblad Bluf! v. The Netherlands*, 9 Feb. 1995 (No 306A), 20 E.H.R.R. 189 in which the Court reviewed an order requiring the withdrawal from publication of a journal containing a confidential security service report. This action was held incompatible with Art. 10 in part because 2,500 copies had already been distributed. (See *id.* paras. 43–6). See also *Fressoz & Roire v. France*, 21 Jan. 1999 para. 53 finding a violation of Art. 10 in connection with the applicant's criminal conviction for the publication of income information that was already available to the public and might already have been known to a large number of people. *Sürek v. Turkey*, (No. 2), 8 July 1999 (not yet reported), finding a violation in punishing the identification of police officers accused of misconduct claimed to be justified by the risk of terrorist reprisals. The information was not in a form inciting to violence and the same material had already been published in other newspapers.

earlier period, of the disclosure of the material the government wished to keep secret. Judge Marten noted that it was undisputed that *Spycatcher* could and would be published in the United States. Therefore, it was 'unlikely that Mr. Wright could effectively be stopped'. More generally, as Judge Pettiti stated, given modern technology, once information is available in one country, 'it is impossible to partition territorially thought and its expression'.

Both the Court's judgment and the dissents which have been noted, therefore, depend on an assessment of the *effectiveness* of the attempted suppression of information. The prohibition of publication was not necessary to prevent injury to national security, on this view, because the information would almost certainly become public and the injury would arise notwithstanding the restriction. A futile measure cannot be a necessary one. Certain aspects of the dissenting opinions, however, take a somewhat broader view. Judge DeMeyer, in an opinion joined by four other judges, argued that prior restraints on expression could almost never be deemed necessary. He conceded that the publication of secret information could be punished after the fact:

Under no circumstances, however, can prior restraint, even in the form of judicial injunctions, either temporary or permanent, be accepted, except in what the Convention describes as a 'time of war or other public emergency threatening the life of the nation' and even then, only 'to the extent strictly required by the exigencies of the situation' [citing Article 15].[35]

This position implicitly emphasizes that phrase of Article 10(2) that demands that interferences on rights be justified by measures 'necessary *in a democratic society*'. A democratic society, it may be argued, depends so crucially on the free exchange of information and ideas that its national interests can almost never be served by measures that limit expression.

C. COMPARISONS

Allowing states to interfere with rights protected by the Convention, so long as there is an important enough reason, entails a recognition that, as a practical matter, few restrictions on state behaviour can be absolute. (But see Article 3, the right to be free of torture or inhuman or degrading treatment. Article 2, the right to life, and Article 4 the prohibition on slavery, are also phrased in absolute terms, but some kinds of conduct are defined out of the prohibition.) Most national constitutions also provide, either expressly or as a result of judicial interpretation, for expansion or contraction of their rules for sufficient reason. If these reservations are not to swallow the rules, however, some specification of a limited class of permissible reasons for deviation must be developed. Equally important, some method must be employed to assure that

---

[35] 26 Nov. 1991 (No. 216). 14 E.H.R.R. 1 153. But See *Wingrove v. United Kingdom*, 25 Nov. 1996 Reports, 1996–V 1937 24 E.H.R.R. where the Court found no violation in the refusal of the British Board of Film Classification to grant a licence for the distribution of an allegedly blasphemous videotape. *Id.* paras, 58–65. See also the dissenting opinion of Judge DeMeyer emphasizing this point.

a particular measure is sufficiently related to the privileged objective—whether, in the words of the Convention, the governmental action is 'necessary'. The following definition of 'necessary' from American constitutional law is often cited. How does it compare with that of the European Court?

[T]he argument on which most reliance is placed, is drawn from the peculiar language of this clause. Congress is not empowered . . . to make all laws, which may have relation to the powers conferred on the government, but such only as may be 'necessary and proper' for carrying them into execution. The word 'necessary' is considered as controlling the whole sentence, and as limiting the right to pass laws for the execution of the granted powers, to such as are indispensable, and without which the power would be nugatory. That it excludes the choice of means, and leaves to Congress, in each case, that only which is most direct and simple.

Is it true, that this is the sense in which the word 'necessary' is always used? Does it always import an absolute physical necessity, so strong that one thing, to which another may be termed necessary, cannot exist without that other? We think it does not. If reference be had to its use, in the common affairs of the world, or in approved authors, we find that it frequently imports no more than that one thing is convenient, or useful, or essential to another. To employ the means necessary to an end, is generally understood as employing any means calculated to produce the end, and not as being confined to those single means, without which the end would be entirely unattainable. . . .[36]

Justifications for infringement of constitutional rights are provided for explicitly in the 1982 Canadian Charter of Rights and Freedoms, Section 1 of which prefaces the specification of rights in the other sections:

The Canadian Charter of Rights and Freedoms guarantees the rights and freedoms set out in it subject only to such reasonable limits prescribed by law as can be demonstrably justified in a free and democratic society.

The 1980 draft charter prepared by the Federal government made the rights subject 'only to such reasonable limits as are generally accepted in a free and democratic society with a parliamentary system of government'. The changes are generally understood to have narrowed the permissible grounds of justification.

In a series of cases, beginning with *Regina v. Oakes*[37] the Supreme Court of Canada has developed a test for deciding whether a particular limitation of a right was 'demonstrably justified' under Section 1. In *Oakes* the Court dealt with a statute that placed on a person possessing a narcotic the burden of showing that he did not possess it for the purpose of trafficking. The Court found this inconsistent with the right to be presumed innocent:

The onus of proving that a limit on a right or freedom guaranteed by the Charter is reasonable and demonstrably justified in a free and democratic society rests upon the party seeking to uphold the limitation . . .

The standard of proof under s. 1 is the civil standard, namely, proof by a preponderance of

---

[36] *McCulloch v. Maryland*. 17 U.S. (4 Wheat.) 316, 413–14 (1819).
[37] [1986] 1 S.C.R. 103.

probability. The alternative criminal standard, proof beyond a reasonable doubt, would, in my view, be unduly onerous on the party seeking to limit. Concepts such as 'reasonableness', 'justiciability' and 'free and democratic society' are simply not amenable to such a standard. Nevertheless, the preponderance of probability test must be applied rigorously. . . .

. . . Where evidence is required in order to prove the constituent elements of a s. I inquiry, and this will generally be the case, it should be cogent and persuasive and make clear to the court the consequences of imposing or not imposing the limit: A court will also need to know what alternative measures for implementing the objective were available to the legislators when they made their decisions. I should add, however, that there may be cases where certain elements of the s. I analysis are obvious or self-evident.

To establish that a limit is reasonable and demonstrably justified in a free and democratic society, two central criteria must be satisfied. First, the objective, which the measures responsible for a limit on a Charter right or freedom are designed to serve, must be 'of sufficient importance to warrant overriding a constitutionally protected right or freedom': The standard must be high in order to ensure that objectives which are trivial or discordant with the principles integral to a free and democratic society do not gain s. 1 protection. It is necessary, at a minimum, that an objective relate to concerns which are pressing and substantial in a free and democratic society before it can be characterized as sufficiently important.

Second, once a sufficiently significant objective is recognized, then the party invoking s. 1 must show that the means chosen are reasonable and demonstrably justified. This involves 'a form of proportionality test': Although the nature of the proportionality test will vary depending on the circumstances, in each case courts will be required to balance the interests of society with those of individuals and groups. There are, in my view, three important components of a proportionality test. First, the measures adopted must be carefully designed to achieve the objective in question. They must not be arbitrary, unfair or based on irrational considerations. In short, they must be rationally connected to the objective. Secondly, the means, even if rationally connected to the objective in this first sense, should impair 'as little as possible' the right or freedom in question . . . Third, there must be a proportionality between the *effects* of the measures which are responsible for limiting the Charter right or freedom, and the objective which has been identified as of 'sufficient importance'.

With respect to the third component, it is clear that the general effect of any measure impugned under s. 1 will be the infringement of a right or freedom guaranteed by the Charter, this is the reason why resort to s. 1 is necessary. The inquiry into effects must, however, go further. A wide range of rights and freedoms are guaranteed by the Charter, and an almost infinite number of factual situations may arise in respect of these. Some limits on rights and freedoms protected by the Charter will be more serious than others in terms of the nature of the right or freedom violated, the extent of the violation and the degree to which the measures which impose the limit trench upon the integral principles of a free and democratic society. Even if an objective is of sufficient importance, and the first two elements of that proportionality test are satisfied, it is still possible that, because of the severity of the deleterious effects of a measure on individuals or groups, the measure will not be justified by the purposes it is intended to serve. The more severe the deleterious effects of a measure, the more important the objective must be if the measure is to be reasonable and demonstrably justified in a free and democratic society.

The Court concluded that the statute at issue served a sufficient interest—restricting drug traffic—but that there was no rational connection between the presumption created and the governmental objective. Therefore the statute was not saved under Section 1.

The *Oakes* test, particularly its requirements that the means chosen should impair the right as little as possible and should be proportionate to the severity of the infringement of the right in question, poses, on its face, extremely rigorous requirements for the validity of any action limiting a Charter right. As one astute commentator has observed 'a strict application of the least drastic means requirement would allow only one legislative response to an objective that involved the limiting of a charter right'[38] Such an interpretation would work a drastic reduction of legislative discretion. For reasons similar to those underlying the 'margin of appreciation' in European human rights law, the Supreme Court soon found it necessary to restate the test. In *Irwin Toy Ltd. v. Attorney-General (Quebec)*[39] the Court upheld a sweeping statutory limitation of broadcast advertising aimed at children. The Court found the measure was demonstrably justified in a free and democratic society:

The party seeking to uphold the limit must demonstrate on a balance of probabilities that the means chosen impair the freedom or right in question as little as possible. What will be 'as little as possible' will of course vary depending on the government objective and on the means available to achieve it. . . .

When striking a balance between the claims of competing groups, the choice of means, like the choice of ends, frequently will require an assessment of conflicting scientific evidence and differing justified demands on scarce resources. Democratic institutions are meant to let us all share in the responsibility of these difficult choices. Thus as courts review the results of the legislature's deliberations, particularly with respect to the protection of vulnerable groups, they must be mindful of the legislature's representative function. . . .

. . . The question is whether the government had a reasonable basis, on the evidence tendered, for concluding that the ban on all advertising directed at children impaired freedom of expression as little as possible given the government's pressing and substantial objective. . . .[40]

While evidence exists that other less intrusive options reflecting more modest objectives were available to the government, there is evidence establishing the necessity of a ban to meet the objectives the government had reasonably set. The Court will not in the name of minimal impairment take a restrictive approach to social science evidence and require the legislature to choose the least ambitious means to protect vulnerable groups. . . .[41]

. . . [A] legislature mediating between the claims of competing groups will be forced to strike a balance without the benefit of absolute certainty concerning how that balance is best struck.[42]

The application of the *Oakes* test has continued to stir debate in the Court with respect to the degree of deference to be accorded legislative judgments in different circumstances. In *RJR-MacDonald v. Canada (Attorney-General)*[43] the Court found

---

[38] P. Hogg, *Constitutional Law of Canada*, s. 35 11(b) (3d ed., 1992).
[39] [1989] 1 S.C.R. 927.
[40] *Id.* at 993–4.
[41] *Id.* at 999.
[42] *Id.* at 993.
[43] [1995] 3 S.C.R. 199.

that a sweeping ban on advertisement of cigarettes violated section 2(b) of the Charter guaranteeing freedom of expression. The justices agreed unanimously that the regulation infringed that right. They divided five to four, however, in deciding that the measure was not justified under section 1. The Court had been presented with massive amounts of conflicting evidence on the relationship between advertising and tobacco consumption. In dissenting, Justice LaForest relied on the reasoning of the *Irwin Toy* case just quoted. He concluded that when the legislature was adjusting the competing claims of different social interests, Courts were incompetent to overrule its necessarily uncertain policy choices. He argued that it was wrong in such cases 'to apply rigorously the criterion of civil proof on the balance of probabilities—.' To do so would make it 'impossible to govern' and to confer on the judiciary 'a supervisory role over a state itself essentially inactive'.[44] For the majority, however, this approach was an abdication of the Court's duty to see that the standards of section 1 were met in cases where a Charter infringement was present. Justice MacLachlan insisted on the civil standard of proof. This standard, she said, 'does not require scientific demonstration; the balance of probabilities may be established by the application of common sense to what is known'. A more deferential attitude by the courts 'to the point of accepting Parliament's view simply on the basis that the problem is serious and the solution difficult, would be . . . to weaken the structure of rights upon which our constitution and our nation is [sic] founded'.[45]

D. LEVELS OF JUSTIFICATION

The jurisprudence of the European Court of Human Rights on whether or not infringements of protected rights are justified under provisions like Article 10(2) evidences a tendency to vary the strictness with which such justification will be demanded depending on the circumstances of the particular case. These differences turn sometimes on the particular public aim that the challenged measure seeks to achieve and sometimes on the character of the violation of the right that is complained of. Thus, in an article reviewing the Court's application of the 'margin of appreciation' Judge Macdonald concludes that '[t]he exact width of the margin of appreciation in any particular case is difficult to specify in advance . . . because it varies in accordance with the precise balance of the . . . principles that the Court thinks is appropriate in the case at hand. Nevertheless, it is possible to say that the margin is probably at its widest when the Court is considering whether derogations are strictly required at a time of grave public emergency and at its narrowest when there is alleged violation of a person's very private and personal life'.[46]

One aspect of the factors influencing the Court's definition of the margin of

---

[44] *Id.* at para. 67.

[45] *Id.* at paras. 136–7. See also *id.* at paras. 182–8 (reasons of Iacobucci, J).

[46] Ronald St. John McDonald, '*The Margin of Appreciation in the Jurisprudence of the European Court of Human Rights*' in '*International Law at the Time of Its Codification: Essays in Honor of Roberto Ago* 187, 207 (1987).

appreciation is illustrated by the way the Court has dealt with two different objectives listed in Article 10(2) which justify limitations on the right of free expression, the protection of morals and the maintenance of the authority and impartiality of the judiciary. In *Handyside*, the Court stressed that, given the great variation in different countries on the requirements of morality, it was particularly appropriate for the court to defer to domestic legislative judgments as to what measures were necessary to protect morals.[47] The court applied the same reasoning in *Müller and Others v. Switzerland*.[48] The cantonal authorities in that case had prosecuted an artist and the promoters of an art show for display of obscene materials. The Criminal Cassation Division of the Federal Court of Switzerland summarized the paintings at issue as showing 'an orgy of unnatural sexual practices (sodomy, bestiality, petting), which is crudely depicted in large format'. The applicants were fined and the paintings were ordered held by a museum for inspection only by 'specialists'. The paintings were returned to the owner on his motion eight years later. The European Court found no violation of Article 10:

35. The applicants' conviction on the basis of Article 204 of the Swiss Criminal Code was intended to protect morals. Today, as at the time of the *Handyside* judgment . . . , it is not possible to find in the legal and social orders of the Contracting States a uniform European conception of morals. The view taken of the requirements of morals varies from time to time and from place to place, especially in our era, characterised as it is by a far-reaching evolution of opinions on the subject. By reason of their direct and continuous contact with the vital forces of their countries, State authorities are in principle in a better position than the international judge to give an opinion on the exact content of these requirements as well as on the 'necessity' of a 'restriction' or 'penalty' intended to meet them.

36. In the instant case, it must be emphasised that—as the Swiss courts found both at the cantonal level at first instance and on appeal and at the federal level—the paintings in question depict in a crude manner sexual relations, particularly between men and animals. . . . They were painted on the spot—in accordance with the aims of the exhibition, which was meant to be spontaneous—and the general public had free access to them, as the organizers had not imposed any admission charge or any age-limit. Indeed, the paintings were displayed in an exhibition which was unrestrictedly open to—and ought to attract—the public at large.

The Court recognises, as did the Swiss courts, that conceptions of sexual morality have changed

---

[47] Similarly, a wide margin of appreciation is sometimes recognized when the state is acting 'in the interests of national security'. *See Leander v. Sweden*, 25 Mar. 1987 (No. 116), 9 E.H.R.R. 433, para. 59. *See also* the partly dissenting opinion of Judge Morenilla in *The Observer and Guardian v. United Kingdom (Spycatcher)* discussed *supra*: 'It is true that the state's margin of appreciation is wider when it is a question of protecting national security than when it is a question of maintaining the authority of the judiciary. . . . ' 26 Nov. 1991 (No. 216), 14 E.H.R.R. 153, para. 3. In *Hadjianastassiou v. Greece*, 16 Dec. 1992 (No. 252), 16 E.H.R.R. 219, the Court held the applicant's conviction by a military tribunal for disclosing classified information did not violate Article 10. The applicant claimed that the information was unimportant to national security, but the Court held that the Greek courts could not 'be said to have overstepped the limits of the margin of appreciation in matters of national security'. *Id.* at para. 47. *See also* Leigh, *Spycatcher in Strasbourg*, [1990] Public Law 200, 203–4, characterizing the Court's attitude toward claimed violations justified in the name of national security concerns as 'largely non-interventionist'.

[48] 24 May 1988 (No. 133), 13 E.H.R.R. 212.

in recent years. Nevertheless, having inspected the original paintings, the Court does not find unreasonable the view taken by the Swiss courts that those paintings, with their emphasis on sexuality in some of its crudest forms, were 'liable grossly to offend the sense of sexual propriety of persons of ordinary sensitivity' . . . In the circumstances, having regard to the margin of appreciation left to them under Article 10 §2, the Swiss courts were entitled to consider it 'necessary' for the protection of morals to impose a fine on the applicants for publishing obscene material.

Judge Spielman, dissenting, argued that states should have greater regard to the relativity of values in the expression of ideas. He also noted that the Court's approach to the state's superior ability to judge the protection of morals could make it 'impossible for an international court to find any violation of Article 10 as the second paragraph of that Article would always apply'.

Clearly, judicial review of the sufficiency of moral justifications for limitations of expression raises acute questions of definition. It may be noted, for example, that the House of Lords, in construing the English obscenity statute's requirement that the article in question must tend to 'deprave or corrupt', has held that such an effect may be found even when the individuals exposed to it have exhibited no objectionable behaviour manifesting such depravity. Rather the evil in the materials is their 'effect . . . on the mind, including the emotions' so as to induce 'thoughts of a most impure and libidinous character'.[49] Some attempt to objectify the moral evil may be perceived in the definition of obscenity in United States constitutional law that denies protection to matters that, *inter alia*, 'the average person applying contemporary community standards' would find appeals, as a whole, to the prurient interest.[50] This standard allows a state to judge obscenity, at least in part, on the basis of local standards, although there are apparently limits to the extent that idiosyncratically intolerant local standards may apply.[51] Likewise, the English statute on obscenity specifically refers to material that tends 'to deprave and corrupt persons who are likely, having regard to all relevant circumstances to read, see or hear the matter'. This has been interpreted as adopting 'a relative conception of obscenity. An article cannot be considered obscene in itself; it can only be so in relation to its likely readers'. In particular, a court ought to apply 'different tests to teenagers, members of men's clubs or men in various occupations or localities'.[52] On the other hand, the judicial application of Canadian statutes for the control of indecency and obscenity has been notable for its studious avoidance of a strictly moral understanding of such laws. The Supreme

---

[49] *Director of Public Prosecutions v. Whyte* [1972] A.C. 849, 864, [1972] 3 All E.R. 12, 21 (Lord Pearson) (quoting *R. v. Hicklin*, (1868) L.R. 3 Q.B. 360). It should be noted that English law also still allows criminal prosecution for the common law crime of 'outraging public decency'. In such a case there is no need for the Court to show that anyone is at risk of 'depravity' or 'corruption'. Nor is there any defence that the publication serves some literary, scientific or artistic public good. See *R. v. Gibson*, [1990] 2 Q.B. 619. [1991] All E.R. 439. Indecency 'includes anything which an ordinary decent man or woman would find to be shocking, disquieting and revolting'. *Knuller (Publishing, Printing and Promotions) Ltd. v. Director of Public Prosecutions* [1973] A.C. 435, 458, [1972] All E.R. 818, 905 (Lord Reid).

[50] *Miller v. California*, 413 U.S. 15, 24 (1973).

[51] *Jenkins v. Georgia*, 418 U.S. 153 (1974).

[52] Obscene Publications Act 1959.

Court of Canada has, on the contrary, emphasized the 'social harms' associated with such expression and particularly the 'degradation and objectification of women'.[53]

In contrast to its treatment of the public goal of protecting morals, the European Court has shown less deference to national judgments as to what is needed 'for maintaining the authority and impartiality of the judiciary'. Consider the following from *Sunday Times v. United Kingdom*.[54]

Again, the scope of the domestic power of appreciation is not identical as regards each of the aims listed in Article 10 §2. The *Handyside case* concerned the 'protection of morals'. The view taken by the Contracting States of the 'requirements of morals', observed the Court, 'varies from time to time and from place to place, especially in our era', and 'State authorities are in principle in a better position than the international judge to give an opinion on the exact content of these requirements'. Precisely the same cannot be said of the far more objective notion of the 'authority' of the judiciary. The domestic law and practice of the Contracting States reveal a fairly substantial measure of common ground in this area. This is reflected in a number of provisions of the Convention, including Article 6, which have no equivalent as far as 'morals' are concerned. Accordingly, here a more extensive European supervision corresponds to a less discretionary power of appreciation.[55]

In response to this approach, the joint dissenting opinion of nine judges included the following:

Even though there might exist a fairly broad measure of common ground between the Contracting States as to the substance of Article 6, it nevertheless remains the fact that the judicial institutions and the procedure can vary considerably from one country to another. Thus, contrary to what the majority of the Court holds, the notion of the authority of the judiciary is by no means divorced from national circumstances and cannot be determined in a uniform way.

. . . It is thus for the national authorities to make the initial assessment of the danger threatening the authority of the judiciary and to judge what restrictive measures are necessary to deal with that danger. The relevant restrictions may vary according to the legal system and the traditions of the country in question.

This cannot be taken to the point of allowing that every restriction on freedom of expression adjudged by the domestic courts to be necessary for observance of the law of contempt must also be considered necessary under the Convention.

And Judge Zekia in his concurring opinion stated:

Whenever it considers it reasonable and feasible, this Court should work out a uniform international European standard for the enjoyment of the rights and freedoms included in the Convention. This could be done gradually when the occasion arises and after giving the appropriate full consideration to national legal systems. . . .

In the legal systems of those continental States which are the original signatories of the Conven-

---

[53] *R. v. Mara*, [1997] 2 S.C.R. 630, 647.

[54] 26 Apr. 1979 (No. 30), 2 E.H.R.R. 245, reproduced in part in Chapter 2, *supra*.

[55] *Id.* at para. 59. See also *Weber v. Switzerland*, 22 May 1990 (No. 177), 12 E.H.R.R. 508 where the Court states that a justification based on 'maintaining the authority and impartiality of the judiciary has to be 'convincingly established'. *Id.* at para. 47.

tion there is, as far as my information and knowledge go, nothing similar to the branch of the common law of contempt of court—with its summary procedure—touching publications which refer to pending civil proceedings. Notwithstanding this fact these countries manage to maintain the authority and impartiality of their judiciary. Am I to accept any submission to the effect that conditions in England are different and that they have to keep alive unaltered the common law of contempt of court under discussion, which is over two centuries old, in order to safeguard the authority and impartiality of the judiciary? My knowledge and experience gained from long years of association with English judges and courts prompt me to say unreservedly that the standard of the judiciary in England is too high to be influenced by any publication in the press . . .

In *Worm v. Austria*[56] the Court found that Article 10 had not been violated when a journalist was convicted of 'influencing the outcome' of judicial proceedings based on an article describing the trial of a high profile political figure for tax evasion. The Court repeated its dictum from *Sunday Times* that the margin of appreciation might be narrower when a state is attempting to maintain the 'authority and impartiality of the judiciary' in light of its 'objective character'. It went on, however, to say that the applicant's conviction could not be held 'contrary to Article 10 of the Convention simply because it might not have been obtained under a different legal system'.[57]

Another category of variations in the level of justification involves the kind (or extent) of violation of the protected right at issue. With respect to the right to respect for one's 'home' in Article 8, the Court has stated that '[t]he importance of such a right to the individual must be taken into account in determining the scope of the margin of appreciation allowed to the government'.[58] In the *Spycatcher* case, the Court noted that freedom of expression was 'one of the foundations of a democratic society', and that, consequently, the exceptions in Article 10(2) 'must be narrowly interpreted and the necessity for any restrictions must be convincingly established'.[59] Given the special role of the press as 'public watchdog' this approach was 'of particular importance,[60] when its rights were involved. Some dissenting opinions were even more explicit in providing especially stringent criteria for what is 'necessary' in free expression cases. For example, Judge Pekkanen argued that, given the 'vital importance' of freedom of expression and freedom of the press 'the state's margin of appreciation in these cases is very narrow indeed'.[61]

Another indication that the limitation of certain rights may be harder to justify than others may be found in a comparison of *Handyside* and *Müller* with *Dudgeon v. United Kingdom*[62] In that case, the Court refused to find the protection of morals an adequate justification for criminal laws directed at homosexual activity. It distinguished its more liberal attitude toward state judgments on morals in *Handyside* by

[56] 29 Aug. 1997, Reports, 1997–V 153, 25 E.H.R.R. 454.
[57] *Id.* at para. 49.
[58] *Gillow v. United Kingdom*, 24 Nov. 1986 (No. 109), 11 E.H.R.R. 335, para. 55.
[59] *Observer and Guardian v. United Kingdom*, 26 Nov. 1991 (No. 216), 14 E.H.R.R. 153, para. 59.
[60] *Id.* at para. 59.
[61] *Id.* (separate opinion).
[62] 23 Sept. 1981 (No. 45), 45 E.H.R.R. 149, reproduced in Chapter 6 *infra*.

noting that the margin of appreciation depends not only on the state interest being advanced, but also on the nature of the particular interference. In *Dudgeon*, the law in question concerned 'a most intimate aspect of private life'. Therefore, a particularly pressing justification was required. Notwithstanding the different results in *Handyside* and *Dudgeon*, the Court subsequently denied that it used different standards in cases involving Article 8 and Article 10.[63]

Unlike the European Convention the United States Constitution declares most of its individual rights in absolute terms. Nevertheless, by judicial interpretation these rights have usually been redefined to assure that serious governmental interests may be pursued notwithstanding their impact on otherwise protected activities. And, as has been the case with the European Court the strength of the justification demanded has varied with the importance of the interest pursued and the right being limited. Thus, like the Court in *Handyside* the United States Supreme Court has been particularly sensitive to the propriety of regulation to provide protection of the morals of children. In *Ginsberg v. New York*,[64] the Supreme Court upheld a statute prohibiting the sale of sexually oriented literature to minors under 17. The Court agreed that since the material was not obscene, its sales to adults could not be forbidden. The state's interest in preventing the distribution of the same material to children, however was sufficient to support the law in question. This case was distinguishable from *Butler v. Michigan*[65] where the United States Supreme Court held unconstitutional a statute prohibiting generally the sale of material unsuitable for children.[66] 'Surely', the Court stated, 'this is to burn the house to roast the pig . . . [The] incidence of this enactment is to reduce the adult population of Michigan to reading only what is fit for children'. Similarly, in *Reno v. American Civil Liberties Union*,[67] the Court found that the Communications Decency Act of 1996, in its attempt to protect children from inappropriate material on the Internet, inhibited too much protected speech intended for adults. The Act prohibited transmission of any 'obscene or indecent' material if a recipient was known to be under 18 years of age. The effect of the law was to 'suppress [. . .] a large amount of speech that adults have a constitutional right to receive and address to one another'.[68] In an opinion concurring in part and dissenting in part, Justice O'Connor raised questions about the viability, given current technology, of a legal model that supposed it was possible to restrict communication to children while maintaining its availability to adults. With physical media 'the twin characteristics of geography and identity enable the establishment's proprietor to prevent children from entering the establishment but to let adults inside'.[69] But electronic communication is 'fundamentally different. . . . Since users can transmit and receive messages on

---

[63] *Norris v. Ireland*, 26 Oct. 1988 (No. 142), 13 E.H.R.R. 186, discussed in Chapter 6 *infra*.

[64] 390 U.S. 629 (1968).

[65] 352 U.S. 380 (1962).

[66] *See also Sable Communications v. F.C.C.*, 492 U.S. 115 (1989) (holding protection of children insufficient to justify a blanket ban on 'dial-a-porn' telephone services).

[67] 521 U.S. 844 (1997).

[68] *Id.* at 874.

[69] *Id.* at 889 (O'Connor J concurring and dissenting).

the Internet without revealing anything about their identities or ages . . . it is not currently possible to exclude persons from accessing certain messages on the basis of their identity.[70]

In this connection it should be noted that while *Handyside* justified the interference with expression by the special need to protect children, the Court did not appear to regard the government's action, and the statute under which it acted, as restricted to communication with children. The government's action was not limited to such particularly objectionable distribution. In that sense, the decision to review the state's action leniently is less persuasive.

In fact, as noted above, English law has been interpreted to require courts to ascertain, as a matter of fact, the likely readers of material, and to adjust its holdings on obscenity to the relative vulnerability of such readers to 'depravity and corruption' by the material in question.[71] The reference in the obscenity statute to the likely readership was inserted exactly to prevent an application to all challenged material of 'literary standards [on] the level of something suitable for the decently brought up female aged 14'.[72] Under the relevant statute '[t]he age and kind of person to whom indecent photographs or books are shown or sold is of the greatest importance'.[73]

The United States Supreme Court has tended to demand different levels of justification for constitutional infringements depending on the exact character of the right infringed. This has been a prominent aspect of its decisions applying the equal protection clause of the Fourteenth Amendment. In recognition of the omnipresent need for government to treat people unequally, it will usually hold a classification invalid only if 'the varying treatment of different groups or persons is so unrelated to the achievement of any combination of legitimate purposes that [it] can only conclude that the legislature's actions were irrational'.[74] If, however, the classification turns on a factor that, for historical or political reasons, the Court has deemed 'suspect' (racial classifications are the paradigm), or impinges on the exercise of a fundamental right (for example, the exercise of the vote) a far more stringent test of justification is called for. In such cases, the government must show 'that such laws are *necessary* to promote a *compelling* governmental interest'. The word necessary is used in that test in a strict way so that 'if there are other, reasonable ways to achieve these goals with a lesser burden on constitutionally protected activity, a State may not choose the way of greater interference'. If it acts at all, it must choose 'less drastic means'.[75]

A similar variation has developed in Canadian constitutional law through inter-

---

[70] *Id.* at 889–90.

[71] *See Director of Public Prosecutions v. Whyte* [1972] A.C. 849: [1972] 3 All E.R. 12: A. W. Bradley & K.D. Ewing *Constitutional and Administrative Law* 522–5 (12th ed. 1999).

[72] *R. v. Secker Warburg Ltd.* [1954] 2 All E.R. 683, 686 (Stable, J.).

[73] *Director of Public Prosecutions v. Whyte* [1972] A.C. 849, 875; [1972] 3 All E.R. 12, 30 (Lord Salmon).

[74] *Vance v. Bradley*, 440 U.S. 93, 97(1979).

[75] *Dunn v. Blumstein*, 405 U.S. 330 (1972). Certain classifications, most prominently those based on gender, have been held to call for a third, intermediate level of scrutiny. In these cases the Court will uphold such laws if they 'serve important governmental objectives and [are] substantially related to the achievement of those objectives'. *Craig v. Boren*, 429 U.S. 190, 197 (1976).

pretation of the *Oakes* test for justifying limitations of rights under Section 1 of the Canadian Charter of Rights and Freedoms. It will be recalled that satisfaction of this test required that a sufficient justification must serve a pressing social need and must demonstrate that the measures taken were proportional to the violation of protected rights they involved. The third 'prong' of this proportionality test called for some balance between the advancement of the legislative goal and the interference with Charter rights. The Supreme Court of Canada has held that this inquiry will sometimes turn on the specific exercise of the right that is claimed to be infringed. Thus, when the state takes action inhibiting free expression, the Court has found it proper to ask what the nature and content of the disfavoured expression is. The Court held that the Canadian Parliament could, under Section 1, make criminal the publication of pornography, defined as sexually explicit material involving violence or degrading or dehumanizing to women. The Court decided the legislative response to this expression was appropriately proportional since the material involved 'lies far from the core of the guarantee of freedom of expression. It appeals only to the most base aspect of individual fulfillment, and it is primarily economically motivated'.[76]

As the cases in this chapter illustrate, the idea of a margin of appreciation, while clear and sensible in concept, has proven highly malleable in application. The numerous factors surveyed which have the capacity to widen or narrow the margin of appreciation may appear in multiple combinations with unpredictable results. One example from the jurisprudence of Article 8(2) arose when a challenge was brought to the policy of the United Kingdom excluding homosexuals from the armed forces. In that case the Court recognized that in pursuing the aim of national security a state was entitled to a broader margin. But it reiterated that when a state infringes 'a most intimate aspect of an individual's private life, particularly serious reasons by way of justification [are] required'.[77] The Court, however, did little more than state these two opposite influences and then proceeded to make an *ad hoc* evaluation of the strength of each of the state's claimed justifications.[78] The variability of the margin of appreciation has sometimes provoked strong reactions from judges frustrated by its imprecision. In a recent case Judge De Meyer expressed his dissatisfaction in a dissenting opinion:

[W]here human rights are concerned, there is no room for a margin of appreciation which would enable the States to decide what is acceptable and what is not.

On that subject the boundary not to be overstepped must be as clear and precise as possible. It is for the Court, not each state individually, to decide that issue, and the Court's views must apply to everyone within the jurisdiction of each state.

The empty phrases concerning a State's margin of appreciation—repeated in the Court's judgments for too long already—are unnecessary circumlocutions, serving only to indicate

---

[76] *R. v. Butler* [1992] 1 S.C.R. 452.

[77] *Smith & Grady v. United Kingdom*, 27 Sept. 1999, para. 90.

[78] *See id.* at paras. 91–110.

abstrusely that the States may do anything the Court does not consider incompatible with human rights.

Such terminology, as wrong in principle as it is pointless in practice, should be abandoned without delay.[79]

The kind of categorization of expression according to the worth of its content for the purpose of determining the extent of constitutional protection afforded, is also common in the constitutional law of the United States,[80] and, as the next section will illustrate, appears to be a prominent feature of adjudication under Article 10 of the European Convention.

C. CATEGORIES OF EXPRESSION

1. POLITICAL EXPRESSION

A. LINGENS V. AUSTRIA

Judgment of 8 July 1986
(No. 103), 8 E.H.R.R. 40

8. Mr. Lingens, an Austrian journalist born in 1931 resides in Vienna and is editor of the magazine *Profil*.

[Shortly after the Austrian general elections of 1975 Simon Wiesenthal, President of the Jewish Documentation Centre, accused Friedrick Peter, head of the Austrian Liberal Party of having served in an SS brigade during the Second World War. Bruno Kreisky, the Chancellor and head of the Austrian Socialist Party vigorously defended Peter in a televised interview and accused Wiesenthal of 'mafia methods'.]

11. At this juncture, the applicant published two articles in the Vienna magazine *Profil*.

12. The first was published on 14 October 1975 under the heading 'The Peter Case'. It related the above events and in particular the activities of the first SS infantry brigade; it also drew attention to Mr. Peter's role in criminal proceedings instituted in Graz (and later abandoned) against persons who had fought in that brigade. It drew the conclusion that although Mr. Peter was admittedly entitled to the benefit of the presumption of innocence, his past nevertheless rendered him unacceptable as a politician in Austria. The application went on to criticise the attitude of Mr. Kreisky whom he accused of protecting Mr. Peter and other former members of the SS for political reasons. With regard to Mr. Kreisky's criticisms of Mr. Wiesenthal, he wrote 'had they been made by someone else this would probably have been described as the basest opportunism', but added that in the circumstances the position was more complex because Mr. Kreisky believed what he was saying. . . .

---

[79] *Z v. Finland*, 25 Feb. 1997, Reports, 1997–I 323, 25 E.H.R.R. 371 (partly dissenting opinion of Judge De Meyer).

[80] *See* L. Tribe. *American Constitutional Law* 928–44 (2d edn. 1988).

13. The second article, published on 21 October 1975, was entitled 'Reconciliation with the Nazis, but how?'. . . .

14. . . . With regard to the then Chancellor, he added: 'In truth Mr. Kreisky's behaviour cannot be criticised on rational grounds but only on irrational grounds: it is immoral, undignified'. It was, moreover, unnecessary because Austrians could reconcile themselves with the past without seeking the favours of the former Nazis, minimising the problem of concentration camps or maligning Mr. Wiesenthal by exploiting anti-Semitism.

Finally, Mr. Lingens criticised the lack of tact with which Mr. Kreisky treated the victims of the Nazis.

16. . . . After a long disquisition on various types of responsibility, [Lingens] stressed that at the time it had in fact been possible to choose between good and evil and gave examples of persons who had refused to collaborate. He concluded that 'if Bruno Kreisky had used his personal reputation, in the way he used it to protect Mr. Peter, to reveal this other and better Austria, he would have given this country—thirty years afterwards—what it most needed to come to terms with its past: a greater confidence in itself'. . . .

18. . . . [In the article Lingens declared that the] 'monstrosity' was not, in his opinion, the fact that Mr. Wiesenthal had raised the matter, but that Mr. Kreisky wished to hush it up.

19. The article ended with a section criticizing the political parties in general owing to the presence of former Nazis among their leaders. The applicant considered that Mr. Peter ought to resign, not to admit his guilt but to prove that he possessed a quality unknown to Mr. Kreisky, namely tact. . . .

20. On 29 October and 12 November 1975, the then Chancellor brought two private prosecutions against Mr. Lingens. He considered that certain passages in the articles summarized above were defamatory and relied on Article III of the Austrian Criminal Code, which reads:

1. Anyone who in such a way that it may be perceived by a third person accuses another of possessing a contemptible character or attitude or of behaviour contrary to honour or morality and of such a nature as to make him contemptible or otherwise lower him in public esteem shall be liable to imprisonment not exceeding six months or a fine.

2. Anyone who commits this offence in a printed document, by broadcasting or otherwise in such a way as to make the defamation accessible to a broad section of the public shall be liable to imprisonment not exceeding one year or a fine.

3. The person making the statement shall not be punished if it is proved to be true. As regards the offence defined in paragraph I, he shall also not be liable if circumstances are established which gave him sufficient reason to assume that the statement was true.

Under Article 112, 'evidence of the truth and of good faith shall not be admissible unless the person making the statement pleads the correctness of the statement or his good faith . . . .'

37. In their respective submissions the Commission the Government and the applicant concentrated on the question whether the interference was 'necessary in a democratic society' for achieving the above mentioned aim.

The applicant invoked his role as a political journalist in a pluralist society: as such he considered that he had a duty to express his views on Mr. Kreisky's condemnations of Mr. Wiesenthal. He also considered—as did the Commission—that a politician who was himself accustomed to attacking his opponents had to expect fiercer criticism than other people.

The Government submitted that freedom of expression could not prevent national courts from exercising their discretion and taking decisions necessary in their judgment to ensure that political debate did not degenerate into personal insult. It was claimed that some of the expressions used by Mr. Lingens overstepped the limits. Furthermore, the applicant had been able to make his views known to the public without any prior censorship; the penalty subsequently imposed on him was therefore not disproportionate to the legitimate aim pursued . . .

39. The adjective 'necessary', within the meaning of Article 10(2), implies the existence of a 'pressing social need'. The Contracting States have a certain margin of appreciation in assessing whether such a need exists, but it goes hand in hand with a European supervision, embracing both the legislation and the decisions applying it, even those given by an independent court . . .

40. In exercising its supervisory jurisdiction, the Court cannot confine itself to considering the impugned court decisions in isolation; it must look at them in the light of the case as a whole, including the articles held against the applicant and the context in which they were written. The Court must determine whether the interference at issue was 'proportionate to the legitimate aim pursued' and whether the reasons adduced by the Austrian courts to justify it are 'relevant and sufficient'.

41. In this connection, the Court has to recall that freedom of expression, as secured in paragraph 1 of Article 10, constitutes one of the essential foundations of a democratic society and one of the basic conditions for its progress and for each individual's self-fulfillment. subject to paragraph 2, it is applicable not only to 'information' or 'ideas' that are favourably received or regarded as inoffensive or as a matter of indifference, but also to those that offend, shock or disturb. Such are the demands of that pluralism, tolerance and broadmindedness without which there is no 'democratic society'.

These principles are of particular importance as far as the press is concerned. Whilst the press must not overstep the bounds set, *inter alia*, for the 'protection of the reputation of others', it is nevertheless incumbent on it to impart information and ideas on political issues just as on those in other areas of public interest. Not only does the press have the task of imparting such information and ideas: the public also has a right to receive them. In this connection, the Court cannot accept the opinion, expressed in the judgment of the Vienna Court of Appeal, to the effect that the task of the press was to impart information, the interpretation of which had to be left primarily to the reader.

42. Freedom of the press furthermore affords the public one of the best means of discovering and forming an opinion of the ideas and attitudes of political leaders. More generally, freedom of political debate is at the very core of the concept of a democratic society which prevails throughout the Convention.

The limits of acceptable criticism are accordingly wider as regards a politician as such than as regards a private individual. Unlike the latter, the former inevitably and knowingly lays himself open to close scrutiny of his every word and deed by both journalists and the public at large, and he must consequently display a greater degree of tolerance. No doubt Article 10(2) enables the reputation of others—that is to say, of all individuals—to be protected, and this protection extends to politicians too, even when they are not acting in their private capacity; but in such cases the requirements of such protection have to be weighed in relation to the interests of open discussion of political issues.

43. The applicant was convicted because he had used certain expressions ('basest opportunism', 'immoral' and 'undignified') apropos of Mr. Kreisky, who was Federal Chancellor at the time,

in two articles published in the Viennese magazine *Profil* on 14 and 21 October 1975. The articles dealt with political issues of public interest in Austria which had given rise to many heated discussions concerning the attitude of Austrians in general—and the Chancellor in particular—to National Socialism and to the participation of former Nazis in the governance of the country. The content and tone of the articles were on the whole fairly balanced but the use of the afore-mentioned expressions in particular appeared likely to harm Mr. Kreisky's reputation.

However, since the case concerned Mr. Kreisky in his capacity as a politician, regard must be had to the background against which these articles were written. They had appeared shortly after the general election of October 1975. Many Austrians had thought beforehand that Mr. Kreisky's party would lose its absolute majority and, in order to be able to govern, would have to form a coalition with Mr. Peter's party. When, after the elections, Mr. Wiesenthal made a number of revelations about Mr. Peter's Nazi past, the Chancellor defended Mr. Peter and attacked his detractor, whose activities he described as 'mafia methods'; hence Mr. Lingens' sharp reaction.

The impugned expressions are therefore to be seen against the background of a post-election political controversy; as the Vienna Regional Court noted in its judgment of 26 March 1979, in this struggle each used the weapons at his disposal; and these were in no way unusual in the hard-fought tussles of politics.

44. On final appeal the Vienna Court of Appeal sentenced Mr. Lingens to a fine; it also ordered confiscation of the relevant issues of *Profil* and publication of the judgment.

As the Government pointed out, the disputed articles had at the time already been widely disseminated, so that although the penalty imposed on the author did not strictly speaking prevent him from expressing himself, it nonetheless amounted to a kind of censure, which would be likely to discourage him from making criticisms of that kind again in the future; the Delegate of the Commission rightly pointed this out. In the context of political debate such a sentence would be likely to deter journalists from contributing to public discussion of issues affecting the life of the community. By the same token, a sanction such as this is liable to hamper the press in performing its task as purveyor of information and public watchdog . . .

46. . . . [The Austrian Courts] held in substance that there were different ways of assessing Mr. Kreisky's behaviour and that it could not logically be proved that one interpretation was right to the exclusion of all others; they consequently found the applicant guilty of defamation.

In the Court's view, a careful distinction needs to be made between facts and value judgments. The existence of facts can be demonstrated, whereas the truth of value judgments is not suscep-tible of proof. The Court notes in this connection that the facts on which Mr. Lingens founded his value judgments were undisputed, as was also his good faith.

Under paragraph 3 of Article III of the Criminal Code, read in conjunction with paragraph 2, journalists in a case such as this cannot escape conviction for the matters specified in paragraph 1 unless they can prove the truth of their statements.

As regards value judgments this requirement is impossible of fulfillment and it infringes free-dom of opinion itself, which is a fundamental part of the right secured by Article 10 of the Convention . . .

47. From the various foregoing considerations it appears that the interference with Mr. Lin-gens' exercise of the freedom of expression was not 'necessary in a democratic society . . . for the protection of the reputation . . . of others'; it was disproportionate to the legitimate aim pursued . . .

[The Court held unanimously that there had been a violation of Article 10.]

B. BARFOD V. DENMARK

Judgment of 22 February 1989
(No. 149), 13 E.H.R.R. 493

[The applicant wrote an article for the magazine *Gronland Dansk* criticizing a judgment of the High Court of Greenland upholding a tax on Danish citizens working on American bases. That Court was composed of a professional judge and two 'lay judges', part time judges who happened to be employed by the Greenland local government. The article made clear that the author thought the lay judges' votes were influenced by their employment by the government. On a complaint initiated by the professional judge the applicant was prosecuted for defamation, convicted and fined.]

25. As was not disputed, the applicant's conviction clearly amounted to an interference by a public authority with his right to freedom of expression as enshrined in Article 10. Such interferences will not however contravene the Convention provided the conditions laid down in the Article's second paragraph are fulfilled.

26. The applicant did not contest either that the interference was 'prescribed by law' or that its aims were those invoked by the Government, namely the protection of the reputation of others and, indirectly, the maintenance of the authority of the judiciary. Like the Commission, the Court has no cause to doubt that the interference satisfied the requirements of Article 10 §2 in these respects.

27. The sole issue debated before the Court was whether the interference was 'necessary in a democratic society' for achieving the above-mentioned aims.

28. The Court has consistently held that the Contracting States have a certain margin of appreciation in assessing the existence and extent of such a necessity, but this margin is subject to a European supervision, embracing both the legislation and the decisions applying it, even those given by an independent court. . . .

30. The applicant's article contained two elements: firstly, a criticism of the composition of the High Court in the 1981 tax case and, secondly, the statement that the two lay judges 'did their duty', which in this context could only mean that they cast their votes as employees of the Local Government rather than as independent and impartial judges.

31. The interference with the applicant's freedom of expression was prompted by the second element alone. However, in the opinion of the Commission this statement concerned matters of public interest involving the functioning of the public administration, including the judiciary. According to the Commission, the test of necessity had to be particularly strict in such matters: thus, even if the article could be interpreted as an attack on the two lay judges, the general interest in allowing public debate about the functioning of the judiciary weighed more heavily than the interest of the two lay judges in being protected against criticism of the kind expressed in the applicant's article. . . .

. . . The Government . . . disagreed with the Commission's interpretation of the test of necessity: they laid great stress on the national authorities' margin of appreciation. According to the Government, the applicant's accusations were defamatory, unsupported by any evidence and in fact false; furthermore, regardless of whether or not the lay judges were effectively disqualified in the 1981 tax case, the accusations did not constitute a contribution to the formation of public opinion worthy of safeguarding in a democratic society.

32. The basis of the Greenland High Court's judgment was its finding, made in the proper exercise of its jurisdiction, that 'the words of the article to the effect that the two . . . lay judges did their duty—namely their duty as employees of the Local Government to rule in its favour—represent a serious accusation which is likely to lower them in public esteem'. Having regard to this and to the other circumstances of the applicant's conviction, the Court is satisfied that the interference with his freedom of expression did not aim at restricting his right under the Convention to criticise publicly the composition of the High Court in the 1981 tax case. Indeed, his right to voice his opinion on this issue was expressly recognised by the High Court in its judgment of 3 July 1984.

33. Furthermore, the applicant's conviction cannot be considered even to have had the result of effectively limiting this right.

It was quite possible to question the composition of the High Court without at the same time attacking the two lay judges personally. In addition, no evidence has been submitted to the effect that the applicant was justified in believing that the two elements of criticism raised by him were so closely connected as to make the statement relating to the two lay judges legitimate. The High Court's finding that there was no proof of the accusations against the lay judges remains unchallenged; the applicant must accordingly be considered to have based his accusations on the mere fact that the lay judges were employed by the Local Government, the defendant in the 1981 tax case. Although this fact may give rise to a difference of opinion as to whether the court was properly composed, it was certainly not proof of actual bias and the applicant cannot reasonably have been unaware of that.

34. The State's legitimate interest in protecting the reputation of the two lay judges was accordingly not in conflict with the applicant's interest in being able to participate in free public debate on the question of the structural impartiality of the High Court . . .

35. The applicant alleged that, having regard to the political background to the 1981 tax case, his accusations against the lay judges should be seen as part of political debate, with its wider limits for legitimate criticism.

The court cannot accept this argument. The lay judges exercised judicial functions. The impugned statement was not a criticism of the reasoning in the judgment of 28 January 1981, but rather, as found by the High Court in its judgment of 3 July 1984, a defamatory accusation against the lay judges personally, which was likely to lower them in public esteem and was put forward without any supporting evidence. In view of these considerations, the political context in which the tax case was fought cannot be regarded as relevant for the question of proportionality . . .

[The Court held by six votes to one that there had been no violation of Article 10.]

Dissenting opinion of Judge Gölcüklü . . .

3. . . . It is in my opinion not possible to extract an *a contrario* argument from the *Lingens* case in which the Court held that 'politicians' must be ready to accept more criticism than non-politicians . . . The Court did not of course mean by this that public criticism in political matters could be directed solely against politicians or that the assessment of State institutions and the position of those who, although not politicians in the strict sense, nevertheless take part in public affairs should be excluded from the arena of free discussion and democratic debate.

4. Democracy is an open system of government in which the freedom of expression plays a

fundamental role, as the Court stated in its judgment in the *Handyside case* . . . I am in full agreement with the opinion of the European Commission of Human Rights when it states: '. . . For the citizen to keep a critical control of the exercise of public power it is essential that particularly strict limits be imposed on interferences with the publication of opinions which refer to activities of public authorities, including the judiciary'; and '. . . even if the article in question could be interpreted as an attack on the integrity or reputation of the two lay judges, the general interest in allowing a public debate about the functioning of the judiciary weights more heavily than the interest of the two judges in being protected against criticism of the kind expressed in the applicant's article'. . . .

C. THE SPECIAL PROTECTION OF POLITICAL EXPRESSION AND THE PRESS

Article 10 refers to 'freedom of expression' generally without specifying particular kinds of expression as more or less deserving of protection. Nevertheless, as we have seen, judicial application of Article 10 has effectively varied the strictness with which the Convention will be applied, depending on the specific kind of expression involved. As *Lingens* illustrates, the Court has argued that speech involving political issues and political figures serves a central role in the functioning of democratic societies. Consequently, arguments that a restriction of such discussion is necessary in such a society will be harder to maintain. For example, in *Bowman v. United Kingdom*[80] the Court found a breach of Article 10, when section 75 of the Representation of the People Act 1983 was applied to the applicant who had printed and distributed 25,000 copies of a leaflet stating the positions of the candidates in a parliamentary constituency on issues relating to abortion. The statute prohibited expenditures in excess of £5 by any person other than the candidate 'with a view to promoting or procuring the election of a candidate'. The prohibition did not apply to print or broadcast media. The Court found this restriction disproportionate to the legitimate aim of promoting equality among candidates since it 'operated for all practical purposes as a total barrier to [the applicant's] publishing information with a view to influencing the voters'.[81]

This preference for political speech has its counterparts in other systems of law. In the United States, such expression is at the 'core' of the constitutional guarantee of the First Amendment. Communication on matters of public interest is of a kind 'entitled to the most exacting degree of First Amendment protection'.[82] In a dissenting opinion, Justice McLachlin of the Supreme Court of Canada captured the reasons for this focus

---

[80]   19 Feb. 1998, Reports 1998–1 175, 26 E.H.R.R. 1.

[81]   *Id.* at para. 47. Six judges dissented in three opinions, stressing the importance of maintaining balanced and fair election campaigns. Judge Valticos found 'something slightly ridiculous in seeking to give the British government lessons in how to hold elections'. Partly dissenting opinion of Judge Valticos. American constitutional decisions under the First Amendment have significantly limited the possibility of state-imposed restrictions on campaign expenditures. *See, e.g., Buckley v. Valeo*, 424 U.S. 1 (1970); *Federal Election Commission v. National Conservative Political Action Committee*, 470 U.S. 480 (1985).

[82]   *FCC v. League of Women Voters*, 468 U.S. 364, 375–6 (1984).

in terms that seem equally applicable to the judgments of the European Convention of Human Rights:

The right to fully and openly express one's views on social and political issues is fundamental to our democracy and hence to all the other rights and freedoms guaranteed by the Charter. Without free expression, the vigorous debate on policies and values that underlies participatory government is lacking. Without free expression, rights may be trammelled with no recourse in the court of public opinion. Some restrictions on free expression may be necessary and justified and entirely compatible with a free and democratic society. But restrictions which touch the critical core of social and political debate require particularly close consideration because of the dangers inherent in state censorship of such debate. This is of particular importance under §1 of the Charter which expressly requires the court to have regard to whether the limits are reasonable and justified in a free and democratic society.[83]

Of course, it is not always obvious whether or not a particular instance of conduct amounts to political expression. In *Thorgeir Thorgeirsan v. Iceland*,[84] the Strasbourg Court held that a conviction for defamation based on a publication charging unspecified police officers with acts of brutality violated Article 10. The government argued that the strict rule of *Lingens* applicable to limitations of 'political discussion' did not apply to 'other matters of public interest', namely matters that did not concern 'direct or indirect participation of citizens in the decision making process'. The Court rejected this distinction with no discussion other than to state that it was not warranted by the Court's case-law.[85]

In *Janowski v. Poland*,[86] on the other hand, the Court found that prosecution for 'insult[ing] a civil servant . . . during and in connection with carrying out of his official duties' did not violate Article 10. The applicant had publicly upbraided police officers whom he believed to be misusing their authority, calling them 'oafs' and 'dumb'. Since his statements were directed to the officers and were witnessed by only a few bystanders, they did not 'form part of an open discussion of matters of public concern'.[87] The Court agreed that the limits of criticism:

may in some circumstances be wider with regard to civil servants exercising their powers than in relation to private individuals. However, it cannot be said that civil servants knowingly lay themselves open to close scrutiny of their every word and deed to the extent to which politicians do and should therefore be treated on an equal footing with the latter when it comes to the criticism of their actions. . . . What is more, civil servants must enjoy public confidence in conditions free of undue perturbation if they are to be successful in performing their tasks and it may therefore prove necessary to protect them from offensive and abusive verbal attacks when on duty.[88]

As the *Barfod* case indicates, the special role and characteristics of the judiciary

---

[83] *R. v. Keegstra* [1990] 3 S.C.R. 697, 849–50.
[84] 25 June 1992 (No. 239), 14 E.H.R.R. 843.
[85] *Id.* at paras. 61, 64.
[86] 21 Jan. 1999.
[87] *Id.* at para. 32.
[88] *Id.* at para. 33.

raise different questions with respect to public discussions of the actions of courts. In particular it may not be appropriate to treat such expression in the same way as criticism of other public agencies. This difference is highlighted by Article 10(2)'s designation of 'maintaining the authority and impartiality of the judiciary' as one of the public aims for which expression may properly be limited. In the 1979 *Sunday Times* case the Court's discussion considered the risks to fair adjudication arising from a public discussion of the issues in litigation:

If the issues arising in litigation are ventilated in such a way as to lead the public to form its own conclusion thereon in advance, it may lose its respect for and confidence in the courts. Again, it cannot be excluded that the public's becoming accustomed to the regular spectacle of pseudotrials in the news media might in the long run have nefarious consequences for the acceptance of the courts as the proper forum for the settlement of legal disputes.[89]

The Court went on, however, to state that the courts 'cannot operate in a vacuum' and that 'it is incumbent on [the media] to impart information and ideas concerning matters that come before the courts just as in other areas of public interest'.[90] In balancing the state interest against the right of expression the extent of the public attention devoted to a particular matter was a proper factor to be considered.[91]

The same considerations were brought to bear in *Worm v. Austria*[92] in which the applicant had written an article about the trial of a public figure for tax evasion, strongly suggesting that the defendant was guilty. The writer was convicted of attempting to influence the outcome of a criminal proceeding and sentenced to pay a fine. The European Court held that the conviction was justified under Article 10(2). It did not expressly distinguish its holding in *Sunday Times* but it emphasized that 'public figures are entitled to the enjoyment of the guarantees of a fair trial set out in Article 6, which in criminal proceedings include the right to an impartial tribunal, on the same basis as every other person'.[93] It held, moreover, that such prosecutions were compatible with the Convention even when the state had not demonstrated 'an actual result of influence on the particular proceedings'.[94]

The importance of protecting the authority of the judiciary has been stressed by the Court not merely in cases concerning comments on on-going proceedings but also, as illustrated by *Barfod*, in critical statements on judicial decisions after the fact. In *Präger & Oberschlick v. Austria*[95] the applicants were a writer and publisher who had been convicted of criminal defamation on the complaint of a judge who, among others, had been harshly criticized in a magazine article. The article had condemned the judge's courtroom behaviour describing him as 'rabid' and prone to 'arrogant bullying'. While agreeing that press criticism of the courts was proper and protected,

---

[89] *Sunday Times v. United Kingdom*, 26 Apr. 1979 (No. 30), 2 E.H.R.R. 245, para. 63.
[90] *Id.* at para. 65.
[91] *Id.*
[92] 29 Aug. 1997, Reports, 1997–V 1534, 25 E.H.R.R. 464.
[93] *Id.* at para. 50.
[94] *Id.* at para. 54.
[95] 26 Apr. 1995 (No. 313), 21 E.H.R.R. 1.

the Strasbourg Court also stressed that the judiciary, 'as the guarantor of justice . . . must enjoy public confidence if it is to be successful in carrying out its duties. It may therefore prove necessary to protect such confidence against destructive attacks that are essentially unfounded, especially in view of the fact that judges who have been criticized are subject to a duty of discretion that precludes them from replying'.[96] The state's actions in this case were not directed to criticism of the system of justice in general but to the 'excessive breadth of the accusations, which, in the absence of a sufficient factual basis, appeared unnecessarily prejudicial'.[97]

Press criticism of the courts was found to be protected by Article 10 in *De Haes & Gijsels v. Belgium*.[98] The applicants were the editor and author of a series of articles criticizing the Antwerp Court of Appeal in a controversial child custody case. Three of the judges and the Advocate General of the court brought a civil defamation action. The articles had accused the judges of bias and suggested that they were swayed by sympathy for the father because they were of the same social class and held similar political views. The European Court repeated its language in *Präger & Oberschlik* about the special protection needed for the courts to maintain public confidence. In this case, however, the journalist had engaged in extensive research and the account published was generally accurate. On the personal attacks the Court noted that they constituted only one aspect among many of the applicant's argument. They amounted to an opinion which, in light of the factual basis of the whole series of articles, was not 'excessive'.[99] The state's interference in these circumstances was not 'necessary' under Article 10(2).

The central place of political discussion in freedom of expression has naturally led to a special emphasis on the need to protect the press from regulation and censorship. The press is separately mentioned in the First Amendment to the United States Constitution, although that clause has not been interpreted to provide any preferred status for the press over other speakers.[100] The European Court has frequently stressed the importance of the press in realizing the values Article 10 was intended to safeguard. The discussion in paragraphs 41 and 42 of the *Lingens* case are illustrative. In the *Spycatcher Case*, discussed above, the Court referred to the press 'vital role of "public watchdog"'.[101]

The importance of an independent press suggests the possibility that Article 10 may prohibit more than direct regulation of the actual publication of material. It might

---

[96] *Id.* at para. 34. In dissent Judge Martens said: 'I agree that public confidence in the judiciary is important . . . but rather doubt whether that confidence is to be maintained by resorting to criminal proceedings to condemn criticism which the very same judiciary may happen to consider as "destructive".' *Id.* at para. 3 (dissenting opinion of Judge Martens joined by Judges Pekkanen and Makarczyk, para. 3).

[97] *Id.* at para. 37.

[98] 24 Feb. 1997, Reports, 1997–I 198, 25 E.H.R.R. 1.

[99] *Id.* at paras. 39, 44–9.

[100] See *First National Bank v. Bellotti*, 435 U.S. 765, 795–802 (1978) (Burger C.J. concurring).

[101] *Observer & Guardian v. United Kingdom*, 26 Nov. 1991 (No. 216), 14 E.H.R.R. 153, para. 59 (b).

also bar actions which interfere with the ordinary information-gathering and disseminating function of newspapers and other media. The Strasbourg Court dealt with
such a case in *Goodwin v. United Kingdom*.[102] In that case a reporter had received
confidential information about the financial condition of a company. The company
obtained an injunction preventing the publication of the information and an order
requiring the reporter to reveal his source. The Court emphasized that freedom of the
press depended on more than a right to publish:

Protection of journalistic sources is one of the basic conditions for press freedom, as is reflected in
the laws and the professional codes of conduct in a number of Contracting States . . . Without
such protection, sources may be deterred from assisting the press in informing the public on
matters of public interest. As a result the vital public watchdog role of the press may be undermined and the ability of the press to provide accurate and reliable information may be adversely
affected. Having regard to the importance of the protection of journalistic sources for press
freedom in a democratic society and the potentially chilling effect an order of source disclosure
has on the exercise of that freedom, such a measure cannot be compatible with Article 10 of the
Convention unless it is justified by an overriding requirement of public interest.[103]

In the case at hand the Court agreed that preventing economic injury to the company and its employees was a legitimate public interest. But, given the injunction
against publication, identifying the source would only deal with the 'residual threat of
damage through dissemination of the confidential information otherwise than by the
press', and aid 'in obtaining compensation and in unmasking a disloyal employee or
collaborator . . . [E]ven if considered cumulatively [these interests were not] sufficient
to outweigh the vital public interest in the protection of the applicant journalist's
source.'[104]

Within months of this judgment the English Court of Appeal affirmed another
disclosure order in a remarkably similar case. The Court of Appeal held that English
law and the standard of the *Goodwin* case were more or less identical but its interpretation of the facts caused it to come to a different conclusion. It highlighted additional
reasons why identification of the leaking employee might be important to the complaining company, the operator of the National Lottery. It noted the 'unease and
suspicion' among employees that would follow from the presence of the unidentified
source and the 'risk that an employee who had proved untrustworthy in one regard
may be untrustworthy in a different respect and reveal the name of, say, a public figure
who has won a huge lottery prize'.[105]

The case-by-case approach to this question employed in both the European Court
and the English courts may be contrasted with that adopted by Judge Walsh in his

---

[102]   27 Mar. 1996, Reports, 1996–II 483, 22 E.H.R.R. 123.

[103]   *Id.* at para. 39.

[104]   *Id.* at para. 45.

[105]   *Camelot Group P.L.C. v. Centaur Communications Ltd.* [1998] 1 All E.R. 251 (C.A.). For a discussion of
English law on the protection of journalistic sources see D. Feldman, *Civil Liberties and Human Rights in
England and Wales* 616–31 (1993).

dissenting judgment in *Goodwin*. In contrast to another dissenting opinion joined by seven judges which accepted the Court's conclusion that it was necessary to assess the competing interests, Judge Walsh questioned whether any Article 10 right could be asserted in these circumstances:

[I]t appears to me that the Court in its decision has decided in effect that under the Convention a journalist is by virtue of his profession to be afforded a privilege not available to other persons. Should not the ordinary citizen writing a letter to the paper for publication be afforded an equal privilege even though he is not by profession a journalist? . . .

In the present case the applicant did not suffer any denial of expressing himself. Rather he has refused to speak. In consequence a litigant seeking the protection of the law for his interests which were wrongfully injured is left without the remedy the courts had decided he was entitled to.[106]

A plurality of the United States Supreme Court came to a similar conclusion in deciding that the First Amendment to the United States Constitution does not shield a journalist from the obligation to answer questions concerning his or her sources from a grand jury. The Court noted that no issue arose as to any inhibition on publication nor on the use of any investigative method. Like Judge Walsh, it also noted that ordinary citizens had no right to withhold confidential information from a grand jury.[107]

It is clear that the First Amendment does not invalidate every incidental burdening of the press that may result from the enforcement of civil or criminal statutes of general applicability. Under prior cases, otherwise valid laws serving substantial public interests may be enforced against the press as against others, despite the possible burden that may be imposed . . .

Nothing before us indicates that a large number or percentage of all confidential news sources . . . would in any way be deterred by our holding that the Constitution does not, as it never has, exempt the newsman from performing the citizen's normal duty of appearing and furnishing the information relevant to the grand jury's task . . .

[W]e cannot accept the argument that the public interest in possible future news about crime from undisclosed unverified sources must take precedence over the public interest in pursuing and prosecuting those crimes reported to the press by informants and in thus deterring the commission of such crimes in the future.[108]

Justice Powell, whose vote provided the majority in the five to four decision, however, took a narrower position, similar to that employed by the Strasbourg Court in *Goodwin*. He stated that '[t]he asserted claim to privilege should be judged on its facts by the striking of a proper balance between freedom of the press and the obligation of all

---

[106] *Goodwin, supra* n. 102 (separate dissenting opinion of Judge Walsh, paras. 1–2).
[107] *Branzburg v. Hayes*, 408 U.S. 665, 681–2 (1972).
[108] *Id.* at 682–3, 691, 695.

citizens to give relevant testimony with respect to criminal conduct'. Such a balance should be undertaken on a 'case-by-case basis'.[109]

2. FREEDOM OF EXPRESSION AND PROTECTION AGAINST DEFAMATION

Article 12 of the Universal Declaration of Human Rights, upon which Article 8 of the European Convention is patterned, declares that 'no one shall be subjected . . . to attack upon his honour and reputation'.[110] No such language appears in the Convention but Article 10(2) in setting out the grounds justifying some interference with freedom of expression includes 'protection of the reputation or rights of others'.

Naturally, an approach which stresses the importance of speech concerning political issues will be especially solicitous of criticisms of public officials, acting as such. But, at some point, such criticism may implicate a state's right to act for 'the protection of others' specified in Article 10(2). Almost every legal system provides redress for individuals whose reputations have been injured by the speech of other people. The Court in *Lingens* agreed that 'this protection extends to politicians too'. But, as the Court's judgment in that case indicates, the case for restricting expression is less compelling when the injured party is a public figure. This is because of the critical social interest in discussing the behaviour and character of such persons which has already been discussed. But, beyond this, it may be that legal measures are less necessary to protect the reputations of public figures than they are in the case of private persons. Public figures might be thought to have invited such comment by assuming a public role, thus, in a sense, 'waiving' the full measure of 'protection' contemplated in Article 10(2).[111] Moreover, a public figure may have superior means at his disposal to respond to unfair criticism. Thus, the private citizen would be more injured by the expression than the public figure. Exactly this distinction has shaped the American constitutional doctrine which limits actions of defamation against publications that have published allegedly libelous statements about public officials and other 'public figures'. To succeed in such an action the plaintiff must prove that the statements were made with 'actual malice', that is with knowledge of their falsity or with a reckless disregard of whether they were true or false.[112] But the constitutionally minimum fault necessary to support a defamation action by 'private' plaintiffs is much lower. They need only show some fault. The distinction was explained in *Gertz v. Robert Welch, Inc.*:[113]

[W]e have no difficulty in distinguishing among defamation plaintiffs. The first remedy of any victim of defamation is self-help—using available opportunities to contradict the lie or correct the

---

[109] *Id.* at 710 (Powell J concurring).
[110] U.N.G.A. Resolution 217A (III), U.N. Doc. A/810, at 71 (1948).
[111] *See* para. 42 of *Lingens v. Austria, supra.*
[112] *See New York Times v. Sullivan*, 376 U.S. 254 (1964); *Curtis Publishing Co. v. Butts*, 388 U.S. 130 (1967).
[113] 418 U.S. 323 (1974).

error and thereby to minimize its adverse impact on reputation. Public officials and public figures usually enjoy significantly greater access to the channels of effective communication and hence have a more realistic opportunity to counteract false statements than private individuals normally enjoy. Private individuals are therefore more vulnerable to injury, and the state interest in protecting them is correspondingly greater. . . .

. . . [T]he communications media are entitled to act on the assumption that public officials and public figures have voluntarily exposed themselves to increased risk of injury from defamatory falsehoods concerning them. No such assumption is justified with respect to a private individual. He has not accepted public office nor assumed an 'influential role in ordering society' . . . He has relinquished no part of his interest in the protection of his own good name, and consequently he has a more compelling call on the courts for redress of injury inflicted by defamatory falsehood. Thus, private individuals are not only more vulnerable to injury than public officials and public figures; they are also more deserving of recovery.

The European Court has observed the same distinction as indicated by its reference in the *Lingens* case to the special situation of public figures. It has not, however, been especially deferential to national judgments as to the measures necessary to protect the reputation of private persons, at least where such persons are involved in matters of legitimate public concern. In *Bladet Tromsø and Stensaas v. Norway*[114] 'the Court found a violation in the imposition of liability on a newspaper for publishing what turned out to be inaccurate and defamatory statements about the practices of certain seal hunters. It noted that methods of seal hunting were a matter of public debate in Norway. A dissenting opinion emphasized that the individuals whose reputations had been injured were 'private persons *par excellence*'.[115]

Although in the United Kingdom there is no constitutional restraint on the extent to which speech concerning public issues and public figures may be subject to defamation actions, the common law has developed a number of doctrines which are sensitive to the importance of open debate on public questions in the functioning of a democratic system of government. Thus, an absolute defence of privilege is available for statements made in parliamentary proceedings.[116] Other statements have the benefit of a 'qualified privilege', which serves as a defence to a libel action unless the plaintiff can show that the statement was made with 'express malice'. Included in this category are a variety of reports of official proceedings. Moreover, statements are qualifiedly privileged if made pursuant to a legal, social or moral duty. Thus, the House of Lords has held that false defamatory statements made at a meeting of a local council are privileged. It is important that, on such occasions the members 'should be able to speak freely and frankly, boldly and bluntly on any matter which affects the interests or welfare of the inhabitants'.[117] When qualified privilege does exist, proof of express malice requires evidence that the speaker knew the statement was false, recklessly ignored its truth or falsity or misused the occasion justifying the claim of privilege out

---

[114] 25 May 1999, 29 E.H.R.R. 125.

[115] *Id.* paras. 62–3; Joint dissenting opinion of Judges Palm, Fuhrmann and Baka.

[116] *See* A. W. Bradley & K. D. Ewing, *Constitutional and Administrative Law*, 235–6 (12th ed. 1999).

[117] *See Horrocks v. Lowe* [1975] A.C. 135, 152 [1974] 1 All E.R. 662, 671 H.L. (Diplock, L.J.).

of personal spite.[118] While those with a special duty to report to officials or with a special need to know are so privileged, the mere fact that the subject matter of a statement is a matter of public interest does not, by itself, give rise to a privilege.[119] One aspect of qualified privilege has limited its usefulness in protecting speech on matters of public concern. Historically, it has been confined to communication made by persons with some kind of duty to report and made to persons with a particular interest in receiving the information. It has thus been restricted to 'information arising in the conduct of quite intimate professional and personal relationships'.[120] Consequently it has been hard to invoke qualified privilege in actions directed at communications made to the public at large.[121] In *Reynolds v. Times Newspapers Ltd.*[122] However, the Court of Appeal approved a distinctly broader definition of the occasions for invoking the privilege. The Court cited, *inter alia*, Article 10 of the Convention as evidence of the need for 'an ample flow of information to the public concerning, and . . . vigorous public discussion of, matters of public interest to the community'.[123] Accordingly the Court agreed that the privilege could attach to statements on matters of public interest made to the general public.[124] It also, however, required a publisher invoking the privilege to show 'the nature, status, and source of the material and the circumstances of the publication [were] such that [it] should in the public interest be protected'.[125] In *Reynolds* this requirement came down to showing that the publisher had received its information from reasonably reliable sources.[126]

The High Court of Australia similarly widened the defence of qualified privilege, acting under what it saw as an implicit constitutional requirement that expression on 'political or government matters which enables the people to exercise a free and informed choice as electors' be permitted.[127] Communication within this category could claim the protection of privilege but, in light of the fact that the defamatory aspects of such speech might now reach thousands of people, the Court added to the conditions for claiming the privilege a showing that the publisher had acted 'reasonably'. This requires evidence that the publisher had 'reasonable grounds for believing the imputation was true, took proper steps . . . to verify the accuracy of the material and did not believe the imputation to be untrue'. Moreover, the defendant's conduct will not be reasonable unless the defendant (when practicable) has sought a response from the person defamed and published the response.[128]

---

[118] *Id.* at 150 (Diplock, L.J.).

[119] A. W. Bradley & K. D. Ewing, *Constitutional and Administrative Law*, 235–6, (12th ed. 1999); M. Brazier, *Street on Torts*, 415–22 (8th edn. 1988).

[120] I. Loveland, 'The Constitutionalisation of Public Libels in English Common Law?' [1998] *Public Law* 633, 638.

[121] *Id.*

[122] [1998] 3 All E.R. 961.

[123] *Id.* at 1004.

[124] *Id.*

[125] *Id.* at 995.

[126] Loveland, *supra* n. 120, at 644.

[127] *Lange v. Australia Broadcasting Corp.* (1997) 145 A.L.R. 96.

[128] *Id.* The *Lange* case is discussed in Loveland, *supra* n. 120.

A potentially broader defence to defamation actions which has developed in light of the interest in free political speech is that of 'fair comment'. Under this doctrine, it is an adequate defence to an action for defamation that the statement complained of was the expression of an honestly held opinion on a matter of public interest and particularly on the conduct of public officials.[129] The connection of this defence to freedom of expression values has been made explicit. Lord Justice Scott in the Court of Appeal noted that the defence promoted the 'public interest to have free discussion of matters of public interest', and that this right was 'one of the fundamental rights of free speech and writing which are so dear to the British nation, and it is of vital importance to the rule of law upon which we depend for our personal freedom. . . .'[130]

More recently, the House of Lords has further emphasized the value of free expression in matters of public concern in holding that governmental institutions had no right to maintain an action for defamation. The House cited both American constitutional cases and judgements of the European Court of Human Rights although it expressly declined to base its decision on the Convention. Lord Keith held:

> It is of the highest public importance that a democratically elected governmental body, or indeed any governmental body, should be open to uninhibited public criticism. The threat of a civil action for defamation must inevitably have an inhibiting effect on freedom of speech.[131]

And, in keeping with the rationale for limiting defamation actions by public figures elaborated in the *Gertz Case* discussed above, Lord Keith noted that '[t]he normal means by which the Crown protects itself against attacks upon its management of the country's affairs is political action and not litigation. . . .'[132] The House, however, did not take this reasoning as far as the American cases. Individuals who felt defamed for criticism of their performance as public officials could still seek legal redress.[133]

Notwithstanding these developments, recent debate in the United Kingdom has centered on the abuses associated with press coverage of the private lives of public figures. Hitherto the only limits on such activity have resulted from a system of media self-regulation. A Code of Practices prohibits unjustified intrusion by the press into private life. It forbids long lens photography into private places or 'persistent pursuit'. It enjoins 'sympathy' and 'discretion' in cases involving 'personal grief or shock'.[134] The Code is administered by a Press Complaints Commission which lacks legal authority to punish or to require corrective actions for violations. When the Human Rights Act 1998,[135] incorporating the Convention right of respect for private and family life, was

---

[129] A. W. Bradley & K. D. Ewing, *Constitutional and Administrative Law* 599 (12th ed. 1999), M. Brazier, *Street on Torts* 479–84 (10th edn. 1988).

[130] *Lyon v. Daily Telegraph Ltd.* [1943] K.B. 746, 752–3, [1943] 2 All E.R. 316, 319–20.

[131] *Derbyshire County Council v. Times Newspapers Ltd.* [1993] A.C. 534, [1993] 1 All E.R. 1011.

[132] *Id.* at 549, [1993] 1 All E.R. at 1019 (quoting Schreiner, J. A. in *Die Spoorbond v. South African Railways* [1946] A.D. 999, 1012–13.).

[133] *Id.* at 549–50, [1993] 1 All E.R. at 1019–20. This rule was expanded to ban libel action by political parties in *Goldsmith v. Bhoyrul* [1997] 4 All. E.R. 268 (Q.B.). For a criticism of the limited character of these holdings see Loveland, *supra.* n. 120.

[134] D. Feldman, *Civil Liberties and Human Rights in England and Wales*, 587–90 (1993).

introduced in Parliament, concerns were raised that this right of privacy might be asserted against the press. In response the Bill was amended by adding section 12 to apply whenever a judicial action under the Act 'might affect the exercise of the Convention right to freedom of expression'. In such cases no relief is to be granted 'to restrain publication before trial unless the Court is satisfied that the applicant is likely to establish that publication should not be allowed'. The Court in such cases must also 'have particular regard to the importance of the Convention right to freedom of expression'. Where 'journalistic, literary or artistic material' is involved, the court must also consider the extent to which the material is already available to the public or any public interest in publication.[136]

Other constitutional systems protecting free expression have also had to balance that right with the desire to protect private matters from public exposure. In *Time, Inc. v. Hill*[137] the United States Supreme Court held that the First Amendment limited the extent to which a publication on a matter of public concern could be subject to a tort action for disclosing private information and placing the plaintiff in a 'false light'. In such cases recovery could only be had if the publication were knowingly false or published with reckless disregard as to its truth or falsity. However in *Zacchini v. Scripps-Howard Broadcasting Co.*[138] the Court held constitutional a damages judgment against a television station for broadcasting, in its entirety, an entertainer's 'human cannonball' act. The action in this case was based on a state law tort of 'appropriation' or 'right of publicity'. The Court stressed that the economic value of the plaintiff's performance was similar to that accorded protection by copyright and patent laws.

The Supreme Court of Canada discussed the reconciliation of privacy and freedom of expression in *Aubry v. Editions Vice-Versa Inc.*[139] in which the plaintiff sought damages for the publication of her photograph in a magazine article about contemporary urban life. The Court noted that everyone has a presumptive right not to have his or her image published without consent as an aspect of the right to private life. That right, however, must yield in some circumstance to the public right to information and the concomitant right of free expression. No liability for violation of a privacy right should arise, for example, if the plaintiff were 'engaged in a public activity or has acquired a certain notoriety'. This is true, in particular, of artists and politicians but also more generally of all those whose professional success depends on 'public opinion'. This would also be the case when an otherwise unknown person becomes involved, wittingly or unwittingly, with important matters of public interest.[140]

Legal remedies for injuries to reputation usually turn critically on the truth or falsity of the statement. Logically, the truth of a statement might be irrelevant if the

---

[135] Human Rights Act 1998, s. 12. See App. C *infra*.
[136] *Id.* See R. Singh, 'Privacy and the Media After the Human Rights Act' [1998] *Europ. Hum. Rights L. Rev.* 712.
[137] 385 U.S. 374, 380–91 (1987).
[138] 433 U.S. 562, 569–79 (1977).
[139] [1998] 1 S.C.R. 591.
[140] *Id.* at paras. 53–9.

sole value at stake were the harm to the good name of the complainant. Indeed, the English common law once held that truth could not be a defence, and, in prosecutions for criminal libel, the rule was 'the greater the truth the greater the libel'.[141] The rule is now, almost everywhere, to the contrary. Therefore, in considering the extent of constitutional protection for arguably libellous speech, we ordinarily are dealing with statements that are false. It may not be obvious why false statements deserve the protection of the Convention or of constitutions. In deciding that falsity does not bar such protection, the United States Supreme Court has emphasized the need for uninhibited expression in public discussion. It stressed that 'erroneous statement is inevitable in free debate and it must be protected if the freedoms of expression are to have the 'breathing space' that they 'need . . . to survive'.[142] Whether such false statements should be privileged has turned on the degree of fault attributable to the speaker in making the incorrect statement. The 'actual malice' standard, cited above, allows a sanction for such speech about a public figure, only when the falsehood was intentional or the result of 'reckless' judgment.[143] The same standard, as noted, must be met before a defamation judgement is allowed based on a statement accorded 'qualified privilege' under English law.) And in the *Gertz Case*, quoted above, even statements about private persons concerning matters of public interest, were held to be constitutionally redressable only on proof that the speaker had acted, at least, negligently.

The truth or falsity of a defamatory statement is associated with the question, discussed in the previous section, of the necessity of restriction of expression for the protection of others in a democratic society. In *Castells v. Spain*[144] the applicant had been convicted of violating a Spanish statute against '[t]hose who seriously insult . . . the Government. . . .' The European Court noted that, in Spanish law, the offence of proffering insults, unlike that of false accusation, was not subject to a defence of truth. Indeed, the applicant had, without success, offered evidence in the national courts to show that the facts about the government in his statement were true. The European Court acknowledged that, under Article 10(2), a State was competent to adopt as necessary for public order, 'measures, even of a criminal law nature, intended to react appropriately and without excess to defamatory accusations devoid of foundation or formulated in bad faith'. However, the interference with the applicant's expression in this case, one that was oblivious to the truth or good faith of the statement was too sweeping to be 'necessary in a democratic society'.[145]

---

[141] W. Prosser, *Handbook of the Law of Torts*, 797 (4th edn. 1971).

[142] *New York Times v. Sullivan*, 376 U.S. 254, 271–2 (1964) (quoting *N.A.A.C.P. v. Button*, 371 U.S. 415 (1963)).

[143] *Id.* at 279–80. The Supreme Court of Canada has held that even intentionally false statements may be protected constitutionally. The Court noted the difficulty of identifying 'the essence of [a] communication and determin[ing] that it is false' since a 'given expression may offer many meanings, some which seem false, others of a metaphysical or allegorical nature, which may possess some validity'. Moreover, even a plainly deliberate exaggeration or falsehood may further a social interest by stimulating useful social action or discussion. *R. v. Zundel* [1992] 2 S.C.R. 731, 756.

[144] 23 Apr. 1992 (No. 236), 14 E.H.R.R. 445.

[145] *Id.* at paras. 46–8.

What, however, of instances like that in *Lingens v. Austria*, where the fault of the speaker in making false or dishonest statements cannot arise since the statements are mere matters of opinion, not subject to a determination of their accuracy? For the Austrian courts this was grounds for denying Lingens the possibility of defending by showing the truth of his article. For the European Court, however, the impossibility of establishing the truth of 'value judgments' meant that he was convicted for the mere dissemination of his opinions, a restriction which could not be necessary, at least in the absence of a showing of bad faith.[146] The Court, has, however, agreed that a state may punish the publication of value judgments not published in good faith. It has not fully explained what, in these circumstances, good faith entails, but its opinions suggest that it requires some minimum effort on the part of the writer or publisher to inform himself about the facts on which such an opinion, ought to be based.[147]

This reasoning suggests that there is no easy distinction between fact and opinion. The same confusion has troubled other jurisdictions. In *Milkovich v. Lorain Journal Co.*,[148] the United States Supreme Court rejected an argument that there should be an absolute constitutional defence to any defamation action based on a published statement of opinion. Since certain statements of opinion (for example, 'In my opinion John Jones is a liar.') imply knowledge of false and defamatory facts, they may cause as much damage to reputation as all-out falsehoods. The Court held a libel action could, consistent with the First Amendment, be maintained if the plaintiff could prove a 'false factual connotation' and show the defendant acted with the degree of fault necessary under the particular circumstances. On the other hand, where a statement 'cannot "reasonably [be] interpreted as stating actual facts" about an individual' as a matter of constitutional law, no action could lie.[149] The English courts have reached a similar conclusion when dealing with the libel defence of 'fair comment', discussed above. More particularly that defence is applicable only to expressions of opinion. To the extent that an ostensible statement of opinion may reasonably be read as implying defamatory facts, the defence is unavailable and liability may be imposed. In *Telnikoff v. Matusevitch*[150] the House of Lords held that, in deciding whether or not a statement should be understood as containing defamatory statements of fact rather than mere comment, it was appropriate to look only at the alleged libel itself without regard to the context in which it was attended since possible readers might not have the benefit of that context in interpreting it. 'The writer of a letter to a newspaper', wrote Lord

---

[146] *See also Oberschlik v. Austria*, 23 May 1991 (No. 204), 19 E.H.R.R. 389, para. 63; *Schwabe v. Austria*, 28 Aug. 1992 (No. 242B), para. 34.

[147] *See De Haes & Gijsels v. Belgium*, 27 Feb. 1997, Reports, 1997–I 198, 25 E.H.R.R. 1, para. 47; *Oberschlick v. Austria (No. 2)*, 1 July 1997, Reports, 1997–IV 1266, 25 E.H.R.R. 357, para. 33; *Bladet Tromsø & Stensaas v. Norway*, 20 May 1999, 29 E.H.R.R. 125, paras. 67–71. In none of these cases did the Court find that the opinions were so unsupported as to permit prosecution consistent with Art. 10. However, this reasoning does appear to support, in, part, the refusal to find a violation in an earlier case. *See Prager & Oberschlick v. Austria*, 26 Apr. 1995 (No. 313), 21 E.H.R.R. 1, para. 37.

[148] 497 U.S. 1 (1990).

[149] *Id.* at 17 (quoting *Hustler Magazine, Inc. v. Falwell*, 485 U.S. 46, 50 (1988)).

[150] [1992] 2 A.C. 343, [1991] 4 All E.R. 817 (H.L.).

Keith, 'has a duty to take reasonable care to make clear that he is writing comment, and not making misrepresentations about the subject upon which he is commenting'.[151]

> There is all the difference in the world between saying that you disapprove of the character of a work, and that you think it has an evil tendency, and saying that a work treats adultery cavalierly, when in fact there is no adultery at all in the story. A jury would have a right to consider the latter beyond the limits of fair criticism.[152]

In Lord Ackner's judgment, he differed with this approach, arguing that it would unduly restrict the right of fair comment and thus impair the public interest in free and open discussion.[153]

The European Court's jurisprudence on the compatibility of defamation actions with Article 10 has extended beyond the permissible elements of such actions. The Court has also expressed concern that damages in certain amounts may not be justified, given their inhibiting effect on expression. In *Tolstoy Miloslavsky v. United Kingdom*[154] the applicant wrote a pamphlet charging Lord Aldington with responsibility for atrocities during the Second World War. He suffered a judgment in a libel action of £1,500,000, a sum three times larger than the highest amount previously awarded by an English jury. The applicant's claim in Strasbourg was limited to the quantum of damages. The Court stated that under Article 10 'an award of damages for defamation must bear a reasonable relationship of proportionality to the injury to reputation suffered'.[155] It concluded that controlling English law did not provide adequate machinery to assure such proportionality, noting particularly the amount of the verdict could not be set aside on appeal unless it 'was so unreasonable that it could not have been made by sensible people and must have been arrived at capriciously, unconscionably or irrationally'.[156] The tension between this wide jury discretion and a regime of free expression had, the Court noted, been recognized by subsequent English cases widening the reviewing power of appellate courts and expressing a hope that such appeals would, over time, establish standards for calculating appropriate awards.[157]

The European Court's judgment in *Tolstoy Miloslavsky* may be compared with that of the Supreme Court of Canada in *Hill v. Church of Scientology*.[158] In that case a libel judgment of $1,600,000 was made to a Crown Attorney who had been accused of professional misconduct by the defendants. Appellate review of such judgments in Canada was determined by 'whether the verdict is so exorbitant or so grossly out of proportion to the libel as to shock the Court's conscience and sense of justice'.[159] The

---

[151] *Id.* at 353; [1991] 4 All E.R. at 823.
[152] *Id.* at 354; [1991] 4 All E.R. at 824 quoting *Merivale v. Carson* (1887) 20 Q.B.D. 275, 284, [1886–90] All E.R. 261, 265.
[153] *Id.* at 361, [1991] 4 All E.R. at 830.
[154] 13 July 1995 (No. 316B), 20 E.H.R.R. 442.
[155] *Id.* at para. 49.
[156] *Id.* at para. 50.
[157] *Id.*
[158] [1995] 2 S.C.R. 1130.
[159] *Id.* at para. 159.

jury in this case had requested guidelines on the range of proper awards but had been refused. The Supreme Court emphasized, however, that jury discretion in the calculation of libel damages was particularly appropriate. Nothing that a 'defamatory statement can seep into the crevasses of the subconscious and lurk there ever ready to spring forth and spread its cancerous evil', it concluded that it 'is members of the community in which the defamed person lives who will be best able to assess the damages'.[160] The Court also declined to impose a cap on non-pecuniary damages as it had done in personal injury/cases. 'If it were known in advance what amount the defamer would be required to pay . . . a defendant might look upon that sum as the maximum cost of a license to defame.'[161] The Court also upheld that part of the verdict consisting of punitive damages although it argued that, with respect to this element, a more searching appellate review was called for. In this regard a reviewing Court should ask whether 'the misconduct of the defendant [was] so outrageous that punitive damages were rationally required to act as deterrence'.[162]

The United States Supreme Court has taken a somewhat more rigorous line with respect to damages in defamation actions when the defamatory material concerned matters of public interest. It will be recalled that American decisions have held that public officials and 'public figures' may only recover for libels published with 'actual malice', that is with knowledge of their falsity or with reckless disregard of their truth or falsity. Private plaintiffs, on the other hand, need only show some 'fault' to recover consistent with the First Amendment. In the *Gertz* case establishing the latter proposition, however, the Supreme Court held that the state's interest in permitting recovery in this kind of case 'extends no further than compensation for actual injury'.[163] Consequently it limited the damages in such cases unless the plaintiff proved actual malice. First, it held unconstitutional the longstanding rule that injury was to be presumed from the mere fact of publication. Any recovery would have to be based on proof of actual injury although the Court recognized that such injury may include much more than pecuniary loss, mentioning 'impairment of reputation and standing in the community, personal humiliation and mental anguish and suffering'.[164] Furthermore (absent proof of actual malice) punitive damages were impermissible since, as the Court noted, they were 'wholly irrelevant to the state interest that justifies a negligence standard for private defamation actions'.[165] With respect to both presumed and punitive damages the Court's concerns were the same. Each doctrine allowed the jury a more or less uncontrollable discretion, 'invit[ing] juries to punish unpopular opinion rather than to compensate individuals for injury sustained by the publication of a false fact'. This practice would 'unnecessarily compound [. . .] the potential of

---

[160] *Id.* at para. 166.
[161] *Id.* at para. 170.
[162] *Id.* at para. 197.
[163] *Gertz v. Robert Welch, Inc.*, 418 U.S. 333, 356 (1974).
[164] *Id.* at 350.
[165] *Id.*

any system of liability ... to inhibit the vigorous exercise of First Amendment freedoms'.[166]

3. FREEDOM OF EXPRESSION AND NATIONAL SECURITY

Necessarily states feel a particular need to put restrictions on expression in situations affecting military, diplomatic or intelligence matters. When such restrictions have been challenged under the Convention, the European Court has considered them under Article 10(2) which permits limitations on expression 'necessary in a democratic society in the interests of public safety [and] for the prevention of disorder or crime'. We have already examined one case where such a justification was offered. In *Observer & Guardian v. United Kingdom*,[167] the Spycatcher case, the Court dealt with an injunction against publication of the memoirs of a British intelligence officer. It held this action to be justified before the book had become widely available in other countries and unjustified thereafter.

One might expect the Court to be unusually reluctant to overturn national determinations on matters so central to state interests.[168] The United States Supreme Court has stated that even prior restraint of expression might be proper to 'prevent actual obstruction to [the government's] recruiting service or the publication of the sailing dates of transports or the number and location of troops'.[169] Nevertheless that Court has continued to scrutinize limitations on expression imposed on members of the military insisting that while the character of permissible restrictions may differ in that context, citizens do not lose their first amendment rights on entry into military service.[170] The European Court of Human Rights has adopted the same approach. In *Grigoriades v. Greece*[171] the Court found a violation of Article 10 when an officer was convicted of 'insulting the armed forces' when he sent a letter to his commanding officer sharply critical of the army. The Court stated that Article 10 'does not stop at the gates of army barracks'. It acknowledged, however, that restrictions on expressions might be allowed when there is 'a real threat to military discipline, as the proper functioning of an army is hardly imaginable without legal rules designed to prevent servicemen from undermining it'.[172] But claims of this kind of justification have been

---

[166] *Id.* at 349. The Court made no reference to the proper quantum of damages in actions brought by public officials and public figures who must prove actual malice for any recovery. One commentator has argued that the logic of *Gertz* indicates that such plaintiffs may not recover presumed or punitive damages under any circumstances. J.E. Nowak & R.D. Rotunda, *Constitutional Law* 1095–6 (5th edn. 1995).

[167] 26 Nov. 1991 (No. 216), 14 E.H.R.R. 153.

[168] Thus the Court has extended a wide margin of appreciation to state determinations of the need for a state of emergency permitting the suspension of rights under Article 15. See Chapter 7(H), *infra*.

[169] *Near v. Minnesota*, 283 U.S. 697, 716 (1931); but see *New York Times Co. v. United States*, 403 U.S. 713 (1971) (holding unconstitutional an injunction against publication of a government report on the Vietnam War over a claim that such publication would be contrary to the interests of national security).

[170] *Parker v. Levy*, 417 U.S. 733 (1974).

[171] 25 Nov. 1997, Reports, 1997–VII 2575, 27 E.H.R.R. 464.

[172] *Id.* at para. 45.

examined critically. In *Vereinigung Demokratischer Soldaten Osterreichs & Gubi v. Austria.*[173] It held there was a breach of Article 10 when the Austrian military refused to distribute on a military base a magazine critical of the Army. The Court did not accept the state's assertion that the publication presented a threat to discipline:

> It is the Court's opinion that such an assertion must be illustrated and substantiated by specific examples. None of the issues of [the magazine] submitted in evidence recommend disobedience or violence, or even question the usefulness of the army . . . [D]espite their often polemical tenor, it does not appear they overstepped the bounds of what is permissible in the context of a mere discussion of ideas, which must be tolerated in the army of a democratic State just as it must be in the society that such an army serves.[174]

The Court again made an independent examination of the threat to national security created by publication of a six-year-old report of the activities of the Dutch internal security service. In *Vereniging Weekblad Bluf! v. The Netherlands* it found that the seizure of the publication violated Article 10.[175]

The armed conflict between Kurdish nationalists and the Turkish state has presented the Court with opportunities to illuminate the limits of free expression in a period of serious threat to the established government. Its response has been to evaluate the degree of danger presented by the expression in each instance and to measure it against the standards justifying limits on expression developed under Article 10(2). So, in one of the first cases on this issue, the Court held Turkey in violation of the Convention when it interfered with and punished the distribution of a leaflet in Izmir charging the authorities with discrimination against Kurds.[176] But it exhibited a far more deferential attitude to the national authorities when they punished a speaker whose words could be interpreted as supporting the Kurdish insurgents in *Zana v. Turkey.*[177] The applicant was prosecuted for a statement made to a journalist in which he said: 'I support the PKK [Kurdish] national liberation movement; on the other hand, I am not in favour of massacres. Anyone can make mistakes, and the PKK kills women and children by mistake.' The Court noted that, at the time the statement was made, the PKK had carried out a number of 'murderous attacks' in the region. The applicant was a former mayor of Diyarbakir, the most important city in south east Turkey. He had made the statement to a major national newspaper. In these circumstances the treatment of the applicant was proportionate to the important social need for maintaining peace and order and was thus justified under Article 10(2).[178]

---

[173] 19 Dec. 1994 (No. 302), 20 E.H.R.R. 56.

[174] *Id.* at para. 38.

[175] 9 Feb. 1995 (No. 306A), 20 E.H.R.R. 189. See also *Smith & Grady v. United Kingdom*, 27 Sept. 1999 (not yet reported), and *Lustig-Prean and Beckett v. United Kingdom*, 27 Sept. 1999, holding that the wide margin of appreciation granted states with respect to matters of national security and military discipline did not extend to justifying the exclusion of homosexuals from military service. See Chapter 6 (B)(4).

[176] *Incal v. Turkey*, 9 June 1998, Reports, 1998–IV 1547.

[177] 25 Nov. 1997, Reports, 1997–VII 2533, 27 E.H.R.R. 667.

[178] *Id.* at paras. 56–62.

In thirteen cases decided on 8 July 1999 the European Court gave some further indications of the factors tending to the finding of a violation of the Convention in this context. All of the cases dealt with written, spoken or broadcast language critical of the Turkish government's Kurdish policies and actions. The expression included academic treatises, histories, poetry, interviews, published letters and editorials. In many of the cases the speakers had employed highly charged language. But, as long as the Court did not find the communications to contain 'incitements to violence', it held the state restrictions incompatible with Article 10.[179] In two cases, however, it declined to find a violation.[180] In one of them the subject was an article about the 'national liberation struggle' of the Kurds and the 'active front of armed violence'. It described the situation as a 'war directed against the forces of the Republic of Turkey' and concluded 'we want to wage a total liberation struggle'. The second case concerned the publication of letters accusing the Turkish authorities of massacres and torture but which did not exhort the readers to violent action. In both cases the Court found the texts 'capable of inciting to further violence . . . Indeed the message which is communicated to the reader is that recourse to violence is a necessary and justified measure of self-defense in the face of the aggressor.'[181] It characterized the article in the first case as an 'incitement to violence'[182] and the letters in the second as 'hate speech and the glorification of violence'.[183]

The Court's interpretation of Article 10 in these cases—permitting the suppression of speech when it contains incitement to violence—has a parallel in the constitutional history of the United States. The great American jurist, Learned Hand, in a case dealing with regulation of expression attacking national policies during World War I, interpreted the controlling statute to reach only the advocacy of illegal action.

[W]ords are not only the keys of persuasion but the triggers of action and those which have no purpose but to counsel the violation of law cannot by any latitude of interpretation be a part of that public opinion which is the final source of government in a democratic state . . . Yet to assimilate agitation, legitimate as such, with direct incitement to violent resistance is to disregard that tolerance of all methods of political agitation which in normal times is a safeguard of the government.[184]

Since none of the texts at issue directly counselled violation of the law, their prohibition was held to be outside the statute.[185]

---

[179] *Arsian v. Turkey*, 8 July 1999; *Beskeya & Okçuoglu v. Turkey*, 8 July 1999; *Ceylan v. Turkey*, 8 July 1999; *Erdogdu & Ince v. Turkey*, 8 July 1999; *Gerger v. Turkey*, 8 July 1999; *Karatas v. Turkey*, 8 July 1999; *Okçuoglu v. Turkey*, 8 July 1999; *Öztürk v. Turkey*, 8 July 1999; *Polat v. Turkey*, 8 July 1999; *Sürek v. Turkey (No. 2)*, 8 July 1999; *Sürek v. Turkey (No. 4)* 8 July 1999; *Sürek & Ödemir v. Turkey*, 8 July 1999 (none yet reported).

[180] *Sürek v. Turkey (No. 1)*, 8 July 1999; *Sürek v. Turkey (No. 3)*, 8 July 1999 (not yet reported).

[181] *Sürek v. Turkey (No. 1)*, *supra.*, n. 180, para. 62; *Sürek v. Turkey (No. 2)*, *supra* n. 179, para 40.

[182] *Sürek v. Turkey (No. 3)*, para. 40.

[183] *Sürek v. Turkey (No. 1)*, *supra* n. 180, para. 62.

[184] *Masses Publishing v. Patten*, 244 Fed. 535, 540 (S.D.N.Y. 1917).

[185] *Id.* at 541–2.

Hand's approach, which has a strong resemblance to that of the Strasbourg Court under Article 10, may be contrasted with that expounded in the same period in the United States Supreme Court in separate opinions of Justices Holmes and Brandeis and, ultimately adopted by a majority of the Court.[186] This is the well-known 'clear and present danger' test according to which expression is within the protection of the First Amendment unless its utterance could be said to create a risk of serious illegal behavior which was both highly probable and immediate. It differs from the 'incitement' inquiry in that it demands consideration of more than the content of the communication. Even exhortations to violence are protected if, in the circumstances, they are not likely to produce imminent harm. So, Holmes dissented from the affirmance of a conviction based on the publication of leaflets concededly encouraging workers to frustrate military production. He doubted that 'enough can be squeezed from these poor and puny anonymities to turn the color of litmus paper.'[187] He went on, in much quoted language, to state that 'we should be eternally vigilant against the attempts to check the expression of opinions that we loathe and believe to be fraught with death unless they so imminently interfere with the lawful and pressing purposes of law that an immediate check is required to save the Country'.[188]

In several dissenting and concurring opinions in the European Court's Turkish judgments members of the Court urged an approach similar to the 'clear and present danger' test. Judge Palm urged the Court to go beyond the 'admittedly harsh and vitriolic language' to focus on the 'general context in which the words were used and their likely impact'.[189] Judge Bonello explicitly advocated adoption of the American approach. Thus 'when the invitation to the use of force is intellectualized, abstract and removed in time and space from the facts of actual or impending violence, then the fundamental right to freedom of expression should generally prevail'.[190]

It should be noted, however, that, in practice, the Court's decisions have not ignored the context in which regulated expression has arisen. In the Turkish judgments the opinions of the Court routinely recited that the evaluation of justifications for the government actions had to take into account the dangerous circumstances in south east Turkey.[191] In one of these decisions it took account of the fact that the message in question had only been read out at a commemorative ceremony 'which considerably restricted its potential impact'.[192] The same recognition of context is evident in the judgment in *Grigoriades v. Greece*[193] where the applicant had been punished because of a letter he had written containing a vitriolic attack on the armed forces

---

[186] *Brandenburg v. Ohio*, 395 U.S. 444 (1969).

[187] *Abrams v. United States*, 250 U.S. 616–629 (1919). (Holmes J, dissenting).

[188] *Id.* at 630 (Holmes J, dissenting).

[189] *Sürek v. Turkey (No 1)*, *supra* n. 180 (partly dissenting opinion of Judge Palm).

[190] See *id.* (partly dissenting opinion of Judge Bonello). Judge Bonello went on to quote from the separate opinions of Justices Holmes and Brandeis noted in the text.

[191] See, e.g., *Baskeya & Okçguoglu v. Turkey*, *supra* n. 179, para. 65.

[192] *Gerger v. Turkey*, *supra* n. 179, para. 50.

[193] 25 Nov. 1997, Reports, 1997–VII 2575, 27 E.H.R.R. 667.

declaring them to be 'a criminal and terrorist apparatus'.[194] Since the letter had merely been delivered to an officer and not published generally, the Court regarded its possible effect on military discipline to be 'insignificant'.[195]

4. OFFENSIVE SPEECH

The Court's jurisprudence on the protection of defamatory speech, examined above, may be illustrative of its treatment of other categories of expression, which by their very utterance can be deemed incompatible with one or more of the goals listed in Article 10(2). One category which has taken on special prominence in recent years is expression denigrating ethnic groups. The European experience with racist regimes in the twentieth century has resulted in an acute sensitivity to the dangers of this kind of expression. International law has been developed to regulate such matters. The International Convention on the Elimination of All Forms of Racial Discrimination (1965)[196] has now been ratified by more than 150 countries. Article 4 of that Convention obliges states to make punishable 'all dissemination of ideas based on racial superiority or hatred' and to prohibit organizations 'which promote and incite racial discrimination'.[197] The Convention also states that these duties are to be carried out 'with due regard to the principles embodied in the Universal Declaration of Human Rights', and several member states entered declarations and reservations to Article 4 limiting their obligations to actions compatible with freedom of expression.[198]

The European Court of Human Rights has twice dealt with claims that expression punishable under laws limiting racist speech is protected under Article 10 and in each case it has found a violation. The Court's judgments make clear, however, that, in general, laws regulating 'hate speech' are compatible with the Convention. In *Jersild v. Denmark*[199] the applicant was a broadcaster who had produced and presented a public affairs television programme about a racist youth gang in Copenhagen. Part of the programme was an interview in which the subjects made crude and vicious remarks about blacks and other minorities. The applicant was convicted under a Danish Penal Code provision prohibiting the dissemination 'to a wide circle' of statements 'threatening, insulting or degrading a group of persons on account of their race, colour, national or ethnic origins or belief'. The Strasbourg Court stressed the 'vital importance of combating racial discrimination' and stated that the 'object and purpose pursued by the U.N. Convention are of great weight in determining whether the applicant's conviction . . . was "necessary" within the meaning of Article 10'. But the applicant's conduct of including those statements in a general news programme

---

[194] *Id.* para. 14.

[195] *Id.* para. 47.

[196] 5 I.L.M. 352 (1966).

[197] *Id.* at 355.

[198] A complete listing of parties and the character of their ratification may be found at http://www.unher.ch/tbs/doc.nsf.

[199] 23 Sept. 1994 (No. 298), 19 E.H.R.R. 1.

which could not itself be understood as intended to promote racism was protected. The Court, consistent with the cases already discussed, was especially mindful of the need to protect the press in its judgments as to the content and form of its presentation of information. 'The punishment of a journalist for assisting in the dissemination of statements made by another person in an interview would seriously hamper the contribution of the press to discussion of matters of public interest.'[200]

In *Lehideux & Isorni v. France*[201] the applicant published an advertisement in *Le Monde* consisting of a defence of the actions of Philippe Pétain, the head of the Vichy government during the second World War. They were prosecuted on the complaint of an organization of former members of the resistance under a statute making it unlawful to make a 'public defense of . . . the crimes of collaboration with the enemy'. Again the Court was at pains to make clear that the Convention offered no protection for expression glorifying racist and totalitarian policies. For example, it stated that the 'negation' of the Holocaust would be unprotected by Article 10[202] and that 'the justification of a pro-Nazi policy would not be allowed to engage the protection afforded by Article 10'.[203] Its finding of a violation was premised on a variety of particular circumstances. These included the fact that the state prosecutor had first declined to proceed, that the passing of time since the relevant events had reduced the risks associated with such assertions, and that less drastic civil remedies were not resorted to. It concluded that the criminal conviction (although a fine of only one franc had been levied) was 'disproportionate and as such unnecessary in a democratic society'.[204] Several dissenting judges were persuaded by the government's argument that the state should be accorded a wide margin of appreciation since it was dealing with a 'very specific field – the history of a state. That issue, by its very nature, was impossible to define objectively in European terms'. Therefore, there could be no 'uniform conception of the requirements' arising from Article 10.[205]

The Supreme Court of Canada has upheld criminal laws prohibiting the promotion of hatred against ethnic, racial or religious groups.[206] It held that although such laws restricted the freedom of expression protected by section 2(b) of the Charter of Rights and Freedom, they were 'demonstrably justified in a free and democratic society' and were permissible under section 1. Like the Strasbourg Court, the Supreme Court relied, in part, on Canada's obligation under the International Convention in calculating the importance of the law's objective.[207] It also agreed that the goals of suppressing

---

[200] *Id.* at paras. 30–5.

[201] 23 Sept. 1998, Reports, 1998–VII 2864.

[202] *Id.* at para. 47.

[203] More specifically the Court held that such expression would be 'removed from the protection of Article 10 by Article 17' (which states that nothing in the Convention gives anyone the 'right to engage in any activity or perform any act aimed at the destruction of any of the rights or freedoms set forth herein'). *Id.*

[204] *Id.* at para. 58.

[205] *Id.* at para. 43. See Joint dissenting opinion of Judges Foighel, Loizu and Freeland, para. 4.; dissenting opinion of Judge Morenilla, para. 2.

[206] *R. v. Keegstra* [1990] 3 S.C.R. 697.

[207] *Id.* at 747–55. The Court also cited a number of reports of the European Commission on Human Rights to the effect that the regulation of such speech was justified under Art. 10 (2). *Id.* at 753–4.

the harmful individual and social effects of hate propaganda should not be left to the ordinary process of public debate:

While holding that, over the long run, the human mind is repelled by blatant falsehood and seeks the good, it is too often true, in the short run, that emotion displaces reason and individuals perversely reject the demonstrations of truth put before them and foresake the good they know. The successes of modern advertising, the triumphs of impudent propaganda such at Hitler's, have qualified sharply our belief in the rationality of man. We know that under strain and pressure in times and of irritation and frustration the individual is swayed and even swept away by hysterical, emotional appeals. We act irresponsibly if we ignore the way in which emotion can drive reason from the field.[208]

The United States Supreme Court has upheld against a First Amendment challenge a state 'group libel' law prohibiting any publication of material adversely depicting any 'class of citizens of any race, color, creed or religion'. The Court analogized such expression to defamatory speech which has been held to be outside the protection of the First Amendment.[209] In 1992, however, the Court held unconstitutional a municipal ordinance making criminal the burning of crosses, the display of Nazi swastikas or other expressions or acts which could cause 'anger, alarm or resentment in others on the basis of race, color, creed, religion or gender'. The state court had characterized the law as limited to acts which created a risk of imminent violence. Such speech generally has been held by the Supreme Court to be outside the protection of the First Amendment. In this case, however, the Court held that the ordinance impermissibly distinguished between different categories of incitements to violence based on the content of the expression.[210]

Selectivity of this sort creates the possibility that the city is seeking to handicap the expression of particular ideas. . . . An ordinance not limited to the favored topics . . . would have precisely the same beneficial effect. In fact the only interest distinctively served by the content limitation is that of displaying the city council's special hostility towards the particular biases thus singled out. That is precisely what the First Amendment forbids[211]

A somewhat different category of expression has historically been regulated for very similar reasons—speech especially offensive to religious feelings. In two cases the Strasbourg Court has declined to find a violation of Article 10 when blasphemy laws were applied in one case to seize a film[212] and, in the second, to deny a licence to distribute a videotape.[213] In each case the expression at issue depicted religious subjects, including Jesus Christ, engaged in apparent sexual activities. The Court held that the regulation of this material was undertaken for the 'protection of the rights of others', particularly the 'right not to be insulted in their religious feelings'.[214] The Court held

---

[208] *Id.* at 747.

[209] *Beauharnais v. Illinois*, 343 U.S. 250 (1952).

[210] *R.A.V. v. City of Saint Paul*, 505 U.S. 377 (1992).

[211] *Id.* at 393, 396.

[212] *Otto-Preminger-Institut v. Austria*, 20 Sept. 1994 (No 295A), 19 E.H.R.R. 34, para. 48.

[213] *Wingrove v. United Kingdom*, 25 Nov. 1996, Reports, 1996–V 1937, 24 E.H.R.R. 1.

[214] *Otto-Preminger Institut*, *supra* n. 212, at para. 48.

that states were entitled to a wide margin of appreciation given the absence of a uniform approach to the subject in European states.[215] It stressed, moreover, that in neither case was the state attempting to suppress critical discussion of religious subjects. It was only the highly offensive manner of presentation that justified the state's actions.[216] In this respect the judgments may be contrasted with its earlier statement that 'Article 10 protects not only the substance of the ideas and information expressed but also the form in which they are conveyed'.[217] A fuller statement of the latter view was given in the judgment of the United States Supreme Court in *Cohen v. California* in which the profane expression of a political view was held protected by the First Amendment:

We cannot overlook the fact . . . that much linguistic expression serves a dual communicative function: it conveys not only ideas capable of relatively precise, detached explication, but otherwise inexpressible emotions as well. In fact, words are often chosen as much for their emotive as their cognitive force. We cannot sanction the view that the Constitution, while solicitous of the cognitive content of individual speech, has little or no regard for that emotive function which, practically speaking, may often be the more important element of the overall message sought to be communicated.[218]

5. COMMERCIAL SPEECH

A. MARKT INTERN AND BEERMANN V. GERMANY

Judgment of 20 November 1989
(No. 164), 12 E.H.R.R. 161

8. The first applicant, Markt Intern, is a publishing firm, whose registered office is at Dusseldorf. The second applicant, Mr. Klaus Beermann, is its editor-in-chief.

9. Markt Intern, which was founded and is run by journalists, seeks to defend the interests of small and medium-sized retail businesses against competition from large-scale distribution companies, such as supermarkets and mail-order firms. It provides the less powerful members of the retail trade with financial assistance in test cases, lobbies public authorities, political parties and trade associations on their behalf and has, on occasion, made proposals for legislation to the legislature.

However, its principal activity in their support is the publication of a number of bulletins aimed at specialised commercial sectors such as that of chemists and beauty product retailers. These are weekly news-sheets which provide information on developments in the market and in particular on the commercial practices of large-scale firms and their suppliers. They are printed by offset and

---

[215] *Id.* at paras. 49–50; *Wingrove, supra* n. 213, at paras. 57–8. See generally S. Ghandi & J. James, 'The English Law of Blasphemy and the European Convention on Human Rights' [1998] *Eur. Hum R.L. Rev.* 430.

[216] *Wingrove, supra* n. 213, at para. 60

[217] *Oberschlick v. Austria*, 23 May 1991 (No. 204), 19 E.H.R.R. 389.

[218] 403 U.S. 15, 25–6 (1971).

are sold by open subscription. They do not contain any advertising or any articles commissioned by the groups whose cause they espouse.

Markt Intern claims to be independent. Its income is derived exclusively from subscriptions. It also publishes other series of bulletins containing more general consumer information, such as 'Steuertip', 'Versicherungstip' and 'Flugtip', which are aimed respectively at taxpayers, holders of insurance policiescies and air travelers. . . .

11. On 20 November 1975 an article by Mr. Klaus Beermann appeared in the information bulletin for chemists and beauty product retailers. It described an incident involving an English mail-order firm, Cosmetic Club International ('the Club'), in the following terms:

> ' "I ordered the April beauty set . . . from Cosmetic Club International and paid for it, but returned it a few days later because I was not satisfied. Although the order form clearly and expressly stated that I was entitled to return the set if I was dissatisfied, and that I would be reimbursed, I have not yet seen a pfennig. There was also no reaction to my reminder of 18 June, in which I gave them until 26 June to reply." This is the angry report of Maria Lachau, a chemist at Celle, concerning the commercial practices of this English Cosmetic Club.
>
> On 4 November we telexed the manager of the Club, Doreen Miller, as follows: "Is this an isolated incident, or is this part of your official policy?" In its swift answer of the following day, the Club claimed to have no knowledge of the set returned by Mrs. Lachau or of her reminder of June. It promised however to carry out a prompt investigation of the case and to clarify the matter by contacting the chemist in Celle.
>
> Notwithstanding this provisional answer from Ettlingen, we would like to put the following question to all our colleagues in the chemist and beauty product trade; Have you had similar experiences to that of Mrs. Lachau with the Cosmetic Club? Do you know of similar cases? The question whether or not this incident is an isolated case or one of many is crucial for assessing the Club's policy.' . . .

15. . . . [The Club began proceedings against Markt Intern under several statutes, claiming the publication unfairly injured it. The Hamburg Regional Court gave judgment for the club.] The Court concluded that the applicants' conduct was punishable. Markt Intern ought not to have generalised from the case of Mrs. Lachau, the circumstances of which had not yet been clarified, and used it to formulate criticism of the Club. This method of proceeding could not be reconciled with the obligations incumbent on journalists. The defendants ought to have begun by taking their enquiries further, but not in the form of their request for information from the retailers. . . .

16. On 31 March 1977 the Hanseatic Court of Appeal found for the applicants and quashed the Regional Court's judgment. . . .

17. The Club appealed to the Federal Court of Justice which on 16 January 1980 set aside the Hanseatic Court of Appeal's judgment and, varying the Hamburg Regional Court's judgment, ordered the applicants to refrain from publishing in their information bulletin the statements disseminated by Markt Intern on 20 November 1975 in the form referred to by the Club in its heads of claim at first instance.

For each contravention, the applicants were liable to a fine or detention to be fixed by the court, but not exceeding 500,000 DM or six months, respectively.

18. The Federal Court of Justice based its judgment on section 1 of the [Unfair Competition Act of 1909], according to which:

> 'Any person who in the course of business commits, for purposes of competition, acts contrary to honest practices may be enjoined from further engaging in those acts and held liable in damages.' . . .

. . . Notwithstanding the lack of a competitive relationship between Markt Intern and the Club, the 1909 Act was said to apply because it was sufficient in this respect that the conduct in question was objectively advantageous to an undertaking, to the detriment of a competitor. That was exactly the aim pursued in this instance . . .

. . . Having regard in particular to the previous reports on the Club published by Markt Intern, the Court of Appeal ought to have found that the applicants had not merely provided information as an organ of the press, but had embraced the interests of the specialised chemists trade and, in order to promote those interests, had attacked the Club's commercial practices. The Court of Appeal ought consequently to have concluded that Markt Intern Intended to act in favour of the specialized trade and to the detriment of the Club. . . .

[In part of its judgment the Federal Court of Justice stated:] 'By their publication of the article complained of . . . , the respondents acted in a way contrary to honest practices within the meaning of section 1 of the 1909 Act. It is immaterial in this connection whether the statements regarding the witness Lachau (first head of claim) were true. The mere fact that a commercially damaging statement is true does not necessarily constitute a defence against a charge of acting in breach of the principles of fair competition. According to the rules of competition, such statements are acceptable only if they are based on sufficient grounds and if the manner and extent of the criticism in question remains within the limits of what is required by the situation because it is contrary to honest practices to engage in competition by making disparaging statements about competitors. In this case, at the time of the publication there was not sufficient cause to report this incident. The exact circumstances had not yet been clarified. The appellant in its reply had agreed to undertake an immediate investigation and to contact Mrs. Lachau in order to clarify the position. The respondents were aware that criticism of the appellant could not be fully justified before further clarification had been sought, as they themselves had described the appellant's reply as a provisional answer. Accordingly, they should have taken into consideration that any such premature publication of this incident was bound to have adverse effects on the appellant's business, because it gave the specialised retailers an effective argument which was capable of being used against the appellant with their mutual customers, and one which could be used even if the incident should turn out to be an isolated mishap from which no conclusion could be drawn as to the appellant's business policy. In these circumstances, at all events at the time of the publication, there were not sufficient grounds for reporting this isolated incident. Such conduct is, moreover, very unusual in business competition.' . . .

19. The applicants then appealed to the Federal Constitutional Court, claiming a violation of the freedom of the press. (Article 5(1) of the Constitution.)

Sitting as a committee of three judges, the Constitutional Court decided, on 9 February 1983, not to entertain the appeal. . . .

20. Mrs. Lachau was not the only customer to complain about the Club. Two others informed the applicants that they had encountered similar difficulties; the first approached them before the publication of the bulletin of 20 November 1975 and the second after it.

According to its own statements, the Club sold 157,929 beauty sets between 1 December 1974 and 30 November 1975. In 1975, 11,870 identifiable persons returned the sets and were reimbursed. . . .

22. The Commission declared the application admissible on 21 January 1986. In its report of 18 December 1987 (Article 31), it expressed the opinion, by twelve votes to one, that there had been a violation of Article 10. . . .

25. The Government primarily disputed the applicability of Article 10. Before the Court it

argued that if the case were examined under that provision, it would fall, by reason of the contents of the publication of 20 November 1975 and the nature of Markt Intern's activities, at the extreme limit of Article 10's field of application. The wording and the aims of the information bulletin in question showed that it was not intended to influence or mobilize public opinion, but to promote the economic interests of a given group of undertakings. In the Government's view, such action fell within the scope of the freedom to conduct business and engage in competition, which is not protected by the Convention.

The applicants did not deny that they defended the interests of the specialised retail trade. However, they asserted that Markt Intern did not intervene directly in the process of supply and demand. The undertaking depended exclusively on its subscribers and made every effort, as was proper, to satisfy the requirements of its readers, whose preoccupation the mainstream press neglected. To restrict the freedom of expression to news items of a political or cultural nature would result in depriving a large proportion of the press of any protection. . . .

26. . . . It is clear that the article in question was addressed to a limited circle of trades people and did not directly concern the public as a whole; however, it conveyed information of a commercial nature. Such information cannot be excluded from the scope of Article 10(1) which does not apply solely to certain types of information or ideas or forms of expression. . . .

31. . . . According to the actual wording of the judgment of 16 January 1980, the article in question was liable to raise unjustified suspicions concerning the commercial policy of the Club and thus damage its business. The Court finds that the interference was intended to protect the reputation and the rights of others, legitimate aims under Article 10(2). . . .

32. The applicants argued that the injunction in question could not be regarded as 'necessary in a democratic society'. The Commission agreed with this view.

The Government, however, disputed it. In its view, the article published on 20 November 1975 did not contribute to a debate of interest to the general public, but was part of an unlawful competitive strategy aimed at ridding the beauty products market of an awkward competitor for specialist retailers. The writer of the article had sought, by adopting aggressive tactics and acting in a way contrary to usual practice, to promote the competitiveness of those retailers. The Federal Court of Justice and the Federal Constitutional Court had ruled in accordance with well established case law, having first weighed all the interests at stake.

In addition, in the field of competition, States enjoyed a wide discretion in order to take account of the specific situation in the national market and, in this case, the national notion of good faith in business. The statements made 'for purposes of competition' fell outside the basic nucleus protected by freedom of expression and received a lower level of protection than other 'ideas' or 'information'.

33. The Court has consistently held that the Contracting States have a certain margin of appreciation in assessing the existence and extent of the necessity of an interference, but this margin is subject to a European supervision as regards both the legislation and the decisions applying it, even those given by an independent court. Such a margin of appreciation is essential in commercial matters and, in particular, in an area as complex and fluctuating as that of unfair competition. Otherwise, the European Court of Human Rights would have to undertake a re-examination of the facts and all the circumstances of each case. The Court must confine its review to the question whether the measures taken on the national level are justifiable in principle and proportionate. . . .

34. . . . The national courts did weigh the competing interests at stake. In their judgments of 2

July 1976 and 31 March 1977, the Hamburg Regional Court and the Hanseatic Court of Appeal explicitly referred to the right to freedom of expression and of the press, as guaranteed by Article 5 of the Constitution and the Federal Constitutional Court, in its decision of 9 February 1983, considered the case under that provision. The Federal Court of Justice based its judgment of 16 January 1980 on the premature nature of the publication in question and on the lack of sufficient grounds for publicising in the information bulletin an isolated incident and in doing so took into consideration the rights and legal interests meriting protection.

35.　In a market economy an undertaking which seeks to set up a business inevitably exposes itself to close scrutiny of its practices by its competitors. Its commercial strategy and the manner in which it honours its commitments may give rise to criticism on the part of consumers and the specialised press. In order to carry out this task, the specialised press must be able to disclose facts which could be of interest to its readers and thereby contribute to the openness of business activities.

However, even the publication of items which are true and describe real events may under certain circumstances be prohibited: the obligation to respect the privacy of others or the duty to respect the confidentiality of certain commercial information are examples. In addition, a correct statement can be and often is qualified by additional remarks, by value judgments, by suppositions or even insinuations. It must also be recognised that an isolated incident can give the false impression that the incident is evidence of a general practice. All these factors can legitimately contribute to the assessment of statements made in a commercial context, and it is primarily for the national courts to decide which statements are permissible and which are not.

36.　In the present case, the article was written in a commercial context; Markt Intern was not itself a competitor in relation to the Club but it intended—legitimately—to protect the interests of chemists and beauty product retailers. The article itself undoubtedly contained some true state-ments, but it also expressed doubts about the reliability of the Club, and it asked the readers to report 'similar experiences' at a moment when the Club had promised to carry out a prompt investigation of the one reported case.

According to the Federal Court of Justice, there was not sufficient cause to report the incident at the time of the publication. The Club had agreed to undertake an immediate investigation in order to clarify the position. Furthermore, the applicants had been aware that criticisms of the Club could not be fully justified before further clarification had been sought, as they themselves had described the reply of the Club as a provisional answer. In the opinion of the Federal Court they should therefore have taken it into consideration that any such premature publication of the incident was bound to have adverse effects on the Club's business because it gave the specialized retailers an effective argument capable of being used against the Club and their customers, and one which could be used even if the incident should turn out to be an isolated mishap from which no conclusion could be drawn as to the Club's business policy.

37.　In the light of these findings and having regard to the duties and responsibilities attaching to the freedoms guaranteed by Article 10, it cannot be said that the final decision of the Federal Court of Justice—confirmed from the constitutional point of view by the Federal Constitutional Court—went beyond the margin of appreciation left to the national authorities. It is obvious that opinions may differ as to whether the Federal Court's reaction was appropriate or whether the statements made in the specific case by Markt Intern should be permitted or tolerated. However, the European Court of Human Rights should not substitute its own evaluation for that of the national courts in the instant case, where those courts, on reasonable grounds, had considered the restrictions to be necessary . . .

[The Court held by nine votes to nine with the casting vote of the President, that there had been no violation of Article 10.]

Joint Dissenting Opinion of Judges Gölcüklü, Pettiti, Russo, Spielmann, De Meyer, Carrillo, Salcedo and Valticos: . . .

It is just as important to guarantee the freedom of expression in relation to the practices of a commercial undertaking as it is in relation to the conduct of a head of government, which was at issue in the *Lingens Case*.[219] Similarly the right thereto must be able to be exercised as much in the interests of the purchasers of beauty products as in those of the owners of sick animals, the interests at stake in the *Barthold Case*.[220] In fact, freedom of expression serves, above all, the general interest.

The fact that a person defends a given interest, whether it is an economic interest or any other interest, does not, moreover, deprive him of the benefit of freedom of expression.

In order to ensure the openness of business activities, it must be possible to disseminate freely information and ideas concerning the products and services proposed to consumers. Consumers, who are exposed to highly effective distribution techniques and to advertising which is frequently less than objective, deserve, for their part too, to be protected, as indeed do retailers.

In this case, the applicants had related an incident which in fact occurred, as has not been contested (Moreover, it was not an 'isolated' case, because in 1975 the undertaking in question had to reimburse 11,870 of its clients, and requested retailers to supply them with additional information.) They had exercised in an entirely normal manner their basic right to freedom of expression.

This right was, therefore, violated in their regard by the contested measures . . .

We find the reasoning set out therein with regard to the 'margin of appreciation' of States a cause for serious concern. As is shown by the result to which it leads in this case, it has the effect in practice of considerably restricting the freedom of expression in commercial matters . . .

[The individual dissenting opinions of Judges Pettiti and DeMeyer are omitted.]

Dissenting Opinion of Judge Martens, approved by Judge Macdonald: . . .

4. The law on unfair competition governs the relationships between competitors on the market. It is based on the assumption that in engaging in competition the competitors seek only to serve their own interests, while attempting to harm those of others. This is why (as the Federal Court notes in its judgment) the German law on unfair competition prohibits persons from engaging in competition by making denigrating statements about their competitors. It is permissible for a competitor to criticise another publicly only if he has sufficient reasons for so doing and if the nature and scope of his criticism remain within the limits required by the situation. In this field, the prohibition on publishing criticism is therefore the norm and it falls to the person who takes the risk of publishing such criticism to show that there were sufficient grounds for his criticism and that it remains within the strictest limits. In considering whether this proof has been furnished, the court weights up only the interests of the two competitors.

---

[219] Reproduced in Section (B)(1) (footnote by editors).
[220] Discussed in the notes following (footnote by editors).

In the field of freedom of expression the converse is true. In this field the basic assumption is that this right is used to serve the general interest, in particular as far as the press is concerned, and that is why in this context the freedom to criticise is the norm. Thus in this field it falls to the person who alleges that the criticism is not acceptable to prove that his claim is well-founded. In determining whether he has done so, the court must weight up the general interest, on the one hand, and the individual interests of the party who claims to have been injured, on the other.

5. It follows that to classify under the law on unfair competition the question whether an article published by an organ of the press is acceptable is to place that organ of the press in a legal position which is fundamentally different from that to which it is entitled under Article 10 of the Convention and one which is clearly unfavourable to it. That is why, in my view, for that organ of the press, such a classification constitutes a considerable restriction on the exercise of the freedoms guaranteed to it under Article 10. It should therefore be asked whether it can be necessary in a democratic society to restrict the rights and fundamental freedoms of an organ of the press in this way solely because that organ has espoused the cause of specific economic interests, namely those of a particular sector of a specialised trade. I am in no doubt that this question must be answered in the negative. This is clear from the fact that, as far as I know, such a rule extending the scope of the law on unfair competition to the detriment of freedom of the press is unknown in the other member states of the Council of Europe, and rightly so because, in certain respects, all newspapers may be regarded as partisan, having espoused the cause of certain specific interests.

6. In my view, it follows from the foregoing that the Court ought to have considered that in this instance it had to examine a case in which the assessment of the national authorities suffered from a fundamental defect and that, accordingly, it ought itself to have determined whether the interference was necessary in a democratic society. Indeed, in such circumstances the margin of appreciation plays no role because this margin cannot justify assessments incompatible with the freedoms guaranteed under the Convention. I emphasize this point because, for my part, I do not deny that in the field of freedom of expression the European Court can limit the scope of its review by leaving the States a certain margin of appreciation.

7. In this context I should like to make clear that I cannot agree, either, with the opinion of the Court in so far as it considers that in this instance, in order to determine whether the interference was proportionate, it is necessary to weigh up the requirements of the protection of the reputation and rights of others, on the one hand, and the publication of the information in question on the other.

In my view—and here too I find myself in agreement with the joint dissenting opinion—it is necessary to ask whether it was established convincingly that the private interests of the Club were more important than the general interest, in accordance with which not only the specialised reader but also the public as a whole should have been able to acquaint themselves with facts having a certain importance in the context of the struggle of small and mediumsized retail undertakings against the large-scale distribution companies. In answering this question, I, like the authors of the joint dissenting opinion, reach the conclusion that the reply must be negative. Like the Court, I take into account the fact that in a market economy an undertaking which seeks to set up a business inevitably exposes itself to close scrutiny of its practices. That is why the Club, which was in that situation, cannot in principle complain that the specialised press, which has given itself the task of defending the interests of its competitors on that market, analyses its commercial strategy and publishes its criticisms thereof. Such criticism contributes, as the Court stressed, to the openness of business activities. Since the freedom of expression also applies to 'statements' which hurt, care should be taken not to find such criticism unacceptable too quickly simply because it harms the undertaking criticized. In this instance, it cannot be denied that the article published by Markt Intern is unfavourable to the Club and reveals a very critical attitude in the latter's regard. On the other hand, it reported an incident which, as has not been contested, in fact occurred and it did not purport to offer a definitive assessment of the Club's commercial practices, but invited retailers to supply additional information. For my part, I am not convinced that it is truly necessary to prohibit such an article in a democratic society. . . .

B. COMPARISONS

There are at least two reasons why expressions directed at commercial or economic interests ought to receive less protection than speech involving political decision-making. First, as a matter of social policy, it might be argued that regulation of such speech poses less of a danger to a central value of the constitutional guarantee, its relation to the democratic process. Second, there is a pervasive and well-established practice of economic regulation which necessarily includes restriction of speech related to economic transactions. In *Markt Intern* the Court accommodated these concerns by espousing a particularly deferential version of the margin of appreciation, noting that, at least with respect to matters of unfair competition, the Court is in a poor position to evaluate decisions in such a 'complex and fluctuating' area. Its general description of the margin of appreciation is consistent with that put forth in other cases. But the judgment insists that, in these circumstances, the European Court of Human Rights 'should not substitute its own evaluation for that of the national Courts . . . when those courts on reasonable grounds had considered the restriction to be necessary'.

In a subsequent case, *Casado Coca v. Spain*,[221] the Strasbourg Court relied on *Markt Intern* in holding that an almost total ban on lawyer advertising did not violate Article 10. In its formulation of the proper standards, however, it adopted language somewhat less deferential to the regulating state. It reiterated that a wide margin of appreciation was appropriate in the 'complex and fluctuating area of unfair competition', and that advertising may sometimes properly be restricted to prevent unfair competition. It went on, however, to state that '[a]ny such restrictions must . . . be closely scrutinized by the court which must weigh the requirements of those particular features against the advertising in question'.[222] In the case at hand, the Court noted the special status and responsibility of the legal profession and the fact that the regulation of lawyer advertising varied greatly in the various states of the members of the Council of Europe. Only in light of its independent evaluation of these factors, did the Court conclude that 'the Bar authorities and the country's courts are in a better

---

[221] 24 Feb. 1994 (No. 285), 18 E.H.R.R. 1.
[222] *Id.* at para. 51.

position than an international court to determine how at a given time the right balance can be struck between the various interests involved'.[223]

In American constitutional law, 'commercial speech', that is speech merely proposing a commercial transaction, was once held to be wholly outside the scope of the First Amendment.[224] More recently, however, it has been found to enjoy some constitutional protection. As was the case in *Markt Intern*, however, regulation of such speech has been subject to less demanding scrutiny than political expression. The justification for applying the First Amendment to this category of expression was summarized in *Virginia State Board of Pharmacy v. Virginia Citizens Consumer Council*[225] in which a statute prohibiting the advertisement of prices of prescription drugs was held unconstitutional:

As to the particular consumer's interest in the free flow of commercial information, that interest may be as keen, if not keener by far, than his interest in the day's most urgent political debate. Appellees' case in this respect is a convincing one. Those whom the suppression of prescription drug price information hits the hardest are the poor, the sick, and particularly the aged. A disproportionate amount of their income tends to be spent on prescription drugs; yet they are the least able to learn, by shopping from pharmacist to pharmacist, where their scarce dollars are best spent. When drug prices vary as strikingly as they do, information as to who is charging what becomes more than a convenience. It could mean the alleviation of physical pain or the enjoyment of basic necessities. . . .

. . . Advertising, however tasteless and excessive it sometimes may seem, is nonetheless dissemination of information as to who is producing and selling what product, for what reason, and at what price. So long as we preserve a predominantly free enterprise economy, the allocation of our resources in large measure will be made through numerous private economic decisions. It is a matter of public interest that those discussions, in the aggregate, be intelligent and well informed. To this end, the free flow of commercial information is indispensable . . . And, if it is indispensable to the proper allocation of resources in a free enterprise system, it is also indispensable to the formation of intelligent opinions as to how that system ought to be regulated or altered. Therefore, even if the First Amendment were thought to be primarily an instrument to enlighten public decision making in a democracy, we could not say that the free flow of information does not serve that goal.

Still, the Supreme Court, recognizing the public interest in regulation of commercial advertising, has formulated a somewhat more relaxed test for its validity. This was summed up in a 'four-part' examination expounded in *Central Hudson Gas and Electric Corp. v. Public Service Commission*:[226]

---

[223] *Id.* at paras. 50–51. The Court also failed to cite the highly deferential language from *Market Intern* in its judgment in *Jacubowski v. Germany*, 23 June 1994 (No. 291–A), 19 E.H.R.R. 64, in which it held there was no violation of Article 10 when the applicant was ordered to desist from circulating material critical of his former employer. The applicant who was hoping to start a new business had distributed the information to potential clients. 'The Court confined itself to the question of "whether the measures taken at the national level [were] justifiable in principle and proportionate".'

[224] *Valentine v. Chrestensen*, 316 U.S. 52 (1942).

[225] 425 U.S. 748, 763–5 (1976).

[226] 447 U. S. 557, 566 (1980).

At the outset we must determine whether the expression is protected by the First Amendment. For commercial speech to come within that provision, it at least must concern lawful activity and not be misleading. Next we ask whether the asserted governmental interest is substantial. If both inquiries yield positive answers, we must determine whether the regulation directly advances the governmental interest asserted, and whether it is not more extensive than is necessary to serve that interest.

The United States Supreme Court has also held that the First Amendment limits the extent to which states may restrict the advertising of attorneys.[227] It has prohibited restriction of non-fraudulent, non-coercive advertising. Thus while states have been held to have authority to limit in-person solicitation, at least in certain circumstances[228] solicitation by letter has been held to be constitutionally protected.[229] The American doctrine on this question should be compared to the European Court's holding in *Casado Coca*, discussed above, in which a sweeping ban on almost all lawyer advertising was held to be compatible with Article 10.

In *Ford v. Quebec (Attorney General)*[230] the Supreme Court of Canada held invalid a law prohibiting the use of languages other than French on commercial signs. It rejected an argument that commercial expression was not included in the protection of Section 2(b) of the Canadian Charter of Rights and Freedoms. It noted the 'significant role' such expression plays in 'enabling individuals to make informed economic choices, an important aspect of individual self-fulfillment and personal autonomy'. It declined, however, to discuss 'the distinct issue of the permissible scope of regulation of advertising (for example to protect consumers) when different governmental interests come into play, particularly when assessing the reasonableness of limits on such commercial expression pursuant to Section 1 of the Canadian Charter'. Indeed, the next year, in *Irwin Toy Ltd. v. Quebec (Attorney-General)*[231] it upheld, under Section 1, a sweeping ban on advertising directed at children, holding it was justifiable under the *Oakes* test, discussed above. In a subsequent five to four decision, however, the Court held invalid a near total ban on tobacco advertising. In explaining the reasons for her judgment, Justice Mclachlin disagreed with the claim that advertising was only entitled to a reduced degree of protection because it was motivated by a desire for profit: '[b]ook sellers, newspaper owners, toy sellers—all are linked by their shareholders' desire to profit from the corporation's business activity, whether the expression sought to be protected is closely linked to the core values of freedom of expression or not'.[232]

---

[227] *Bates v. State Bar*, 433 U. S. 350 (1977).

[228] *Ohralik v. Ohio State Bar*, 436 U. S. 477 (1978). But see *Edenfield v. Fane*, 507 U. S. 761 (1993) (holding unconstitutional a ban on in-person solicitation by certified public accountants).

[229] *Shapero v. Kentucky Bar Assoc.* 486 U. S. 466 (1988). But see *Florida Bar v. Went For It Inc.*, 515 U. S. 618 (1995) (upholding a prohibition on mail solicitation by lawyers targeted specifically at accident victims within 30 days after an accidents).

[230] [1988] 2 S. C. R. 712.

[231] [1989] 1 S. C. R. 927.

[232] *RJR-MacDonald Inc. v. Canada (Attorney-General)* [1995] 3 S.C.R. 199, para. 171. Maclachlan J. was responding to these remarks in the dissenting reasons of LaForest J:

The English Court of Appeal has explicitly upheld a ban on advertising by medical practitioners. It held that the rules formulated by the General Medical Council were a proper exercise of the power conferred on it by statute to provide advice and guidance on questions of ethical professional conduct. The litigant in that case had been refused permission to publish factual, non-promotional information about his practice in the general press. The Court held that the restriction was a reasonable regulation in light of the policy to discourage commercial competition among doctors, since such competition might impair the ability of patients to choose physicians on sensible grounds. The Court rejected an argument that it should interpret the governing statute to allow only such restrictions as are consistent with Article 10 of the European Convention on Human Rights.[233]

While the European Court of Human Rights, as illustrated by its judgment in *Markt Intern*, is reluctant to find a violation of the Convention when mere commercial speech is at issue, the European Court of Justice of the European Union has required that expression have a commercial aspect if its restriction is to raise a question under the mainly economic treaties under which it operates. The contrast is illustrated by the reactions of these courts to an Irish prohibition on publication in Ireland of information on abortion services available in the United Kingdom. In *Society for the Protection of Unborn Children v. Grogan*[234] the Court of Justice refused to find this prohibition incompatible with European Community law. In the particular case in controversy, the information had been provided by student groups unrelated to the clinics whose services were described. Therefore, it was 'not distributed on behalf of an economic operator established in another member state. On the contrary, the information constitutes a manifestation of freedom of expression and of the freedom to impart and receive information, which is independent of the economic activity carried on by clinics established in another member-state'.[235] The link between the information distributed and the economic activity was, thus, 'too tenuous' to regard the Irish prohibition as a restriction on the freedom to supply services guaranteed by Article 59 of the Treaty of Rome. Although the Court agreed that it also had the power, in a proper case, to assess the compatibility of national legislation with fundamental rights, and particularly those laid down in the European Convention on Human Rights, it could do so only with respect to legislation within the scope of Community law. The absence of an economic aspect to the case at hand, therefore, also precluded the Court from pronouncing on the application of Article 10 of the

---

It must be kept in mind that tobacco advertising serves no political, scientific or artistic ends; nor does it promote participation in the political process. Rather, its sole purpose is to inform consumers about, and promote the use of, a product that is harmful, and often fatal, to the consumers who use it. The main, if not sole, motivation for this advertising is, of course, profit.

Id. at para. 75.

[233] *R. v. General Medical Council. ex parte Colman* [1990] 1 All E.R. 489 C.A.
[234] [1991] 3 C.M.L.R. 849.
[235] *Id.* at 891.

Convention.[236] When the same restriction came before the Court of Human Rights in *Open Door Counselling and Dublin Woman v. Ireland*,[237] a violation of Article 10 was found. The information suppressed was, the Court noted, information about services lawful in Britain, access to which by Irish women was not contrary to Irish law. The restriction on this information created a risk to the health of women seeking abortions. Notwithstanding the 'moral implications', this limitation 'call[ed] for careful scrutiny . . . as to their conformity with the tenets of democratic society'.[238] Note that the absence of an economic motivation, which was fatal to the claim in the Court of Justice, saved the claim in Strasbourg from the very lenient standard of *Markt Intern*.

Although identification of regulated speech as commercial in character may alter the treatment of the restriction under the Convention, Community Law, or a domestic constitution, it is often not at all clear when a statement should be designated as 'commercial' rather than 'political'. In *Barthold v. Germany*[239] the applicant, a veterinarian, was subject to professional discipline for making statements, quoted in a newspaper article, about the lack of night service by veterinarians in Hamburg. The German court held that the applicant had violated established standards against professional advertising. Since the restriction imposed on the applicant prevented him from expressing opinions and imparting information on 'a topic of general interest', the European Court of Human Rights held that Article 10 applied without 'needing to inquire . . . whether or not advertising as such comes within [its] scope'. Since, the Court found, the commercial and professional aspects to the applicant's statements were 'altogether secondary, having regard to the principal content of the article and to the nature of the issue being put to the public at large', the German Court did not 'achieve a fair balance between the two interests at stake'. The judgment of the national courts, the Court felt, risked 'discouraging members of the liberal professions from contributing to debate on topics affecting the life of the community if ever there is the slightest likelihood of these utterances being treated as entailing, to some degree, an advertising effect.[240] Even the regulation of matters as far removed from

---

[236] See also Case C–299/95 *Kremzow v. Austria* [1997] 3 C.M.L.R. 1289, where the European Court of Justice considered a reference from the Austrian courts. Those courts were dealing with a claim for reduced sentence and for compensation by a criminal defendant whose sentence had already been held incompatible with Art. 6 of the Convention by the European Court of Human Rights (21 Sept. 1993 (No. 268B), 17 E.H.R.R. 322). The reference sought a ruling on whether national courts were bound by judgments of the European Court of Human Rights. The European Court of Justice noted that the convictions at issue, for murder and illegal possession of firearms, were for violations of law not fairly within the field of application of European Community law. While the detention following conviction did restrain the 'free movement' of the defendant, this did not create a sufficient connection with Community law to support the jurisdiction of the Court.

[237] 29 Oct. 1992 (No. 246), 15 E.H.R.R. 244.

[238] *Id.* at para. 72.

[239] 25 Mar. 1985 (No. 90), 7 E.H.R.R. 383.

[240] 20 Nov. 1989 (No. 165), 12 E.H.R.R. 161, para. 37. The problem of characterizing speech also arose in *Jacubowski v. Germany*, Judgment of 23 June 1994 (No. 291–A), 19 E.H.R.R. 64, in which the Court found no violation where the applicant was ordered to stop circulating information critical of his former employer. Although the applicant's action was in response to public statements of the employer commenting adversely on the applicant's competence as a manager, the Court treated the case mainly as one

issues of public policy as a highly eccentric commentary on the safety of microwave ovens has been held properly examinable on a stricter standard then that applied to commercial speech. In *Hertel v. Switzerland*,[241] the Court held such expression was not 'purely "commercial" statements' but was participation in a debate affecting the general interest, for example, over public health.[242] 'It matters little that [the] opinion is a minority one and may appear to be devoid of merit since, in a sphere in which it is unlikely that any certainty exists, it would be particularly unreasonable to restrict freedom of expression only to generally accepted ideas.'[243]

In United States constitutional law, the extension of First Amendment protection to commercial speech was, prompted, in part, by a recognition that the categories of commercial and political speech could not be obviously distinguished. In *Bigelow v. Virginia*[244] the U.S. Supreme Court considered a state statute prohibiting the publication of an advertisement for a 'profit-making' abortion clinic:

The advertisement published in appellant's newspaper did more than simply propose a commercial transaction. It contained factual material of clear 'public interest'. Portions of its message, most prominently the lines, 'Abortions are now legal in New York. There are no residency requirements', involve the exercise of the freedom of communicating information and disseminating opinion.

Viewed in its entirety, the advertisement conveyed information of potential interest and value to a diverse audience—not only to readers possibly in need of the services offered, but also to those with a general curiosity about, or genuine interest in, the subject matter or the law of another State and its development, and to readers seeking reform in Virginia. The mere existence of the Women's Pavilion in New York City, with the possibility of its being typical of other organizations there, and the availability of the services offered, were not unnewsworthy. Also, the activity advertised pertained to constitutional interests. *See Roe v. Wade*, 410 U.S. 113 (1973), and *Doe v. Bolton*, 410 U.S. 179 (1973). Thus, in this case, appellant's First Amendment interests coincided with the constitutional interests of the general public. . . .

Advertising, like all public expression, may be subject to reasonable regulation that serves a legitimate public interest. To the extent that commercial activity is subject to regulation, the relationship of speech to that activity may be one factor, among others, to be considered in weighing the First Amendment interest against the governmental interest alleged. Advertising is not thereby stripped of all First Amendment protection. The relationship of speech to the marketplace of products or of services does not make it valueless in the marketplace of ideas.

The Court has stated that 'a State cannot foreclose the exercise of constitutional rights by mere labels'. Regardless of the particular label asserted by the State—whether it calls speech 'commercial' or 'commercial advertising' or 'solicitation'—a court may not escape the task of assess-

---

where the applicant was seeking a competitive advantage in connection with the initiation of his own business. *Id.* at para. 28. Three dissenting judges, on the other hand, emphasized that the applicant 'had an obvious and pressing interest in trying to protect his impugned reputation without delay' and that '[t] here was a parallel public interest to learn whether the applicant would defend himself against his former employer'. *Id.* (dissenting opinion of Judges Walsh, McDonald and Wildhaber).

[241] 25 Aug. 1998, Reports, 1998–VI 2298, 28 E.H.R.R. 534.
[242] *Id.* at para. 47.
[243] *Id.* at para. 50.
[244] 421 U.S. 809 (1977).

ing the First Amendment interest at stake and weighing it against the public interest allegedly served by the regulation. . . .

6. ARTISTIC EXPRESSION

While questions of freedom of expression are usually associated with restrictions on political speech, they may also arise in connection with attempts to suppress what the state views as offensive artistic or literary works. 'Beauty has constitutional status too, [and] the life of the imagination is as important to the human adult as the life of the intellect'.[245] As the *Handyside* and *Markt Intern* cases indicate, the European Court has readily applied Article 10 to speech which is not 'political' in any obvious sense. Indeed, it has explicitly held that the protection of Article 10 extends to 'artistic expression':

The applicants indisputably exercised their right to freedom of expression—the first applicant by painting and then exhibiting the works in question, and the nine others by giving him the opportunity to show them in public at the 'Fri-Art 81' exhibition they had mounted.

Admittedly, Article 10 does not specify that freedom of artistic expression, in issue here, comes within its ambit; but neither, on the other hand, does it distinguish between the various forms of expression. As those appearing before the Court all acknowledged, it includes freedom of artistic expression—notably within freedom to receive and impart information and ideas—which affords the opportunity to take part in the public exchange of cultural, political and social information and ideas of all kinds. Confirmation, if any were needed, that this interpretation is correct, is provided by the second sentence of paragraph 1 of Article 10, which refers to 'broadcasting, television or cinema enterprises', media whose activities extend to the field of art. Confirmation that the concept of freedom of expression is such as to include artistic expression is also to be found in Article 19 §2 of the International Covenant on Civil and Political Rights, which specifically includes within the right of freedom of expression information and ideas 'in the form of art'.[246]

Notwithstanding suggestions by some commentators that the First Amendment ought to be restricted in its coverage to political speech[247] the Supreme Court of the United States has reviewed regularly restrictions on artistic expression under the First Amendment. In *Miller v. California*, discussed above,[248] the Court stated explicitly that the Constitution 'protects words which, taken as a whole, have serious literary, artistic or in political value'. Similarly, in *R. v. Butler*[249] the Canadian Supreme Court hald that the guarantee of Section 2(b) of the Canadian Charter of Rights and Freedoms applies not only to written words but to films, even films portraying solely physical activity, since 'the creation of the film is attempting to convey some meaning'.

[245] Kalven, '*The Metaphysics of the Law of Obscenity*,' 1960 *Sup. Ct. Rev.* 1 15–16. *See also* Nahmod, 'Artistic Expression and Aesthetic Theory: The Beautiful, The Sublime and the First Amendment, [1987] *Wisc. L. Rev.* 221.

[246] *Müller and Others v. Switzerland*, 24 May 1988 (No. 130), 13 E.H.R.R. 212, para. 27.

[247] *See* Bork, 'Neutral Principles and Some First Amendment Problems', (1971) 47 *Ind. L.J.* 1.

[248] Discussed in Section (A)(2)(d).

[249] [1992] 1 S.C.R. 452.

The actual character of the protection extended to artistic expression, however, may be different from that accorded political speech. Public regulation of such work typically stems from a desire to suppress material that offends social standards of decency, often standards relating to the proper scope of public discussion or depiction of sexual activity. As has already been discussed, American constitutional law deals with the issue by removing a category of 'obscene' speech from the ambit of First Amendment protection. The case law of the European Convention and the Canadian Charter accord such expression *prima facie* protection, but acknowledge the possibility of regulation justified by other pressing social needs. As we have already seen, the justification invoked may well alter the strictness with which the challenged material is reviewed.[250]

7. BROADCASTING

Article 10 makes special reference to the right of states to license 'broadcasting television or cinema enterprises'. Significantly, this caveat is contained in paragraph 1, rather than being included, or merely left by implication, in paragraph 2, which specifies the various justifications for limitation of the right. This placement implies that broadcast licensing should not be considered an infringement of the right of expression at all.[251]

The Court has, however, held to the contrary. In *Groppera Radio AG and Others v. Switzerland*,[252] the Court held that no violation of Article 10 occurred when Swiss authorities prohibited the re-transmission by Swiss cable transmission companies of the signal from a radio station broadcasting from Italy but aimed exclusively at a Swiss audience. The direct broadcasts of the station were in violation of the International Telecommunications Convention to which Switzerland and Italy were both parties.

Although the Court found no violation, it did not rely solely on the third sentence of Article 10(1) in so doing. Rather, it held that the exception to freedom of expression in that sentence was 'of limited scope'. It was directed at licensing systems dealing with 'the way in which broadcasting is organized in [the individual states'] territories, particularly in its technical aspects. It does not, however, provide that licensing measures shall not otherwise be subject to the requirements of paragraph 2, for that would lead to a result contrary to the object and purpose of Article 10 taken as a whole'. Therefore, although the Court found the measure in question was part of a proper licensing scheme, it proceeded to examine it under paragraph 2. The Court concluded that the prohibition was necessary for the 'prevention of disorder', which might follow from the unregulated use of the broadcasting spectrum, and for the 'protection of others' in allowing for the fair allocation of the limited number of broadcast frequencies, both nationally and internationally.

[250] *See* Section B(2)(A).
[251] *See* P. van Dijk & G.J.H. van Hoof, *Theory and Practice of the European Convention on Human Rights*, 419 (1990).
[252] 28 Mar. 1990 (No. 173), 12 E.H.R.R. 321.

In a concurring opinion, Judge Pinheiro Farinha argued that the Court's approach made the third sentence of paragraph 1 redundant. Under that approach, every licensing measure, like any other restriction on speech, will have to satisfy the criteria of paragraph 2. He would have made the holding 'solely on the basis of the third sentence'. Indeed, in *Autronic AG v. Switzerland*,[253] the Court found that Switzerland's prohibition of a company's reception of Russian satellite transmissions intended for the general public, could not be justified under paragraph 2 and, therefore, violated the Convention. The Court found that international radio agreements did not preclude such reception and, since the signal was intended for the general public in Russia, no issue of privacy was involved. The Court gave no indication that the third sentence of paragraph 1 called for a more generous view of the national regulation. On the contrary, it cited its established case law in non-broadcasting contexts that, when the rights of Article 10 were involved, the Court's supervision of a state's margin of appreciation 'must be strict' and the 'necessity for restricting [those rights] must be convincingly established'.

Subsequently, in *Informationsverein Lentia v. Austria*,[254] the Court further clarified its view of the relationship between the third sentence of paragraph (1) and paragraph (2). The authorization of broadcast licensing by a state might be:

made conditional on [technical or] other considerations including such matters as the nature and objectives of a proposed station, its potential audience at national, regional or local level, the rights and needs of a specific audience and the obligations deriving from international legal instruments . . . This may lead to interferences whose aims will be legitimate under the third sentence of paragraph 1, even though they do not correspond to any of the aims set out in paragraph 2.[255]

Thus, the licensing provision was held to expand the purposes for which broadcasting could be regulated through the licence procedure beyond those of paragraph 2, but the scheme would still have to satisfy the other requirements of paragraph 2, namely that the restriction be 'prescribed by law' and be 'necessary in a democratic society'.[256]

Using this model, the Court determined that Article 10 was violated when Austria legislated a public monopoly on broadcasting. The critical question for the Court was whether such a monopoly was necessary for one of the permissible objectives of a licensing scheme. The Court concluded that it was not necessary to guarantee objective impartiality, balance and diversity in broadcasting. The Court noted that most other European countries achieved this objective not by restricting licences but through the grant of numerous competitive broadcasting licences subject to specified criteria.[257] The Austrian monopoly was an extreme example of the pervasive control

---

[253] 22 May 1990 (No. 178), 12 E.H.R.R. 485.

[254] 24 Nov. 1993 (No. 276), 17 E.H.R.R. 93.

[255] *Id.* at para. 32.

[256] *Id.*

[257] *Id.* at para. 39. The Court's holding was made notwithstanding the conceded fact that government monopoly of broadcasting was common among the signatory states at the time of the drafting of the Convention. *Id.* at para. 36.

and regulation of broadcast media. As a practical matter, all broadcast communication requires some public regulation to limit signal interference that could frustrate all such activity. Beyond this, however, there is a widely shared understanding that radio and television programming have an especially powerful influence on public opinion and culture and that some social control of the content of the material broadcast is appropriate. As the Court noted in *Informationsverein Lentia*, the initial response to this perception was the creation of state broadcasting monopolies.[258] This approach has gradually given way to a regime of controlled competition. The United Kingdom has followed this pattern. The British Broadcasting Corporation held such a monopoly until 1954, when commercial broadcasting was permitted under a licensing system that has extended its scope to cover many radio and television channels. Both the B.B.C. and the independent broadcasters, however, are subject to an elaborate scheme of regulation. It aims to maintain standards of public service and decency, while preserving editorial independence. The British courts have been reluctant to second-guess the various agencies charged with balancing these concerns.[259]

Consistent with this approach the First Amendment to the United States Constitution has not been applied to regulation of broadcast expression with the same rigour with which it has been invoked of behalf of print media. Although its factual premise may have been undermined by technical developments[260] the Supreme Court has reasoned that the scarcity of broadcast frequencies justifies a more active public interference with content decisions by radio and television stations.[261] Thus, the Court has upheld regulation requiring the presentation of both sides of controversial issues,[262] the sale of advertising time to political candidates[263] and prohibiting sexually explicit material at certain times of day.[264] On the other hand, there are constitutional limits to broadcast regulation. The Supreme Court has held that Congress acted unconstitutionally in prohibiting publicly funded television stations from broadcasting editorial opinions. The Court stated that the regulation of broadcasts must be related to a narrowly defined and substantial public interest.[265] More recently the Court held unconstitutional a federal regulation whereby cable television operators were required to carry local broadcasting channels on their service. The Court concluded that it was permissible to promote over the air broadcasting by such means, but, in this case, there was no showing that local broadcasting was in real jeopardy. Therefore, the requirement was not shown to be sufficiently related to the stated objectives to be justified under the First Amendment.[266]

---

[258] *Id.* at paras. 38–9.

[259] See D. Feldman, *Civil Liberties and Human Rights in England and Wales*, 590–602 (1993).

[260] *See* Lucas A. Powe, *American Broadcasting and the First Amendment* (1987).

[261] *Red Lion Broadcasting Co. v. Federal Communications Commission*, 395 U.S. 367 (1969).

[262] *Id.*

[263] *CBS v. Federal Communications Commission*, 453 U.S. 367 (1981). On the Strasburg Court's approach to limitations of election expenditures see *Bowman v. United Kingdom*, 19 Feb. 1998, Reports, 1998–I 175, 26 E.H.R.R. 1 discussed at section (C)(1)(c) *supra*.

[264] *Federal Communication Commission v. Pacifica Foundation*, 438 U.S. 726 (1978).

[265] *Federal Communication Commission v. League of Women Voters*, 468 U.S. 364 (1984).

[266] *Turner Broadcasting System, Inc. v. Federal Communications Commission*, 512 U.S. 622 (1994).

It is worth noting that the Supreme Court has recently declined to extend its somewhat relaxed approach to broadcast regulation to regulation of the Internet. It struck down the federal Communications Decency Act of 1991 which prohibited the Internet transmission of obscene, indecent or patently offensive material which would be available to persons under 18 years of age. In rejecting the government's argument that it should follow its broadcast jurisprudence, the Court listed some of the relevant differences between the two media:

Neither before nor after the enactment of the CDA have the vast democratic fora of the Internet been subject to the type of government supervision and regulation that has attended the broadcast industry. Moreover . . . communications over the Internet do not 'invade' an individual's home or appear on one's computer screen unbidden. Users seldom encounter content 'by accident' . . . Finally, . . . the Internet can hardly be considered a 'scarce' expressive commodity. It provides relatively unlimited, low cost capacity for communication of all kinds . . . Through the use of chat rooms, any person with a phone line can become a town crier with a voice that resonates farther than it could from any soapbox. Through the use of web pages, mail exploders, and news groups the same individual can become a pamphleteer[267]

D. EXPRESSION AND PUBLIC EMPLOYMENT

In a well-known remark, Justice Oliver Wendell Holmes (then on the Massachusetts Supreme Judicial Court) said: 'Petitioner may have a constitutional right to talk politics but he has no constitutional right to be a policeman'.[268] The United States Supreme Court has, however, now moved toward a significantly more expansive, though somewhat ill-defined, view of the free speech rights of public employees. A fairly good summary is found in *Pickering v. Board of Education*:[269]

To the extent that the Illinois Supreme Court's opinion may be read to suggest that teachers may constitutionally be compelled to relinquish the First Amendment rights they would otherwise enjoy as citizens to comment on matters of public interest in connection with the operations of the public schools in which they work, it proceeds on a premise that has been unequivocally rejected in numerous prior decisions of this Court . . . At the same time it cannot be gain-said that the State has interests as an employer in regulating the speech of its employees that differ significantly from those it possesses in connection with regulation of the speech of the citizenry in general. The problem in any case is to arrive at a balance between the interests of the teacher, as a citizen, in commenting upon matters of public concern and the interest of the State, as an employer, in promoting the efficiency of the public services it performs through its employees. . . .

While criminal sanctions and damage awards have a somewhat different impact on the exercise

---

[267] *Reno v. American Civil Liberties Union*, 521 U.S. 844, 868–70 (1997) (internal citations and quotation marks omitted).

[268] *McAuliffe v. New Bedford*, 155 Mass. 216, 220 (1892).

[269] 391 U.S. 563, 568 (1968).

of the right to freedom of speech from dismissal from employment, it is apparent that the threat of dismissal from public employment is nonetheless a potent means of inhibiting speech. We have already noted our disinclination to make an across-the-board equation of dismissal from public employment for remarks critical of superiors with awarding damages in a libel suit by a public official for similar criticism. However, in a case such as the present one, in which the fact of employment is only tangentially and insubstantially involved in the subject matter of the public communication made by a teacher, we conclude that it is necessary to regard the teacher as the member of the general public he seeks to be.

In sum, we hold, in a case such as this, absent proof of false statements knowingly or recklessly made by him, a teacher's exercise of his right to speak on issues of public importance may not furnish the basis for his dismissal from public employment.[270]

When this issue first arose in the European Court of Human Rights it took a very different view. In two judgments delivered in 1986 the Court reviewed the refusal to renew the appointments of two teachers, one in the university and one in a secondary school. Neither applicant had yet earned permanent tenure. The actions were motivated by the teachers' associations with right- or left-wing political parties. The Court held there was no interference with Article 10 rights. Rather these matters fell 'within the sphere of rights of access to the civil service, a right not secured in the Convention'.[271] But in 1995 when a similar case came to the Court in *Vogt v. Germany*, the Court found a violation when another teacher was dismissed because of her active membership in the Communist Party. The state maintained that such membership was a breach of the teacher's duty of political loyalty to the constitutional order, a duty imposed on all civil servants. The applicant had, in contrast to the 1986 cases, achieved the status of a permanent member of the civil service. The Court reaffirmed that:

the refusal to appoint a person as a civil servant cannot as such provide the basis for a complaint under the Convention. This does not mean however, that a person who has been appointed as a civil servant cannot complain on being dismissed if that dismissal violates his or her rights under the Convention.[272]

The Court went on to hold that the dismissal of a civil servant for the kind of activity at issue in that case was not 'necessary in a democratic society' for the protection of the rights of others, preventing disorder or preserving national security:

The Court proceeds on the basis that a democratic State is entitled to require civil servants to be loyal to the constitutional principles on which it is founded. In this connection it takes into account Germany's experience under the Weimar Republic and during the bitter period that followed the collapse of that regime up to the adoption of the Basic Law in 1949. Germany

---

[270] *Id.* at 568, *see also Connick v. Meyers*, 461 U.S. 138 (1983). The Court has held that the same considerations govern the legality of public decisions to terminate at will contracts in response to statements on political activities by the contractors: *Board of County Comm'rs. Wabaunsee County Kansas v. Umbehr*, 518 U.S. 668 (1996).

[271] *Kosiek v. Germany*, 28 Aug. 1986 (No. 105), 9 E.H.R.R. 328, para. 36; *Glasenapp v. Germany*, 28 Aug. 1986 (No. 104), 9 E.H.R.R. 25.

[272] 26 Sept. 1995 (No 323), 21 E.H.R.R. 205, para. 43.

wished to avoid a repetition of those experiences by founding its new State on the idea that it should be a 'democracy capable of defending itself'. Nor should Germany's position in the political context of the time be forgotten. These circumstances understandably lent extra weight to this underlying notion and to the corresponding duty of political loyalty imposed on civil servants.

Even so, the absolute nature of that duty as construed by the German courts is striking. It is owed equally by every civil servant, regardless of his or her function and rank. It implies that every civil servant, whatever his or her own opinion on the matter, must unambiguously renounce all groups and movements which the competent authorities hold to be inimical to the Constitution. It does not allow for distinctions between service and private life; the duty is always owed, in every context.

* * *

[T]here are several reasons for considering dismissal of a secondary-school teacher by way of disciplinary sanction for breach of duty to be a very severe measure. This is firstly because of the effect that such a measure has on the reputation of the person concerned and secondly because secondary-school teachers dismissed in this way lose their livelihood, at least in principle, as the disciplinary court may allow them to keep part of their salary. Finally, secondary-school teachers in this situation may find it well nigh impossible to find another job as a teacher, since in Germany teaching posts outside the civil service are scarce. Consequently, they will almost certainly be deprived of the opportunity to exercise the sole profession for which they have a calling, for which they have been trained and in which they have acquired skills and experience.

A second aspect that should be noted is that Mrs. Vogt was a teacher of German and French in a secondary school, a post which did not intrinsically involve any security risks.

The risk lay in the possibility that, contrary to the special duties and responsibilities incumbent on teachers, she would take advantage of her position to indoctrinate or exert improper influence in another way on her pupils during lessons. Yet no criticism was leveled at her on this point. On the contrary, the applicant's work at school had been considered wholly satisfactory by her superiors and she was held in high regard by her pupils and their parents and also by her colleagues; the disciplinary courts recognised that she had always carried out her duties in a way that was beyond reproach. Indeed the authorities only suspended the applicant more than four years after instituting disciplinary proceedings, thereby showing that they did not consider the need to remove the pupils from her influence to be a very pressing one.

Since teachers are figures of authority to their pupils, their special duties and responsibilities to a certain extent also apply to their activities outside school. However, there is no evidence that Mrs. Vogt herself, even outside her work at school, actually made anti-constitutional statements or personally adopted an anti-constitutional stance.[273]

The special interest that a state may have even in the non-classroom statements of public school teachers was explored by the Supreme Court of Canada in *Ross v. New*

---

[273] *Id.* at paras. 59–60.

Brunswick School District No. 15.[274] In that case the Court held that it was allowable under the Charter of Rights and Freedoms for a school board to remove from teaching duties a high school teacher who had frequently expressed anti-Semitic opinions both in speech and in published writing. It agreed the board's action infringed freedom of expression but found it was a permissible limitation of that right under section 1 of the Charter:

Young children are especially vulnerable to the messages conveyed by their teachers. They are less likely to make an intellectual distinction between comments a teacher makes in the school and those the teacher makes outside the school. They are, therefore, more likely to feel threatened and isolated by a teacher who makes comments that denigrate personal characteristics of a group to which they belong. Furthermore, they are unlikely to distinguish between falsehoods and truth and more likely to accept derogatory views espoused by a teacher . . .

[T]he state, as employer, has a duty to ensure that the fulfilment of public function is undertaken in a manner that does not undermine public trust and confidence. The appellant Commission submits that the 'standard of behaviour which a teacher must meet is greater than the minimum standard of conduct otherwise tolerated, given the public responsibilities which a teacher must fulfil and the expectations which the community holds for the educational system . . .'

The Board held that the fact that the respondent publicly made anti-Semitic statements contributed to the 'poisoned environment' in the school system and that it was reasonable to anticipate that his statements and writings had influenced the anti-Semitic sentiment in the schools . . . It is thus necessary to remove the respondent from his teaching position to ensure that no influence of this kind is exerted by him upon his students and to ensure that the educational services are discrimination-free.[275]

The Court held, however, that the Charter prohibited outright termination of employment on account of off-duty statements made by the teacher. His retention in a non-teaching position would not compromise the ability of the school board to maintain the appropriate environment in the schools.[276]

The context-specific character of the European Court's judgment in *Vogt* was clarified by its decision in *Ahmed and Others v. United Kingdom.*[277] In that case it upheld, six to three, a prohibition on partisan political activity by senior civil servants in local government. The Court found the limitation justified by the government's interest in maintaining a politically neutral civil service which could act loyally and impartially on behalf of the democratically chosen authority. The Court noted that the prohibition was limited to those officers whose duties demanded strict non-partisanship and that these amounted at most to 2 per cent of 2,300,000 such officers and even for these an exemption process was available.[278] The affected persons, moreover, were not com-

---

274 [1996] 1 S.C.R. 825.
275 *Id.* at paras. 82–4, 101.
276 *Id.* at paras. 106–7.
277 2 Sept. 1998, Reports, 1998–VI 2356, 29 E.H.R.R. 1.
278 *Id.* at paras. 50–3, 59.

pelled to be silent on all political matters, but merely actions that could reasonably be judged as 'espousing or opposing a party political view'.[279] Given the state's margin of appreciation the restrictions were found not disproportionate to the aim pursued. Similarly in *Rekvényi v. Hungary*[280] It found a limit on political activities by the police to be compatible with Article 6. The Court noted particularly that Hungary was in a period of transition from totalitarianism to democracy and that the prior regime had employed the political co-optation of the police to maintain control. Moreover, as in *Ahmed*, the limits actually imposed left open substantial opportunities for political expression.[281]

E. INTERFERENCES 'PRESCRIBED BY LAW'

Under Article 10(2) and other parallel provisions a valid interference with a Convention right must not only be necessary to a specified public interest, but it must also exist in a particular form. It must be 'prescribed by law'. The value protected by this requirement is often summarized as the value of the 'rule of law'. For similar reasons, in the United States, otherwise properly punishable behaviour may not, consistent with due process of law, be dealt with by an unduly vague statute. The reasons for this doctrine were summed up in *Grayned v. Rockford*:[282]

It is a basic principle of due process that an enactment is void for vagueness if its prohibitions are not clearly defined. Vague laws offend several important values. First, because we assume that man is free to steer between lawful and unlawful conduct, we insist that laws give the person of ordinary intelligence a reasonable opportunity to know what is prohibited, so that he may act accordingly. Vague laws may trap the innocent by not providing fair warning. Second, if arbitrary and discriminatory enforcement is to be prevented, laws must provide explicit standards for those who apply them. A vague law impermissibly delegates basic policy matters to policemen, judges, and juries for resolution on an *ad hoc* and subjective basis, with the attendant dangers of arbitrary and discriminatory application. Third, but related, where a vague statute 'abut[s] upon sensitive areas of basic First Amendment freedoms', it 'operates to inhibit the exercise of [those] freedoms'. Uncertain meanings inevitably lead citizens to 'steer far wider of the unlawful zone' . . . than if the boundaries of the forbidden areas were clearly marked.

The same requirement as that in the Convention appears in Section 1 of the Canadian Charter of Rights and Freedoms, which states that the rights and freedoms specified in the Charter are 'subject only to such reasonable limits prescribed by law as can be demonstrably justified in a free and democratic society'. The phrase 'prescribed by

---

[279] *Id.* at para 63.

[280] 20 May 1999 (not yet reported).

[281] *Id.* at paras. 44–9. The United States Supreme Court has also upheld limits on the political activities of civil servants as consistent with the First Amendment. *United States Civil Service Comm'n v. National Association of Letter Carriers*, 413 U.S. 548 (1973).

[282] 408 U.S. 104, 108 (1972).

law' was absent from the original draft of the Charter prepared by the Canadian government but was inserted during parliamentary consideration. The French version of the Charter uses the phrase 'par un règle de droit'. This should be compared with the French version of Article 10(2) of the Convention which uses the term 'prévues par la loi'. It has been suggested that the Canadian usage more clearly encompasses a wider field including, in addition to statutes, regulations and common law decisions.[283]

The Supreme Court of Canada has not yet had the occasion to examine a common law rule under Section 1, but has expressed the view that a common law limitation could be one 'prescribed by law'.[284]

The European Court addressed the relation of the phrase to common law decisions in *Sunday Times v. United Kingdom*,[285] in which it considered whether judicial citations for contempt of court could be justified as interferences 'prescribed by law . . . for maintaining the authority and impartiality of the judiciary':

46. The applicants argue, *inter alia*, that the law of contempt of court, both before and after the decision of the House of Lords, was so vague and uncertain and the principles enunciated by that decision so novel that the restraint imposed cannot be regarded as 'prescribed by law'. The Government maintain that it suffices, in this context, that the restraint was in accordance with the law; they plead, in the alternative, that on the facts of the case the restraint was at least 'roughly foreseeable'.

47. The Court observes that the word 'law' in the expression 'prescribed by law' covers not only statute but also unwritten law. Accordingly, the Court does not attach importance here to the fact that contempt of court is a creature of the common law and not of legislation. It would clearly be contrary to the intention of the drafters of the Convention to hold that a restriction imposed by virtue of the common law is not 'prescribed by law' on the sole ground that it is not enunciated in legislation: this would deprive a common-law State which is Party to the Convention of the protection of Article 10 §2 and strike at the very roots of that State's legal system. . . .

49. In the Court's opinion, the following are two of the requirements that flow from the expression 'prescribed by law'. First, the law must be adequately accessible: the citizen must be able to have an indication that is adequate in the circumstances of the legal rules applicable to a given case. Secondly, a norm cannot be regarded as a 'law' unless it is formulated with sufficient precision to enable the citizen to regulate his conduct: he must be able—if need be with appropriate advice—to foresee, to a degree that is reasonable in the circumstances, the consequences which a given action may entail. Those consequences need not be foreseeable with absolute certainty: experience shows this to be unattainable. Again, whilst certainty is highly desirable, it may bring in its train excessive rigidity and the law must be able to keep pace with changing circumstances. Accordingly, many laws are inevitably couched in terms which, to a greater or lesser extent, are vague and whose interpretation and application are questions of practice.

The Court found that the common law rule of contempt of court had been developed with sufficient certainty that a finding of contempt could be considered 'prescribed by

---

[283]   *See* P. Hogg, *Constitutional Law of Canada* 684 (2nd edn. 1986).
[284]   *R. v. Thomsen* [1988] 1 S.C.R. 640, 650–1.
[285]   *See* Chapter 3(B)(2) *supra*.

law'. Prior cases gave a clear enough indication to enable the applicants to foresee a risk that publication might result in contempt.

This conclusion may be compared with the Court's judgment in *Kruslin v. France*,[286] dealing with a complaint that wiretapping by French authorities was in violation of Article 8. In interpreting the language of Article 8(2) stating that limitations on the rights to privacy and family life must be 'in accordance with law', the Court had previously held that any such law must, as in the case of Article 10(2), be accessible and its application foreseeable.[287] In *Kruslin*, the Court held that, even in a civil law system, interception of telephone conversations was not prevented from being 'in accordance with the law', merely because the governing legal rule had been developed in judicial decisions. Notwithstanding the greater emphasis on enacted law in such systems, 'case-law has traditionally played a major role in Continental countries'. But, in the case at issue, many of the rules governing telephone tapping, including some of the limitations on the investigative authorities, had been 'laid down piecemeal in judgments given over the years, the great majority of them after the interception complained of by Mr. Kruslin . . . Some have not yet been expressly laid down in case-law at all . . . [but are said to be inferable] from general enactments or principles or else from an analogical interpretation of legislative provisions—or Court decisions—concerning investigative measures different from telephone tapping'. Moreover, many questions about the scope of authorized wiretapping remained unanswered. Since French law 'written and unwritten, [did] not indicate with reasonable clarity the scope and manner of exercise of the relevant discretion conferred on the public authorities', the interference with his privacy was not 'in accordance with law'.

The Court has also indicated that an interference may or may not be 'prescribed by law' depending on the capacity of the particular applicant to discover the relevant legal authority and rules. Most clearly, the Court has stated that where restrictions on prisoners' correspondence were governed by prison 'orders and instructions', which were not available to prisoners, such interferences could not be 'in accordance with law' in the sense required by Article 8(2).[288] On the other hand, in *Groppera Radio and Others v. Switzerland*[289] the Court held that a Swiss decision to limit the retransmission of broadcasts that was based on administrative regulations promulgated under the International Telecommunications Convention was 'prescribed by law'. This was so even though the regulations had not been published by the Swiss authorities and were 'highly technical and complex'. The Court reasoned that broadcasters who might be affected by the decision should be expected to inform themselves about the relevant rules, which, although not published, had been made available for inspection.

---

[286] 24 Apr. 1990 (No. 176A), 12 E.H.R.R. 547. *See also Huvig v. France*, 24 Apr. 1990 (No. 176B), 12 E.H.R.R. 528.

[287] Article 8(2) uses the English term 'in accordance with law' instead of 'prescribed by law' which is found in articles 9(2), 10(2) and 11(2). The French usage, 'prévues par la loi' is identical in all four articles and the Court has held that they should be given an 'identical interpretation'. *Silver v. United Kingdom*, 25 Mar. 1983 (No. 61), 5 E.H.R.R. 347, para. 85.

[288] *Id.* at para. 89.

[289] 28 Mar. 1990 (No. 173), 12 E.H.R.R. 321.

The Canadian Supreme Court found one type of restriction that was *not* prescribed by law where an accused was stopped for speeding and required to submit to a 'breathalyzer' test without having been informed of his right to counsel in violation of Section 10(b) of the Charter. The procedure on stopping the driver was neither prescribed by statute nor in common law. A majority of the Justices appeared to agree that, in such circumstances, a justification under Section 1 of the Charter could not be shown. The limit on the respondent's right to consult counsel was imposed by the conduct of the police officers and not by a rule of law.[290]

The Canadian Supreme Court has held that interference with a Charter right under a broadly drawn statute does not, by itself, mean that the interference is not 'prescribed by law'. In *Irwin Toy v. Quebec (Attorney-General)*,[291] it found the criteria of Section 1 met when a regulation provided that an advertisement came within a statutory prohibition if it were aimed at children. The regulation also set forth three general and non-conclusive guidelines for making that determination:

Absolute precision in the law exists rarely, if at all. The question is whether the legislature has provided an intelligible standard according to which the judiciary must do its work. The task of interpreting how that standard applies in particular instances might always be characterized as having a discretionary element, because the standard can never specify all the instances in which it applies. On the other hand, where there is no intelligible standard and where the legislature has given a plenary discretion to do whatever seems best in a wide set of circumstances, there is no 'limit prescribed by law'.

The Court elaborated its reasons for assuming that the creation of discretionary authority did not prevent its exercise from being 'prescribed by law' in *Osborne v. Canada (Treasury Board)*.[292] It noted that the vagueness of a statute was relevant to the Section 1 inquiry not only with respect to this 'threshold' requirement, but also in connection with the question of whether the interference was a reasonable limitation 'demonstrably justified', since imprecision 'may fail to confine the invasion of a Charter right within reasonable limits'.

This Court has shown a reluctance to disentitle a law to §1 scrutiny on the basis of vagueness which results in the granting of wide discretionary powers. Much of the activity of government is carried on under the aegis of laws which, of necessity, leave a broad discretion to government officials. Since it may very well be reasonable in the circumstances to confer a wide discretion, it is preferable in the vast majority of cases to deal with vagueness in the context of a §1 analysis rather than disqualifying the law *in limine*.

A question may also arise as to whether a limitation of a right is 'prescribed by law' when the *sanction* for the exercise of a right is uncertain. The English Court of Appeal, in *Rantzen v. Mirror Group Newspapers, Ltd.*,[293] reversed an award of £250,000 in damages in a civil action for libel against a newspaper that had been found to have

---

[290] *R. v. Therens* [1985] 1 S.C.R. 613, 621.

[291] [1989] 1 S.C.R. 927.

[292] [1989] 1 S.C.R. 927.

[293] [1993] 4 All E.R. 975 C.A.

defamed a well known television presenter and child welfare activist. The Court held that appellate courts should carefully scrutinize such awards, noting that the prior practice, where juries were free to award damages, without clear instructions, could, in such case, amount to a limitation of freedom of expression protected by Article 10 of the Convention, and such a limitation was not sufficiently certain to be 'prescribed by law'. '[U]nder the present practice no one, and certainly not a newspaper, had any means whereby, even with appropriate advice, he could foresee the consequences of the exercise by him of his right to freedom of expression.'[294]

F. ARTICLE 11: FREEDOM OF ASSOCIATION

Closely related to the right of expression provided in Article 10 is freedom of association provided in Article 11. That Article reads:

(1) Everyone has the right to freedom of peaceful assembly and to freedom of association with others, including the right to form and to join trade unions for the protection of his interests.

(2) No restrictions shall be placed on the exercise of these rights other than such as are prescribed by law and are necessary in a democratic society in the interests of national security or public safety, for the prevention of disorder or crime, for the protection of health or morals or for the protection of the rights and freedoms of others. This Article shall not prevent the imposition of lawful restrictions on the exercise of these rights by members of the armed forces, of the police or of the administration of the State.

The right of association is often recognized as an essential means to effect expression. The United States Supreme Court has identified a right of association in the United States Constitution even though there is no explicit mention of the right in the text. It has found it to be a logical corollary of the first amendment right of free speech.[295] It has noted that individual expression 'could not be vigorously protected from interference by the State unless a correlative freedom to engage in group effort toward these [desired] ends were not also guaranteed'.[296] The European Court of Human Rights, while dealing with an express right, has also mentioned its affinity with the right of expression, referring to Article 11 as *lex specialis* in relation to the *lex generalis* of Article 10.[297] It has, consequently, invoked the general principles associated with the latter article in dealing with claims under the former.[298]

The most obvious application of this understanding of the right of association is in

[294] *Id.* at 990. In reaching this conclusion, Neill, L.J. cited the case law of the Court at Strasbourg as well as that of the United States Supreme Court, notably *New York Times v. Sullivan*, 376 U.S. 254 (1964) and *Gertz v. Robert Welch, Inc.*, 418 U.S. 323 (1974) discussed at Section (C)(2) *supra*.

[295] *NAACP v. Alabama ex rel Patterson*, 357 U.S. 449 (1958).

[296] *Roberts v. United States Jaycees*, 468 U.S. 609, 622 (1984).

[297] *Ezelin v. France*, 26 Apr. 1991 (No. 202), 14 E.H.R.R. 362, para. 62.

[298] *United Communist Party of Turkey v. Turkey*, 30 Jan. 1998, Reports, 1998–I 1, 26 E.H.R.R. 121, para. 42.

connection with political parties. When the Constitutional Court of Turkey ordered the dissolution of the United Communist Party, the European Court examined the action with particular intensity, noting that 'political parties are a form of association essential to the proper functioning of democracy'.[299] Given that critical role,

the exceptions set out in Article 11 are, where political parties are concerned, to be construed strictly; only convincing and compelling reasons can justify restrictions or such parties' freedom of association. In determining whether a necessity within the meaning of Article 11(2) exists, the Contracting States possess only a limited margin of appreciation, which goes hand in hand with rigorous European supervision embracing both the law and the decisions applying it, including those given by independent courts.[300]

In the *United Communist Party* case the Court found neither of two offered justifications for the dissolution adequate under this standard. It dealt quickly with the fact that there was a prior Turkish law prohibiting the word 'communist' in party names. There was no evidence that the party in question, whatever its name, was going to engage in activities 'that represented a real threat to Turkish society or the Turkish State'.[301] The second ground relied on by the Constitutional Court was the party's program which called for rectifying the grievances of the Kurdish minority in Turkey. The Turkish court inferred that the party was, thereby, a threat to the unity of the Turkish state. The European Court noted that the party programme did not endorse any special treatment for, much less secession of, the Kurds and that it coupled its position with an insistence on peaceful and democratic means to deal with Kurdish aspiration:

Democracy thrives on freedom of expression. From that point of view there can be no justification for hindering a political group solely because it seeks to debate in public the situation of part of the State's population and to take part in the nation's political life in order to find, according to democratic rules, solutions capable of satisfying everyone considered.[302]

The Court's strict approach to limitation on political parties was extended to other kinds of associations in *Sidiropoulos v. Greece*.[303] The European Court found that the refusal to register an organization named 'Home of Macedonian Civilisation' was a violation of Article 11. The Greek court dealing with the case had gone outside the judicial record and relied on secondary accounts to conclude that the association aimed to promote a separate Macedonian state. It therefore meant to undermine the territorial integrity of Greece. The European Court noted that the organization had not yet begun functioning and, therefore, these conclusions were based on 'mere suspicion'. The refusal to register it on these grounds was an excessive response to whatever threat the group might pose. It did not, however, 'rule out that, once

---

[299] *Id.* at para. 25.
[300] *Id.* at para. 46.
[301] *Id.* at para. 54.
[302] *Id.* at para. 57.
[303] 10 July 1998, Reports, 1998–IV 1594, 27 E.H.R.R. 633.

founded, the association might, under cover of the aims mentioned in its memo-randum of association, have engaged in activities incompatible with those aims'. In such case the authorities 'would not have been powerless' to deal with it.[304]

The Court's solicitude for the right of association has extended even further than protection for such rather traditional voluntary groups. In *Chassagnou and Others v. France*[305] landowners complained about a legislative scheme whereby the regulation of hunting rights on their property was put in the hands of a statutorily created 'hunter's association'. All affected landowners were made members of this association thereby giving them some influence over its policies. The applicants were philosophically opposed to hunting. The European Court decided the law violated Article 1 of Proto-col 1 as a disproportionate interference with the right to peaceful enjoyment of property. It also held the compulsory membership of the hunter's association violated Article 11. That membership was essentially formal. It was conceded that membership required no payment of dues nor any other participation in the affairs of the organ-ization. Without further explanation the Court declared that this 'takes nothing away from the compulsory nature of their membership'. It characterized the law in ques-tion as one requiring 'an association . . . fundamentally contrary to [the applicant's] own convictions' and found the objects of the legislation did not require such a measure.[306] On the other hand, when an applicant could avoid joining an employer's association by concluding a substitute collective bargaining agreement, the Court held there was no violation of Article 11 rights.[307]

Article 11 mentions one form of association expressly—trade unions. Several cases deal with claims that Article 11 requires governments to deal with unions and to refrain from actions that may penalize membership in a union or participation in union activities. The European Court has been unsympathetic to such a broad inter-pretation of the right of association. In *National Union of Belgian Police v. Belgium*[308] the applicant, a police union not recognized by the government, asserted that Article 11 included an implicit right of a union to be recognized by the government. The Court found that while Article 11 does contain a right to join and form trade unions, there is no inherent right to particular treatment by the government. In *Schmit and Dahlström v. Sweden*[309] the government refused to deal with or recognize a union independently of a larger federation of unions. The individual union subsequently called a strike and the government a lockout in connection with a contract dispute with the union federation. When a contract with the federation was agreed upon, it denied retroactive benefits to members of this striking union, even members like the applicants, who did not take part in the strike. The Court found no violation of applicants' freedom to join trade unions. There was no intent on the part of the

---

[304] *Id.* at paras. 44–6.
[305] 29 Apr. 1999 (not yet reported).
[306] *Id.* at paras. 115–17.
[307] *Gustafsson v. Sweden*, 25 Apr. 1996, Reports, 1996–II 637, 22 E.H.R.R. 409, at para. 52.
[308] 27 Oct. 1975 (No. 19), 1 E.H.R.R. 578.
[309] 6 Feb. 1976 (No. 21), 1 E.H.R.R. 632.

government to discourage membership in the applicant union. Even non-striking members of the union by their status, lent financial and moral support to the strike.

These cases did not expressly address the question of whether or not the right 'to form and join trade unions for the protection of his interests' includes a right to strike. In response to such a claim in *Schmidt and Dahlström*, the Court only noted that, when such a right exists under national law, it may be limited without infringing Article 11. The Court held that the right to form and join unions includes a right to be 'enabled, in conditions not at variance with Article 11, to strive, through the medium of their organizations, for the protection of their occupational interests'. A right to strike, the court noted, is one means to this end but not the only one.

The Canadian Supreme Court has also considered claims that the right to strike is encompassed in the right of association. The Canadian Charter of Rights and Freedoms, like the European Convention, contains an explicit protection of 'freedom of association' (Section 2(d)) but provides no definition of that freedom. More particularly it makes no mention of trade unions. In *Reference Re Public Service Employee Relations Act (Alta.)*,[310] the Supreme Court of Canada considered the nature of the right in connection with challenged provincial statutes which required that certain terms of employment for public service employees, firefighters, and police be settled by compulsory arbitration and which prohibited strikes by such employees. The unions contended these provisions infringed upon the right of association. The Court held, four to two, that the statutes were valid. Three members of the majority held that a union's right to associate does not include a right to bargain collectively or to strike. Justice McIntyre agreed that the statute was constitutional, holding only that the right of association did not include a right to strike. His judgment, part of which follows, contains an illuminating discussion of the right of association:

Various theories have been advanced to define freedom of association guaranteed by the Constitution. They range from the very restrictive to the virtually unlimited. To begin with, it has been said that freedom of association is limited to a right to associate with others in common pursuits or for certain purposes. Neither the objects nor the actions of the group are protected by freedom of association. . . .

A second approach provides that freedom of association guarantees the collective exercise of constitutional rights or, in other words, the freedom to engage collectively in those activities which are constitutionally protected for each individual. This theory has been adopted in the United States to define the scope of freedom of association under the American Constitution. . . .

A third approach postulates that freedom of association stands for the principle that an individual is entitled to do in concert with others that which he may lawfully do alone and, conversely, that individuals and organizations have no right to do in concert what is unlawful when done individually. . . .

A fourth approach would constitutionally protect collective activities which may be said to be

---

[310] [1987] 1 S.C.R. 313. In 1999 the Supreme Court held that s. 2(d) did not require the Federal government to extend the same rights of collective bargaining to employee associations of the Royal Canadian Mounted Police that is provided for other federal employees. *Delisle v. Canada (Attorney General)* [1999] 2 S.C.R. 989.

fundamental to our culture and traditions and which by common assent are deserving of protection . . .

A fifth approach rests on the proposition that freedom of association, under s. 2(d) of the Charter, extends constitutional protection to all activities which are essential to the lawful goals of an association. This approach was advanced in *Re Service Employees' Int'l Union, Loc. 204 and Broadway Manor Nursing Home* (1983), 4 D.L.R. (4th) 231, 44 O.R. (2d) 392, 10 C.R.R. 37, by the Ontario Divisional Court. The court held that freedom of association included the freedom to bargain collectively and to strike, since, in its view, these activities were essential to the objects of a trade union and without them the association would be emasculated . . .

Justice McIntyre concluded that the fourth, fifth and sixth approaches do not provide acceptable definitions of freedom of association. The fourth approach is unacceptable, since it focuses on whether the nature of the activity involves pursuit of a fundamental right. But freedom of association is concerned with the manner in which a group chooses to advance its goals and not at all with the particular goals that they are attempting to advance. The fifth and sixth approaches are also unacceptable, because they both give greater constitutional rights to members of a group than to individuals. An activity could not become constitutionally protected simply because it is performed by a group. Rather, the basic purpose of freedom of association is to insure that an activity, protected if done by an individual, is also protected if done collectively.

Of the remaining approaches, it must surely be accepted that the concept of freedom of association includes at least the right to join with others in lawful, common pursuits and to establish and maintain organizations and associations as set out in the first approach . . . It is, I believe, equally clear that, in accordance with the second approach, freedom of association should guarantee the collective exercise of constitutional rights. Individual rights protected by the Constitution do not lose that protection when exercised in common with others. People must be free to engage collectively in those activities which are constitutionally protected for each individual. . . .

One enters upon more controversial ground when considering the third approach which provides that whatever action an individual can *lawfully* pursue as an individual, freedom of association ensures he can pursue with others. Conversely, individuals and organizations have no constitutional right to do in concert what is unlawful when done alone. This approach is broader than the second, since constitutional protection attaches to all group acts which can be lawfully performed by an individual, whether or not the individual has a constitutional right to perform them. It is true, of course, that in this approach the range of Charter-protected activity could be reduced by legislation, because the legislature has the power to declare what is and what is not lawful activity for the individual. The legislature, however, would not be able to attack directly the associational character of the activity, since it would be constitutionally bound to treat groups and individuals alike. A simple example illustrates this point: golf is a lawful but not constitutionally protected activity. Under the third approach, the legislature could prohibit golf entirely. However, the legislature could not constitutionally provide that golf could be played in pairs but in no greater number, for this would infringe the Charter guarantee of freedom of association. This contrasts with the second approach, which would provide no protection against such legislation, because golf is not a constitutionally protected activity for the individual. . . .

When this definition of freedom of association is applied, it is clear that it does not guarantee the right to strike. . . .

[T]here is no analogy whatever between the cessation of work by a single employee and a strike conducted in accordance with modern labour legislation. The individual has, by reason of the cessation of work, either breached or terminated his contract of employment. It is true that the law will not compel the specific performance of the contract by ordering him back to work . . . But, this is markedly different from a lawful strike. An employee who ceases work does not contemplate a return to work. In recognition of this fact, the law does not regard a strike as either a breach of contract or a termination of employment, . . .

As illustrated by the *Chassagnout* case discussed above, a number of European cases have concerned an asserted right *not* to associate in a given organization. In *Young, James, and Webster v. United Kingdom*[311] a British law permitted closed shop agreements, requiring all British rail workers to be members of a union. Young and Webster objected for political reasons, while James did not feel that the union protected the workers' interests. All were denied exemption by a review board. The applicants claimed the Article 11 freedom of association necessarily contained some freedom from association. The Court agreed with the applicants. In addition, the Court did not find the membership requirement to be necessary in a democratic society (Article 11(2)). The benefits of keeping down confusion in bargaining and in aiding the formation of trade unions were not sufficiently advanced by the restriction. For similar reasons, the Court held that requiring membership in a private association, as a condition to obtaining and holding a taxi licence was not 'necessary' for the efficient regulation of taxi cabs.[312] In *Gustafsson v. Sweden*[313] the Court considered a trade union boycott against an employee who had refused either to join the employer's association or to conclude a substitute collective bargaining agreement with his employees. Although the applicant's difficulties had not been caused by direct action of the state, the Court found implicit in Article 11 a positive obligation to protect individuals from coerced association. Since, however, the applicant could have avoided this result by concluding a substitute agreement, it held that any burden on the right was not disproportionate to the boycotting union's interest in promoting the collective bargaining system.[314]

The existence of a right not to associate depends on the characterization of the organization in which membership is compelled. In *LeCompte, VanLeuven and Demeyere v. Belgium*,[315] the state required that all doctors be members of the Ordre des Medicins. The Court found no violation of Article 11, because the Order performed important public regulatory functions and was, thus, 'not an Association within the meaning of Article 11'. Moreover, the applicants were not prevented from joining other societies. On the other hand, in *Sigudur A. Sigurjónnson v. Iceland*,[316] the Court

---

[311] 13 Aug. 1981 (No. 44), 4 E.H.R.R. 38.

[312] *Sigudur A. Sigurjónnson v. Iceland*, 30 June 1993 (No. 264), 16 E.H.R.R. 462.

[313] 25 Apr. 1996, Reports, 1996–II 637, 22 E.H.R.R. 409.

[314] *Id.* at paras. 51–5.

[315] 23 June 1981 (No. 43), 4 E.H.R.R. 1.

[316] 30 June 1993 (No. 264), 16 E.H.R.R. 462.

held that a privately organized and operated association of taxi cab drivers was not a 'public-law association' but a private association and thus within Article 11. Although the organization did perform certain public functions, the primary responsibility for public regulation of taxi cabs was in another public agency.[317]

A similar issue has divided the Supreme Court of Canada. An employee complained about compulsory due payments to a union that expended funds for political causes with which the employee disagreed. The Court was unanimous in upholding the compulsory payments. Three justices so held on the ground that Section 2(d) of the Charter did not include a right to refrain from compulsory association. Three judges held there was such a right since both free association and non-association were essential to an individual's potential for 'self-actualization'. They found, however, that the compelled association in this case was demonstrably necessary for the proper end of allowing unions to participate in political and economic debate and, therefore, there was no violation under Section 1. A seventh judge did not decide if Section 2(d) encompassed a right not to associate since she concluded that, if there were such a right, the interference would be permissible under Section 1.[318]

While the United States Supreme Court has stated that the right of association merited protection whenever it advanced beliefs that 'pertain to political, economic or religious matters',[319] it has been quite tolerant of legislative restrictions on associations for mere economic purposes, such as labour unions. Thus, the Court has upheld a Federal law requiring union officials to attest that they were not members or supporters of the Communist Party, since Congress' concerns were found to be with protecting the economy and not with direct regulation of expression or belief.[320] The Supreme Court, like the European Court, has also found that the right of association entails some right to refuse to associate with groups with which one disagrees. The Court has held that a State may not require a public employee to contribute funds to a union to support its political activities, although compulsory contributions may be proper to support its collective bargaining activities.[321]

In an important decision which settled a number of contested questions of British constitutional law, the House of Lords upheld a decision by the competent minister to prohibit the civilian employees of the Government Communications Headquarters, an agency concerned with national security and intelligence, from being members of independent trade unions. The House, however, did not address any arguments directly based on a claim of freedom of association.[322] A subsequent application to the European Commission of Human Rights did raise a claim of violation of Article 11,

---

[317] *See also Chassagnou v France, supra* n. 305.

[318] *Lavigne v. Ontario Public Service Employees' Union* [1991] 2 S.C.R. 211.

[319] *Id.* at 461.

[320] *American Communications Association v. Douds*, 339 U.S. 382 (1950).

[321] *Abood v. Board of Education*, 431 U.S. 209 (1977). But see *Glickman v. Wileman Bros. & Elliot Inc.*, 521 U.S. 457 (1996) (holding that requiring producer to contribute to an advertising programme does not violate the First Amendment where the producers did not object to the message financed on political or ideological grounds).

[322] *Council of Civil Service Unions v. Minister for Civil Service* [1985] 1 A.C. 374, [1984] 3 All E.R. 935 (H.L.)

but the Commission found the issue governed by the last sentence of Article 11(2), allowing lawful restrictions on the exercise of these rights 'by . . . members of the . . . administration of the states'. In light of the wide leeway granted to a state in dealing with matters of national security,[323] the Commission found the application 'manifestly ill-founded' and, therefore, inadmissible.[324] In 1989, Parliament enacted a statute which made it an offence simply to be a member of the Irish Republican Army.[325]

[323] *See* Section (C)(3) *supra.*

[324] *Council of Civil Service Unions v. United Kingdom,* Application No. 11603/85, 10 E.H.R.R. 269. On the criteria of admissibility *see* Chapter 2, (B)(1)(a) *supra.* In *Rekvényi v. Hungary,* 20 May 1999 1999, the Court upheld a ban on police joining a political party citing, *inter alia* the last sentence of Art. 11(2). *Id.* paras. 58–62.

[325] *See* A. W. Bradley & K. D. Ewing, *Constitutional and Administrative Law,* 682 (12th ed. 1999).

6

RESPECT FOR PRIVATE AND FAMILY LIFE

ARTICLE 8

1. Everyone has the right to respect for his private and family life, his home and his correspondence.

2. There shall be no interference by a public authority with the exercise of this right except such as is in accordance with the law and is necessary in a democratic society in the interests of national security, public safety or the economic well-being of the country, for the prevention of disorder or crime, for the protection of health or morals, or for the protection of the rights and freedoms of others.

A. FAMILY LIFE

Like so much of the Convention, the protection of private and family life in Article 8 reflects Europe's terrifying experience with fascism in the 1930s and 40's. Numerous references in the debates of the Consultative Assembly refer to the intrusion of the fascist state into the intimate decisions of the family, including the racially restrictive Nazi laws on marriage and the policy of totalitarian governments to alienate children from their parents for the purpose of political indoctrination.[1]

The phrasing in which this protection was stated, however, is unique in the Convention. Whereas Article 10 declares 'the right to freedom of expression' and Article 11, the 'right to freedom of peaceful assembly', Article 8 refers directly to no particular protected action. Rather it speaks of a right to 'respect for . . . private and family life'. Respect, as J. E. S. Fawcett pungently observed, 'belongs to the world of manners rather than the law'.[2] This choice of expression strongly suggests an intention to leave the contracting states considerable leeway in the regulation of private and family

---

[1] *See Travaux Préparatoires*, vol. II at 90, 96, 100, 114.

[2] J. E. S. Fawcett, *The Application of the European Convention on Human Rights*, 211 (2nd edn. 1987). See also Art. 2 of Protocol 1 to the Convention requiring the State to 'respect the right of parents to ensure . . . education and teaching in conformity with their own religious and philosophical convictions'.

relations. That inference is reinforced by the drafting history of Article 8. The first draft put before the Consultative Assembly merely incorporated Article 12 of the Universal Declaration of Human Rights which stated that 'no one should be subject to arbitrary and unlawful interference with his privacy, family, home or correspondence'.[3] A subsequent draft altered this formulation to a declaration that a right to 'privacy in respect of family, home and correspondence, shall be recognized'.[4] This provision was further attenuated into the version finally adopted. These changes indicate that there may, for example, be interferences with the family which do not amount to an infringement of the right to respect for family life so as to raise a *prima facie* violation of the Convention.

The current text also represents a narrowing of the concerns evinced in Article 12 of the Universal Declaration. That provision, in addition to privacy, family, home and correspondence, stated a right to legal protection for 'attacks on [one's] honour and reputation'. While the state's interest in protecting reputations now appears in the European Convention among the justifications for limiting free expression in Article 10(2), it is not stipulated as an affirmative duty of the state as it is in the Universal Declaration.

While the complex of interests described in the text of Article 8 might plausibly be read to concern only the unjustified exposure to public view of matters properly confined to the knowledge of an individual or family group, subsequent interpretation has been premised on a far broader principle. Respect for 'private life' has been held to require non-interference with an individual's decisions on ways to live his or her own life. An early commentator on Article 8 stated this view in especially sweeping terms, saying it should protect against 'attacks upon physical or mental integrity or intellectual freedom'.[5] While the European Court of Human Rights has never embraced a definition this broad, as will be seen, it has understood the right to include the freedom to make particularly personal life choices, notably those involving sexual conduct.[6] Indeed, on occasion, the Court has held that respect for private life may require highly

---

[3] *See* Chapter 1(B) *supra*.

[4] *Travaux Préparatoires*, vol. IV, p. 278.

[5] F. Jacobs, *The European Convention on Human Rights* 126 (1975).

[6] *See* Section (B) *infra*. As an extension of this idea the Court has stated that assaults upon or restraints on an individual's person may, since they affect his or her 'personal integrity', give rise to issues under Art. 8. See *X v. Y*, 26 Mar. 1985 (No. 91), 8 E.H.R.R. 235 (reproduced in part in section (A)(5)(A) *infra*) para. 22; *Costello-Roberts v. United Kingdom*, 25 Mar. 1993, (No. 247C), 19 E.H.R.R. 112, para. 36. This understanding creates a significant overlap between Art. 8 and other articles of the Convention. In *Raninen v. Finland*, 16 Dec. 1997, Reports, 197–VIII 2804, 26 E.H.R.R. 563, discussed in Chapter 4, section (A)(2), the applicant complained of being handcuffed during an arrest. He alleged violations of Arts. 3, 5 and 8. In discussing the claim under Art. 8 the Court 'recognize[d] that . . . aspects of the concept [of private life] extend to situations of deprivation of liberty. Moreover, it does not exclude the possibility that there might be circumstances in which Article 8 could be regarded as affording a protection in relation to conditions during detention which do not attain the level of severity recognized by Article 3'. *Id.* at para. 63. In that case, however, the Court found the handcuffing did not have 'such adverse effects on his physical or moral integrity as to constitute an interference with the applicant's right to respect for private life'. *Id.* at para. 64.

formal and public actions. In *Gaskin v. United Kingdom*[7] the Court held that Article 8 was violated by an agency's refusal to disclose to the applicant the contents of confidential records relating to his childhood while he was under state care.

The transformation of Article 8 into a general charter of individual autonomy is clearly fraught with difficulties. Any restraint on individual choice may be assailed as raising a possible violation of this right. Such an omnibus right is in marked contrast to the apparently modest ambitions for this provision implied by the drafting process. The Convention, itself, may be seen as an enumeration of *particular* ways in which free choice and action are protected, and the supplementing of that specification with such a broad presumption of liberty threatens to make the other rights redundant. One of the most vexing problems confronting the Court is finding ways (short of justification under Article 8(2), of elaborating some special, narrowing characteristics of the right to respect for private life.[8] As the materials in this chapter illustrate, claims under Article 8 present the questions of interpretation and definition of Convention rights in their most acute form.

1. JOHNSTON *V.* IRELAND

Judgment of 18 December 1986
(No. 112), 9 E.H.R.R. 203

. . .

10. The first applicant is Roy H. W. Johnston, who was born in 1930 and is a scientific research and development manager. He resides at Rathmines, Dublin, with the second applicant, Janice Williams-Johnston, who was born in 1938; she is a school-teacher by profession and used to work as director of a play-group in Dublin, but has been unemployed since 1985. The third applicant is their daughter Nessa Doreen Williams-Johnston, who was born in 1978.

11. The first applicant married a Miss M. in 1952 in a Church of Ireland ceremony. Three children were born of this marriage, in 1956, 1959 and 1965.

---

[7] *Gaskin v. United Kingdom*, 7 July 1989 (No. 160), 12 E.H.R.R. 36. Compare *R. v. Mid-Glamorgan Family Health Services, ex parte Martin* [1995] 1 All. E.R. 356 holding that a health authority may deny a psychiatric patient access to his records on the grounds that such information would be harmful to him. In *McGinley & Egan v. United Kingdom*, 9 June 1998, Reports 1998–III 1334, 27 E.H.R.R. 1 the applicants complained that the government had not informed them of the dangers to their health created by their exposure to radiation during tests of nuclear weapons. The Court stated that where a state engages in activities hazardous to health, respect for private and family life requires an effective and accessible procedure to enable affected persons to discover all relevant and appropriate information. *Id.* at para. 101. In this case, the Court determined that such a procedure had been put in place and there was no violation. *Id.* at para. 102.

[8] Defining private life is even more problematic when taking into account the Count's doctrine that Art. 8 also imposes 'positive obligations on the state to facilitate the development of family and private life'. See Section (A)(5) *infra*. In response to the potentially limitless reach of such positive obligations the Court has held that they do not require fostering 'interpersonal relations of such broad and indeterminate scope that there can be no conceivable direct link between the measure the State was urged to take . . . and the applicants' private life.' *Botta v. Italy*, 24 Feb. 1998. Reports, 1998–I 412 26, E.H.R.R. 24, para. 35.

In 1965, it became clear to both parties that the marriage had irretrievably broken down and they decided to live separately at different levels in the family house. Several years later both of them, with the other's knowledge and consent, formed relationships and began to live with third parties. By mutual agreement, the two couples resided in self-contained flats in the house until 1976, when Roy Johnston's wife moved elsewhere.

In 1978, the second applicant, with whom Roy Johnston had been living since 1971, gave birth to Nessa. He consented to his name being included in the Register of Births as the father. . . .

[The Court cited various provisions of the Irish Constitution including s. 41.3.2, ('No law shall be enacted providing for the grant of a dissolution of marriage') and s. 41.3.3 prohibiting remarriage by Irish residents who were single by virtue of a foreign divorce. It also noted provisions of Irish law allowing legal separation on proof of adultery, cruelty or unnatural offenses. Under Irish law Williams-Johnston had no right to maintenance from Johnston. While each could make testamentary dispositions to the other, such bequests were subject to certain statutory rights of the spouse or any legitimate children. Unmarried couples also could not take advantage of certain statutory benefits and public services and could not adopt a child.]

[Under Irish law the child was deemed illegitimate. The Court canvassed the legal situation of illegitimate children and their parents. The mother of an illegitimate child was given full guardianship, but the father's rights were limited to matters of custody and access. While illegitimate children could be legitimated by the parents' subsequent marriage this ability was not given to parents who could not have been lawfully married at the time of the child's birth. An illegitimate child had no rights of intestate succession from the estate of the father and had such rights with respect to the estate of the mother only if she had left no legitimate issue. Taxes on inheritance were more favorable to legitimate than to illegitimate children of the decedent.]

52. The Court agrees with the Commission that the ordinary meaning of the words 'right to marry' [in Article 12] is clear, in the sense that they cover the formation of marital relationships but not their dissolution. Furthermore, these words are found in a context that includes an express reference to 'national laws'; even if, as the applicants would have it, the prohibition on divorce is to be seen as a restriction on capacity to marry, the Court does not consider that, in a society adhering to the principle of monogamy, such a restriction can be regarded as injuring the substance of the right guaranteed by Article 12.

Moreover, the foregoing interpretation of Article 12 is consistent with its object and purpose as revealed by the *travaux préparatoires*. The text of Article 12 was based on that of Article 16 of the Universal Declaration of Human Rights, paragraph 1 of which reads:

> Men and women of full age, without any limitation due to race, nationality or religion, have the right to marry and to found a family. They are entitled to equal rights as to marriage, during marriage and at its dissolution.

In explaining to the Consultative Assembly why the draft of the future Article 12 did not include the words found in the last sentence of the above-cited paragraph, Mr. Teitgen, Rapporteur of the Committee on Legal and Administrative Questions, said:

> In mentioning the particular Article [of the Universal Declaration], we have used only that part of the paragraph of the Article which affirms the right to marry and to found a family, but not the subsequent provisions of the Article concerning equal rights after marriage, since we only guarantee the right to marry.

In the Court's view, the *travaux préparatoires* disclose no intention to include in Article 12 any guarantee of a right to have the ties of marriage dissolved by divorce.

53. The applicants set considerable store on the social developments that have occurred since the Convention was drafted, notably an alleged substantial increase in marriage breakdown.

It is true that the Convention and its Protocols must be interpreted in the light of present-day conditions. However, the Court cannot, by means of an evolutive interpretation, derive from these instruments a right that was not included therein at the outset. This is particularly so here, where the omission was deliberate.

54. The Court thus concludes that the applicants cannot derive a right to divorce from Article 12. That provision is therefore inapplicable in the present case, either on its own or in conjunction with Article 14.

55. The principles which emerge from the Court's case law on Article 8 include the following:

(a) By guaranteeing the right to respect for family life, Article 8 presupposes the existence of a family.

(b) Article 8 applies to the 'family life' of the 'illegitimate' family as well as to that of the 'legitimate' family.

(c) Although the essential object of Article 8 is to protect the individual against arbitrary interference by the public authorities, there may in addition be positive obligations inherent in an effective 'respect' for family life. However, especially as far as those positive obligations are concerned, the notion of 'respect' is not clear-cut: having regard to the diversity of the practices followed and the situations obtaining in the Contracting States, the notion's requirements will vary considerably from case to case. Accordingly, this is an area in which the Contracting Parties enjoy a wide margin of appreciation in determining the steps to be taken to ensure compliance with the Convention with due regard to the needs and resources of the community and of individuals.

56. In the present case, it is clear that the applicants, the first and second of whom have lived together for some fifteen years, constitute a 'family' for the purposes of Article 8. They are thus entitled to its protection, notwithstanding the fact that their relationship exists outside marriage.

The question that arises, as regards this part of the case, is whether an effective 'respect' for the applicants' family life imposes on Ireland a positive obligation to introduce measures that would permit divorce.

57. It is true that, on this question, Article 8, with its reference to the somewhat vague notion of 'respect' for family life, might appear to lend itself more readily to an evolutive interpretation than does Article 12. Nevertheless, the Convention must be read as a whole and the Court does not consider that a right to divorce, which it has found to be excluded from Article 12, can, with consistency, be derived from Article 8, a provision of more general purpose and scope. The Court is not oblivious to the plight of the first and second applicants. However, it is of the opinion that, although the protection of private or family life may sometimes necessitate means whereby spouses can be relieved from the duty to live together[9] the engagements undertaken by Ireland under Article 8 cannot be regarded as extending to an obligation on its part to introduce measures permitting the divorce and the remarriage which the applicants seek.

58. On the point, there is therefore no failure to respect the family life of the first and second applicants . . .

---

[9] *See Airey v. Ireland* (discussed at Section (A)(2) *infra*).

[The Court found no violations of Article 14 taken in conjunction with Article 8 or of Article 9.]

64. The Court thus concludes that the complaints related to the inability to divorce and re-marry are not well-founded.

65. The first and second applicant further alleged that, in violation of Article 8, there had been an interference with, or lack of respect for, their family life [in connection with matters other than the ability to divorce and remarry] on account of their status under Irish law . . .

66. In the Court's view, there has been no interference by the public authorities with the family life of the first and second applicants: Ireland has done nothing to impede or prevent them from living together and continuing to do so and, indeed, they have been able to take a number of steps to regularise their situation as best they could. Accordingly, the sole question that arises for decision is whether an effective 'respect' for their family life imposes on Ireland a positive obligation to improve their status.

68. It is true that certain legislative provisions designed to support family life are not available to the first and second applicants. However, like the Commission, the Court does not consider that it is possible to derive from Article 8 an obligation on the part of Ireland to establish for unmarried couples a status analogous to that of married couples . . .

71. Roy Johnston and Janice Williams-Johnston have been able to take a number of steps to integrate their daughter in the family. However, the question arises whether an effective 'respect' for family life imposes on Ireland a positive obligation to improve her legal situation.

72. Of particular relevance to this part of the case, in addition to the principles recalled above, are the following passages from the Court's case law:

> . . . when the State determines in its domestic legal system the regime applicable to certain family ties such as those between an unmarried mother and her child, it must act in a manner calculated to allow those concerned to lead a normal family life. As envisaged by Article 8, respect for family life implies in particular, in the Court's view, the existence in domestic law of legal safeguards that render possible as from the moment of birth the child's integration in his family. In this connection, the State has a choice of various means, but a law that fails to satisfy this requirement violates paragraph 1 of Article 8 without there being any call to examine it under paragraph 2.[10]
>
> In determining whether or not a positive obligation exists, regard must be had to the fair balance that has to be struck between the general interest of the community and the interests of the individual, the search for which balance is inherent in the whole of the Convention . . . In striking this balance the aims mentioned in the second paragraph of Article 8 may be of a certain relevance, although this provision refers in terms only to interferences with the right protected by the first paragraph—in other words is concerned with the negative obligations flowing therefrom . . .[11]

74. As is recorded in the Preamble to the European Convention of 15 October 1975 on the Legal Status of Children born out of Wedlock, 'in a great number of member States [of the Council of Europe] efforts have been, or are being, made to improve the legal status of children born out of wedlock by reducing the differences between their legal status and that of children born in wedlock which are to the legal or social disadvantage of the former'. Furthermore, in Ireland itself this trend is reflected in the Status of Children Bill recently laid before Parliament.

---

[10] *See Marckx v. Belgium* (discussed in Section (A)(3) *infra*).

[11] *See Rees v. United Kingdom* (discussed in section (C)(1)(B) *infra*).

In its consideration of this part of the present case, the Court cannot but be influenced by these developments. As it observed in its above mentioned *Marckx* judgment, 'respect' for family life, understood as including the ties between near relatives, implies an obligation for the State to act in a manner calculated to allow these ties to develop normally. And in the present case the normal development of the natural family ties between the first and second applicants and their daughter requires, in the Court's opinion, that she should be placed, legally and socially, in a position akin to that of a legitimate child.

75. Examination of the third applicant's present legal situation, seen as a whole, reveals, however, that it differs considerably from that of a legitimate child; in addition, it has not been shown that there are any means available to her or her parents to eliminate or reduce the differences. Having regard to the particular circumstances of this case and notwithstanding the wide margin of appreciation enjoyed by Ireland in this area, the absence of an appropriate legal regime reflecting the third applicant's natural family ties amounts to a failure to respect her family life.

Moreover, the close and intimate relationship between the third applicant and her parents is such that there is of necessity also a resultant failure to respect the family life of each of the latter. Contrary to the Government's suggestion, this finding does not amount, in an indirect way, to a conclusion that the first applicant should be entitled to divorce and re-marry; this is demonstrated by the fact that in Ireland itself it is proposed to improve the legal situation of illegitimate children, whilst maintaining the constitutional prohibition on divorce.

76. There is accordingly, as regards all three applicants, a breach of Article 8 under this head.

77. It is not the Court's function to indicate which measures Ireland should take in this connection; it is for the State concerned to choose the means to be utilised in its domestic law for performance of its obligation under Article 53.[12] In making its choice, Ireland must ensure that the requisite fair balance is struck between the demands of the general interest of the community and the interests of the individual.

> [The Court held, 16 to one, that the unavailability of divorce did not violate Article 8. It held unanimously that the other aspects of Irish law affecting the adult applicants did not violate Article 8. I: held unanimously that the legal disabilities of the child-applicant violated Article 8.]

Declaration by Judge Pinheiro Farinha . . .

Separate Opinion, Partly Dissenting and Partly Concurring, of Judge de Meyer . . .

5. We are thus faced with a situation in which, by mutual consent and a considerable time ago, two spouses separated, regulated their own and their children's rights in an apparently satisfactory fashion and embarked on a new life, each with a new partner.

In my view, the absence of any possibility of seeking, in such circumstances, the civil dissolution of the marriage constitutes, first and of itself, a violation, as regards each of the spouses, of the rights guaranteed in Article 8, 9 and 12 of the Convention. Secondly, in that it perforce means that neither spouse can re-marry in a civil ceremony so long as his wife or husband is alive, it constitutes a violation of the same rights as regards each of the spouses and each of the new partners. . . .

[12] *See Airey v. Ireland* (discussed at Section (A)(2) *infra*); *Marckx v. Belgium* (discussed at Section (A)(3) *infra*).

On more than one occasion, the Court has pointed out that there can be no such society without pluralism, tolerance and broadmindedness: these are hallmarks of a democratic society.

In a society grounded on principles of this kind, it seems to me excessive to impose, in an inflexible and absolute manner, a rule that marriage is indissoluble, without even allowing consideration to be given to the possibility of exceptions in cases of the present kind.

For so draconian a system to be legitimate, it does not suffice that it corresponds to the desire or will of a substantial majority of the population: the Court has also stated that 'although individual interests must on occasion be subordinated to those of a group, democracy does not simply mean that the views of a majority must always prevail: a balance must be achieved which ensures the fair and proper treatment of minorities and avoids any abuse of a dominant position'. . . .

6. The foregoing considerations do not imply recognition of a right to divorce or that such a right, to the extent that it exists, can be classified as a fundamental right.

They simply mean that the complete exclusion of any possibility of seeking the civil dissolution of a marriage is not compatible with the right to respect for private and family life, with the right to freedom of conscience and religion and with the right to marry and to found a family. . . .

However, it seems to me that it is not sufficient to say that the third applicant should be placed 'in a position akin to that of a legitimate child': in my view, we ought to have stated more clearly and more simply that the legal situation of a child born out of wedlock must be identical to that of a child of a married couple and that, by the same token, there cannot be, as regards relations with or concerning a child, any difference between the legal situation of his parents and of their families that depends on whether he was the child of a married couple or a child born out of wedlock. . . .

2. MARRIAGE

The European Court has addressed the limitations Article 8 and 12 impose on regulation of the martial relationship in two other cases. In *Airey v. Ireland*,[13] the applicant was the wife of an alcoholic and violent husband. Irish law allowed recourse to the High Court for obtaining a legal separation, but the applicant was unable to afford the expense of such an action. The Court held there was a violation of Article 6(1), since the applicant had effectively been denied access to a court for determination of her civil rights. The Court also held that, under Article 8, protection of family or private life sometimes requires 'being relieved of the duty to live together', and the means for accomplishing this relief must be provided to anyone who needs it. In dissent, Judge Vilhjamsson said: 'It is a farfetched interpretation of Article 8 to come to the conclusion that the duty to respect Mrs. Airey's private and family life included the duty to help her seek judicial dissolution'. Compare *Boddie v. Connecticut*,[14] in which the United States Supreme Court held that a $60 service and filing fee for initiation of a divorce action amounted to a deprivation of liberty without due process of law in violation of the Fourteenth Amendment. In the case of divorce, the Court noted,

---

[13] 9 Oct. 1979 (No. 32), 2 E.H.R.R. 305.
[14] 401 U.S. 371 (1971).

access to court was 'the exclusive precondition to the adjustment of the fundamental human relationship. The requirement that the appellant resort to the judicial process is entirely a state created matter.'

In *Johnston* the Court held that Article 12 does not include a right to a dissolution of marriage, even though the applicants' inability to marry stemmed solely from state created legal rules. But marriage itself is largely a creature of legal rules precluding divorce and prohibiting bigamy. Thus, Article 12 allows restrictions 'according to the national laws'. In *F v. Switzerland*,[15] the Court considered Swiss law which imposed a three year ban on remarriage after the applicant's third divorce where he had been found guilty of adultery and particularly offensive behaviour. The Court held that, notwithstanding the reference to national law, a state may not 'restrict or reduce the right in such a way or to such an extent that the very essence is impaired'.[16] It noted that restrictions on marriage elsewhere in Europe related only to procedures, capacity or consent. It rejected Switzerland's arguments that the law was necessary for the protection of possible future spouses or that it compelled reflection benefiting the person who wished to remarry. The Court concluded that the measure 'affected the very essence of the right to marry, was disproportionate to the very aim pursued' and therefore violated Article 12.

3. ILLEGITIMACY

In deciding that Irish law violated the rights of the child applicant and her parents under Article 8 in *Johnston v. Ireland*, the Court did not consider possible justifications under paragraph 2. It followed its judgment in *Marckx v. Belgium*,[17] where the Court did discuss the state's interests in deciding what obligations arose from the duty to respect the family life of a mother and her illegitimate daughter and whether differential treatment of legitimate and illegitimate families was justifiable under Article 14:

39. The Government, relying on the difference between the situations of the unmarried and the married mother, advance the following arguments; whilst the married mother and her husband 'mutually undertake . . . the obligation to feed, keep and educate their children' (Article 203 of the Civil Code), there is no certainty that the unmarried mother will be willing to bear on her own the responsibilities of motherhood; by leaving the unmarried mother the choice between recognising her child or dissociating herself from him, the law is prompted by a concern for protection of the child, for it would be dangerous to entrust him to the custody and authority of someone who has shown no inclination to care for him; many unmarried mothers do not recognise their child.

In the Court's judgment, the fact that some unmarried mothers, unlike Paula Marckx, do not wish to take care of their child cannot justify the rule of Belgian law whereby the establishment of

---

[15] 18 Dec. 1987 (No. 128), 10 E.H.R.R. 411. *See also Vermeire v. Belgium,* 29 Nov. 1991 (No. 214C), 15 E.H.R.R. 488.

[16] Citing *Rees v. United Kingdom* (discussed in section (C)(1)(B) *infra.* (4)).

[17] 13 June 1979 (No. 31), 2 E.H.R.R. 330.

their maternity is conditional on voluntary recognition or a court declaration. In fact, such an attitude is not a general feature of the relationship between unmarried mothers and their children; besides, this is neither claimed by the Government nor proved by the figures which they advance. As the Commission points out, it may happen that also a married mother might not wish to bring up her child, and yet as far as she is concerned, the birth alone will have created the legal bond of affiliation. . . .

40. The Government do not deny that the present law favours the traditional family but they maintain that the law aims at ensuring that family's full development and is thereby founded on objective and reasonable grounds relating to morals and public order (*order public*).

The Court recognises that support and encouragement of the traditional family is in itself legitimate or even praiseworthy. However, in the achievement of this end recourse must not be had to measures whose object or result is, as in the present case, to prejudice the 'illegitimate' family, the members of the 'illegitimate' family enjoy the guarantees of Article 8 on an equal footing with the members of the traditional family. . . .

In the United States legislation disfavouring the relationship between illegitimate children and their natural parents was quite common well into the twentieth century. In a series of decisions in the 1960s and 1970s, however, the Supreme Court held many of these statutes unconstitutional as violating the Equal Protection clause of the Fourteenth Amendment. For the most part, the Supreme Court's principal focus (unlike that of the European Court) was not on the injury done to the family. Rather, the emphasis was on the individual right of the illegitimate child and the legal disadvantages imposed on it in comparison with the legal status of legitimate children. The Court has never made clear what degree of scrutiny is appropriate for classification based on illegitimacy, but it has expressed doubts about the utility of such classifications in serving proper objectives. In one of the earliest cases, *Levy v. Louisiana*[18] the Court held invalid a wrongful death statute which denied to illegitimate children an action based on the wrongful death of their mother:

Legitimacy or illegitimacy of birth has no relation to the nature of the wrong allegedly inflicted on the mother. These children, though illegitimate, were dependent on her, she cared for them and nurtured them; they were indeed hers in the biological and in the spiritual sense; in her death they suffered wrong in the sense that any dependent would.

We conclude that it is invidious to discriminate against them when no action, conduct, or demeanor of theirs is possibly relevant to the harm that was done the mother.

The judgments of the American and European Courts should be contrasted with that of the Irish Supreme Court in *O'B v. S*,[19] where the exclusion of illegitimate children from the definition of 'issue' entitled to shares in the estate of a person who died intestate, was challenged as a violation of the provision of the Irish Constitution that 'all citizens shall, as human persons, be held equal before the law'. The Court held that the intestacy provisions, while discriminatory, were justified as a proper means of fulfilling the state's responsibility under another constitutional article to protect 'the

18 391 U.S. 68 (1968).
19 [1984] I.R. 316.

Family'. The Court emphasized that the 'family' referred to in the Constitution was the 'family based upon marriage'. The distinction in the succession law served this purpose by assuring that 'the family patrimony will be kept within the family on intestacy'. 'It can scarcely be doubted that the [challenged provision] was designed to strengthen the family as required by the Constitution and, for that purpose, to place members of a family based on marriage in a more favourable position than other persons . . .'

4. LEGAL DEFINITIONS OF THE FAMILY

The protection of 'family life' from intrusive legal regulation presents an immediate problem. To a very substantial degree a 'family' (like a marriage)[20] is defined by rules of law. How can such rules, at the same time, interfere with the very institution they define?[21] In his dissent in *Levy v. Louisiana* and in a companion case, *Glona v. American Guarantee Co.*,[22] (in the United States Supreme Court), Justice Harlan emphasized the legal definition of family relationships:

The Court today, for some reason which I am at a loss to understand, rules that the State must base its arbitrary definition of the plaintiff class on biological rather than legal relationships . . . [N]either a biological relationship nor legal acknowledgment is indicative of the love or economic dependence that may exist between two persons . . . The rights at issue here stem from the existence of a family relationship, and the State has decided only that it will not recognize the family relationship unless the formalities of marriage, or of the acknowledgment of children by the parent in question, have been complied with.

In *Johnston v. Ireland*, the Court found that Article 8 governed the state's regulation of a family unit consisting of the child and both unmarried parents. It thereby relied on an 'autonomous interpretation' of the term, family, in Article 8. In *Marckx* the Court found that a mother and her illegitimate daughter constituted a family entitled to respect under Article 8.

The Supreme Court of Ireland, in contrast, has limited the term 'family' in the Irish Constitution to those relationships conforming to positive rules of law. The Court has held that provisions providing that the state must guarantee the protection of the family and affirming the rights of parents to control the education of their children, do not extend to parents becoming such outside of wedlock. Both references, the Court held, refer to:

the family which is founded on the institution of marriage and, in [this] context . . . marriage means valid marriage under the law for the time being in force in the State. While it is true that unmarried persons cohabitating together and the children of their union may often be referred to

---

[20] *See* Section 2, *supra*.
[21] *See* Frances E. Olsen, 'The Myth of State Intervention in the Family' (1985) 8 Mich. L. Rev. 835; Note, 'Looking for a Family Resemblance: The Unity of the Functional Approach to the Legal Definition of Family' (1992) 104 Harv. L. Rev. 1640.
[22] 391 U.S. 68 (1968); 391 U.S. 73 (1968).

as family and have many, if not all, of the outward appearances of a family, and may indeed for the purpose of a particular law be regarded as such. Nevertheless, so far as [these constitutional provisions are] concerned the guarantees therein contained are confined to families based upon marriage.[23]

The European Court confronted other dimensions of family life in *Berrehab v. The Netherlands*.[24] There the applicant complained that the Netherlands had violated Article 8 by separating him from his daughter when it refused to extend his visa and deported him. Berrehab, a Moroccan national, had while residing in the Netherlands, married a Dutch wife. Their child was born almost two years later, days after the marriage had been dissolved. For four years thereafter, Berrehab contributed to the child's support and saw her four times a week for several hours each time. The government refused to extend his permission to remain in the Netherlands which had been granted 'for the sole purpose of enabling him to live with his Dutch wife'. After extended appeals and reviews, he was deported. The Court held that even an entirely formal legal relationship could create, *prima facie*, a protected family unit.

[A] child born of a [lawful] union is *ipso jure* part of that relationship; hence from the moment of the child's birth and by the very fact of it, there exists between him and his parents a bond amounting to 'family life', even if the parents are not then living together . . . Subsequent events, of course, may break that tie, but this was not so in the instant case [referring to the regular visits between the applicant and his daughter.][25]

The Court held that the deportation was an interference with the right protected in Article 8(1), and, although the immigration policies at issue had a legitimate aim, *viz* 'the economic well-being of the country', these measures were not 'necessary in a democratic society'. In making that determination the Court considered how important deportation of Berrehab was to the state and how seriously his family life was injured. The facts of the applicant's continued relationship with his daughter were considered by the Court principally in connection with that determination, and not in deciding whether an interference with family life occurred in the first place.

The results of the *Marckx, Johnston*, and *Berrehab* cases imply that a substantive family relationship is protected, even if unaccompanied by legal form, and that a formal, legal family relation is protected, even if without substantive content. In *X, Y and Z v. United Kingdom*[26] the Court held that a family relationship existed between a female-to-male transsexual and the child (conceived by artificial insemination) of the woman with whom he had lived in a stable relationship for more than 10 years. The Court noted that the couple had applied jointly for the fertilization treatment and that

---

[23]　*State (Nicolaou) v. An Bord Uchtala* [1966] 1.R. 567, 643.

[24]　21 June 1988 (No. 138), 11 E.H.R.R. 322.

[25]　*Id.* at para. 21. Similarly, the Court has ruled that the contracting of a legal marriage, even absent cohabitation, is sufficient to engage Article 8. *Abdulaziz Cabules and Balkandali v. United Kingdom*, 28 May 1985 (No. 94), 7 E.H.R.R. 471.

[26]　22 Apr. 1997, Reports, 1997–II 619, 24 E.H.R.R. 143.

'X was involved throughout that process and has acted as Z's father in every respect since the birth'.[27]

In all of the cases discussed the claim of family life, whether based on legal or biological ties, was evidenced by a sustained social relationship. But even this is not essential. In *Keegan v. Ireland*,[28] the Court held the adoption of an infant without the knowledge or consent of the natural father was a violation of Article 8. This was so even where there had been no marriage between mother and father and where the father had established no personal relationship with the child. The child in *Keegan*, who was born after its parents had cohabited for about two years and separated, had been placed with prospective adoptive parents at the age of seven weeks. The applicant father had seen the baby the day after it was born but had not been allowed to see it thereafter. The European Court noted that *de facto* as well as marriage-based relationships could qualify as family life within Article 8, citing *Johnston*. It concluded that the parents' relationship before the birth had all the characteristics of a family. 'A child born out of such a relationship is *ipso iure* part of the "family" unit from the moment of its birth and by the very fact of it' (citing *Berrehab*). The fact that the family relationship had broken down shortly before the birth 'does not alter this conclusion any more than it would for a couple who were lawfully married in a similar situation'.[29] Similarly, in *Söderbäck v. Sweden*,[30] the Court assumed that the adoption of the applicant's daughter by her stepfather was an interference with his family life. This was supposed even though he had never been married to the mother and his contact with the 4-year-old child had been extremely limited.[31] The Court held, however, that the adoption was justified under Article 8(2) as a decision within the state's margin of appreciation.[32]

The United States Supreme Court has held that the natural father of children born outside of marriage, who had established a parental relationship with them, had a right under the due process clause of the Fourteenth Amendment to notice and hearing before his children could be made wards of the state.[33] However, an unmarried father who had failed to establish such a relationship and had neglected to register himself on a state-maintained 'putative father registry' was not entitled to notice and hearing in connection with adoption proceedings.[34]

The Constitutional Court of South Africa held unconstitutional the provision of the Child Care Act which allowed an illegitimate child to be adopted with the sole consent of the mother.[35] The Court found this arrangement inconsistent with the equality provision of the Constitution. It recognized that, at least in early childhood,

---

[27] *Id.* para. 37.

[28] 26 May 1994 (No. 290), 18 E.H.R.R. 342.

[29] *Id.*

[30] 28 Oct. 1998, Reports, 1998–VII 3086, 29 E.H.R.R. 95.

[31] *Id.* at paras. 24–5.

[32] *Id.* at paras. 32–5.

[33] *Stanley v. Illinois*, 406 U.S. 645 (1972).

[34] *Lehr v. Robertson*, 463 U.S. 248 (1983). *See also Michael H. v. Gerald D.*, 491 U.S. 110 (1989) in which the Supreme Court upheld a statute creating presumption that a child born to a married woman was the child of her husband against a claim that the presumption violated the rights of the natural father.

[35] *Fraser v. The Children's Court* [1997] **2** S.A.L.R. 261

the 'biological relationship' between mother and child was 'very direct and not comparable to that of a father.' But, it noted, there could be circumstances where the relationship of the child with the father was as strong or stronger.[36] It also found the law to discriminate between married and unmarried fathers, noting that it was impossible to make a universally valid presumption that the latter class was uninterested or unfit.[37] The Court declined, however, to order a remedy which would require the consent of both parents in every adoption. Rather it left Parliament to craft a law which responded to the various rights relevant in different circumstances.[38]

The House of Lords has held that controlling statutes denied the unmarried father of children any right of notice and, indeed, any right to contest proceedings by local authorities for placement and adoption of his children. Such procedural rights were extended only to parents, guardians and custodians. But, under the relevant statute parental rights for children born outside of marriage were vested exclusively in the mother. The speech of Lord Brandon (delivered before the Strasbourg court's judgment in *Keegan*) entertained the possibility that this result might contravene Articles 6 and 8 of the Convention but concluded that 'while English courts will strive when they can to interpret statutes as conforming with the obligations of the United Kingdom under the Convention, they are nevertheless bound to give effect to statutes which are free from ambiguity in accordance with their terms, even if those statutes may be in conflict with the Convention'.[39]

The European Court further developed its understanding of the factors relevant to the creation of family life in *Kroon v. The Netherlands*[40] in which the competing interests associated with recognition of legal, biological and social families were brought into especially sharp focus. The applicants were a biological mother, father and child. The child had been born while the mother was married to another man from whom she was later divorced. The father and mother never lived together although they had three more children. Under Dutch law a child born to a married woman was presumed to be the issue of her husband. The mother was not permitted to rebut that presumption. The applicant mother and father had been refused in their request to alter the birth records to allow the father to recognize the child. The government disputed the claim that the applicants, who lived in separate households, had a 'family life'. The Court held Article 8 applicable.

Although, as a rule, living together may be a requirement for such a relationship, exceptionally other factors may also serve to demonstrate that a relationship has sufficient constancy to create *de facto* 'family ties': such is the case here, as since 1983, four children have been born [to the applicants].[41]

---

[36] *Id.* at para. 25.

[37] *Id.* at para. 26.

[38] *Id.* at paras. 27–30. The transitional South African Constitution s. 98(5) expressly granted the court the authority to order such a remedy. See also Constitution of the Republic of South Africa 1996, 172(1)(b).

[39] *In re M and H* [1988] 3 All E.R. 5, 15.

[40] 27 Oct. 1994 (No. 297C), 19 E.H.R.R. 263.

[41] *Id.* at para. 30.

In dissent Judge Misful Bonnici argued:

In my opinion 'family life' necessarily implies 'living together as a family.' The exception to this refers to circumstances related to necessity, i.e. separation brought about by reasons of work, illness or other necessities of the family itself. . . . But, equally clearly this does not apply when the separation is completely voluntary. When it is voluntary then, clearly, the member or members of the family who do so have opted against family life, against living together as a family. And since these are the circumstances of the instant case, where the first two applicants have voluntarily opted not to have a 'family life,' I cannot understand how they can call upon Netherlands law to respect something which they have wilfully opted against. The artificiality of this approach is in strident contradiction with the natural value of family life which the Convention guarantees.[42]

The Court held that the Netherlands had failed to respect the family life so recognized. It declared that such respect 'requires that biological and social realities prevail over a legal presumption which, as in the present case, flies in the face of both established fact and the wishes of those concerned without actually benefitting anyone'.[43]

The United States Supreme Court has held that the father of a child born to a woman married to another man may be denied parental rights. In *Michael H. v. Gerald D.*[44] it declared constitutional a state statute creating a presumption similar to that in *Kroon*. The Court determined that, although the father had established a continuing parental relationship with the child, his interest in being recognized as a parent did not amount to a 'fundamental right' so as to require strict protection under the Fourteenth Amendment. Justice Scalia noted that, traditionally, the father of the child of a woman married to another man had not been recognized as part of 'a protected family unit under the historic practices of our society'.[45]

The Supreme Court of Canada has extended constitutional protection to *de facto* families under section 15 of the Charter of Rights and Freedoms, mandating equal treatment before the law. In *Miron v. Trudel*[46] the Court ruled that a failure to extend statutory insurance benefits to unmarried as well as married couples violated the Charter. The plurality opinion held that discrimination based on the absence of a formal marriage was on a ground 'analogous' to those expressly listed in section 15— race, national or ethnic origin, colour, religion, sex, age or mental or physical disability:

[D]iscrimination on the basis of marital status touches the essential dignity and worth of the individual in the same way as other recognized grounds of discrimination are violative of fundamental human rights norms. Specifically, it touches the individual's freedom to live life with the

---

[42] *Id.* (dissenting opinion).
[43] *Id.* para. 40.
[44] 491 U.S. 110 (1989).
[45] *Id.* at 124.
[46] [1995] 2 S.C.R. 418.

mate of one's choice in the fashion of one's choice. This is a matter of defining importance to individuals.[47]

In addition, the plurality found that unmarried couples had suffered historical disadvantage and social opprobrium and that their status, while not strictly immutable, was often beyond the practical power of individuals to change. It cited recent developments premised on the idea that 'distinguishing between cohabiting couples on the basis of whether they are legally married or not fails to accord with current social values or realities.[48] The dissenting justices insisted that a distinction, at least in this context, between married and unmarried couples was an appropriate means of advancing the legislative goal of fostering and protecting the institution of marriage.[49]

In *M v H*[50] the Court held invalid Ontario's distinction between opposite-sex and same-sex couples in creating obligations of spousal support. The Family Law Act included unmarried persons in its definition of 'spouse' but limited it to relationships between a man and a woman. The Supreme Court had already held that sexual orientation was an 'analogous ground' to those traits expressly listed in section 15.[51] Since, *inter alia*, the exclusion of same-sex couples implied 'that they are judged to be incapable of forming intimate relationships of economic interdependence as compared to opposite-sex couples' a *prima facie* violation of section 15 was made out.[52] The majority declined to find the distinction justifiable under section 1 of the Charter. Since the statute had already been extended to unmarried couples, the province could not rely on the special protection of marriage. The Court found unconvincing the argument that the limited scope of the statute was intentionally related to cases when economic dependence was more of a problem or that it was meant to protect children.[53] But it held that, in any event, these objectives were not rationally furthered by excluding same-sex couples.[54]

In *Marckx*, the Court also found a violation of Article 8 with respect to the child's grandmother whose legal relations were affected by the child's status as illegitimate. This raises yet another question as to the definition of the 'family' whose life is protected by Article 8. Near relatives, such as a grandmother the Court stated, 'may play a considerable part in family life'.[55] Decisions of the United States Supreme Court have defined a sphere of family autonomy which is protected from interference under the due process clauses of the Fifth and Fourteenth Amendments. It also has determined that the grandparent-grandchild relationship is protected. In *Moore v. East Cleveland*,[56] The Supreme Court held invalid a zoning ordinance which had the

---

[47] *Id.* para. 151.

[48] *Id.* paras. 152–5.

[49] *Id.* paras. 40–5.

[50] [1999] 2 S.C.R. 3.

[51] See *Egan v. Canada* [1995] 2 S.C.R. 513.

[52] [1999] 2 S.C.R. 3 at paras. 73–4.

[53] *Id.* at paras. 86–107.

[54] *Id.* at paras. 109–17.

[55] *Id.* at para. 55. *See also Bronda v. Italy*, 9 June 1998, Reports 1998–IV 1476 (right of grandparents to contest public care order).

[56] 431 U.S. 494 (1977).

effect of preventing a grandchild from sharing a single family dwelling with his grandmother. The plurality noted that the tradition 'of uncles, aunts, cousins, and especially grandparents sharing a household along with parents and children has roots equally venerable and equally deserving of constitutional recognition'.[57]

5. POSITIVE OBLIGATIONS

In *Johnston v. Ireland*, the Court noted that, in addition to protecting individuals from arbitrary interference (in paragraph 2), 'there may . . . be positive obligations inherent in [the] 'respect for family life' mandated by paragraph 1'. A state must, according to the court, 'act in a manner calculated to allow [family] ties to develop naturally'. The extent of these positive obligations has never been defined with any precision. To the extent they have been found to exist, they have been interpreted to require a legal environment which allows family or private life to develop normally. The ability to transmit property on death, one of the legal capacities limited in *Johnston*, might be seen as an essential attribute of the maintenance of family relations over time.

A. X AND Y *v.* THE NETHERLANDS

Judgment of 26 March 1985
(No. 91), 8 E.H.R.R. 235

7. Mr. X and his daughter Y were born in 1929 and on 13 December 1961 respectively. The daughter, who is mentally handicapped, had been living since 1970 in a privately-run home for mentally handicapped children.

8. During the night of 14 to 15 December 1977, Miss Y was woken up by a certain Mr. B, the son-in-law of the directress; he lived with his wife on the premises of the institution although he was not employed there. Mr. B forced the girl to follow him to his room, to undress and to have sexual intercourse with him.

This incident, which occurred on the day after Miss Y's sixteenth birthday, had traumatic consequences for her, causing her major mental disturbance.

9. On 16 December 1977, Mr. X went to the local police station to file a complaint and to ask for criminal proceedings to be instituted.

The police officer said that since Mr. X considered his daughter unable to sign the complaint because of her mental condition, he could do so himself. . . .

10. . . . The officer subsequently informed the public prosecutor's office that in the light of the father's statement and of his own observations concerning the girl's mental condition, she did not seem to him capable of filing a complaint herself. According to the headmaster of the school she was attending and another teacher there, she was unable to express her wishes concerning the institution of proceedings. . . .

---

[57] A survey of the European Court's treatment of various family relationships is found in J. Liddy, 'The Concept of Family Life Under the ECHR [1998] *European Human Rights Law Review* 15.

[Mr. X appealed the public prosecutor's decision not to institute criminal proceedings against Mr. B to the Arnhem Court of Appeal.]

12. ...

The Court of Appeal dismissed the appeal on 12 July 1979. In fact, it considered it doubtful whether a charge of rape (Art. 242 of Criminal Code) could be proved. As for Article 248ter, [making criminal the inducement of indecent acts from a minor by gift, promise, deceit or abuse of dominant position] it would have been applicable in the instant case, but only if the victim herself had taken action. [Under Art. 64(1) of the Criminal code a legal representative could lodge the complaint only if the victim were under sixteen years old or under legal guardianship. Guardianship, however, was available only for persons of twenty-one or older.] In the Court of Appeal's view, the father's complaint could not be regarded as a substitute for the complaint which the girl, being over the age of sixteen, should have lodged herself, although the police had regarded her as incapable of doing so; since in the instant case no one was legally empowered to file a complaint, there was on this point a gap in the law, but it could not be filled by means of a broad interpretation to the detriment of Mr. B. ...

17. At the hearings, counsel for the Government informed the Court that the Ministry of Justice had prepared a Bill modifying the provisions of the Criminal Code that related to sexual offences. Under the Bill, it would be an offence to make sexual advances to a mentally handicapped person. ...

22. There was no dispute as to the applicability of Article 8: the facts underlying the application to the Commission concern a matter of 'private life', a concept which covers the physical and moral integrity of the person, including his or her sexual life.

23. The Court recalls that although the object of Article 8 is essentially that of protecting the individual against arbitrary interference by the public authorities, it does not merely compel the State to abstain from such interference: in addition to this primarily negative undertaking, there may be positive obligations inherent in an effective respect for private on family life, these obligations may involve the adoption of measures designed to secure respect for private life even in the sphere of the relations of individuals between themselves.

24. The applicants argued that for a young girl like Miss Y, the requisite degree of protection against the wrongdoing in question would have been provided only by means of the criminal law. In the Government's view, the Convention left it to each State to decide upon the means to be utilised and did not prevent it from opting for civil-law provisions.

The Court, which on this point agrees in substance with the opinion of the Commission, observes that the choice of the means calculated to secure compliance with Article 8 in the sphere of the relations of individuals between themselves is in principle a matter that falls within the Contracting States' margin of appreciation. In this connection, there are different ways of ensuring 'respect for private life' and the nature of private life that is at issue. Recourse to the criminal law is not necessarily the only answer.

25. The Government cited the difficulty encountered by the legislature in laying down criminal-law provisions calculated to afford the best possible protection of the physical integrity of the mentally handicapped: to go too far in this direction might lead to unacceptable paternalism and occasion an inadmissible interference by the State with the individual's right to respect for his or her sexual life.

The Government stated that under Article 1401 of the Civil Code, taken together with Article 1407, it would have been possible to bring before or file with the Netherlands courts, on behalf of Miss Y:

— an action for damages against Mr. B for pecuniary or non-pecuniary damage;

— an application for an injunction against Mr. B, to prevent repetition of the offence;

— a similar action or application against the directress of the children's home.

The applicants considered that these civil-law remedies were unsuitable. They submitted that, amongst other things, the absence of any criminal investigation made it harder to furnish evidence on the four matters that had to be established under Article 1401, namely a wrongful act, fault, damage and a causal link between the act and the damage. Furthermore, such proceedings were lengthy and involved difficulties of an emotional nature for the victim, since he or she had to play an active part therein . . .

27. The Court finds that the protection afforded by the civil law in the case of wrongdoing of the kind inflicted on Miss Y is insufficient. This is a case where fundamental values and essential aspects of private life are at stake. *Effective deterrence is indispensable* in this area and it can be achieved only by criminal-law provisions; indeed, it is by such provisions that the matter is normally regulated.

Moreover, as was pointed out by the Commission, this is in fact an area in which the Netherlands has generally opted for a system of protection based on the criminal law. The only gap, so far as the Commission and the Court have been made aware, is as regards persons in the situation of Miss Y; in such cases, this system meets a procedural obstacle which the Dutch legislature had apparently not foreseen. . . .

29. Two provisions of the Criminal Code are relevant to the present case, namely Article 248ter and Article 239(2).

Article 248ter requires a complaint by the actual victim before criminal proceedings can be instituted against someone who has contravened this provision. The Arnhem Court of Appeal held that, in the case of an individual like Miss Y, the legal representative could not act on the victim's behalf for this purpose. The Court of Appeal did not feel able to fill this gap in the law by means of a broad interpretation to the detriment of Mr. B. It is in no way the task of the European Court of Human Rights to take the place of the competent national courts in the interpretation of domestic law, it regards it as established that in the case in question criminal proceedings could not be instituted on the basis of Article 248ter.

As for Article 239(2) [making criminal indecent acts while another person 'is present against his will', and which had been interpreted by Dutch courts to prohibit sexual advances to mentally handicapped persons], this is apparently designed to penalise indecent exposure and not indecent assault and was not clearly applicable to the present case. Indeed, no one, even the public prosecutor's office, seems to have considered utilising this provision at the time, or even referring to it at the outset of the Strasbourg proceedings.

30. Thus, neither Article 248 nor Article 239(2) of the Criminal Code provided Miss Y with practical and effective protection. It must therefore be concluded, taking account of the nature of the wrongdoing in question, that she was the victim of a violation of Article 8 of the Convention.

[The Court held unanimously that there was a violation of Article 8.]

B. THE LIMITS OF POSITIVE OBLIGATIONS

Many of the cases in which the Court has been asked to find that a state violated Article 8 by failing to discharge a positive obligation have, like the principal case, dealt with some claim of a defect in existing law. So, in *X & Y*, the Netherlands' violation consisted of its failure to allow criminal prosecution of people in the situation of Y's attacker. In *Marckx* and *Johnston* the Court held that the state was obliged to provide machinery for inheritance by children born outside of marriage. The Court has also found that France was required to change its rules of civil status so as to recognize the new gender of a transsexual[58] and that the United Kingdom had a positive obligation to make available to an adult applicant the records of his supervision as a child committed to public care.[59] In contrast to *X & Y*, in *Stubbings and Others v. United Kingdom*[60] the applicants alleged that they had been the victims of sexual abuse as children. They brought civil actions against the claimed abusers but the English courts interpreted applicable law to bar such actions if brought more than six years after the plaintiff's eighteenth birthday. The European Court held that the state had satisfied the positive obligation notwithstanding the applicants' inability to pursue a civil remedy. It noted that the underlying conduct was a serious criminal offence in British law and that such prosecutions were not time-barred. Indeed, one of the persons sued by the applicants had pleaded guilty to such a crime.

Article 8 does not necessarily require that States fulfil their positive obligations to secure respect for private life by the provision of unlimited civil remedies in circumstances where criminal law sanctions are in operation.[61]

The Court also declined to find a breach of positive obligation when Finnish law failed to provide a broadly defined right to change one's surname.[62]

In the context of Article 2's right to life the Court has defined a state's positive obligation to protect human life against attacks by private persons to go beyond 'putting in place effective criminal-law provisions to deter the commission of offences against the person backed up by law-enforcement machinery for the prevention, suppression and sanctioning of breaches of such provisions'.[63] It considered the nature of such an extended duty in *Osman v. United Kingdom*.[64] In that case one of the applicants, a 15-year-old had been wounded and his father had been shot and killed by a former teacher. The applicants claimed that over a number of months the police had been given information which should have made clear the danger of an assault but they had not searched the suspect's home nor arrested him. The Court agreed that there was:

---

[58] *B. v. France*, 25 Mar. 1992 (No. 232), 16 E.H.R.R. 1.
[59] *Gaskin v. United Kingdom*, 7 July 1989 (No. 160 12 E.H.R.R.)
[60] 22 Oct. 1996, Reports 1996–IV 1487, 23 E.H.R.R. 213.
[61] *Id.* para. 64.
[62] *Stjerna v. Finland*, 25 Nov. 1994 (No. 229 B), 4 E.H.R.R. 195.
[63] *Osman v. United Kingdom*, 28 Oct. 1998, Reports 1998–VIII 3124, 29 E.H.R.R. 245, para. 115.
[64] *Id.*

in certain well-defined circumstances a positive obligation on the authorities to take preventive operational measures to protect an individual whose life is at risk from the criminal acts of another individual . . .

For the Court, and bearing in mind the difficulties involved in policing modern societies, the unpredictability of human conduct and the operational choices which must be made in terms of priorities and resources, such an obligation must be interpreted in a way which does not impose an impossible or disproportionate burden on the authorities. Accordingly, not every claimed risk to life can entail for the authorities a Convention requirement to take operational measures to prevent that risk from materializing. Another relevant consideration is the need to ensure that the police exercise their powers to control and prevent crime in a manner which fully respects the due process and other guarantees which legitimately place restraints on the scope of their action to investigate crime and bring offenders to justice, including the guarantees contained in Articles 5 and 8 of the Convention.

In the opinion of the Court where there is an allegation that the authorities have violated their positive obligation to protect the right to life in the context of their above-mentioned duty to prevent and suppress offences against the person, it must be established to its satisfaction that the authorities knew or ought to have known at the time of the existence of a real and immediate risk to the life of an identified individual or individuals from the criminal acts of a third party and that they failed to take measures within the scope of their powers which, judged reasonably, might have been expected to avoid that risk. The Court does not accept the Government's view that the failure to perceive the risk to life in the circumstances known at the time or to take preventive measures to avoid that risk must be tantamount to gross negligence or wilful dis-regard of the duty to protect life. Such a rigid standard must be considered to be incompatible with the requirements of Article 1 of the Convention and the obligations of Contracting States under that Article to secure the practical and effective protection of the rights and freedoms laid down therein, including Article 2. For the Court, and having regard to the nature of the right protected by Article 2, a right fundamental in the scheme of the Convention, it is sufficient for an applicant to show that the authorities did not do all that could be reasonably expected of them to avoid a real and immediate risk to life of which they have or ought to have knowledge. This is a question which can only be answered in the light of all the circumstances of any particular case.[65]

In the case at hand, the Court found no breach of the state's positive obligation since, given the information available to the police at the relevant times, the measures they had taken amounted to a reasonable response.[66]

Outside Article 2, the Court has been unsympathetic to claims that a state has a positive obligation to take actions to facilitate private life that go beyond merely changing its law. It has, however, held that the state's duty to provide opportunities for individuals to develop family and private life and to enjoy their homes, includes an obligation to take action to deal with severe environmental pollution affecting the applicants' homes. In one case it held the state had not acted in a timely fashion to

---

[65] *Id.* at paras. 115–16.
[66] *Id.* at para. 121.

correct a serious problem of smells, fumes and noise from a water treatment plant—even when these emissions were not a significant threat to health.[67] In another case the state's breach consisted of its failure to notify affected residents of the risks associated with the operation of a fertilizer plant, emitting toxic substances and inflammable gases.[68] In contrast, in an earlier case, the Court rejected a claim that the United Kingdom was obliged to regulate more strictly the noise level at Heathrow Airport. While the Court agreed, against the argument of the government, that the applicant's Article 8 rights were affected, it found the government's actions sufficient given a state's wide margin of appreciation in such matters.[69]

Claims that Article 8 requires states to undertake other kinds of actions to facilitate family or private life have been often rejected. The Court found no violation in a state's failure to require facilities for handicapped people at a private beach resort visited by the applicant: '[t]he right to gain access to the beach and the sea at a place distinct from his normal place of residence during his holidays concerns interpersonal relations of such broad and indeterminate shape that there can be no conceivable direct link between the measures the State was urged to take in order to make good the omissions of the private bathing establishment and the applicant's private life'.[70] The Court has also held that the state's positive obligation in connection with respect for the home, does not include a duty to see that each family has its own home.[71]

It is not always clear, of course, when a claim involves a positive obligation and when it alleges a more familiar 'interference' with a right. In the last case mentioned, concerning the right to an individual home, the applicant complained specifically of a legal rule that prohibited him from terminating the lease of a tenant in a house he owned and, thus, prevented him from using it for his own family. It would have been easy to characterize this as an interference with his private and family life but the Court chose to treat the case as involving the positive obligation associated with that right.[72] While one approach or another may make little difference in result, it has been suggested that the decision to treat cases under the rubric of positive obligations rather then interference tends to obscure the Court's analysis of state justifications for the claimed infringement.[73] The problem of state justification arises because the positive obligation is derived from paragraph 1 of Article 8, as distinguished from the prohibition on state *interference* with that right in paragraph 2, and that only the interferences of paragraph 2 are expressly stated to be permissible if necessary for certain stated public objectives. The court has summed up its approach to the question as follows:

In determining whether or not a positive obligation exists, regard must be had to the fair balance

---

[67] *Lopez Ostra v. Spain*, 9 Dec. 1994 (No. 303 C), 20 E.H.R.R. 277.

[68] *Guerra v. Italy*, 19 Feb. 1998, Reports, 1998–I 210, 26 E.H.R.R. 357.

[69] *Powell & Raynor v. United Kingdom*, 21 Feb. 1990 (No. 172), 12 E.H.R.R. 355.

[70] *Botta v. Italy*, 24 Feb. 1998, Reports, 1998–I 412, 26 E.H.R.R. 611, para. 35.

[71] *Velosa Baretta v. Portugal*, 21 Nov. 1995 (No. 334).

[72] *See id.*

[73] *See* C. Warbrick, 'The Structure of Article 8' *European Human Rights Law Rev.* 32, 35–6 (1998).

that has to be struck between the general interest of the community and the interests of the individual, the search for which balance is inherent in the whole of the Convention. In striking this balance the aims mentioned in the second paragraph of Article 8 may be of certain relevance, although this provision refers in terms only to 'interferences' with the right protected by the first paragraph—in other words is concerned with the negative obligations flowing therefrom.[74]

In fact, notwithstanding the absence of an express set of justifications, the Court has held that the discretion accorded to a state in deciding how to meet its positive obligations is especially broad. In *Johnston v. Ireland* the Court concluded:

Although the essential object of Article 8 is to protect the individual against arbitrary interference by the public authorities, there may in addition be positive obligations inherent in an effective 'respect' for family life. However, especially as far as those positive obligations are concerned, the notion of 'respect' is not clear-cut: having regard to the diversity of the practices followed and the situations obtaining in the Contracting States, the notion's requirements will vary considerably from case to case. Accordingly, this is an area in which the Contracting Parties enjoy a wide margin of appreciation in determining the steps to be taken to ensure compliance with the Convention with due regard to the needs and resources of the community and of individuals.

The idea of positive obligations has most often been explicated in cases involving Article 8. However, in one judgment the Court has presumed a similar aspect is inherent in the right of assembly provided in Article 11. In *Platform 'Arzte für das Leben' v. Austria,*[75] the applicants complained that the authorities had not provided sufficient protection for their anti-abortion demonstration which had been disrupted by other private groups. The Commission had found the Article 11 claim inadmissible because 'manifestly ill-founded',[76] but it had found a violation of Article 13 requiring states to provide an effective remedy for violations of Convention rights. The Court, in reviewing the Article 13 determination, had to decide whether the facts revealed an 'arguable' violation of Article 11. With respect to that Article the Court noted:

31. The Court does not have to develop a general theory of the positive obligations which may flow from the Convention, but before ruling on the arguability of the applicant association's claim it has to give an interpretation of Article 11.

32. A demonstration may annoy or give offence to persons opposed to the ideas or claims that it is seeking to promote. The participants must, however, be able to hold the demonstration without having to fear that they will be subject to physical violence by their opponents; such a fear would be liable to deter associations or other groups supporting common ideas or interests from openly expressing their opinions on highly controversial issues affecting the community. In a democracy the right to counter-demonstrate cannot extend to inhibiting the exercise of the right to demonstrate.

Genuine, effective freedom of peaceful assembly cannot, therefore, be reduced to a mere duty on

[74] *Rees v. United Kingdom,* 17 Oct. 1986 (No. 106), 9 E.H.R.R. 203.

[75] 21 June 1988 (No. 139), 13 E.H.R.R. 204. In *Delisle v. Canada (Deputy Attorney General)* [1999] 2 S.C.R. 989 paras. 33–7, the Supreme Court of Canada held that s. 2(a) of the Charter of Rights and Freedoms assuring freedom of association did not oblige the state to include a particular association of public employees within its statutory scheme of collective bargaining.

[76] *See* Chapter 2 (B)(1) *supra.*

the part of the State not to interfere: a purely negative conception would not be compatible with the object and purpose of Article 11. Like Article 8, Article 11 sometimes requires positive measures to be taken, even in the sphere of relations between individuals, if need be.

In the case at issue, however, the Court found the authorities had clearly taken 'reasonable and appropriate measures' and therefore, on these facts, they found no arguable violation of Article 11.

In *Gustafsson v. Sweden*[77] the applicant, a restaurant owner, was subjected to a 'blockade' by unions as a result of his refusal to enter into a collective bargaining agreement. The blockade caused the stoppage of deliveries to his restaurant and the termination of its listing in a catalogue of youth hostels. The applicant claimed that these acts were undertaken to force him into an unwanted association, thus engaging Article 11. Although the pressure of which he complained was not initiated by the state, the European Court held that 'national authorities may, in certain circumstances, be obliged to intervene in the relationships between private individuals by taking reasonable and appropriate measures to secure the effective enjoyment of the negative right to freedom of association'.[78] The Court went on to hold that the state must be accorded a wide margin of appreciation in deciding which measures to that end should be adopted and, in this case, weighing the state's interest in promoting a system of collective bargaining and the economic injuries suffered by the applicant, the state's positive obligation had not been breached.[79]

On the other hand, the Court has refused to find that Article 10's right of expression entailed a positive obligation on the part of the state to collect and disseminate useful information to citizens:

In cases concerning restrictions on freedom of the press [the Court] has on a number of occasions recognized that the public has a right to receive information as a corollary of the specific function of journalists, which is to impart information and ideas on matters of public interest . . . [But the] freedom to receive information referred to in paragraph 2 of Article 10 of the Convention 'basically prohibits a government from restricting a person from receiving information that others wish or may be willing to impart to him.' That freedom cannot be construed as imposing on a State . . . positive obligations to collect and disseminate information of its own motion.[80]

In his dissenting opinion in *Nielsen v. Denmark*,[81] Judge Carillo Salcedo suggested that Article 5 was similar in structure to Article 8 and evinced a similar positive obligation on the state to protect individuals' liberty. In that case, the Court found

---

[77] 25 Apr. 1996, Reports, 1996–II 638, 22 E.H.R.R. 409.

[78] *Id.* at para. 45.

[79] *Id.* at paras. 45–53. In *Young, James & Webster v. United Kingdom*, 26 June 1981 (No. 44), 4 E.H.R.R. 38, the Court suggested that Art. 11 was applicable when employees had been dismissed when they failed to join a union because 'the domestic law in force at the relevant time . . . made lawful the treatment of which the applicants complained'. *Id.* at para. 49. *See also Sibson v. United Kingdom*, 20 Apr. 1993 (No. 258A), 17 E.H.R.R. 193.

[80] *Guerra v. Italy*, 19 Feb. 1998, Reports, 1998–I 210, 26 E.H.R.R. 357, para. 53.

[81] 28 Nov. 1988 (No. 144), 11 E.H.R.R. 175.

that a psychiatric commitment of a child which was approved by his mother, the custodial parent, did not create a violation of Article 5. Judge Carillo Salcedo argued:

Like Mr. Frowein, in his partly concurring, partly dissenting opinion [in the Commission], I think that Article 5 is constructed in a very clear way. The first sentence of paragraph 1 imposes a positive obligation on States to protect the freedom of persons subject to their jurisdiction by legislation and other action, while the second sentence of paragraph 1, and sub-paragraphs (a) to (f), protect individuals against specific deprivations of liberty resulting from the action of the public authorities. . . .

In my view, the issue is not, as the majority of the Commission thought, a child's right to oppose a decision of a parent with custody, but the absence in Danish law of adequate procedures for judicial review in connection with the committal of a child to a psychiatric hospital by the parent with custody, where, as in this case, the child in question is not mentally ill and there are disagreements concerning custody.[82]

The inference by the European Court of 'positive obligations' raises fundamental questions about the character of the Convention and the rights it guarantees. Are the substantive rights listed rights against the state only or also against private individuals? Sometimes, of course, the actions of private persons leading to the violation of Convention rights are the result of cooperation with public officials, in which case, the state may readily be seen to be sufficiently responsible to engage its obligations under the Convention.[83]

The recognition of positive obligations, however, raises the question of the reach of the Convention on a more basic level. To the extent the state has a positive obligation under the Convention to prevent, or at least deter and punish, individual rapists, persons attempting to break up demonstrations, or parents dealing unfairly with their children, the Convention might be understood as setting standards of conduct for these private individuals. There is some support for this view, as a general matter, in the text of the Convention. In Article 1 the contracting parties undertake not merely to refrain from conduct but to 'secure to everyone within their jurisdiction the rights and freedoms defined in Section 1 of this Convention'. Article 13 obliges each state to provide an effective remedy to everyone whose Convention rights have been violated. Such a remedy is to be maintained 'notwithstanding that the violation has been committed by persons acting in an official capacity'. While this latter phrase is, no doubt, meant to counter any official immunity for official violations, it may also suggest that the drafters contemplated both private and public transgressions.

The Court cited the Article 1 obligation of states to secure Convention rights in deciding to hear a case in which the underlying complaint involved the corporal punishment of a seven-year-old boy by the headmaster of his private boarding school,

---

[82] *Id.* (dissenting opinion of Judge Carillo Salcedo). As discussed below the Court has also effectively recognized a positive State obligation to prevent the infliction of inhuman and degrading treatment under Art. 3.

[83] *See*, e.g. *A v. France*, 23 Nov. 1993 (No. 277B), 17 E.H.R.R. 462, para. 36.

which received no financial support from the state. The Court held that the state responsibility of the United Kingdom was engaged in these circumstances, although it concluded that no violation had, in fact, occurred.[84] In an opinion dissenting on the substantive point, four judges emphasized especially the fact that the United Kingdom made primary education compulsory in either a state or private school. These judges expressed the view that the state could not avoid the responsibility that it clearly would have in state schools, by allowing an alternative system for private schools. 'On the other hand', noted the judges, 'it is granted that the Convention is not applicable as such, in all respects to relations between private persons'.[85]

This reasoning was carried further in a case holding that the state's positive obligations obliged it to prohibit parental mistreatment of their children in ways which contravene the standards of Article 3. The United Kingdom was found in violation of the Convention on the complaint of a child who had been repeatedly beaten by his stepfather with a garden cane. The stepfather had been acquitted in a prosecution for assault after the jury had been instructed that a parent had the right to use 'moderate' measures to discipline a child. In the European Court's view English law did not provide adequate protection against treatment contrary to Article 3.[86] This decision evoked a strong reaction in Britain, in part, because it was seen as wrongly imposing legal standards on distinctly private conduct. The leader of the parliamentary opposition complained at 'court rulings about what people can do to their own children in their own homes on things like this. It's up to parents to decide whether they want to smack their children. They don't need a European judge to tell them whether they're allowed to do that.'[87]

The constitutional laws of Canada and the United States have dealt with very similar questions concerning the possible application of constitutional rules to private conduct. In the United States, the state or government action doctrines have been applied to limit the reach of most constitutional provisions to actions that could be attributed to decisions of the state and federal governments. The distinction between constitutionally regulated public conduct and constitutionally unregulated private conduct has been referred to by the United States Supreme Court as resting on an 'essential dichotomy'.[88] It has been justified as necessary for marking out an area of flexibility and discretion as to the proper extent and character of legislation governing private conduct. A necessary extension of this idea is that there is no general affirmative duty on the government to assure that private conduct conforms to a constitutional norm. The purpose of the Constitution, the Court has suggested, was 'to protect people from the state, not to ensure that the state protected them from each

---

[84] *Costello-Roberts v. United Kingdom*, 25 Mar. 1993 (No. 247), 19 E.H.R.R. 112, para. 26.

[85] *Id.* (Joint partly Dissenting Opinion of Judges Ryssdal, Thór Vilhjálmsson, Matscher and Wildhaber).

[86] *A v. United Kingdom*. 23 Sept. 1998, Reports, 1998–VI 2692, 27 E.H.R.R. 611, paras. 9–10, 24. Neither the applicability of the Convention nor the finding of a violation was contested by the United Kingdom. *Id.* at para. 18.

[87] T. Shaw & C. Randall, 'Government Defends Right of Parents to Smack', *The Daily Telegraph*, 24 Sept. 1998, 1.

[88] *Jackson v. Metropolitan Edison Co.*, 419 U.S. 345, 349 (1974).

other. The Framers were content to leave the extent of governmental obligation in the latter area to the democratic political process'.[89]

Similarly, in Canada, the Supreme Court has affirmed the idea that the Charter of Rights and Freedoms is, in general, a restraint only on governments and legislatures, and not on private individuals. In *RWDSU v. Dolphin Delivery Ltd.*, the Court held that the securing of an injunction by a private employer against secondary picketers on a common law claim of inducing a breach of contract did not implicate the freedom of expression protected by the Charter.[90] In making that determination the Court cited commentary which declared that the application of the Charter to private action:

would be tantamount to setting up an alternative tort system. In the area of private discrimination, an entirely new system of civil liability in competition with the dispute mechanisms tested by human rights legislation would result.[91]

The Court emphasized this distinction in *Hill v. Church of Scientology*, in which it held that a defamation action did not trigger the protections of the Charter even when the plaintiff was a Crown Attorney who was reacting to charges of misconduct in the exercise of his public duty.[92]

With respect to the extension of Convention rights to control private conduct, the European Court may be influenced by the German doctrine of 'drittwirkung' or 'horizontal effect' of constitutional norms. The German Constitutional Court has held that the Basic Law's specification of rights creates an 'objective ordering of values' that permeates the legal system as a whole. Thus, while the constitutional rules do not directly restrain private behaviour they have an indirect influence on the interpretation and application of private law rules even in cases in which no state agency is a party.[93]

Insofar as the rules of the Convention have been incorporated into national law, either on a constitutional or subconstitutional level, the courts of the states involved may find the Convention might also have a *drittwirkung* on the resolution of private litigation, and a number of legal systems have done just that.[94] Insofar as the European Court of Human Rights is concerned, however, the question must have a very different dimension. To the extent applications have been expressly directed at private

---

[89] *DeShaney v. Winnebago County Dept. of Social Services*, 489 U.S. 189, 197 (1989).

[90] [1986] 2 S.C.R. 573.

[91] *Id.* at 597, quoting Anne McLellan and Bruce P. Elman, 'To Whom Does the Charter Apply? Some Recent Cases on s. 32' (1986) 2 *Alta. L. Rev.* 361, 367.

[92] [1995] 2 S.C.R. 1130, paras. 72–9. The Court did hold, however, that the common law of defamation was to be applied with regard to the values of free expression protected in the Charter. *Id.* at para. 95. *See also Dagenais v. Canadian Broadcasting Corp.* [1994] 3 S.C.R. 835, at paras. 67–79 (applying Charter values to the exercise of discretion by judges in issuing publication bans).

[93] *See Lüth Case*, (1958) 7 BVerfGE 198 translated and edited in Donald P. Kommers, *The Constitutional Jurisprudence of the Federal Republic of Germany* 368 (1989) and Commentary in *id.* at 376. A very valuable discussion is Peter E. Quint, 'Free Speech and Private Law in German Constitutional Theory' (1989) 48 *Md. L. Rev.* 247. On those questions in the context of the new United Kingdom Human Rights Act *see* M. Hunt, 'The Horizontal Effect of the Human Rights Act' [1998] *Public Law* 423.

[94] *See* Andrew Z. Drzemczewski, *European Human Rights Convention in Domestic Law*, 199–218 (1983).

persons, the Commission has declared then inadmissible *ratione personae*, that is by reason of a lack of personal jurisdiction.[95] But, as has been noted, the enforcement of a positive obligation on the part of the *state* to bring a certain state of affairs among private persons into existence will often come to the same thing, as it will require the state to deter or punish certain private actions (such as those of B in the principal case) that might interfere with the exercise of protected rights.

Similarly, the Court has held that a judicial order with respect to the relative rights of contending parents in a custody dispute may represent an 'interference with the ... right to respect for family life', and the fact that it came out of 'a dispute between private individuals makes no difference in this respect'.[96] In connection with a similar dispute, the Canadian Supreme Court has held that judicial orders in a custody dispute do not engage the limitations of the Canadian Charter of Rights and Freedoms, under the logic of the *Dolphin Delivery Case* discussed above. Such cases 'are essentially private in nature and there exists no state action to be impugned'.[97]

As is the case where constitutional norms are applied against private individuals by national courts, the elaboration of the relative right of individuals and states in these circumstances will raise some peculiar problems. The standard form of analysis in determining the presence or absence of violations of the Convention includes an inquiry into whether or not the infringement of the right is justified by pertinent state interests. When the effective cause of the violation is a private action a question arises how these concerns are to be balanced. In *Gustafsson v. Sweden*[98] the Court held that a business owner's right of association under Article 11 was infringed when the business was subjected to a boycott organized by a trade union. Although Article 11 was held applicable, the Court did not apply Article 11(2) justifications directly. But it found relevant the fact that 'the applicant ha[d] not substantiated his submission to the effect that the terms of employment which he offered were more favourable than those required under a collective agreement'. Therefore, it concluded that the union's actions were directed to 'legitimate interests consistent with Article 11'.[99] In partial dissent Judge Jambrek argued that

the industrial action giving rise to the applicant's complaint must be subject to the very same restrictions as would apply to direct interference by the state. If the union action was not justified under paragraph 2 of Article 11, the respondent State was under a positive

---

[95] *See* Drzemczewski, *supra* n. 94 at 221; P. van Dijk & G. J. H. van Hoof, *Theory and Practice of the European Convention on Human Rights*, 76–8 (2d edn. 1990). See generally A. Clapham, *Human Rights in the Private Sphere* (1993).

[96] *Hoffmann v. Austria*, 23 June 1993 (No. 255C), 17 E.H.R.R. 293. Compare the dissenting opinions of Judges Matscher and Mifsud Bounici.

[97] *Young v. Young* [1993] 4 S.C.R. 391. On the general question of the existence of constitutional limits to private actions in the United States, see R. Kay, *The State Action Doctrine, the Public-Private Distinction and the Independence of Constitutional Law*, 10 *Constitutional Commentary*, 329 (1993).

[98] 25 Apr. 1996, Reports 1996–II 638, 22 E.H.R.R. 409.

[99] *Id.* at para. 53.

obligation to take action to secure the applicant's enjoyment of his right to freedom of association.[100]

He concluded that, in this case, the union action was directed at the 'protection of the rights and freedoms of others'. He focused exclusively on the *union*'s interest, discounting the Court's reliance on 'the corporate aim' of promoting the system of collective bargaining. Since there was no evidence that the applicant's employees were at a serious disadvantage relative to unionized employees, the union's action 'did not correspond . . . to any pressing social need'.[101]

The evaluation of the justification for infringements effected by private parties presents additional difficulty. The Court has traditionally only considered justifications on the basis of collectively held interests. The promotion of interests such as the protection of order or of morals raises rather different questions when undertaken by individuals. Moreover, as Judge Jambrek also noted in his separate opinion in *Gustafsson*, since the private actors whose interests are being considered will not normally be parties to the proceedings in Strasbourg, the Court will be faced with special problems in identifying and measuring those interests.[102]

This problem may be especially acute where the individuals whose actions are claimed to require state control may, themselves, have plausible arguments that such restrictions on their behaviour infringe *their* rights under the Convention.[103] For example, to the extent an employer's actions with respect to labour unions are held to be limited by Article 11 of the Convention,[104] such an employer may assert an interference with its right to hold and use property under Article 1 of Protocol 1 or with its right of expression under Article 10. An interpretation of the Convention insisting on a general observance of the values it protects by private person, as well as states, therefore, has the potential vastly to enlarge the field of conduct subject to an uncertain supervision by the European Court. The implications of such a development for the rule of law are far from clear. To date, the relatively limited enforcement of 'positive obligations' by the Court provides no plain indication of how it will approach these general questions.[105]

---

[100] *Id.* (dissenting opinion of Judge Jambrek, at para. 2).

[101] *Id.* at para. 10.

[102] *Id.* at para 5.

[103] *See* E. Alkema. *The Third-Party Application or 'Drittwirkung' of the European Convention on Human Rights, in Protecting Human Rights: The European Dimension*, 33 (Matscher & Petzold eds. 1985).

[104] *See* van Dijk & van Hoof, *supra* n. 95 at 19–20. On this point see the discussion in Chapter 5, section F, *supra* on the potential of Art. 8's right of privacy to conflict with Art. 10's right of expression under the United Kingdom's Human Rights Act, in connection with journalists' intrusion into private lives.

[105] *See* Drzemczewski, *supra* n. 94 at 222–5. For a useful summary of the questions raised by the applicability of the Convention rights to private acts see M. Hunt, *supra*. n. 93.

6. ASPECTS OF FAMILY LIFE

A. THE HOME

Among the objects which must be accorded respect under Article 8 is 'the home'. It is difficult to separate rights respecting the home in a physical sense from those associated with 'family life'. A protected private space is essential to the activities which constitute family life. Complaints involving attacks upon or intrusions into a home, therefore, always engage both aspects of the right. Moreover, the Strasbourg Court has usually measured the effect of injuries to a home in connection with their impact on the life of the family who lives there.

Most obviously the intentional destruction of a dwelling house involves a presumptive violation of Article 8 and several cases involving the burning down of houses by Turkish security forces have so held.[106] An unjustified entry into the house by police has also been held to constitute a violation.[107] More difficult issues are presented when the complaint concerns state action or inaction making the use of the home more difficult or dangerous. In *Powell and Raynor v. United Kingdom*[108] the applicants claimed that noise from Heathrow Airport gave rise to a violation of Article 8. The Court agreed that the 'scope for enjoying the amenities of his home have been adversely affected' and that Article 8 is a 'material provision'. It concluded, however, that in light of the public need for the airport and the efforts that had been made to limit noise, no violation of Article 8 had been made out.[109]

In a subsequent case, however, the Court found a violation when an applicant complained about the placement of a waste treatment plant near her home. For several years she and her family had been subjected to smells, noise and fumes. Although no serious health risk had resulted the Court found the injury to the applicant's 'quality of life' was not justified by the public need for the plant and that the response of the state to the applicant's difficulties was insufficient.[110] Similarly, when Italian authorities failed to take effective measures to prevent flammable and toxic emissions from a chemical plant and also failed to inform affected residents, a violation of Article 8 was found.[111]

The protection of an individual's choice of home life by Article 8 was brought before the Court in *Buckley v. United Kingdom*.[112] In that case, the applicant was a gypsy

---

[106] *See Selçuk & Asker v. Turkey*, 24 Apr. 1998, Reports, 1998–II 891, 26 E.H.R.R. 595; *Mentes & Others v. Turkey*, 28 Nov. 1997, Reports 1997–VIII 2689, 26 E.H.R.R. 595; *Akdivar v. Turkey*, 16 Dec. 1996 (not yet reported).

[107] *McLeod v. United Kingdom*, 23 Sept. 1998, Reports, 1998–VII, 2774, 27 E.H.R.R. 493. *See also Larkos v. Cyprus*, 18 Feb. 1999, holding that there was discrimination violating Art. 14 in connection with Art. 8 where the applicant's tenancy in a state-owned house was terminated. It was stipulated that no termination would have been allowed under Cyprus law if the property had been privately owned.

[108] 21 Feb. 1990 (No. 172), 12 E.H.R.R. 355.

[109] *Id.* paras. 40–5.

[110] *Lopez Ostra v. Spain*, 9 Sept. 1994 (No. 303C), 20 E.H.R.R. 277, paras. 44–58.

[111] *Guerra and Others v. Italy*, 19 Feb. 1998, Reports, 1998–I 210, 26 E.H.R.R. 357.

[112] 25 Sept. 1996, Reports, 1996–IV 1271, 23 E.H.R.R. 101.

whose traditional lifestyle required living in caravans. The local authorities ordered removal of the applicant's caravan as contrary to planning regulations intended to preserve the rural character of the countryside. The Court held Article 8 applicable over the governmental objection that 'home' referred to a 'legally established' home only.

[T]he applicant bought the land to establish her residence there. She has lived there almost continuously since 1988—save for an absence of two weeks for family reasons in 1993—and it has not been suggested that she has established, or intends to establish another residence elsewhere. The case, therefore, concerns the applicant's right to respect for her 'home'.[113]

The Court held, however, that the interference did not give rise to a violation since it was 'necessary' to public safety, economic wellbeing, protection of health and the protection of the rights of others. In particular, the Court found that the environmental goals of the planning regulations had been pursued in a reasonable and balanced fashion, and had taken into account the special residential practices of the gypsy population. The applicant had been offered an alternative site for her caravan in the same area. Although she had adduced several reasons why that site was undesirable, the Court concluded that 'Article 8 does not reasonably go so far as to allow individuals' preference as to their place of residence to override the general interest'.[114] In light of the broad margin of appreciation properly accorded a state with respect to 'town and country planning schemes', including the exercise of discretionary judgment, the court held (three judges dissenting) that the applicant had been 'afford[ed] due respect under Article 8'.[115]

In *Velosa Baretta v. Portugal*,[116] the Court held that the right to respect for family life does not entail a duty on the part of the state 'to enable each family to have a home for themselves alone'.[117] In that case it upheld Portugal's refusal to allow a property owner to evict a tenant in order to use the house for his own family, thus making it necessary for the applicant's family to continue living with his in-laws.

B. LANGUAGE RIGHTS

Article 8 was first construed by the Court in 1968 in the *Belgian Linguistic Case*,[118] in which French-speaking parents challenged the Belgian school system which divided the country into various regions for the purpose of determining the language of instruction. The principal ground of the challenge was incompatibility with Article 2 of the First Protocol to the Convention which guarantees, *inter alia*, respect for the 'right of parents to ensure such education and teaching in conformity with their own religious and philosophical convictions'. A separate claim was made under Article 8.

---

113 *Id.* para. 54.
114 *Id.* para. 81.
115 *Id.* paras. 74–84.
116 21 Nov. 1995 (No. 334).
117 *Id.* para. 24.
118 23 July 1968 (No. 6), 1 E.H.R.R. 252.

The Court's judgment is long and detailed, discussing the specific rules in effect in each region. It held the entire system was in violation of the Convention insofar as it denied the children of French-speaking families access to French language education solely on the basis of the parents' residency. This holding was based on a discrimination forbidden by Article 14 in conjunction with Article 2 of the First Protocol. Otherwise the laws at issue were found proper. In its discussion of Article 8, the Court (in paragraph 7) stated:

It is true that one result of the Acts of 1932 and 1963 has been the disappearance in the Dutch unilingual region of the majority of schools providing education in French. Consequently French-speaking children living in this region can now obtain their only education in Dutch, unless their parents have the financial resources to send them to private French-language schools. This clearly has a certain impact upon family life when parents do not have sufficient means to enrol their children in private school. . . .

Harsh though such consequences may be in individual cases, they do not involve any breach of Article 8. This provision in no way guarantees the right to be educated in the language of one's parents by the public authorities or with their aid. Furthermore, in so far as the legislation leads certain parents to separate themselves from their children, such a separation is not imposed by this legislation: it results from the choice of the parents who place their children in schools situated outside the Dutch unilingual region with the sole purpose of avoiding their being taught in Dutch, that is to say in one of Belgium's national languages.

In 1993, the Parliamentary Assembly of the Council of Europe recommended the addition to the Convention of a Protocol on the rights of minorities. Article 8 of the draft Protocol provides that each member of a national minority 'shall have the right to learn his/her mother tongue at an appropriate number of schools and state educational and training establishments located in accordance with the geographic distribution of the minority'. Commentary to the Protocol made clear the right to learn the mother language did not automatically include a right that such language be the principal medium of instruction.

The holding of the European Court in the *Belgian Linguistic Case* is to be contrasted with that of the United States Supreme Court in *Meyer v. Nebraska*,[119] in which a Nebraska law forbidding instruction in any language other than English, in a school, public or private, was held invalid as a deprivation of liberty without due process of law. The Court held this liberty included a right 'to marry, establish a home and bring up children'. It went on to say:

That the State may do much, go very far, indeed, in order to improve the quality of its citizens, physically, mentally and morally, is clear, but the individual has certain fundamental rights which must be respected. The protection of the Constitution extends to all, to those who speak other languages as well as to those born with English on the tongue. Perhaps it would be highly advantageous if all had ready understanding of our ordinary speech, but this cannot be coerced by methods which conflict with the Constitution—a desirable end cannot be promoted by prohibited means.

For the welfare of his Ideal Commonwealth, Plato suggested a law which should provide: 'That

---

[119] 262 U.S. 390, 401–403 (1923) (citations omitted).

the wives of our guardians are to be common, and their children are to be common, and no parent is to know his own child; not any child his parent. The proper officers will take the offspring of the good parents to the pen or fold, and there they will deposit them with certain nurses who dwell in a separate quarter, but the offspring of the inferior, or of the better when they chance to be deformed, will be put away in some mysterious unknown place, as they should be.' In order to submerge the individual and develop ideal citizens. Sparta assembled the males at seven into barracks and intrusted their subsequent education and training to official guardians. Although such measures have been deliberately approved by men of great genius, their ideas touching the relation between individual and State were wholly different from those upon which our institutions rest; and it hardly will be affirmed that any legislature could impose such restrictions upon the people of a State without doing violence to both letter and spirit of the Constitution.

The desire of the legislature to foster a homogeneous people with American ideals prepared readily to understand current discussions of civic matters is easy to appreciate. Unfortunate experiences during the late war and aversion toward every characteristic of traculent adversaries were certainly enough to quicken that aspiration. But the means adopted we think exceed the limitations upon the power of the State and conflict with rights assured to plaintiff in error. The interference is plain enough and no adequate reason therefore in time of peace and domestic tranquility has been shown.

Unlike many other judgments of the 'substantive due process' era, *Meyer* has continued to be cited with approval by the Supreme Court. It has taken on particular importance in light of modern cases creating a special constitutional protection for autonomous private decisions regarding matters of sex, procreation and child-rearing.

The matter of language rights is especially critical in countries like Belgium with more than one significant language group. Rather than deal with this issue through ordinary legislation or by invoking more general guarantees of equality, privacy, education and so forth, some of these countries have enacted rather specific constitutional rules on the right to use the minority language in defined situations. Since confederation, the Canadian Constitution has provided that either English or French may be used in legislative or judicial proceedings in the federal government and in the province of Quebec.[120] A similar provision was enacted for the province of Manitoba when it was created in 1870,[121] and for New Brunswick in 1982.[122] Furthermore, in the Constitution Act 1982, very specific rules were included governing minority language education rights for qualifying citizens of Canada in any province 'where numbers warrant'.[123] This provision was relied on by the Supreme Court of Canada to strike down parts of the Quebec Charter of the French Language in 1984, insofar as it denied English language education to certain children.[124] In subsequent cases, that Court has held that linguistic minority communities are entitled to some degree of management and control of the minority language instruction, as well as to a 'distinct physical setting' for the instruction. The exact character and extent of these latter

[120] Constitution Act 1867, §133.
[121] Manitoba Act 1870, §33.
[122] Constitution Act 1982, §§16–20.
[123] Constitution Act 1982, §23.
[124] *Attorney-General of Quebec v. Quebec Association of Protestant School Boards* [1984] 2 S.C.R. 66.

rights should be determined on a 'sliding scale' relating to the number of students involved so that the larger the minority population the more independent its educational establishment must be.[125]

C. IMMIGRATION AND DEPORTATION

In a number of cases applicants have relied on Article 8's insistence on respect for family life as the basis for contesting a decision to refuse entry to or to deport aliens, when the excluded person has family connections in the relevant state. This has presented a difficult problem for states that wish to use their immigration laws to maintain an economic preference for their own citizens or to deport a person who has engaged in disruptive criminal activities. In *Abdulaziz Cabales and Balkandali v. United Kingdom*[126] the Court staked this area out as subject to secrutiny for compliance with Article 8. It rejected a suggestion that the Fourth Protocol to the Convention was an exhaustive statement of the limits put on national decisions on matters concerning movement and immigration.[127] It stated, moreover, that a state's 'positive obligations' were relevant in determining whether it had acted in conformity with the Convention. It warned, however, that a wide margin of appreciation was in order in light, *inter alia*, of the fact that it is 'well-established international law' that a state has the right to control the entry of non-nationals into its territory. In *Abdulaziz*, the Court held that the refusal of the United Kingdom to allow the husbands of legally settled aliens to join them did not, itself, violate Article 8[128] but that the disparate treatment for entry of husbands and wives violated Article 14 in conjunction with Article 8.[129]

In reviewing expulsions argued to amount to interferences in an applicant's private life, the European Court has accepted the view that a *prima facie* infringement arises whenever the applicant has a substantial connection with the deporting state. But it has also assumed such actions generally pursue a legitimate interest such as the prevention of disorder or the protection of health or morals. Thus most cases come down to the question whether the interference is 'necessary in a democratic society' to serve the relevant public interest. This has been treated as an inquiry into whether, in the factual circumstances of each case, the state had 'struck a fair balance between the relevant interests'.[130]

These cases naturally evaluate the interests in family life that are subject to disruption—the time in which the family has been in place, the number and proxim-

---

[125] *See Reference Re Public Schools, Act (Man.)* [1993] 1 S.C.R. 839; *Mahe v. Alberta*, [1990] 1 S.C.R. 342. The impact of the European Convention on a number of aspects of language rights is summarized in A. Connelly, *The European Convention on Human Rights and the Protection of Linguistic Minorities*, 2 Irish Journal of European Law 277 (1993).

[126] 28 May 1985 (No. 94), 7 E.H.R.R. 471.

[127] *Id.* at para. 60.

[128] *Id.* at para. 68.

[129] *Id.* at paras. 70–85.

[130] *See*, e.g., *Dalia v. France*, 19 Feb. 1998, Reports, 1998–I 76.

ity of relatives involved, and the quality of the relationships.[131] In *Nasri v. France*[132] the applicant was deaf-mute and had lived in France almost his entire life. He had been convicted of numerous offences including participation in a gang rape. Notwithstanding the seriousness of his crimes, the Court was persuaded that the impact of deportation on the applicant's family life was so severe as to support the finding of a violation:

Above all it is necessary to take account of Mr. Nasri's handicap. He has been deaf and dumb since birth and this condition has been aggravated by an illiteracy which was the result in particular of largely inadequate schooling, even though this was to a certain extent attributable to the applicant, since on account of his behaviour he was expelled from the establishments he attended . . . [T]he Court is inclined to the view that, for a person confronted with such obstacles, the family is especially important, not only in terms of providing a home, but also because it can help to prevent him from lapsing into a life of crime, all the more so in this instance inasmuch as Mr. Nasri has received no therapy adapted to his condition. . . .

In view of this accumulation of special circumstances, notably his situation as a deaf and dumb person, capable of achieving a minimum psychological and social equilibrium only within his family, the majority of whose members are French nationals with no close ties to Algeria, the decision to deport the applicant, if executed, would not be proportionate to the legitimate aim pursued. . . .[133]

In *Abdulaziz*, in deciding that Article 8 alone was not violated by the refusal to admit the spouses of the applicants, the Court took note of the fact that the family life which was claimed to be impeded by the state's policy might have been established in the resident state of the alien spouse or in some third county. To hold that each relevant state must be open to the family would be equivalent to finding a Convention right to choose the state in which the family might live.[134] Of course, when there existed serious obstacles to uniting the family in any other place, Article 8 might be more directly implicated. On this basis, the Court found a violation in the *Berrehab Case*[135] when the Netherlands attempted to deport the father of a small child resident in that country with her mother, and with whom the father had maintained close ties, when, as a practical matter, the applicant could not be expected to travel frequently between the Netherlands and Morocco.[136] A consistent factor in the Court's examination of this question has been the extent to which the applicant might be able to reestablish family relationships in his or her country of origin. A violation is more likely to be found when the applicant was born in the deporting state or has lived there from an early age. The same would be true where the applicant did not speak

---

[131] *See*, e.g., *Beldjoudi v. France*, 26 Mar. 1992 (No. 234A), 14 E.H.R.R. 801.
[132] 13 July 1995 (No. 324), 21 E.H.R.R. 458.
[133] *Id.* at paras. 43, 46.
[134] *Id.* at para. 68. See also *Cruz Varas v. Sweden*, 20 Mar. 1991 (No. 201), 14 E.H.R.R. 1, para. 88.
[135] 21 June 1988 (No. 138), 11 E.H.R.R. 322.
[136] *Id.* at para. 23.

the language of his formal nationality or where he or she had few relatives still living there.[137]

In examining these claims, the Court has weighed the hardships involved in maintaining family life, against the urgency of the state's reasons for exclusion, in order to determine whether the state had struck a 'proper balance' between the Convention rights of the affected family and the aims specified in Article 8(2). In *Moustaquim v. Belgium*[138] the applicant, a Moroccan national, was 20 years old when he was ordered deported on the basis of a long series of offences committed as a juvenile and as an adult. He had arrived in Belgium at the age of one. His father, mother and seven siblings were in Belgium. The Court, in finding a violation of Article 8, stressed that most of the applicant's difficulties had occurred while he was an adolescent, and the most serious charges had been brought over a fairly short period. The applicant had committed no offence in the 39 months prior to the deportation order (although admittedly he had been in detention for 16 months of that time). On these facts, the deportation constituted a disproportionate interference with the applicant's family life. The Court has recognized that the elimination of certain social evils notably commerce in illegal drugs, raises an unusually strong need for action by the state.[139] But even a record of serious offences does not create a *per se* justification for exclusion. In *Beldjoudi v. France*,[140] the applicant's criminal record was, the Court agreed, 'much worse than that of Mr. Moustaquim'. He had been convicted of a large number of very serious crimes as an adult over a 15-year period, and, at the time the case was heard in Strasbourg, the applicant was being held on a fresh offence. Although these facts strengthened France's claim that it was necessary to deport Beldjoudi to maintain public order, the Court also noted that the impact of a deportation on the applicant's family life was extreme. He had been born in France (of Algerian parents), had spent his whole life in France and knew no Arabic. 'He [did] not seem to have any links with Algeria apart from that of nationality'.[141] Most important, the Court noted that he had been married for 20 years to a Frenchwoman who, as a practical matter, could not be expected to uproot herself and move to Algeria. Based on all these factors the Court found the deportation decision 'not ... proportionate to the legitimate aim pursued'.[142]

It is apparent that the close individualized examination of the applicant's family life in the deporting and destination countries, and of the applicant's record of criminal behaviour, has resulted in a jurisprudence about which few generalizations are possible. This problem is aggravated by the fact that the Court's balance of factors is more

---

[137] Compare *Beldjoudi v. France*, 26 Nov. 1992 (No. 234A); *Moustaquim v. Belgium*, 18 Feb. 1991 (No. 193), 13 E.H.R.R. 802; *Nasri v. France*, 13 July 1995 (No. 324), 21 E.H.R.R. 458 (violations) with *C v. Belgium*, 7 Aug. 1996, Reports, 1996–III 915; *Boughanemi v. France*, 24 Apr. 1996, Reports, 1996–II 593, 22 E.H.R.R. 228; *Dalia v. France*, 19 Feb. 1998, Reports, 1998–I 76 (no violations).

[138] 18 Feb. 1991 (No. 193), 13 E.H.R.R. 802.

[139] See *C v. Belgium*, 7 Aug. 1996, Reports, 1996–III 915; *Dalia v. France*, 19 Feb. 1998, Reports, 1998–I 716.

[140] 26 March 1992 (No. 234A), 14 E.H.R.R. 801.

[141] *Id.* at para. 77.

[142] *Id.* at para. 79.

often merely stated than defended. The *ad hoc* quality of these judgments has disturbed some of the judges. In one case Judge Martens expressed his dissatisfaction in a dissenting opinion:

The majority's case-by-case approach is a lottery for national authorities and a source of embarrassment for the Court. A source of embarrassment since it obliges the Court to make well-nigh impossible comparisons between the merits of the case before it and those which it has already decided. It is—to say the least—far from easy to compare the cases of Moustquim, Beldjoudi, Nasri and Boughanemi. Should one just make a comparison based on the number of convictions and the severity of sentences or should it also take into account personal circumstances? The majority has, obviously, opted for the latter approach and has felt able to make the comparison, but—with due respect—I cannot help feeling the outcome is necessarily tainted with arbitrariness.[143]

An extreme example of this difficulty is *Boujlifa v. France*.[144] The Court merely recited the applicant's experience and family connection in France and the nature of his criminal offenses and stated without further explanation: '[the Court] considers that in the instant case the requirements of public order outweighed the personal considerations which prompted the application'.[145] A number of judges writing individual opinions have proposed that the Court should adopt a heavy presumption that deportation of any alien who has spent all or almost all of his or her life in a state ('integrated aliens' or 'second generation aliens') would violate Article 8.[146]

D. GÜL *v.* SWITZERLAND

Judgment of 19 February 1996
Reports, 1996–I 159, 22 E.H.R.R. 93

6. Mr. Gül is a Turkish national who was born in January 1947 and now lives with his wife at Pratteln in the canton of Basle Rural, Switzerland.

7. Until 1983 he lived with his wife and their two sons, Tuncay (born on 12 October 1971) and Ersin (born on 20 January 1983), in the town of Gumushane in Turkey. On 25 April 1983 he travelled to Switzerland, where he applied for political asylum as a Kurd and former member of the Turkish Social Democratic Party (the 'CHP'). He worked in a restaurant there until 1990, when he fell ill. Since then he has been in receipt of a partial-invalidity pension.

8. In 1987 the applicant's wife, who had remained in Turkey with their two sons, seriously burned herself during a fit brought on by her epilepsy, from which she had suffered since 1982. In December 1987, having found that it was impossible for her to obtain proper treatment in the area where she was then living, she joined her husband in Switzerland, where she was taken into hospital as an emergency case. Two of the fingers of her left hand were amputated.

---

[143] *Boughanemi v. France*, 24 Apr. 1996, Reports, 1996–II 593, 22 E.H.R.R. 228 (dissenting opinion of Judge Martens, at para. 4).

[144] 21 Oct. 1997, Reports, 1997–IV 2250.

[145] *Id.* at para. 44.

[146] *Boughanemi v. France*. 24 Apr. 1996, Reports, 1996–II 593, 22 E.H.R.R. 228 (dissenting opinion of Judge Martens); *Boujlifa v. France*, 21 Oct. 1997, Reports 1997–IV 2250 (dissenting opinions of Judges Baka and Van Dijk). *See also* C. Warbrick, 'The Structure of Article 8' [1998] *European Human Rights Law Rev.* 32.

9. On 19 September 1988 in Switzerland Mrs. Gül gave birth to her third child, Nursal, a daughter. As she still suffered from epilepsy, she could not take care of the baby, who was placed in a home in Switzerland, where she has remained ever since. In a written declaration dated 31 March 1989, a Prattelin specialist in internal medicine stated that a return to Turkey would be impossible for Mrs. Gül and might even prove fatal to her, given her serious medical condition. . . .

11. [The applicant's application for political asylum was refused but] [i]n view of the length of time Mr. Gül had been living in Switzerland and his wife's precarious state of health, the police considered that the conditions for the issue of such a permit laid down in Article 13(f) of the Federal Council's Order Limiting the Number of Aliens (the 'OLNA') had been satisfied. The final decision to grant a residence permit was given by the Federal Aliens Office on 15 February 1990. . . .

13. On 14 May 1990 Mr. Gül asked the Basle Rural Cantonal Aliens Police for permission to bring to Switzerland his two sons, Tuncay and Ersin, who had remained in Turkey.

14. In a decision of 19 September 1990 the Aliens Police rejected Mr. Gül's request, on the ground that the conditions for family reunion had not been satisfied. (Art 39 of the OLNA.) Firstly, the Gül family's flat did not conform to the standards laid down and, secondly, the applicant did not have sufficient means to provide for his family. In any event, Tuncay was already 18 and was therefore ineligible for a residence permit under the rules governing family reunion. [The applicant's appeals of these decisions was rejected by cantonal government and the Swiss Federal Court]. . . .

19. Ersin has lived in Turkey since his birth, at first in Gumushane until 1993 (with his mother until 1987), and then in Istanbul.

According to the Government, he is at present living, as is his grandfather, with the family of his elder brother Tuncay, and has been visited several times by his father.

The applicant maintained that Ersin frequently moved from one home to another and spent two or three days staying with various Kurdish families who used to live in the village where he was born, including the family of his elder brother. Owing to his grandfather's limited financial resources and the distance between the homes of some of these families and the school it was not possible for the boy to attend school on a regular basis.

As is evidenced by an article which appeared in the Turkish newspaper Sabah on 25 July 1995, Mr. and Mrs. Gül visited their son in Turkey in July and August 1995. . . .

[The Commission by a vote of fourteen to ten expressed its opinion that there had been a violation of Article 8.]

29. It is first necessary to determine whether there is a 'family life' within the meaning of Article 8.

30. The Government's primary submission was that Article 8 was not applicable, since in the instant case the element of intention inherent in the concept of family life was missing. Mr. Gül had left Turkey when his younger son Ersin was three months old, and had never attempted to develop a family life in his country of origin. In addition, the focus of that son's family life was in Turkey since, even after his mother's departure, the child had been taken in as a member of his elder brother's family. Furthermore, the fact that Mr. and Mrs. Gül's daughter Nursal had been placed in a home in Switzerland showed that they were in any event incapable of assuming their parental responsibilities with regard to the boy.

32. The Court reiterates that it follows from the concept of family on which Article 8 is based that a child born of a marital union is ipso facto part of that relationship; hence, from the moment of the child's birth and by the very fact of it, there exists between him and his parents a bond amounting to 'family life' which subsequent events cannot break save in exceptional circumstances. . . .

33. Admittedly, Mr. Gül left Turkey in 1983, when his son Ersin was only three months old; Mrs. Gül left Ersin in 1987 because of her accident.

However, after obtaining a residence permit on humanitarian grounds in Switzerland in 1990, the applicant asked the Swiss authorities for permission to bring the boy, who was then six years old, to Switzerland. Subsequently, he repeatedly asked the Swiss courts to allow his son to join him, before bringing his case before the Convention institutions. Despite the distance, in geographical terms, between them, the applicant has made a number of visits to Turkey, the last of those being in July and August 1995. It cannot therefore be claimed that the bond of 'family life' between them has been broken.

34. Secondly, it is necessary to ascertain whether there was interference by the Swiss authorities with the applicant's right under Article 8.

35. Mr. Gül submitted that the result in practice of the authorities' persistent refusal to allow Ersin to join him in Switzerland had been to separate the family and make it impossible, owing to lack of sufficient financial resources, for the parents to maintain regular contacts with their son, whereas, according to the Court's case law, contacts between parents and child were of capital importance. In addition, the length of time Mr. Gül had lived in Switzerland, his invalidity and his wife's ill health made family reunion in Turkey an unrealistic prospect, so that the family could only be brought together again in Switzerland.

36. The Government submitted that the applicant could not rely on a right to family reunion in Switzerland, as he had only a humanitarian permit, which was not a true settlement permit but merely a document authorising residence that could be withdrawn from him. In addition, Switzerland had fully discharged the positive obligations arising under Article 8(1), as the invalidity pension the applicant was in receipt of enabled him to make occasional visits to Turkey. In any event, Switzerland was in no way responsible for the situation the Gül family was in. Lastly, the Swiss authorities were not under any obligation to ensure that the applicant led an optimal family life in Switzerland. . . .

38. The Court reiterates that the essential object of Article 8 is to protect the individual against arbitrary action by the public authorities. There may in addition be positive obligations inherent in effect 'respect' for family life. However, the boundaries between the State's positive and negative obligations under this provision do not lend themselves to precise definition. The applicable principles are, none the less, similar. In both contexts regard must be had to the fair balance that has to be struck between the competing interests of the individual and of the community as a whole; and in both contexts the State enjoys a certain margin of appreciation.

The present case concerns not only family life but also immigration, and the extent of a State's obligation to admit to its territory relatives of settled immigrants will vary according to the particular circumstances of the persons involved and the general interest. As a matter of well established international law and subject to its treaty obligations, a State has the right to control the entry of non-nationals into its territory.

Moreover, where immigration is concerned, Article 8 cannot be considered to impose on a State a general obligation to respect the choice by married couples of the country of their matrimonial residence and to authorise family reunion in its territory. In order to establish the scope of the State's obligations, the facts of the case must be considered.

39. In this case, therefore, the Court's task is to determine to what extent it is true that Ersin's move to Switzerland would be the only way for Mr. Gül to develop family life with his son. . . .

41. By leaving Turkey in 1983, Mr. Gül caused the separation from his son, and he was unable to prove to the Swiss authorities—who refused to grant him political refugee status—that he personally had been a victim of persecution in his home country. In any event, whatever the applicant's initial reasons for applying for political asylum, the visits he has made to his son in recent years tend to show that they are no longer valid. His counsel, moreover, expressly confirmed this at the hearing. In addition, according to the government, by virtue of a social security convention concluded on 1 May 1969 between Switzerland and Turkey, the applicant could continue to receive his ordinary invalidity pension and half of the supplementary benefit he receives at present in respect of his wife, his son Ersin and his daughter Nursal if he returned to his home country.

Mrs. Gül's return to Turkey is more problematic, since it was essentially her state of health that led the Swiss authorities to issue a residence permit on humanitarian grounds. However, although her state of health seemed particularly alarming in 1987, when her accident occurred, it has not been proved that she could not later have received appropriate medical treatment in specialist hospitals in Turkey. She was, moreover, able to visit Turkey with her husband in July and August 1995.

Furthermore, although Mr. and Mrs. Gül are lawfully resident in Switzerland, they do not have a permanent right of abode, as they do not have a settlement permit but merely a residence permit on humanitarian grounds, which could be withdrawn, and which under Swiss law does not give them a right to family reunion.

42. In view of the length of time Mr. and Mrs. Gül have lived in Switzerland, it would admittedly not be easy for them to return to Turkey, but there are, strictly speaking, no obstacles preventing them from developing family life in Turkey. That possibility is all the more real because Ersin has always lived there and has therefore grown up in the cultural and linguistic environment of his country. On that point the situation is not the same as in the *Berrehab Case*,[147] where the daughter of a Moroccan applicant had been born in the Netherlands and spent all her life there.

43. Having regard to all these considerations, and while acknowledging that the Gül family's situation is very difficult from the human point of view, the Court finds that Switzerland has not failed to fulfil the obligations arising under Article 8(1), and there has therefore been no interference in the applicant's family life within the meaning of that Article.

[The Court held by seven votes to two that there had been no breach of Article 8.]

Dissenting Opinion of Judge Martens, approved by Judge Russo

. . .

6. 'According to the Court's well established case law, "the mutual enjoyment by parent and child of each other's company constitutes a fundamental element of family life" ', as the Court pointed out in paragraph 86 of the McMichael Judgment.[148] Consequently, decisions of State

---

[147] 21 June 1988 (No. 138), 11 E.H.R.R. 322.
[148] 24 Feb. 1995 (No. 307 B), 20 EHRR 205.

authorities hindering such enjoyment in principle amount to an infringement of the State's obligation to respect the family life of those concerned. It follows that the refusal of the Swiss authorities to grant the applicant's son Ersin authorization to reside in Switzerland in principle entails their responsibility under Article 8.

Before it is possible to assess whether the refusal was justified, it is—alas—necessary to give some consideration to the question whether or not Switzerland's obligation under Article 8 is a positive or a negative one.

7. The Court's case law distinguishes between positive and negative obligations. Negative obligations require Member States to refrain from action, positive to take action. The Court has repeatedly stressed that the boundaries between the two types 'do not lend themselves to precise definition'. The present case well illustrates the truth of this proposition since the question whether the Swiss decision violated a positive or a negative obligation, if either, seems hardly more than one of semantics: the refusal of the Swiss authorities to let Ersin and his parents be reunited may be considered as an action from which they should have refrained, whereas it could arguably also be viewed as failing to take an action which they were required to take, *viz* making a reunion possible by granting the authorisation. If one takes the view that if there is a violation at all, it must be of a positive obligation . . . then one has to put up with the rather awkward systematic inconsistency that exclusion of a person from a state where his family lives does not fall into the same category of breaches as expulsion of a person from a state where his family lives: the former decision may be in breach of a positive obligation under Article 8, whereas the latter may be in breach of a negative obligation.

8. These and other difficulties in distinguishing between cases where positive and cases where negative obligations are at stake would be immaterial if both kinds of obligation were treated alike. There was a time, however, when the Court's case law did treat them differently.

The Abdulaziz, Cabales and Balkandali judgment[149] is a striking instance: see paragraph 67 of that judgment. Under the pretext of the vagueness of the notion 'respect' in Article 8 the Court held that its requirements will vary from case to case, thus creating for itself the possibility of taking into account, when establishing whether or not there is a positive obligation, whether or not there is a consensus between Member States and, moreover, a wide margin of appreciation for the State concerned. This approach has been rightly criticized both outside and inside the Court. One of the main objections was that under this doctrine, in the context of positive obligations, the margin of appreciation might already come into play at the stage of determining the existence of the obligation, whilst in the context of negative obligations it only plays a role, if at all, at the stage of determining whether a breach of the obligation is justified.

The Court's doctrine on this point has, however, evolved considerably since the *Abdulaziz* judgment. The aforementioned difference in treatment between positive and negative obligations has gradually dwindled away. The Court now holds that the applicable principles are similar, adding that in both contexts regard must be had to the fair balance that has to be struck between the competing interests of the individual and the community. (See, inter alia, *Keegan v. Ireland*,[150] *Hokkanen v. Finland*[151] and *Stjerna v. Finland*.[152]

---

[149] *Abdulaziz v. United Kingdom*, 28 May 1995 (No. 94), 7 E.H.R.R. 471.
[150] 26 May 1994 (No. 290), 18 E.H.R.R. 342.
[151] 23 Sept. 1995 (No. 299 A), 19 E.H.R.R. 139, para. 55.
[152] 25 Nov. 1995 (No. 299 B), 24 E.H.R.R. 195.

9. . . . It follows that the refusal of the Swiss authorities to grant the applicant's son Ersin authorisation to reside in Switzerland amounts to a violation of Article 8, unless it is deemed justified under paragraph 2 of that article or under similar principles to those enshrined therein.

10. Was it 'necessary in a democratic society' to refuse the applicant's seven year old son Ersin authorisation to come and live in Switzerland with his parents? In other words, did that decision of the Swiss authorities strike a fair balance between the competing interests of the applicant, his wife and their son on the one hand and those of the community as a whole on the other?

11. In explaining the interests of the community the Government have stressed that Switzerland has a very high percentage of foreigners living within its borders. Hence, as counsel for the Government put it at our hearing, 'in Switzerland immigration is a particularly sensitive subject'. Against this background the Government are, understandably, afraid of creating a precedent and therefore emphasise—rightly—that what is at stake is their right to control the entry of non-nationals into their territory and that, accordingly, we should leave them a wide margin of appreciation. In this context they stress that they have only granted the applicant and his wife a temporary residence permit on humanitarian grounds, that as a consequence of that generosity they have already to bear the costs of subsistence of the applicant, his wife and their daughter Nursal and that it is therefore asking too much to expect them to do the same for Ersin.

12. So much for the one scale of the balance. What lies in the other? First and foremost, of course, a fundamental element of an elementary human right, the right to care for your own children. It was only natural that the applicant and his wife, as soon as their residence situation was regularised, wanted their seven year old son to live with them. There is a dispute as to Ersin's living conditions, but I need not go deeply into that. It suffices to note that the Government have not convincingly established that those conditions were satisfactory, let alone that, at the decisive moment, it was more in the interest of Ersin to remain in Turkey than to be reunited with his father and mother.

13. The Government do not argue that these are not weighty interests. But they seek to diminish their relevance by contending that the applicant—on whom, they add, is the burden—has not shown that there are obstacles to re-establishing the family—father, mother and Ersin—in Turkey. It is clear that the Government are thus relying on paragraph 68 of the *Abdulaziz* judgment. However, they choose to ignore the fact that the Court, in the first sentence of that paragraph, explicitly distinguishes 'the present proceedings'—viz the cases of the three wives that were before the Court—from the case of 'immigrants who already had a family which they left behind in another country until they had achieved settled status in the United Kingdom' (= the country of settlement).

That is an important proviso, for it strongly suggests that in a case of 'immigrants who already had a family which they left behind'—such as the present applicant—different norms should be applied.

14. Which norms? The Court does not answer that question, but it is natural to infer that it intended to make it clear that in respect to such cases it might possibly hold that, in the context of the issue of family reunion, the State of settlement should respect the choice of the immigrants who have achieved settled status there and, accordingly, must accept members of their family which they had left behind for settlement.

In other words, contrary to the Government's suggestion, the *Abdulaziz* judgment is no authority for their allegation that Switzerland may refuse Ersin entry—although he is a member of the family which the applicant and his wife left behind—on the mere ground that if the applicant and his wife want family reunion they should go back to Turkey, there being a violation of Switzerland's obligations under Article 8 only if the applicant proves that there are obstacles to doing so or other special reasons why that could not be expected of him.

On the contrary, the *Abdulaziz* judgment supports the proposition that in cases where a father and mother have achieved settled status in a country and want to be reunited with their child which for the time being they have left behind in their country of origin, it is per se unreasonable, if not inhumane to give them the choice between giving up the position which they have acquired in the country of settlement or to renounce the mutual enjoyment by parent and child of each other's company which constitutes a fundamental element of family life.

15. It remains, of course, to be considered whether the latter principle applies in the present case, where the applicant has not 'achieved settled status' in Switzerland, in so far as he and his wife have not been granted a 'settlement permit', but have to base their right of residence on a permit which has, in principle, a temporary character and, consequently, a lower legal status than a settlement permit.

It cannot be denied that, from a point of view of State interest—that is from a point of view of immigration and residence—there is a good case for answering this question in the negative. However, the European Court of Human Rights has to ensure, in particular, that State interests do not crush those of an individual, especially in situations where political pressure—such as the growing dislike of immigrants in most Member States—may inspire State authorities to harsh decisions. As we stressed in paragraph 29 of our aforementioned *Berrehab* judgment, the Court must examine cases like this not only from the point of view of immigration and residence, but also with regard to the mutual interests of the applicant, his wife and Ersin.

Whether he came as a refugee or as a job seeker, at the material time the applicant has been living in Switzerland for seven years and his wife for four years. During these years he had been legally employed, apparently by the same employer, until an unspecified date in 1990 when he fell ill. The Swiss authorities have taken this time element into consideration, since their decision to grant a residence permit was partly based on the time the applicant had been living in Switzerland. Rightly so, for generally speaking it may be assumed that after a period of between three and five years immigrants become rooted in the country of settlement. By then they have formed new social ties there and have definitively begun to adapt themselves to their new homeland. In assessing the humaneness of the choice with which the Swiss authorities confronted the applicant and his wife this element, the fact that they have become integrated in their new homeland—an element which, incidentally, is closely connected with their private life—is of far more importance than the formal status of their permit.

There are some further, specific elements to be taken into account.

The first is that for the applicant and his wife the choice in question was not only between renouncing their son or renouncing the position which they had acquired in Switzerland, but also between renouncing their son Ersin or their little daughter Nursal who was being educated in a home in Switzerland and whose interests almost certainly would have required that she should be left behind.

The second is that the applicant's wife is dependent on medical care which she can certainly get in Switzerland, whilst it is in debate to what extent, if at all, she will be able to get it in Turkey.

The third is that the mere fact that the Turkish authorities did not immediately arrest the applicant when he entered the country as a visitor does not imply that he would not get into trouble if he tried to settle there again on a permanent basis.

The fourth is that the applicant and his wife deserve compassion: whilst his wife had been suffering from epilepsy since 1982 and had a terrible accident in 1987, the applicant himself became disabled in 1990.

Under these circumstances it could not reasonably be required of the applicant and his wife that in order to be reunited with Ersin they should leave Switzerland and return to Turkey.

It follows that a proper balance was not achieved between the interests involved, that the refusal of the Swiss authorities is disproportionate and, as such, not necessary in a democratic society. I thus conclude that there was a violation of Article 8.

The Court in *Ahmut v. The Netherlands*[153] was again confronted with a claim based on the refusal of a state to admit the family of a resident, in this case, one who had acquired local nationality. The applicant, when he applied for a residence permit for his son, had lived in the Netherlands for four years and had acquired Dutch nationality two months previously. The son, who was 10 years old, had been raised in Morocco by his mother. After the death of the mother he had been cared for by his maternal grandmother. He then moved to the Netherlands and lived with the applicant but, at the time of the Court's hearing, had been expelled and was enrolled in a boarding school in Morocco. A brother and two uncles remained in Morocco. The European Court viewed the case as raising the state's positive obligation to respect the applicant's family life. It cited the *Gül* case as setting forth the controlling principles. Since the son had a strong linguistic and cultural connection to Morocco and still had family there, he was 'not prevented from maintaining the degree of family life which he himself had opted for when moving to the Netherlands in the first place, nor is there any obstacle to his returning to Morocco . . . Article 8 does not guarantee a right to choose the most suitable place to develop family life.'[154]

Judge Martens noted that the case 'could have easily been distinguished from that of Gül' but that the chamber had 'chosen to follow that unfortunate precedent'. He was concerned that the case showed 'an increasing preparedness to condone harsh decisions, in the field of immigration'.[155]

E. PARENTAL RIGHTS

In five judgments issued on 8 July 1987, the European Court of Human Rights considered alleged violations of the Convention in connection with the legal scheme in the United Kingdom for restricting and terminating parental rights in the interests of the welfare of children.[156] In each case, the child had been placed in the care of the

---

[153] 28 Nov. 1996, Reports, 1996–VI 2017, 24 E.H.R.R. 62.

[154] *Id.* at paras. 70–1.

[155] *Id.* (dissenting opinion of Judge Martens, at para. 2).

[156] *O & H v. United Kingdom*, 8 July 1987 (No. 120), 10 E.H.H.R. 82; *W, B & R v. United Kingdom*, 8 July 1987 (No. 121), 10 E.H.R.R. 29.

local authority. While that status continued, the authority made a decision to terminate the access of the parent to the child and, in some cases, to place the child for
adoption. These decisions were made without formal notice or an opportunity for the
parent to present objections. The Court held that these were interferences with the
right to respect for family life and that, although they were for a legitimate aim, it was
not necessary in a democratic society so to limit the parent's involvement.[157] The Court
also held that the termination of access was a determination of a civil right and,
therefore, Article 6(1) was applicable.[158] The absence of consultation amounted to a
violation of that Article. American constitutional law also requires notice and hearing
before terminating parental rights.[159]

The European Court further examined the extent of permissible interference with
parental rights in 1988 in *Olsson v. Sweden*.[160] There it found that the Swedish
authority's decision to take temporary custody of three children was 'necessary in a
democratic society' to protect the rights of the children when there had been a good
faith and reasonable determination that the parents were unable to satisfy the children's need for 'care, stimulation and supervision'. It also found, however, that, in light
of the fact that the state's custody was understood by all to be temporary, the placement of the children at a great distance from their parents and from each other, and
severe restriction on the access of the parents to the children, could not be so justified.
The state's explanation, that these circumstances were made necessary by administrative difficulties and by the parents' uncooperative attitude, was insufficient to prevent
a violation. The Court stressed that, in these circumstances, state actions should be
'consistent with the ultimate aim of reuniting the family'.[161]

That aim also was central to the Court's holdings in three cases in which Swedish
authorities had delayed the taking of custody by biological parents, even after the
termination of public care. The child welfare authorities, in these cases, alleged that an
abrupt transfer of custody would be harmful to the children who had spent many
years in foster homes. In *Eriksson v. Sweden*[162] the child had spent her first few years in a
foster home before the care order was terminated. The biological mother was prohibited from removing her daughter from the foster home and restricted in her
contacts with her. The Court, noting the absence of serious efforts to facilitate the
reunification of the family, held these interferences were not 'necessary in a democratic society'. In two subsequent cases, however, the Court held that the delay in
return of custody was justifiable in light of such factors as the genuineness of the

---

[157] *See also McMichael v. United Kingdom*, 24 Feb. 1995 (307 B), 20 E.H.R.R. 205.

[158] *See* Chapter 8, *infra*.

[159] *See Santosky v. Kramer*, 455 U.S. 745 (1982). The Supreme Court of Canada has held that the Charter of
Rights and Freedoms may require the state to supply legal representation to indigent parents in proceedings
affecting custody. Whether such representation must be provided in a given case depends on 'the seriousness
of the interests at stake, the complexity of the proceedings and the capacities of the [parent]'. *New Brunswick
(Minister of Health) v. G. (J)* [1999] 3 S.C.R. 46.

[160] 24 Mar. 1988 (No. 130), 11 E.H.R.R. 259.

[161] *Id.* at para. 81. *See also Margareta and Roger Andersson v. Sweden*, 25 Feb. 1992 (No. 226A), 14 E.H.R.R.
615.

[162] 22 June 1989 (No. 156), 12 E.H.R.R. 183.

state's efforts at restoring the parent-child relationship, the seriousness of the risk to the child and the degree of cooperation of the biological parents.[163]

Consistently with these judgments, the Court has drawn a distinction between decisions to take a child into care or to maintain that care, and decisions to restrict parental access or to limit parental rights while the child is in public custody. Those in the former category, being in principle temporary, and aimed at ultimate reunification, are accorded a wide margin of appreciation. The latter kind of decisions, however, carry the risk that 'family relations between the parents and a young child [will be] effectively curtailed'.[164] These will be examined more carefully. This approach makes it more difficult to defend the termination of parental status on the ground that contact between child and parent had been reduced or eliminated.[165]

In all of these cases the general structure of the European Court's approach has been the same. It has assumed that Article 8(1) protects a right to 'the mutual enjoyment by parent and child of each other's company'.[166] Removal of the child by the state, however, may be justified under Article 8(2) insofar as necessary for the protection of the 'health' and 'the rights and freedoms' of the child.[167]

The approach may be contrasted with the fundamentally different one taken by English courts with respect to questions of parental right and child custody. In *Re K.D.*[168] the House of Lords recognized that normally 'the recognized bond and relationship between parent and child gives rise to universally recognized norms which ought not to be gratuitously interfered with; and which, if interfered with at all, ought to be so only if the welfare of the child dictates it'. But, according to the judgment of Lord Oliver, it was unhelpful to treat this fact as giving rise to a 'right' of access in the parent. He rejected an argument that 'the starting point in every case should be that a parent has a right of access which should be given effect to by the court and curtailed and inhibited only if the court is satisfied that the exercise of the right will be positively inimical to the interests of the child'.[169] He quoted approvingly a trial judge's conclusion that:

> So far as access to a child is concerned, there are no rights in the sense in which lawyers understand the word. It is a matter to be decided always entirely on the footing of the best interests of the child, either by agreement between the parties, or by the Court if there is no agreement.[170]

The Law Lords considered that there was nothing in their view incompatible with the judgments of the European Court of Human Rights.[171]

---

[163] See *Rieme v. Sweden*, Judgment of 22 Apr. 1992 (No. 226), 16 E.H.R.R. 155; *Olsson v. Sweden* (No. 2), Judgment of 27 Nov. 1992 (No. 250), 17 E.H.R.R. 134.

[164] *Johansen v. Norway*, Judgment of 7 Aug. 1996, Reports, 1996–II 979, 23 E.H.R.R. 33, para. 64.

[165] See, e.g., *id.* at para. 84.

[166] *Andersson v. Sweden*, 25 Feb. 1992 (No. 226), 14 E.H.R.R. 615, para. 72.

[167] *Rieme v. Sweden*, 22 Apr. 1992 (No. 226B), 16 E.H.R.R. 155, para. 66.

[168] [1988] 1 All E.R. 577.

[169] *Id.* at 590.

[170] *Id.* at 589 quoting *A. v. C.* [1985] F.L.R. 445, 455.

[171] *Id.* at 588.

The Strasbourg Court has also held that Article 8 may restrict custody decisions in disputes between parents. In *Hoffman v. Austria*,[172] the Court considered a case in which the Austrian Supreme Court held that the parental rights over the children of divorced parents should be granted to the father, because the applicant-mother, who had prevailed in earlier proceedings, was raising the children according to the principles of Jehovah's Witnesses. The Supreme Court held that this was compelled by Austrian law which prohibited changing the religion of the children without the consent of both parents. It also declared that the religious training by the mother would be detrimental to the welfare of the children, noting it might result in delay of necessary blood transfusions (which were contrary to the beliefs of Jehovah's Witnesses) and would make them 'social outcasts'. The European Court held the decision resulted in a violation of Article 14 in conjunction with Article 8, because it involved discrimination on the basis of religion in the exercise of Article 8 rights. The Court held that the Supreme Court's order amounted to a difference in treatment based on the applicant's religion and that this difference was not based on an 'objective and reasonable justification'. The Court agreed that the interests of the child are paramount but, without elaboration, concluded that '[n]otwithstanding any argument to the contrary, a distinction based essentially on a difference in religion alone is not acceptable'.[173] In dissent, Judge Walsh denied that the Austrian court's judgments were properly understood as based on religion. Noting particularly the risk to the children posed by applicant's views on blood transfusions, he insisted that '[t]he fact that the hazard was brought into existence by a religious belief . . . does not create a situation where removal of the hazard must necessarily, if at all, be regarded as discrimination on the grounds of religious belief'.[174]

The European Court's holding may be contrasted with the decisions of the Supreme Court of Canada on a related question—judicial restrictions on the right of a non-custodial parent to influence his or her child on religious matters. Like the House of Lords in *K.D.* the Court has de-emphasized the notion of parental 'rights' in the determination of these questions. The sole criterion applied to access orders is the 'best interests of the child', and any resulting limitations on the religious activities of the parent do not infringe his or her right of religious freedom or expression under Section 2 of the Canadian Charter of Rights and Freedoms: '[W]hile parents are free to engage in religious practices themselves, those activities may be curtailed when they interfere with the best interests of the child without thereby infringing the parent's religious freedom'.[175] In applying the best interests test to the question, however, a majority of the Court has concluded that the value of an open and honest relationship with the noncustodial parent may be as important, and more important, than avoiding any discomfort and stress that the introduction of the religious differences of the parents may create. Thus, the Court overturned a decree barring a non-custodial parent from 'discuss[ing] the Jehovah's Witness religion with the children,[176] but

---

[172] 23 June 1993 (No. 255C), E.H.R.R.

[173] Para. 36. The Court also took note of Article 5 of Protocol 7, which entered into force in Austria after the relevant events, which provides for the equality of spouses with respect to parental rights. Para. 35.

[174] *Id.* (partly dissenting opinion of Judge Walsh).

[175] *Young v. Young* [1993] 4 S.C.R. 3, 94.

[176] *Id.* at 112.

upheld an order (issued after a finding that the non-custodial parent's "religious fanaticism was disturbing to such a young girl") providing that he could 'teach the child the Jehovah's Witness religion but does not have the right to indoctrinate her continually with the precepts and religious practices of Jehovah's Witnesses'.[177]

B. PRIVATE LIFE

1. DUDGEON *v.* UNITED KINGDOM

Judgment of 22 October 1981
(No. 45), 4 E.H.R.R. 149

13. Mr. Jeffrey Dudgeon, who is 35 years of age, is a shipping clerk resident in Belfast, Northern Ireland.

Mr. Dudgeon is a homosexual and his complaints are directed primarily against the existence in Northern Ireland of laws which have the effect of making certain homosexual acts between consenting adult males criminal offences. . . .

[A governmental proposal to liberalize the law by decriminalizing homosexual acts in private between two consenting males over the age of 21 had been withdrawn in 1978 in the face of intense opposition by a number of groups and especially from religious groups including the Roman Catholic and Presbyterian churches.]

32. The applicant has, on his own evidence, been consciously homosexual from the age of 14. For some time he and others have been conducting a campaign aimed at bringing the law in Northern Ireland into line with that in force in England and Wales and, if possible, achieving a minimum age of consent lower than 21 years. . . .

37. The applicant complained that under the law in force in Northern Ireland he is liable to criminal prosecution on account of his homosexual conduct and that he has experienced fear, suffering and psychological distress directly caused by the very existence of the laws in question—including fear of harassment and blackmail. He further complained that, following the search of his house in January 1976, he was questioned by the police about certain homosexual activities and that personal papers belonging to him were seized during the search and not returned until more than a year later.

He alleged that, in breach of Article 8 of the Convention he has thereby suffered, and continues to suffer, an unjustified interference with his right to respect for his private life. . . .

39. Although it is not homosexuality itself which is prohibited but the particular acts of gross indecency between males and buggery . . . , there can be no doubt but that male homosexual practices whose prohibition is the subject of the applicant's complaints come within the scope of the offences punishable under the impugned legislation; it is on that basis that the case has been

---

[177] *D.P. v. C.S.* [1993] 4 S.C.R. 141, 142 (translation of order).

argued by the Government, the applicant and the Commission. Furthermore, the offences are committed whether the act takes place in public or in private, whatever the age or relationship of the participants involved, and whether or not the participants are consenting. It is evident from Mr. Dudgeon's submissions, however, that his complaint was in essence directed against the fact that homosexual acts which he might commit in private with other males capable of valid consent are criminal offences under the law of Northern Ireland. . . .

41. The Court sees no reason to differ from the views of the Commission: the maintenance in force of the impugned legislation constitutes a continuing interference with the applicant's right to respect for his private life (which includes his sexual life) within the meaning of Article 8 §1. In the personal circumstances of the applicant, the very existence of this legislation continuously and directly affects his private life (see, *mutatis mutandis*, the *Marckx* judgment) . . . either he respects the law and refrains from engaging—even in private with consenting male partners—in prohibited sexual acts to which he is disposed by reason of his homosexual tendencies, or he commits such acts and thereby becomes liable to criminal prosecution. . . .

45. It next falls to be determined whether the interference is aimed at 'the protection of morals' or 'the protection of the rights and freedoms of others', the two purposes relied on by the Government. . . .

49. There can be no denial that some degree of regulation of male homosexual conduct, as indeed of other forms of sexual conduct, by means of the criminal law can be justified as 'necessary in a democratic society'. The overall function served by the criminal law in this field is, in the words of the Wolfenden report, 'to preserve public order and decency [and] to protect the citizen from what is offensive or injurious'. Furthermore, this necessity for some degree of control may even extend to consensual acts committed in private, notably where there is call—to quote the Wolfenden report once more—'to provide sufficient safeguards against exploitation and corruption of others, particularly those who are specially vulnerable because they are young, weak in body or mind, inexperienced, or in a state of special physical, official or economic dependence'. In practice there is legislation on the matter in all the member States of the Council of Europe, but what distinguishes the law in Northern Ireland from that existing in the great majority of the member States is that it prohibits generally gross indecency between males and buggery whatever the circumstances. It being accepted that some form of legislation is 'necessary' to protect particular sections of society as well as the moral ethos of society as a whole, the question in the present case is whether the contested provisions of the law of Northern Ireland and their enforcement remain within the bounds of what, in a democratic society, may be regarded as necessary in order to accomplish those aims.

50. A number of principles relevant to the assessment of the 'necessity', 'in a democratic society', of a measure taken in furtherance of an aim that is legitimate under the Convention have been stated by the Court in previous judgments.

51. Firstly, 'necessary' in this context does not have the flexibility of such expressions as 'useful', 'reasonable', or 'desirable', but implies the existence of a 'pressing social need' for the interference in question (see the . . . *Handyside* judgment) . . .

52. In the second place, it is for the national authorities to make the initial assessment of the pressing social need in each case; accordingly, a margin of appreciation is left to them (*ibid*). However, their decision remains subject to review by the Court (*ibid*) . . .

As was illustrated by the *Sunday Times* judgment, the scope of the margin of appreciation is not identical in respect of each of the aims justifying restrictions on a right . . . The Government inferred from the *Handyside* judgment that the margin of appreciation will be more extensive where the protection of morals is in issue. It is an indisputable fact, as the Court stated in the *Handyside* judgment, that 'the view taken . . . of the requirements of morals varies from time to time and from place to place, especially in our era', and that 'by reason of their direct and continuous contact with the vital forces of their countries, State authorities are in principle in a better position than the international judge to give an opinion on the exact content of those requirements'. . . .

However, not only the nature of the aim of the restriction but also the nature of the activities involved will affect the scope of the margin of appreciation. The present case concerns a most intimate aspect of private life. Accordingly, there must exist particularly serious reasons before interferences on the part of the public authorities can be legitimate for the purposes of paragraph 2 of Article 8.

53. Finally, in Article 8 as in several other Articles of the Convention, the notion of 'necessity' is linked to that of a 'democratic society'. According to the Court's case-law, a restriction on a Convention right cannot be regarded as 'necessary in a democratic society'—two hallmarks of which are tolerance and broadmindedness—unless, amongst other things, it is proportionate to the legitimate aim pursued. [citing *inter alia Handyside*]

54. The Court's task is to determine on the basis of the aforestated principles whether the reasons purporting to justify the 'interference' in question are relevant and sufficient under Article 8 §2 (see the . . . *Handyside* judgment,) . . . The Court is not concerned with making any value-judgment as to the morality of homosexual relations between adult males. . . .

56. In the first place, the Government drew attention to what they described as profound differences of attitude and public opinion between Northern Ireland and Great Britain in relation to questions of morality. Northern Irish society was said to be more conservative and to place greater emphasis on religious factors, as was illustrated by more restrictive laws even in the field of heterosexual conduct.

Although the applicant qualified this account of the facts as grossly exaggerated, the Court acknowledges that such differences do exist to a certain extent and are a relevant factor. As the Government and the Commission both emphasised, in assessing the requirements of the protection of morals in Northern Ireland, the contested measures must be seen in the context of Northern Irish society.

The fact that similar measures are not considered necessary in other parts of the United Kingdom or in other member States of the Council of Europe does not mean that they cannot be necessary in Northern Ireland . . . Where there are disparate cultural communities residing within the same State, it may well be that different requirements, both moral and social, will face the governing authorities. . . .

59. Without any doubt, faced with these various considerations, the United Kingdom Government acted carefully and in good faith; what is more, they made every effort to arrive at a balanced judgment between the differing viewpoints before reaching the conclusion that such a substantial body of opinion in Northern Ireland was opposed to a change in the law that no further action should be taken. Nevertheless, this cannot of itself be decisive as to the necessity for the interference with the applicant's private life resulting from the measures being challenged (see the above-mentioned *Sunday Times* judgment) . . . Notwithstanding the margin of appreciation left to the national authorities, it is for the Court to make the final evaluation as to whether the reasons it

has found to be relevant were sufficient in the circumstances, in particular whether the interference complained of was proportionate to the social need claimed for it.

60. The Convention right affected by the impugned legislation protects an essentially private manifestation of the human personality.

As compared with the era when that legislation was enacted, there is now a better understanding, and in consequence an increased tolerance, of homosexual behaviour to the extent that in the great majority of the member States of the Council of Europe it is no longer considered to be necessary or appropriate to treat homosexual practices of the kind now in question as in themselves a matter to which the sanctions of the criminal law should be applied; the Court cannot overlook the marked changes which have occurred in this regard in the domestic law of the member States . . . In Northern Ireland itself, the authorities have refrained in recent years from enforcing the law in respect of private homosexual acts between consenting males over the age of 21 years capable of valid consent. No evidence has been adduced to show that this has been injurious to moral standards in Northern Ireland or that there has been any public demand for stricter enforcement of the law.

It cannot be maintained in these circumstances that there is a 'pressing social need' to make such acts criminal offences, there being no sufficient justification provided by the risk of harm to vulnerable sections of society requiring protection or by the effects on the public. On the issue of proportionality, the Court considers that such justifications as there are for retaining the law in force unamended are outweighed by the detrimental effects which the very existence of the legislative provisions in question can have on the life of a person of homosexual orientation like the applicant. Although members of the public who regard homosexuality as immoral may be shocked, offended or disturbed by the commission by others of private homosexual acts, this cannot on its own warrant the application of penal sanctions when it is consenting adults alone who are involved.

61. Accordingly, the reasons given by the Government, although relevant, are not sufficient to justify the maintenance in force of the impugned legislation in so far as it has the general effect of criminalising private homosexual relations between adult males capable of valid consent. In particular, the moral attitudes towards male homosexuality in Northern Ireland and the concern that any relaxation in the law would tend to erode existing moral standards cannot, without more, warrant interfering with the applicant's private life to such an extent. 'Decriminalisation' does not imply approval, and a fear that some sectors of the population might draw misguided conclusions in this respect from reform of the legislation does not afford a good ground for maintaining it in force with all its unjustifiable features.

To sum up, the restriction imposed on Mr. Dudgeon under Northern Ireland law, by reason of its breadth and absolute character, is, quite apart from the severity of the possible penalties provided for, disproportionate to the aims sought to be achieved.

62. . . . The Court has already acknowledged the legitimate necessity in a democratic society for some degree of control over homosexual conduct notably in order to provide safeguards against the exploitation and corruption of those who are specially vulnerable by reason, for example, of their youth. However, it falls in the first instance to the national authorities to decide on the appropriate safeguards of this kind required for the defence of morals in their society and, in particular, to fix the age under which young people should have the protection of the criminal law.

63. Mr. Dudgeon has suffered and continues to suffer an unjustified interference with his right to respect for his private life. There is accordingly a breach of Article 8. . . .

[The Court held, 15 to four, that there was a violation of Article 8.]

Dissenting opinion of Judge Walsh . . .

9. This raises the age-old philosophical question of what is the purpose of law. Is there a realm of morality which is not the law's business or is the law properly concerned with moral principles? In the context of United Kingdom jurisprudence and the true philosophy of law this debate in modern times has been between Professor H. L. A. Hart and Lord Devlin. Generally speaking the former accepts the philosophy propounded in the last century by John Stuart Mill while the latter contends that morality is properly the concern of the law. Lord Devlin argues that as the law exists for the protection of society it must not only protect the individual from injury, corruption and exploitation but it

'must protect also the institutions and the community of ideas, political and moral, without which people cannot live together, Society cannot ignore the morality of the individual any more than it can his loyalty; it flourishes on both and without either it dies.'

10. It would appear that the United Kingdom claim that in principle it can legislate against immorality. In modern United Kingdom legislation a number of penal statues appear to be based upon moral principles. Cruelty to animals is illegal because of a moral condemnation of enjoyment derived from the infliction of pain upon sentient creatures. The laws restricting or preventing gambling are concerned with the ethical significance of gambling which is confined to the effect that it may have on the character of the gambler as a member of society. The legislation against racial discrimination has as its object the shaping of people's moral thinking by legal sanctions and the changing of human behaviour by having the authority to punish.

11. The opposing view, traceable in English jurisprudence to John Stuart Mill, is that the law should not intervene in matters of private moral conduct more than necessary to preserve public order and to protect citizens against what is injurious and offensive and that there is a sphere of moral conduct which is best left to the individual conscience just as if it were equatable to liberty of thought or belief. . . .

14. If it is accepted that the State has a valid interest in the prevention of corruption and in the preservation of the moral ethos of its society, then the State has a right to enact such laws as it may reasonably think necessary to achieve these objects. The rule of law itself depends on a moral consensus in the community and in a democracy the law cannot afford to ignore the moral consensus of the community. If the law is out of touch with the moral consensus of the community, whether by being either too far below it or too far above it, the law is brought into contempt. Virtue cannot be legislated into existence but non-virtue can be if the legislation renders excessively difficult the struggle after virtue. Such a situation can have an eroding effect on the moral ethos of the community in question. The ultimate justification of law is that it serves moral ends. It is true that many forms of immorality which can have a corrupting effect are not the subject of prohibitory or penal legislation. However such omissions do not imply a denial of the possibility of corruption or of the erosion of the moral ethos of the community but acknowledge the practical impossibility of legislating effectively for every area of immorality. Where such legislation is enacted it is a reflection of the concern of the 'prudent legislator'. . . .

16. In my view, the Court's reference to the fact that in most countries in the Council of Europe homosexual acts in private between adults are no longer criminal does not really advance the argument. The twenty-one countries making up the council of Europe extend geographically from Turkey to Iceland and from the Mediterranean to the Arctic Circle and encompass considerable

diversities of culture and moral values. The Court states that it cannot overlook the marked changes which have occurred in the laws regarding homosexual behaviour throughout the member States. It would be unfortunate if this should lead to the erroneous inference that a Euro-norm in the law concerning homosexual practices has been or can be evolved.

17. Religious beliefs in Northern Ireland are very firmly held and directly influence the views and outlook of the vast majority of persons in Northern Ireland on questions of sexual morality. In so far as male homosexuality is concerned, and in particular sodomy, this attitude to sexual morality may appear to set the people of Northern Ireland apart from many people in other communities in Europe, but whether that fact constitutes a failing is, to say the least, debatable. Such views on unnatural sexual practices do not differ materially from those which throughout history conditioned the moral ethos of the Jewish, Christian and Muslim cultures. . . .

19. Even if it should be thought, and I do not so think, that the people of Northern Ireland are more 'backward' than the other societies within the Council of Europe because of their attitude towards homosexual practices, that is very much a value judgment which depends totally upon the initial premise. It is difficult to gauge what would be the effect on society in Northern Ireland if the law were now to permit (even with safeguards for young people and people in need of protection) homosexual practices of the type at present forbidden by law. I venture the view that the Government concerned, having examined the position, is in a better position to evaluate that than this Court, particularly as the Court admits the competence of the State to legislate in this matter but queries the proportionality of the consequences of the legislation in force.

20. The law has a role in influencing moral attitudes and if the respondent Government is of the opinion that the change sought in the legislation would have a damaging effect on moral attitudes then in my view it is entitled to maintain the legislation it has. The judgment of the Court does not constitute a declaration to the effect that the particular homosexual practices which are subject to penalty by the legislation in question virtually amount to fundamental human rights. However, that will not prevent it being hailed as such by those who seek to blur the essential difference between homosexual and heterosexual activities.

22. In the United States of America there has been considerable litigation concerning the question of privacy and the guarantees as to privacy enshrined in the Constitution of the United States. The United States Supreme Court and other United States courts have upheld the right of privacy of married couples against legislation which sought to control sexual activities within marriage, including sodomy. However, these courts have refused to extend the constitutional guarantee of privacy which is available to married couples to homosexual activities or to hetero-sexual sodomy outside marriage. The effect of this is that the public policy upholds as virtually absolute privacy within marriage and privacy of sexual activity within the marriage.

It is a valid approach to hold that, as the family is the fundamental unit group of society, the interests of marital privacy would normally be superior to the State's interest in the pursuit of certain sexual activities which would in themselves be regarded as immoral and calculated to corrupt. Outside marriage there is no such compelling interest of privacy which by its nature ought to prevail in respect of such activities.

23. It is to be noted that Article 8 §1 of the Convention speaks of 'private and family life'. If the *ejusdem generis* rule is to be applied, then the provision should be interpreted as relating to private life in that context as, for example, the right to raise one's children according to one's own philosophical and religious tenets and generally to pursue without interference the activities which

are akin to those pursued in the privacy of family life and as such are in the course of ordinary human and fundamental rights. No such claim can be made for homosexual practices.

24. In my opinion there has been no breach of Article 8 of the Convention. . . .

2. THE DEFINITION OF 'PRIVATE LIFE'

The particular circumstances of Jeffrey Dudgeon, the applicant in the principal case raise an issue as to the meaning of the term, 'private' life. The Court found that '[f]or some time [Dudgeon] and others have been conducting a campaign aimed at bringing the law in Northern Ireland into line with that in force in England and Wales. . . .'[178] Although it made no finding on Dudgeon's own sexual orientation, in a subsequent case dealing with the sodomy law of Ireland, the applicant, a member of the Irish Senate, was described as 'an active homosexual and . . . a campaigner for homosexual rights'.[179] Thus, the interference with privacy involved here could not consist of activities of the state in disclosing to public view facts which the applicants wished to keep secret. Rather, the Court holds that respect for private life includes respect for the applicant's sexual life by which, of course, the Court must mean a sexual life of the applicant's own choosing. Thus, 'private' must be read to refer not to questions of disclosure or nondisclosure but to the right to choose certain intimate aspects of one's life, free of government regulation.

Such a definition, of course, requires some sense of the scope of activity in which individual autonomy is protected. The Court has not addressed this question in any comprehensive fashion. In a slightly different context, however, it has suggested an idea of 'private life' that is quite broad. The Court has held that Article 8 controls searches not merely of individual's 'homes', which are specifically mentioned in Article 8, but of business premises as well. The latter category is included because such searches represent an interference with the right to respect for 'private life'.

29. The Court does not consider it possible or necessary to attempt an exhaustive definition of the notion of 'private life'. However, it would be too restrictive to limit the notion to an 'inner circle' in which the individual may live his own personal life as he chooses and to exclude therefrom entirely the outside world not encompassed within that circle. Respect for private life must also comprise to a certain degree the right to establish and develop relationships with other human beings.

There appears, furthermore, to be no reason of principle why this understanding of the notion of 'private life' should be taken to exclude activities of a professional or business nature since it is, after all, in the course of their working lives that the majority of people have a significant, if not the greatest, opportunity of developing relationships with the outside world. This view is supported by the fact that, as was rightly pointed out by the Commission, it is not always possible to distinguish clearly which of an individual's activities form part of his professional or business life and which do not. Thus, especially in the case of a person exercising a liberal profession, his work in

---

[178] Para. 32.

[179] *Norris v. Ireland*, 26 Oct. 1988 (No. 142), 13 E.H.R.R. 186, para. 9.

that context may form part and parcel of his life to such a degree that it becomes impossible to know in what capacity he is acting at a given moment of time . . .

31. More generally, to interpret the words 'private life' and 'home' as including certain professional or business activities or premises would be consonant with the essential objects and purpose of Article 8, namely to protect the individual against arbitrary interference by the public authorities. Such an interpretation would not unduly hamper the Contracting States, for they would retain their entitlement to 'interfere' to the extent permitted by paragraph 2 of article 8: that entitlement might well be more far-reaching where professional or business activities or premises were involved than would otherwise be the case.[180]

In subsequent dicta, however, the Court has suggested that the number of people involved in an activity and the degree of secrecy attached to it may be relevant in determining whether it involved 'private life'. In considering whether prosecution of group sado-masochistic practices violated Article 8 the Court observed:

[A] considerable number of people were involved in the activities in question which included, *inter alia*, the recruitment of new 'members' the provision of several specially equipped 'chambers' and the shooting of many video-tapes which were distributed among the 'members.' . . . It may thus be open to question whether the sexual activities of the applicants fell entirely within the notion of 'private life' in the particular circumstances of the case.[181]

3. PRIVATE ACTS AND THE PROTECTION OF MORALS

Article 8(2) contemplates that privacy rights may be infringed, to some extent, for the 'protection of morals'. The *Dudgeon* case indicates, however, that the state's power in this regard may be strictly construed. It is not clear from the judgment what private consensual acts, if any, may be regulated on that basis. Put another way, it is not clear whether there are any instances of private conduct which are proscribable *just* because they are offensive to public morality. The Court affirms the propriety of legislation against homosexual conduct insofar as necessary to protect against exploitation of vulnerable people—those 'young, weak in body or mind, inexperienced, or in a state of physical, official, or economic dependence'.[182] But, such narrower legislation would not be applicable to truly consensual behaviour. Consequently it would be supportable under the Article 8(2) exception for legislation necessary for the 'protection of the rights and freedoms of others' and thus does not require the invocation of the Article 8(2) exemption for interference necessary for the 'protection of . . . morals'.

---

[180] *Niemietz v. Germany*, 16 Dec. 1992 (No. 251B), 16 E.H.R.R. 97.

[181] *Laskey, Jaggard & Brown v. United Kingdom*, 19 Feb. 1997, Reports, 1997–I 120, 24 E.H.R.R. 39, para. 36. In *Halford v. United Kingdom*, 25 June 1997, Reports, 1997–III 1004, 24 E.H.R.R. 523, the Court found Art. 8 applicable when a police officer's office telephone, part of a separate police communication system, was tapped by police authorities. The Court pointed out that the phone was one of two in the applicant's office and had been designated for personal use. *Id.* at paras. 44–5.

[182] Para. 49 quoting the Wolfenden Report. *See also* para. 61.

The Court seems unable to avoid adopting Hart's position in the Hart-Devlin debate adverted to in Judge Walsh's dissenting opinion. But it is hard to reconcile that stance with the right of the state to protect morals specified in Article 8(2). Perhaps moral regulation in general is proper but Northern Ireland's legislation on homosexuality is not interference 'necessary in a democratic society for the protection of morals'. But if homosexual conduct is, itself, immoral it is difficult to argue that its prohibition is not necessary for the protection of morality. The only other argument would be that the state's judgment as to the morality of the conduct is erroneous. Still, the Court says that it 'is not concerned with making any value-judgment as to the morality of homosexual relations between adult males'.[183]

A serious evaluation of the 'protection of morals' authority of Article 8(2) requires some identification of relevant moral standards. In *Dudgeon*, the government presented evidence, which the Court accepted, that the prevalent moral sentiment in Northern Ireland was that 'a change in the law would be seriously damaging to the moral fabric of society'.[184] But the Court did not regard that fact as conclusive. The Court did seem to rely on an evolving tolerance for homosexual behaviour and its decriminalization in many European states. This opposition raises the problem of reconciling national moral views with the hypothetical 'Euro-norm' referred to by Judge Walsh.

The European Court has only rarely relied on a state's power to protect morals to justify an interference with Convention rights. In the *Handyside Case*, reprinted in the previous chapter, the Court noted that given the variation in moral views, a particularly generous margin of appreciation was appropriate. It relied on this rationale in refusing to find a violation in that case, as well as in the Case of *Müller and Others*, where it found permissible a decision to prosecute an artist for a display of obscenity.[185]

It is noteworthy, however, that the court gave no consideration to this justification in connection with its holding that families with illegitimate children were entitled to equal legal status with other families. This was, at least in form, because the claims in those cases arose under Article 8's, 'positive obligations' to which the justifications in paragraph 2 are not strictly applicable.[186] In any event, the promotion of moral conduct by means of a penalty inflicted on illegitimate children is, at best, problematic.[187]

The Court's reluctance to rely on the justification of protection of morals was particularly evident in *Laskey, Jaggard & Brown v. United Kingdom*.[188] The applicants had been prosecuted for committing acts of violence, including infliction of wounds, while engaging in homosexual sado-masochistic activities. The government argued that the prosecution was justified for the protection of health and of morals: the former because the activities created a risk of physical injury and the latter because

---

[183] Para. 54.

[184] Para. 57.

[185] *See* Chapter 5(C)(6) *supra*.

[186] See Section (A)(5) *supra*.

[187] In this connection *see Weber v Aetna Casualty & Surety Co.* 406 U.S. 164, 175 (1972) ('[V]isting this condemnation [of extra-marital sexual elations] on the head of an infant is illogical and unjust.').

[188] 19 Feb. 1997, Reports, 1997–I 120, 24 E.H.R.R. 39.

they 'undermine the respect which human beings should confer upon each other'.[189]
The Court held there was no violation but relied solely on the risk of physical harm.
In the judgment of the House of Lords, in contrast, the moral aspects of the prosecution had been prominent. Lord Templeton insisted that '[s]ociety is entitled and
bound to protect itself against a cult of violence. Pleasure derived from the infliction
of pain is an evil thing. Cruelty is uncivilized.'[190] Although the European Court quoted
this language in setting out the history of the case, in its own reasons for judgment the
physical dangers were emphasized. In a concurring opinion Judge Pettiti criticized the
majority for failing to recognize a state's right to 'regulate and punish practices of
sexual abuse that are demeaning even if they do not involve infliction of physical
harm'. He concluded that the 'protection of private life means the protection of a
person's intimacy and dignity, not the protection of his baseness or the promotion of
criminal immoralism'.[191]

The Supreme Court of Canada declined to rely on the protection of morals in
upholding the constitutionality of a law criminalizing the sale and distribution of
obscene material against a charge that it violated freedom of expression. The Court
construed the statute at issue to prohibit only materials depicting sexual violence or
cruelty, or which could be said to dehumanize men or women in a sexual context.
With respect to the proposition that such a law incorporated 'a particular conception
of morality', Justice Sopinka, writing for the Court, found such an aim 'no longer
defensible' in view of the Charter. 'To impose a certain standard of public and sexual
morality solely because it reflects the values of a given community is inimical to the
exercise and enjoyment of individual freedoms, which form the basis of our social
contract.' He rejected the idea that a majority could decide 'what values should
inform individual lives and then coercively impose those values on minorities'.[192] The
statute was justifiable, however, not on the basis of 'moral disapprobation but the
avoidance of harm to society', citing the exploitation of women and children depicted
in the material, and the need to promote gender equality which was threatened by the
proliferation of degrading and violent material.[193] In his majority decision holding that
omission of sexual orientation as a prohibited ground of discrimination in a provincial human rights statute was unconstitutional, Justice Iacobucci stated, in dicta, that
an argument that moral disapproval of homosexual relations could amount to a
'pressing and substantial objective' was 'a position which I find difficult to accept in
this case'.[194] In holding a sodomy law invalid the Constitutional Court of South Africa
was direct in declining to consider moral values present in society: '[t]he enforcement
of the private moral views of a portion of the community, which are based to a large
extent on nothing more than prejudice, cannot qualify as such a legitimate purpose

---

[189] *Id.* at para. 40.
[190] *R. v. Brown* [1993] 2 All E.R. 75, 84.
[191] 19 Feb. 1997, Reports, 1997–I 120, 24 E.H.R.R. 39 (concurring opinion).
[192] *R. v. Butler* [1992] 1 S.C.R. 452, 497.
[193] *Id.* at 466–7.
[194] *Vriend v. Alberta* [1997] 1 S.C.R. 493.

[as to justify legislation limiting rights]. There is accordingly nothing in the proportionality enquiry, to weigh against the extent of the limitation and its harmful impact on gays.'[195]

4. PRIVATE LIFE AND SEXUAL PREFERENCES

The European Court reaffirmed its holding in *Dudgeon* in 1988 in *Norris v. Ireland.*[196] There a challenge was posed to the very same statutes insofar as they were continued in Ireland after independence from Great Britain. In that case, the government urged the Court to adopt a more deferential approach to a state's determination that challenged measures were necessary for the protection of morals. It argued that '[w]ithin broad parameters the moral fibre of a democratic nation is a matter for its own institutions'. The Court rejected this suggestion concluding that to accept it would result in the state's 'discretion in the field of morals [being] unfettered'.[197]

Norris had previously challenged the sodomy laws in the Irish courts claiming that they were an interference with rights of privacy implicit in the Irish Constitution's general guarantee of personal rights. In his majority opinion rejecting that claim, Chief Justice O'Higgins of the Irish Supreme Court noted:

The Preamble [to the Irish Constitution] proudly asserts the existence of God in the Most Holy Trinity and recites the People of Ireland as humbly acknowledging their obligation to 'Our Divine Lord Jesus Christ'. It cannot be doubted that a people so asserting and acknowledging their obligation to Our Divine Lord Jesus Christ were proclaiming a deep religious conviction and faith and an intention to adopt a Constitution consistent with that conviction and faith and with Christian beliefs. Yet it is suggested that in the very act of so doing the People rendered inoperative laws which had existed for hundreds of years prohibiting unnatural sexual conduct which Christian teaching held to be gravely sinful. It would require very clear and express provisions in the Constitution itself to convince me that such took place. When one considers that the conduct in question had been condemned consistently in the name of Christ for almost two thousand years, and at the time of the enactment of the Constitution was prohibited as criminal by the laws in force in England, Wales, Scotland and Northern Ireland the suggestion becomes more incomprehensible and difficult of acceptance.[198]

Chief Justice O'Higgins further asserted that homosexuality had been shown to create psychological injury, to increase venereal disease and to undermine the institution of marriage. These were evils the state was entitled to combat.

Two Justices dissented. In his dissenting opinion, Justice Henchy reviewed the evidence of the plaintiff's witnesses, including a Catholic and a Protestant clergyman,

---

[195] *National Coalition for Gay and Lesbian Equality and Another v. Minister for Justice and Other* [1999] S.A.L.R. 6 para. 37.

[196] 26 Oct. 1988 (No. 142), 13 E.H.R.R. 186.

[197] The extent of a state's 'margin of appreciation'—especially with regard to the protection of morals—is discussed in Chapter 5 (B)(2)(D) *supra*.

[198] *Norris v. Attorney General* [1984] I.R. 36 (Ir. S.C. 1983).

both of whom testified that the challenged laws were not necessary to reinforce the Christian morality of the State and were, indeed, contrary to Christian teaching insofar as they showed a lack of love and charity toward homosexuals.

In 1993 the European Court ruled that the criminal prohibition on homosexual activity in Cyprus violated the Convention, notwithstanding the government's argument that no prosecutions had been brought under the law for a long time and there were no plans to do so. The Court noted that there was no assurance that prosecutions might not be brought or police investigations undertaken in the future.[199] It took Cyprus another five years to comply with the judgment by decriminalizing consensual homosexual conduct.[200]

The Strasbourg Court held that the United Kingdom's policy of excluding and discharging homosexuals from the armed forces violated Article 8 in *Smith and Grady v. United Kingdom*.[201] The principal argument of the government was that in military service 'cohesion and morale had to withstand the internal rigours of normal and corporate life, close physical and shared living conditions together with external pressures such as grave danger and work'.[202] In such circumstances the fact of entrenched attitudes of hostility, suspicion or discomfort directed towards homosexuals could compromise the operational effectiveness and 'fighting power' of the forces.[203] The Court held that to the extent such consequences were a result of negative attitudes they could not provide a sufficient justification under Article 8(2), 'any more than similar negative attitudes towards those of a different race, origin or colour'.[204] The Court noted that a strict code of conduct, such as that already in place with respect to discrimination or harassment based on race or gender, was an alternative to the exclusionary policy, with a much less severe impact on the private life of homosexuals.[205]

The constitutional law of Canada has dealt with interference with expression of sexual identity under the equality provision of the Charter which prohibits discrimination 'in particular . . . based on race, national or ethnic origin, colour, religion, sex, age or mental or physical disability'. In *Egan v. Canada*[206] the Supreme Court held that discrimination against homosexuals was discrimination on a ground 'analogous' to those listed and, therefore, required justification under section 1 of the Charter. Some of the justices based this finding on the personal and practically immutable nature of sexual orientation[207] and some on the history of discrimination suffered by

---

[199] *Modinos v. Cyprus*, 22 Apr. 1993 (No. 259), 16 E.H.R.R. 485.

[200] 'Cyprus Parliament Approves "Gay Sex" Law,' Agence France Press, 21 May 1998 (available in Lexis/ Nexis, News Library).

[201] 27 Sept. 1999 (not yet reported). An almost identical judgment was given in *Lustig-Prean & Beckett v. United Kingdom*, Judgment of 27 Sept. 1999 (not yet reported).

[202] *Id.* at para. 77.

[203] *Id.* at para. 95.

[204] *Id.* at para. 97.

[205] *Id.* at para. 102.

[206] [1995] 2 S.C.R. 513.

[207] *Id.* at 528 (La Forest J).

homosexuals.[208] The practice challenged in *Egan*, the exclusion of same-sex couples from old age security benefits, was upheld as justifiable under section 1. But in *Vriend v. Alberta*[209] the Court held that the exclusion of sexual orientation as a prohibited ground of private discrimination in the Alberta Individual Rights Protection Act constituted discrimination against homosexuals and was unjustified under section 1.

In *M v. H*[210] the Court held invalid under section 15 the Ontario Family Law Act which limited spousal support rights and obligations to participants in heterosexual relationships. The Court reasoned that same-sex relationships could involve the same problems of economic dependence which the Court took to be the target of the law. It held the statutory limitation in no way contributed to the alleviation of this problem.[211]

There is no explicit provision protecting privacy, intimate decisions or family life in the United States Constitution. The courts, however, have found a right to be free of government coercion in these areas to be part of the 'liberty' protected by the Fifth and Fourteenth Amendments of which a person may not be deprived without due process of law.[212] Modern cases have translated this into a doctrine which requires that governmental interference in this sphere of private life is not permissible in the absence of a particularly strong governmental justification.

In 1986 in *Bowers v. Hardwick*,[213] the Supreme Court refused to extend that doctrine to invalidate anti-homosexuality laws of the type considered in *Dudgeon*:

Accepting the decisions in these cases and the above description of them, we think it evident that none of the rights announced in those cases bears any resemblance to the claimed constitutional right of homosexuals to engage in acts of sodomy that is asserted in this case. No connection between family, marriage, or procreation on the one hand and homosexual activity on the other has been demonstrated, either by the Court of Appeals or by respondent. Moreover, any claim that these cases nevertheless stand for the proposition that any kind of private sexual conduct between consenting adults is constitutionally insulated from state proscription is unsupportable. . . .

. . . Sodomy was a criminal offense at common law and was forbidden by the laws of the original thirteen States when they ratified the Bill of Rights. In 1868, when the Fourteenth Amendment was ratified, all but 5 of the 37 States in the Union had criminal sodomy laws. In fact, until 1961, all 50 States outlawed sodomy, and today, 24 States and the District of Columbia continue to provide criminal penalties for sodomy performed in private and between consenting adults . . . Against this background, to claim that a right to engage in such conduct is 'deeply rooted in this Nation's history and tradition' or 'implicit in the concept of ordered liberty' is, at best, facetious.

Even if the conduct at issue here is not a fundamental right, respondent asserts that there must be a rational basis for the law and that there is none in this case other than the presumed belief of a majority of the electorate in Georgia that homosexual sodomy is immoral and unacceptable. This is said to be an inadequate rationale to support the law. The law, however is constantly based on notions of morality, and if all laws representing essentially moral choices are to be invalidated

---

[208] *Id.* at 599–603 (Cory J).
[209] [1997] 1 S.C.R. 493.
[210] [1999] 2 S.C.R. 3.
[211] *Id.* at paras. 108–35.
[212] *See Meyer v. Nebraska*, discussed at Section (A)(6)(B) *supra*.
[213] 478 U.S. 186 (1986).

under the Due Process Clause, the courts will be very busy indeed. Even respondent makes no such claim, but insists that majority sentiments about the morality of homosexuality should be declared inadequate. We do not agree, and are unpersuaded that the sodomy laws of some 25 States should be invalidated on this basis.

In *Romer v. Evans*,[214] however, the Supreme Court held that an amendment to the Colorado Constitution prohibiting any state or municipal measure forbidding discrimination on the basis of sexual orientation, violated the Equal Protection Clause of the Fourteenth Amendment. The Court noted that the amendment disadvantaged homosexuals alone from seeking legal protection of this kind. As such, it constituted discrimination against homosexuals. Without deciding that such discrimination was analogous to racial or gender discrimination, it still, like any classification, had to be justified by showing it was rationally related to a legitimate state interest. In this case the majority found such a showing had not been made. Rather the 'disadvantage imposed is born of animosity toward the class of persons affected. . . . [I]t is a classification of persons undertaken for its own sake.'[215] The opinion of the Court failed to cite the *Bower* case, an omission noted by the dissent which contended that '[i]f it is constitutionally permissible for a state to make homosexual conduct criminal, surely it is constitutionally permissible for a state to enact other laws merely disfavoring homosexual conduct'.[216]

In a case brought before the Constitutional Court of the Federal Republic of Germany, in 1957, two male homosexuals claimed that Section 175 of the Penal Code punishing homosexual acts violated Article 2(1) of the Basic Law which states: 'Everyone should have the right to the free development of his personality insofar as he does not infringe the rights of others or offend against the constitutional order or the moral code'. The Court agreed that this constitutional provision provided some protection for personal decisions regarding sexual conduct. It found, however, that the 'moral code' unequivocally condemned homosexual behaviour. It relied upon the attitude of the two dominant Christian denominations and a long history of anti-homosexuality laws which were rooted in public aversion to such acts. It was not dissuaded from this conclusion by the existence of more liberal laws elsewhere in Western Europe, noting that such changes might be for reasons unrelated to moral judgment and that, in any event, German moral disapproval was decisive.[217]

On the other hand, the Constitutional Court of South Africa has held invalid the criminal prohibition of homosexual acts. It invoked section 9, the equality provision, section 9(3) explicitly listing sexual orientation as a prohibited ground of discrimination. The Court went on to hold that the criminal law was also invalid under section

---

[214] 517 U.S. 620 (1996).

[215] *Id.* at 634–5.

[216] *Id.* at 641 (Scalia J. dissenting).

[217] BVerfGE 389 (1957) reported in part in Murphy & Tanehous, *Comparative Constitutional Law: Cases and Commentaries* 403 (1977). The German law criminalizing consensual homosexual acts was repealed in 1994. StGB §175 repealed as of 31 May 1994, by Art. 1, No. 1, BGBl–I, 1168.

10 stating a right to 'dignity' and under section 14, the right to privacy. In connection with its holding on section 10 it said the law's

symbolic effect is to state that in the eyes of our legal system all gay men are criminals. The stigma thus attached to a significant proportion of our population is manifest. But the harm imposed by the criminal law is far more than symbolic. As a result of the criminal offence gay men are at risk of arrest, prosecution and conviction of the offence of sodomy simply because they seek to engage in sexual conduct which is part of their experience of being human. Just as apartheid legislation rendered the lives of couples of different racial groups perpetually at risk, the sodomy offence builds insecurity and vulnerability into the daily lives of gay men . . . [The law] degrades and devalues gay men in our broader society. As such it is a palpable invasion of their dignity and a breach of section 10 of the Constitution.[218]

5. PRIVACY RIGHTS AND ABORTION

The best known application of the modern American doctrine protecting the right of privacy has involved the right of a woman to procure an abortion. *Roe v. Wade*[219] held that a state could not proscribe abortions in the first trimester of pregnancy and that it could regulate abortions in the second trimester only insofar as reasonably related to maternal health. Subsequent cases applied this test to various state laws, permitting some, striking down others.[220]

In its most recent decision on abortion, the Supreme Court reformulated the critical test for the validity of restrictions on abortions. Three justices, holding the essential votes for any determination, rejected the trimester analysis of the question. The test throughout a pregnancy was to be the same: 'Only where state regulation imposes an undue burden on a women's ability to make this [abortion] decision does the power of the state reach into the heart of this liberty.'[221] These justices defined 'undue burden' as one having the purpose or effect of 'placing a substantial obstacle in the path of a woman's choice'. The state's interest in protecting health and potential life would be evaluated within this framework. Four justices joined a separate opinion which would have overruled *Roe*. These justices condemned the 'undue burden' test as 'inherently manipulable [which] will prove hopelessly unworkable in practice'.[222]

In 1988 the Supreme Court of Canada declared invalid Section 251 of the Canadian Criminal Code which limited the performance of abortions to those performed in

---

[218] *Nation Coalition for Gay & Lesbian Equality and Another v. Minister for Justice and Another* [1999] 1 S.A.C.R. 6 (10 Sept. 1998).

[219] 410 U.S. 113 (1973).

[220] *See*, e.g. *Akron v. Akron Center for Reproductive Health, Inc.*, 462 U.S. 416 (1983).

[221] *Planned Parenthood of Southeastern Pennsylvania v. Casey*, 505 U.S. 833 (1992) (joint opinion of O'Connor, Kennedy and Souter, JJ.)

[222] *Id.* at 986 (Scalia, J. concurring in the judgment in part and dissenting in part).

approved hospitals and certified by a hospital committee as necessary to terminate a pregnancy that would be likely to endanger the life or health of the pregnant woman. The Court found that the provision violated Section 7 of the Canadian Charter of Rights and Freedoms which prohibits deprivation of 'life, liberty or security of the person ... except in accordance with the principles of fundamental justice'. The Court concluded first that a ban on abortion could constitute a substantial threat to 'security of the person'. It then found that the statute was not in accordance with 'principles of fundamental justice', because the procedures it provided had the effect of preventing abortions even for those women who, under the standard set out, Parliament had determined had a sufficient reason for the abortion. The majority did not find it necessary to decide whether Parliament's substantive reasons for restricting abortions were in accord with 'fundamental justice'.[223]

The European Commission of Human Rights considered several applications concerning national laws regulating abortion. Some claimed those laws were too strict, others that they were too liberal. The Commission's reports treated as relevant both Article 2 on the right to life and Article 8. Indeed both articles were invoked by both opponents and defenders of abortion.[224] The Court has not yet adjudicated a case involving a claimed right to an abortion. The Court has, however, made clear that Article 8 protects a person's physical and moral integrity'.[224A] In *Open Door Counselling and Dublin Woman v. Ireland*,[225] the Court did hold that the issuance of an injunction by the Irish courts against communicating information about the availability of abortions in the United Kingdom was an unjustified interference with the right of free expression under Article 10. In that case, however, the Court carefully avoided expressing an opinion as to 'whether a right to abortion is guaranteed under the Convention or whether the foetus is encompassed by the right to life as contained in Article 2'.[226] Similarly, it refused to decide whether the protection of the right of 'others mentioned in Article 10, paragraph 2 extended to the unborn. It did hold, however, that the Irish prohibition of abortion pursued a legitimate aim under that provision—'the protection of morals of which the protection, in Ireland, of the right to life of the unborn is one aspect'. This conclusion was based on the 'profound moral values concerning the nature of life which were reflected in the stance of the majority of the Irish people'[226A]

---

[223] *Morgentaler v. R.* [1988] 1 S.C.R. 60.

[224] *X v. Norway*, Application No. 867/60, 6 C.D. 39 (1961); *X v. Austria*, Application No. 7045/75, 7 D.R. 87 (1976); *Bruggeman & Scheuten v. Germany*, Application No. 6959/75, 10 D.R. 100 (1977); *X. v. United Kingdom*, Application No. 8416/79 19 D.R. 244 (1980); *H v. Norway*, Application No. 17004/90, 73 D.R. 155 (1992).

[224A] *Costello-Roberts v. United Kingdom*, 25 Mar. 1993 (No. 274C), para. 34.

[225] 29 Oct. 1992 (No. 246), 15 E.H.R.R. 244.

[226] *Id.* at para. 66.

[226A] *Id.* at para. 63.

C. PRIVATE LIFE AND PERSONAL IDENTITY

1. SEXUAL IDENTITY

A. SHEFFIELD AND HORSHAM *V.* UNITED KINGDOM

Judgment of 30 July 1998,
Reports, 1998–V 2011, 27 E.H.R.R. 163

12. The first applicant, Miss Kristina Sheffield, is a British citizen, born in 1946 and currently resident in London. At birth the applicant was registered as being of the male sex. Prior to her gender re-assignment treatment she was married. She has one daughter from that marriage, which is now dissolved.

13. In 1986 the first applicant began treatment at a gender identity clinic in London and on a date unspecified, successfully underwent sex re-assignment surgery and treatment. She changed her name by deed poll to her present name. The change of name was recorded on her passport and driving licence.

14. Miss Sheffield refers to the difficulties which she has encountered as a result of her decision to undergo gender re-assignment surgery and her subsequent change of sex.

15. She states that she was informed by her consultant psychiatrist and her surgeon that she was required to obtain a divorce as a pre-condition to surgery being carried out. Following the divorce, the applicant's former spouse applied to the court to have her contact with her daughter terminated. The applicant states that the judge granted the application on the basis that contact with a transsexual would not be in the child's interests. The applicant has not seen her daughter since then, a period of some twelve years.

16. Although her new name has been entered on her passport and driving licence, her birth certificate and various records including social security and police records continue to record her original name and gender. As to her passport, she maintains that if there is a need for further enquiries about the bearer, this will inevitably lead to her former name and gender being disclosed. She cites by way of example her experience when applying for a visa to the United States Embassy in London.

17. On 7 and 16 April 1992 Miss Sheffield attended court to stand surety in the sum of GBP 2,000 for a friend. On both occasions she was required, to her great embarrassment, to disclose to the court her previous name. She has also been dissuaded from acting as an alibi witness for a friend who was tried on criminal charges in March 1994 for fear of adding an element of sensationalism to the proceedings through the disclosure to the court of her original gender as inscribed on her birth certificate.

18. In June 1992 Miss Sheffield was arrested for breach of firearms regulations. The charges were dropped when it was established that the pistol was a replica. Following comments of police officers indicating that they were aware that the applicant had undergone a sex change operation, the applicant sought to discover whether these personal details were held on police computer files. She discovered that the official request for information made under the provisions of the Data

Protection Act 1984 required her to state her sex and other names. She did not pursue the enquiry.

19. On 20 December 1992 the applicant entered into an insurance contract in respect of her car. The form which she was required to fill in as the basis of the contract required her to state her sex. Since she continues under United Kingdom law to be regarded as male she was obliged to give her sex as male. She also notes that she is obliged under the Perjury Act 1911 to disclose her former sexual identity in certain contexts under pain of criminal sanction.

20. The applicant maintains that her decision to undergo gender re-assignment surgery has resulted in her being subjected to discrimination at work or in relation to obtaining work. She is a pilot by profession. She states that she was dismissed by her employers in 1986 as a direct consequence of her gender re-assignment and has found it impossible to obtain employment in the respondent State in her chosen profession. She attributes this in large part to the legal position of transsexuals in that State.

21. The second applicant, Miss Rachel Horsham, is a British citizen born in 1946. She has been living in the Netherlands since 1974 and acquired Dutch citizenship by naturalization in September 1993. The second applicant was registered at birth as being of the male sex. She states that from an early age she began to experience difficulties in relating to herself as male and when she was twenty-one she fully understood that she was a transsexual. She left the United Kingdom in 1971 as she was concerned about the consequences of being identified as a transsexual. Thereafter she led her life abroad as a female.

22. From 1990, Miss Horsham received psychotherapy and hormonal treatment and finally underwent gender re-assignment surgery on 21 May 1992 at the Free University Hospital, Amsterdam.

23. On 26 June 1992, following earlier refusals, she applied to the British Consulate in Amsterdam seeking a change of photograph and the inscription of her new name in her passport. She was informed that this could only be carried out in accordance with an order from the Dutch courts. On 24 August 1992 Miss Horsham obtained an order from the Amsterdam Regional Court that she be issued a birth certificate by the Registrar of Births in The Hague recording her new name and the fact that she was of the female sex. The birth certificate was issued on 12 November 1992. In the meantime, on 11 September 1992 and on production of the court order, the British Consulate issued a new passport to the applicant recording her new name and her sex as female.

24. On 15 November 1992 the second applicant requested that her original birth certificate in the United Kingdom be amended to record her sex as female. By letter dated 20 November 1992, the Office of Population Censuses and Surveys (OPCS) replied that there was no provision under United Kingdom law for any new information to be inscribed on her original birth certificate.

25. Miss Horsham states that she is forced to live in exile because of the legal situation in the United Kingdom. She has a male partner whom she plans to marry. She states that they would like to lead their married life in the United Kingdom but has been informed by the OPCS by letter dated 4 November 1993 that as a matter of English law, if she were to be held to be domiciled in the United Kingdom, she would be precluded from contracting a valid marriage whether that marriage 'took place in the Netherlands or elsewhere'.

26. Under English law, a person is entitled to adopt such first names or surname as he or she wishes. Such names are valid for purposes of identification and may be used in passports, driving

licences, medical and insurance cards etc. The new names are also entered on the electoral roll.

27. Under English law, marriage is defined as the voluntary union between a man and a woman. In the case of *Corbett v. Corbett* [1971] (Probate Reports 83), Mr Justice Ormrod ruled that sex for that purpose is to determined by the application of chromosomal, gonadal and genital tests where these are congruent and without regard to any surgical intervention. This use of biological criteria to determine sex was approved by the Court of Appeal in *R. v. Tan* [1983] (Queen's Bench Reports 1053) and given more general application, the court holding that a person born male had been correctly convicted under a statute penalizing men who live on the earnings of prostitution, notwithstanding the fact that the accused had undergone gender re-assignment therapy.

Under section 11(b) of the Matrimonial Causes Act 1973 any marriage where the parties are not respectively male and female is void. The test applied as to the sex of the partners to a marriage is that laid down in the above-mentioned case of Corbett v. Corbett. According to that same decision a marriage between a male-to-female transsexual and a man might also be avoided on the basis that the transsexual was incapable of consummating the marriage in the context of ordinary and complete sexual intercourse (obiter per Ormrod J).

28. Registration of births is governed by the Births and Deaths Registration Act 1953 ('the 1953 Act'). Section 1 (1) of that Act requires that the birth of every child be registered by the Registrar of Births and Deaths for the area in which the child is born. An entry is regarded as a record of the facts at the time of birth. A birth certificate accordingly constitutes a document revealing not current identity but historical facts.

29. The sex of the child must be entered on the birth certificate. The criteria for determining the sex of a child at birth are not defined in the Act. The practice of the Registrar is to use exclusively the biological criteria (chromosomal, gonadal and genital) as laid down by Mr Justice Ormrod in the above-mentioned case of *Corbett v. Corbett*.

30. The 1953 Act provides for the correction by the Registrar of clerical errors or factual errors. The official position is that an amendment may only be made if the error occurred when the birth was registered. The fact that it may become evident later in a person's life that his or her 'psychological' sex is in conflict with the biological criteria is not considered to imply that the initial entry at birth was a factual error. Only in cases where the apparent and genital sex of a child was wrongly identified or where the biological criteria were not congruent can a change in the initial entry be made. It is necessary for that purpose to adduce medical evidence that the initial entry was incorrect. No error is accepted to exist in the birth entry of a person who undergoes medical and surgical treatment to enable that person to assume the role of the opposite sex.

31. The Government point out that the use of a birth certificate for identification purposes is discouraged by the Registrar General, and for a number of years birth certificates have contained a warning that they are not evidence of the identity of the person presenting it. However, it is a matter for individuals whether to follow this recommendation.

32. A transsexual continues to be recorded for social security, national insurance and employment purposes as being of the sex recorded at birth. A male to female transsexual will accordingly only be entitled to a State pension at the state retirement age of 65 and not the age of 60 which is applicable to women.

33. In its judgment of 30 April 1996, in the case of *P. v. S. and Cornwall County Council*, the

European Court of Justice (ECJ) held that discrimination arising from gender re-assignment constituted discrimination on grounds of sex. . . . The ECJ held, rejecting the argument of the United Kingdom Government that the employer would also have dismissed P. if P. had previously been a woman and had undergone an operation to become a man, that

> . . . Where a person is dismissed on the ground that he or she intends to undergo or has undergone gender re-assignment, he or she is treated unfavourably by comparison with persons of the sex to which he or she was deemed to belong before undergoing gender re-assignment.
>
> To tolerate such discrimination would be tantamount, as regards such a person, to a failure to respect the dignity and freedom to which he or she is entitled and which the Court has a duty to safeguard.

* * *

35. In their written observations on the legal recognition of transsexuals in comparative law Liberty suggested that over the last decade there has been an unmistakably clear trend in the member States of the Council of Europe towards giving full legal recognition to gender re-assignment. According to the study carried out by Liberty [a civil liberties organization,] the majority of member States now make provision for such recognition. For example, out of thirty-seven countries analysed, only four (including the United Kingdom) do not permit a change to be made to a person's birth certificate in one form or another to reflect the re-assigned sex of that person.

42. The applicants stated that under English law they continue to be regarded as being of the male sex and to suffer prejudice on that account. The failure to give legal recognition to their new gender has serious consequences for the way in which they conducted their lives, compelling them to identify themselves frequently in public contexts in a gender which they had renounced. This was a matter of profound hurt and distress and an affront to their dignity. Miss Sheffield's experiences provided a convincing account of the extreme disadvantages which beset post-operative transsexuals and of how the current legal situation operated to the detriment of their privacy and even exposed them to the risk of penalties for the offence of perjury. For her part, Miss Horsham claimed that she had to abandon her residence in the United Kingdom in order to avoid the difficulties which she encountered there as a transsexual.

43. They contended that the law of the respondent State continued to be based on a restrictive and purely biological approach to the determination of an individual's gender. In their view, the conclusive nature of that approach must now be reviewed in light of recent medical research findings which demonstrated convincingly that the sex of a person's brain is also to be considered one of the decisive indices of his or her gender. According to Professor L.J.G. Gooren, a distinguished and recognized authority on this subject, the brain's ability to differentiate between the male and female sex occurs when an individual is between three and four years old. A problem arises if the brain differentiates sex in a manner which is contradictory to the nature of the external genitalia. This dysfunction explains the feelings which transsexuals like the applicants have about their bodies.

* * *

45. The applicants recalled that the Court in its *Rees v. the United Kingdom* judgment had stated that the respondent State should keep the need for appropriate legal measures in the area

of transsexualism under review having regard in particular to scientific and societal developments. The Court reiterated that view in its *Cossey v. United Kingdom* judgment. Notwithstanding
new medical findings on the cause of transsexualism and the increased legal recognition of
a transsexual's post-operative gender at the level of the European Union and in the member
States of the Council of Europe, the respondent State has still not reviewed its domestic law in this
area.

46. The Government replied that Article 8 of the Convention does not require a Contracting
State to recognise generally for legal purposes the new sexual identity of an individual who has
undergone gender re-assignment surgery. With reference to the above-mentioned Rees and Cossey
judgments, they pleaded that a Contracting State properly enjoys a wide margin of appreciation in
respect of its positive obligations under Article 8, especially so in the area of transsexualism where
there is no sufficiently broad consensus within the member States on how to address the complexity of the legal, ethical, scientific and social issues which arise. They argued that Professor
Gooren's research findings on the notion of a person's psychological sex cannot be considered
conclusive of the issue and required further verification (see, for example, S. M. Breedlove's
article in Nature vol 378, p. 15, 2 November 1995); nor was the applicants' reliance on the
European Court of Justice's ruling in P.v.S. and Cornwall Country Council of support to their case
that a European-wide consensus existed on the need to give legal recognition to the situation of
transsexuals. That case was not concerned with the legal status of transsexuals. Moreover, much of
the comparative material submitted by Liberty had already been considered by the Court at the
time of its judgment in the Rees case.

47. The Government further submitted that the applicants had not adduced any evidence of
having suffered any substantial practical detriment on a day-to-day basis which would suggest
that the authorities had exceeded their margin of appreciation. The applicants are only obliged to
reveal their pre-operative gender on rare occasions and only when it is justified to do so. Further,
to allow the applicants' birth certificates to be altered so as to provide them with official proof of
their new sexual status would undermine the function of the birth register as an historical record
of fact; nor could the civil liberties implications of allowing a change of sex to be entered on the
register be discounted.

* * *

51. . . . [A]s in the above-mentioned Rees and Cossey cases, the issue raised by the applicants
before the Court is not that the respondent State should abstain from acting to their detriment but
that it has failed to take positive steps to modify a system which they claim operates to their
prejudice. . . .

52. The Court reiterates that the notion of 'respect' is not clear-cut, especially as far as the
positive obligations inherent in that concept are concerned: having regard to the diversity of the
practices followed and the situations obtaining in the Contracting States, the notion's requirements will vary considerably from case to case. In determining whether or not a positive obligation
exists, regard must be had to the fair balance that has to be struck between the general interest of
the community and the interests of the individual, the search for which balance is inherent in the
whole of the Convention.

53. It is to be noted that in applying the above principle in both the Rees and Cossey cases, the
Court concluded that the same respondent State was under no positive obligation to modify its

system of birth registration in order to allow those applicants the right to have the register of birth updated or annotated to record their new sexual identities or to provide them with a copy birth certificate or a short-form certificate excluding any reference to sex at all or sex at the time of birth. Although the applicants in the instant case have formulated their complaints in terms which are wider than those invoked by Mr Rees and Miss Cossey since they contend that their rights under Article 8 of the Convention have been violated on account of the failure of the respondent State to recognize for legal purposes generally their post-operative gender, it is nonetheless the case that the essence of their complaints concerns the continuing insistence by the authorities on the determination of gender according to biological criteria alone and the immutability of the gender information once it is entered on the register of birth.

54. The Government have relied in continuing defence of the current system of births registration on the general interest grounds which were accepted by the Court in its Rees and Cossey judgments as justification for preserving the register of births as an historical record of facts subject neither to alteration so as to record an entrant's change of sex nor to abridgement in the form of an extract containing no indication of the bearer's registered gender as well as to the wide margin of appreciation which they claim in respect of the treatment to be accorded in law to post-operative transsexuals. It is the applicants' contention that that defence is no longer tenable having regard to significant scientific and legal developments and to the clear detriment which the maintenance in force of the current system has on their personal situation, factors which, in their view, tilt the balance away from the defence of public interest considerations in favour of the need to take action to safeguard their own individual interests.

55. The Court notes that in its Cossey judgment it considered that there had been no noteworthy scientific developments in the area of transsexualism in the period since the date of adoption of its Rees judgment which would compel it to depart from the decision reached in the latter case. This view was confirmed subsequently in the Court's B. v. France judgment in which it observed that there still remained uncertainty as to the essential nature of transsexualism and that the legitimacy of surgical intervention in such cases is sometimes questioned.

As to legal developments occurring since the date of the Cossey judgment, the Court in the B. case stated that there was, as yet, no sufficiently broad consensus among the member States on how to deal with a range of complex legal matters resulting from a change of sex.

56. In the view of the Court, the applicants have not shown that since the date of adoption of its Cossey judgment in 1990 there have been any findings in the area of medical science which settle conclusively the doubts concerning the causes of the condition of transsexualism. While Professor Gooren's research into the role of the brain in conditioning transsexualism may be seen as an important contribution to the debate in this area, it cannot be said that his views enjoy the universal support of the medico-scientific profession. Accordingly, the non-acceptance by the authorities of the respondent State for the time being of the sex of the brain as a crucial determinant of gender cannot be criticised as being unreasonable. The Court would add that, as at the time of adoption of the Cossey judgment, it still remains established that gender re-assignment surgery does not result in the acquisition of all the biological characteristics of the other sex despite the increased scientific advances in the handling of gender re-assignment procedures.

57. As to legal developments in this area, the Court has examined the comparative study which has been submitted by Liberty. However, the Court is not fully satisfied that the legislative trends outlined by amicus suffice to establish the existence of any common European approach to the problems created by the recognition in law of post-operative gender status. In particular, the

survey does not indicate that there is as yet any common approach as to how to address the repercussions which the legal recognition of a change of sex may entail for other areas of law such as marriage, filiation, privacy or data protection, or the circumstances in which a transsexual may be compelled by law to reveal his or her pre-operative gender.

* * *

59. Nor is the Court persuaded that the applicants' case histories demonstrate that the failure of the authorities to recognise their new gender gives rise to detriment of sufficient seriousness as to override the respondent State's margin of appreciation in this area (cf the above-mentioned B. v. France judgment). It cannot be denied that the incidents alluded to by Miss Sheffield were a source of embarrassment and distress to her and that Miss Horsham, if she were to return to the United Kingdom, would equally run the risk of having on occasions to identify herself in her pre-operative gender. At the same time, it must be acknowledged that an individual may with justification be required on occasions to provide proof of gender as well as medical history. This is certainly the case of life assurance contracts which are uberrimae fidei. It may possibly be true of motor insurance where the insuror may need to have regard to the sex of the driver in order to make an actuarial assessment of the risk. Furthermore, it would appear appropriate for a court to run a check on whether a person has a criminal record, either under his or her present name or former name, before accepting that person as a surety for a defendant in criminal proceedings. However, quite apart from these considerations the situations in which the applicants may be required to disclose their pre-operative gender do not occur with a degree of frequency which could be said to impinge to a disproportionate extent on their right to respect for their private lives. The Court observes also that the respondent State has endeavoured to some extent to minimise intrusive inquiries as to their gender status by allowing transsexuals to be issued with driving licences, passports and other types of official documents in their new name and gender, and that the use of birth certificates as a means of identification is officially discouraged.

60. Having reached those conclusions, the Court cannot but note that despite its statements in the Rees and Cossey cases on the importance of keeping the need for appropriate legal measures in this area under review having regard in particular to scientific and societal developments, it would appear that the respondent State has not taken any steps to do so. The fact that a transsexual is able to record his or her new sexual identity on a driving licence or passport or to change a first name are not innovative facilities. They obtained even at the time of the Rees case. Even if there have been no significant scientific developments since the date of the Cossey judgment which make it possible to reach a firm conclusion on the aetiology of transsexualism, it is nevertheless the case that there is an increased social acceptance of transsexualism and an increased recognition of the problems which post-operative transsexuals encounter. Even if it finds no breach of Article 8 in this case, the Court reiterates that this area needs to be kept under review by Contracting States.

* * *

62. The applicants submitted that any marriage which a male-to-female post-operative transsexual contracted with a man would be void under English law having regard to the fact that a male-to-female transsexual is still considered for legal purposes as male. While they addressed the prejudice which they suffered in respect of their right to marry in the context of their more general

complaint under Article 8 of the Convention, before the Commission they [also] relied on Article 12. . . .

* * *

66. The Court recalls that the right to marry guaranteed by Article 12 refers to the traditional marriage between persons of opposite biological sex. This appears also from the wording of the Article which makes it clear that Article 12 is mainly concerned to protect marriage as the basis of the family. Furthermore, Article 12 lays down that the exercise of this right shall be subject to the national laws of the Contracting States. The limitations thereby introduced must not restrict or reduce the right in such a way or to such an extent that the very essence of the right is impaired. However, the legal impediment in the United Kingdom on the marriage of persons who are not of the opposite biological sex cannot be said to have an effect of this kind.

67. The Court recalls further that in its Cossey judgment it found that the attachment to the traditional concept of marriage which underpins Article 12 of the Convention provides sufficient reason for the continued adoption by the respondent State of biological criteria for determining a person's sex for the purposes of marriage, this being a matter encompassed within the power of the Contracting States to regulate by national law the exercise of the right to marry

[The Court's discussion of Article 14 in which it found no violation of the Convention and Article 13, which they found unnecessary to consider, is omitted.]

The joint Concurring Opinion of Judges DeMeyer, Valticos and Morenilla, the concurring opinion of Judge Freeland, the partly dissenting opinion Judge Casedevall, are omitted.

Joint partly dissenting opinion of Judges Bernhardt, Thor Vilhjalmsson, Spielmann, Palm, Wildhaber, Makarczyk and Voicu.

We are of the conviction that in the almost twelve years since the Rees case was decided important developments have occurred in this area. However, notwithstanding these changes and the above cautionary remarks, United Kingdom law has remained at a standstill. No review of the legal situation of transsexuals has taken place.

* * *

We are convinced therefore in light of the evolution of attitudes in Europe towards the legal recognition of the post-operative transsexual that the States' margin of appreciation in this area can no longer serve as a defence in respect of policies which lead inevitably to embarrassing and hurtful intrusions into the private lives of such persons. If the State can make exceptions in the case of driving licences, passports and adoptive children solutions can be found which respect the dignity and sense of privacy of post-operative transsexuals. As the Commission has pointed out, it must be possible for the law to provide for transsexuals to be given prospective legal recognition of their new sexual identity without necessarily destroying the historical nature of the birth register as a record of fact. It is of relevance in this context that the applicants are not claiming that their former identity should, for all purposes, be completely effaced. In short, protecting the applicants from being required to make embarrassing revelations as to their sexual persona need not involve such a root and branch overhaul of the system of birth registration as thought necessary in the Rees and Cossey judgments. The margin of appreciation may come into play in a wider manner as regards the specific choices exercised by the State in conferring legal recognition. . . .

Dissenting Opinion of Judge Van Dijk.

* * *

3. As far as the legal status of transsexuals is concerned, one cannot say that landslide changes have taken place in the member States of the Council of Europe since the Court gave judgment in the Cossey case. However, at the very least, there has been a steady development in the direction of fuller legal recognition and there is no sign of any retreat in that respect. Among the member States of the Council of Europe which allow the surgical re-assignment of sex to be performed on their territories, the United Kingdom appears to be the only State that does not recognize the legal implications of the result to which the treatment leads. The recommendations and resolutions of the Parliamentary Assembly of the Council of Europe and the European Parliament, although not legally binding, are also indicative of the same trend towards legal recognition and of the growing awareness that post-operative transsexuals are entitled to such recognition.

5. [I]t is my firm belief that the applicants in the present case have sufficient, and even major, grounds to seek the protection of the Convention. . . . In applying the fair-balance test, and as an element thereof the proportionality test, the majority should have taken stock of the whole picture. In particular, they should have taken into account, on the one hand, that the detriment to the first applicant is not limited to the specific incidents advanced by her (to be considered quite serious in themselves), but consists of a continuous risk of being forced to reveal her pre-operative gender which she deliberately and at great cost has abandoned and, on the other hand, that the Government have not made out any plausible argument that the interests of third parties referred to by the majority cannot be met in another less distressing way for the applicant and without destroying the historical nature of the births register. The second applicant, Miss Horsham, can avoid the same measures and continuity of detriment only at the cost of having to choose as her country of residence a country other than her own country.

6. . . . Even if one accepts that full legal recognition of gender re-assignment poses certain problems for the English legal system and for society at large, and in specific situations for certain third parties, keeping the system as it is now, with its serious and continuous consequences for the private lives of post-operative transsexuals and the distress involved, in my opinion cannot be considered as an attitude on the part of the British Government that is proportionate to the aims pursued: legal certainty and consistency for the protection of the rights of others; society and individual third parties may be required to accept a certain inconvenience to enable their fellow citizens to live in dignity and worth in the same society in accordance with the sexual identity chosen by them at great personal cost. . . .

7. In conclusion I am of the opinion that the Court should have revised its previous case-law on the matter in relation to the United Kingdom, and should have found a violation of Article 8. Indeed, I deem it highly regrettable that the present Court has not used this very last opportunity to do so, thus giving clear guidance on what I consider to be the right direction in this area to the new Court. The concluding observation by which the majority reiterates that this area needs to be kept under review by Contracting States sounds rather gratuitous and will hardly impress the new Court, given the weight which the present Court has attached to that need.

8. With respect to Article 12 of the Convention I can be quite brief. Since, in my opinion, Article 8 requires legal recognition of gender re-assignment following a surgical operation, this implies that the applicants have to be considered as persons of the new sex for legal purposes,

including for the application of Article 12. Therefore, even if one starts from the presumption that Article 12 has to be considered to refer to marriages between persons of the opposite sex—a presumption which still seems to be justified in view of the clear wording of the provision, although it has the unsatisfactory consequence that it denies to, or at least makes illusive for, homosexuals a right laid down in the Convention—the applicants should be treated as women under Article 12, and should be allowed to marry men. Only in that way is their choice of a new sexual identity socially respected and legally recognized. The fact that, biologically, the medical treatment may not have changed their sex to that of women is, in my opinion, not relevant as that fact does not stand in the way of a marriage and the applicants are in any case not (or no longer) in any better disposition—psychologically or physically—to marry women. I cannot see any reason why legal recognition of re-assignment of sex requires that biologically there has also been a (complete) re-assignment; the law can give an autonomous meaning to the concept of 'sex', as it does to concepts like 'person', 'family', 'home', 'property' et cetera. . . .

B. PERSONAL IDENTITY AND GENDER RE-ASSIGNMENT

The English Court of Appeal has held that local health authorities, acting under the National Health Service Act, may not implement what amounts to a blanket prohibition on the funding of gender re-assignment treatment. While agreeing that it might be appropriate to restrict such funding, the Court decided that an authority must take as a starting point in setting its policy that transsexualism is an illness suitable for treatment. Two judges went out of their way to make clear that the judgment was based on English law principles of judicial review and not on any obligation inferable from the European Convention.[227]

Barely mentioned in the principal case is the European Court's judgment in *B. v. France*,[228] the only decision in which a transsexual successfully invoked Article 8 to oblige the state to extend official recognition of altered gender. In that case, the Court noted several differences between the balance of considerations in French law and the English law found consistent with the Convention in the *Rees* and *Cossey* judgments cited in *Sheffield*. The consequences of non-recognition were deemed more onerous in France. For example, the applicant in *B*, treated according to birth gender, was strictly limited in choice of names. The applicant's birth gender was also encoded in a personal identity number essential for an assortment of transactions with government and private entities. Moreover, accommodating the new gender was deemed to involve less of a public burden in France than in Britain since the former already employed a fairly comprehensive personal identity system which could effect the necessary changes in a relatively simple way.[229]

The *B* case, however, was not based on a conclusion that a European consensus was emerging on the subject of gender re-assignment. As in *Rees*, *Cossey* and the principal case, the Court maintained that there were still significant differences in the way

---

[227] *North West Lancashire Health Authority v. A, D. & G* (Transcript, 29 July 1999) (C.A.).

[228] 25 Mar. 1992 (No. 232C), 16 E.H.R.R. 1.

[229] *Id.* at paras. 51–63.

transsexuals were treated in various states.[230] It seems clear, however, as the Court acknowledged, that a more generous attitude toward accommodating these changes is developing. As noted in the judgment, a large majority of European countries now allow birth certificates to be altered to indicate the new sex of the registered person. A number of American states have enacted similar provisions.[231] In *P v. S*, cited by the applicant in *Sheffield*, the European Court of Justice held that discrimination in employment against a transsexual was sex discrimination prohibited by European Communities directives: '[w]here a person is dismissed on the ground that he or she intends to undergo, or has undergone, gender reassignment, he or she is treated unfavourably by comparison with persons of the sex to which he or she was deemed to belong before undergoing gender reassignment'.[232]

The rights of transsexuals have sometimes been asserted in connection with attempts by such persons to marry someone of their former gender. The most prominent precedent in English law is *Corbett v. Corbett*[233] which held such marriages void as not being a union between a man and a woman. The sex of the relevant individuals moreover was to be determined by biological factors present at birth. The result in *Corbett* appeared to have been confirmed by an Act of Parliament that declared a marriage void if 'the parties are not respectively male and female'.[234] But in dicta in a subsequent case, two judges of the Court of Appeal suggested that, in light of changes in scientific understanding and social attitudes, the statutory language might be construed to yield a result differing from *Corbett*.[235] Some European countries have legislated to recognize the right of post-operative transsexuals to marry.[236] In Singapore after the High Court followed *Corbett*, the Parliament legalized such marriages prospectively.[237]

2. PERSONAL IDENTITY AND CHOICE OF NAME

The European Court has assumed that obstacles to or limitations on a person's right to choose his or her name implicate the Article 8 right to respect for private life. In *Stjerna v. Finland*[238] the authorities denied the applicant's request to change his name to Tawaststjerna. The Court held that, while this did not constitute an interference with

---

[230] *Id.* at para. 48.

[231] *See*, e.g., La. Rev. Stat. art. 40, sec. 62; Mass. Ann. Laws ch. 46, sec. 13. *See also* Revised Statutes of Ontario (1990), Ch. V. 4, S 36.

[232] [1996] 2 C.M.L.R. 247, 263.

[233] [1971] P. 83, [1970] 2 All E.R. 33.

[234] Matrimonial Causes Act 1973 s. 11(c).

[235] *J. v. S-T* [1998] 1 All E.R. 431, 449–50 (Ward LJ), 476 (Sir Brian Neill). The law in Scotland is the same as the rule of *Corbett*. Marriage (Scotland) Act 1977, s. 5(4)(e); *X, Petitioner* 1957 S.L.T. (Sh. Ct.) 61.

[236] *See* C. Hamilton, K. Stanley, & D. Hodson, *Family Law in Europe* (1995) at 168 (Germany), 305 (Netherlands).

[237] Women's Charter (Amendment) Act 1986, s.11A. *See Lim v. Hiok* [1991] Singapore J. Legal Stud. 509. These developments are discussed in K.L. Ter, 'Transsexual Marriages in Singapore', (1998) 148. *New L.J.* 202.

[238] 25 Nov. 1994 (No. 299B), 4. E.H.R.R. 195.

private life under Article 8 (2), it did raise questions about the state's positive obligations under Article 8 (1), noting that a name 'constitutes a means of personal identification and a link to a family'.[239] In striking the appropriate balance in this regard the
Court recognized that the state had an interest in restricting the choice of name 'for
example in order to ensure accurate population registration or to safeguard the means
of personal identification and of linking the bearers of a given name to a family'.[240] The
Court, taking into account the diversity of regulation of member states, also decided
that the state should be accorded a wide margin of appreciation. In that light it found
neither the inconvenience caused to the applicant in requiring him to use his old
name, nor his partiality to the chosen new name substantial enough to conclude there
was a lack of respect for his private life.[241] It reached the same result in *Guillot v. France*[242]
in which the Registrar of Births, Deaths and Marriages refused the applicants' request to
name their new daughter 'Fleur de Marie', the name of the heroine in a novel by Eugene
Sue. Under French law parents were generally required to choose from names of saints
and historical figures. Conceding that this limitation imposed some burden, the Court
found this did not amount to a failure to respect the applicant's family and private life.
The Court took note of the fact that the preferred name could still be used for social
purposes. Where the legal name was required the applicants were permitted to give the
very similar name, Fleur-Marie.[243] The Court, therefore, did not have to evaluate the
reasons given by French authorities for rejecting the applicant's choice—that it was
'excessively whimsical and so eccentric that the child is likely to be the first victim'.[244]

While the Court appears to give the state considerable latitude in regulating individual names it has set limits on the extent to which regulations may differ for men
and women. In *Burghartz v. Switzerland*,[245] it held that the Swiss Civil Code's provisions
on names of married persons constituted a violation of Article 14 in conjunction with
Article 8. The applicant wished to use, as his surname, a hyphenated name, consisting
of his and his wife's surnames. The code allowed for married couples to use either
husband's or wife's name as the family name but only allowed hyphenated names to a
wife who wished to add her surname to the family name. Since the choice of names
was restricted more for husbands than wives, the Swiss law represented a discrimination based on sex in the enjoyment of Article 8 rights. The Court held, moreover, that
no reasonable justification for the difference had been shown. The Court held that the
injury was not mitigated by the fact that the husband could use the name he preferred
informally, since only the legal name could be used 'in a person's official papers'.[246]

---

[239] *Id.* at para. 37.
[240] *Id.* at para. 39.
[241] *Id.* at paras. 39–45.
[242] 24 Oct. 1996, Reports, 1996–V 1593.
[243] *Id.* at para. 27.
[244] *Id.* at para. 10.
[245] 22 Feb. 1994 (No. 280B), 18 E.H.R.R. 101.
[246] *Id.* at paras. 26–8. On the Court's Art. 8 name jurisprudence *see* A. Gross, 'Rights and Normalization;
A Critical Study of European Human Rights Case Law on the Choice and Change of Name', 9 *Harv. Hum. Rts.
J.* 269 (1996).

D. PUBLIC DISCLOSURE OR INVESTIGATION OF PRIVATE INFORMATION

The expansive reading of the term in the European case law apart, privacy, in its most obvious sense, connotes the capacity to keep certain information secret. The state, as a result of the extensive field of regulation entrusted to it, has a constant need to obtain, monitor and evaluate information.[247] The most acute confrontation of these conflicting tendencies occurs in the investigation and prosecution of criminal offences. Article 8, by insisting on respect for private life, home and correspondence, appears to limit the investigative reach of public authorities. Of course, paragraph 2 recognizes the legitimate need for such measures 'in the interest of national security, public safety [or] for the prevention of disorder or crime'.

In its judgments, the Court has sought to reconcile the genuine needs of public officials with individual privacy, by insisting that searches be controlled by some process of independent prior approval and supervision. In *Funke v. France*,[248] the Court found the law governing searches by customs officials defective in this regard:

Above all, in the absence of any requirement of a judicial warrant the restrictions and conditions provided for in law . . . appear too lax and full of loopholes for the interferences with the applicant's rights to have been strictly proportionate to the legitimate aim pursued.

In a subsequent case the Court stated that it 'must be particularly vigilant where . . . the authorities are empowered under national law to order and effect searches without a judicial warrant'. In such cases 'a legal framework and very strict limits on such power are called for.'[249]

It should be noted that, although Article 8 names only one *place*—the home, the Court has interpreted that term broadly to include, as well, a person's business, noting, among other things, that the French text uses the word 'domicile' which has 'a broad connotation'. In any event, a person's business is protected from searches, in light of the Court's generous view of the term 'private life'.[250]

The Fourth Amendment to the United States Constitution affirms the 'right of the people to be secure in their persons, houses, papers and effects against unreasonable searches or seizures'. What constitutes a search depends, under modern judicial interpretations, on whether or not the person aggrieved had a 'reasonable expectation of

---

[247] *See* e.g., *M.S. v. Sweden*, 27 Aug. 1997, Reports, 1997–IV 1437, 28 E.H.R.R. 313 and *Z v. Finland*, 25 Feb. 1997, Reports, 1997–I 323, 25 E.H.R.R. 371, concerning the disclosure of medical records to public officials for various purposes.

[248] 25 Feb. 1993 (No. 256A), 16 E.H.R.R. 297, para. 57. *See also, Miailhe v. France*, 25 Feb. 1993 (No. 256C), 16 E.H.R.R. 332, para. 38.

[249] *Camenzind v. Switzerland*, 16 Dec. 1997, Reports, 1997–VIII 2880, 28 E.H.R.R. 458, para. 45.

[250] *See Niemetz v. Germany*, 16 Dec. 1992 (No. 251B), 16 E.H.R.R. 97, paras. 29–31; *Miailhe v. France*, 25 Feb. 1993 (No. 119), 10 E.H.R.R. 333, para. 28. The Court's discussion of 'private life' in the *Niemetz* case is reproduced, in part, at Section (B)(2) *supra*.

privacy' in the place searched.[251] Thus merely looking at or listening outside a house is not within the Amendment, while, ordinarily, entry into an occupied dwelling is.[252] Like the European Court, the United States Supreme Court has held, moreover, that a person may have a reasonable expectation of privacy in places outside the home, including commercial premises.[253] A search or seizure is not 'unreasonable', under the Amendment, if it is authorized by a warrant after determination by a 'neutral and detached magistrate', that 'probable cause' exists to believe that contraband or evidence of a crime will be found.[254] There are, however, numerous exceptions to the warrant requirement based on the exigencies of the situation. Thus, police may search an automobile, which might otherwise be quickly removed, without a warrant. Even then, however, the officers must be shown to have had probable cause for the search. The Supreme Court has held that evidence obtained from an unconstitutional search may not be introduced in a criminal trial,[255] although again there are many exceptions. The most important exception holds that evidence from a search undertaken in good faith on the basis of a warrant issued by a competent authority may be used, even if it turns out the approval of the warrant was made without probable cause.[256]

Section 8 of the Canadian Charter of Rights and Freedoms also prohibits unreasonable searches and seizures, and like the American Court, the Supreme Court of Canada has held that the critical determination in finding an unconstitutional search is the invasion of a person's reasonable expectation of privacy. Thus, something less than probable cause could justify a border search where travellers' expectations of privacy were unlikely to be substantial.[257] Also, the Canadian Court has followed the United States Supreme Court in holding that the principal way to prevent unreasonable searches is to require prior approval by an independent magistrate based on a finding of probable cause.[258] The use of unlawfully obtained evidence in Canada is governed by Section 24(2) of the Charter which stipulates that such evidence is to be excluded only where its admission would 'bring the administration of justice into disrepute'. In making that determination, the Supreme Court has held that courts should consider the character of the evidence itself, the nature of the conduct by which it was obtained and the effect of excluding the evidence. Again

---

[251] *Katz v. United States*, 389 U.S. 147 (1967).

[252] *See See v. City of Seattle*, 387 U.S. 541 (1967).

[253] *Id.*

[254] *See*, e.g. *Coolidge v. New Hampshire*, 403 U.S. 443 (1971); *Sandwich v. City of Tampa*, 407 U.S. 345 (1967).

[255] *Mapp v. Ohio*, 367 U.S. 643 (1961) (state courts); *Weeks v. United States*, 232 U.S. 383 (1914) (federal courts). The fact that evidence is obtained as a result of a search or other action that violates Art. 8 does not by itself make it a violation of the Convention to use that evidence in a subsequent trial. In each case this question is to be examined under Art. 6 and the question is 'whether the trial as a whole [is] fair'. *Schenk v. Switzerland*, 12 July 1988 (No. 140), 13 E.H.R.R. 242, para. 53.

[256] *United States v. Leon*, 486 U.S. 397 (1984).

[257] *See R v. Simmons* [1988] 2 S.C.R. 495; *see also R. v. McKinley Transport* [1990] 1 S.C.R. 627 (diminished expectation of privacy in taxpayer's records concerning income).

[258] *Hunter v. Southam* [1984] 2 S.C.R. 145. As in the United States, Canadian courts have recognized a number of exceptions to the warrant requirement. *See*, e.g. *R. v. Rao* (1984) O.R. (2d) 80, 109 (Ontario Court of Appeals) (search of an automobile).

echoing the American law, the Canadian courts have held that, in weighing the second factor, the good faith belief of the police that they were acting lawfully should be taken into account.[259]

The European Court of Human Rights has also made it clear that interception of telephone communications may create an interference with private life and correspondence and thus a violation of Article 8. In *Klass and Others v. Germany*,[260] however, the Court found that the German scheme for authorizing such wiretaps, although it did not provide for judicial review, had strict administrative procedures for the approval of such activity and the use to which the information gathered could be put, and was consistent with Article 8. On the other hand, in *Malone v. United Kingdom*,[261] the Court found a violation in the claimed wiretapping of the applicant's telephone conversations. Unlike the situation in Germany, the government of the United Kingdom did not operate under a single comprehensive set of regulations. Various statutes and common law doctrines governed. Indeed, it was not clear to the Court what legal standards were applicable to the alleged wiretapping in the applicant's case. This being so, the Court found that the interference with Article 8 rights could not be justified under Article 8(2) because it was not 'in accordance with law'. The Court reached a similar conclusion with respect to the French law on wiretapping which was the product of a number of judicial decisions and where there was no comprehensive and explicit scheme regulating the subject.[262] The Court has been especially demanding of national regulations in this regard. In *Valenzuela Contreras v. Spain*,[263] a domestic court had approved a wiretap on the basis of very broad statutory and constitutional provisions but had also attempted to impose safeguards on the activity. This kind of *ad hoc* judicial protection was insufficient to prevent a violation of Article 8:

The requirement that the effects of the 'law' be foreseeable means, in the sphere of monitoring telephone communications, that the guarantees stating the extent of the authorities discretion and the manner in which it is to be exercised must be set out in detail in domestic law so that it has a binding force which circumscribes the judges' discretion in the application of such measures.[264]

The United Kingdom responded to the *Malone* judgment by enacting the Interception of Communications Act 1985, which defined the criteria for permissible wiretapping

---

[259] *See* Peter W. Hogg. *Constitutional Law of Canada*, 1067–8 (3rd edn., 1992).

[260] 6 Sept. 1978, (No. 28), 2 E.H.R.R. 214.

[261] 2 Aug. 1984 (No. 282), 4 E.H.R.R. 330.

[262] *Kruslin v. France*, 24 Apr. 1990 (No. 176B), 12 E.H.R.R. 547; *Huvig v. France*, 24 Apr. 1990 (No. 176B). 12 E.H.R.R. 528. *See also Kopp v. Switzerland*, 25 Mar. 1998, Reports, 1998–II 524, 27 E.H.R.R. 91 where the wiretapping of a law office was carried out under a fairly detailed set of regulations. These regulations, however, made no explicit provision for excluding lawyer–client communications although the surveillance was carried out with the intention of respecting the confidentiality of this material. Since the relevant definitions and procedures were not spelled out in the rules, the interference was held not in accordance with law'.

[263] 30 July 1998, Reports, 1998–V 1901, 28 E.H.R.R. 483.

[264] *Id.* at para. 60.

and procedures for challenging such decisions. In *Halford v. United Kingdom*[265] the Strasbourg Court found a violation of Article 8 when a police department wiretapped the office telephone of one of its own officers. The 1985 Act did not apply to internal communications systems such as the one involved in this case. The Court held Article 8 applied to such interceptions since the applicant had a 'reasonable expectation of privacy' with respect to the calls made on that telephone, one that had been assigned to her expressly for private use. Since these actions were unregulated by the 1985 Act the interferences were not in 'accordance with the law' under Article 8 (2).[266] For similar reasons several Law Lords have decided that police surveillance of conversations using a hidden microphone were also outside the 1985 Act and would violate Article 8.[267]

Although it was, for some time, a doubtful question, it is now clear that interceptions of telephone communications in the United States are treated as 'searches' and thus are subject to the Fourth Amendment.[268] In particular, in normal circumstances it is necessary that a wiretap be approved in advance by a neutral and detached magistrate. In *United States v. United States District Court*, the Supreme Court held improper a wiretap approved only by the Attorney-General in a case allegedly involving a threat to national security.[269] The government had argued that in such cases the President's constitutional authority supported such a power (granted in the statute governing wiretaps). The Supreme Court, like the European Court in the cases cited, focussed on the crucial requirement of an independent review of the decision.

These Fourth Amendment freedoms cannot properly be guaranteed if domestic security surveillance may be conducted solely within the discretion of the Executive Branch. The Fourth Amendment does not contemplate the executive officers of Government as neutral and disinterested magistrates. Their duty and responsibility are to enforce the laws, to investigate, and to prosecute . . . But those charged with this investigative and prosecutorial duty should not be the sole judges of when to utilize constitutionally sensitive means in pursuing their tasks. The historical judgment, which the Fourth Amendment accepts, is that unreviewed executive discretion may yield too readily to pressures to obtain incriminating evidence and overlook potential invasions of privacy and protected speech. . . .

We cannot accept the government's argument that internal security matters are too subtle and complex for judicial evaluation. Courts regularly deal with the most difficult issues of our society. There is no reason to believe that federal judges will be insensitive to or uncomprehending of the issues involved in domestic security cases. Certainly courts can recognize that domestic security surveillance involves different considerations from the surveillance of 'ordinary crime'. If the threat is too subtle or complex for our senior law enforcement officers to convey its significance to a court, one may question whether there is probable cause for surveillance.

[265] 25 June 1997, Reports, 1997–III 1004, 24 E.H.R.R. 523.

[266] *Id.* para. 51.

[267] *R. v. Khan* [1997] A.C. 558.

[268] *Katz v. United States*, 389 U.S. 347 (1967).

[269] 407 U.S. 297 (1972). An exception to the general requirements of a prior warrant is an interception or recording occurring with the consent of a party to the conversation. *See e.g. U.S. v White*, 401 U.S. 745 (1971). Whether consent of one party to a telephonic communication prevents the interception of the conversation from constituting a violation of Article 8, was raised before the Court but not addressed, in its judgment in *A. v. France*, 23 Nov. 1993 (No. 277B), 17 E.H.R.R. 462.

The Supreme Court made clear that its decision was limited to matters of *domestic* security. Investigations touching foreign relations might involve different considerations.

American constitutional doctrine has distinguished between the risks to privacy involved in wiretaps and that involved in other types of searches and seizures. In *Berger v. New York*,[270] the Supreme Court held invalid a New York statute providing for authorization of wiretaps for certain periods. It found such authorizations similar to general warrants in their broad sweep:

. . . The purpose of the probable-cause requirement of the Fourth Amendment, to keep the state out of constitutionally protected areas until it has reason to believe that a specific crime has been or is being committed, is thereby wholly aborted. . . . [T]he statute's failure to describe with particularity the conversations sought gives the officer a roving commission to 'seize' any and all conversations. . . . [A]uthorization of eavesdropping for a two-month period is the equivalent of a series of intrusions, searches, and seizures pursuant to single showing of probable cause. . . . During such a long and continuous (24 hours a day) period the conversations of any and all persons coming into the area covered by the device will be seized indiscriminately and without regard to their connection with the crime under investigation. . . . [T]he statute places no termination date on the eavesdrop once the conversation sought is seized. This is left entirely in the discretion of the officer. Finally, the statute's procedure, necessarily because its success depends on secrecy, has no requirement for notice as do conventional warrants, nor does it overcome this defect by requiring some showing of special facts. On the contrary, it permits unconsented entry without any showing of exigent circumstances. Such a showing of exigency, in order to avoid notice, would appear more important in eavesdropping, with its inherent dangers, than that required when conventional procedures of search and seizure are utilized. . . . In short, the statute's blanket grant of permission to eavesdrop is without adequate judicial supervision or protective procedures.

The Supreme Court of Canada has followed the American decisions in holding that electronic surveillance is a search or seizure within Section 8 of the Canadian Charter of Rights and Freedoms.[271] The Court has held that the purpose of the prohibitions on unreasonable search and seizure is to protect a reasonable expectation of privacy, and such an expectation is violated when a third party intercepts a telephone conversation without the knowledge or consent of the participants.[272] In contrast to the United States Supreme Court, which has held that surveillance agreed to by a participant is not a search or seizure within the Fourth Amendment,[273] the Supreme Court of Canada has refused to draw this distinction.[274]

Article 8's protection of private life has been held to limit the state's use of private

---

[270] 388 U.S. 41 (1967).

[271] *R. v. Duarte* [1990] 1 S.C.R. 30.

[272] *R. v. Thompson* [1990] 2 S.C.R. 1111.

[273] *United States v. White*, 401 U.S. 745 (1971).

[274] *R. v. Duarte* [1990] 1 S.C.R. 30; *R. v. Wiggins* [1990] 1 S.C.R. In these cases the recordings were, in fact, admitted because the police acted in good faith and the evidence was held not to bring the administration of justice into disrepute, thus satisfying Section 24(2) of the Charter. *See also A. v. France*, 23 Nov. 1993 (No. 277B), 17 E.H.R.R. 462, in which the issue was presented to the Strasbourg Court but not decided.

information in judicial proceedings and thereafter. In *Z v. Finland*[275] the applicant was the wife of X who was prosecuted for a series of rapes and for attempted manslaughter. The latter charge was based on the claim that X was infected with HIV virus at the time of the rapes. The prosecution theory was that X knew he had contracted the disease from his wife. Z refused to provide information to the prosecutors citing a privilege against giving testimony against one's spouse. The prosecution then had Z's hospital records seized and the City Court ordered Z's doctors to provide information on her condition. The European Court held these actions to be justifiable for the prevention of crime and the protection of others. It noted the serious nature of the crimes charged and the limitations that had been placed on further dissemination of the information gathered. Two other actions, however, were not so justified: the refusal of the Finnish courts to extend the confidentiality of the information beyond 10 years and the identification of the applicant by name in the judgment of the Court of Appeals (a judgment the Court had immediately forwarded to a large national newspaper). Since there were ways of proceeding which would have served the public need for information without imposing so great a burden on the applicant, these actions were a 'disproportionate' interference with her rights under Article 8.[276]

In *Z* the Court emphasized that the margin of appreciation varied, in part, based on the severity of the interference with the right. The importance of confidentiality of medical information was deemed 'crucial not only to respect the sense of privacy of a patient but also to preserve his or her confidence in the medical profession and in the health services in general'.[277] When the medical condition in question was HIV infection this concern was even greater:

In view of the highly intimate and sensitive nature of information concerning a person's HIV status, any state measures compelling communication or disclosure of such information without the consent of the patient call for the most careful scrutiny on the part of the Court, as do the safeguards designed to secure effective protection.[278]

Article 8 makes explicit reference to respect for correspondence. Indeed, the Court has based its wiretap judgments partly on the protection of private life, and partly on its conclusion that telephone communication represents a form of correspondence.[279] The Court has addressed this aspect of the Article in several cases dealing with limits on the correspondence of people detained by the State. In *DeWilde, Ooms and Versyp v. Belgium*,[280] the Court held that in the case of a person detained for vagrancy, the general right of the authorities to supervise and censor prisoners' mail was justifiable as necessary for the 'prevention of disorder crime, for the protection of health or morals or for the protection of rights of freedom of others' under Article 8(2). In

[275] 25 Feb. 1997, Reports, 1997–I 323, 25 E.H.R.R. 371.
[276] *Id.* at paras. 43, 102–14.
[277] *Id.* at para. 95.
[278] *Id.* at para. 96.
[279] *Klass and Others v. Germany*, 6 Sept. 1978 (No. 28), 2 E.H.R.R. 214.
[280] 18 June 1971 (No. 12), 1 E.H.R.R. 373.

Golder v. United Kingdom,[281] however, it found a violation in official refusal to allow a prisoner to contact a solicitor for purpose of initiating a libel action:

In order to show why the interference complained of by Golder was 'necessary', the Government advanced the prevention of disorder or crime and, up to a certain point, the interests of public safety and the protection of the rights and freedoms of others. Even having regard to the power of appreciation left to the contracting States, the Court cannot discern how these considerations, as they are understood 'in a democratic society', could oblige the Home Secretary to prevent Golder from corresponding with a solicitor with a view to suing Laird for libel. The Court again lays stress on the fact that Golder was seeking to exculpate himself of a charge made against him by that prison officer acting in the course of his duties and relating to an incident in prison. In these circumstances, Golder could justifiably wish to write to a solicitor. It was not for the Home Secretary himself to appraise—no more than it is for the court today—the prospects of the action contemplated; it was for a solicitor to advise the applicant on his rights and then for a court to rule on any action that might be brought.

The Home Secretary's decision proves to be all the less 'necessary in a democratic society' in that the applicant's correspondence with a solicitor would have been a preparatory step to the institution of civil legal proceedings and, therefore, to the exercise of a right embodied in another Article of the Convention, that is, Article 6.

Similarly, in *Schönenberger and Durmaz v. Switzerland*,[282] the Court found a violation of Article 8 where the prosecutor refused to deliver to a prisoner held in detention on remand, a letter in which a lawyer offered his services and advised the prisoner of his right to refuse to answer questions. The Court held that, given the fact that the prisoner undoubtedly had such a right under Swiss law, this interference with correspondence posed no threat to the normal conduct of the prosecution and, therefore, the prosecutor's action was not necessary for 'the prevention of disorder or crime'. The Court reinforced its strict view of any interference with correspondence between prisoners and their legal advisers in *Campbell v. United Kingdom*[283] in which it held that officials may only open a letter from a lawyer to a prisoner when they have reasonable cause to believe it contains an illicit enclosure. Even then, a letter may not be *read* unless 'the authorities have reasonable cause to believe that the privilege is being abused in that the contents of the letter endanger prison security or the safety of others or are otherwise of a criminal nature'.

As was the case with surveillance of telephone conversations, the Court has also insisted that restriction on correspondence must be stated with some clarity in advance. In *Herczegfalvy v. Austria* it held that a restriction on delivery of letters from the applicant who had been committed to a psychiatric institution was invalid under Article 8. While such a limitation could be appropriate to protect the health of the appellant, in this case the decision on which letters to forward was made in the sole discretion of the appellant's 'curator' or legal guardian. Such unguided authority

---

[281] 21 Feb. 1975 (No. 18), 1 E.H.R.R. 524.
[282] 20 June 1988 (No. 137), 11 E.H.R.R. 202.
[283] 25 Mar. 1992 (No. 233), 15 E.H.R.R. 137, para. 48.

meant the limitation was not 'in accordance with the law'.[284] In *Petra v. Romania*[285] a statute giving prison governors the right to stop any correspondence unsuited to the process of rehabilitating a prisoner and implemented by unpublished regulations was held to provide insufficient guidance on its scope and administration and thus to fail 'the requirement of accessibility.'[286]

Finally, in *Silver and Others v. United Kingdom*[287] the Court undertook a letter-by-letter examination of the interferences by English officials with the correspondence of prisoners under various prison regulations finding some (e.g. concerning letters containing threats of violence) necessary under Article 8(2) and others (e.g. concerning letters to a journalist) unjustified.[288]

In the United States it has been held that sealed letters or packages committed to the mails are fully protected under the Fourth Amendment.[289] With respect to prisoners' mail, the Supreme Court has held that official censorship may violate the First Amendment rights of the non-prison *addressee*.[290]

---

[284] 24 Sept. 1992 (No. 244), 15 E.H.R.R. 437, paras. 87–91. *See also Calogero Diana v. Italy*, 15 Nov. 1996, Reports, 1996–V 1765.

[285] 23 Sept. 1998, Reports, 1998–VII 2844.

[286] *Id.* paras. 37–8.

[287] 25 Mar. 1983 (No. 61), Reports, 1998–VIII 2844, 5 E.H.R.R. 347.

[288] *See also Boyle and Rice v. United Kingdom*, 27 Apr. 1988 (No. 131), 10 E.H.H.R. 425.

[289] *Ex parte Jackson*, 96 U.S. 727, 730 (1877).

[290] *Procunier v. Martinez*, 416 U.S. 396 (1974).

7

THE RIGHT TO LIBERTY AND SECURITY OF PERSON

ARTICLE 5

1. Everyone has the right to liberty and security of person. No one shall be deprived of his liberty save in the following cases and in accordance with a procedure prescribed by law:

(a) the lawful detention of a person after conviction by a competent court;

(b) the lawful arrest or detention of a person for non-compliance with the lawful order of a court or in order to secure the fulfilment of any obligation prescribed by law;

(c) the lawful arrest or detention of a person effected for the purpose of bringing him before the competent legal authority on reasonable suspicion of having committed an offence or when it is reasonably considered necessary to prevent his committing an offence or fleeing after having done so;

(d) the detention of a minor by lawful order for the purpose of educational supervision or his lawful detention for the purpose of bringing him before the competent legal authority;

(e) the lawful detention of persons for the prevention of the spreading of infectious diseases, of persons of unsound mind, alcoholics or drug addicts or vagrants;

(f) the lawful arrest or detention of a person to prevent his effecting an unauthorised entry into the country or of a person against whom action is being taken with a view to deportation or extradition.

2. Everyone who is arrested shall be informed promptly, in a language which he understands, of the reasons for his arrest and of any charge against him.

3. Everyone arrested or detained in accordance with the provisions of paragraph (1)(c) of this Article shall be brought promptly before a judge or other officer authorized by law to exercise judicial power and shall be entitled to trial within a reasonable time or to release pending trial. Release may be conditioned by guarantees to appear for trial.

4. Everyone who is deprived of his liberty by arrest or detention shall be entitled to take proceedings by which the lawfulness of his detention shall be decided speedily by a court and his release ordered if the detention is not lawful.

5. Everyone who has been the victim of arrest or detention in contravention of the provisions of this Article shall have an enforceable right to compensation.

A. INTRODUCTION

The individual's right to physical liberty and the security of his or her person is such a manifestly desirable right that in secure democracies which proclaim liberal values it is sometimes taken for granted. Yet the right lies at the heart of any governmental system that claims to observe the rule of law. In Magna Carta in 1215, the celebrated Chapter 39 proclaimed: 'No free man shall be taken or imprisoned . . . except by the lawful judgment of his peers or by the law of the land' (*Nullus liber homo capiatur, vel imprisonetur, . . . nisi per legale judicium parium suorum vel per legem terrae*). In the Petition of Right of 1628, the English Parliament reversed a decision by the judges that upheld the right of the King by his special command to detain individuals: the Petition recited Chapter 39 of Magna Carta and declared that 'no free man, in any such manner as is before mentioned, [may] be imprisoned or detained'. Under the Fifth Amendment to the United States Constitution ratified in 1791, no person 'shall be deprived of life, liberty, or property, without due process of law'. In the Canadian Charter of Rights and Freedoms 1981, by Section 7: 'Everyone has the right to life, liberty and security of the person and the right not to be deprived thereof except in accordance with the principles of fundamental justice'; and by Section 9: 'Everyone has the right not to be arbitrarily detained or imprisoned'.

Such provisions serve to reinforce the fundamental duty of state organs to respect the right of all human beings to their physical security.

1. CYPRUS *V.* TURKEY

Resolution DH (92) 12 of 2 April 1992
(1992), 15 E.H.R.R. 509

[In 1992 the European Commission of Human Rights reported on an interstate complaint from Cyprus against Turkey (both states being parties to the Convention) that up to 2,000 Greek Cypriots who had been in Turkish custody from the time of the Turkish invasion of North Cyprus in 1974 were years later still missing and unaccounted for.]

117. In its evaluation of [the] evidence the Commission has found it established in three of the five cases investigated, and has found sufficient indications in an indefinite number of cases that Greek Cypriots, who are still missing, were in Turkish custody in 1974. It considers that this creates a presumption of Turkish responsibility for the fate of these persons and notes with concern that no relevant information has been provided by the Turkish authorities.

118. The Commission notes that the families of these missing persons have been without news from them for nearly nine years and that this is due to the respondent Government's failure to account for the fate of these persons in their custody. It finds that the resulting uncertainty has caused severe suffering to these families who are entitled under the Convention to be informed of the situations of their close relatives. . . .

119. The wording of Article 5 . . . shows in the Commission's view that any deprivation of liberty must be subject to law and that any unaccounted disappearance of a detained person must be considered as a particularly serious violation of the Article, which can also be understood as a guarantee against such disappearances. . . .

121. The Commission cannot exclude that missing persons found to have been in Turkish detention in 1974 have died in the meanwhile but, on the material before it, it cannot make any finding as to the circumstances in which such deaths may have occurred. . . .

123. The Commission, having found it established in three cases, and having found sufficient indications in an indefinite number of cases, that Greek Cypriots who are still missing were unlawfully deprived of their liberty, in Turkish custody in 1974, noting that Turkey has failed to account for the fate of these persons, concludes by 16 votes against one that Turkey has violated Article 5 of the Convention. . . .

2. KURT *v.* TURKEY

Judgment of 25 May 1998
Reports, 1998–III 1152, 27 E.H.R.R. 373

[During several days in November 1993, security operations were carried out in Agilli, a village in south-east Turkey, and houses were burnt down, including that of the applicant. On 24 November, the villagers were required to gather in the village school while soldiers and village guards searched for the applicant's son, Üzeyir Kurt. On the next day, the applicant saw Üzeyir surrounded by soldiers and village guards; his face was bruised and swollen, as if he had been beaten. She fetched him a jacket as he complained of feeling cold, but she was not permitted to stay with him. She never saw him again and could discover no evidence that he had been seen elsewhere. Having failed in all the inquiries that she made, she contacted a human rights association who gave her assistance in approaching the Turkish authorities and in making an application to the European Commission of Human Rights at Strasbourg. Subsequently, the applicant asserted that a public prosecutor in Turkey had attempted to get her to withdraw her allegations that her son had been maltreated. She also made two statements before a notary in which (inter alia) she purported to withdraw her application to Strasbourg, although subsequently she complained that the withdrawal had been forced upon her.

In proceedings at Strasbourg, the Turkish government accepted that there had been a security operation in Agilli at the relevant time against those who were suspected of being terrorist members of the PKK (Kurdish Workers' Party). Denying responsibility for Üzeyir's disappearance, the government contended that he had joined or been kidnapped by the PKK, that his mother had been manipulated by the human rights association and that her account of her events had been distorted.]

118. The applicant submitted that the disappearance of her son gave rise to multiple violations of Article 5 of the Convention . . .

119. The applicant reasoned that the very fact that her son's detention was unacknowledged meant that he was deprived of his liberty in an arbitrary manner contrary to Article 5(1). She contended that the official cover-up of his whereabouts and fate placed her son beyond the reach of the law and he was accordingly denied the protection of the guarantees contained in Article 5(2), (3), (4) and (5).

120. The Government reiterated that the applicant's contention regarding the disappearance of her son was unsubstantiated by the evidence and had been disproved by the investigation which the authorities had conducted. In its submission, no issue could therefore arise under Article 5. . . .

122. The Court notes at the outset the fundamental importance of the guarantees contained in Article 5 for securing the right of individuals in a democracy to be free from arbitrary detention at the hands of the authorities. It is precisely for that reason that the Court has repeatedly stressed in its case law that any deprivation of liberty must not only have been effected in conformity with the substantive and procedural rules of national law but must equally be in keeping with the very purpose of Article 5, namely to protect the individual from arbitrariness.[1] This insistence on the protection of the individual against any abuse of power is illustrated by the fact that Article 5(1) circumscribes the circumstances in which individuals may be lawfully deprived of their liberty, it being stressed that these circumstances must be given a narrow interpretation having regard to the fact that they constitute exceptions to a most basic guarantee of individual freedom.[2]

123. It must also be stressed that the authors of the Convention reinforced the individual's protection against arbitrary deprivation of his or her liberty by guaranteeing a corpus of substantive rights which are intended to minimise the risks of arbitrariness by allowing the act of deprivation of liberty to be amenable to independent judicial scrutiny and by securing the accountability of the authorities for that act. The requirements of Article 5(3) and (4) with their emphasis on promptitude and judicial control assume particular importance in this context. Prompt judicial intervention may lead to the detection and prevention of life-threatening measures or serious ill treatment which violate the fundamental guarantees contained in Articles 2 and 3 of the Convention.[3] What is at stake is both the protection of the physical liberty of individuals as well as their personal security in a context which, in the absence of safeguards, could result in a subversion of the rule of law and place detainees beyond the reach of the most rudimentary forms of legal protection.

124. The Court emphasises in this respect that the unacknowledged detention of an individual is a complete negation of these guarantees and a most grave violation of Article 5. Having assumed control over that individual it is incumbent on the authorities to account for his or her whereabouts. For this reason, Article 5 must be seen as requiring the authorities to take effective measures to safeguard against the risk of disappearance and to conduct a prompt effective investigation into an arguable claim that a person has been taken into custody and has not been seen since.

125. Against that background, the Court recalls that it has accepted the Commission's finding that Üzeyir Kurt was held by soldiers and village guards on the morning of 25 November 1993. His detention at that time was not logged and there exists no official trace of his subsequent whereabouts or fate. That fact in itself must be considered a most serious failing since it enables those responsible for the act of deprivation of liberty to conceal their involvement in a crime, to cover their tracks and to escape accountability for the fate of the detainee. In the view of the

---

[1] *See*, among many other authorities, *Chahal v. United Kingdom* 15 Nov. 1996, Reports, 1996–V 1831, 23 E.H.R.R. 413, para. 118) reprinted at (E)(3)(b) *infra*.

[2] *See, mutatis mutandis, Quinn v. France* (No. A/311) (1996) 21 E.H.R.R. 529, para. 42.

[3] See, *mutatis mutandis, Aksoy v. Turkey* 18 Dec. 1996, Reports, 1996–IV 2260, 23 E.H.R.R. 553, para. 76; reprinted at (H)(4) *infra*.

Court, the absence of holding data recording such matters as the date, time and location of detention, the name of the detainee as well as the reasons for the detention and the name of the person effecting it must be seen as incompatible with the very purpose of Article 5 of the Convention.

126. Furthermore, the Court considers that having regard to the applicant's insistence that her son was detained in the village the public prosecutor should have been alert to the need to investigate more thoroughly her claim. He had the powers under the Code of Criminal Procedure to do so. However, he did not request her to explain why she was so adamant in her belief that he was in detention. She was neither asked to provide a written statement nor interviewed orally. Had he done so he may have been able to confront the military personnel involved in the operation in the village with her eyewitness account. However, that line of inquiry was never opened and no statements were taken from any of the soldiers or village guards present in the village at the time. The public prosecutor was unwilling to go beyond the gendarmerie's assertion that the custody records showed that Üzeyir Kurt had neither been held in the village nor was in detention. He accepted without question the explanation that Üzeyir Kurt had probably been kidnapped by the PKK during the military operation and this explanation shaped his future attitude to his inquiries and laid the basis of his subsequent non-jurisdiction decision.

127. The Court, like the Commission, also considers that the alleged PKK involvement in the disappearance of the applicant's son lacked any firm and plausible evidentiary basis. As an explanation it was advanced too hastily by the gendarmerie in the absence of any corroborating evidence; nor can it be maintained that the statements given by the three villagers to the gendarme officers on 28 February 1994 lent credence to what was in effect mere supposition as to the fate of Üzeyir Kurt. The questions put to the villagers can only be described as formulated in a way designed to elicit responses which could enhance the credibility of the PKK kidnapping theory. Furthermore, and as noted earlier, the Government's other contention that the applicant's son had left the village to join the PKK also lacks any firm evidentiary basis.

128. Having regard to these considerations, the Court concludes that the authorities have failed to offer any credible and substantiated explanation for the whereabouts and fate of the applicant's son after he was detained in the village and that no meaningful investigation was conducted into the applicant's insistence that he was in custody and that she was concerned for his life. They have failed to discharge their responsibility to account for him and it must be accepted that he has been held in unacknowledged detention in the complete absence of the safeguards contained in Article 5.

129. The Court, accordingly, like the Commission, finds that there has been a particularly grave violation of the right to liberty and security of person guaranteed under Article 5 raising serious concerns about the welfare of Üzeyir Kurt.

[The Court reached its decision on Article 5 by a majority of 6 to 3.[4] Judge Petiti explained why he disagreed with the majority's reasoning on the application of Article 5]:

The *Kurt* case concerns a presumed disappearance. Under the ordinary criminal law, disappearances may involve cases of running away, false imprisonment or abduction.

Under public international law, a policy of systematic political disappearances may exist, as occurred in Brazil, Chile and Argentina.

---

[4] For the Court's decision on Art. 13, *see* Chapter 9, Section B.1.d, *infra*.

In such cases, especially where they have been verified by the European Committee for the Prevention of Torture, it is for one or more Member States of the Council of Europe to lodge an application against the state concerned. It would be cowardly to avoid the problem by leaving the court to decide on the basis of an application by an individual. An application by a state would occasion an international regional inquiry enabling the situation to be assessed objectively and thoroughly. I could have found that there had been a violation if the case had concerned instructions given by the army, gendarmerie or the police, both with regard to the security operations and to the verification of their implementation and follow up. . . .

In the system of the European Convention on Human Rights, the fact that states are liable for the failings of the authorities of which they are composed means that the court must identify the authorities and police or army units responsible. The *Kurt* case was in any event deficient in that there was no investigation of the type performed in cases before the Hague International Criminal Court and one of the main witnesses and the commanding officers of the gendarmerie units did not give evidence at the trial. The Commission itself acknowledged that it had doubts. The majority of the Court speculates on the basis of a hypothesis of continued detention relying on their personal conviction. That to my mind, is 'heresy' in the international sphere, since the instant case could have been decided on the basis of the case law under Article 5 requiring objective evidence and documents that convince the judges beyond all reasonable doubt; but both documents and witnesses were lacking in the present case. . . .

Even such a fundamental right as the right to physical liberty is not absolute. Within every legal system there exist situations in which one's liberty must, if necessary, give way in the face of some other vital interest of the community. These situations arise pre-eminently (but not exclusively) in the system of criminal justice. The exercise of powers of arrest and detention by state organs is tolerable only if it is governed by the need to observe due process of law. Article 5 of the Convention has three aims; (a) to proclaim the right of individual liberty; (b) to define the range of situations in which the right may be curtailed by exercise of the state's coercive power; and (c) to lay down the essential conditions which must be observed if that power is to be controlled by law. The power to ensure that those conditions are observed is primarily a matter for the national courts as the custodians of liberty under the law. As a secondary safeguard where a state is a party to the Convention, the national laws and the manner in which national judges act as custodians of liberty are subject to supervision and review by organs of the Convention.

There is an evident overlap between the emphasis in Article 5 on due process of law in relation to the deprivation of liberty, and the more general protection for procedural due process granted by Article 6 (see Chapter 8). The main overlap is between Article 5(3) (the arrested person's right to be brought promptly before a judge and the right to trial within a reasonable time or to release on bail) and Article 6(1) (an accused person's right to a trial of his or her case within a reasonable time). Many cases of delay in the criminal process raise questions under both Articles 5 and 6. The selection of cases made in this chapter seeks to avoid duplication with Chapter 8(D), but in their application the two Articles complement each other in an important way.

In contrast to the fairly elaborate limitation in Article 5 of the reasons and manner in which liberty may be restricted, the Fifth and Fourteenth amendments to the United States Constitution merely specify that the state may not deprive any person of 'life, liberty, or property without due process of law'. The content of the terms 'life, liberty and property' and 'due process of law' is discussed in Chapter 8 below in connection with the Article 6 right to a fair procedure in civil and criminal proceedings. While the meaning of 'liberty' in this sense has been much contested in American constitutional law, and while the paradigm deprivation of liberty remains incarceration after criminal conviction, that term has been given a far broader meaning than mere freedom of personal movement. As one standard commentary has summarized it:

While the required procedures may differ depending on the type of action, the government can never impose substantial physical restraints on an individual without establishing a procedure to determine the factual basis and legality of such actions.[5]

Thus it is clear that, under American law, the restrictions dealt with in the principal cases could be imposed only after a procedure consistent with due process of law.

We have seen that Section 7 of the Canadian Charter of Rights and Freedoms declares that no person can be deprived of 'life, liberty and the security of the person . . . except in accordance with the principles of fundamental justice'. As has been the case with 'due process', the meaning of 'fundamental principles of justice' has been controversial. But there is complete agreement that it at least requires a fair and impartial procedure before the state may deprive someone of the protected interests. Unlike the United States courts, the Canadian courts have restricted the term, 'deprivation of liberty', to some form of physical restraint. The nature of that restraint, however, has been widely construed to include, among other things, compelling a person to provide fingerprints or to produce evidence. In calling these impositions deprivations of liberty, the Supreme Court of Canada has emphasized that they involve elements of physical restraint.[6]

B. HAS THERE BEEN A DEPRIVATION OF LIBERTY?

The right to liberty under Article 5 is protected by the duty laid on organs of the state to deprive no-one of their liberty except in cases provided for by Article 5(1) and in accordance with a procedure prescribed by law. Thus the first issue to be answered where Article 5 is invoked, is whether there has on the facts been a deprivation of

---

[5] J. Nowak and R. Rotunda, *Constitutional Law* (4th edn., 1991), 498.

[6] *See Thompson Newspapers v. Canada* [1990] 1 S.C.R. 425 (dissenting reasons of Wilson J at 446, on which point, however, a majority of the judges concurred). *See also* P. W. Hogg. *Constitutional Law of Canada* (4th edn, 1997), §44 (7).

liberty. If so, the second issue for decision is whether the deprivation of liberty is for one of the purposes stated in Article 5(1).

1. GUZZARDI V. ITALY

Judgment of 6 Nov. 1980
(No. 39), 3 E.H.R.R. 333

[Under legislation dating from 1956 and 1965, the courts in Italy could order preventive measures to be taken against persons who presented a danger to security and public morality, including idlers, habitual vagrants who were fit for work, those regularly involved in illicit dealings and those suspected of belonging to mafia-type organizations. The measures included power to impose an order to reside in a specified district. In 1975, Guzzardi was ordered by a court in the city of Milan to reside on Asinara, a small island off Sardinia, where the residence area (Cala Reale) measured 2.5 square kilometres. He had a prison record and was in the course of being prosecuted on serious charges for which he was later sentenced to a long period in prison. However, the power to make a residence order was separate from the criminal proceedings. Having found that the conditions of life on Asinara did not constitute inhuman or degrading treatment within Article 3, the Court considered whether Guzzardi had been deprived of his liberty and, if so, whether there had been a breach of Article 5.]

90. The Commission was of the view that on Asinara the applicant suffered a deprivation of liberty within the meaning of the Article; it attached particular significance to the extremely small size of the area where he was confined, the almost permanent supervision to which he was subject, the all but complete impossibility for him to make social contacts and the length of his enforced stay at Cala Reale.

91. The Government disputed the correctness of this analysis. It reasoned as follows. The factors listed above were not sufficient to render the situation of persons in compulsory residence on the island comparable to the situation of prisoners as laid down by Italian law; there existed a whole series of fundamental differences that the Commission had wrongly overlooked. The distinguishing characteristic of freedom was less the amount of space available than the manner in which it could be utilised; a good many districts in Italy and elsewhere were less than 2.5 sq km in area. The applicant was able to leave and return to his dwelling as he wished between the hours of 7 a.m. and 10 p.m. His wife and son lived with him for 14 of the some 16 months he spent on Asinara; the inviolability of his home and of the intimacy of his family life, two rights that the Convention guaranteed solely to free people, were respected. Even as regards his social relations, he was treated much more favourably than someone in penal detention: he was at liberty to meet, within the boundaries of Cala Reale, the members of the small community of free people—about 200 individuals—living on the island, notably at Cala d'Oliva; to go to Sardinia or the mainland if so authorised; to correspond by letter or telegram without any control; to use the telephone, subject to notifying the *carabinieri* of the name and number of his correspondent. The supervision of which he complained constituted the *raison d'être* of the measure ordered in his respect. . . .

92. The Court recalls that in proclaiming the 'right to liberty', paragraph 1 of Article 5 is contemplating the physical liberty of the person; its aim is to ensure that no one should be dispossessed of this liberty in an arbitrary fashion. As was pointed out by those appearing before

the Court, the paragraph is not concerned with mere restrictions on liberty of movement; such restrictions are governed by Article 2 of Protocol No. 4 which has not been ratified by Italy. In order to determine whether someone has been 'deprived of his liberty' within the meaning of Article 5, the starting point must be his concrete situation and account must be taken of a whole range of criteria such as the type, duration, effects and manner of implementation of the measure in question.[7]

93. The difference between deprivation of and restriction upon liberty is nonetheless merely one of degree of intensity, and not one of nature or substance. Although the process of classification into one or other of these categories sometimes proves to be no easy task in that some borderline cases are a matter of pure opinion, the Court cannot avoid making the selection upon which the applicability or inapplicability of Article 5 depends.

94. As provided for under the 1956 Act . . . special supervision accompanied by an order for compulsory residence in a specified district does not of itself come within the scope of Article 5. . . .

It does not follow that 'deprivation of liberty' may never result from the manner of implementation of such a measure, and in the present case the manner of implementation is the sole issue that falls to be considered. . . .

95. The Government's reasoning (see para. 91 above) is not without weight. It demonstrates very clearly the extent of the difference between the applicant's treatment on Asinara and classic detention in prison or strict arrest imposed on a serviceman.[8] Deprivation of liberty may, however, take numerous other forms. Their variety is being increased by developments in legal standards and in attitudes; and the Convention is to be interpreted in the light of the notions currently prevailing in democratic States.[9]

Whilst the area around which the applicant could move far exceeded the dimensions of a cell and was not bounded by any physical barrier, it covered no more than a tiny fraction of an island to which access was difficult and about nine-tenths of which was occupied by a prison. Mr. Guzzardi was housed in part of the hamlet of Cala Reale which consisted mainly of the buildings of a former medical establishment which were in a state of disrepair or even dilapidation, a *carabinieri* station, a school and a chapel. He lived there principally in the company of other persons subjected to the same measure and of policemen. The permanent population of Asinara resided almost entirely at Cala d'Oliva, which Mr. Guzzardi could not visit, and would appear to have made hardly any use of its right to go to Cala Reale. Consequently, there were few opportunities for social contacts available to the applicant other than with his near family, his fellow 'residents' and the supervisory staff. Supervision was carried out strictly and on an almost constant basis. Thus, Mr. Guzzardi was not able to leave his dwelling between 10 p.m. and 7 a.m. without giving prior notification to the authorities in due time. He had to report to the authorities twice a day and inform them of the name and number of his correspondent whenever he wished to use the telephone. He needed the consent of the authorities for each of his trips to Sardinia or the mainland, trips which were rare and, understandably, made under the strict supervision of the *carabinieri*. He was liable to punishment by 'arrest' if he failed to comply with any of his obligations. Finally, more than 16 months elapsed before his arrival at Cala Reale and his departure for Force. . . .

---

[7] *See Engel v. The Netherlands*, 8 June 1976 (No. 22), 1 E.H.R.R. 647, paras. 58–59; reprinted at Section (B)(2) *infra*.

[8] *See id.* at para. 63.

[9] *See* notably *Tyrer v. United Kingdom* 25 Apr. 1978 (No. 26), 2 E.H.R.R. I, reprinted at Chapter 4 (B)(1) *supra*.

It is admittedly not possible to speak of 'deprivation of liberty' on the strength of any one of these factors taken individually, but cumulatively and in combination they certainly raise an issue of categorisation from the viewpoint of Article 5. In certain respects the treatment complained of resembles detention in an 'open prison' or committal to a disciplinary unit.[10] . . .

The Court considers on balance that the present case is to be regarded as one involving deprivation of liberty.

96. It remains to be determined whether the situation was one of those exhaustively listed in Article 5(1) of the Convention,[11] in which the contracting States reserve the right to arrest or detain individuals.

97. The Government relied, in the alternative, on sub-paragraph (e) of Article 5(1), maintaining that *mafiosi* like the applicant were 'vagrants' and 'something else besides'. . . . In the Government's opinion, the imposition on a 'vagrant' of preventive measures restricting, or even depriving him of, his liberty was justified, under the Convention and Italian law, not so much by his lack of fixed abode as by the absence of any apparent occupational activity . . . and, hence, the impossibility of identifying the source of his means of subsistence. The existence of this danger factor, the Government continued, was recognised by the Milan Regional Court in its decision of 30 January 1975 . . . ; in addition and above all, that Court took notice of the far more serious risk stemming from the applicant's links with mafia associations which engaged in kidnapping with a view to extracting ransoms. According to the Government, provision could not be made in an international instrument for the typically Italian phenomenon of the mafia, yet it would be an absurd conclusion to regard Article 5(1)(e) as allowing vagrants but not presumed *mafiosi* to be deprived of their liberty.

98. The Court concurs with the Commission's contrary view. . . .

[In a series of reports made on Guzzardi by the Italian police, prosecutor and courts, there had been no reference to the 'vagrancy' provision in the 1956 Act.]

These authorities relied on the 1956 Act solely in combination with the 1965 Act which concerns individuals whom there are strong reasons to suspect of belonging to mafia-type associations . . . What is more, they in no way described or depicted Mr. Guzzardi as a vagrant. Admittedly, they noted, in passing, that there were serious doubts as to whether he really worked as a mason as he claimed, but they laid much greater stress on his record, his illegal activities, his contacts with habitual criminals and still more his links with the mafia.

The Government's argument is open to a further objection. In addition to vagrants, sub-paragraph (e) refers to persons of unsound mind, alcoholics and drug addicts. The reason why the Convention allows the latter individuals, all of whom are socially maladjusted, to be deprived of their liberty is not only that they have to be considered as occasionally dangerous for public safety but also that their own interests may necessitate their detention. One cannot therefore deduce from the fact that Article 5 authorises the detention of vagrants that the same or even stronger reasons apply to anyone who may be regarded as still more dangerous.

---

[10] *See Engel v. The Netherlands*, 8 June 1976 (No. 22), 1 E.H.R.R. 647, para. 64, reprinted at section (B)(2) *infra*.

[11] *See Winterwerp v. The Netherlands*, 24 Oct. 1979 (No. 33), 2 E.H.R.R. 387, 401–2, para. 37; reprinted at section (D)(2) *infra*.

[The Court examined the matter under the other sub-paragraphs of Article 5(1), and held that the compulsory residence order was 'not a punishment for a specific offence but a preventive measure taken on the strength of indications of a propensity to crime'. The measure thus did not constitute detention 'after conviction by a competent court'.

   The Court held by ten votes to eight that Article 5(1) had been breached. Matscher J. was one of the dissenting judges:]

2. ... The nature of the Convention system is such that in the first place it is left to the governments of the contracting States to take the measures they deem appropriate for the accomplishment of their tasks. Amongst those tasks, the protection of the fundamental rights of the general public plays a pre-eminent role. At the same time, it is for the Convention institutions to review those measures in order to determine whether or not they are in conformity with the requirements of the Convention. In the course of this review, the provisions of the Convention should not be interpreted in a vacuum; the measures complained of must always be put back in the general setting to which they belong.

The principle that account must be taken of the general context of the case when examining an application concerning the alleged violation of a fundamental right does not in any way mean that—save for the possibility referred to in Article 15 of the Convention—exceptional circumstances allow the contracting States to take measures that are not compatible with the requirements of the Convention. On the other hand, I do deduce from this principle that certain measures which, from the viewpoint of the Convention, might be seen as open to considerable criticism in a so-called normal situation are less open to criticism and can be considered as being in conformity with the Convention when there is a crisis overshadowing public order and notably when rights of others, which are also guaranteed by the Convention, are being threatened by the activities of certain dangerous and anti-social elements. Such a crisis was obtaining in Italy at the time when the present case began. . . .

3. . . . It is obvious to me that the concept of 'deprivation of liberty' is not a matter for formal and precise criteria; quite the contrary—it is a concept of some complexity, having a core which cannot be the subject of argument but which is surrounded by a 'grey zone' where it is extremely difficult to draw the line between 'deprivation of liberty' within the meaning of Article 5(1) and mere restrictions on liberty that do not come within the ambit of that provision.

In fact, the Convention system has itself introduced (in Article 2 of Protocol No. 4), alongside the concept of 'deprivation of liberty', the concept of 'restriction on liberty of movement' and, as the Court has rightly observed (see para. 93 of the present judgment) the difference between the two is merely one of degree or intensity, and not one of nature or substance. In addition, the bounds that Article 5 requires the contracting States not to exceed in their judicial, disciplinary and police systems may vary from one situation to another.

Accordingly, only a careful analysis of the various factors which together made up Mr. Guzzardi's situation on Asinara can provide an answer to the question whether or not that situation fell within the concept of 'deprivation of liberty' within the meaning of Article 5(1). Clearly, since this is a matter of opinion, different views are tenable.

Personally, I do not attach quite the same weight as the majority of the Court to these various factors . . . taken individually and together. In addition, I take the 'general context of the case' into account. The whole leads me to the conclusion that the measure applied to Mr. Guzzardi amounted to a serious restriction on his liberty, which was motivated by perfectly understandable reasons and was also in conformity with Italian law, but that it did not attain the level and intensity that would cause it necessarily to be classified as a deprivation of liberty within the meaning of Article 5(1) of the Convention. . . .

2. ENGEL AND OTHERS *v.* THE NETHERLANDS

Judgment of 8 June 1976
(No. 22), 1 E.H.R.R. 647

[Engel and four others were conscript soldiers serving in the Dutch armed forces. On separate occasions, they were sentenced under military law to be punished for breaches of discipline and had been held under various forms of detention. Having appealed unsuccessfully to the Supreme Military Court, they complained to Strasbourg of various breaches of the Convention, including Articles 5 and 6. The Court held first that the Convention applies in principle to members of the armed forces and not only to civilians.]

54. . . . Nevertheless, when interpreting and applying the rules of the Convention in the present case, the court must bear in mind the particular characteristics of military life and its effects on the situation of individual members of the armed forces. . . .

1. The right to liberty in the context of military service

57. During the preparation and subsequent conclusion of the Convention, the great majority of the Contracting States possessed defence forces and, in consequence, a system of military discipline that by its very nature implied the possibility of placing on certain of the rights and freedoms of the members of these forces limitations incapable of being imposed on civilians. The existence of such a system, which those States have retained since then, does not in itself run counter to their obligations.

Military discipline, nonetheless, does not fall outside the scope of Article 5(1). Not only must this provision be read in the light of Article 1 and 15 . . . but the list of deprivations of liberty set out therein is exhaustive, as is shown by the words 'save in the following cases'. A disciplinary penalty or measure may in consequence constitute a breach of Article 5(1). The Government, moreover, acknowledge this.

58. In proclaiming the 'right to liberty', paragraph 1 of Article 5 is contemplating individual liberty in its classic sense, that is to say the physical liberty of the person. Its aim is to ensure that no one should be dispossessed of liberty in an arbitrary fashion. As pointed out by the Government and the Commission, it does not concern mere restrictions upon liberty of movement (Art. 2 of Protocol No. 4). . . .

59. In order to determine whether someone has been 'deprived of his liberty' within the meaning of Article 5, the starting point must be his concrete situation. Military service, as encountered in the Contracting States, does not on its own in any way constitute a deprivation of liberty under the Convention, since it is expressly sanctioned in Article 4(3)(b). In addition, rather wide limitations upon the freedom of movement of the members of the armed forces are entailed by reason of the specific demands of military service so that the normal restrictions accompanying it do not come within the ambit of Article 5 either.

Each State is competent to organise its own system of military discipline and enjoys in the matter a certain margin of appreciation. The bounds that Article 5 requires the State not to exceed are not identical for servicemen and civilians. A disciplinary penalty or measure which on analysis would unquestionably be deemed a deprivation of liberty were it to be applied to a civilian may not possess this characteristic when imposed upon a serviceman. Nevertheless, such penalty or measure does not escape the terms of Article 5 when it takes the form of restrictions that clearly deviate from the normal conditions of life within the armed forces of the Contracting States. In order to establish whether this is so, account should be taken of a whole range of factors such as the nature, duration, effects and manner of execution of the penalty or measure in question.

2. The existence of deprivations of liberty in the present case

61. No deprivation of liberty resulted from the three and four days' *light arrest* awarded respectively against Mr. Engel . . . and Mr. van der Wiel . . . Although confined during off-duty hours to their dwellings or to military buildings or premises, as the case may be, servicemen subjected to such a penalty are not locked up and continue to perform their duties (Art. 8 of the 1903 Act) . . . They remain, more or less, within the ordinary framework of their army life.

62. *Aggravated arrest* differs from light arrest on one point alone: in off-duty hours, soldiers serve the arrest in a specially designated place which they may not leave in order to visit the canteen, cinema or recreation rooms, but they are not kept under lock and key (Art. 9-B of the 1903 Act . . .). Consequently, neither does the court consider as a deprivation of liberty the twelve days' aggravated arrest complained of by Mr. de Wit. . . .

63. *Strict arrest*, abolished in 1974, differed from light arrest and aggravated arrest in that non-commissioned officers and ordinary servicemen served it by day and by night locked in a cell and were accordingly excluded from the performance of their normal duties (Art. 10-B of the 1903 Act . . .). It thus involved deprivation of liberty. It follows that the *provisional arrest* inflicted on Mr. Engel in the form of strict arrest . . . had the same character despite its short duration (20–22 March 1971).

64. *Committal to a disciplinary unit*, likewise abolished in 1974 but applied in 1971 to Mr. Dona and Mr. Schul, represented the most severe penalty under military disciplinary law in the Netherlands. Privates condemned to this penalty following disciplinary proceedings were not separated from those so sentenced by way of supplementary punishment under the criminal law, and during a month or more they were not entitled to leave the establishment. The committal lasted for a period of three to six months; this was considerably longer than the duration of the other penalties, including strict arrest which could be imposed for one to 14 days. Furthermore it appears that Mr. Dona and Mr. Schul spent the night locked in a cell . . . For the various reasons, the court considers that in the circumstances deprivation of liberty occurred. . . .

66. The court thus comes to the conclusion that neither the light arrest of Mr. Engel and Mr. van der Wiel, nor the aggravated arrest of Mr. de Wit, . . . call for a more thorough examination under paragraph 1 of Article 5.

The punishment of two days' strict arrest inflicted on Mr. Engel on 7 April 1971 and confirmed by the Supreme Military Court on 23 June 1971 coincided in practice with an earlier measure: it was deemed to have been served beforehand, that is from 20 to 22 March 1971, by the applicant's period of provisional arrest. . . .

On the other hand, the court is required to determine whether the lastmentioned provisional arrest, as well as the committal of Mr. Dona and Mr. Schul to a disciplinary unit, complied with Article 5(1).

3. The compatibility of the deprivations of liberty found in the present case with Article 5(1)

67. The Government maintained, in the alternative, that the committal of Mr. Dona and Mr. Schul to a disciplinary unit and the provisional arrest of Mr. Engel satisfied, respectively, the requirements of sub-paragraph (a) and of sub-paragraph (b) of Article 5(1). . . .

68. Sub-paragraph (a) of Article 5(1) permits the 'lawful detention of a person after conviction by a competent court'. . . .

The court, like the Government . . . notes that this provision makes no distinction based on the legal character of the offence of which a person has been found guilty. It applies to any 'conviction' occasioning deprivation of liberty pronounced by a 'court', whether the conviction be classified as criminal or disciplinary by the internal law of the State in question.

Mr. Dona and Mr. Schul were indeed deprived of their liberty 'after' their conviction by the Supreme Military Court. Article 64 of the 1903 Act conferred a suspensive effect upon their appeals against the decisions of their commanding officer (8 October 1971) and the complaints officer (19 October 1971) . . . Consequently, their transfer to the disciplinary barracks at Nieuwersluis occurred only by virtue of the final sentences imposed on 17 November 1971. . . .

It remains to be ascertained that the said sentences were passed by a 'competent court' within the meaning of Article 5(1)(a).

The Supreme Military Court, whose jurisdiction was not at all disputed, constitutes a court from the organisational point of view. Doubtless, its four military members are not irremovable in law, but like the two civilian members they enjoy the independence inherent in the Convention's notion of a 'court'.[12]

Furthermore, it does not appear . . . that Mr. Dona and Mr. Schul failed to receive before the Supreme Military Court the benefit of adequate judicial guarantees under Article 5(1)(a), an autonomous provision whose requirements are not always co-extensive with those of Article 6. The guarantees afforded to the two applicants show themselves to be 'adequate' for the purposes of Article 5(1)(a) if account is taken of 'the particular nature of the circumstances' under which the proceedings took place. . . .

Finally, the penalty inflicted was imposed and then executed 'lawfully' and 'in accordance with a procedure prescribed by law'. In short, it did not contravene Article 5(1).

69. The provisional arrest of Mr. Engel for its part clearly does not come within the ambit of sub-paragraph (a) of Article 5(1).

The Government have derived argument from sub-paragraph (b) insofar as the latter permits 'lawful arrest or detention' intended to 'secure the fulfilment of any obligation prescribed by law'.

The court considers that the words 'secure the fulfilment of any obligation prescribed by law' concern only cases where the law permits the detention of a person to compel him to fulfil a specific and concrete obligation which he has until then failed to satisfy. A wide interpretation would entail consequences incompatible with the notion of the rule of law from which the whole Convention draws its inspiration.[13] It would justify, for example, administrative internment meant to compel a citizen to discharge, in relation to any point whatever, his general duty of obedience to the law.

---

[12] *See De Wilde, Ooms and Versyp v. Belgium (No. 1)*, 18 June 1971 (No. 12), 1 E.H.R.R. 373, para. 78.
[13] *See Golder v. U.K.*, 21 Feb. 1975 (No. 18), 1 E.H.R.R. 524, para. 34.

In fact, Mr. Engel's provisional arrest was in no way designed to secure the fulfilment in the future of such an obligation. Article 44 of the 1903 Act, applicable when an offer has 'sufficient indication to suppose that a subordinate has committed a serious offence against military discipline', refers to past behaviour. The measure thereby authorised is a preparatory stage of military disciplinary proceedings and is thus situated in a punitive context. Perhaps this measure also has on occasions the incidental object or effect of inducing a member of the armed forces to comply henceforth with his obligations, but only with great contrivance can it be brought under sub-paragraph (b). If the latter were the case, this sub-paragraph could moreover be extended to punishments *stricto sensu* involving deprivation of liberty on the ground of their deterrent qualities. This would deprive such punishments of the fundamental guarantees of sub-paragraph (a).

The said measure really more resembles that spoken of in sub-paragraph (c) of Article 5(1) of the Convention. However in the present case it did not fulfil one of the requirements of that provision since the detention of Mr. Engel from 20 to 22 March 1971 had not been 'effected for the purpose of bringing him before the competent legal authority'. . . .

In conclusion, the applicant's deprivation of liberty from 20 to 22 March 1971 occurred in conditions at variance with this paragraph. . . .

[The differing opinions of the judges on several issues in the case are omitted.]

In *Raninen v Finland*,[14] compulsory military service led to a specific breach of Article 5 when the applicant, who objected on grounds of conscience to military service, was subject to a series of arrests, detentions on remand, and convictions. In June 1992, after a court had ordered his release, he was returned to a civil prison and was there handcuffed and driven to army barracks where he spent the night in a military hospital. On the next day, he was again arrested. The Government accepted that until that further arrest, his detention overnight had been contrary to Finnish law. The Strasbourg Court held that Article 5(1) had been breached but also, as we have seen,[15] that the handcuffing did not constitute 'inhuman or degrading treatment' for purposes of Article 3. Like the European Court, American courts have recognized that while persons in military service do not lose their constitutional rights,[16] the expression of those rights may be more limited in the military context. Thus, in a decision defining the First Amendment rights of military personnel, the United States Supreme Court noted that '[the] fundamental necessity for imposition of discipline may render permissible within the military that which would be constitutionally impermissible outside it'.[17]

---

[14] 16 Dec. 1997, Reports, 1997–VIII 2804, 26 E.H.R.R. 563.

[15] *See* Chapter 4 Section (A)(2) *supra*.

[16] *See* in this connection (in Chapter 8 below) the discussion of the judicial attempts to differentiate criminal charges and disciplinary proceedings.

[17] *Parker v. Levy*, 417 U.S. 733, 758 (1954).

C. DETENTION AFTER CONVICTION

In the ordinary case where a person is convicted of criminal charges and receives a prison sentence that is lawful in national law, the Convention is not infringed. The prisoner may have rights of appeal by national law against the conviction and/or against sentence. However, if the sentence is for life or for an indeterminate period, further decisions may have to be made as to how long the prisoner must be detained and when he/she can be released. Practice in European countries varies in this respect, some countries providing for further preventive detention for persistent offenders. Often the release of long-term prisoners is regarded more as an executive than a judicial function. Do such decisions involve a breach of Article 5 as an impermissible deprivation of liberty? Or are they consistent with Article 5 since the original custodial sentence will have taken effect 'after' a decision by the criminal court?

1. VAN DROOGENBROECK *V.* BELGIUM

Judgment of 24 June 1982
(No. 50), 4 E.H.R.R. 443

[Acting under Section 23 of the 'Social Protection' Act of 1 July 1964, the Belgian criminal court in 1970 sentenced Mr. van Droogenbroeck to two years' imprisonment for theft. The court also ordered that he be 'placed at the Government's disposal' for ten years, on the basis that he was a recidivist who manifested a persistent tendency to crime. After serving his principal sentence, he was in 1972 placed by the Ministry of Justice in semi-custodial care intended to secure his rehabilitation, but he quickly absconded and was later arrested on further charges of theft. Other attempts at rehabilitation having failed, he was committed by the Ministry, acting under the 1964 Act, to prison in a block reserved for recidivists. After he was once more released, similar events were repeated, and several times he appeared before an executive body known as the Body for Recidivists. He complained to Strasbourg that, *inter alia*, he had for several years been detained by ministerial order and not by order of a court.]

34. As regards paragraph 1(a), there is no dispute as to the 'competence' of the 'court' which ordered the measure complained of, namely the Ghent Court of Appeal by its judgment of 20 October 1970.

The same is true of the question whether any deprivation of liberty occurred. In this connection, it should be recalled that according to Belgian case law the placing of recidivists and habitual offenders at the Government's disposal is to be classified as a penalty involving deprivation of liberty; this is so irrespective of the form which implementation of the order may take in a given case or at a given time, be it detention, semi-custodial care, or remaining at liberty under supervision or on probation. However, the Court will take into account solely the first of such forms, this being the only one of which Mr. van Droogenbroeck complained. . . . [The] Court will confine its examination to the periods of detention which were the subject of Mr. van Droogenbroeck's application . . . namely those running from 21 January 1976 to 1 June 1977 and from 21 December 1977 to 18 March 1980.

35. The Court has to determine whether those periods of detention occurred 'after conviction' by the Ghent Court of Appeal.

Having regard to the French text, the word 'conviction', for the purposes of Article 5(1)(a), has to be understood as signifying both a 'finding of guilt', after 'it has been established in accordance with the law that there has been an offence'[18] and the imposition of a penalty or other measure involving deprivation of liberty. These conditions are satisfied in the instant case.

The word 'after' does not simply mean that the 'detention' must follow the 'conviction' in point of time: in addition, the 'detention' must result from, 'follow and depend upon' or occur 'by virtue of' the 'conviction.'[19]

36. According to the applicant, the deprivations of liberty complained of stemmed not from a sentence imposed by a 'competent court' but from decisions taken by the Minister of Justice.

The respondent State, on the other hand, maintained that detention occurred 'by operation of law' following the judicial decision placing a recidivist at the Government's disposal and represented 'the principal method of implementing' such a decision; it was only release that required 'a Ministerial decision'. The 'task entrusted to the Minister . . . by the Act of 1 July 1964' was said to be confined 'to determining the modalities for the execution of a sentence involving deprivation of liberty', for example 'by suspending', on such conditions as he determined, 'the detention entailed by such a penalty . . . ' Accordingly, so it was argued, 'by not deciding to release, the Minister does not decide to detain'.

37. This is a controversial point in Belgian law. . . .

Even when an offender is not set free after serving his initial sentence—something which did not occur in the instant case and is nowadays exceptional—this is apparently the result of Ministerial instructions to the effect that he should be detained. At any rate, that such is the position emerges from paragraph 6 of a circular of 20 December 1930, which was supplied by the Government.

In any event, the Ministerial decisions of 11 January and 11 September 1975 revoking the conditional release granted to Mr. van Droogenbroeck did order that he be 'detained'.

38. Be that as it may, one must look beyond the appearances and the language used and concentrate on the realities of the situation.

This is a matter in which the Government enjoy a wide measure of discretion . . . In a judgment of 4 April 1978, the Belgian Court of Cassation observed that 'execution of the penalty' in question 'is to a large extent a matter for the discretion of the Minister of Justice. . . . ' In short, to adopt the language used by the Commission's delegate, 'the court decision does not order the detention' of recidivists and habitual offenders: it 'authorises' it.

39. In these circumstances, the Court has to consider whether there was a sufficient connection, for the purposes of Article 5, between the last-mentioned decision and the deprivation of liberty at issue.

This question must receive an affirmative reply since the Minister's discretion is exercised within a framework set both by the Act and by the sentence pronounced by the 'competent court'. In this respect, the Court notes that, according to Belgian case law, a judgment which sentences the person concerned to imprisonment and, by way of a supplementary or accessory penalty,

[18] *See Guzzardi v. Italy,* 6 Nov. 1980 (No. 39), 3 E.H.R.R. 333, para. 100.

[19] *See X v. United Kingdom,* 24 Oct. 1981 (No. 46), 4 E.H.R.R. 188, para. 39 (reprinted at Section (D)(2) *infra; Engel v. The Netherlands* (No. 1), Judgment of 8 June 1976 (No. 22), 1 E.H.R.R. 647 (reprinted at Section (B)(2) *supra.*)

places him at the Government's disposal pursuant to section 22 or section 23 of the 1964 Act constitutes 'an inseparable whole'. There are two components to the judgment: the first is a penalty involving deprivation of liberty which the offender must undergo for a period specified in the court decision, and the second is the placing of the offender at the Government's disposal, the execution of which may take different forms ranging from remaining at liberty under supervision to detention.

The choice between these forms of execution is a matter for the discretion of the Minister of Justice. Nevertheless he does not enjoy an unlimited power in making his decision: within the bounds laid down by the Act, he must assess the degree of danger presented by the individual concerned and the short- or medium-term prospects of reintegrating him into society.

40. In fact, sight must not be lost of what the title and general structure of the 1964 Act, the drafting history and Belgian case law show to be the objectives of this statute that is to say not only 'to protect society against the danger presented by recidivists and habitual offenders' but also 'to provide [the Government] with the possibility of endeavouring to reform [them]'. Attempting to achieve these objectives requires that account be taken of circumstances that, by their nature, differ from case to case and are susceptible of modification. At the time of its decision, the court can, in the nature of things, do no more than estimate how the individual will develop in the future. The Minister of Justice, for his part, is able, through and with the assistance of his officials, to monitor that development more closely and at frequent intervals but this very fact means that with the passage of time the link between his decisions not to release or to re-detain and the initial judgment gradually becomes less strong. The link might eventually be broken if a position were reached in which those decisions were based on grounds that had no connection with the object-ives of the legislature and the court or on an assessment that was unreasonable in terms of those objectives. In those circumstances, a detention that was lawful at the outset would be transformed into a deprivation of liberty that was arbitrary and, hence, incompatible with Article 5.

Such a situation did not obtain in the present case. The Belgian authorities showed patience and trust towards Mr. van Droogenbroeck: notwithstanding his conduct, they gave him several opportunities to mend his ways. The manner in which they exercised their discretion respected the requirements of the Convention, which allows a measure of indeterminacy in sentencing and does not oblige the Contracting States to entrust to the courts the general supervision of the execution of sentences.

[The Court therefore found that there had been no violation of Article 5(1). However, the Court found a violation of Article 5(4), by which someone who is deprived of their liberty is entitled to take proceedings by which the lawfulness of the detention may be decided speedily by a court. Although the original decision to sentence Mr. van Droogenbroeck had been taken by a court, the statutory duty of the Minister of Justice thereafter was to consider whether con-tinued detention was needed on such grounds as a 'persistent tendency to crime' or 'danger to society'. In the Court's opinion, 'the very logic of the Belgian system' required subsequent judicial review, at reasonable intervals, of the justification for the continuing deprivation of liberty.[20] The reason for this was to ensure that detention decisions taken by the Minister of Justice were not arbitrary and that the conditions initially justifying indefinite detention had not ceased to exist.]

[20] Para. 47.

2. WEEKS *v.* UNITED KINGDOM

Judgment of 2 March 1987
(No. 114), 10 E.H.R.R. 293

[In 1966, when aged 17, Mr. Weeks pleaded guilty to armed robbery: with the aid of a starting pistol loaded with blank cartridges, he had stolen 35 pence (less than 1 U.S. $) from a small shop. He was sentenced to life imprisonment, the Court of Appeal stating that this might enable him to be released much sooner than if a fixed term of imprisonment had been imposed. He was released on licence in 1976 by the Home Secretary, who under the Criminal Justice Act 1967 acted on the recommendation of an advisory body, the Parole Board. Thereafter he committed various criminal acts and his licence was revoked more than once, so that he was reimprisoned in 1977 and again in 1985 under the sentence imposed in 1966. He complained that there had been breaches of Article 5(1) and 5(4).]

38. The applicant did not dispute that his original detention following his conviction in 1966 was justified under Article 5(1) of the Convention. He contended, however, that his detention subsequent to the revocation of his licence in June 1977 was not in accordance with this provision . . .

39. In what it described as its central submission, the Government argued that the applicant's recall to prison in 1977 had not deprived him of his liberty because both his liberty and his right to liberty had been taken away from him for the rest of his life by virtue of the sentence of life imprisonment imposed on him in 1966. The applicant was on this ground alone said to be precluded from claiming a breach of Article 5, whether paragraph 1 or paragraph 4. The Government drew a distinction between liberty, properly understood, and a life prisoner being permitted to live on licence outside prison. In the latter case, the Government explained, the prisoner was still serving his sentence, albeit outside prison as a result of a privilege granted to him by the Home Secretary, but his right to liberty had not been restored to him. In sum, it was one and the same deprivation of liberty in June 1977 as in December 1966, based on his original conviction and sentence, and no new issue arose under Article 5.

40. The Court is not convinced by such reasoning.

It is true that in terms of English law, except in the event of a free pardon or an exercise of the Royal Prerogative commuting the sentence, a person sentenced to life imprisonment never regains his right to liberty, even when released on licence. This is not to say, however, that Mr. Weeks lost his 'right to liberty and security of person', as guaranteed by Article 5 of the Convention, as from the moment he was sentenced to life imprisonment in December 1966. Article 5 applies to 'everyone'. All persons, whether at liberty or in detention, are entitled to the protection of Article 5. . . .

Whether Mr. Weeks regained his 'liberty', for the purposes of Article 5 of the Convention, when released on licence in March 1976 is a question of fact, depending upon the actual circumstances of the régime to which he was subject. . . . Admittedly, for persons sentenced to life imprisonment, any release under the 1967 Act is granted as an act of clemency and is always conditional . . . Nevertheless, the restrictions to which Mr. Weeks' freedom outside prison was subject under the law are not sufficient to prevent its being qualified as a state of 'liberty' for the purposes of Article 5. Hence, when recalling Mr. Weeks to prison in 1977, the Home Secretary was ordering his removal from an actual state of liberty, albeit one enjoyed in law as a privilege and not as of right, to a state of custody. . . .

41. Following his 'conviction by a competent court' in December 1966, Mr. Weeks was sentenced to life imprisonment. The issue in the present case is whether his re-detention on recall to prison some ten years later was 'in accordance with a procedure prescribed by law', 'lawful' and undergone 'after' that conviction.

42. It was not contested that Mr. Weeks' re-detention as from 30 June 1977 was in accordance with a procedure prescribed by English law and otherwise lawful under English law. That, however, is not necessarily decisive. The 'lawfulness' required by the Convention presupposes not only conformity with domestic law but also, as confirmed by Article 18, conformity with the purposes of the deprivation of liberty permitted by sub-paragraph (a) of Article 5(1).[21] Furthermore, the word 'after' in sub-paragraph (a) does not simply mean that the detention must follow the 'conviction' in point of time: in addition, the 'detention' must result from, 'follow and depend upon' or occur 'by virtue of' the 'conviction'.[22] In short, there must be a sufficient causal connection between the conviction and the deprivation of liberty at issue.[23]

43. The contested decision of the Home Secretary was taken within the legal framework set by the life sentence passed by the 'competent court' in 1966, taken together with the provisions in the 1967 Act governing the release on licence and recall to prison of persons sentenced to life imprisonment. A life sentence can never be terminated, save by pardon or in the event of being commuted, and except in those circumstances any release after sentence will always be conditional. The 1967 Act confers on the Home Secretary the power to order both release on licence and recall, but the discretion granted is not unfettered, as it was under the system in force when the applicant was sentenced. The Home Secretary can only release on the recommendation of the Parole Board and, in the case of a life prisoner, only after consulting the Lord Chief Justice and the trial judge if available. Similarly, he may revoke the licence if recommended to do so by the Parole Board. He also has the power to revoke the licence without consulting the Board 'where it appears to him that it is expedient in the public interest to recall [the] person before such consultation is practicable'. However, a further constraint upon his power of recall is that his decision may be overruled by the Parole Board. The revocation of the licence reactivates the original sentence of life imprisonment by making the recalled prisoner 'liable to be detained in pursuance of his sentence'. . . .

45. In the submission of the Government, the lawfulness of any action taken by the Home Secretary in the present case derived from the immutable fact of Mr. Weeks' conviction and sentence in 1966. This in itself was sufficient to justify, under Article 5(1)(a), his re-detention after a period of conditional release. Whilst recognising that the instability of Mr. Weeks' personality undoubtedly did influence the choice of sentence, the Government maintained that this is not material to the issue under Article 5(1) since, in its view, it is not legitimate to distinguish one life sentence from another. . . .

46. As the Delegate of the Commission pointed out, it may be extremely difficult, if not impossible, to disentangle different elements underlying a particular sentence in a given case and to determine which of those elements was accorded more importance by the sentencing judge; in the present case, however, it was the trial court itself and the Court of Appeal that explained in detail the reasons why Mr. Weeks received a life sentence as opposed to a determinate sentence.

[21] *See Bozano v. France*, 18 Dec. 1986 (No. 111), 9 E.H.R.R. 297, para. 54.

[22] *Id.* at para. 53 and *Van Droogenbroeck v. Belgium* 24 June 1982 (No. 50), 4 E.H.R.R. 443, para. 35 reprinted at section (C)(1) *supra*.

[23] *See Van Droogenbroeck, supra* n. 22, para. 39.

The Court agrees with the Commission and the applicant that the clearly stated purpose for which Mr. Weeks' sentence was imposed, taken together with the particular facts pertaining to the offence for which he was convicted, places the sentence in a special category.

Mr. Weeks was convicted of armed robbery and, aged only 17, was sentenced to life imprisonment, the severest sentence known to English law. . . . Armed with a starting pistol loaded with blank cartridges, he had entered a pet shop and stolen 35 pence, which sum was later found on the shop floor. Later the same day, he had telephoned the police to announce that he would give himself up. It emerged from the evidence that he had committed the robbery because he owed his mother £3. What otherwise would appear a 'terrible' sentence in relation to these pathetic circumstances was seen by the trial judge and the Court of Appeal as appropriate in the light of the purpose intended to be achieved.

The intention was to make the applicant, who was qualified both by the trial judge and by the Court of Appeal as a 'dangerous young man', subject to a continuing security measure in the interests of public safety. The sentencing judges recognised that it was not possible for them to forecast how long his instability and personality disorders would endure. . . . [They] accordingly had recourse to an 'indeterminate sentence': this would enable the appropriate authority, namely the Home Secretary, to monitor his progress and release him back into the community when he was no longer judged to represent a danger to society or to himself, and thus hopefully sooner than would have been possible if he had been sentenced to a long term of imprisonment . . . In substance, Mr. Weeks was being put at the disposal of the State because he needed continued supervision in custody for an unforeseeable length of time and, as a corollary, periodic reassessment in order to ascertain the most appropriate manner of dealing with him.

The grounds expressly relied on by the sentencing courts for ordering this form of deprivation of liberty against Mr. Weeks are by their very nature susceptible of change with the passage of time, whereas the measure will remain in force for the whole of his life. In this, his sentence differs from a life sentence imposed on a person because of the gravity of the offence.

47. In this sense, the measure ordered against Mr. Weeks is thus comparable to the Belgian measure at issue in the *Van Droogenbroeck* case, that is the placing of a recidivist or habitual offender at the disposal of the Government—although in the present case the placement was for a whole lifetime and not for a limited period. The legitimate aim (of social protection and the rehabilitation of offenders) pursued by the measure and its effect on the convicted person are substantially the same in both cases. . . .

49. Applying the principles stated in the *Van Droogenbroeck* judgment, the formal legal connection between Mr. Weeks' conviction in 1966 and his recall to prison some ten years later is not on its own sufficient to justify the contested detention under Article 5(1)(a). The causal link required by sub-paragraph (a) might eventually be broken if a position were reached in which a decision not to release or to re-detain was based on grounds that were inconsistent with the objectives of the sentencing court. 'In those circumstances, a detention that was lawful at the outset would be transformed into a deprivation of liberty that was arbitrary and, hence, incompatible with Article 5'.[24]

50. In the submission of the applicant, the objectives of the courts in 1966 and 1967 as regards the length of his loss of liberty were satisfied on his release in March 1976; the requisite link was broken at that stage, so that his full rights under Article 5 were restored to him and his redetention fifteen months later was no longer justified under Article 5(1)(e).

[24] *Van Droogenbroek v. Belgium, supra* n. 22, para. 40.

The Court does not accept this contention. As a matter of English law, it was inherent in Mr. Weeks' life sentence that, whether he was inside or outside prison, his liberty was at the discretion of the executive for the rest of his life (subject to the controls subsequently introduced by the 1967 Act, notably the Parole Board). This the sentencing judges must be taken to have known and intended. It is not for the Court, within the context of Article 5, to review the appropriateness of the original sentence, a matter which moreover has not been disputed by the applicant in the present proceedings.

It remains to examine the sufficiency of the grounds on which his re-detention in June 1977 and thereafter was based. In this area, as in many others, the national authorities are to be recognized as having a certain discretion since they are better placed than the international judge to evaluate the evidence in a particular case. . . .

The Court reviewed the evidence as to Mr. Weeks' behaviour in 1977, found that it was still 'unstable, disturbed and aggressive' and concluded that his recall to prison in 1977 and subsequent detention were compatible with Article 5(1).

Mr. Weeks also complained of a breach of Article 5(4). The Court again emphasized that his 'indeterminate' sentence was in a special category because it was imposed for the stated purpose of social protection and rehabilitation: 'unlike the case of a person sentenced to life imprisonment because of the gravity of the offence committed, the grounds relied on by the sentencing judge for deciding that the length of the deprivation of Mr. Weeks' liberty should be subject to the discretion of the executive for the rest of his life are by their nature susceptible of change with the passage of time'.[25]

For the purposes of Article 5(4), Weeks was therefore entitled to a decision by a court as to the lawfulness of his detention. The Court reviewed the constitution and powers of the Parole Board which had considered his case. Could the Board be regarded as a judicial body for the purposes of Article 5(4)? The Court held that while the Board's members were independent and impartial, it lacked the power to do more than advise the Home Secretary to release a prisoner; and its procedure did not require the Board to disclose to the prisoner any adverse material which it held about him (which a judicial body would be required to do). The Court further held that the scope of judicial review of the Board's advice and the Home Secretary's decisions was not wide enough to ensure that an individual's detention was 'consistent with and therefore justified by the objectives of the indeterminate sentence imposed on him'.[26] There had thus been a breach of Mr. Weeks' rights under Article 5(4).

While the circumstances of Mr. Weeks' sentence and subsequent history were exceptional, the principles adopted by the Court have been applied in the context of the most serious criminal conduct.[27]

---

[25] *Weeks v. United Kingdom*, 2 Mar. 1987 (No. 114), 10 E.H.R.R. 293, para. 58.

[26] *Id.* at para. 69.

[27] *See Hussain v. United Kingdom*, 21 Feb. 1996, Reports, 1996–I 252, 22 E.H.R.R. I and *T and V v. United Kingdom*, 16 Dec. 1999 (not yet reported).

3. THYNNE, WILSON AND GUNNELL *V.* UNITED KINGDOM

Judgment of 25 Oct. 1990
(No. 190), 13 E.H.R.R. 666

[In English law, the maximum sentence that can be imposed for serious offences such as rape is life imprisonment. Each of the three applicants had committed grave sexual offences and assaults and was sentenced to life imprisonment. In each case psychiatric evidence indicated that the applicant was suffering from a mental or personality disorder. As in *Weeks v. United Kingdom*, the effect of a life sentence was to give the Home Secretary the power to decide when a prisoner can be released. The European Court had already decided, in *Van Droogenbroeck v. Belgium* and in *Weeks*, that the taking of discretionary decisions as to whether a life prisoner should be released was a matter which, under Article 5(4), must be subject to an adequate level of judicial control. But the British government had not changed the system, so the same issues again came before the Strasbourg Court.]

A. Whether the requisite judicial control was incorporated in the original conviction

65. The applicants claimed that a discretionary life sentence is composed of a punitive element—i.e. a period of imprisonment to satisfy the needs of retribution and deterrence (the 'tariff' period)—and a security element based on the need to protect the public. They maintained that they had received discretionary life sentences because, as in the *Weeks* case,[28] the courts considered them to be mentally unstable and dangerous and that such a sentence would enable the Secretary of State to monitor their progress and decide when it was safe to release them. Since these factors were susceptible to change with the passage of time a right to judicial review at reasonable intervals of the continued lawfulness of their detention was required.

66. The Government argued that the present cases did not fall into the same category as the *Weeks* case. In that case, as perceived by the Court, the facts relating to the offence could not be described as grave and the sole purpose of the sentence as stated by the courts was to detain the offender because he might present a danger to the public for an indeterminate period in the future. The need for punishment was not a factor in the stated purpose of the life sentence in that case. In contrast, the present applicants had committed particularly serious offences and the sentencing courts had emphasised the need for punishment.

The Government contended that in a normal discretionary life sentence no clear dividing line can be drawn by reference to the 'tariff' period between the punitive and security purposes for which the sentence is imposed. In its submission there is no clearly identifiable point after which the sole justification of the sentence is protective detention.

In the first place it stated that the purpose of the tariff has been wrongly understood by both the applicants and the Commission as providing support for such a division. The 'tariff' was a notional period communicated by the judges to the Secretary of State in both mandatory and discretionary life sentences to enable him to fix the first review date by the Local Review Committee. It represented the judges' views as to the minimum period of detention necessary to satisfy the requirements of retribution and deterrence. The judges' recommendation in this respect, however, was relevant only to the fixing of the date for the first review. When considering release, the

---

[28] See section (C)(2) *supra.*

Secretary of State was not bound by the judicial view on 'tariff', but had to take into account a variety of factors which it was impossible to subject to finite analysis. . . .

In the second place the gravity of the offences was relevant at all times throughout the sentence, especially when the Secretary of State was called on to assess the risk factor when considering release. Gravity also remained the immutable justification in a discretionary life sentence — although not the sole justification — for the continued detention or recall of the life prisoner.

67. In proceedings originating in an individual application, the Court has, without losing sight of the general context, to confine its attention as far as possible to the issues raised by the concrete case before it. Accordingly, it will limit its examination to the application of Article 5(4) to the particular circumstances of the present applicants.

68. It was held in the *De Wilde, Ooms and Versyp* judgment of 18 June 1971 that where a sentence of imprisonment is imposed after 'conviction by a competent court', the supervision required by Article 5(4) is incorporated in the decision of the court.[29] In subsequent cases the Court made it clear that this finding related only to 'the initial decision depriving a person of his liberty' and did not purport 'to deal with an ensuing period of detention in which new issues affecting the lawfulness of the detention might arise'.[30] In this connection the concept of lawfulness under Article 5(4) requires that the detention be in conformity not only with domestic law but also with the text of the Convention, the general principle embodied therein and the aim of the restrictions permitted by Article 5(1).

69. In cases concerning detention of persons of unsound mind under Article 5(1)(e) where the reasons initially warranting detention may cease to exist the Court has held that 'it would be contrary to the object and purpose of Article 5 . . . to interpret paragraph 4 . . . as making this category of confinement immune from subsequent review of lawfulness merely provided that the initial decision issued from a court . . .'[31] This interpretation of Article 5(4) has also, in certain circumstances, been applied to detention 'after conviction by a competent court' under Article 5(1)(a).[32] What is of importance in this context is the nature and purpose of the detention in question, viewed in the light of the objectives of the sentencing court, and not the category to which it belongs under Article 5(1).[33]

[Citing its earlier decisions in *Weeks* and *Van Droogenbroeck*, the Court summarized the psychiatric evidence relating to the three applicants when they were convicted, and continued:]

Each of the applicants was thus sentenced to life imprisonment because, in addition to the need for punishment, he was considered by the courts to be suffering from a mental or personality disorder and to be dangerous and in need of treatment. Life imprisonment was judged to be the most appropriate sentence in the circumstances since it enabled the Secretary of State to assess their progress and to act accordingly. Thus the courts' sentencing objectives were in that respect similar to those in *Weeks*, but also took into account the much greater gravity of the offences committed.

73. As regards the nature and purpose of the discretionary life sentence under English law, the

[29] (No. 12), 1 E.H.R.R. 373.

[30] *See, inter alia, Weeks* (reprinted at section (C)(2) *supra*).

[31] *See X v. United Kingdom*, 24 Oct. 1981 (No. 46), 4 E.H.R.R. 188 (reprinted at section (D)(2) *infra*).

[32] *See, inter alia, Van Droogenbroeck v. Belgium*, 24 June 1982 (No. 50), 4 E.H.R.R. 443 (reprinted at section (C)(2) *supra*) *Weeks v. United Kingdom*, 2 Mar. 1987 (No. 114), 10 E.H.R.R. 293 (reprinted at section (C)(2) *supra*) and *E. v. Norway*, 29 Aug. 1990 (No. 181A), 17 E.H.R.R. 30, para. 50.

[33] See *Van Droogenbroeck, supra* n. 32.

Government's main submission was that it is impossible to disentangle the punitive and security components of such sentences. The Court is not persuaded by this argument: the discretionary life sentence has clearly developed in English law as a measure to deal with mentally unstable and dangerous offenders; numerous judicial statements have recognized the protective purpose of this form of life sentence. Although the dividing line may be difficult to draw in particular cases, it seems clear that the principles underlying such sentences, unlike mandatory life sentences, have developed in the sense that they are composed of a punitive element and subsequently of a security element designed to confer on the Secretary of State the responsibility for determining when the public interest permits the prisoner's release. This view is confirmed by the judicial description of the 'tariff' as denoting the period of detention considered necessary to meet the requirements of retribution and deterrence.

74. The Court accepts the Government's submissions that the 'tariff' is also communicated to the Secretary of State in cases of mandatory life imprisonment; that the Secretary of State in considering release may not be bound by the intimation of the 'tariff'; and that in the assessment of the risk factor in deciding on release the Secretary of State will also have regard to the gravity of the offences committed.

However, in the Court's view this does not alter the fact that the objectives of the discretionary life sentence as seen above are distinct from the punitive purposes of the mandatory life sentence and have been so described by the courts in the relevant cases.

75. It is clear from the judgments of the sentencing courts that in their view the three applicants, unlike Mr. Weeks, had committed offences of the utmost gravity meriting lengthy terms of imprisonment. Nevertheless, the Court is satisfied that in each case the punitive period of the discretionary life sentence has expired. . . .

76. Having regard to the foregoing, the Court finds that the detention of the applicants after the expiry of the punitive periods of their sentences is comparable to that at issue in the *Van Droogenbroeck* and *Weeks* cases: the factors of mental instability and dangerousness are susceptible to change over the passage of time and new issues of lawfulness may thus arise in the course of detention. It follows that at this phase in the execution of their sentences, the applicants are entitled under Article 5(4) to take proceedings to have the lawfulness of their continued detention decided by a court at reasonable intervals and to have the lawfulness of any re-detention determined by a court. . . .

B. Whether the available remedies satisfied the requirements of Article 5(4)

79. Article 5(4) does not guarantee a right to judicial control of such scope as to empower the 'court' on all aspects of the case, including questions of expediency, to substitute its own discretion for that of the decision-making authority; the review should, nevertheless, be wide enough to bear on those conditions which, according to the Convention, are essential for the lawful detention of a person subject to the special type of deprivation of liberty ordered against these three applicants.

80. The Court sees no reason to depart from its finding in the *Weeks* judgment that neither the Parole Board nor judicial review proceedings—no other remedy of a judicial character being available to the three applicants—satisfy the requirements of Article 5(4). Indeed, this was not disputed by the Government. . . .

4. WYNNE *V.* UNITED KINGDOM

Judgment of 18 July 1994 (294A),
19 E.H.R.R. 333

[Wynne was convicted of murder in 1964 and received the mandatory sentence of life imprisonment. After being released on a life licence in 1980, he committed a further killing, pleaded guilty to manslaughter on the basis of diminished responsibility and was sentenced to a discretionary life sentence. His life licence in respect of the 1964 conviction was revoked. Having served the punitive part (tariff) in respect of that conviction, he claimed a breach of Article 5(4) in that the continued lawfulness of his detention could not be reviewed by a court, arguing that he should have the benefit of the ruling in *Thynne, Wilson and Gunnell v. United Kingdom* (above).]

28. The applicant submitted . . . that it is the discretionary life sentence which has become the real and effective basis for his detention since his conviction in 1982. It was this sentence, imposed on him because of his dangerousness, which was intended by the trial judge to be the primary authority for this detention from then on. . . .

In the alternative, he maintained that the judicial finding in 1982 that he was suffering from a long-standing mental disorder broke the chain of causation between the original mandatory life sentence and his subsequent re-detention under that sentence. His legal status was altered to that of someone who was not fully responsible for his actions who needed to be left in preventive detention.

He was—he claimed—thus entitled under Article 5(4) to have the lawfulness of his continued detention determined by a court.

29. For both the Government and the Commission the mandatory life sentence continued to be operative following the revocation of his life licence.

30. The Court notes that the applicant received a mandatory life sentence in 1964 and was released on life licence in 1980. This, however, was revoked by the trial judge in 1982 following the applicant's conviction for manslaughter. As a result his detention thereafter was based on both the mandatory sentence, which remained in force, and the new discretionary life sentence. The fact that he committed a further offence in 1981 and was judged to be suffering from a mental disorder at that time in no way affected under English law the continued validity of the original sentence or its reactivation on his recall. It merely provided a supplementary legal basis for his detention.

31. The applicant further submitted that Article 5(4) applied to mandatory life sentences in the same way as it applied to discretionary life sentences. He maintained that the distinction made by the Court in the case of *Thynne, Wilson and Gunnell v. United Kingdom*[34] between these two types of life sentence was no longer valid since it was based on the false assumption that a mandatory sentence had as its object the punishment of a murderer for life. In fact the mandatory sentence had not been interpreted in this way by Parliament, the courts, the Parole Board or by successive Home Secretaries. Indeed recent court decisions have described the mandatory sentence as composed, like the discretionary life sentence, of a period of punishment (the 'tariff') to reflect the requirements of retribution and deterrence as well as a period of preventive detention,

---

[34] 25 Oct. 1990 (No. 190), 13 E.H.R.R. 666 (reprinted at section (C)(3) *supra*).

following the expiry of the 'tariff' period. Furthermore, the procedures that have developed to review the mandatory sentence have been founded on the understanding that when the requirements of punishment have been satisfied the only justification for continued detention is dangerousness. In particular, there is a presumption that at this point the prisoner will be released unless he is a danger to the public.

Accordingly, he submitted, it follows from the very nature of the mandatory life sentence that the applicant is entitled to invoke the same protection afforded under Article 5(4) to discretionary life prisoners in the post-tariff stage, namely a review by a court of his continued dangerousness.

[The Government did not accept this argument, submitting that the requirements of Article 5(4) were satisfied by the procedure at the murder trial in 1964.]

33. The court recalls its judgment in *Thynne, Wilson and Gunnell v. United Kingdom* where it held that discretionary life prisoners were entitled under Article 5(4) to take proceedings to have the lawfulness of their continued detention decided by a court at reasonable intervals and to have the lawfulness of any re-detention determined by a court. This view was taken because of the very nature of the discretionary life sentence which, unlike the mandatory sentence, was imposed not because of the inherent gravity of the offence but because of the presence of factors which were susceptible to change with the passage of time, namely mental instability and dangerousness. A clear distinction was drawn between the discretionary life sentence which was considered to have a protective purpose and a mandatory life sentence which was viewed as essentially punitive in nature.

34. The applicant is now asking the Court to reconsider its characterisation of the mandatory sentence in *Thynne, Wilson and Gunnell* on the grounds *inter alia* that recent English judicial pronouncements have tended to assimilate both types of life sentence.

35. The Court notes judicial comments to the effect that the theory and practice of the mandatory sentence are out of tune and that, for purposes of procedures designed to consider the release of the mandatory prisoner as well as the standards of fairness applicable to such procedures, the mandatory sentence should also be seen as containing both a punitive and a preventive element.

However, the fact remains that the mandatory sentence belongs to a different category from the discretionary sentence in the sense that it is imposed automatically as the punishment for the offence of murder irrespective of considerations pertaining to the dangerousness of the offender. That mandatory life prisoners do not actually spend the rest of their lives in prison and that a notional tariff period is also established in such cases—facts of which the Court was fully aware in *Thynne, Wilson and Gunnell*—does not alter this essential distinction between the two types of life sentence.

As observed by the House of Lords in *R. v. Secretary of State, ex parte Doody,*[35] while the two types of life sentence may now be converging there remains nonetheless, on the statutory framework, the underlying theory and the current practice, a substantial gap between them. This is borne out by the very facts *inter alia* relied on by the applicant to support his case, namely that in mandatory life sentences the release of the prisoner is entirely a matter within the discretion of the Secretary of State who is not bound by the judicial recommendation as to the length of the tariff period and who is free under English law to have regard to other criteria than

---

[35] [1994] 1 A.C. 531.

dangerousness, following the expiry of the 'tariff' period, in deciding whether the prisoner should be released. . . .

36. Against the above background, the Court sees no cogent reasons to depart from the finding in the *Thynne, Wilson and Gunnell* case that, as regards mandatory life sentences, the guarantee of Article 5(4) was satisfied by the original trial and appeal proceedings and confers no additional right to challenge the lawfulness of continuing detention or re-detention following revocation of the life licence. . . . Accordingly, in the circumstances of the present case, there are no new issues of lawfulness which entitle the applicant to a review of his continued detention under the original mandatory life sentence.

In *Hussain v. United Kingdom*,[36] the applicant, born in 1962, had been convicted when aged 16 of murdering his two-year-old brother and received a mandatory sentence of detention 'during Her Majesty's pleasure'. Relying on Article 5(4), he claimed that he was entitled at reasonable intervals to have the issue of his continued detention heard by a court. The issue was thus whether a juvenile's sentence 'during pleasure' for murder should be assimilated under the Convention to a mandatory sentence of life imprisonment or to a discretionary sentence. The Court unanimously held that such an indeterminate sentence could be justified only by considerations based on the need to protect the public.

These considerations, centred on an assessment of the young offender's character and mental state and of his or her resulting dangerousness to society, must of necessity take into account any developments in the young offender's personality and attitude as he or she grows older. A failure to have regard to the changes that inevitably occur with maturation would mean that young persons detained ['during pleasure'] . . . would be treated as having forfeited their liberty for the rest of their lives, a situation which . . . might give rise to questions under Article 3 of the Convention.[37]

Since new issues of lawfulness might arise in the course of detention, Article 5(4) entitled Hussain to have those issues decided by a court at reasonable intervals. Moreover, Article 5(4) 'required an oral hearing in the context of an adversarial procedure involving legal representation and the possibility of calling and questioning witnesses.'[38] The same principles were applied by the Court in the much-publicised case of two English juveniles convicted of murdering a two-year-old boy.[39]

The American courts have held that the trial preceding a criminal conviction provides that due process which is constitutionally required to deprive a person of ordinary liberty. Upon conviction, the imprisoned persons may usually be regulated and confined as directed by correctional authorities without providing any particular procedures. Thus, prisoners may be transferred to less favourable conditions of

[36] 21 Feb. 1996, Report, 1996–I 252, 22 E.H.R.R. 1.

[37] *Id.* at para. 53.

[38] *Id.* at para. 60.

[39] *T and V v. United Kingdom*, 16 Dec. 1999 (not yet reported), when (*inter alia*) the Court held unanimously that Art. 5(4) had been breached because English law did not enable decisions regarding the applicants' continuing detention to be taken by a court.

confinement,[40] or subjected to solitary confinement[41] without a prior hearing, on the theory that such changes are all within the ordinary limits of the original sentence. The Supreme Court has also held, however, that even persons properly convicted and confined retain certain liberty interests and certain kinds of treatment which could not reasonably have been contemplated at the time of sentencing may invade those interests. Thus, the state may not transfer a prisoner to a mental hospital or administer anti-psychotic drugs without providing a means in which the legality of those actions could be contested.[42] The Supreme Court has also held that the state may, by its own practices and regulations, create expectations as to the way it will deal with convicted persons so as to give rise to constitutionally protected liberty interests. At one time it determined the existence of such state-created interests by a close analysis of the language of any relevant regulations. More recently, it has held that the proper inquiry is whether or not the changes in the conditions of confinement complained of impose 'atypical and significant hardship on the inmate in relation to the ordinary incidents of prison life.'[43]

The due process clauses have also been interpreted to prohibit the state from continuing the detention of a person properly detained for one purpose when it is conceded that that purpose is no longer served. To the extent the state wishes to justify confinement on some other basis, it is obliged to provide fair procedures for testing the new factual and legal predicates of such an action. Thus, the Supreme Court has stated that a person serving a sentence after conviction may not be detained beyond the time of his sentence on the grounds of mental illness and dangerousness without affording that person the same procedural protections required for civil commitments in general.[44] Along the same lines, in *Foucha v. Louisiana*,[45] a defendant had been committed to a state mental hospital after a verdict of not guilty by reason of insanity. State law provided that he should remain confined, even after he was no longer suffering from a mental illness, until he could show that he was no longer dangerous to himself or others. The Supreme Court held such detention unconstitutional.

It does not follow merely because a person is sentenced to an indeterminate term, that the absence of periodic judicial review violates a right to have the legality of a

---

[40] *Meachum v. Fano*, 427 U.S. 215 (1976). *See also Olim v. Wakinekona*, 461 U.S. 238 (1983) (transfer from Hawaii to California).

[41] *Hewitt v. Helms*, 459 U.S. 460 (1983).

[42] *See Vitek v. Jones*, 445 U.S. 480 (1980); *Washington v. Harper*, 494 U.S. 210 (1990).

[43] *Sandin v. Connor*, 515 U.S. 472, 484 (1995). Illustrations of the Court's jurisprudence on the point include *Morrisey v. Brewer*, 408 U.S. 471 (1972) (parole); *Gagnon v. Scarpelli*, 411 U.S. 778 (1973) (probation); *Wolff v. McDonnell*, 418 U.S. 539 (1974) (good time credit); *Young v. Harper*, 520 U.S. 143 (1997) (pre-parole programme). The Court has held that the initial decision to grant parole must also employ a fair procedure where the state has sufficiently precisely defined the factors of eligibility. *See Greenholz v. Inmates*, 442 U.S. 1 (1979). On the other hand, no particular procedure need be associated with a governor's decision to grant or withhold a pardon or commutation of sentence. *Connecticut Board of Pardons v. Dumschat*, 452 U.S. 458 (1981); *Ohio Adult Parole Authority v. Woodward*, 523 U.S. 272 (1998).

[44] *See Jackson v. Indiana*, 406 U.S. 715, 724–30 (1972) discussing *Baxstrom v. Herald*, 383 U.S. 107 (1966). The standards and procedures for civil commitment under American constitutional law are discussed at section (D)(3) *infra*.

[45] 504 U.S. 71 (1992).

deprivation of liberty determined. The question, as stated by the European Court in the *Thynne, Wilson* and *Gunnell* case (and illustrated by the *Foucha* case) is whether, at some point, there occurs 'a period of detention in which new issues affecting [its] lawfulness might arise'.[46] Where, however, the reasons for the indefinite sentence were fully determined at the original trial, the 'requisite judicial control [may have been] incorporated in the original conviction'.[47] Reasoning like this underlay the judgment of the Supreme Court of Canada in upholding indeterminate sentences for 'dangerous offenders' in *R. v. Lyons*.[48] According to the reasons for judgment of Justice LaForest in which a majority joined, the defendant, in such a case:

is clearly being sentenced for the 'serious personal injury offence' he or she may have been found guilty of committing albeit in a different way than ordinarily would be done . . . Thus the appellant's contention that he is being punished for what he might do rather than for what he has done . . . must be rejected. The punishment, as I noted, flows from the actual commission of a specific crime, the requisite elements of which have been proved beyond a reasonable doubt.[49]

Moreover, Justice LaForest stated that it was appropriate for the trial court, in deciding the appropriateness of such a sentence in the first instance to consider not only the gravity of the offence but the potential risk to the public in the future.[50] The sentence, therefore, was not arbitrary and violated neither Section 7 nor Section 9 of the Charter. The sufficiency of the original determination was made clear by the Court's decision in *R. v. Milne* decided the same day as *Lyons*. In that case, the defendant had been declared a dangerous offender and given an indeterminate sentence after conviction of a crime which was subsequently deleted from the list of offences in the dangerous offender statute. This later legislative judgment that the offence did not provide a predicate for a finding of dangerousness did not affect the constitutionality of the original sentence.[51]

D. DETENTION OF MENTAL PATIENTS

The principles which were applied in *Van Droogenbroeck, Weeks, Thynne, Wilson and Gunnell* and *Hussain* are also relevant to the treatment of mentally disordered persons, who are vulnerable to the risk of being deprived of their liberty over lengthy periods.

---

[46] 25 Oct. 1990 (No. 190), 13 E.H.R.R. 666, para. 68 quoting *DeWilde, Ooms and Versyp v. Belgium*, 18 June 1971 (No. 12), 1 E.H.R.R. 373.

[47] *Id.*.

[48] [1987] 2 S.C.R. 309.

[49] *Id.* at 328.

[50] *Id.*

[51] [1987] 2 S.C.R. 512. The judgments of the Supreme Court of Canada as to the compatibility of indeterminate sentences with the Charter's prohibition of cruel or unusual punishment are discussed in Chapter 4, *supra*.

1. WINTERWERP *v.* THE NETHERLANDS

Judgment of 24 Oct. 1979
(No. 33), 2 E.H.R.R. 387

[Article 5(1)(e) permits the lawful detention of persons of unsound mind. Mr. Winterwerp had been compulsorily detained for a considerable period between 1968 and 1978, originally on his wife's application, under the Mentally Ill Persons Act of 1884. The Act regulated in detail the procedures for detention and the periods for which detention could be authorized. Among the arguments advanced by Mr. Winterwerp before the Court were that he was not a person of unsound mind, that he had been confined solely by administrative action, and that his detention from year to year had been renewed by proceedings in which he played no part.]

A. 'The lawful detention of persons of unsound mind'

36. Mr. Winterwerp maintains in the first place that his deprivation of liberty did not meet the requirements embodied in the words 'lawful detention of persons of unsound mind'. Neither the Government nor the Commission agrees with this contention.

37. The Convention does not state what is to be understood by the words 'persons of unsound mind'. This term is . . . a term whose meaning is continually evolving as research in psychiatry progresses, an increasing flexibility in treatment is developing and society's attitudes to mental illness change, in particular so that a greater understanding of the problems of mental patients is becoming more widespread.

In any event, sub-paragraph (e) of Article 5(1) obviously cannot be taken as permitting the detention of a person simply because his views or behaviour deviate from the norms prevailing in a particular society. To hold otherwise would not be reconcilable with the text of Article 5(1), which sets out an exhaustive list[52] of exceptions calling for a narrow interpretation.[53] Neither would it be in conformity with the object and purpose of Article 5(1), namely, to ensure that no one should be dispossessed of his liberty in an arbitrary fashion.[54] Moreover, it would disregard the importance of the right to liberty in a democratic society.[55]

[The Court examined the provisions of the Mentally Ill Persons Act governing detention, found that in practice only a person whose mental disorder was of such a kind or of such gravity as to be an actual danger to himself or to others was liable to be detained, and concluded that the detention of such a person under the Act 'in principle falls within the ambit of Article 5(1)(e)'.]

39. The next issue to be examined is the 'lawfulness' of the detention for the purposes of Article 5(1)(e). Such 'lawfulness' presupposes conformity with the domestic law in the first place and also, as confirmed by Article 18, conformity with the purpose of the restrictions permitted by

---

[52] See *Engel v. The Netherlands*, 8 June 1976 (No. 22), 1 E.H.R.R. 647, para. 57 reprinted at section (B)(2) *supra* and *Ireland v. United Kingdom*, 18 Jan. 1978 (No. 25), 2 E.H.R.R. 25, para. 194.

[53] See, *mutatis mutandis, Klass v. Germany*, 6 Sept. 1978 (No. 28), 2 E.H.R.R. 214, para. 42 and *The Sunday Times v. United Kingdom*, 26 Apr. 1979 (No. 30), 2 E.H.R.R. 245, para. 65.

[54] See *Lawless v. Ireland (No. 3)*, 1 July 1961, 1 E.H.R.R. 15, 27–8 reprinted at section (H)(1) *infra* and *Engle v. The Netherlands, supra* n. 52, para. 58.

[55] See *De Wilde, Ooms and Versyp v. Belgium*, 18 June 1971 (No. 12), 1 E.H.R.R. 373, para. 65, and *Engel v. The Netherlands, supra* n. 52, para. 82.

Article 5(1)(e); it is required in respect of both the ordering and the execution of the measures involving deprivation of liberty. . . .

As regards the conformity with the domestic law, the Court points out that the term 'lawful' covers procedural as well as substantive rules. There thus exists a certain overlapping between this term and the general requirement stated at the beginning of Article 5(1), namely, observance of 'a procedure prescribed by law' (see para. 45 below).

Indeed, these two expressions reflect the importance of the aim underlying Article 5(1) (see para. 37 above): in a democratic society subscribing to the rule of law, no detention that is arbitrary can ever be regarded as 'lawful'.

The Commission likewise stresses that there must be no element of arbitrariness; the conclusion it draws is that no one may be confined as 'a person of unsound mind' in the absence of medical evidence establishing that his mental state is such as to justify his compulsory hospitalization . . .

The Court fully agrees with this line of reasoning. In the Court's opinion, except in emergency cases, the individual concerned should not be deprived of his liberty unless he has been reliably shown to be of 'unsound mind'. The very nature of what has to be established before the competent national authority—that is, a true mental disorder—calls for objective medical expertise. Further, the mental disorder must be of a kind or degree warranting compulsory confinement. What is more, the validity of continued confinement depends upon the persistence of such a disorder.[56]

40. The Court undoubtedly has the jurisdiction to verify the 'lawfulness' of the detention. Mr. Winterwerp in fact alleges unlawfulness by reason of procedural defects in the making of three of the detention orders under consideration. Those allegations are dealt with below in connection with the closely linked issue of compliance with 'a procedure prescribed by law' . . . In the present context, it suffices to add the following: in deciding whether an individual should be detained as a 'person of unsound mind', the national authorities are to be recognized as having a certain discretion, since it is in the first place for the national authorities to evaluate the evidence adduced before them in a particular case; the Court's task is to review under the Convention the decisions of those authorities.[57]

41. As to the facts of the instant case, the medical evidence submitted to the courts indicated in substance that the applicant showed schizophrenic and paranoiac reactions, that he was unaware of his pathological condition and that, on several occasions, he had committed some fairly serious acts without appreciating their consequences. In addition, various attempts at his gradual rehabilitation into society have failed. . . .

42. Mr. Winterwerp criticises the medical reports as unsatisfactory for the purposes of Article 5(1)(e). In addition, he queries whether the burgomaster's initial direction to detain was founded on psychiatric evidence.

In the Court's view, the events that prompted the burgomaster's direction in May 1968 . . . are of a nature to justify an 'emergency' confinement of the kind provided for at that time under section 14 of the Netherlands Act. While some hesitation may be felt as to the need for such confinement to continue for as long as six weeks, the period is not so excessive as to render the detention 'unlawful'. Despite the applicant's criticisms, the Court has no reason whatsoever to

---

[56] *See, mutatis mutandis, Stögmüller v. Austria,* 10 Nov. 1969 (No. 9), 1 E.H.R.R. 155, para. 4, and *De Wilde, Ooms and Versyp v. Belgium, supra* n. 55 para. 82.

[57] *See* notably, *mutatis mutandis, Handyside v. United Kingdom,* 7 Dec. 1976 (No. 24), 1 E.H.R.R. 737, paras. 48 and 50; *Klass v. Germany, supra* n. 53, para. 49 and *The Sunday Times v. United Kingdom* (1979), *supra* n. 53, para. 59.

doubt the objectivity and reliability of the medical evidence on the basis of which the Netherlands courts from June 1968 onwards, have authorised his detention as a person of unsound mind. Neither is there any indication that the contested deprivation of liberty was effected for a wrongful purpose.

43. The Court accordingly concludes that Mr. Winterwerp's confinement, during all the various phases under consideration, constituted 'the lawful detention of [a person] of unsound mind' within the meaning of sub-paragraph (e) of Article 5(1).

B. 'In accordance with a procedure prescribed by law'

44. The applicant maintains that his deprivation of liberty was not carried out 'in accordance with a procedure prescribed by law'. For the applicant, this expression implies respect for certain elementary principles of legal procedure, such as informing and hearing the person concerned and affording him some kind of participation and legal assistance in the proceedings. In his submission, these principles have not been observed in his case.

The Government reply that the relevant procedure under Netherlands law, in ensuring regular review by an independent judge who bases his decision on medical declarations, undoubtedly meets such requirements as may be made in this respect by Article 5(1). . . .

45. The Court for its part considers that the words 'in accordance with a procedure prescribed by law' essentially refer back to domestic law; they state the need for compliance with the relevant procedure under that law.

However, the domestic law must itself be in conformity with the Convention, including the general principles expressed or implied therein. The notion underlying the term in question is one of fair and proper procedure, namely, that any measure depriving a person of his liberty should issue from and be executed by an appropriate authority and should not be arbitrary. The Netherlands Mentally Ill Persons Act . . . satisfies this condition.

46. Whether the procedure prescribed by that Act was in fact respected in the applicant's case is a question that the Court has jurisdiction to examine. Whilst it is not normally the Court's task to review the observance of domestic law by the national authorities, it is otherwise in relation to matters where, as here, the Convention refers directly back to that law; for, in such matters, disregard of the domestic law entails breach of the Convention, with the consequence that the Court can and should exercise a certain power of review.

However, the logic of the system of safeguard established by the Convention sets limits upon the scope of this review. It is in the first place for the national authorities, notably the courts, to interpret and apply the domestic law, even in those fields where the Convention 'incorporates' the rules of that law: the national authorities are, in the nature of things, particularly qualified to settle the issues arising in this connection.

> [The Court then considered and rejected two allegations of procedural defects made by Mr. Winterwerp. Having found that Article 5(1) had not been violated, the Court considered whether the Dutch legislation satisfied the individual's right under Article 5(4) to take proceedings before a court for a speedy decision as to the lawfulness of his detention. The main issue under Article 5(4) was whether the Dutch courts had been obliged to give Mr. Winterwerp a hearing.]

The judicial proceedings referred to in Article 5(4) need not, it is true, always be attended by the same guarantees as those required under Article 6(1) for civil or criminal litigation. Nonetheless, it is essential that the person concerned should have access to a court and the opportunity to be heard either in person or, where necessary, through some form of representation, failing which he will not have been afforded 'the fundamental guarantees of procedure applied in matters of deprivation of liberty'.[58] Mental illness may entail restricting or modifying the manner of exercise of such a right, but it cannot justify impairing the very essence of the right. Indeed, special procedural safeguards may prove called for in order to protect the interests of persons who, on account of their mental disabilities, are not fully capable of acting for themselves.

61. Under . . . the Mentally Ill Persons Act, . . . neither the District Court nor the Regional Court was obliged to hear the individual whose detention was being sought. . . .

As to the particular facts, the applicant was never associated, either personally or through a representative, in the proceedings leading to the various detention orders made against him: he was never notified of the proceedings or of their outcome; neither was he heard by the courts or given the opportunity to argue his case.

[Accordingly Article 5(4) had been breached. The Court further found that Article 6(1) had been breached, since the Dutch court's decision to divest the applicant of the capacity to deal with his property (in which decision neither he nor a representative had any opportunity to take part) was a 'determination of his civil rights and obligations' (see Chapter 8 below).]

2. X v. UNITED KINGDOM

Judgment of 24 Oct. 1981
(No. 46), 4 E.H.R.R. 188

[Under English law, certain convicted criminals may be treated as mental patients and kept in custody in a secure hospital rather than be sent to prison. X was in 1968 convicted of wounding with intent to cause grievous bodily harm and because of his mental condition was sent to such a hospital. In 1971 the Home Secretary approved his conditional discharge and X returned to live with his wife at home and got a job. In 1974, his wife complained to a probation officer of X's conduct; he was arrested and taken back to the same hospital. Two years later, he was again released. His claim, similar to those made in *Van Droogenbroeck* and *Weeks*, was that the decision to recall him to hospital was an administrative one and subject to no judicial safeguards.]

40. In its *Winterwerp* judgment, the Court stated three minimum conditions which have to be satisfied in order for there to be 'the lawful detention of a person of unsound mind' within the meaning of Article 5(1)(e): except in emergency cases, the individual concerned must be reliably shown to be of unsound mind, that is to say, a true mental disorder must be established before a competent authority on the basis of objective medical expertise; the mental disorder must be of a kind or degree warranting compulsory confinement; and the validity of continued confinement depends upon the persistence of such a disorder.

41. The applicant's counsel argued that the recall procedures established under section 66 of the [Mental Health Act 1959], since they do not lay down any minimum conditions comparable to those stated in the *Winterwerp* judgment, and in particular the need for objective medical

---

[58] *De Wilde, Ooms and Versyp v. Belgium, supra.* n. 55, para. 76.

evidence, were incompatible with Article 5(1)(e). The unfettered discretion vested in the Home Secretary meant, so it was submitted, that any recall decision, even one taken in good faith, must by its very nature be arbitrary.

Section 66(3) is, it is true, framed in very wide terms; the Home Secretary may at any time recall to hospital a 'restricted patient' who has been conditionally discharged. Nevertheless, it is apparent from other sections in the Act that the Home Secretary's discretionary power under section 66(3) is not unlimited. Section 147(1) defines a 'patient' as 'a person suffering or appearing to be suffering from mental disorder' and section 4(1) defines 'mental disorder' as 'mental illness, arrested or incomplete development of mind, psychopathic disorder, and any other disorder or disability of mind'. According to the Government, it is implicit in section 66(3) that unless the Home Secretary on the medical evidence available to him decides that the candidate for recall falls within this statutory definition, no power of recall can arise.

Certainly, the domestic law itself must be in conformity with the Convention, including the general principles expressed or implied therein. However, section 66(3), it should not be forgotten, is concerned with the recall, perhaps in circumstances when some danger is apprehended, of patients whose discharge from hospital has been restricted for the protection of the public. The *Winterwerp* judgment expressly identified 'emergency cases' as constituting an exception to the principle that the individual concerned should not be deprived of his liberty 'unless he has been reliably shown to be of "unsound mind"'; neither can it be inferred from the *Winterwerp* judgment that the 'objective medical expertise' must in all conceivable cases be obtained before rather than after confinement of a person on the ground of unsoundness of mind. . . . A wide discretion must in the nature of things be enjoyed by the national authority empowered to order such emergency confinements. . . .

42. It is not disputed that the applicant's deprivation of liberty was effected 'in accordance with a procedure prescribed by law' and that throughout it was 'lawful' in the sense of being in conformity with the relevant domestic law. However, it was submitted on behalf of the applicant that his deprivation of liberty was arbitrary and unlawful, and thus not justified under Article 5(1)(e), because he had not been 'reliably' shown to be of unsound mind by objective medical evidence existing at the time of his recall.

43. The object and purpose of Article 5(1) is precisely to ensure that no one should be deprived of his liberty in an arbitrary fashion; consequently, quite apart from conformity with domestic law, 'no detention that is arbitrary can ever be regarded as "lawful"'.[59] Three minimum conditions required for 'the lawful detention of a person of unsound mind' are set out above (at para. 40). Whilst the Court undoubtedly has the jurisdiction to verify the fulfilment of these conditions in a given case, the logic of the system of safeguard established by the Convention places limits on the scope of this control; since the national authorities are better placed to evaluate the evidence adduced before them, they are to be recognized as having a certain discretion in the matter and the Court's task is limited to reviewing under the Convention the decisions they have taken.[60]

44. The applicant was a man with a history of psychiatric troubles. He was first committed to Broadmoor Hospital after his conviction for an offence involving a violent attack on a workmate. His discharge was made conditional upon, *inter alia*, his being subject to medical supervision at a psychiatric outpatients' clinic. The consultant psychiatrist who treated him during the period of his

---

[59] *See Winterwerp v. The Netherlands, supra* n. 55, paras. 37, 39.

[60] *See id.*, paras. 40, 46.

conditional discharge considered him to be 'a querulous suspicious person liable to paranoid ideation [who] inevitably presents a risk to the community'; in a letter written in 1971 to the Sheffield probation service, the consultant psychiatrist spoke of the need to 'steer [X] clear of depressed situations which could lead to murder or serious bodily harm to other people'. Lastly, X's wife visited the probation officer and told him that, contrary to what she had stated earlier, her husband remained deluded and threatening.

... On being informed of the wife's complaints, the responsible medical officer at Broadmoor, who had copies of the psychiatric reports prepared concerning the applicant during the period of his conditional release, became alarmed at the possibility of a recurrence of violent behaviour by the applicant, especially if he came to know of his wife's intention to leave him. The responsible medical officer therefore referred the matter to the Home Office and, acting on the doctor's advice, the Home Secretary issued a warrant in pursuance of which the applicant was recalled to hospital the same day, without prior medical examination or verification of the wife's allegations. ...

45. Regard must also be had to the overall system under the 1959 Act governing the discharge and recall of restricted patients. Under section 65(1), a court may direct that a hospital order against an offender be made subject to restrictions in respect of discharge only where it appears necessary for the protection of the public ... When the Home Secretary, pursuant to section 66(2), discharges a patient from hospital while a restriction order is in force ... he is thus suspending a measure taken to protect the public. As was stated by one of the Divisional Court judges at the hearing on 21 June 1974 in the habeas corpus proceedings brought by X, very often the only way patients of this kind can be allowed back into the community is by releasing them on licence, with very careful supervision and an immediate reaction in the event of a sign of new danger. ...

In such circumstances, the interests of the protection of the public prevail over the individual's right to liberty to the extent of justifying an emergency confinement in the absence of the usual guarantees implied in Article 5(1)(e) ... On the facts of the present case, there was sufficient reason for the Home Secretary to have considered that the applicant's continued liberty constituted a danger to the public, and in particular to his wife.

46. While these considerations were enough to justify X's recall as an emergency measure and for a short duration, his further detention in hospital until February 1976 must, for its part, satisfy the minimum conditions described above (at para. 40). These conditions were satisfied in the case of X. ...

47. In conclusion, there was no breach of Article 5(1).

[The Court proceeded to consider whether there had been a breach of X's rights under Article 5(4). Having first held, in accordance with precedent, that a person of unsound mind was entitled in principle to take proceedings at reasonable intervals to review the lawfulness of his detention, the Court considered whether this right had been satisfied by habeas corpus proceedings which X had taken—unsuccessfully—in the English High Court. Referring to those proceedings, the Court said:]

56. ... The case was considered by the Divisional Court on the basis of affidavits, including one by the applicant. Such medical evidence as there was before the Divisional Court ... was obtained by X's solicitors. The Home Secretary was himself under no obligation to produce material justification for X's detention.

All this, however, followed from the nature of the remedy provided. In habeas corpus proceedings, in examining an administrative decision to detain, the court's task is to enquire whether the detention is in compliance with the requirements stated in the relevant legislation and with the applicable principles of the common law. According to these principles, such a decision (even though technically legal on its face) may be upset, *inter alia*, if the detaining authority misused its powers by acting in bad faith or capriciously or for a wrongful purpose, or if the decision is supported by no sufficient evidence or is one which no reasonable person could have reached in the circumstances. Subject to the foregoing, the court will not be able to review the grounds or merits of a decision taken by an administrative authority to the extent that under the legislation in question these are exclusively a matter for determination by that authority. . . .

In the present case, once it was established that X was a patient who had been conditionally discharged whilst still subject to a restriction order, the statutory requirements for recall by warrant under section 66(3) of the 1959 Act were satisfied . . . This being so, it was then effectively up to X to show, within the limits permitted by English law, some reason why the apparently legal detention was unlawful. The evidence adduced by X did not disclose any such reason and the Divisional Court had no option but to dismiss the application. . . .

58. Notwithstanding the limited nature of the review possible in relation to decisions taken under section 66(3) of the 1959 Act, the remedy of habeas corpus can on occasions constitute an effective check against arbitrariness in this sphere. It may be regarded as adequate, for the purposes of Article 5(4), for emergency measures for the detention of persons on the ground of unsoundness of mind. . . .

On the other hand, in the Court's opinion, a judicial review as limited as that available in the habeas corpus procedure in the present case is not sufficient for a continuing confinement such as the one undergone by X. Article 5(4), the Government are quite correct to affirm, does not embody a right to judicial control of such scope as to empower the court, on all aspects of the case, to substitute its own discretion for that of the decision-making authority. The review should, however, be wide enough to bear on those conditions which, according to the Convention, are essential for the 'lawful' detention of a person on the ground of unsoundness of mind, especially as the reasons capable of initially justifying such a detention may cease to exist . . . This means that in the instant case Article 5(4) required an appropriate procedure allowing a court to examine whether the patient's disorder still persisted and whether the Home Secretary was entitled to think that a continuation of the compulsory confinement was necessary in the interests of public safety.

59. The habeas corpus proceedings brought by X in 1974 did not therefore secure him the enjoyment of the right guaranteed by Article 5(4); this would also have been the case had he made any fresh application at a later date. . . .

The Court examined other procedures available to X and decided that certain bodies known as mental health review tribunals, created by the Mental Health Act 1959, were not judicial bodies for the purposes of article 5(4) since they had advisory functions only. In consequence of the decision in *X's Case*, the British legislation was amended to give to a review tribunal power in such cases to release the detained patient from custody (see now Part V of the Mental Health Act 1983).

3. JOHNSON *V.* UNITED KINGDOM

Judgment of 24 October 1997, Reports, 1997–VII 2391,
27 E.H.R.R. 296

[The applicant had been charged with a criminal assault in 1984, was found to be suffering from mental illness and was detained in a secure state hospital. In June 1989, a mental health review tribunal found that he was no longer suffering from mental illness. Although this finding was confirmed by three successive tribunals, the applicant was not released from the hospital until January 1993. The reason for the delayed release was that the tribunals took the view that he was not immediately ready to lead an independent life and that his release should be conditional upon residence for the purpose of rehabilitation in an approved hostel under psychiatric and social worker supervision. No place for him at such a hostel could be found.]

51. Johnson in his primary submission maintained that the June 1989 Tribunal should have ordered his immediate and unconditional discharge. Having regard to the strength of the psychiatric evidence before it and to its own assessment of his condition, that Tribunal was satisfied that he was no longer suffering from mental illness . . . Relying on the Court's *Winterwerp v. The Netherlands* judgment of 24 October 1979[61] he asserted that the authorities could not invoke any margin of appreciation to justify his continued detention beyond 15 June 1989 leaving aside any short period of time which might be needed to implement arrangements for his discharge. . . . The Tribunal had not been justified in denying him an immediate and unconditional discharge on account of a possible risk of recurrence of mental illness given that any such risk had been neutralised by reason of the treatment he had received in Rampton Hospital.

52. While acknowledging by way of an alternative submission that the discharge of a person who is found to be no longer of unsound mind may be made subject to conditions, the applicant contended that any such conditions must not hinder immediate or near immediate release and certainly not delay it excessively as occurred in his case. The imposition of the hostel residence condition was not only an onerous, unnecessary and disproportionate requirement which could in itself be considered to be a breach of Article 5(1) of the Convention if implemented, it was also causative of a delay of three years and seven months before he was eventually released. . . .

53. While disputing the lawfulness of the hostel requirement and the benefit which he would have gained from it, the applicant asserted that it was for the authorities to ensure that a placement in a hostel could be guaranteed if not immediately then within a matter of weeks, if they considered such a course of action necessary. In no event could a deferral of discharge for three and a half years pending the finding of a placement be justified. . . .

54. The Government contended that Article 5(1)(e) of the Convention should not be interpreted in a way which requires the authorities in all cases to order the immediate and unconditional release of a patient who is no longer suffering from mental illness. Such an approach in the instant case would have prevented the 1989 Tribunal from assessing whether or not the applicant's own interests and those of the community would be best served by ordering his immediate and unconditional release because of his apparent recovery. The Tribunal needed to

---

[61] See Section D(1) *supra*.

have sufficient flexibility or discretion to assess those twin interests having regard to the applicant's previous history of unprovoked and indiscriminate violence and to the unpredictable nature of mental illness especially where, as in the applicant's case, it manifested itself in violent behaviour. . . .

56. The Government maintained that the authorities had made considerable efforts to secure a suitable hostel, . . . but the applicant's intransigence and lack of co-operation, especially after October 1990, did not facilitate their task. . . .

In view of the applicant's case history particular care was required in finding him an appropriate hostel. Given that he had still not complied with the hostel requirement, the 1990 and 1991 Tribunals were justified in continuing to defer his discharge. . . .

[The Court examined the detention after 15 July 1989 under Article 5(1)(e) alone, and without regard to Article 5(1)(a), since the applicant was detained on the basis of an order under the Mental Health Act 1989 made without limit in time to undergo psychiatric treatment. It was not contested by the applicant that the continued detention was lawful in domestic law, in view of the tribunal's statutory power to impose conditions on the discharge of patients who are no longer mentally ill and to delay discharge until the conditions are fulfilled.]

60. The Court stresses, however, that the lawfulness of the applicant's continued detention under domestic law is not in itself decisive. It must also be established that his detention after 15 June 1989 was in conformity with the purpose of Article 5(1) of the Convention, which is to prevent persons from being deprived of their liberty in an arbitrary fashion and with the aim of the restriction contained in sub-paragraph (e). In this latter respect the Court recalls that, according to its established case law, an individual cannot be considered to be of 'unsound mind' and deprived of his liberty unless the following three minimum conditions are satisfied: first, he must reliably be shown to be of unsound mind; secondly, the mental disorder must be of a kind or degree warranting compulsory confinement; thirdly, and of sole relevance to the case at issue, the validity of continued confinement depends upon the persistence of such a disorder.[62]

61. By maintaining that the 1989 Tribunal was satisfied that he was no longer suffering from the mental illness which led to his committal to Rampton Hospital, Johnson is arguing that the abovementioned third condition as to the persistence of mental disorder was not fulfilled and he should as a consequence have been immediately and unconditionally released from detention.

The Court cannot accept that submission. In its view it does not automatically follow from a finding by an expert authority that the mental disorder which justified a patient's compulsory confinement no longer persists, that the latter must be immediately and unconditionally released.

Such a rigid approach to the interpretation of that condition would place an unacceptable degree of constraint on the responsible authority's exercise of judgment to determine in particular cases and on the basis of all the relevant circumstances whether the interests of the patient and the community into which he is to be released would in fact be best served by this course of action. It must also be observed that in the field of mental illness the assessment as to whether the disappearance of the symptoms of the illness is confirmation of complete recovery is not an exact science. Whether or not recovery from an episode of mental illness which justified a patient's confinement is complete and definitive or merely apparent cannot in all cases be measured with

---

[62] See *Winterwerp v. The Netherlands*, 24 Oct. 1979, (No. 33), 2 E.H.R.R. 387 reprinted at section (D)(1) *supra*, para. 40, and *Luberti v. Italy*, 23 Feb. 1984 (No. 75A), 6 E.H.R.R. 440, para. 27.

absolute certainty. It is the behaviour of the patient in the period spent outside the confines of the psychiatric institution which will be conclusive of this.

62. [The] Court in its *Luberti v. Italy* judgment accepted that the termination of the confinement of an individual who has previously been found by a court to be of unsound mind and to present a danger to society is a matter that concerns, as well as that individual, the community in which he will live if released. Having regard to the pressing nature of the interests at stake, and in particular the very serious nature of the offence committed by Luberti when mentally ill, it was accepted in that case that the responsible authority was entitled to proceed with caution and needed some time to consider whether to terminate his confinement, even if the medical evidence pointed to his recovery.

63. In the view of the Court it must also be acknowledged that a responsible authority is entitled to exercise a similar measure of discretion in deciding whether in the light of all the relevant circumstances and the interests at stake it would in fact be appropriate to order the immediate and absolute discharge of a person who is no longer suffering from the mental disorder which led to his confinement. That authority should be able to retain some measure of supervision over the progress of the person once he is released into the community and to that end make his discharge subject to conditions. . . . It is however of paramount importance that appropriate safeguards are in place so as to ensure that any deferral of discharge is consonant with the purpose of Article 5(1) . . . and, in particular, that discharge is not unreasonably delayed.

64. Having regard to the above considerations, the Court is of the opinion that the 1989 Tribunal could in the exercise of its judgment properly conclude that it was premature to order Johnson's absolute and immediate discharge from Rampton Hospital. While it was true that the Tribunal was satisfied on the basis of its own assessment and the medical evidence before it that the applicant was no longer suffering from mental illness, it nevertheless considered that a phased conditional discharge was appropriate in the circumstances. . . . As an expert review body which included a doctor who had interviewed the applicant, the Tribunal could properly have regard to the fact that as recently as 10 February 1988 the applicant was still found to be suffering from mental illness and that his disorder had manifested itself prior to his confinement in acts of spontaneous and unprovoked violence against members of the public. . . . The Tribunal was also in principle justified in deferring the applicant's release in order to enable the authorities to locate a hostel which best suited his needs and provided him with the most appropriate conditions for his successful rehabilitation.

66. However . . . the Tribunal lacked the power to guarantee that the applicant would be relocated to a suitable post-discharge hostel within a reasonable period of time. The onus was on the authorities to secure a hostel willing to admit the applicant. It is to be observed that they were expected to proceed with all reasonable expedition in finalising the arrangements for a placement. While the authorities made considerable efforts to this end these efforts were frustrated by the reluctance of certain hostels to accept the applicant as well as by the latter's negative attitude. . . . Admittedly a suitable hostel may have been located within a reasonable period of time had the applicant adopted a more positive approach to his rehabilitation. However, this cannot refute the conclusion that neither the Tribunal nor the authorities possessed the necessary powers to ensure that the condition could be implemented within a reasonable time. Furthermore, the earliest date on which the applicant could have had his continued detention reviewed was 12 months after the review conducted by the June 1989 Tribunal. . . .

67. In these circumstances it must be concluded that the imposition of the hostel residence

condition by the June 1989 Tribunal led to the indefinite deferral of the applicant's release from Rampton Hospital especially since the applicant was unwilling after October 1990 to co-operate further with the authorities in their efforts to secure a hostel. . . . While the 1990 and 1991 Tribunals considered the applicant's case afresh, they were obliged to order his continued detention since he had not yet fulfilled the terms of the conditional discharge imposed by the June 1989 Tribunal.

Having regard to the situation which resulted from the decision taken by the latter Tribunal and to the lack of adequate safeguards including provision for judicial review to ensure that the applicant's release from detention would not be unreasonably delayed, it must be considered that his continued confinement after 15 June 1989 cannot be justified on the basis of Article 5(1)(e) of the Convention.

[The Court found it unnecessary to deal with issues relating to Article 5(4). The applicant had claimed £100,000 compensation under Article 41 for his detention between June 1989 and January 1993, basing this claim on awards made by English courts in cases where an individual's detention had been unlawful. Ruling that some delay was inevitable while the search was made for a suitable hostel, and noting the applicant's refusal to co-operate in the search, the Court awarded £10,000 as compensation for non-pecuniary damage.]

Under the Fifth and Fourteenth Amendments to the United States Constitution, a person may be committed involuntarily to a mental hospital only on a showing by 'clear and convincing' evidence that that person suffers from a mental illness and is likely to be dangerous to him or herself or to others. This standard of proof requires that the state show more than a mere preponderance of the evidence, but given the inevitable 'lack of certainty and the fallibility of psychiatric diagnosis', these facts need not be proven beyond a reasonable doubt, the constitutionally required standard of proof for criminal conviction.[63] The Supreme Court has never held squarely

---

[63] *Addington v. Texas*, 441 U.S. 418, 429 (1979). *See also Heller v. Doe*, 509 U.S. 312 (1998) holding constitutional against an equal protection challenge a state law requiring a higher standard of proof for committals based on 'mental illness' than for those based on 'mental retardation'. In *Jones v. United States*, 463 U.S. 354 (1983), however, the Court held that a criminal defendant, acquitted by reason of insanity, could on that basis alone be committed even though his mental condition had been proven by a mere preponderance of the evidence. But *see Foucha v. Louisiana*, 507 U.S. 71 (1992) discussed at section C above, holding that after such a person has been found no longer to suffer from mental illness his or her release may not be conditioned on such a person affirmatively proving that he or she is no longer dangerous. In *R v. Swain* [1991] 1 S.C.R. 933, the Supreme Court of Canada held unconstitutional as improper interference with liberty under s.7 of the Charter, the Criminal Code provisions requiring every insanity acquittee to be detained without hearing at the pleasure of the Lieutenant Governor. The Court held that the safeguards of the criminal trial alone were not sufficient protection against the post-acquittal detention. In response to this decision, the Canadian Parliament introduced a new verdict of 'not criminally responsible', described by the Supreme Court as neither a conviction nor an acquittal. After such a verdict the court and, periodically, a review board would consider whether the individual should be detained, released on conditions or released absolutely (Canadian Criminal Code, s.672.54). On each occasion the court or review board is to consider the safety of the public but, in that light, it is also to make the disposition 'least onerous and least restrictive to the accused'. The Supreme Court, taking constitutional principles into account, has interpreted the statute to require an absolute discharge unless there is evidence of a 'significant threat to the safety of the public'. The hearings are not to be adversarial and 'there is never any legal burden on the [not criminally responsible] accused to show that he or she does not pose a significant threat to the safety of the public': *Winko v. British Columbia (Forensic Psychiatric Institute)* [1999] 2 S.C.R. 625, paras. 31–2, 48, 52, 62.

that persons committed civilly are entitled as a matter of constitutional law to periodic review of the propriety of their confinement.[64] Certain state courts, however, extending the logic of the holdings discussed above on the need for new hearings where the basis of detention has changed, have so held under their state constitutions.[65]

E. OTHER PERMITTED GROUNDS OF DETENTION

1. LAWFUL ARREST OR DETENTION ON REASONABLE SUSPICION OF HAVING COMMITTED AN OFFENCE

In the ordinary course of criminal justice, it frequently occurs that someone suspected of an offence is arrested and detained by the police, only to be released later when it is decided on further inquiry that there are insufficient grounds to justify his or her detention. The right to liberty under Article 5 is not infringed merely because the individual is never prosecuted for the suspected offence, or because he or she is acquitted after a trial. Ordinarily the police and other investigative authorities have a wide discretion in how they use their powers of arrest, subject to limits imposed by national law. But the arrest or detention of an individual may lead to a breach of Article 5, if for instance the arrest is unlawful by national law and no redress is obtainable by recourse to national remedies, or if the arrest although lawful by national law is nonetheless 'arbitrary' according to the jurisprudence of the Strasbourg Court.

The following cases illustrate aspects of that jurisprudence, arising from situations in which the Court has decided whether an arrest or detention was justified under Article 5(1)(c). Thus the individual must be suspected of having committed an offence in national law, and the offence must not itself be such as to impinge unduly on rights or freedoms protected under the Convention. Mere suspicion is not enough; reasonable grounds for suspicion must exist, but the police need not have evidence sufficient to use in a criminal trial to overcome the presumption of innocence under Article 6(2). The Court has summarized the relevance of reasonable suspicion to a prolonged detention in this way:

The persistence of reasonable suspicion that the person arrested has committed an offence is a condition *sine qua non* for the lawfulness of the continued detention, but after a certain lapse of

---

[64] It has suggested as much, however, in dicta. *See Parham v. J.R.* 442 U.S. 584, 617 (1979).
[65] *See Fasulo v. Arafeh*, 378 A.2d 553 (Conn. 1977); *State v. Fields*, 390 A.2d 574 (N.J. 1978).

time it no longer suffices: the Court must then establish whether the other grounds given by the judicial authorities continued to justify the deprivation of liberty.[66]

Thus even if an arrest for reasonable suspicion is justified at an early stage of a case, this does not authorize detention throughout a protracted inquiry. In such cases, Article 5(3) guarantees both the right to be brought promptly before a judge and the right to trial within a reasonable time or to release pending trial. In respect of release on bail, the Court has long applied the principle that unless the national authorities justify continued detention by reasons that in the opinion of the Court are relevant and sufficient, the detention will be in breach of Article 5(3).[67]

Although the Strasbourg Court repeatedly insists that national courts are better placed than an international court to make detailed assessments of the facts and norms that apply to an individual's detention in relation to criminal justice, the Court will intervene when it considers that a national decision is 'arbitrary' in the sense that there is no reasonable basis for it if the national law is properly understood. One instance of this is given by *Tsirlis and Kouloumpas v. Greece*,[68] where a Greek military court breached Article 5(1)(a) by sending two Jehovah's Witness ministers to prison for refusing to perform military service, having 'blatantly ignored' case law that made it clear that the applicants were ministers of a 'known religion' and thus entitled to be exempted from service in the army. Another example is provided by *Loukanov v. Bulgaria*.

A. LOUKANOV *V.* BULGARIA

Judgment of 20 March 1997, Reports, 1997–II 529,
24 E.H.R.R. 121

[Mr. Loukanov was a former Prime Minister of Bulgaria who on 9 July 1992 was arrested on suspicion of having misappropriated public funds, in that while in office he had taken part in collective decisions to provide aid by way of grants and loans to various developing countries. He was released from detention on 30 December 1992, some three months after Bulgaria had ratified the European Convention on Human Rights and recognized the compulsory jurisdiction of the Court. While the case was pending before the Court, Mr. Loukanov was shot dead; his widow and children were permitted by the Court to pursue the application on his behalf.]

37. The applicant, with whom the Commission agreed, was of the opinion that the facts which had been invoked against him at the time of his arrest and during his continued detention could not, in the eyes of an objective observer, be construed as misappropriation of funds or as a breach of official duties aimed at facilitating the commission of such an offence. Accordingly, there had been no 'reasonable suspicion of [his] having committed an offence' within the meaning of Article

---

[66] *W v. Switzerland*, 26 Jan. 1993 (No. 254), 17 E.H.R.R. 60, para. 30. See also Chapter 8, (D) *infra*.

[67] *Wemhoff v. Germany*, 27 June 1968 (No. 7), 1 E.H.R.R. 55; and *Letellier v. France*, 26 June 1991 (No. 207), 14 E.H.R.R. 83. On aspects of Art. 5(3), see section F below.

[68] 29 May 1997, Reports, 1997–III 909, 25 E.H.R.R. 198.

5(1)(c). Nor could the detention be 'reasonably considered necessary to prevent his committing an offence or fleeing after having done so' . . .

The applicant, for his part, stressed that the decisions leading to the charges against him and his being detained on remand had been taken collectively by the Government at the time and in a manner which was consistent with the relevant law, including the then Bulgarian Constitution; the allocation of the funds in question had been effected in accordance with the national budget as adopted by the National Assembly and had subsequently been approved by the latter. The measures had been in keeping not only with the policies of the Government at the time but also with relevant United Nations resolutions on development assistance. They had not benefited any members of the Government or any third parties; the funds had been received in their entirety by the addressee countries.

38. The Government maintained before the Commission that the applicant's detention had been effected on the grounds of suspicion of his having committed a crime and had been in conformity with Bulgarian law. Although it was true that the allocation of development aid had not as such constituted a criminal offence, the charges in question had been brought because the transfers of funds had, under the cover of development assistance, involved improper 'deals' causing damage to Bulgaria's economic interests. The Government were, however, not in a position to provide any details of such 'deals' as it would adversely affect the confidentiality of the criminal proceedings instituted against the applicant and eight other former Government members.

Before the Court the Government stated that they were prepared to accept the Commission's opinion that there had been a violation of Article 5(1) of the Convention, whilst at the same time informing the Court of the views of the Prosecutor General, the authority which had ordered the applicant's detention on remand. In this regard the Government pointed out that it was not within its powers to assess the measures taken in this case by the prosecution and the Supreme Court which, under the Constitution, were both independent judicial authorities.

[The Prosecutor-General observed to the Court that in Bulgarian law guilt did not depend on whether the offender had obtained an advantage for himself or for a third party and that because of the complex circumstances, the issue of criminal intent could be determined only during preliminary investigations. The decision to detain the applicant on remand had been taken in view of such factors as who he was, the gravity of the offences, his opportunities of absconding and the fact that he had appealed against the withdrawal of his passport, which according to the Bulgarian Supreme Court had justified the suspicion that he might commit further offences.]

40. The Court observes at the outset that it has jurisdiction to examine the facts and circumstances of the applicant's complaints in so far as they related to the period after 7 September 1992, when Bulgaria ratified the Convention and recognised the Court's compulsory jurisdiction. In doing so, it will take into account the state of the proceedings as of that date,[69] in particular the fact that the grounds for his detention, stated in the detention order of 9 July and the Supreme Court judgment of 13 July upholding the order, remained the same until his release on 30 December 1992. . . .

As to the observations made by the Government concerning the independence of the authorities which had taken the measures giving rise to the applicant's Convention complaints, it should be

[69] See, for instance *Benham v. United Kingdom* 10 June 1996, Reports, 1996–II 738, 22 E.H.R.R. 293, para. 40; reprinted at section (E)(2)(a) *infra*.

emphasised that the Governments are answerable under the Convention for the acts of such authorities as they are for those of any other State agency. In all cases before the Court, what is in issue is the international responsibility of the State.

41. ... The Court is of the view that the central issue in the case under consideration is whether the applicant's detention from 7 September to 30 December 1992 was 'lawful' within the meaning of Article 5(1), including whether it was effected 'in accordance with a procedure prescribed by law'. The Court reiterates that the Convention here refers essentially to national law, but it also requires that any measure depriving the individual of his liberty must be compatible with the purpose of Article 5, namely to protect the individual from arbitrariness.

Where the Convention refers directly back to domestic law, as in Article 5, compliance with such law is an integral part of the obligations of the Contracting States and the Court is accordingly competent to satisfy itself of such compliance where relevant; the scope of its task in this connection, however, is subject to limits inherent in the logic of the European system of protection, since it is in the first place for the national authorities, notably the courts, to interpret and apply domestic law.[70]

42. Turning to the particular circumstances of the case, . . . it is undisputed that the applicant had, as a member of the Bulgarian Government, taken part in the decisions—granting funds in assistance and loans to certain developing countries—which had given rise to the charges against him.

43. However, none of the provisions of the Criminal Code relied on to justify the detention . . . specified or even implied that anyone could incur criminal liability by taking part in collective decisions of this nature. Moreover, no evidence has been adduced to show that such decisions were unlawful, that is to say contrary to Bulgaria's constitution or legislation, or more specifically that the decisions were taken in excess of powers or were contrary to the law on the national budget.

In the light of the above, the Court is not persuaded that the conduct for which the applicant was prosecuted constituted a criminal offence under Bulgarian law at the relevant time.

44. What is more, the Public Prosecutor's order of detention of 9 July 1992 and the Supreme Court's decision of 13 July upholding the order, referred to Articles 201 to 203 of the Criminal Code. As appears from the case law supplied to the Court, a constituent element of the offence of misappropriation under Articles 201 to 203 of the Criminal Code was that the offender had sought to obtain for himself or herself or for a third party an advantage. . . .

However, the Court has not been provided with any fact or information capable of showing that the applicant was at the time reasonably suspected of having sought to obtain for himself or a third party an advantage from his participation in the allocation of funds in question.[71] . . . Indeed, it was not contended before the Convention institutions that the funds had not been received by the States concerned.

45. In these circumstances, the Court does not find that the deprivation of the applicant's liberty during the period under consideration was 'lawful detention' effected 'on reasonable suspicion of [his] having committed an offence'.

---

[70] See, *inter alia, Bozano v. France*, 18 Dec. 1986 (No. 111), 9 E.H.R.R. 297, para. 58; and *Kemmache v. France (No. 3)*, 24 Nov. 1994 (No. 296C), 19 E.H.R.R. 349, para. 42.

[71] *See*, for instance, *Murray v. United Kingdom*, 28 Oct. 1994 (No. 300A), 19 E.H.R.R. 193, para. 51.

Having reached this conclusion, the Court does not need to examine whether the detention could reasonably be considered necessary to prevent his committing an offence or fleeing after having committed one.

46. Accordingly, there has been a violation of Article 5(1) in the present case.

The facts of *Loukanov* illustrate difficulties that may occur when a country such as Bulgaria moves from an authoritarian system of government in which there is recourse to criminal law as a sanction for political behaviour, to a more democratic system in which rule of law values are applied to criminal justice. As well as making an award of legal expenses to Mr Loukanov's family, the Court awarded the sum of 40,000 French francs to the family by way of just satisfaction for that period of his detention (115 days) that occurred after Bulgaria's ratification of the Convention.

B. STEEL AND OTHERS *V.* UNITED KINGDOM

Judgment of 23 September 1998, Reports, 1998–VII 2719
(1998), 28 E.H.R.R. 603

[The first applicant, Helen Steel, took part in a protest against a grouse shoot on a Yorkshire moor; despite police warnings, she walked in front of a member of the party as he lifted his shotgun to aim, thus preventing him from enjoying his sport. She was arrested and held in a police station for 44 hours before being brought before a magistrate and released on bail. She was later convicted of an offence against section 5 of the Public Order Act 1986, for which she was fined £70, and found to have committed a breach of the peace, for which she was ordered to be bound over to keep the peace for 12 months in the sum of £100. Refusing to be bound over, she was sent to prison for 28 days. The second applicant, Rebecca Lush, had protested against the extension of a motorway in Wanstead, London; while standing under the bucket of an earth-digging machine, she was arrested and detained for 17 hours before being released on bail. She was convicted of conduct likely to cause a breach of the peace and was ordered to be bound over for 12 months in the sum of £100. Refusing to be bound over, she was sent to prison for seven days. The other applicants (Needham, Polden and Cole) attended a peaceful protest in London outside premises where a conference to promote the sale of military helicopters was being held. Distributing leaflets and holding banners, they were arrested by the police and detained for seven hours before being released on bail. Subsequently no evidence was offered against them.

These applications raised a variety of issues, including issues under Article 10 (right to freedom of expression). Having set out the relevant rules of English law, the Court dealt with the arrests and initial detention of all five applicants.]

47. The Court recalls that each applicant was arrested for acting in a manner which allegedly caused or was likely to cause a breach of the peace and detained until he or she could be brought before a magistrates' court.

48. Breach of the peace is not classed as a criminal offence under English law. However, the Court observes that the duty to keep the peace is in the nature of a public duty; the police have powers to arrest any person who has breached the peace or who they reasonably fear will breach the peace; and the magistrates may commit to prison any person who refuses to be bound over not

to breach the peace where there is evidence beyond reasonable doubt that his or her conduct caused or was likely to cause a breach of the peace and that he or she would otherwise cause a breach of the peace in the future.

49. Bearing in mind the nature of the proceedings in question and the penalty at stake, the Court considers that breach of the peace must be regarded as an 'offence' within the meaning of Article 5(1)(c).[72]

50. The court therefore finds that each applicant was arrested and detained with the purpose of bringing him or her before the competent legal authority on suspicion of having committed an 'offence' or because it was considered necessary to prevent the commission of an 'offence'.

[The Court proceeded to consider whether that suspicion was reasonable in connection with the issue of lawfulness]

52. The applicants contended that their arrests and initial periods of detention had not been 'lawful', since the concept of breach of the peace and the attendant powers of arrest were insufficiently certain under English law.

First, they submitted that if, as appeared from the national case law, an individual committed a breach of the peace when he or she behaved in a manner the natural consequence of which was that others would react violently, it was difficult to judge the extent to which one could engage in protest activity, in the presence of those who might be annoyed, without causing a breach of the peace. Secondly, the power to arrest whenever there were reasonable grounds for apprehending that a breach of the peace was about to take place granted too wide a discretion to the police. Thirdly, there had been conflicting decisions at Court of Appeal level as to the definition of breach of the peace. . . .

53. The Commission found that there had been no violation of Article 5(1) since the arrests and initial detention had not been arbitrary and there had been no suggestion of any lack of conformity with domestic law.

54. The Court recalls that the expressions 'lawful' and 'in accordance with a procedure prescribed by law' in Article 5(1) stipulate not only full compliance with the procedural and substantive rules of national law, but also that any deprivation of liberty be consistent with the purpose of Article 5 and not arbitrary.[73] In addition, given the importance of personal liberty, it is essential that the applicable national law meets the standard of 'lawfulness' set by the Convention, which requires that all law, whether written or unwritten, be sufficiently precise to allow the citizen—if need be, with appropriate advice—to foresee, to a degree that is reasonable in the circumstances, the consequences which a given action may entail.[74]

55. In this connection, the Court observes that the concept of breach of the peace has been clarified by the English courts over the last two decades, to the extent that it is now sufficiently established that a breach of the peace is committed only when an individual causes harm, or appears likely to cause harm, to persons or property or acts in a manner the natural consequence of which would be to provoke others to violence. It is also clear that a person may be arrested for

---

[72] See, mutatis mutandis, Benham v. United Kingdom, supra n. 69, para. 56.

[73] See id. at para. 40.

[74] S.W. v. United Kingdom, 22 Nov. 1995 (No. 335C) 21 E.H.R.R. 363, paras. 35–36 and, mutatis mutandis, The Sunday Times v. United Kingdom, 26 Apr. 1979 (No. 30), 2 E.H.R.R. 245, para. 49 and Halford v. United Kingdom, 25 June 1997, Reports, 1997–III 1004, 24 E.H.R.R. 523, para. 49.

causing a breach of the peace or where it is reasonably apprehended that he or she is likely to cause a breach of the peace.

Accordingly, the Court considers that the relevant legal rules provided sufficient guidance and were formulated with the degree of precision required by the Convention.[75]

56. When considering whether the arrest and detention of each applicant was carried out in accordance with English law, the Court recalls that it is in the first place for the national authorities, notably the courts, to interpret and apply domestic law. However, since failure to comply with domestic law entails a breach of Article 5(1), the Court can and should exercise a certain power of review in this matter.[76]

57. The Court has already noted that under English law there is a power to arrest an individual who causes a breach of the peace or who is reasonably apprehended to be likely to cause a breach of the peace. It will therefore examine the circumstances of each applicants' arrest to determine whether one of these criteria applied.

[In respect of Helen Steel and Rebecca Lush:]

60. The Court notes that the national courts which dealt with these cases were satisfied that each applicant had caused or had been likely to cause a breach of the peace.

The Court, having itself examined the evidence before it, finds no reason to doubt that the police were justified in fearing that these applicants' behaviour, if persisted in, might provoke others to violence. It follows that the arrest and initial detention of the first and second applicants complied with English law. Moreover, there is no evidence to suggest that these deprivations of liberty were arbitrary.

61. In conclusion, there has been no violation of Article 5(1) in respect of the arrests and initial detention of the first and second applicants.

[In respect of Steel and Lush, the Court found that their detention for refusing to be bound over to keep the peace amounted to detention for non-compliance with the order of a court, and was within Article 5(1)(b); further, the detention was lawful since the applicants could reasonably have foreseen that if they acted in a manner the natural consequence of which would be to provoke others to violence, they might be bound over to keep the peace. The Court reached a different conclusion in respect of the other applicants, Needham, Polden and Cole:]

63. The Court notes that there is no ruling of a national court on the question whether the arrests and detention of these applicants accorded with English law, since the prosecution decided to withdraw the allegations of breach of the peace from the magistrates and since the applicants did not bring any civil claim for false imprisonment against the police. It observes that the government has not raised any preliminary objection in respect of this omission by the applicants, and, in the absence of such a plea, it is not necessary for the Court to consider whether the complaint should have been declared inadmissible for non-exhaustion of domestic remedies.[77]

64. Having itself considered the evidence available to it relating to the arrests of these three applicants, the Court sees no reason to regard their protest as other than entirely peaceful. It does not find any indication that they significantly obstructed or attempted to obstruct those attending

---

[75] *See*, e.g., *Larissis v. Greece* (1998) 4 B.H.R.C. 370, para. 34.

[76] *See Benham v. United Kingdom, supra* n. 69, para. 41.

[77] *See Olsson v. Sweden (No. 1)*, 24 Mar. 1988 (No. 130), 11 E.H.R.R. 259, para. 56 and *Open Door Counselling and Dublin Woman v. Ireland*, 29 Oct. 1992 (No. 246), 15 E.H.R.R., para. 46.

the conference, or took any other action likely to provoke these others to violence. Indeed it would not appear that there was anything in their behaviour which could have justified the police in fearing that a breach of the peace was likely to be caused.

For this reason, in the absence of any national decision on the question, the Court is not satisfied that their arrests and subsequent detention for seven hours complied with English law so as to be 'lawful' within the meaning of Article 5(1).

65. It follows that there has been a violation of Article 5(1) in respect of the third, fourth and fifth applicants.

In respect of Article 10, the Court found against Steel (by five to four) and Lush (by seven to two), but upheld unanimously the complaints by Needham, Polden and Cole. In their partly dissenting opinion in respect of Steel, Judges Valticos and Makarczyk said that it was debatable whether the vague power of the magistrates to bind persons over to be of good behaviour was compatible with the letter and spirit of the Convention, and continued:

What is not in any event debatable is that to detain for 44 hours and then sentence to 28 days imprisonment a person who, albeit in an extreme manner, jumped up and down in front of a member of the shoot to prevent him from killing a feathered friend is so manifestly extreme, particularly in a country known for its fondness for animals, that it amounted, in our view, to a violation of the Convention.

C. FOX, CAMPBELL AND HARTLEY *v.* UNITED KINGDOM

Judgment of 30 August 1990
(No. 182), 13 E.H.R.R. 157

[Under the same legislation that gave rise to *Brogan v. United Kingdom*,[78] three persons had been detained in Northern Ireland as suspected terrorists for periods ranging between 30 and 48 hours. They complained *inter alia* that they had been detained in breach of Article 5(1)(c), since the police had no 'reasonable suspicion' that they had committed an offence and had in fact arrested them to gain information about terrorist activities generally without necessarily intending to charge them with criminal offences. In this case, the Court revisited an important matter of interpretation which in *Brogan* it had resolved in favour of the security forces.]

32. The 'reasonableness' of the suspicion on which an arrest must be based forms an essential part of the safeguard against arbitrary arrest and detention which is laid down in Article 5(1)(c). The Court agrees with the Commission and the Government that having a 'reasonable suspicion' presupposes the existence of facts or information which would satisfy an objective observer that the person concerned may have committed the offence. What may be regarded as 'reasonable' will however depend upon all the circumstances.

In this respect, terrorist crime falls into a special category. Because of the attendant risk of loss of life and human suffering, the police are obliged to act with utmost urgency in following up all information, including information from secret sources. Further, the police may frequently have to arrest a suspected terrorist on the basis of information which is reliable but which cannot, without

[78] Section (F)(2)(A) *infra*.

putting in jeopardy the source of the information, be revealed to the suspect or produced in court to support a charge.

As the Government pointed out, in view of the difficulties inherent in the investigation and prosecution of terrorist-type offences in Northern Ireland, the 'reasonableness' of the suspicion justifying such arrests cannot always be judged according to the same standards as are applied in dealing with conventional crime. Nevertheless, the exigencies of dealing with terrorist crime cannot justify stretching the notion of 'reasonableness' to the point where the essence of the safeguard secured by Article 5(1)(c) is impaired.

33. . . . The Government argued that it was unable to disclose the acutely sensitive material on which the suspicion against the three applicants was based because of the risk of disclosing the source of the material and thereby placing in danger the lives and safety of others. In support of its contention that there was nevertheless reasonable suspicion, it pointed to the facts that the first two applicants had previous convictions for serious acts of terrorism connected with the Provisional IRA and that all three applicants were questioned during their detention about specific terrorist acts of which they were suspected. In the Government's submission these facts were sufficient to confirm that the arresting officer had a *bona fide* or genuine suspicion and it maintained that there was no difference in substance between a *bona fide* or genuine suspicion and a reasonable suspicion. The Government observed moreover that the applicants themselves did not contest that they were arrested and detained in connection with acts of terrorism.

The Government also stated that, although it could not disclose the information or identify the source of the information which led to the arrest of the applicants, there did exist in the case of the first and second applicants strong grounds for suggesting that at the time of their arrest the applicants were engaged in intelligence gathering and courier work for the Provisional IRA and that in the case of the third applicant there was available to the police material connecting him with the kidnapping attempt about which he was questioned.

34. Certainly Article 5(1)(c) of the Convention should not be applied in such a manner as to put disproportionate difficulties in the way of the police authorities of the Contracting States in taking effective measures to counter organised terrorism. It follows that the Contracting States cannot be asked to establish the reasonableness of the suspicion grounding the arrest of a suspected terrorist by disclosing the confidential sources of supporting information or even facts which would be susceptible of indicating such sources or their identity.

Nevertheless the Court must be enabled to ascertain whether the essence of the safeguard afforded by Article 5(1)(c) has been secured. Consequently the respondent government has to furnish at least some facts or information capable of satisfying the Court that the arrested person was reasonably suspected of having committed the alleged offence. This is all the more necessary where, as in the present case, the domestic law does not require reasonable suspicion, but sets a lower threshold by merely requiring honest suspicion.

35. The Court accepts that the arrest and detention of each of the present applicants was based on a *bona fide* suspicion that he or she was a terrorist, and that each of them, including Mr. Hartley, was questioned during his or her detention about specific terrorist acts of which he or she was suspected.

The fact that Mr. Fox and Ms. Campbell both have previous convictions for acts of terrorism connected with the IRA, although it could reinforce a suspicion linking them to the commission of terrorist-type offences, cannot form the sole basis of a suspicion justifying their arrest in 1986, some seven years later. . . .

The aforementioned elements on their own are insufficient to support the conclusion that there was 'reasonable suspicion.' The Government has not provided any further material on which the suspicion against the applicants was based. Its explanations therefore do not meet the minimum standard set by Article 5(1)(c) for judging the reasonableness of a suspicion for the arrest of an individual.

[The Court by a majority of four to three held that the British government had not shown that the police had 'reasonable suspicion' within the meaning of Article 5(1)(c). The applicants' rights had thus been breached.]

While the Court's power to intervene in a national system of criminal justice was illustrated in the three preceding cases, the Court will not intervene merely because the national authorities have made what to the persons detained may seem a harsh or unnecessary decision. In *Kemmache v. France (No 3)*[79] the applicant had been released on bail pending trial on charges concerning counterfeit currency; he surrendered to bail on the eve of the trial, but the trial was adjourned on the request of a co-accused. When Kemmache sought release on bail once again, this was refused by the Assize Court. In deciding by eight to one that there had been no breach of Article 5(1), the Strasbourg Court said:

In principle, and without prejudice to its power to examine the compatibility of national decisions with the Convention, it is not the Court's role to assess itself the facts which have led a national court to adopt one decision rather than another. If it were otherwise, the Court would be acting as a court of third or fourth instance, which would be to disregard the limits imposed on its action.[80]

In *Kemmache*, the Court found that the decisions of the French courts disclosed neither abuse of authority, bad faith nor arbitrariness. They could not therefore be held unlawful, especially in view of the right to apply for release still open to Kemmache in French law. Judge Walsh, dissenting, considered that the reasons advanced by the French court for refusing to release Kemmache were 'entirely based on a speculative and intuitive approach on the part of the national judicial authorities. Such an approach cannot be a substitute for evidence'.[81]

---

[79] 24 Nov. 1994 (No. 296C), 19 E.H.R.R. 349.

[80] *Id.*, at para. 44.

[81] *Id.*, dissenting judgment, para. 3. In *K-F v. Germany*, 27 Nov. 1997 Reports, 1997–VII 2657, 26 E.H.R.R. 390, the Court took a similar approach to that in *Kemmache*, in holding that detention of the applicant overnight on suspicion of fraud was lawful, and that, since the detention exceeded the statutory period of 12 hours, to that extent only had Art. 5(1)(c) been breached. In *Scott v. Spain*, 18 Dec. 1996, Reports, 1996–VI 2382, 24 E.H.R.R. 39, the facts relating to a detention lasting for four years were complex: there were at various times grounds for detention under both Art. 5(1)(c) and 5(1)(f), since while Scott was detained in respect of an alleged rape in Spain of a foreign tourist, the United Kingdom was seeking his extradition on a charge of murder. The Court by 8–1, by reasoning that is unclear, found no breach of Art. 5(1)(c), but unanimously found a breach of Art. 5(3) in respect of delay before Scott was tried for rape. The majority's reasoning on Art. 5(1)(c) was forcefully criticized by Judge Repik, who found that the power to detain in relation to extradition had been used improperly for purposes of the rape charge.

2. ARREST OR DETENTION TO SECURE THE FULFILMENT OF AN OBLIGATION PRESCRIBED BY LAW

A. BENHAM *v.* UNITED KINGDOM

Judgment of 10 June 1996, Reports, 1996–II 738,
22 E.H.R.R. 293

[In 1990, a new form of local tax, known in law as the community charge but popularly called the 'poll tax', was imposed upon all adults in England and Wales, the amount due being a fixed sum that had no regard to the taxpayer's resources. Benham was a young unemployed man who failed to pay the sum of £325 due in 1990–1. The legislation empowered local magistrates to commit a poll-tax debtor to prison for up to three months where non-payment was due to his 'wilful failure or culpable neglect'. Remarking that Benham could have made greater efforts to find work, the magistrates sent him to prison for 30 days, without his having been legally represented before them. Eleven days later, the English High Court ordered his release on bail; the High Court later held that the magistrates ought not to have sent him to prison when there was no evidence either that he had the resources to pay or that there had been 'wilful failure or culpable neglect'. At Strasbourg, Benham claimed that there had been breaches of Article 5(1) and 5(5) (duty to compensate for unlawful detention) and of Article 6.]

39. The Court first observes that this case falls to be examined under subparagraph (b) of Article 5(1), since the purpose of the detention was to secure the fulfilment of B's obligation to pay the community charge owed by him.

40. The main issue to be determined in the present case is whether the disputed detention was 'lawful', including whether it complied with 'a procedure prescribed by law'. The Convention here essentially refers back to national law and states the obligation to conform to the substantive and procedural rules thereof, but it requires in addition that any deprivation of liberty should be consistent with the purpose of Article 5, namely to protect individuals from arbitrariness.[82]

41. It is in the first place for the national authorities, notably the courts, to interpret and apply domestic law. However, since under Article 5(1) failure to comply with domestic law entails a breach of the Convention, it follows that the Court can and should exercise a certain power to review whether this law has been complied with.[83]

42. A period of detention will in principle be lawful if it is carried out pursuant to a court order. A subsequent finding that the court erred under domestic law in making the order will not necessarily retrospectively affect the validity of the intervening period of detention. For this reason, the Strasbourg organs have consistently refused to uphold applications from persons convicted of criminal offences who complain that their convictions or sentences were found by the appellate courts to have been based on errors of fact or law.[84]

43. It was agreed by those appearing before the Court that the principles of English law which should be taken into account in this case distinguished between acts of a magistrates' court which

---

[82] See *Quinn v. France*, 22 Mar. 1995 (No. 311), 21 E.H.R.R. 529, para. 47.

[83] See *Bouamar v. Belgium*, 29 Feb. 1988 (No. 129) 11 E.H.R.R. 1, para. 49.

[84] See *Bozano v. France*, 18 Dec. 1986 (No. 111), 9 E.H.R.R. 297, para. 55.

were within its jurisdiction and those which were in excess of jurisdiction. The former were valid and effective unless or until they were overturned by a superior court, whereas the latter were null and void from the outset.

> [The Court reviewed the authorities in national law on the question whether the magistrates had exceeded their jurisdiction in sending Benham to prison, and examined the reasons given by the English High Court for deciding that the magistrates had acted wrongly.]

46. Against the above background, it cannot be said with any degree of certainty that the judgment of the [High] Court was to the effect that the magistrates acted in excess of jurisdiction within the meaning of English law. It follows that the Court does not find it established that the order for detention was invalid, and thus that the detention which resulted from it was unlawful under national law. The mere fact that the order was set aside on appeal did not in itself affect the lawfulness of the detention.

47. Nor does the Court find that the detention was arbitrary. It has not been suggested that the magistrates who ordered B's detention acted in bad faith, nor that they neglected to attempt to apply the relevant legislation correctly. It considers the question of the lack of legal aid to be less relevant to the present head of complaint than to that under Article 6.

Accordingly, the Court finds no violation of Article 5(1) of the Convention.

Since there was no breach of Article 5(1), the Court also rejected the applicant's claim under Article 5(5) (right to compensation for unlawful detention). However, the Court held that Benham's rights under Article 6 had been breached.[85]

Another instance of detention within Article 5(1)(b) (power 'to secure the fulfilment of any obligation prescribed by law') is afforded by *Steel v. United Kingdom*[86] where, as we have seen, the Court upheld the power of English magistrates to require persons convicted of public order offences to agree to be bound over to keep the peace, failing which they would be sent to prison.

3. ARREST OR DETENTION TO PREVENT AN UNAUTHORIZED ENTRY INTO THE COUNTRY OR WITH A VIEW TO DEPORTATION OR EXTRADITION

For a state to be able to enforce its immigration laws, whether by refusing entry to illegal entrants or by removing from its territory those subject to deportation or extradition, detention of the individuals concerned may be necessary. The purpose of such detention may be to give time for inquiries to be made, to prevent the detainees absconding and (as with proposed deportation or extradition) to enable the individual to challenge the proposed action in national courts. Lawful authority for a

---

[85] Although in English law the proceedings before the magistrates were viewed as civil and not criminal, the Court held that Benham had in essence been 'charged with a criminal offence' within Art. 6(1) and (3); as the magistrates could impose a prison sentence of up to three months, the interests of justice required that Benham should have had legal aid before the magistrates.

[86] Section (E)(1)(B) *supra*.

detention must exist and questions may arise as to the conditions of detention, its duration and the extent of judicial protection for the detainee. It may be argued that those who seek without permission to enter the country and are then detained bring the detention upon themselves, since they may at any time go free by deciding to leave the country. The first of two cases, both concerning those seeking asylum as refugees, indicates how the Strasbourg Court has responded to this argument; the second exemplifies how individual liberty is eroded when factors of national security cause an individual to be detained for a long period of time.

A. AMUUR *v.* FRANCE

Judgment of 25 June 1996, Reports, 1996–III 826,
22 E.H.R.R. 533

[The applicants (three brothers and a sister) were Somali nationals who arrived at Orly airport, Paris, on a flight from Syria and claimed that they had fled Somalia where their lives were at risk following the overthrow of the President. The French authorities detained them for 20 days at the airport and in a secure section of the Arcade Hotel nearby. The Somalis had no access to legal advice for 15 days, but shortly thereafter challenged their detention in the French courts. They were returned to Syria two days before the French court held that the detention was unlawful. When the Somalis claimed under the Convention that Article 5(1) had been breached, the Commission by 16–10 rejected the claim, the majority stating that the applicants could at any time have left France for Syria, where their lives were not in danger, and the necessary 'deprivation of liberty' was lacking.]

38. The applicants complained of the physical conditions of their 'detention' in the transit zone. . . . In addition, these conditions had been aggravated by the excessive length of their 'detention'. . . . They also emphasised that under the relevant international conventions and national legislation they should, as asylum seekers, have enjoyed special protection and more favourable treatment than unlawful immigrants. The detention of asylum seekers could not be justified unless their application for asylum was considered manifestly ill-founded, which was clearly not so in the applicants' case, as the other members of their family were granted refugee status by the French Office for the Protection of Refugees and Stateless Persons.

39. According to the Government, the applicants' stay in the transit zone was not comparable to detention. They had been lodged in part of the Hôtel Arcade where the 'physical conditions' of the accommodation were described as satisfactory. . . . The original reason why they were held and for the length of time they were held had been their obstinacy in seeking to enter French territory despite being refused leave to enter. They could not therefore 'validly complain of a situation which they had largely created', as the Court itself had held in the *Kolumpar v. Belgium* judgment of 24 September 1992.[87]

41. The Court notes in the first place that in the fourth paragraph of the Preamble to its Constitution of 27 October 1946 (incorporated into that of 4 October 1958). France enunciated the right to asylum in 'the territories of the Republic' for 'everyone persecuted on account of his action in the cause of freedom'. France is also party to the 1951 Geneva Convention Relating to

---

[87] *Kolumpar v. Belgium* 24 Sept. 1992 (No. 235C), 16 E.H.R.R. 197.

the Status of Refugees . . .

The Court also notes that many Member States of the Council of Europe have been confronted for a number of years now with an increasing flow of asylum seekers. It is aware of the difficulties involved in the reception of asylum seekers at most large European airports and in the processing of their applications. . . .

Contracting States have the undeniable sovereign right to control aliens' entry into and residence in their territory. The Court emphasizes, however, that this right must be exercised in accordance with the provisions of the Convention, including Article 5.

42. In proclaiming the right to liberty, Article 5(1) contemplates the physical liberty of the person; its aim is to ensure that no one should be dispossessed of this liberty in an arbitrary fashion. On the other hand, it is not in principle concerned with mere restrictions on the liberty of movement; such restrictions are governed by Article 2 of Protocol No. 4.

[On whether the applicants had been deprived of their liberty, the Court referred to *Guzzardi v Italy*[88] and continued:]

43. Holding aliens in the international zone does indeed involve a restriction upon liberty, but one which is not in every respect comparable to that which obtains in centres for the detention of aliens pending deportation. Such confinement, accompanied by suitable safeguards for the persons concerned, is acceptable only in order to enable States to prevent unlawful immigration while complying with their international obligations, particularly under the 1951 Geneva Convention . . . States' legitimate concern to foil the increasingly frequent attempts to get round immigration restrictions must not deprive asylum seekers of the protection afforded by these Conventions.

Such holding should not be prolonged excessively, otherwise there would be a risk of it turning a mere restriction on liberty—inevitable with a view to organising the practical details of the alien's repatriation or, where he has requested asylum, while his application for leave to enter the territory for that purpose is considered—into a deprivation of liberty. In that connection account should be taken of the fact that the measure is applicable not to those who have committed criminal offences but to aliens who, often fearing for their lives, have fled from their own country.

Although by the force of circumstances the decision to order holding must necessarily be taken by the administrative or police authorities, its prolongation requires speedy review by the courts, the traditional guardians of personal liberties. Above all, such confinement must not deprive the asylum seeker of the right to gain effective access to the procedure for determining refugee status . . .

[The Court summarized the facts relating to the detention of the applicants between 9 and 29 March 1992, found that they were sent back to Syria before being able to make an effective application to the authority with jurisdiction to rule on their refugee status, and continued:]

46. In concluding that there was no deprivation of liberty, the Government and the Commission attached particular weight to the fact that the applicants could at any time have removed themselves from the sphere of application of the measure in issue. More particularly, the Government argued that although the transit zone is 'closed on the French side', it remains 'open to the

---

[88] *Guzzardi v. Italy*, 6 Nov. 1980 (No. 39), 3 E.H.R.R. 333, para. 92 reprinted at section (B)(1) *supra*.

outside', so that the applicants could have returned of their own accord to Syria, where their safety was guaranteed, in view of the assurances which the Syrian authorities had given the French Government. . . .

47. The applicants maintained that such reasoning would amount to binding the application of Article 5 to that of Article 3 of the Convention, this would be to ignore the specific object of Article 5, and its wording, which had to be strictly construed; it would also deprive Article 5 of any useful effect, particularly with regard to asylum applications.

48. The mere fact that it is possible for asylum seekers to leave voluntarily the country where they wish to take refuge cannot exclude a restriction on liberty, the right to leave any country, including one's own, being guaranteed, moreover, by Protocol No. 4 to the Convention. Further-more, this possibility becomes theoretical if no other country offering protection comparable to the protection they expect to find in the country where they are seeking asylum is inclined or prepared to take them in.

Sending the applicants back to Syria only became possible, apart from the practical problems of the journey, following negotiations between the French and Syrian authorities. As for the assurances of the latter, these were dependent on the vagaries of diplomatic relations, regard being had to the fact that Syria was not bound by the Geneva Convention relating to the Status of Refugees.

49. The Court concludes that holding the applicants in the transit zone of Paris-Orly Airport was equivalent in practice, in view of the restrictions suffered, to a deprivation of liberty. Article 5(1) is therefore applicable to the case.

50. It remains to be determined whether the deprivation of liberty found to be established in the present case was compatible with paragraph 1 of Article 5. Where the 'lawfulness' of deten-tion is in issue, . . . the Convention refers essentially to national law and lays down the obligation to conform to the substantive and procedural rules of national law, but it requires in addition that any deprivation of liberty should be in keeping with the purpose of Article 5, namely to protect the individual from arbitrariness. . . .

In order to ascertain whether a deprivation of liberty has complied with the principle of compatibility with domestic law, it therefore falls to the Court to assess not only the legislation in force in the field under consideration, but also the quality of the other legal rules applicable to the persons concerned. Quality in this sense implies that where a national law authorizes depriv-ation of liberty—especially in respect of a foreign asylum seeker—it must be sufficiently access-ible and precise, in order to avoid all risk of arbitrariness. These characteristics are of funda-mental importance with regard to asylum seekers at airports, particularly in view of the need to reconcile the protection of fundamental rights with the requirements of States' immigration policies.

51. The applicants asserted that their detention had no legal basis, whether under the French legislation in force at the time or under international law. They had found themselves in a legal vacuum in which they had neither access to a lawyer nor information about exactly where they stood at the time. In support of the above argument, they rely on the reasons for the judgment of the Créteil tribunal de grande instance, ruling on their application for an interim order.

52. The Court notes that even though the applicants were not in France within the meaning of the Ordinance of 2 November 1945, holding them in the international zone of Paris-Orly Airport made them subject to French law. . . .

[The Court examined the executive rules that at the relevant time governed the holding of persons in the transit zone of airports in France.]

53. The Court emphasises that from 9 to 29 March 1992 the applicants were in the situation of asylum seekers whose application had not yet been considered. In that connection, neither the Decree of 27 May 1982 nor the—unpublished—circular of 26 June 1990 (the only text at the material time which specifically dealt with the practice of holding aliens in the transit zone) constituted a 'law' of sufficient 'quality' within the meaning of the Court's case law; there must be adequate legal protection in domestic law against arbitrary interferences by public authorities with the rights safeguarded by the Convention[89] . . . The abovementioned circular consisted, by its very nature, of instructions given by the Minister of the Interior to Prefects and Chief Constables concerning aliens refused leave to enter at the frontiers. . . . At the material time none of these texts allowed the ordinary courts to review the conditions under which aliens were held or, if necessary, to impose a limit on the administrative authorities as regards the length of time for which they were held. They did not provide for legal, humanitarian and social assistance, nor did they lay down procedures and time-limits for access to such assistance so that asylum seekers like the applicants could take the necessary steps.

54. The French legal rules in force at the time, as applied in the present case, did not sufficiently guarantee the applicants' right to liberty.

There has accordingly been a breach of Article 5(1).

B. CHAHAL *V.* UNITED KINGDOM

Judgment of 15 November 1996, Reports, 1996–V 1831,
23 E.H.R.R. 413

[This case has already been considered[90] in relation to issues under Article 3 (degrading and inhuman treatment) that arose when the British government sought to deport to India a Sikh nationalist who was considered to be a threat to national security. By the date of the Court's decision, the applicant had been detained for over six years and his attempts to secure release in the United Kingdom had failed. Having decided that his deportation to India would involve a breach of Article 3, the Court considered whether breaches of Article 5(1) and 5(4) had occurred in respect of his lengthy detention.]

112. The Court recalls that it is not in dispute that Mr. Chahal has been detained 'with a view to deportation' within the meaning of Article 5(1)(f). Article 5(1)(f) does not demand that the detention of a person against whom action is being taken with a view to deportation be reasonably considered necessary, for example to prevent his committing an offence or fleeing; in this respect Article 5(1)(f) provides a different level of protection from Article 5(1)(c).

Indeed, all that is required under this provision is that 'action is being taken with a view to deportation'. It is therefore immaterial, for the purposes of Article 5(1)(f), whether the underlying decision to expel can be justified under national or Convention law.

113. The Court recalls, however, that any deprivation of liberty under Article 5(1)(f) will be justified only for as long as deportation proceedings are in progress. If such proceedings are not

---

[89] *Malone v. United Kingdom* 2 Aug. 1984 (No. 82), 7 E.H.R.R. 14, para. 67.
[90] Chapter 4(C)(2) *supra.*

prosecuted with due diligence, the detention will cease to be permissible under Article 5(1)(f).[91]

It is thus necessary to determine whether the duration of the deportation proceedings was excessive.

114. The period under consideration commenced on 16 August 1990, when Mr. Chahal was first detained with a view to deportation. It terminated on 3 March 1994, when the domestic proceedings came to an end with the refusal of the House of Lords to allow leave to appeal. Although he has remained in custody until the present day, this latter period must be distinguished because during this time the Government have refrained from deporting him in compliance with the request made by the Commission. . . .

[The Court examined the various stages of the administrative and judicial proceedings taken in the applicant's case in the United Kingdom.]

117. As the Court has observed in the context of Article 3, Mr. Chahal's case involves considerations of an extremely serious and weighty nature. It is neither in the interests of the individual applicant nor in the general public interest in the administration of justice that such decisions be taken hastily, without due regard to all the relevant issues and evidence.

Against this background, . . . none of the periods complained of can be regarded as excessive, taken either individually or in combination. Accordingly, there has been no violation of Article 5(1) of the Convention on account of the diligence, or lack of it, with which the domestic procedures were conducted.

118. It also falls to the Court to examine whether Mr. Chahal's detention was 'lawful' for the purposes of Article 5(1)(f), with particular reference to the safeguards provided by the national system. . . .

119. There is no doubt that Mr. Chahal's detention was lawful under national law and was effected 'in accordance with a procedure prescribed by law'. However, in view of the extremely long period during which Mr. Chahal has been detained, it is also necessary to consider whether there existed sufficient guarantees against arbitrariness.

120. In this context, the Court observes that the applicant has been detained since 16 August 1990 on the ground, essentially, that successive Secretaries of State have maintained that, in view of the threat to national security represented by him, he could not safely be released. The applicant has, however, consistently denied that he posed any threat whatsoever to national security, and has given reasons in support of this denial.

121. The Court further notes that, since the Secretaries of State asserted that national security was involved, the domestic courts were not in a position effectively to control whether the decisions to keep Mr. Chahal in detention were justified, because the full material on which these decisions were based was not made available to them.

122. However, in the context of Article 5(1) of the Convention, the advisory panel procedure provided an important safeguard against arbitrariness. This panel, which included experienced judicial figures was able fully to review the evidence relating to the national security threat

---

[91] In *Quinn v. France*, 22 Mar. 1995 (No. 31), 21 E.H.R.R. 529, there had been a breach of Art. 5(1)(f) during a period of almost two years that Quinn was held in France pending extradition to Switzerland. The proceedings had not been conducted with due diligence, separate delays of three months and 10 months having occurred during the period.

represented by the applicant. Although its report has never been disclosed, at the hearing before the Court the Government indicated that the panel had agreed with the Home Secretary that Mr. Chahal ought to be deported on national security grounds. The Court considers that this procedure provided an adequate guarantee that there were at least *prima facie* grounds for believing that if Mr. Chahal were at liberty, national security would be put at risk and thus, that the executive had not acted arbitrarily when it ordered him to be kept in detention.

123. In conclusion, the Court recalls that Mr. Chahal has undoubtedly been detained for a length of time which is bound to give rise to serious concern. However, in view of the exceptional circumstances of the case and the facts that the national authorities have acted with due diligence throughout the deportation proceedings against him and that there were sufficient guarantees against the arbitrary deprivation of his liberty, this detention complied with the requirements of Article 5(1)(f).

It follows that there has been no violation of Article 5(1).

[This decision was reached by a majority of 13 votes to six. The Court then considered whether the proceedings that Mr. Chahal had been able to take in the British courts satisfied Article 5(4), by which every detained person is entitled to take proceedings by which the lawfulness of the detention shall be decided speedily by a court. The Court commented generally on Article 5(4) before dealing with the specific circumstances of Mr. Chahal:]

127. The Court . . . recalls that the notion of 'lawfulness' under paragraph 4 of Article 5 has the same meaning as in paragraph 1, so that the detained person is entitled to a review of his detention in the light not only of the requirements of domestic law but also of the text of the Convention, the general principles embodied therein and the aim of the restrictions permitted by Article 5(1).[92]

The scope of the obligations under Article 5(4) is not identical for every kind of deprivation of liberty;[93] this applies notably to the extent of the judicial review afforded. Nonetheless, it is clear that Article 5(4) does not guarantee a right to judicial review of such breadth as to empower the court, on all aspects of the case including questions of pure expediency, to substitute its own discretion for that of the decision-making authority. The review should, however, be wide enough to bear on those conditions which are essential for the 'lawful' detention of a person according to Article 5(1). . . .[94]

129. The notion of 'lawfulness' in Article 5(1)(f) does not refer solely to the obligation to conform to the substantive and procedural rules of national law; it requires in addition that any deprivation of liberty should be in keeping with the purpose of Article 5. The question therefore arises whether the available proceedings to challenge the lawfulness of Mr. Chahal's detention and to seek bail provided an adequate control by the domestic courts.

130. The Court recollects that, because national security was involved, the domestic courts were not in a position to review whether the decisions to detain Mr. Chahal and to keep him in detention were justified on national security grounds. Furthermore, although the procedure before the advisory panel undoubtedly provided some degree of control, bearing in mind that Mr. Chahal was not entitled to legal representation before the panel, that he was only given an outline of the grounds for the notice of intention to deport, that the panel had no power of decision and that its

---

[92] *See E. v. Norway*, 29 Aug. 1990 (No. 181A), 17 E.H.R.R. 30, para. 49.

[93] *See, inter alia, Bouamar v. Belgium*, 29 Feb. 1988 (No. 129), 11 E.H.R.R., 1, reprinted at section (F)(2) *infra*.

[94] *See E. v. Norway, supra* note 92, para. 50.

advice to the Home Secretary was not binding and was not disclosed, the panel could not be considered as a 'court' within the meaning of Article 5(4).[95]

131. The Court recognises that the use of confidential material may be unavoidable where national security is at stake. This does not mean, however, that the national authorities can be free from effective control by the domestic courts whenever they choose to assert that national security and terrorism are involved. . . .

In the Court's unanimous view, such effective control did not exist and Article 5(4) had been breached, since neither the proceedings in the British courts nor the hearing before the advisory panel satisfied Article 5(4). In regard to Article 5(1), judges in the minority differed sharply from the majority. Judge de Meyer considered that it was 'clearly excessive' for Chahal to have been detained for over six years. Judge Pettiti held that it was clear from past cases (such as *Amuur v. France*)[96] that if proceedings for deportation were not conducted by the state with due diligence or if there had been a misuse of authority, detention might cease to be justifiable; in his view, Chahal had been treated by the British authorities even more severely than a convicted criminal, since his detention amounted to an indefinite sentence and the authorities had 'clearly refused to seek a means of expelling him to a third country'.

F. RIGHT TO BE BROUGHT PROMPTLY BEFORE A JUDGE OR OTHER OFFICER AUTHORIZED TO EXERCISE JUDICIAL POWER

Two aspects of this right are examined below. The first concerns the nature of the 'judge or other officer authorized to exercise judicial power' before whom the arrested person has the right to be brought. The second concerns the meaning of 'promptly': what period of time is allowed to the police between arresting a suspect and bringing him or her before a 'judge or other officer authorized to exercise judicial power'?

1. WHO MAY EXERCISE JUDICIAL POWER FOR THE PURPOSES OF ARTICLE 5(3)?

Many European legal systems have commonly provided for the public prosecutor, a salaried lawyer in the public service, to exercise investigatory functions into particular crimes before deciding whether and whom to prosecute and, in the course of the investigation, to have power to release a suspect on bail or to order that he or she be

---

[95] See, *mutatis mutandis, X. v. United Kingdom*, 24 Oct. 1981 (No. 46), 4 E.H.R.R. 188, para. 61.

[96] See Section (E)(3)(A) *supra*.

held in custody. In *Schiesser v. Switzerland*,[97] Mr. Schiesser was arrested on charges of theft and was at once brought before the District Attorney for Winterthur, who ordered that he be detained on remand. Schiesser's appeal against detention was later rejected both by the Zurich Public Prosecutor and by the prosecution chamber of the Zurich Court of Appeal. In the Swiss legal system, the District Attorney is both an investigating and a prosecuting authority. When Schiesser alleged a breach of Article 5(3), the Strasbourg Court decided (by five to two) that the District Attorney was 'an officer authorised by law to exercise judicial power'. The Court observed that Article 5(3) left a state a choice between entrusting decisions as to bail to a judge sitting in court or to a category of 'other officers'. This second category was capable of including officials in public prosecutors' departments. Since the purpose of Article 5 was to ensure that no one should be dispossessed arbitrarily of his liberty, the 'officer' referred to in Article 5(3) must 'offer guarantees befitting the "judicial" power conferred on him by law'. Amongst the essential conditions were that the officer must be independent of the executive and of the parties; that the officer must hear the individual; and that the officer must review the substantive grounds relied on that should determine whether or not the detainee could be released. The Court examined in detail the status of the District Attorney in Swiss law and concluded that in practice the District Attorney acted in complete independence of the Public Prosecutor and exercised a personal discretion conferred by law. The Court emphasized that in Mr. Schiesser's case:

the District Attorney intervened exclusively in his capacity as an investigating authority, that is, in considering whether Mr. Schiesser should be charged and detained on remand and, subsequently, in conducting enquiries with an obligation to be equally thorough in gathering evidence in his favour and evidence against him . . . He did not assume the mantle of prosecutor: he neither drew up the indictment nor represented the prosecuting authorities before the trial court . . . He therefore did not exercise concurrent investigating and prosecuting functions, with the result that the Court is not called upon to determine whether the converse situation would have been in conformity with Article 5(3).[98]

Judges Ryssdal and Evrigenis dissented. In the course of his judgment, Judge Ryssdal stated:

The purpose of Article 5(3) is to establish a system of judicial review and, by that means, to give specific guarantees to persons deprived of their liberty. If a contracting State leaves such judicial power to an 'officer' other than a judge, it is necessary that this 'other officer' should not be dependent on or controlled by the administration and also that he can be regarded as independent and impartial. Depriving a person of his liberty is a very serious measure, and the purpose of Article 5(3) is to give the utmost protection to individual liberty.[99]

Accepting that Article 5(3) allowed the power of decision regarding detention on

---

[97] 4 Dec. 1979 (No. 34), 2 E.H.R.R. 417.
[98] *Id.* at para. 34.
[99] *Id.* at para. 4.

remand to be entrusted to an authority which holds judicial power concurrently with other power, Judge Evrigenis said:

> Nevertheless, such a combination of judicial and non-judicial power must not entail fundamental contradictions as to the nature and the purpose of the diverse powers so combined. . . . To entrust the power of decision regarding detention on remand to an authority which numbers amongst its powers that of a prosecuting authority would be contrary to the Convention. It is immaterial whether or not in a given case this authority is called on to exercise the two kinds of power. Their incompatibility is inherent in the system itself and divests the authority in question of the legal and psychological attributes of independence, objectivity and impartiality that must be possessed by the authority to which Article 5(3) entrusts the fate of a person deprived of his liberty.[100]

In 1990, the decision of the majority in *Schiesser* came up for re-consideration by the Court.

A. HUBER *V.* SWITZERLAND
Judgment of 23 Oct. 1990
(No. 188)

> [The applicant, Mrs. Huber, had been taken before the District Attorney in Zurich for questioning as a witness and at the end of his examination the District Attorney ordered that she be held in custody on grave suspicion of having given false evidence. Subsequent proceedings against her led to her being fined 4,000 Swiss francs for attempting to give false evidence. She complained in the Federal Court that, in breach of Article 5(3) of the Convention, the same District Attorney (Mr. J.) had both ordered her detention and drawn up the indictment. The Federal Court applied the judgment of the European Court in *Schiesser*, and held that the Attorney's independence and impartiality 'must be considered exclusively at the time of the arrest and not in the light of the mere possibility that he may play a role later in the proceedings and draw up the indictment'. When Mrs. Huber's complaint of a breach of Article 5(3) reached the European Court, a plenary court of 22 judges was convened and again examined the legal position of the District Attorney in Zurich.]

37. . . . Mrs. Huber argued further that in general a prosecutor (*Ankläger*) could never be regarded as an 'officer' within the meaning of Article 5(3). In the present case, of the various functions a District Attorney was called upon to perform, that of prosecution predominated: the duty to establish incriminating and exonerating evidence with equal care made no difference in this respect.

38. The Commission took the view that Mr. J. could not be regarded as independent of the parties to the trial because he could be one of them and indeed was.

Its Delegate invited the Court to depart from the *Schiesser* judgment of 4 December 1979.[101] . . . In the Delegate's view, the Court's case-law has moved towards the principle that prosecution and judicial functions must be completely separated; such separation was, he considered, necessary at this stage in the development of the protection of human rights in Europe.

In this connection he noted a difference between the *Schiesser* and *Huber* cases. In the former

---

[100] *Id.* at para. C.
[101] 4 Dec. 1979 (No. 34), 2 E.H.R.R. 417 discussed at Section (F)(1) *supra*.

the District Attorney had not assumed the role of prosecuting authority, whereas in the latter he drew up the indictment. The Delegate did not attach decisive importance to this, since circumstances of this nature were determined by the subsequent course of the criminal proceedings and the lawfulness of the Attorney's action in relation to Article 5(3) should, in his opinion, be clear at the outset.

39. The Government contended that the District Attorney was in substance, despite his title, an investigating judge. In this, he could be clearly distinguished from the officers of the prosecuting authority whom the Court had to consider in the cases of *Skoogström v. Sweden* and *Pauwels v. Belgium*.[102] Clearly it fell to him to draw up the indictment, but cantonal law required him to take into account exonerating evidence as well as incriminating evidence, without setting out the grounds of suspicion or any legal considerations . . .

In the present case he had ordered Mrs. Huber's arrest in complete independence and at that stage he was in no way called upon to express an opinion on her guilt. The mere fact that, fourteen months later, he had submitted the indictment could not compromise his independence retrospectively: the Government fully endorsed the reasoning of the Federal Court in its judgment of 14 March 1989, according to which the position of the District Attorney had to be considered exclusively at the time of the arrest without taking into account the possibility that he might subsequently play a role as prosecuting authority. . . .

Moreover, the applicant had not contested the detention order, or the lawfulness of her detention on remand, under Article 5(4) or challenged the investigative measures. Yet she had not been unaware that Mr. J. could subsequently play another role. Nor had she ever claimed that he was prejudiced against her. In general, it was, in the Government's opinion, hard to see what an accused person might gain from having the indictment drawn up by a different judicial officer from the official responsible for his arrest.

The *Schiesser* judgment had, according to the Government, left open the question of the compatibility with the Convention of the combination of the functions of investigation (*instruction*) and prosecution. Furthermore, the Commission and the Court had based their decision at the time on a number of factors taken together; an isolated circumstance—the drawing up of the indictment—could not justify overruling their case-law. The Swiss authorities were therefore entitled to rely on the above-mentioned judgment in such circumstances, unless there were compelling reasons to the contrary such as a manifest failure on the part of the District Attorney to fulfil his duties or action by him which was *ultra vires*. . . .

40. The Court notes in the first place that the only issue in dispute is the impartiality of the Zürich District Attorney when the detention order was made. Mrs. Huber did not deny that he was independent of the executive, that he heard her himself before placing her in detention on remand and that he examined with equal care the circumstances militating for and against such detention.

41. In the present case Mr. J. first intervened at the stage of the investigation. He considered whether it was necessary to charge the applicant and ordered her detention on remand, then conducted the investigation. . . .

Subsequently, fourteen months after the arrest, he acted as prosecuting authority in drawing up the indictment. However, he did not assume the role of prosecuting counsel in the trial court, the Zürich District Court, although he could have done so because the Cantonal Code of Criminal Procedure attributed to him the status of a party in the trial proceedings. . . .

---

[102] Respectively, 2 Oct. 1984 (No. 83), 7 E.H.R.R. 263 and 26 May 1988 (No. 135), 11 E.H.R.R. 238.

42. In several judgments which post-date the *Schiesser* judgment of 4 December 1979 and which concern Netherlands legislation on the arrest and detention of military personnel,[103] the Court found that the *auditeur-militair,* who had ordered the detention of the applicants, could also be called upon to assume, in the same case, the role of prosecuting authority after referral of the case to the Military Court. It concluded from this that he could not be 'independent of the parties' at that preliminary stage precisely because he was 'liable' to become one of the parties at the next stage in the procedure.

43. The Court sees no grounds for reaching a different conclusion in this case as regards criminal justice under the ordinary law. Clearly the Convention does not rule out the possibility of the judicial officer who orders the detention carrying out other duties, but his impartiality is capable of appearing open to doubt[104] if he is entitled to intervene in the subsequent criminal proceedings as a representative of the prosecuting authority.

Since that was the situation in the present case (. . .) there has been a breach of Article 5(3).

In *Brincat v. Italy,*[105] the Court was invited by the Italian government to depart from the position laid down in *Huber v. Switzerland* (namely that legitimate doubt is raised about a judicial officer's impartiality if he is entitled to intervene in subsequent proceedings) and to return to *Schiesser v. Switzerland* (no breach of Article 5(3) if the judicial officer had not sought to exercise his prosecutorial functions at the time he decided to detain a suspect in custody). The Court saw no reason for departing from the position which it adopted in *Huber* and in many other cases, such as *De Jong, Baljet* and *Van Den Brink v. The Netherlands.*[106] In *Hood v. United Kingdom,*[107] which was one of many cases against the United Kingdom finding that the British system of courts martial did not meet the minimum standards for an independent and impartial court set by Article 6(1), the Court applied *Huber v. Switzerland* in holding that Article 5(3) had been breached in respect of the applicant's pre-trial detention by decision of his commanding officer.

2. THE MEANING OF 'PROMPTLY' IN ARTICLE 5(3)

The requirement in Article 5(3) that an arrested person be brought promptly before a judge or other officer was interpreted in *McGoff v. Sweden.*[108] Under a warrant of arrest issued in Stockholm, McGoff, an Irish citizen, was extradited from Switzerland to

---

[103] *See, e.g., De Jong, Baljet and Van den Brink v. Netherlands,* 22 May 1984 (No. 77), 8 E.H.R.R. 20, discussed at Section (F)(2)(B) *infra.*

[104] *See Pauwels v. Belgium,* 26 May 1988 (No. 135), 11 E.H.R.R. 238, para. 38 and *mutatis mutandis, Piersack v. Belgium* 1 Oct. 1982 (No. 53), 5 E.H.R.R. 169, para. 31; *De Cubber v. Belgium,* 26 Oct. 1984 (No. 86), 7 E.H.R.R. 236, para. 30; and *Hauschildt v. Denmark,* 24 May 1989 (No. 154), 12 E.H.R.R. 266, para. 52 *in fine.*

[105] 26 Nov. 1992 (No. 249A), 16 E.H.R.R. 591.

[106] See *supra* n. 103.

[107] 18 Feb. 1999 (not yet reported). See also *Findlay v. United Kingdom,* 27 Feb. 1997, Reports, 1997–I 263, 24 E.H.R.R. 221; *Coyne v. United Kingdom,* 24 Sept. 1997, Reports, 1997–V 1848; and *Cable and Others v. United Kingdom,* 18 Feb. 1999 (not yet reported). The law relating to courts martial in the United Kingdom has already been amended by the Armed Forces Act 1996 in response to these challenges.

[108] 26 Oct. 1984 (No. 83), 8 E.H.R.R. 246.

Sweden on charges of smuggling narcotics. He was brought to Stockholm on 24 January 1980 and held in prison, appearing before a court only on 8 February 1980. After his subsequent trial, conviction and imprisonment, the main issue before the European Court was whether he had been brought promptly before a judge. Under the Swedish law at that time, the Swedish court had to be notified immediately when an arrest warrant had been executed and could then order the detained person to be tried within two weeks. If the trial could not be held within two weeks, the court had at least once every two weeks to decide in a public hearing whether detention should be continued. The Court had no difficulty in dealing with the question of delay:

27. The Court, like the Commission, notes that the Stockholm District Court did not hear Mr. McGoff in person when it issued a warrant for his arrest in October 1977 and that his detention began more than two years later. This being so, the arrest warrant did not preclude the subsequent application of the guarantees in Article 5(3). However, fifteen days elapsed between the time when Mr. McGoff was placed in custody in Sweden (24 January 1980) and when he was brought before the District Court (8 February 1980). An interval of this length cannot be regarded as consistent with the required 'promptness'. By way of comparison, reference may be made to the *De Jong, Baljet and Van Den Brink* judgment of 22 May 1984[109] where the Court held that, six days after arrest, the limits laid down by the Convention had already been exceeded.

Accordingly, there has been a breach of Article 5(3).

(A) BROGAN *V.* UNITED KINGDOM

Judgment of 24 Nov. 1988
(No. 145B), 11 E.H.R.R. 117

[During and after the 1970s, because of the commission of acts of terrorism arising from events in Northern Ireland, the British Parliament conferred on the police special powers for detaining those suspected of IRA membership or other terrorist activities. Under the Prevention of Terrorism (Temporary Provisions) Act 1984, the police could hold those suspected of being concerned in terrorism for up to 48 hours and, with authority from the Secretary of State, for a further five days. By contrast, under the general criminal law, suspects might be detained by the police for 36 hours at most before being brought into court for a decision as to whether they should continue to be detained pending the bringing of charges.

Brogan and three others from Northern Ireland were held by the police under the 1984 Act for periods ranging between four days six hours, and six days 16 hours, authority for their detention beyond 48 hours having been obtained from the Secretary of State. Each was then released without being charged with any offences. At Strasbourg they claimed breaches of paragraphs 1, 3, 4 and 5 of Article 5.]

48. The government has adverted extensively to the existence of particularly difficult circumstances in Northern Ireland, notably the threat posed by organized terrorism.

The Court, having taken notice of the growth of terrorism in modern society, has already recognised the need, inherent in the Convention system, for a proper balance between the defence of the institutions of democracy in the common interest and the protection of individual rights . . . Examination of the case must proceed on the basis that the Articles of the Convention in respect

---

[109] See *supra* n. 103.

of which complaints have been made are fully applicable. This does not, however, preclude proper account being taken of the background circumstances of the case. In the context of Article 5, it is for the Court to determine the significance to be attached to those circumstances and to ascertain whether, in the instant case, the balance struck complied with the applicable provisions of that Article in the light of their particular wording and its overall object and purpose.

[In respect of the claimed breach of Article 5(1), the applicants argued that they had been detained on suspicion of involvement in unspecified acts of terrorism, not on suspicion of having committed a specific offence. They argued that they had been subjected to administrative detention exercised for the purpose of gathering information, as was corroborated by the use in practice of the special powers. The Court rejected these arguments by a majority of 16–3, holding that the detention fell within Article 5(1)(c). The Court said that the fact that the applicants were neither charged nor brought before a court did not necessarily mean that the purpose of their detention was inconsistent with Article 5(1)(c). There was no reason to believe that the police investigation was not in good faith or that the detention of the applicants was not intended to further that investigation. On whether there had been a breach of Article 5(3), the Court was also divided.]

55. Under the 1984 Act, a person arrested under section 12 on reasonable suspicion of involvement in acts of terrorism may be detained by police for an initial period of 48 hours, and, on the authorisation of the Secretary of State for Northern Ireland, for a further period or periods of up to five days. . . .

The applicants noted that a person arrested under the ordinary law of Northern Ireland must be brought before a Magistrates' Court within 48 hours and that under the ordinary law in England and Wales (Police and Criminal Evidence Act 1984) the maximum period of detention permitted without charge is four days, judicial approval being required at the 36 hour stage. In their submission, there was no plausible reason why a seven-day detention period was necessary, marking as it did such a radical departure from ordinary law and even from the three-day period permitted under the special powers of detention embodied in the Northern Ireland (Emergency Provisions) Act 1978. Nor was there any justification for not entrusting such decisions to the judiciary of Northern Ireland.

56. The government has argued that in view of the nature and extent of the terrorist threat and the resulting problems in obtaining evidence sufficient to bring charges, the maximum statutory period of detention of seven days was an indispensable part of the effort to combat that threat . . . In particular, they drew attention to the difficulty faced by the security forces in obtaining evidence which is both admissible and usable in consequence of training in anti-interrogation techniques adopted by those involved in terrorism. Time was also needed to undertake necessary scientific examinations, to correlate information from other detainees and to liaise with other security forces. The government claimed that the need for a power of extension of the period of detention was borne out by statistics. For instance, in 1987 extensions were granted in Northern Ireland in respect of 365 persons. Some 83 were detained in excess of five days and of this number 39 were charged with serious terrorist offences during the extended period.

As regards the suggestion that extensions of detention beyond the initial 48-hour period should be controlled or even authorised by a judge, the government pointed out the difficulty, in view of the acute sensitivity of some of the information on which the suspicion was based, of producing it in court. Not only would the court have to sit *in camera* but neither the detained person nor his legal advisers could be present or told any of the details. This would require a fundamental and undesirable change in the law and procedure of the United Kingdom . . .

In all the circumstances, the Secretary of State was better placed to take such decisions and to ensure a consistent approach. Moreover, the merits of each request to extend detention were personally scrutinised by the Secretary of State or, if he was unavailable, by another Minister. . . .

58. The fact that a detained person is not charged or brought before a court does not in itself amount to a violation of the first part of Article 5(3). No violation of Article 5(3) can arise if the arrested person is released 'promptly' before any judicial control of his detention would have been feasible. If the arrested person is not released promptly, he is entitled to a prompt appearance before a judge or judicial officer.

The assessment of 'promptness' has to be made in the light of the object and purpose of Article 5. The Court has regard to the importance of this Article in the Convention system: it enshrines a fundamental human right, namely the protection of the individual against arbitrary interferences by the State with his right to liberty. . . .

59. The obligation expressed in English by the word 'promptly' and in French by the word '*aussitôt*' is clearly distinguishable from the less strict requirement in the second part of paragraph 3 ('reasonable time'/'*délai raisonnable*') and even from that in paragraph 4 of Article 5 ('speedily'/'*à bref délai*'). . . .

Whereas promptness is to be assessed in each case according to its special features, the significance to be attached to those features can never be taken to the point of impairing the very essence of the right guaranteed by Article 5(3), that is the point of effectively negativing the State's obligation to ensure a prompt release or a prompt appearance before a judicial authority. . . .

61. The investigation of terrorist offences undoubtedly presents the authorities with special problems. . . . The Court takes full judicial notice of the factors adverted to by the government in this connection. It is also true that in Northern Ireland the referral of police requests for extended detention to the Secretary of State and the individual scrutiny of each police request by a Minister do provide a form of executive control. In addition, the need for the continuation of the special powers has been constantly monitored by Parliament and their operation regularly reviewed by independent personalities. The Court accepts that, subject to the existence of adequate safeguards, the context of terrorism in Northern Ireland has the effect of prolonging the period during which the authorities may, without violating Article 5(3), keep a person suspected of serious terrorist offences in custody before bringing him before a judge or other judicial officer.

The difficulties, alluded to by the government, of judicial control over decisions to arrest and detain suspected terrorists may affect the manner of implementation of Article 5(3), for example in calling for appropriate procedural precautions in view of the nature of the suspected offences. However, they cannot justify, under Article 5(3), dispensing altogether with 'prompt' judicial control.

62. As indicated above, the scope for flexibility in interpreting and applying the notion of 'promptness' is very limited. In the court's view, even the shortest of the four periods of detention namely the four days and six hours spent in police custody by Mr. McFadden, falls outside the strict constraints as to time permitted by the first part of Article 5(3). To attach such importance to the special features of this case as to justify so lengthy a period of detention without appearance before a judge or other judicial officer would be an unacceptably wide interpretation of the plain meaning of the word 'promptly'. An interpretation to this effect would import into Article

5(3) a serious weakening of a procedural guarantee to the detriment of the individual and would entail consequences impairing the very essence of the right protected by this provision. The Court thus has to conclude that none of the applicants was either brought 'promptly' before a judicial authority or released 'promptly' following his arrest. The undoubted fact that the arrest and detention of the applicants were inspired by the legitimate aim of protecting the community as a whole from terrorism is not on its own sufficient to ensure compliance with the specific requirements of Article 5(3).

There has thus been a breach of Article 5(3) in respect of all four applicants . . .

This decision that Article 5(3) had been breached was taken by a majority of twelve votes to seven. The Court held unanimously that there had been no breach of Article 5(4), since the remedy of habeas corpus was available to the applicants, although they had not made use of it; and, further, (by thirteen votes to six) that Article 5(5) had been breached, since the violations of Article 5(3) had not given rise to an enforceable right to compensation in the Northern Ireland courts. A short account of the sequel to this important decision will be found in the final section of this Chapter. What was decided in *Brogan* as regards Article (5)(1)(c) was, as we have seen, reconsidered by the Court in *Fox, Campbell and Hartley v. United Kingdom*.[110]

In *Sakik v. Turkey*,[111] six applicants, members of the Democratic Party, were former members of the Turkish National Assembly and of a political party which had been dissolved on account of its unconstitutional activities. In March 1994, they were arrested (two of them while leaving the Parliament building in Ankara on 2 March and the rest on 4 March) and detained on charges of having committed terrorist activities. Their detention was authorised by the prosecutor attached to the Ankara National Security Court until 16 March 1994. Only on 17 March was their continued detention authorised by the court. The applicants complained *inter alia* of breaches of Article 5(3) and 5(4). As regards Article 5(3), the Court said, citing decisions such as *Brogan v. United Kingdom*:

The Court has already accepted on several occasions that the investigation of terrorist offences undoubtedly presents the authorities with special problems. This does not mean, however, that the investigating authorities have *carte blanche* under Article 5 to arrest suspects for questioning, free from effective control by the domestic courts and, ultimately, by the Convention supervisory institutions, whenever they choose to assert that terrorism is involved.

What is at stake here is the importance of Article 5 in the Convention system: it enshrines a fundamental human right, namely the protection of the individual against arbitrary interferences by the State with his right to liberty . . . [paragraph 44]

. . . Even supposing that the activities of which the applicants stood accused were linked to a terrorist threat, the Court cannot accept that it was necessary to detain them for 12 or 14 days without judicial intervention [paragraph 45].

The Court also held that there had been breaches of Article 5(4) (in the absence of

---

[110] See Section (E)(1)(C) *supra*.
[111] 26 Nov. 1997, Reports, 1997–VII 2609, 26 E.H.R.R. 662.

an available remedy to enable a court to rule on the legality of the detention) and of Article 5(5), since the applicants had no realistic prospect in national law of obtaining compensation for detention in breach of their Convention rights. The Turkish government relied unsuccessfully on a derogation filed under Article 15 of the Convention relating to the security situation in south-east Turkey.[112]

G. THE RIGHT TO A DECISION BY A COURT AS TO THE LEGALITY OF DETENTION

An all-pervasive theme in Article 5 is that an act interfering with individual liberty must not only be for one of the stated grounds but must also be 'lawful'. Article 5 requires at the least that such an act must be authorized in national law, both as to the grounds and as to the procedure involved. Where someone has been deprived of their liberty, he or she is entitled by Article 5(4) to a 'speedy' decision by a national court as to whether the deprivation is lawful and to an order for his or her release if it is not.

It is one thing for a national constitution to contain finely phrased guarantees of individual liberty. It is another thing for a legal system, through the decisions of its courts, to provide a prompt and effective remedy against any official body that has taken away someone's liberty. It is such a remedy which English law has for long sought to provide by means of the writ of habeas corpus. As the nineteenth-century jurist A. V. Dicey wrote:

There is no difficulty, and there is often very little gain, in declaring the existence of a right to personal freedom. The true difficulty is to secure its enforcement. The Habeas Corpus Acts have achieved this end, and have therefore done for the liberty of Englishmen more than could have been achieved by any declaration of rights.[113]

And, even more sweepingly, Dicey proclaimed:

The Habeas Corpus Acts declare no principle and define no rights, but they are for practical purposes worth a hundred constitutional articles guaranteeing individual liberty.

Under the Convention, Article 5(4) is the 'habeas corpus' clause. It recognizes that the deprivation of an individual's liberty may well be disputed, and requires such disputes to be resolved speedily by the national courts.

One distinction drawn in the case-law (as we saw in *Winterwerp v. The Netherlands*, above) is that where the decision depriving the individual of liberty is taken by an administrative body, Article 5(4) requires a state to make available a right of recourse to a court; but if the initial decision is itself taken by a court, the requirements of Article 5(4) may be incorporated in that decision, provided that an adequate pro-

---

[112] See Section H, *infra*.
[113] A. V. Dicey, *Law and the Constitution* (10th edn., by E. C. S. Wade, 1959), 221.

cedure, respecting the rights of the individual, has been observed.[114] However, even if judicial procedure appears to have been observed initially, a decision by an inferior court affecting individual liberty ought to be subject to possible review and supervision by a superior court. Such review must itself be made 'speedily', i.e. without excessive delay.[115] Article 5(4) 'does not guarantee a right to judicial control of all aspects or details of the detention',[116] but does require a review of the essential grounds of a detention. It is somewhat ironic, as we have already seen (in *X v. United Kingdom* and in *Chahal v. United Kingdom*, above), that the habeas corpus procedure in English law does not always meet this requirement. The Court has also laid down the minimum procedural requirements which such hearings must observe.

In *De Jong, Baljet and Van Den Brink v. The Netherlands*,[117] three conscripts to the Dutch army refused to obey orders on grounds of conscientious objection. They were arrested and kept in custody pending trial before a military court. The Court decided that paragraphs 3 and 4 of Article 5 could be applied concurrently, since, in the Court's words, 'the guarantee assured by paragraph 4 is of a different order from, and additional to, that provided by paragraph 3'.[118] With respect to Article 5(4), the Court said:

58. The two remedies relied on by the Government in connection with paragraph 4 of Article 5 were those available under Articles 13 and 34 of the Military Code.

Article 13, which is applicable in the period prior to referral for trial, allows a suspected serviceman who has been in custody on remand for 14 days to petition the Military Court to fix a term within which the commanding general must either decide whether the case is to be referred for trial or else terminate the detention. The fact that this remedy could not be exercised until at least two weeks after the arrest prevented the applicants from being able to obtain a 'speedy' decision, even having regard to the exigencies of military life and military justice.

Following referral and prior to the commencement of the trial, Article 34 permits the detained serviceman to address a request for release to the Military Court. It was not disputed in the present case that the Military Court could be regarded as a 'court' for the purposes of Article 5(4), in the sense of enjoying the necessary independence and offering sufficient procedural safeguards appropriate to the category of deprivation of liberty being dealt with. In addition, Article 34 of the Military Code is capable in practice of leading to a 'speedy' decision, depending upon how rapidly the referral for trial occurs in the particular circumstances. Mr. de Jong was seven days, Mr. Baljet 11 days and Mr. van den Brink six days in custody, before being referred for trial and hence without a remedy. In the Court's view, even having regard to the exigencies of military life and military justice, the length of absence of access to a court was in each case such

---

[114] See *De Wilde, Ooms and Versyp v. Belgium*, 18 June 1971 (No. 12), 1 E.H.R.R. 373, para. 73.

[115] See e.g. *Luberti v. Italy*, 23 Feb. 1984 (No. 75), 6 E.H.R.R. 440, 451–4: undue delay where, in 'an urgent case involving deprivation of liberty', it took the superior courts over 18 months to review the decision of committal; and *E v. Norway* 29 Aug. 1990 (No. 181A), 17 E.H.R.R. 30 discussed at Section (G)(1) *infra*.

[116] *Ashingdane v. United Kingdom*, 28 May 1985 (No. 93), 7 E.H.R.R. 528, para. 52.

[117] 22 May 1984 (No. 77), 8 E.H.R.R. 20.

[118] *Id.* at para. 57. The Court also held that the '*auditeur-militair*', an officer in the Dutch army with prosecutorial functions, was not an officer 'authorised by law to exercise judicial power for the purposes of Article 5(3): *id.* paras. 46–50, 23 Oct. 1990 (No. 188). And *see Huber v. Switzerland*, reprinted at Section (F)(1)(A) *supra*, and *Hood v. United Kingdom*, 18 Feb. 1999 (not yet reported), discussed at Section (F)(1)(A) *supra*.

as to deprive the applicant of his entitlement to bring proceedings to obtain a 'speedy' review of the lawfulness of his detention.

1. SANCHEZ-REISSE *v.* SWITZERLAND

Judgment of 21 Oct. 1986
(No. 107), 9 E.H.R.R. 71

[An Argentinian citizen, Mr. Sanchez-Reisse, was alleged to have been involved in a kidnapping conspiracy in Argentina. He was arrested in Lausanne and held in prison while the Argentine government instituted proceedings for his extradition from Switzerland. Two requests for release made to the Swiss authorities were refused after some delay in each case. He complained both of the nature of the procedure by which his requests for release were considered and of the delays that occurred.]

44. In the first place, he complained of the fact that he had not been able to apply directly to a court. Being obliged, like anyone who was detained with a view to extradition, to turn first of all to an administrative body, he did not have, so he maintained, direct access to the judicial authority competent to hear a request by him for provisional release. . . .

45. As Mr. Sanchez-Reisse had stated that he objected to being extradited, the Federal Court had exclusive jurisdiction to rule on the question of release. Although, legally speaking, the request was addressed solely to the Federal Court, the practice—since enshrined in the 1981 Act—was that the request went first to the [Federal Police] Office, which examined it and gave an opinion thereon.

The Court considers that the intervention of the Office did not impede the applicant's access to the Federal Court or limit the latter's power of review. Moreover, it may meet a legitimate concern: as extradition, by its very nature, involves a State's international relations, it is understandable that the executive should have an opportunity to express its views on a measure likely to have an influence in such a sensitive area.

46. The applicant made a second complaint, concerning the impossibility of conducting one's own defence, due to the fact that the exclusively written nature of the procedure necessitated the assistance of a lawyer. He alleged that a detainee needed to be able to check the action taken by the lawyer, in particular by attending the oral proceedings, especially as the latter might have been appointed by the Office. . . .

47. In the Court's view, the allegation of the applicant—who in fact chose his lawyer himself—does not stand up to examination. It has no basis in the actual text of Article 5(4). What is more, it loses sight of the fact that Swiss law, by requiring the assistance of a lawyer, affords an important guarantee to the person concerned by an extradition procedure. The detainee is, by definition, a foreigner in the country in question and therefore often unfamiliar with its legal system. Furthermore, Mr. Sanchez-Reisse furnished no evidence that his legal knowledge was sufficient to enable him to present his requests effectively in writing.

48. Mr. Sanchez-Reisse also alleged that he should have had an opportunity of replying to the Office's opinion, which was *ex hypothesi* negative since its very existence presupposed a refusal on the part of the administrative authority to grant release.

At the same time he complained of the fact that he had not been able to appear—either as of right or on his application—before a court in order to argue the case for his release. In his view, this was the cause of the worsening of his state of health, which was the main ground of his requests for release. The lack of any contact with a court was, he said, incompatible with the very nature of habeas corpus. It was all the harsher as detention with a view to extradition afforded the detainee fewer points of reference than ordinary pretrial detention: in Switzerland a court hearing extradition cases confined itself to reviewing compliance with the conditions of the treaty and thus did not consider the merits of the charge.

49. The Government maintained that the Office's opinion was the counterpart of the reasons adduced by the detainee in support of his request for release. There was thus equality of arms.

The Government also disputed the existence of any right to appear in person. They advocated a systematic interpretation of Article 5, stressing notably a contrast between paragraphs 3 and 4; they relied in this connection on the Court's case law, in particular the *Winterwerp* judgment of 24 October 1979[119] and the judgment of 5 November 1981 in the case of *X v. United Kingdom*.[120] In the Government's submission, to deprive a person against whom extradition proceedings were being taken of his liberty was a measure of international co-operation, and this made the particular circumstances of the individual of secondary importance. . . .

51. In the Court's opinion, Article 5(4) required in the present case that Mr. Sanchez-Reisse be provided, in some way or another, with the benefit of an adversarial procedure.

Giving him the possibility of submitting written comments on the Office's opinion would have constituted an appropriate means, but there is nothing to show that he was offered such a possibility. Admittedly, he had already indicated in his request the circumstances which, in his view, justified his release, but this of itself did not provide the 'equality of arms' that is indispensable: the opinion could subsequently have referred to new points of fact or of law giving rise, on the detainee's part, to reactions or criticisms or even to questions of which the Federal Court should have been able to take notice before rendering its decision.

The applicant's reply did not, however, necessarily have to be in writing: the result required by Article 5(4) could also have been attained if he had appeared in person before the Federal Court.

The possibility for a detainee 'to be heard either in person or, where necessary, through some form of representation' features in certain instances among the 'fundamental guarantees of procedure applied in matters of deprivation of liberty'.[121] Despite the difference in wording between paragraph 3 (right to be brought before a judge or other officer) and paragraph 4 (right to take proceedings) of Article 5, the Court's previous decisions relating to these two paragraphs have hitherto tended to acknowledge the need for a hearing before the judicial authority. These decisions concerned, however, only matters falling within the ambit of sub-paragraphs (c) and (e) *in fine* of paragraph 1. And, in fact, 'the forms of the procedure required by the Convention need not . . . necessarily be identical in each of the cases where the intervention of a court is required'.[122]

In the present case, the Federal Court was led to take into consideration the applicant's worsening state of health, a factor which might have militated in favour of his appearing in person,

---

[119] *Winterwerp v. The Nethlands*, 24 Oct. 1979 (No. 33), 2 E.H.R.R. 387 reprinted at Section (D)(1) *supra*.

[120] (No. 46), 4 E.H.R.R. 188.

[121] *De Wilde, Ooms and Versyp v. Belgium* 18 June 1971 (No. 12), 1 E.H.R.R. 373, para. 76 reprinted at Section (D)(2) *supra*.

[122] See *Winterwerp v. The Netherlands*, *supra*, n. 119 and *Schiesser v. Switzerland* 4 Dec. 1979 (no. 34), 2 E.H.R.R. 417 discussed at Section (F)(1) *supra*.

but it had at its disposal the medical certificates appended to the third request for provisional release from custody. There is no reason to believe that the applicant's presence could have convinced the Federal Court that he had to be released.

Nevertheless, it remains the case that Mr. Sanchez-Reisse did not receive the benefit of a procedure that was really adversarial.

52. To sum up, the procedure followed in the two cases in dispute did not, viewed as a whole, fully comply with the guarantees afforded by Article 5(4).

[Judges Ganshof van der Meersch and Walsh concurred, but differed from the majority judgment on a significant point of principle:]

. . . In our view, an exclusively written procedure does not satisfy the requirements of Article 5(4) of the Convention, even if the person concerned does have the benefit of the assistance of a lawyer and of the opportunity to challenge the legality of his detention before competent courts.

Despite the silence of the provision in question, it seems to us that only the opportunity for the prisoner to be heard in person provides a complete answer to Article 5(4). This latter is inspired by the institution of habeas corpus which fundamentally consists of appearing in flesh and blood before the court.

Moreover, the same solution is woven into the thread of the Court's case law which has hitherto, as the Court's judgment mentions, tended to acknowledge the necessity of a hearing by a judicial authority. It is true that the case law so far only concerns hypotheses relevant to letters (c) and (e) *in fine* of paragraph 1, but we cannot see any reasons why a person 'against whom action is being taken with a view to deportation of extradition' (letter (f)) should be so deprived.

In brief, the personal appearance of the applicant before the court was necessary.

The Court also considered whether the Swiss authorities had in two instances complied with the requirement in Article 5(4) that the question of whether a detention was lawful must be 'decided speedily'. Delays had occurred both while the Federal Police Office processed the papers (21 and 20 days) and while the matter was before the court (10 and 26 days). The Court held (by six to one) that, in what was a straightforward case, these delays were excessive. For this reason too, there had been a breach of Article 5(4).

The requirement that judicial proceedings reviewing the legality of detention be 'decided speedily' was considered in *E v. Norway*.[123] E, who had repeatedly been convicted of crimes of violence, and was considered to be an untreatable psychopath, was subject to a decision by the Ministry of Justice that for a short but indefinite time he should be held in a secure institution. E sought judicial review of that decision, but it was over eight weeks before the Oslo court upheld the detention. E claimed that Article 5(4) had been infringed, contending *inter alia* that the lawfulness of his detention had not been decided 'speedily'. His detention had been authorized on 21 July 1988, proceedings to challenge the detention were instituted on 3 August, a hearing held on 7 September and judgment was delivered on 27 September. The Strasbourg Court found that one reason for initial delay in Oslo was that the challenge had been instituted during the vacation period, and observed that the Convention requires states:

[123] 29 Aug. 1990 (No 181A), 17 E.H.R.R. 30.

to organise their legal systems so as to enable the courts to comply with its various require-ments. It is incumbent on the judicial authorities to make the necessary administrative arrangements, even during a vacation period to ensure that urgent matters are dealt with speedily, and this is particularly necessary when the individual's personal liberty is at stake [paragraph 66].

Even after the hearing, it took the judge three weeks to deliver judgment. The Court concluded that Article 5(4) had been breached, since E had not received the speedy decision to which he was entitled.

2. BOUAMAR *V.* BELGIUM

Judgment of 29 Feb. 1988
(No. 129), 11 E.H.R.R. 1

[Naim Bouamar, a Moroccan boy living in Belgium, had a disturbed personality owing mainly to family problems. He was suspected of various criminal offences and on no less than nine occasions in 1980, when he was aged 16, he was detained in a remand prison for adults for periods not exceeding 15 days, after which he would return to an open juvenile institution or to his family home. In all, he spent 119 days in prison during 1980. A succession of appeals against the commitments to prison were unsuccessful. The European Court rejected the main submission by the Belgian government that the successive detentions were within Article 5(1)(d) (detention of a minor by lawful order for the purpose of educational supervision) and then considered whether there had been breaches of Article 5(4).]

56. The Government submitted that the review required in Article 5(4) was incorporated in the decision to deprive a person of his liberty where, as in the instant case, it was taken by a judicial body.

57. The Juvenile Court, which is a single-judge section of the Liège *Tribunal de Première Instance*, is undoubtedly a 'court' from the organisational point of view, but the European Court has consistently held that the intervention of a single body of this kind will satisfy Article 5(4) only on condition that 'the procedure followed has a judicial character and gives to the individual concerned guarantees appropriate to the kind of deprivation of liberty in question; in order to determine whether a proceeding provides adequate guarantees, regard must be had to the particu-lar nature of the circumstances in which such proceeding takes place'.

58. That being so, it must be determined whether the applicant enjoyed such guarantees before the Juvenile Court.

The 1965 Act does contain some of them. Section 62 lays down that the provisions relating to proceedings in respect of lesser criminal offences normally apply also to proceedings against juveniles. Furthermore, sections 54 and 55 permit juveniles to be represented by a lawyer, who will be allowed access to all the documents in the file.

59. The applicant, however, complained of the informal nature of these proceedings. The 1965 Act made no provision for any hearing *inter partes* where the Juvenile Court judge had to make an interim custody order in chambers. He was free to take his decision on the basis of what he considered to be adequate information.

The Government contended that the informal nature of the proceedings was justified by the youth of the persons concerned, the urgency of the measures to be taken and the short duration of their effects. . . . At all events, the Government maintained, Mr. Bouamar had been given a hearing by a judge before each placement was ordered and his lawyer had had every opportunity to plead his case.

The young man's lawyers stated, however, that as they had never been given notice to attend, they had never been present at the hearings in chambers which had taken place each time before the juvenile was sent to the remand prison, whereas they had sometimes appeared before the juvenile courts in this case on other occasions. In addition, they had not been enabled to comment on the submissions of Crown Counsel—when the latter made an application to the Juvenile Court—or on the welfare reports, to which they had had no access.

60. The Court reiterates that the scope of the obligation under Article 5(4) is not identical in all circumstances or for every kind of deprivation of liberty. Nevertheless, in a case of the present kind, it is essential not only that the individual concerned should have the opportunity to be heard in person but that he should also have the effective assistance of his lawyer. The impugned orders make it clear that the juvenile was given a hearing by the Juvenile Court, except in one instance when he refused to be heard. However, they do not give any indication that one of his lawyers was present; counsel for the applicant moreover denied that one of them was present, and the Government did not dispute their statements. The mere fact that Mr. Bouamar—who was very young at the time—appeared in person before the court did not, in the circumstances of the case, afford him the necessary safeguards.

61. The Court must consequently ascertain whether the remedies available against the aforementioned placement orders satisfied the conditions in Article 5(4), as was argued by the Government but disputed by the applicant. In the first place, an ordinary appeal (*appel*) could be lodged and, in the second place, where appropriate, an appeal lay on points of law (*pourvoi en cassation*). It was also possible both for the Juvenile Court and for the Juvenile Court of Appeal in further interim proceedings to revoke or vary the initial decision, either on an application by Crown Counsel or of their own motion.

62. In the instant case, several of the orders for provisional placement in a remand prison were varied or revoked, expressly or by implication, by further interim orders made either on appeal . . . or by the Juvenile Court.

However, most of the further interim proceedings before the Juvenile Court and the Juvenile Court of Appeal suffered from the same defect as the earlier proceedings: they took place in the absence of Mr. Bouamar's lawyers.

63. At the hearings of the applicant's appeals against the orders of 18 January, 4 March, 7 May and 4 July 1980, the juvenile chamber of the Court of Appeal heard one or other of Mr. Bouamar's lawyers. But it did not give its decision until 29 April 1980 on the appeals against the orders of 18 January and 4 March 1980; 30 June 1980 on the appeal against the order of 7 May 1980; and 3 February 1981 on the appeal against the order of 4 July 1980. Such lapses of time are scarcely compatible with the speed required by the terms of Article 5(4) of the Convention.

Furthermore, the appellate court did not really 'decide' the 'lawfulness' of the placement measures which were challenged before it, although it did go into the issue of lawfulness in some of the reasons given in two of its three decisions: following established case law, it held in the operative part of its judgments of 29 April 1980, 30 June 1980 and 3 February 1981, that the appeals were inadmissible because devoid of purpose, since Mr. Bouamar had in the meantime been released pursuant to interim orders.

The Court of Cassation held likewise . . .

The applicant's ordinary appeals and appeals on points of law thus had not practical effect.

64. In sum, there was a breach of Article 5(4). . . .

The opportunity to participate in the procedure leading to a judicial decision is fundamental to Article 5(4). Thus in *Toth v. Austria*,[124] the applicant had been arrested on charges of having committed a series of bank frauds and detained on remand for over two years before his trial and conviction. His applications for release on bail had been dealt with in a judicial manner by the court of first instance, but his appeals against refusal of bail had not been accorded due process by the Linz Court of Appeal. That court ruled on his appeals against the refusal of bail without giving either him or his lawyer a hearing, whereas the public prosecutor had been represented before the court. The Strasbourg Court observed that Article 5(4) did not compel a state to provide a second level of jurisdiction to deal with applications for release from detention. But if a state chose to do so, it must afford to detainees the same guarantees on appeal as at first instance. The Court has repeatedly ruled that the question of whether Article 5(4) has been observed must be determined in the light of the circumstances of each case. Thus in *RMD v. Switzerland*,[125] the applicant was detained on suspicion of having committed thefts in seven cantons. Within a period of two months, he was moved from prison to prison in those cantons; attempts by his lawyers to obtain his release were frustrated as by Swiss law an application for release had to be struck out when the detainee was no longer within the canton.

The explanation for that situation lies in the federal structure of the Swiss Confederation, in which each canton has its own code of criminal procedure, and it is not for the Court to express a view on the system as such. Like the Commission, however, the Court considers that those circumstances cannot justify the applicant's being deprived of his rights under Article 5(4). Where . . . a detained person is continually transferred from one canton to another, it is for the State to organise its judicial system in such a way as to enable its courts to comply with the requirements of that Article [paragraphs 53, 54].

The necessity for legal representation and fair procedure has also been emphasized in cases involving mental illness.

---

[124] 12 Dec. 1991 (No. 224), 14 E.H.R.R. 551. See also *Kampanis v. Greece*, 13 July 1995 (No. 325), 21 E.H.R.R. 43 (breach of Art. 5(4) where applicant has been denied the opportunity of hearing and replying to the prosecutor's oral submissions to the court).

[125] 26 Sept. 1997, 28 E.H.R.R. 224.

3. MEGYERI v. GERMANY

Judgment of 12 May 1992
(No. 237A), 15 E.H.R.R. 584

[A Hungarian citizen resident in Germany was found by a German court, at which he was represented by appointed counsel, to have committed criminal offences while suffering from a schizophrenic psychosis with signs of paranoia. He was committed to a psychiatric hospital and his detention was at intervals reviewed by a criminal court, in proceedings for which no counsel were assigned to represent him.]

22. The principles which emerge from the Court's case law on Article 5(4) include the following.

(a) A person of unsound mind who is compulsorily confined in a psychiatric institution for an indefinite or lengthy period is in principle entitled, at any rate where there is no automatic periodic review of a judicial character, to take proceedings at reasonable intervals before a court to put in issue the 'lawfulness'—within the meaning of the Convention—of his detention.

(b) Article 5(4) requires that the procedure followed has a judicial character and gives to the individual concerned guarantees appropriate to the kind of deprivation of liberty in question; in order to determine whether a proceeding provides adequate guarantees, regard must be had to the particular nature of the circumstances in which such proceeding takes place.

(c) The judicial proceedings referred to in Article 5(4) need not always be attended by the same guarantees as those required under Article 6(1) for civil or criminal litigation. Nonetheless, it is essential that the person concerned should have access to a court and the opportunity to be heard either in person or, where necessary, through some form of representation. Special procedural safeguards may prove called for in order to protect the interests of persons who, on account of their mental disabilities, are not fully capable of acting for themselves.

(d) Article 5(4) does not require that persons committed to care under the head of 'unsound mind' should themselves take the initiative in obtaining legal representation before having recourse to a court.

23. It follows from the foregoing that where a person is confined in a psychiatric institution on the ground of the commission of acts which constituted criminal offences but for which he could not be held responsible on account of mental illness, he should—unless there are special circumstances—receive legal assistance in subsequent proceedings relating to the continuation, suspension or termination of his detention. The importance of what is at stake for him—personal liberty—taken together with the very nature of his affliction—diminished mental capacity—compels this conclusion.

24. As regards Mr. Megyeri's state of mental health, the Court recalls that the origin of his confinement was the finding by the Cologne Regional Court on 14 March 1983—in criminal proceedings in which he had been represented by officially-appointed counsel—that he could not be held responsible for his acts because he was suffering from a schizophrenic psychosis with signs of paranoia.

In July 1986 the Aachen Regional Court had before it expert evidence to the effect that there had been a further deterioration in his condition, that he was not willing to undergo treatment and that he showed a distinct propensity towards aggressive behaviour and violence. There had, in addition, been previous court judgments which pointed in the same direction: the applicant was incapable of conducting court proceedings and his mental illness was so obvious that no expert's opinion on the point was necessary; his delusions had become more severe and guardianship proceedings should be instituted.

25. One of the issues falling to be determined in the 1986 review was whether, if Mr. Megyeri were released on probation, he would be likely to commit illegal acts similar to those that had occasioned the original confinement order. In this connection, the Aachen Regional Court not only considered a report by three experts but also heard the applicant in person, in order to form its own impression of him. It is doubtful, to say the least, whether Mr. Megyeri, acting on his own, was able to marshal and present adequately points in his favour on this issue, involving as it did matters of medical knowledge and expertise.

Again, it is even more doubtful whether, on his own, he was in a position adequately to address the legal issue arising: would his continued confinement be proportionate to the aim pursued (the protection of the public), in the sense contemplated in the Federal Constitutional Court's leading judgment of 8 October 1985?

26. Finally, the Court notes that by July 1986 the applicant had already spent more than four years in a psychiatric hospital. As required by German law, his confinement was reviewed by courts at yearly intervals and the 1986 proceedings before the Aachen Regional Court formed part of this series. . . .

27. Nothing in the foregoing analysis reveals that this was a case in which legal assistance was unnecessary, even if it is correct that Mr. Megyeri did not specifically ask the Aachen Regional Court or the Cologne Court of Appeal to assign counsel to him in the proceedings in question. . . .

There has therefore been a breach of Article 5(4). . . .

The United States Supreme Court has held that the determination of the propriety of detention of a person pending criminal trial is governed by the Fourth Amendment to the Constitution which declares that no person may be seized without probable cause. Such cause must be based on 'facts and circumstances sufficient to warrant a prudent man in believing that [the suspect] had committed or was committing an offense'.[126] The Court has held that the decision as to probable cause justifying the initial arrest does not require a prior warrant in every case. It may also be made by a law enforcement officer or a prosecutor. In such cases, however, the detained person is entitled to a judicial determination 'promptly after arrest'.[127] The Supreme Court has refused to set an inflexible rule as to what amount of time may pass before such a hearing. It has held, however, that a hearing within 48 hours is generally sufficient. Beyond that time the state bears the burden of showing a pressing reason for the further delay.[128] While the presence or absence of probable cause is, in many states, decided in a full blown adversary hearing, the Court has held that such a procedure is not constitutionally required. It is sufficient if the question is 'decided by a magistrate in a nonadversary

[126] *Gerstein v. Pugh*, 420 U.S. 103, 111 (1974) quoting *Beck v. Ohio*, 379 U.S. 89, 91 (1964) (internal quotation marks omitted).

[127] 420 U.S. 103, 125 (1974).

[128] *County of Riverside v. McLaughlin*, 500 U.S. 44, 56–7 (1991).

proceeding on hearsay and written testimony . . .'[129] In particular the Constitution does not require the presence of appointed counsel at this stage in the prosecution.[130]

The Canadian Criminal Code provides that a person who is arrested is to be brought before a justice, where a justice is available within a period of 24 hours after the arrest 'without unreasonable delay and in any event within that period'. Some Canadian courts have held that this provision may be violated even when a person is held for less than 24 hours.[131]

Section 9 of the Charter, moreover, prohibits explicitly arbitrary detentions, and a failure to provide a prompt judicial determination of the propriety of the detention might, on reasoning similar to that of the American law discussed, be thought to make it arbitrary, in violation of that provision. Finally, Section 10(c) of the Charter guarantees a right to have the validity of a detention 'determined by way of habeas corpus and to be released if the detention is not lawful'.[132]

The most common guarantee against unjustified detention of a person accused of crime pending trial is the institution of bail, allowing release upon the posting of sufficient security. The English Bill of Rights of 1689 provided that 'excessive bail ought not to be required',[133] and this provided the model for parallel provisions in the Eighth Amendment to the United States Constitution, which states 'excessive bail shall not be required', and in Section 11 of the Canadian Charter of Rights and Freedoms, which declares that every person charged with an offence has the right 'not to be denied reasonable bail without just cause'. All of these formulations, it will be noted, suggest that the *amount* of bail may differ for different cases so long as it is 'reasonable' or not 'excessive'. What is reasonable in a given case depends on the purpose for which the bail is demanded. The central purpose of this requirement has historically been to provide some assurance that the accused will appear for trial. Consequently, the calculation of reasonableness has turned on the risk, in each case, that the defendant may abscond before trial.[134] The factors to be considered in assessing that risk include the severity of the offence charged and the possible punishment, the financial circumstances of the defendant, his history, character and connection to the community where he is to appear.[135]

As there is no right to bail, *per se*, merely a right that the amount set be not

---

[129] *Gerstein v. Pugh*, 420 U.S. 103, 111 (1974) quoting *Beck v. Ohio*, at 120.

[130] *Id.* at 122–3.

[131] R.S.C. 1985, c. C–46, s. 503. *See R v. Koszulap* (1974) 20 C.C.C. (2d) 193 and *R v. Tam* (1995) 100 C.C.C. (3d) 196, paras, 36–57.

[132] *See* generally, P. Hogg, *Constitutional Law of Canada* (3rd edn. 1992), 1069–88. The U.S. Supreme Court has expressly rejected a 24 hour rule as a constitutional requirement; *County of Riverside v. McLaughlin*, n. 128 *supra*.

[133] 1 W. & M. sess. 2, c. 2.

[134] *See Stack v. Boyle*, 342 U.S. 1 (1951).

[135] *See* e.g. *id.*; *Truong Dinh Hung v. United States*, 439 U.S. 1326 (Brennan, Circuit Justice 1978). The Supreme Court of Canada has held valid, as consistent with s. 11 of the Charter provisions that place on a detained person the burden of showing that his or her detention is unjustified if the person is charged with an indictable offence committed while on bail for another indictable offence or with having committed an offence under the Narcotics Control Act: *R. v. Pearson* [1992] 3 S.C.R. 665; *B. v. Morales* [1992] 3 S.C.R. 711.

excessive, it follows that in certain cases no bail may be allowed at all, if, in those circumstances, no amount of money offers sufficient security that the accused will appear for trial. More controversial is the assertion that bail may be denied, not because of doubts about the appearance of the defendant, but because of concerns that his release would create a danger for the community. Statutes of both Canada and the United States provide that such issues are properly considered in deciding whether any bail will be allowed.[136] Although earlier dicta of the Court had indicated that the propriety and amount of bail could, consistent with the presumption of innocence, only be assessed in light of the risk of non-appearance, the United States Supreme Court has held that this procedure does not violate the due process clause of the Fifth Amendment, nor the excessive bail clause of the Eighth Amendment.[137] The Supreme Court of Canada has upheld the constitutionality of provisions authorizing preventive detention for the purpose of protecting public safety. However, it held invalid as impermissibly vague provision for detention when 'in the public interest'.[138]

H. THE CHALLENGE OF TERRORISM AND THE RIGHT OF STATES TO DEROGATE FROM THE CONVENTION

Only some of the duties of states and some individual rights are phrased by the Convention in absolute terms. Thus, while the right not to be tortured is absolute, the rights to respect for private and family life and to freedom of expression (Articles 8 and 10) are subject to qualifications and limitations which are 'prescribed by law and necessary in a democratic society' for stated purposes such as national security or public safety (see Chapters 6 and 5, respectively). Other rights are expressly limited by a test of reasonableness, such as the right of a detained person (under Article 5(3)) to be tried 'within a reasonable time'—the sole right under Article 5 to be qualified in this way. What, then, is the position if a state wishes to impose extraordinary restrictions on individual liberty (for instance, preventive detention for suspected terrorists) which go well beyond ordinary criminal process? Such restrictions are inherently likely to involve breaches of Article 5.

The answer to this question is that a state may secure relief from Article 5 (and certain other duties) by exercising the right to derogate from Convention obligations, which is authorized by Article 15. By this provision, 'in time of war or other emergency threatening the life of the nation', a state may take steps to derogate from those Convention duties which permit derogation.

---

[136] 18 U.S.C. 1342 (g) (1994) (United States); R.S.C. 1985, c. C–46, ss. 515–26.
[137] *United States v. Salerno*, 481 U.S. 739 (1987).
[138] *R v. Pearson, R v. Morales*, both n. 135 *supra*.

The very first case to reach the Court at Strasbourg concerned a derogation by Ireland from Article 5 because of the threat from the IRA.

1. LAWLESS *V.* REPUBLIC OF IRELAND (NO. 3)

Judgment of 1 July 1961
(No. 3), 1 E.H.R.R. 15

[The applicant, an Irish citizen, was detained without trial for five months in 1957 because of his active membership of the IRA. The Court held that detention without trial was a restriction of liberty which was not authorized by Article 5. However, before detaining Mr. Lawless, the Irish government had notified the Secretary-General of the Council of Europe of its intention to use special powers to deal with the threat from the IRA. Did such a derogation exclude the jurisdiction of the Strasbourg Court? In giving its answer to this question, the Court read Article 15, and continued:]

22. It follows from these provisions that, without being released from all its undertakings assumed in the Convention, the Government of any High Contracting Party has the right, in case of war or public emergency threatening the life of the nation, to take measures derogating from its obligations under the Convention other than those named in Article 15(2), provided that such measures are strictly limited to what is required by the exigencies of the situation and also that they do not conflict with other obligations under international law. It is for the Court to determine whether the conditions laid down in Article 15 for the exercise of the exceptional right of derogation have been fulfilled in the present case.

23. The Irish Government, by a Proclamation dated 5 July 1957 and published in the *Official Gazette* on 8 July 1957, brought into force the extraordinary powers conferred upon it by Part II of the Offences against the State (Amendment) Act 1940 'to secure the preservation of public peace and order'.

24. By letter dated 20 July 1957 addressed to the Secretary-General of the Council of Europe, the Irish Government expressly stated that 'the detention of persons under the Act is considered necessary to prevent the commission of offences against public peace and order and to prevent the maintaining of military or armed forces other than those authorized by the Constitution'. . . .

28. In the general context of Article 15 of the Convention, the natural and customary meaning of the words 'other public emergency threatening the life of the nation' is sufficiently clear; they refer to an exceptional situation of crisis or emergency which affects the whole population and constitutes a threat to the organised life of the community of which the State is composed . . . [The] Court must determine whether the facts and circumstances which led the Irish Government to make their Proclamation of 5 July 1957 come within this conception. The Court, after an examination, finds this to be the case; the existence at the time of a 'public emergency threatening the life of the nation' was reasonably deduced by the Irish Government from a combination of several factors, namely in the first place, the existence in the territory of the Republic of Ireland of a secret army engaged in unconstitutional activities and using violence to attain its purposes; secondly, the fact that this army was also operating outside the territory of the State, thus seriously jeopardising the relations of the Republic of Ireland with its neighbour; thirdly, the steady and alarming increase in terrorist activities from the autumn of 1956 and throughout the first half of 1957.

29. Despite the gravity of the situation, the Government had succeeded, by using means available under ordinary legislation, in keeping public institutions functioning more or less normally, but the homicidal ambush on the night of 3 to 4 July 1957 in the territory of Northern Ireland near the border had brought to light, just before 12 July—a date, which, for historical reasons, is particularly critical for the preservation of public peace and order—the imminent danger to the nation caused by the continuance of unlawful activities in Northern Ireland by the IRA and various associated groups, operating from the territory of the Republic of Ireland.

30. In conclusion, the Irish Government were justified in declaring that there was a public emergency in the Republic of Ireland threatening the life of the nation and were hence entitled, applying the provisions of Article 15 (1) of the Convention for the purposes for which those provisions were made, to take measures derogating from their obligations under the Convention.

31. Article 15(1) provides that a High Contracting Party may derogate from its obligations under the Convention only 'to the extent strictly required by the exigencies of the situation'. It is therefore necessary . . . to examine whether the bringing into force of Part II of the 1940 Act was a measure strictly required by the emergency existing in 1957.

32. G. R. Lawless contended before the Commission that even if the situation in 1957 was such as to justify derogation from obligations under the Convention, the bringing into operation and the enforcement of Part II of the Offences against the State (Amendment) Act 1940 were disproportionate to the strict requirements of the situation. . . .

36. However, in the judgment of the Court, in 1957 the application of the ordinary law had proved unable to check the growing danger which threatened the Republic of Ireland. The ordinary criminal courts, or even the special criminal court or military courts, could not suffice to restore peace and order; in particular, the amassing of the necessary evidence to convict persons involved in activities of the IRA and its splinter groups was meeting with great difficulties caused by the military, secret and terrorist character of those groups and the fear they created among the population. The fact that these groups operated mainly in Northern Ireland, their activities in the Republic of Ireland being virtually limited to the preparation of armed raids across the border, was an additional impediment to the gathering of sufficient evidence. The sealing of the border would have had extremely serious repercussions on the population as a whole, beyond the extent required by the exigencies of the emergency.

It follows from the foregoing that none of the above-mentioned means would have made it possible to deal with the situation existing in Ireland in 1957. Therefore, the administrative detention . . . of individuals suspected of intending to take part in terrorist activities, appeared, despite its gravity, to be a measure required by the circumstances.

37. Moreover, the Offences against the State (Amendment) Act of 1940 was subject to a number of safeguards designed to prevent abuses in the operation of the system of administrative detention. The application of the Act was thus subject to constant supervision by Parliament, which not only received precise details of its enforcement at regular intervals but could also at any time, by a resolution, annul the Government's Proclamation which had brought the Act into force. The Offences against the State (Amendment) Act 1940 provided for the establishment of a Detention Commission made up of three members, . . . the members being an officer of the Defence Forces and two judges. Any person detained under this Act could refer his case to that Commission whose opinion, if favourable to the release of the person concerned, was binding upon the Government; moreover, the ordinary courts could themselves compel the Detention Commission to carry out its functions.

In conclusion, immediately after the Proclamation which brought the power of detention into force, the Government publicly announced that it would release any person detained who gave an undertaking to respect the Constitution and the law and not to engage in any illegal activity . . . The persons arrested were informed immediately after their arrest that they would be released following the undertaking in question. In a democratic country such as Ireland, the existence of this guarantee of release given publicly by the Government constituted a legal obligation on the Government to release all persons who gave the undertaking.

Therefore, it follows from the foregoing that the detention without trial provided for by the 1940 Act, subject to the above-mentioned safeguards, appears to be a measure strictly required by the exigencies of the situation within the meaning of Article 15 of the Convention. . . .

In the case of *Ireland v. United Kingdom*, (Chapter 4(A)) it was the British government's decision to introduce detention without trial which enabled the security forces to adopt the methods of interrogation in depth that gave rise to the complaints of torture and inhuman and degrading treatment. Quite apart from the practice of interrogation, the detentions themselves would necessarily have involved breaches of Article 5. As the Court held in *Ireland v. United Kingdom*:

(a) the power to detain without trial is not within the list of permitted grounds in Article 5(1);

(b) those arrested were not informed promptly of the reasons for their arrest (Article 5(2));

(c) they were not brought promptly before a court or other competent judicial authority (Article 5(3)); and

(d) their rights in national law to seek judicial review of the legality of their detention were not sufficient to satisfy Article 5(4).

However, the Court also held (citing *Lawless v. Ireland (No. 3)*, above) that the United Kingdom had derogated validly from its obligations under Article 5, and the government had stayed within the 'margin of appreciation' available to it under Article 15 when it adopted the policy of detention without trial. As the Court stated:

207. . . . It falls in the first place to each Contracting State, with its responsibility for 'the life of [its] nation', to determine whether that life is threatened by a 'public emergency' and, if so, how far it is necessary to go in attempting to overcome the emergency. By reason of their direct and continuous contact with the pressing needs of the moment, the national authorities are in principle in a better position than the international judge to decide both on the presence of such an emergency and on the nature and scope of derogations necessary to avert it. In this matter, Article 15(1) leaves those authorities a wide margin of appreciation.

Nevertheless, the States do not enjoy an unlimited power in this respect. The Court, which, with the Commission, is responsible for ensuring the observance of the States' engagements (Art. 19) is empowered to rule on whether the States have gone beyond the 'extent strictly required by the exigencies' of the crisis. The domestic margin of appreciation is thus accompanied by a European supervision.

2. THE SEQUEL TO *BROGAN V. UNITED KINGDOM*

The derogation under Article 15 which was considered in *Ireland v. United Kingdom* was withdrawn by the British government in August 1984, several years after the government had given up the policy of detaining suspected terrorists without trial (although the legislation permitting detention without trial was not repealed). No derogation under Article 15 was in force at the time of the arrests which gave rise to *Brogan v. United Kingdom*.[139] As we have seen, the Court in *Brogan* held that the legislation authorizing detention by authority of the Secretary of State for up to seven days was incompatible with the rights guaranteed by Article 5. In response to the Court's decision, the United Kingdom legislation could have been amended, either by reducing the period of detention for questioning or by requiring a detainee to be brought promptly before a judge or other officer exercising judicial power. In fact, the government insisted that the ability to hold suspects for up to seven days was necessary in the fight against terrorism and that it was not possible to introduce 'a satisfactory procedure for the review of detention of terrorist suspects involving the judiciary'.[140] Being unwilling to change the law, the government lodged a derogation under Article 15 so that it might continue to detain suspects for up to seven days without any judicial authority being obtained. Was this derogation a proper use of Article 15?

3. BRANNIGAN *V.* UNITED KINGDOM

Judgment of 26 May 1993
(No. 258B), 17 E.H.R.R. 594

[On facts very similar to those in *Brogan v. United Kingdom* above, the two applicants had been held for questioning for periods of six days 14 hours and four days six hours respectively. The main issue for decision was whether the United Kingdom's derogation complied with Article 15. Having held that a public emergency in the United Kingdom existed which threatened the life of the nation, the Court considered whether the measures taken were strictly required by the exigencies of the situation.]

49. For the applicants, the purported derogation was not a necessary response to any new or altered state of affairs but was the Government's reaction to the decision in *Brogan and Others* and was lodged merely to circumvent the consequences of this judgment.

50. The Government and the Commission maintained that, while it was true that this judgment triggered off the derogation, the exigencies of the situation have at all times since 1974 required the powers of extended detention conferred by the Prevention of Terrorism legislation. It was the view of successive governments that these powers were consistent with Article 5(3) and that no derogation was necessary. However, both the measures and the derogation were direct responses to the emergency with which the United Kingdom was and continues to be confronted.

51. The Court first observes that the power of arrest and extended detention has been con-

---

[139] 24 Nov. 1988 (No. 145B), 11 E.H.R.R. 117 reprinted at Section (F)(2)(A) *supra*.
[140] Hansard, HC Deb, 14 Nov. 1989, col. 209, WA.

sidered necessary by the Government since 1974 in dealing with the threat of terrorism. Following the *Brogan and Others* judgment the Government were then faced with the option of either introducing judicial control of the decision to detain under section 12 of the 1984 Act or lodging a derogation from their Convention obligations in this respect. The adoption of the view by the Government that judicial control compatible with Article 5(3) was not feasible because of the special difficulties associated with the investigation and prosecution of terrorist crime rendered derogation inevitable. Accordingly, the power of extended detention without such judicial control and the derogation of 23 December 1988 being clearly linked to the persistence of the emergency situation, there is no indication that the derogation was other than a genuine response.

52. The applicants maintained that derogation was an interim measure which Article 15 did not provide for since it appeared from the notice of derogation communicated to the Secretary General of the Council of Europe on 23 December 1988 that the Government had not reached a 'firm or final view' on the need to derogate from Article 5(3) and required a further period of reflection and consultation. Following this period the Secretary of State for the Home Department confirmed the derogation in a statement to Parliament on 14 November 1989. Prior to this concluded view Article 15 did not permit derogation. Furthermore, even at this date the Government had not properly examined whether the obligation in Article 5(3) could be satisfied by an 'officer authorised by law to exercise judicial power.'

53. The Government contended that the validity of the derogation was not affected by its examination of the possibility of judicial control of extended detention since, as the Commission had pointed out, it was consistent with the requirements of Article 15(3) to keep derogation measures under constant review.

54. The Court does not accept the applicants' argument that the derogation was premature.

While it is true that Article 15 does not envisage an interim suspension of Convention guarantees pending consideration of the necessity to derogate, it is clear from the notice of derogation that 'against the background of the terrorist campaign, and the over-riding need to bring terrorists to justice, the Government did not believe that the maximum period of detention should be reduced.' However it remained the Government's wish 'to find a judicial process under which extended detention might be reviewed and, where appropriate, authorized by a judge or other judicial officer.'

The validity of the derogation cannot be called into question for the sole reason that the Government had decided to examine whether in the future a way could be found of ensuring greater conformity with Convention obligations. Indeed, such a process of continued reflection is not only in keeping with Article 15(3) which requires permanent review of the need for emergency measures but is also implicit in the very notion of proportionality.

55. The applicants further considered that there was no basis for the Government's assertion that control of extended detention by a judge or other officer authorised by law to exercise judicial power was not possible or that a period of seven days' detention was necessary. They did not accept that the material required to satisfy a court of the justification for extended detention could be more sensitive than that needed in proceedings for habeas corpus. They and the Standing Advisory Commission on Human Rights also pointed out that the courts in Northern Ireland were frequently called on to deal with submissions based on confidential information—for example, in bail applications—and that there were sufficient procedural and evidential safeguards to protect confidentiality. Procedures also existed where judges were required to act on the basis of material which would not be disclosed either to the legal adviser or to his client. This was the case, for

example, with claims by the executive to public interest immunity or application by the police to extend detention under the Police and Criminal Evidence (Northern Ireland) Order 1989.

56. On this point the Government responded that none of the above procedures involved both the non-disclosure of material to the detainee or his legal adviser and an executive act of the court. . . .

It was also emphasised that the Government had reluctantly concluded that, within the framework of the common-law system, it was not feasible to introduce a system which would be compatible with Article 5(3) but would not weaken the effectiveness of the response to the terrorist threat. Decisions to prolong detention were taken on the basis of information the nature and source of which could not be revealed to a suspect or his legal adviser without risk to individuals assisting the police or the prospect of further valuable intelligence being lost. Moreover, involving the judiciary in the process of granting or approving extensions of detention created a real risk of undermining their independence as they would inevitably be seen as part of the investigation and prosecution process.

In addition, the Government did not accept that the comparison with habeas corpus was a valid one since judicial involvement in the grant or approval of extension would require the disclosure of a considerable amount of additional sensitive information which it would not be necessary to produce in habeas corpus proceedings. In particular, a court would have to be provided with details of the nature and extent of police inquiries following the arrest, including details of witnesses interviewed and information obtained from other sources as well as information about the future course of the police investigation. . . .

58. The Court notes the opinions expressed in the various Reports reviewing the operation of the Prevention of Terrorism legislation that the difficulties of investigating and prosecuting terrorist crime give rise to the need for an extended period of detention which would not be subject to judicial control. Moreover, these special difficulties were recognized in its above mentioned *Brogan and Others* judgment.[141]

It further observes that it remains the view of the respondent Government that it is essential to prevent the disclosure to the detainee and his legal adviser of information on the basis of which decisions on the extension of detention are made and that, in the adversarial system of the common law, the independence of the judiciary would be compromised if judges or other judicial officers were to be involved in the granting or approval of extensions.

The Court also notes that the introduction of a 'judge or other officer authorized by law to exercise judicial power' into the process of extension of periods of detention would not of itself necessarily bring about a situation of compliance with Article 5(3). That provision—like Article 5(4)—must be understood to require the necessity of following a procedure that has a judicial character although that procedure need not necessarily be identical in each of the cases where the intervention of a judge is required.

59. It is not the Court's role to substitute its view as to what measures were most appropriate or expedient at the relevant time in dealing with an emergency situation for that of the Government which has direct responsibility for establishing the balance between the taking of effective measures to combat terrorism on the one hand, and respecting individual rights on the other. In the context of Northern Ireland, where the judiciary is small and vulnerable to terrorist attacks, public confidence in the independence of the judiciary is understandably a matter to which the Government attaches great importance.

[141] *Supra* n. 139.

60. In the light of these considerations it cannot be said that the Government has exceeded their margin of appreciation in deciding, in the prevailing circumstances, against judicial control.

[The Court then rejected arguments for the applicants which sought to show that there were inadequate safeguards against abuse of the power to detain for questioning and that the government was in breach of its obligations under Article 4 of the International Covenant on Civil and Political Rights. The Court concluded that the derogation lodged by the United Kingdom satisfied the requirements of Article 15, and the complaints of breaches of Article 5(3) were rejected. This decision was reached by a majority of 22 to four. In the course of his dissenting judgment, Judge Walsh said:]

6. One of the suggested remedies for arrested persons in the present case is the ancient writ of habeas corpus. This remedy can only be obtained if there is a proven breach of the national law. A breach of the Convention cannot ground such relief unless it is also a breach of the national law. It is unfortunate that the Court has been allowed to believe otherwise . . . Yet in the present case the Government suggest that in habeas corpus proceedings the genuineness of the 'reasonable belief' may be tested (though I doubt if the secret sources would be required to be disclosed in any court) although that remedy, which fits into Article 5(4) of the Convention, has not been sought to be excluded by the terms of the derogation. A habeas corpus writ can, in theory, be sought within an hour or so after an arrest; in other words well within the period encompassed in the expression 'promptly' in Article 5(3). That procedure, if it is possible to avail of it, could thus impart the disadvantage to the police secrecy which the respondent Government claims it is entitled to avoid; yet the Government has not sought to explain this inconsistency.

7. It appears to me to be an inescapable inference that the Government does not wish any such arrested person to be brought before a judge at any time unless and until they are in a position to and desire to prefer a charge. The real target might appear to be Article 5(1)(c). The admitted purpose of the arrest is to interrogate the arrested person in the hope or expectation that he will incriminate himself. Article 5 makes it quite clear that no arrest can be justified under the Convention if the sole justification for it is the desire to interrogate the arrested person. If an arresting officer has a 'reasonable belief' that is coupled to the knowledge or intention that the grounds will never be revealed to a judge, and that the arrested person must be released if no revealable evidence is forthcoming, such arrest ought not to be regarded as an arrest in good faith for the purposes of Article 5(1)(c) of the Convention.

9. Article 5(3) of the Convention is an essential safeguard against arbitrary executive arrest or detention, failure to observe which could easily give rise to complaints under Article 3 of the Convention which cannot be the subject of derogation. Prolonged and sustained interrogation over periods of days, particularly without a judicial intervention, could well fall into the category of inhuman or degrading treatment in particular cases. In the present case, the applicant Brannigan, during 158 hours of detention, was interrogated forty-three times which means he was interrogated on average every two-and-a-half hours over that period, assuming he was allowed the regulation period of eight hours free from interrogation every 24 hours. The applicant McBride on the same basis was interrogated on average every three hours over his period of detention of 96 hours. The object of these interrogations was to gain 'sufficient admissions' to sustain a charge, or charges.

10. The Government's plea that it is motivated by a wish to preserve public confidence in the independence of the judiciary is, in effect, to say that such confidence is to be maintained or achieved by not permitting them to have a role in the protection of the personal liberty of the

arrested persons. One would think that such a role was one which the public would expect the judges to have. It is also to be noted that neither Parliament nor the Government appears to have made any serious effort to rearrange the judicial procedure or jurisdiction, in spite of being advised to do so by the persons appointed to review the system, to cater for the requirement of Article 5(3) in cases of the type now under review. It is the function of national authorities so to arrange their affairs as not to clash with the requirements of the Convention. The Convention is not to be remoulded to assume the shape of national procedures.

[Another of the dissenting judges was Judge Makarczyk, who had newly joined the Court:]

I regret that I am unable to share the position of the majority of the Court in the present case. This is for three main reasons: the general consequences of the judgment; the question of a time-limit for the derogation and the reasons for the derogation as put forward by the respondent Government.

1. The principle that a judgment of the Court deals with a specific case and solves a particular problem does not, in my opinion, apply to cases concerning the validity of a derogation made by a State under Article 15 of the Convention. A derogation made by any State affects not only the position of that State, but also the integrity of the Convention system of protection as a whole. It is relevant for other Member States—old and new—and even for States aspiring to become Parties which are in the process of adapting their legal systems to the standards of the Convention. For the new Contracting Parties, the fact of being admitted, often after long periods of preparation and negotiation, means not only the acceptance of Convention obligations, but also recognition by the community of European States of their equal standing as regards the democratic system and the rule of law. In other words, what is considered by the old democracies as a natural state of affairs, is seen as a privilege by the newcomers which is not to be disposed of lightly. A derogation made by a new Contracting Party from Eastern and Central Europe would call into question this new legitimacy and is, in my opinion, quite improbable. Any decision of the Court concerning Article 15 should encourage and confirm this philosophy. In any event it should not reinforce the views of those in the new Member States for whom European standards clash with interests which they have inherited from the past. I am not convinced that the reasoning adopted by the majority fulfils these requirements. This is especially so as the derogation concerns a provision of the Convention which, for some, should not be the subject of any derogation at all.

2. I fully recognise the difficulties, and even the impossibility, for the Court in setting a precise time-limit for the derogation as a precondition of its validity under Article 15. However, I believe that the judgment should very clearly and unequivocally indicate that the Court accepts the derogation only as a strictly temporary measure. After all, it recognizes the non-observance of Article 5(3) of the Convention, a basic provision of which the applicants cannot avail themselves because of the derogation. The Court also considers the time factor as essential when speaking of its supervisory role in respect of the margin of appreciation. It is true that the Court emphasises the obligation of the derogating State to review the situation on a regular basis. But this obligation clearly results from the third paragraph of Article 15 and the emphasis does not contribute to reassure the international community that the Court is doing all that is legally possible for the full applicability of the Convention to be restored as soon as practicable. On the contrary, the present wording of the judgment tends rather to perpetuate the status quo and opens, for the derogating State, an unlimited possibility of applying extended administrative detention for an uncertain period of time, to the detriment of the integrity of the Convention system and, I firmly believe, of the derogating State itself.

3. This leads me to the third reason for my dissent which I consider to be of vital importance.

The main point that, in my opinion, the United Kingdom Government should attempt to prove before the Court is that extended administrative detention does in fact contribute to eliminate the reasons for which the extraordinary measures needed to be introduced—in other words the prevention and combatting of terrorism. But, as far as I can see, no such attempt has been made either in the Government's Memorial and the attached documents, or in the pleading before the Court. Instead, the Government's main arguments have centred on the alleged detrimental effects on the judiciary, of control by a judge of extended detention without the normal judicial procedure.

I will not enlarge on this last argument, which has been skilfully called into question by dissenters both in the Commission and in the Court. I can only add that any form of judicial control could be beneficial for all concerned. If the Government had been able to provide valid arguments that extended detention without any form of judicial control does in fact contribute both to the punishment and prevention of the crime of terrorism, I would be ready to accept the legality of the derogation, notwithstanding the first two reasons of my dissent. . . .

The main question raised by *Brannigan* is whether the majority's decision to approve the derogation from Article 5(3) goes too far in permitting a state to cut back on its duties under Article 5. For example, should the Court have scrutinized more rigorously the government's claim that the measures derogated from its obligations 'to the extent strictly required by the exigencies of the situation'? There is a potential danger that a state found to have committed breaches of the Convention (apart from obligations from which no derogation is permitted) may decide that the least onerous course of compliance is to lodge a specific derogation with the Council of Europe, of the kind approved in *Brannigan*. For instance, does the approach of the Court in *Brannigan* permit a state to suspend the the judicial protection of liberty under Article 5(4)?[142] The Court was reluctant to give a positive answer to this question in a case arising from unrest and conflict in areas of Turkey.

4. AKSOY *V.* TURKEY

Judgment of 18 December 1996, Reports, 1996–IV 2260,
23 E.H.R.R. 553

[The applicant had lived in south east Turkey, most of which had been subject to emergency rule since 1987. On a date that he claimed to be 24 November 1992, he was arrested and detained on suspicion of terrorist activities. He was subjected to brutality and torture before being released on 10 December 1992, requiring hospital treatment. He was at a later date shot dead after having been threatened because of his complaint to Strasbourg. The majority of the Court (the Turkish judge dissenting) rejected preliminary objections raised by the Turkish government and held that Aksoy's rights under Article 3 had been violated. In relation to Article 5(3), he had been held for 14 or more days without being brought before a judge. The government relied on the fact that Turkey had on 5 May 1992 derogated from its obligations

---

[142] For extended criticism of *Brannigan*, see S. Marks, 'Civil Liberties at the Margin: the United Kingdom Derogation and the ECHR' 15 *OJLS* 69 (1995).

under Article 5. The Court referred to earlier decisions on Article 15, found that terrorist activity in south east Turkey had created a 'public emergency threatening the life of the nation' and considered whether the government's measures were 'strictly required by the exigencies of the situation'.]

(a) The length of the unsupervised detention

71. The Government asserted that the applicant had been arrested on 26 November 1992 along with 13 others on suspicion of aiding and abetting PKK terrorists . . . He was held in custody for 14 days, in accordance with Turkish law, which allows a person detained in connection with a collective offence to be held for up to 30 days in the state of emergency region.

72. They explained that the place in which the applicant was arrested and detained fell within the area covered by the Turkish derogation. . . . The investigation of terrorist offences presented the authorities with special problems, . . . because the members of terrorist organizations were expert in withstanding interrogation, had secret support networks and access to substantial resources. A great deal of time and effort was required to secure and verify evidence in a large region confronted with a terrorist organisation that had strategic and technical support from neighbouring countries. These difficulties meant that it was impossible to provide judicial supervision during a suspect's detention in police custody. . . .

74. While [the applicant] did not present detailed arguments against the validity of the Turkish derogation as a whole, he questioned whether the situation in South East Turkey necessitated the holding of suspects for 14 days or more without judicial supervision. He submitted that judges in South East Turkey would not be put at risk if they were permitted and required to review the legality of detention at shorter intervals. . . .

[Stressing the importance of Article 5 in the Convention system, the Court continued:].

76. Judicial control of interferences by the executive with the individual's right to liberty is an essential feature of the guarantee embodied in Article 5(3) . . . Furthermore, prompt judicial intervention may lead to the detection and prevention of serious ill-treatment, which . . . is prohibited by the Convention in absolute and non-derogable terms.

77. In the *Brannigan and McBride* judgment, the Court held that the United Kingdom Government had not exceeded their margin of appreciation by derogating from their obligations under Article 5 of the Convention to the extent that individuals suspected of terrorist offences were allowed to be held for up to seven days without judicial control.

In the instant case, the applicant was detained for at least 14 days without being brought before a judge or other officer. The Government have sought to justify this measure by reference to the particular demands of police investigations in a geographically vast area faced with a terrorist organization receiving outside support.

78. Although the Court is of the view . . . that the investigation of terrorist offences undoubtedly presents the authorities with special problems, it cannot accept that it is necessary to hold a suspect for 14 days without judicial intervention. This period is exceptionally long, and left the applicant vulnerable not only to arbitrary interference with his right to liberty but also to torture. Moreover, the Government have not adduced any detailed reasons before the Court as to why the fight against terrorism in South East Turkey rendered judicial intervention impracticable.

(b) Safeguards

79. The Government emphasized that both the derogation and the national legal system provided sufficient safeguards to protect human rights. Thus, the derogation itself was limited to the strict minimum required for the fight against terrorism; the permissible length of detention was prescribed by law and the consent of a Public Prosecutor was necessary if the police wished to remand a suspect in custody beyond these periods. Torture was prohibited by Article 243 of the Criminal Code. . . .

80. The applicant pointed out that long periods of unsupervised detention, together with the lack of safeguards provided for the protection of prisoners, facilitated the practice of torture. Thus, he was tortured with particular intensity on his third and fourth days in detention, and was held thereafter to allow his injuries to heal; throughout this time he was denied access to either a lawyer or a doctor. Moreover, he was kept blindfolded during interrogation, which meant that he could not identify those who mistreated him. The reports of Amnesty International, the European Committee for the Prevention of Torture and the United Nations Committee against Torture, showed that the safeguards contained in the Turkish Criminal Code, which were in any case inadequate, were routinely ignored in the state of emergency region. . . .

82. In its . . . *Brannigan and McBride* judgment,[143] the Court was satisfied that there were effective safeguards in operation in Northern Ireland which provided an important measure of protection against arbitrary behaviour and incommunicado detention. For example, the remedy of habeas corpus was available to test the lawfulness of the original arrest and detention, there was an absolute and legally enforceable right to consult a solicitor 48 hours after the time of arrest and detainees were entitled to inform a relative or friend about their detention and to have access to a doctor.

83. In contrast, however, the Court considers that in this case insufficient safeguards were available to the applicant, who was detained over a long period of time. In particular, the denial of access to a lawyer, doctor, relative or friend and the absence of any realistic possibility of being brought before a court to test the legality of the detention meant that he was left completely at the mercy of those holding him.

84. The Court has taken account of the unquestionably serious problem of terrorism in South East Turkey and the difficulties faced by the State in taking effective measures against it. However, it is not persuaded that the exigencies of the situation necessitated the holding of the applicant on suspicion of involvement in terrorist offences for 14 days or more in incommunicado detention without access to a judge or other judicial officer. . . .

87. In conclusion, the Court finds that there has been a violation of Article 5(3) of the Convention.

In view of the above decision, the Court did not find it necessary to decide whether the Turkish derogation met the formal requirements of Article 15(3). In *Sakik v. Turkey*[144] where the applicants were detained in the capital, Ankara, the government relied on the same derogation. However, the area of the emergency referred to in the derogation did not include Ankara. Rejecting the argument that the terrorist threat in south-east Turkey extended to the whole of Turkey, the Court noted that Article 15 authorizes derogations 'only to the extent strictly required by the exigencies of the situation':

---

[143] Reprinted at Section (H)(3) *supra*.
[144] 26 Nov. 1997, Reports, 1997–VII 2609, 26 E.H.R.R. 662.

In the present case the Court would be working against the object and purpose of that provision if, when assessing the territorial scope of the derogation concerned, it were to extend its effects to a part of Turkish territory not explicitly named in the instrument of derogation. It follows that the derogation in question is inapplicable *ratione loci* to the facts of the case [paragraph 39, 26 E.H.R.R. 662].

Comparison may be made between the approach of the Strasbourg Court towards a state that seeks to derogate from its Convention duties and the position under the Inter-American Convention on Human Rights.

5. HABEAS CORPUS IN EMERGENCY SITUATIONS

Advisory Opinion OC-8/87, Inter-American Court of Human Rights
(1987) 11 E.H.R.R. 33

[The American Convention on Human Rights provides in Article 27(1) (Suspension of Guarantees) that in time of war, public danger or other emergency threatening a state's independence or security, the state may take measures derogating from its Convention obligations to the extent strictly required by the exigencies of the situation. By Article 27(2), such derogation may not authorize suspension of eleven specified articles (including the right to life, the right to humane treatment, and freedom from slavery) nor of 'the judicial guarantees essential for the protection of such rights'. The Inter-American Commission of Human Rights requested an advisory opinion from the Inter-American Court on whether the writ of habeas corpus is one of the 'judicial guarantees' which cannot be suspended in times of national emergency. The Commission stated this reason for its request:

> Some States Parties to the American Convention on Human Rights have assumed that one of the rights that may be suspended in emergency situations is the right to judicial protection afforded by the writ of habeas corpus. Some States have even promulgated special laws or have instituted a practice enabling them to hold a detainee *incommunicado* for a prolonged period of time, in some cases for as long as 15 days. During that time, the detainee may be refused all contact with the outside world, thus preventing resort to the writ of habeas corpus.

[The Court's advisory opinion concluded unanimously that judicial remedies such as habeas corpus, which are essential for the protection of rights and freedoms which under the American Convention are non-derogable, may not be suspended even in time of emergency.]

20. It cannot be denied that under certain circumstances the suspension of guarantees may be the only way to deal with emergency situations and, thereby, to preserve the highest values of a democratic society. The Court cannot, however, ignore the fact that abuses may result from the application of emergency measures not objectively justified in the light of the requirements prescribed in Article 27. . . .

21. It is clear that no right guaranteed in the Convention may be suspended unless very strict conditions—those laid down in Article 27(1)—are met. Moreover, even when these conditions are satisfied, Article 27(2) provides that certain categories of rights may not be suspended under any circumstances. Hence, rather than adopting a philosophy that favours the suspension of rights, the Convention establishes the contrary principle, namely, that all rights are to be guaranteed and

enforced unless very special circumstances justify the suspension of some, and that some rights may never be suspended, however serious the emergency. . . .

24. The suspension of guarantees also constitutes an emergency situation in which it is lawful for a government to subject rights and freedoms to certain restrictive measures that, under normal circumstances, would be prohibited or more strictly controlled. This does not mean, however, that the suspension of guarantees implies a temporary suspension of the rule of law, nor does it authorize those in power to act in disregard of the principle of legality by which they are bound at all times. When guarantees are suspended, some legal restraints applicable to the acts of public authorities may differ from those in effect under normal conditions. These restraints may not be considered to be non-existent, however, nor can the government be deemed thereby to have acquired absolute powers that go beyond the circumstances justifying the grant of such exceptional legal measures. . . .

27. As the Court has already noted, in serious emergency situations it is lawful temporarily to suspend certain rights and freedoms whose free exercise must, under normal circumstances, be respected and guaranteed by the State. However, since not all of these rights and freedoms may be suspended even temporarily, it is imperative that 'the judicial guarantees essential for (their) protection' remain in force. Article 27(2) does not link these judicial guarantees to any specific provision of the Convention, which indicates that what is important is that these judicial remedies have the character of being essential to ensure the protection of those rights. . . .

30. The guarantees must be not only essential but also judicial. The expression 'judicial' can only refer to those judicial remedies that are truly capable of protecting these rights. Implicit in this conception is the active involvement of an independent and impartial judicial body having the power to pass on the lawfulness of measures adopted in a state of emergency. . . .

35. In order for habeas corpus to achieve its purpose, which is to obtain a judicial determination of the lawfulness of a detention, it is necessary that the detained person be brought before a competent judge or tribunal with jurisdiction over him. Here habeas corpus performs a vital role in ensuring that a person's life and physical integrity are respected, in preventing his disappearance or the keeping of his whereabouts secret and in protecting him against torture or other cruel, inhumane, or degrading punishment or treatment.

36. This conclusion is buttressed by the realities that have been the experience of some of the peoples of this hemisphere in recent decades, particularly disappearances, torture and murder committed or tolerated by some governments. This experience has demonstrated over and over again that the right to life and to humane treatment are threatened whenever the right to habeas corpus is partially or wholly suspended. . . .

38. If . . . the suspension of guarantees may not exceed the limits of that strictly required to deal with the emergency, any action on the part of the public authorities that goes beyond those limits, which must be specified with precision in the decree promulgating the state of emergency, would also be unlawful notwithstanding the existence of the emergency situation.

39. The Court should also point out that since it is improper to suspend guarantees without complying with the conditions referred to in the preceding paragraph, it follows that the specific measures applicable to the rights or freedoms that have been suspended may also not violate these general principles. Such violation would occur, for example, if the measures taken infringed the legal régime of the state emergency, if they lasted longer than the time limit specified, if they were manifestly irrational, unnecessary or disproportionate, or if, in adopting them, there was a misuse or abuse of power.

40. If this is so, it follows that in a system governed by the rule of law it is entirely in order for an autonomous and independent judicial order to exercise control over the lawfulness of such measures by verifying, for example, whether a detention based on the suspension of personal freedom complies with the legislation authorized by the state of emergency. In this context, habeas corpus acquires a new dimension of fundamental importance. . . .

The European and American Conventions on Human Rights are not identical in the provision which they make for derogation. Nonetheless, one conclusion which may be drawn from this Opinion of the American Court is that no European state should be permitted to derogate from its duties under Article 5(4) of the European Convention, even though this is not expressly excluded by Article 15(2).

8

RIGHT TO A FAIR AND PUBLIC HEARING IN THE DETERMINATION OF CIVIL RIGHTS AND CRIMINAL CHARGES

ARTICLE 6

1. In the determination of his civil rights and obligations or of any criminal charge against him, everyone is entitled to a fair and public hearing within a reasonable time by an independent and impartial tribunal established by law. Judgment shall be pronounced publicly but the press and public may be excluded from all or part of the trial in the interest of morals, public order or national security in a democratic society, where the interests of juveniles or the protection of the private life of the parties so require, or to the extent strictly necessary in the opinion of the court in special circumstances where publicity would prejudice the interests of justice.

2. Everyone charged with a criminal offence shall be presumed innocent until proved guilty according to law.

3. Everyone charged with a criminal offence has the following minimum rights:

(a) to be informed promptly, in a language which he understands and in detail, of the nature and cause of the accusation against him;

(b) to have adequate time and facilities for the preparation of his defence;

(c) to defend himself in person or through legal assistance of his own choosing or, if he has not sufficient means to pay for legal assistance, to be given it free when the interests of justice so require;

(d) to examine or have examined witnesses against him and to obtain the attendance and examination of witnesses on his behalf under the same conditions as witnesses against him;

(e) to have the free assistance of an interpreter if he cannot understand or speak the language used in court.

A. INTRODUCTION

Article 6 of the Convention deals with the rights of people subjected to or threatened with conviction of a crime, some other deprivation of liberty, and in one significant reference, to a modification of their 'civil rights and obligations'. Predominantly, moreover, it concerns the manner in which these actions are carried out and the fairness of the procedures accompanying them.

The idea that the abuse of government policy may effectively be limited by channelling its exercise through procedures that are regular, impartial and that give affected persons a chance to be heard, is an ancient insight of the law. The Magna Carta in 1215 compelled the King to pledge that '[t]o no one we will sell, to no one will we deny or delay right or justice'; and that '[no] free man shall be taken or imprisoned or disseised . . . or outlawed or exiled or in any wise destroyed, nor will we go upon him, nor will we send upon him, unless by the lawful judgment of his peers, or by the law of the land'. The common law has developed the concept of fair procedure in the doctrine of 'natural justice' under which courts and other official and quasi-official bodies will act only after notice to the affected parties and after an opportunity for them to respond and only when the judges themselves are free of any extraneous bias.[1]

Almost everywhere 'written' constitutions govern, fair procedure has been constitutionalized.[2] In the United States Constitution, governments are barred by the Fifth and Fourteenth Amendments from depriving 'any person of life, liberty or property without due process of law', a requirement which has, first and foremost, been held to involve a fair and impartial procedure.[3] Beyond this general guarantee, the United States Constitution sets out certain specific procedural rights especially for those charged with criminal offences. Similarly, the Canadian Charter of Rights and Freedoms, in Section 7, secures the 'right to life, liberty, and security of the person and the right not to be deprived thereof except in accordance with the principles of fundamental justice'. At the time of enactment the phrase 'fundamental justice' was understood to be a synonym for the common law idea of 'natural justice', which, as noted, is a procedural concept.[4] And, like the United States Constitution, it crystallized this general requirement into certain specific procedural rules applicable to criminal defendants.[5]

The European Convention follows an identical model. In Article 6(1) it mandates that everyone facing criminal conviction or a determination of civil rights is entitled to a 'fair and public hearing within a reasonable time by an independent and

---

[1] *Dr. Bentley's Case*, 1 Stra. 557 (1723); *Dr. Bonham's Case*, Co. Rep. 1135 (1610); *see* A. W. Bradley and K. D. Ewing, *Constitutional and Administrative Law* 786–99 (12th ed. 1999).

[2] H. van Marrseveen & G. von der Tang, *Written Constitutions: A Computerized Comparative Study*, 105–6 (1978).

[3] *See Hurtado v. California*, 110 U.S. 516 (1884); *Joint Anti-Fascist Refugee Committee v. McGrath*, 341 U.S. 123 (1951).

[4] See P. Hogg, *Constitutional Law of Canada*, 1032–3 (3rd edn. 1992).

[5] Canadian Charter of Rights and Freedoms, Canada Act, 1982, Sections 8–14.

impartial tribunal established by law'. Then, in Article 6(2) and 6(3), it particularizes certain aspects of that right for those charged with a criminal offence.

Procedural rights, those provided in Article 6 and those in Article 5, surveyed in the last chapter, have been the rights most commonly invoked before the European Court of Human Rights. Given the volume of jurisprudence, all that can be done here is to give a sample of the way the Court has dealt with some of the questions presented. These materials will focus on two matters that seem central to the matrix of issues involved in Article 6 claims. The first is the definition of the government actions affecting individuals that trigger the procedural guarantees. The second concerns the essential characteristics of a 'fair hearing' in an 'impartial tribunal'.

It is useful in examining Article 6 to keep in mind the extent to which its requirements may overlap with those of Article 5. There may be occasions on which both Articles will have to be satisfied. Article 5 governs the circumstances and procedures which must be associated with a deprivation of personal liberty. Article 6 concerns the procedures which are required in civil and criminal adjudications. For example, Article 6(3) specifies the particular rights of individuals accused of crimes in the preparation and presentation of their defence. To the extent that conviction might lead to a deprivation of liberty, these may also be seen as safeguards against that eventuality. Similarly Article 5(2)–(4), dealing with rights of arrested persons, might be seen as procedural guarantees associated with the criminal adjudicatory process. Articles 5(3) and 6(1) both deal with the promptness with which an adjudication must proceed against criminal defendants.[6]

B. CRIMINAL CHARGES AND CIVIL RIGHTS

1. ADOLF *V.* AUSTRIA

Judgment of 26 March 1982
(No. 49), 4 E.H.R.R. 313

9. The applicant, an Austrian citizen born in 1918, lives in Innsbruck where he practices the profession of accountant and financial consultant.

10. On 15 July 1977, an 85-year-old woman, Mrs. Irmgard Proxauf, acting through a lawyer, reported to the Innsbruck public prosecutor's office that three days earlier during a quarrel Mr. Adolf had thrown at another person, Mrs. Anneliese Schuh, a bunch of keys which had then struck her (i.e. Mrs. Proxauf), causing her injury. In her letter headed 'request to enquire into a set of facts', she called on the prosecutor's office to take criminal proceedings against the applicant and stated that she would be a civil party claiming damages in any such proceedings.

---

[6] These provisions are discussed in Section (D) *infra*.

11. The federal police at Innsbruck, instructed on 12 August by the public prosecutor's office to investigate whether or not a punishable act had been committed, interrogated several persons cited by Mrs. Proxauf as witnesses and, on 22 September, the applicant himself. He denied the facts alleged against him and denounced the complaint as being knowingly false. After pointing out that the object alleged to have caused the injury was, in fact, an envelope containing a single key, he asserted, amongst other things, that he had not thrown it: he had wanted to give it back to Mrs. Proxauf, but it had slipped out of his hand and had touched her arm. Mrs. Schuh, he said, had picked it up and thrown it, just above his head, over a distance of 13 metres in the direction of his house. Mr. Adolf's wife and two employees had written a note setting out what they remembered of the incident, which he stated was available to the court, as an item for inclusion in the case-file. The police accepted the note, but did not question Mrs. Adolf or the employees. . . .

12. . . . On 22 December, the district court notified an associate of the applicant's lawyer that the proceedings had been terminated (on an unspecified date) in pursuance of section 451 (2) of the Code of Criminal Procedure. Following a request made by Mr. Adolf on 4 January 1978, the court served on him on 24 January a decision dated 10 January which reads as follows:

Decision

In the criminal case against Dr. Gustav Adolf for the offence of inflicting bodily harm, within the meaning of section 83 of the Penal Code, the District Court of Innsbruck has decided as follows upon the request of the public prosecutor:

The conditions of section 42 of the Penal Code are met; the proceedings are terminated in accordance with section 451 (2) of the Code of Criminal Procedure.

Reasons

By letter of 15 July 1977, the civil party Irma Proxauf informed the public prosecutor of an incident involving herself and the accused which had happened on 12 July 1977. She alleged that the accused had caused her an injury, namely a bruise on her left arm and another below her left breast, with a bunch of keys. The investigations made thereupon and the expert opinion have shown that in the course of a quarrel the accused flew into a rage and threw an envelope containing a key in the direction of Mrs. Anneliese Schuh who however managed to avoid the missile, while the 85-year-old Irma Proxauf standing behind her was hit. The key first struck the back of the right hand, causing a superficial abrasion, and then bounced against the left side of the above-named person's chest. No injury could be established on the chest.

The injury found is insignificant as it does not exceed the three-day limit; the fault of the accused may be described as insignificant, and his character gives cause to expect that he will conduct himself properly in future.

Therefore the conditions of section 42 of the Penal Code are met, justifying the above decision.

District Court of Innsbruck, Section 9,
10 January 1978.

[Section 42 of the Penal Code reads as follows:

(1) Where an act requiring public prosecution as a matter of course involves liability to no more than a fine, a custodial sentence not exceeding one year or both, the act shall not be punishable if:

1. the guilt of the author of the act is slight;

2. the act has had no or only trifling consequences and if in addition;

3. punishment is not necessary in order to deter the author of the act or other persons from committing criminal offences.

(2) The decision whether or not the conditions of paragraph (1) hereof are met shall be taken by the court; where the court decides in the affirmative, it shall bring the proceedings to a close no matter what state they may have reached.]

13. The applicant challenged this decision before the Regional Court of Innsbruck which, on 23 February 1978, declared the appeal inadmissible on the ground that section 451 (2) of the Code of Criminal Procedure limits the right of appeal to the prosecutor.

14. On 25 January 1980, a little more than six months after the European Commission of Human Rights had accepted the application, the *Generalprokurator* (the public prosecutor attached to the Supreme Court) filed with the Supreme Court, pursuant to section 33 (2) of the Code of Criminal Procedure, an application for annulment of the decision dated 10 January 1978 in the interests of the proper application of the law. . . .

16. The Supreme Court rejected the application for annulment on 28 February 1980 . . .

[The Supreme Court held that] [s]ection 42 simply requires the existence of a suspicion. Even if a court describes the suspect's conduct in terms of findings of fact, any statements to this effect could not be regarded as judicial findings, . . . with the attendant legal consequences. In point of fact, by reason of its basic legal character, any decision taken in pursuance of section 42 of the Penal Code can only be understood in one way: further clarification of, and possible prosecution in, a case which is already recognisable as being a trifling matter is to be avoided, not least in the interests of procedural economy. Howsoever the reasons given therefor may be worded, any such decision contains (if only because of its very nature) a negative ruling on the merits of the case and does not at all amount to a declaration, equivalent to a finding of guilt, that the suspect has (unlawfully and with criminal intent) committed a punishable act.

It would certainly have been preferable had the Innsbruck District Court stated this explicitly and without ambiguity in the decision being challenged. Nonetheless, the more or less apposite choice of wording in the reasoning could not deprive the reasoning of the specific significance it had as a result of the nature of the decision given and could not, therefore, in any way adversely affect the person concerned. . . .

17. The judgment of the Supreme Court was reproduced in an Austrian legal journal but the applicant's identity was not revealed. . . .

The professional association to which Mr. Adolf belongs has not instituted any disciplinary proceedings against him in respect of the facts underlying Mrs. Proxauf's complaint.

According to Mr. Adolf, the file on his case, including the Innsbruck District Court's decision dated 10 January 1978, has been produced in evidence in a civil action between himself and Mrs. Proxauf in the matter of an easement; an order issued by the competent civil court in Innsbruck took the case-file into consideration.

18. The costs of the procedure, and notably the costs of the medical opinion, were borne by the State. The applicant himself had to pay his lawyer's fees and his own expenses . . .

22. . . . Section 42 was introduced into the new Austrian Penal Code which entered into force on 1 January 1975, and is aimed at avoiding criminal trials in trivial cases, notably for reasons of procedural economy; the section is headed 'acts not meriting punishment'. The Supreme Court

and the great majority of legal commentators regard it as a clause which is not concerned with mere procedure but which provides a substantive ground for exonerating the accused.

23. A decision taken by a court in pursuance of section 42 to terminate proceedings is not entered in the criminal record of the person concerned. The file relating to a case closed in this manner may be used in other legal (and disciplinary) proceedings, as may, in principle, the case-file in any legal action whatever its outcome.

According to Mr. Adolf anyone may go to the court and consult the register of cases and the register of names and, at least as far as the former is concerned, ask for an extract. The Government contested these assertions, save apparently as regards the possibility of having access to the register of names. The latter simply contains a reference to the register of cases without giving any indication as to the nature of the litigation. . . .

29. The Government's principal submission was that Article 6 was not applicable in the present case since no criminal charge existed at any time or, at least, at the time when the decision at issue was rendered. This view is not shared by the Commission and is contested by the applicant.

30. The Court thus has to ascertain whether there was a 'criminal charge' ('*accusation en matière pénale*', Article 6(1)) against Mr. Adolf or whether he was 'charged with a criminal offence' ('*accusé d'une infraction*' and '*accusé*', Article 6(2) and (3)).

These expressions are to be interpreted as having an 'autonomous' meaning in the context of the Convention and not on the basis of their meaning in domestic law. The legislation of the State concerned is certainly relevant, but it provides no more than a starting-point in ascertaining whether at any time there was a 'criminal charge' against Mr. Adolf or he was 'charged with a criminal offence'. The prominent place held in a democratic society by the right to a fair trial favours a 'substantive', rather than a 'formal', conception of the 'charge' referred to by Article 6; it impels the Court to look behind the appearances and examine the realities of the procedure in question in order to determine whether there has been a 'charge' within the meaning of Article 6. . . .

33. In the submission of the Government, the fact that the District Court applied section 42 of the Penal Code proved there never was a 'charge' or an 'offence' in this case. The Government pointed out, furthermore, that the Supreme Court and the great majority of Austrian legal commentators regard the section as not being concerned with procedure but as providing a substantive ground for exonerating the accused, its purpose, it is said, being to 'decriminalize' certain acts of a trivial nature by making them non-punishable.

In the first place, the Court observes, as did the Commission's Delegate, that recourse to section 42 cannot affect the existence, or retroactively alter the nature, of the procedures conducted before the court order terminating proceedings. The decision dated 10 January 1978 referred to 'the criminal case against Dr. Gustav Adolf for the offence of inflicting bodily harm, within the meaning of section 83 of the Penal Code' and described him as an 'accused'. In the notification of 22 December 1977, the district court had moreover already mentioned the 'proceedings against Gustav Adolf under section 83 of the Penal Code'.

As regards the concept of a non-punishable act, it is clearly in line with the title and text of section 42. Nevertheless, non-punishable or unpunished criminal offences do exist and Article 6 of the Convention does not distinguish between them and other criminal offences; it applies whenever a person is 'charged' with any criminal offence.

34. To sum up, in 1977 Mr. Adolf was subject to a criminal charge (within the meaning of the

Convention) to which the reasoned decision dated 10 January 1978 related. Article 6 was thus applicable in the present case. . . .

40. According to the Government, the district court's decision should be read in conjunction with the judgment of the Supreme Court; this judgment, the Government submitted, clarified the district court's decision by showing that it was grounded solely on the existence of a 'suspected state of affairs'.

The Court recognizes that the district court's reasoned decision dated 10 January 1978 must be read with the judgment of the Supreme Court and in the light of it. That judgment has cleared Mr. Adolf of any finding of guilt and thus the presumption of his innocence is no longer called into question. By reason of the nature of section 42 of the Penal Code, the proceedings, on that section being applied, did not and could not terminate with any finding of guilt; it was therefore not necessary for the district court to proceed with any hearing in the case or examination of evidence.

[The Court held by four votes to three that there had been no breach of Article 6.]

Joint Dissenting Opinion of Judges Cremona, Liesch and Pettiti:

[4] In our view this reasoning clearly amounts to a judicial finding, in the context of a criminal charge, that the applicant inflicted bodily harm on another person and that he was in a state of guilt in doing so. The net result is that, notwithstanding the applicant's persistent denial of the allegations made against him, and without holding a public trial, hearing any witnesses and giving the applicant the opportunity to challenge the aforesaid expert medical opinion, [the District Court] made findings establishing both the disputed facts and his contested guilt.

[5] It is true that in its decision of 28 February 1980 the Austrian Supreme Court in effect stated that, notwithstanding the infelicitous wording used by the district court in its decision, that decision, inasmuch as it applied section 42 of the Austrian Penal Code, was based solely on the existence of a 'suspected state of affairs'.

[6] But whilst it is clear that, in a case like this, in principle it is not within the province of our Court to review the correctness of the construction put upon section 42 of the Penal Code of Austria by the Austrian Supreme Court, it is equally clear that what was found by the district court in unambiguous and unmistakable language cannot be made to mean other than what it obviously and unavoidably means. The 'fact' of those findings was not erased by mere 'hypothetical' whitewashing.

[7] Indeed the fact remains that the district court's decision, the grounds of which in effect amounted to declaring the applicant guilty of a criminal offence, still stands. The Supreme Court did not set it aside and the construction put upon it in no way erased the positive findings actually made in it. Nor did that Court correct the failure of the district court to respect the requirements of Article 6(1) and (2) of the Convention taken together, which should have been observed before those findings were actually reached.

[8] Clearly, before a person is found guilty of a criminal offence it is essential that he should have the benefit of the guarantees of Article 6 of the Convention. But the decision of the district court, which as already stated still stands, was reached by a procedure under which the applicant did not have the opportunity to exercise his rights under that Article, in particular his right to a fair and public hearing and his right to be presumed innocent until proved guilty according to law. . . .

2. THE INTERESTS PROTECTED BY ARTICLE 6

In the *Adolf Case* the Court had to decide what kind of injury Adolf suffered. Article 6 presupposes certain undesirable consequences from an adverse 'determination of a criminal charge'. An initial question in many Article 6 cases, therefore, must be: did the procedures in issue, in fact, determine a criminal charge? As with many of the other terms in the Convention, the European Court (see, e.g., paragraph 30 of the principal case) has refused to be bound by the particular legal classifications used by respondent states. Rather, the words 'criminal charge' in Article 6 have an 'autonomous meaning'. This means the Strasbourg Court must decide which instances of state decision-making, in response to what kinds of conduct, entailing what consequences, amount to the determination of such a criminal charge. In making that inquiry the Court has formulated a three factor test. It asks:

whether or not the text defining the offence belongs, in the legal system of the respondent State, to the criminal law; next, the nature of the offence and, finally, the nature and degree of severity of the penalty that the person concerned risked incurring.[7]

Moreover,

[T]hese criteria are alternative and not cumulative; for Article 6 to apply by virtue of the words 'criminal charge', it suffices that the offence in question should by its nature be 'criminal' from the point of view of the Convention, or should have made the person concerned liable to a sanction which, by its nature and degree of severity, belongs in general to the 'criminal' sphere. This does not exclude that a cumulative approach may be adopted where the separate analysis of each criterion does not make it possible to reach a clear conclusion as to the existence of a 'criminal charge'.[8]

The Court applied this approach in deciding that the finding of 'minor offences' for unruly public behavior was the determination of a criminal charge even though no imprisonment and only minor fines were employed as sanctions.[9] It was enough that the rules invoked were imposed on all citizens for the protection of public order.[10] In six cases decided on the same day, the Court found that the Austrian procedure for dealing with motor vehicle offences came within Article 6. It took note of the acts prohibited, some of the terminology used in the relevant statutes, and the possible imposition of fines the non-payment of which could result in imprisonment.[11] The Court has also held that the deduction of 'points' leading to possible suspension of driving privileges after conviction for a traffic offence was a procedure subject to

---

[7] *Kadubec v. Slovakia*, 2 Sept. 1998, Reports, 1998–VI 2518, 23 E.H.R.R. 553, para. 50.

[8] *Id.* at para. 51.

[9] *Id.* at paras. 52–3. *See also Lauko v. Slovakia*, 2 Sept. 1998, Reports, 1998–VI 2497.

[10] *Kadubec, supra* n.7, at para. 52.

[11] *Schmautzer v. Austria*, 23 Oct. 1995 (No. 328A), 21 E.H.R.R. 511, para. 28 (seatbelt violation). See also *Umlauft v. Austria*, 23 Oct. 1995 (No. 328B), 22 E.H.R.R. 76; *Gradinger v. Austria*, 23 Oct. 1955 (No. 328C); *Palaoro v. Austria*, 23 Oct. 1995 (No. 329B). Precisely the same reasoning was applied on the same day to proceedings against a contractor for violation of planning regulations. *Pramstaller v. Austria*, 23 Oct. 1995 (No. 329A).

Article 6. Although the procedure was administered separately from the underlying offence, it was found to be a secondary penalty with a punitive or deterrent function.[12]

On the other hand, not every similarity between a nominally administrative procedure and a classic criminal charge suffices to bring it under Article 6. This includes the use of involuntary detention. In an unexplained dictum the Court has stated that such detention in a mental health facility following a violent crime 'did not involve "determination of a criminal charge"'.[13] It did, however, find a violation of Article 6 with respect to the applicant's 'civil rights' and of Article 5(1).[14] Note that in the principal case the applicant was neither imprisoned nor fined. He complained that the information concerning the proceeding was available to the public. An important aspect of a criminal conviction is the 'stigma' that attaches to the defendant.

In *Paul v. Davis*,[15] the United States Supreme Court dealt with an action brought against the local police, who had distributed to merchants the name and picture of the plaintiff on a list of 'active shoplifters'. The Court found that mere injury to reputation did not amount to a deprivation of liberty triggering the procedural requirements of the fourteenth amendment. Justice Brennan dissented. He emphasized the close connection between the kind of injury inflicted on the plaintiff and that associated with criminal conviction:

The Court today holds that police officials [may] on their own initiative and without trial constitutionally condemn innocent individuals as criminals and thereby brand them with one of the most stigmatizing and debilitating labels in our society. If there are no constitutional restraints on such oppressive behavior, the safeguards constitutionally accorded an accused in a criminal trial are rendered a sham, and no individual can feel secure that he will not be arbitrarily singled out for similar ex parte punishment by those primarily charged with fair enforcement of the law. . . . The logical and disturbing corollary of this holding is that no due process infirmities would inhere in a statute constituting a commission to conduct ex parte trials of individuals, so long as the only official judgment pronounced was limited to the public condemnation and branding of a person as a Communist, a traitor, an 'active murderer', a homosexual or any other mark that 'merely' carries social opprobrium. The potential of today's decision is frightening for a free people.[16]

Is the injury in the principal case distinguishable?[17]

Several European cases deal with the consequences of a criminal proceeding which is terminated before a verdict is entered. In *Minelli v. Switzerland*,[18] the applicant was the subject of a criminal defamation action that was discontinued before hearing because of the passage of the limitation period. The Swiss trial court charged the applicant with the bulk of the court costs of the action and part of the costs of the private prosecutors. It made that assessment based on its determination that, had it

---

[12] *Malige v. France*, 23 Sept. 1998, Reports, 1998–VII 2922, 28 E.H.R.R. 578, paras. 37–9.

[13] *Aerts v. Belgium*, 30 July 1998, Reports, 1998–V 1939, 29 E.H.R.R. 50, para. 59.

[14] *Id.* at paras. 59–60, 45–50.

[15] 424 U.S. 693 (1976).

[16] *Id.* at 714, 721.

[17] For a consideration by the European Court of the relation of Art. 6 to state procedures affecting reputation, *see Fayed v. United Kingdom*, 21 Sept. 1994 (No. 294B), 18 E.H.R.R. 393.

[18] 25 Mar. 1983 (No. 62), 5 E.H.R.R. 554.

been possible for the case to go forward, 'he would in all probability have been convicted'. That determination was based on the court's estimate of the evidence that had been submitted and on the outcome of a related case. A subsequent determination on appeal by the federal court added certain nuances to the prior judgment but 'approved the substance of the decision on the essential points'. The European Court found a violation of Article 6(2), the presumption of innocence. After concluding that Article 6 was applicable to private prosecutions it held:

[T]he presumption of innocence will be violated if, without the accused's having previously been proved guilty according to law and, notably, without his having had the opportunity of exercising his rights of defence, a judicial decision concerning him reflects an opinion that he is guilty. This may be so even in the absence of any formal finding; it suffices that there is some reasoning suggesting that the court regards the accused as guilty.[19]

In three judgments rendered on 25 August 1987, the European Court reached a different conclusion when the issue was a claim for reimbursment of costs instead of the initial charging of costs after a criminal action had been discontinued. In *Lutz v. Germany*,[20] the applicant had objected to a finding that he was guilty of a traffic violation (a 'regulatory offence'), but the applicable limitation period expired before a court could consider his objection. The domestic courts refused to order reimbursement of his costs finding that, but for the time bar, the applicant 'would most probably have been convicted'. In *Englert v. Germany*,[21] a prosecution for extortion was discontinued because the prosecutor, acting pursuant to the Criminal Code, determined that any sentence expected would be negligible in comparison with that imposed for a subsequent conviction. Again, the domestic courts refused to reimburse the applicant's costs or to compensate him for time held in detention pending trial stating that 'a conviction is clearly more likely than an acquittal' and that Englert's own actions had given rise to 'the strong suspicion that he had committed an offence'. In *Nolkenbockhuff v. Germany*,[22] the applicant's husband had been convicted of business fraud and had died before the determination of his appeal. The Court refused to reimburse his expenses holding that the conviction 'almost certainly would have been upheld'. In all these cases, the European Court found no violation of Article 6. It was conceded by the applicants that the mere imposition of costs in a criminal proceeding did not offend the presumption of innocence. Moreover, in these cases the reasons for refusing to reimburse costs were not actually findings of guilt. (In the *Lutz* and *Englert* cases, the applicants claimed those reasons amounted to 'a conviction in disguise'.) They were described as a 'state of suspicion' which justified, on an equitable basis, the withholding of public reimbursement of costs. Article 6 does not require a state 'where a prosecution has been discontinued to indemnify a person "charged with a criminal offence" for any detriment he may have suffered'. Judge Cremona dissented,

---

[19] *Id.* at para. 37.
[20] 25 Aug. 1987 (No. 123), 10 E.H.R.R. 182.
[21] 25 Aug. 1987 (No. 123), 13 E.H.R.R. 392.
[22] 25 Aug. 1987 (No. 123), 13 E.H.R.R. 366.

finding the *Minelli* case controlling. He argued that '[w]hat is decisive is that at the end of the day one is left with the impression that the courts did consider that the applicant was in fact guilty'.

Even in cases where a criminal charge is undeniably lodged there may be a question exactly when the requirements of Article 6—and especially the special rights of the accused under Article 6(3)—attach. Again the Court has refused to be bound by the formal definitions of the local legal system, asking instead whether the applicant had, at the relevant time, in fact become the focus of a criminal investigation.[23] As the cases discussed in the previous paragraph indicate, there may also be a question of when an individual ceases to be under a criminal charge. In addition to cases of discontinued prosecution, the Court has assumed that Article 6 applies to proceedings in appellate courts.[24] The Court has not yet addressed the impact of Article 6 on proceedings evaluating applications for pardons. On a related question, the Privy Council has held that judicial review of the fairness of such proceedings is not appropriate. In a recent judgment affirming this position the Judicial Committee quoted Lord Diplock: '[m]ercy is not the subject of legal rights. It begins where legal rights end'.[25]

The definition of a 'criminal charge' also arises in cases where a state attempts to impose punishment for what it asserts are 'disciplinary' rather than 'criminal' reasons. In *Campbell and Fells v. United Kingdom*,[26] this issue was considered in the context of prison discipline. The applicants were involved in a protest which had led to a violent disturbance. They were charged with mutiny and incitement to mutiny. Their penalties included forfeiture of the potential remission of sentence otherwise available to them.

The government submitted that Article 6 was inapplicable to the proceedings. Citing prior case law,[27] the Court set forth the following principles for deciding when a 'criminal charge' was in contest:

70. The first matter to be ascertained is whether or not the text defining the offences in issue belongs, according to the domestic legal system, to criminal law, disciplinary law or both concurrently. . . .

It is clear that, in English law, the offences with which Mr. Campbell was charged belong to disciplinary law: Rule 47 states that conduct of this kind on the part of a prisoner shall be 'an offence against discipline' and the Rules go on to provide how it shall be dealt with under the special prison disciplinary regime. . . .

71. In any event, the indications so afforded by the national law have only a relative value: the very nature of the offence is a factor of greater import.

In this respect, it has to be borne in mind that misconduct by a prisoner may take different forms; certain acts are clearly no more than a question of internal discipline, whereas others

---

[23] *See*, e.g., *Sevres v. France*, 20 Oct. 1997, Reports, 1997–VI 2159, 28 E.H.R.R. 265.

[24] *See*, e.g., *Hadjianastassiou v. Greece*, 16 Dec. 1992 (No. 252), 16 E.H.R.R. 219.

[25] *Reckley v. Minister of Public Safety and Immigration (No. 2)* [1996] 1 A.C. 527, [1996] 1 All E.R. 562.

[26] 28 June 1984 (No. 80), 7 E.H.R.R. 165.

[27] *Engel and Others v. The Netherlands*, 8 June 1976 (No. 22), 1 E.H.R.R. 647; *Ozturk v. Germany*, 21 Feb. 1984 (No. 73), 6 E.H.R.R. 409.

cannot be seen in the same light. Firstly, some matters may be more serious than others; in fact, the Rules grade offences, classifying those committed by Mr. Campbell as 'especially grave'. Secondly, the illegality of some acts may not turn on the fact that they were committed in prison: certain conduct which constitutes an offence under the Rules may also amount to an offence under the criminal law. Thus, doing gross personal violence to a prison officer may correspond to the crime of 'assault occasioning actual bodily harm' and, although mutiny and incitement to mutiny are not as such offences under the general criminal law, the underlying facts may found a criminal charge of conspiracy. It also has to be remembered that, theoretically at least, there is nothing to prevent conduct of this kind being the subject of both criminal and disciplinary proceedings.

The Court considers that these factors, whilst not of themselves sufficient to lead to the conclusion that the offences with which the applicant was charged have to be regarded as 'criminal' for Convention purposes, do give them a certain colouring which does not entirely coincide with that of a purely disciplinary matter.

72. It is therefore necessary to turn to the last criterion stated in the above-mentioned *Engel and Others* judgement and in the above-mentioned *Oztürk* judgment, namely the nature and degree of severity of the penalty that Mr. Campbell risked incurring. The maximum penalties which could have been imposed on him included forfeiture of all of the remission of sentence available to him at the time of the Board's award (slightly less than three years), forfeiture of certain privileges for an unlimited time and, for each offence, exclusion from associated work, stoppage of earnings and cellular confinement for a maximum of 56 days; he was in fact awarded a total of 570 days' loss of remission and subjected to the other penalties mentioned for a total of 91 days. . . .

In its above-mentioned *Engel and Others* judgment, the Court stated that deprivation of liberty liable to be imposed as a punishment was, in general, a penalty that belonged to the 'criminal' sphere. It is true that in the present case the legal basis for the detention remained, even after the Board's award, the original sentence of imprisonment and that nothing was added thereto. However, the Court is of the opinion that the forfeiture of remission which Mr. Campbell risked incurring and the forfeiture actually awarded involved such serious consequences as regards the length of his detention that these penalties have to be regarded, for Convention purposes, as 'criminal'. By causing detention to continue for substantially longer than would otherwise have been the case, the sanction came close to, even if it did not technically constitute, deprivation of liberty and the object and purpose of the Convention require that the imposition of a measure of such gravity should be accompanied by the guarantees of Article 6. . . .[28]

---

[28] The United States Supreme Court has held that certain decisions by prison officials may amount to a deprivation of some 'liberty' retained even by convicted criminals, and therefore that they can only be effected with 'due process of law' entailing minimum procedural safeguards. This reasoning has been applied to revocation of parole, *Morrisey v. Brewer*, 408 U.S. 471 (1972), probation, *Gagnon v. Scarpelli*, 411 U.S. 778 (1973), forfeiture of 'good time credit', *Wolff v. McDonnell*, 418 U.S. 539 (1974), and to involuntary commitment of a prisoner to a mental hospital, *Vitek v. Jones*, 445 U.S. 480 (1980). No liberty interest, however, was found implicated, and no procedural protection required, for transfer of prisoners to different institutions or facilities or for other changes in the conditions of confinement: *Olim v. Wakinekona*, 461 U.S. 238 (1983), or changes in visitation rights, *Kentucky Dept. of Corrections v. Thompson*, 490 U.S. 454 (1989).

In most of these cases the Supreme Court decided the presence of a liberty interest based on an examination of the text of the statute or regulation which appeared to create the entitlement. Thus it held there was a protected interest even in the initial decision to parole where the language seemed to make such release mandatory on the occurrence of certain conditions. *Greenholz v. Inmates*, 472 U.S. 1 (1979) (*see also Hewitt v.*

The Court has attempted to separate disciplinary action from 'criminal charges' in several subsequent cases. In *Weber v. Switzerland*,[29] the Court held that a fine imposed on the complainant in a criminal proceeding for revealing information concerning the case was the result of a criminal charge. The Code of Criminal Procedure in the Swiss Canton of Vaud (an analogous provision in the Criminal Code was not invoked) bound 'parties, their counsel, employees of their counsel and experts and witnesses to maintain the confidentiality of the investigation'. The state argued that this was merely a matter of internal discipline limited to those involved in judicial procedure. The Court found this unconvincing with respect to the restriction imposed on the parties:

> As persons who above all others are bound by the confidentiality of an investigation, judges, lawyers and all those closely associated with the functioning of the courts are liable in such an event, independently of any criminal sanctions, to disciplinary measures on account of their profession. The parties, on the other hand, only take part in the proceedings as people subject to the jurisdiction of the courts and they therefore do not come within the disciplinary sphere of the judicial system. As [the relevant provision], however, potentially affects the whole population, the offence it defines, and to which it attaches a punitive sanction is a 'criminal' one. . . .[30]

On the other hand, the levying of fines on a party for 'improper statements' made in written submissions to the court has been held non-criminal, since they were used only in reaction to statements in judicial proceedings and 'not to such statements made in a different context or by a person falling outside the circle of people covered by that provision'. 'Rules enabling a Court to sanction disorderly conduct in proceedings before it are a common feature of legal systems of the Contracting States' and are 'more akin to the exercise of disciplinary powers than to the imposition of a punishment for commission of a criminal offence'. The amount of the fines (three fines of 1,000 Swedish Krona (about U.S. $150 or £100) each and the fact that the applicant

---

Helms, 459 U.S. 460 (1983) finding a liberty interest against 'administrative segregation' based on 'language of an unmistakably mandatory character'. *Id.* at 471). *In Sandin v. O'Connor*, 515 U.S. 472 (1995), however, the Court rejected a text-based approach holding the imposition of restrictions on prisoners required constitutionally minimum procedural safeguards only when those restrictions 'impos[e] atypical and significant hardship on the inmate in relation to the ordinary incidents of prison life'. *Id.* at 484.

The Supreme Court of Canada has held that under s.7 of the Canadian Charter of Rights and Freedom, a prisoner's 'liberty' is affected by significant changes in the manner of his confinement and in the possibilities for release. Consequently, such changes may only be effected if not 'contrary to the principles of fundamental justice' in both substance and procedure. *Cunningham v. Canada* [1993] 2 S.C.R. 243.

In the United Kingdom the House of Lords has held that while the legality of changes in the circumstances of confinement of a convicted prisoner may be challenged in a public law proceeding for judicial review, *Leech v. Deputy Governor, Parkhurst Prison* [1988] A.C. 533, such a prisoner had no private law remedy for damages. The House found that neither the relevant prison rules, nor the authorizing legislation, contemplated such a right of action. Nor were such acts by prison authorities the basis for an action in tort for false imprisonment since the prisoner had already been lawfully confined. Unlike the United States Supreme Court, the House denied a prisoner had any 'residual liberty' of which he might be deprived. *R. v. Deputy Governor of Parkhurst Prison ex parte Hague* [1992] 1 A.C. 58 H.L.

[29] 22 May 1990 (No. 177), 12 E.H.R.R. 508.

[30] *Id.* at para 33. For the American constitutional law on the characterization of sanctions for noncompliance with judicial orders *see* the discussion of *United Mine Workers v. Bagwell, infra*.

was liable to imprisonment for non-payment did not change the Court's conclusion.[31] The Court reached the same result in a later case involving offensive oral and written statements in which the amount of the fines was considerably higher. In this case the maximum fine was 10,000 Austrian schillings (about $U.S. 950 or £ 475) and the total amount fined was 22,500 schillings.[32] Judge Jungwiert dissented in the second case arguing that the penalties were 'at the level of a criminal punishment'.[33]

The distinction between sanctions directed at a limited number of participants in specified activities and those applied to the public at large was also evident in *Demicoli v. Malta*,[34] where the applicant had been held punishable by the Maltese House of Representatives for a satirical article about the House. In a fairly summary proceeding that body had found the applicant guilty of a defamatory libel, breaching the privileges of the House. While breach of parliamentary privilege was not formally classified as criminal in Maltese law, the Court noted that, in the proceedings against the applicant, certain members of the House equated its judgment with criminal proceedings and that defamatory libel was also a criminal offence in Maltese law. The Court also stressed that the action against the applicant was distinct from matters relating merely to the 'internal regulation and orderly functioning' of the House. Finally, it noted that the whole population was subject to such actions without regard to where the offending action took place.

The assessment of tax surcharges was held to involve the equivalent of a 'criminal charge' in *Bendenoun v. France*.[35] It was not classed as such under domestic law and was vested in administrative, not criminal, courts. Moreover, the amounts involved were calculated on the basis of the tax originally due and, in case of death of the taxpayer, were charged against his estate. Conceding that these factors militated against characterization as criminal, the Court, nonetheless, felt they were outweighed by other aspects of the procedure. As in the *Weber* and *Demicoli* cases, the surcharges were imposed not on a selected group but, potentially, on 'all citizens in their capacity as taxpayers'. They were intended not as compensation for a loss caused, but for their punitive and deterrent effects. Finally, the Court noted that the amounts involved were very large and that, on a nonpayment, a person could be remitted to the criminal courts where he was liable to imprisonment.[36]

The Supreme Court of Canada addresses the distinction between criminal charges

[31] *Ravnsborg v. Sweden*, 23 Mar. 1994 (No. 283B), 18 E.H.R.R. 38, para. 34.

[32] *Putz v. Austria*, 22 Feb. 1996, Reports, 1996–I 312.

[33] *Id.* (Judge Jungwiert dissenting). Compare the holding in *Putz* with that in *Garyfallou AEBE v. Greece*, 24 Sept 1997, Reports, 1997–V 1821, 28 E.H.R.R. 344 in which the Court found a maximum fine of 15,500 Deutsche Marks for violation of trade regulation, with non-payment resulting in possible seizure of property or detention, should be regarded as involving a criminal charge without regard to the nature of the underlying conduct.

[34] 27 Aug. 1991 (No. 210), 14 E.H.R.R. 47.

[35] 24 Feb. 1994 (No. 284), 18 E.H.R.R. 54.

[36] *Id.* at paras. 45–7. To the same effect see *Benham v. United Kingdom*, 10 June 1996, Reports, 1996–III 738, 22 E.H.R.R. 293 (discussed in Chapter 7, Section (E)(2)(a) *supra*); *A.P.M.P. & T.P. v. Switzerland*, 29 Aug. 1997, Reports, 1997–V 1477, 26 E.H.R.R. 541; *E.L., R.L. & J.O.L. v. Switzerland*, 29 Aug. 1997, Reports, 1997–V 1509.

and disciplinary proceedings in the context of actions involving officers of the Royal Canadian Mounted Police. It held that a 'major service offence' amounts to an offence within Section 11 of the Canadian Charter of Rights and Freedoms, and thus must be accompained by a series of procedural safeguards. It sought to distinguish such offences from other disciplinary and regulatory infractions by identifying two characteristics, either of which would be sufficient to create a 'criminal or penal matter', that define such an offence. Note the similarity of these factors to those identified by the Strasbourg Court in addressing the same question under Article 6. First, an offence is present in a matter of 'public nature, intended to promote public order and welfare within a public sphere of activity' as distinguished from 'private, domestic or disciplinary matters which are regulatory, protective or corrective and which are primarily intended to maintain discipline, professional integrity and professional standards or to regulate conduct within a limited private sphere of activity'. Second, any matter is an 'offence' which is accompanied by a 'true penal consequence' defined as 'imprisonment or a fine which, by its magnitude, would appear to be imposed for the purpose of redressing the wrong done to society rather than the maintenance of internal discipline within the limited sphere of activity'. Although, generally, service offences would not meet the first test, as they were imposed to maintain discipline within a limited sphere, in the offence at bar, physical abuse of a suspect, the allowable punishment of one year's imprisonment, entailed a 'true penal consequence'.[37]

Canadian courts have long been called on to characterize legislation as criminal or non-criminal in connection with the distribution of powers under the Constitution Act, 1867. That Act gives exclusive legislative authority over maters of criminal law to the federal Parliament.[38] In these federalism cases the Court has stated the criteria for criminal law somewhat more broadly than in connection with Charter issues. It has noted two requirements: such laws 'must contain prohibitions backed by penalties; and they must be directed at a "legitimate public purpose"'.[39] In a recent case the Supreme Court upheld the Environmental Protection Act against an argument by dissenting justices that the law prohibited no primary conduct. Rather it merely vested in administrative officers a power to prescribe the degree and manner of use of various substances.[40] The majority, noting the special difficulties of environmental regulation, regarded the Act as one in which Parliament made 'provision for carefully tailoring the prohibited action to specified substances used or dealt with in specific circumstances'.[41]

---

[37] R. v. Wigglesworth, [1987] 2 S.C.R. 541. See also R. v. Généreux, [1992] 1 S.C.R. 259, holding that trial in a court martial of a breach of the Military Code of Service Discipline involved an 'offense' under s.11. The Code made a 'service offense' of any violation of the Criminal Code and, in this case, the underlying conduct alleged was a violation of the Narcotics Control Act.

[38] Constitution Act 1867, s. 91(27). See generally P. Hogg, Constitutional Law of Canada (3rd edn. 1992) ss. 18.1–18.11.

[39] R. v. Hydro-Quebec [1997] 3 S.C.R. 213., para. 35 (Lamer & Iacobucci JJ dissenting).

[40] Id. at paras. 45–63 (dissenting opinion).

[41] Id. at para. 151.

The United States Supreme Court has had to grapple with the defining character-istics of criminal proceedings in several contexts. Many of the rights accorded by the Fifth and Sixth amendments to the Constitution are available only to the accused in a criminal prosecution. The Court has stated the essence of such a criminal law to be that the 'sanction . . . [it] impose[s] is punishment'.[42] This is principally a question of legislative intent. In *Kennedy v. Mendoza-Martin*[43] the Court decided that a statute withdrawing citizenship from persons leaving the country to avoid the draft was 'criminal' based on an extensive review of the legislative history, which was replete with references to 'punishments' and 'penalties'.[44] The Court also set forth a more general approach to be used in the absence of such a clear legislative record:

Whether the sanction involves an affirmative disability or restraint, whether it has historically been regarded as punishment, whether it comes into play only on a finding of scienter, whether its operation will promote the traditional aims of punishment—retribution and deterrence, whether the behavior to which it applies is already a crime, whether an alternative purpose to which it may rationally be connected is assignable for it, and whether it appears excessive in relation to the alternative purpose assigned, are all relevant to the inquiry, and may often point in differing directions. Absent conclusive evidence of Congressional intent as to the penal nature of a statute, these factors must be considered in relation to the statute on its face.[45]

In *Allen v. Illinois*[46] the Court considered an Illinois procedure for the civil commit-ment of 'sexually dangerous' persons. It held that the Fifth Amendment's privilege against self-incrimination was not applicable in such proceedings. Under the statute a person could be committed if he was found to suffer from a mental disorder and to possess 'criminal propensities toward acts of sexual assault'. It was a prerequisite to the commitment, which was of indefinite duration, that the person be shown to have committed at least one act or attempt at sexual assault. On commitment he was to be provided with 'care and treatment' and to be released if a court found him to be no longer dangerous. The Supreme Court noted that the legislation expressly declared itself to be 'civil in nature'. It agreed that such labels were not dispositive but required in such cases the 'clearest proof' that 'the statutory scheme [is] so punitive either in purpose or effect as to negate [the state's] intention'.[47] The Court held such proof had not been produced. The requirement of an earlier act of sexual assault need not be understood as a predicate 'to punish past misdeeds, but primarily to show the accused's mental condition and to predict future behavior'.[48]

The Court reached the same conclusion with respect to a similar scheme in *Kansas*

---

[42] 372 U.S. 144, 167 (1963).

[43] *Id.*

[44] *Id.* at 170–85.

[45] *Id.* at 168–9.

[46] 478 U.S. 364 (1986).

[47] *Id.* at 368–9, quoting *United States v. Ward*, 448. U.S. 242, 248–9 (1972) (quotation marks and brackets in original).

[48] *Id.* at 371.

v. Hendricks.[49] In that case, however, the committal, which was to a maximum security institution, was not to be initiated until the subject was ending a prison term for sexual assault and little or no treatment was contemplated after commitment. The Court noted that a state 'may take measures to restrict the freedom of the dangerously mentally ill. This is a legitimate non-punitive governmental objective and has been historically so regarded'.[50] The protection of the public was a sufficient and non-criminal basis for detention even in the absence of treatment.

The American courts have also been called on to draw a constitutional distinction between civil and criminal proceedings in connection with the appropriate procedure to be employed in adjudicating citations of contempt of court where an individual has failed to follow an order of a court. A characterization of contempt as criminal requires elaborate procedure, including a jury trial. In its most recent pronouncement on the issue, the United States Supreme Court (like the European Court in *Bendenoun*) placed considerable emphasis on the punitive, as opposed to compensatory, purpose of an adjudication of contempt. In *United Mine Workers v. Bagwell*,[51] a state court had enjoined a labour union from engaging in certain illegal activities in connection with a strike and associated picketing. It further announced that any violation of its order would result in fines of $20,000 each if the infraction were nonviolent, and $100,000 if it were violent. In a six-month period the court levied fines of more than $64 million. The Supreme Court held these fines could, consistent with the Fourteenth Amendment to the United States Constitution, be imposed only if preceded by a criminal trial. The fines were conceded to be noncompensatory. The Court distinguished fines of increasing daily amounts, intended to coerce compliance with judicial orders. Rather, these were 'analogous to fixed, determinate, retrospective criminal fines which [the contemnors] had no opportunity to purge once imposed'[52]

3. CIVIL RIGHTS AND PUBLIC RIGHTS

The material which follows surveys the attempt of the European Court of Human Rights to delineate the characteristics of those 'civil rights and obligations' the determination of which, under Article 6, must be preceded by fair procedure. The Court has sometimes focused on the distinction between such 'civil rights' and 'public rights'. In the determination of the latter no particular procedure is required. This distinction does not turn on the gravity or potential gravity of the injury to the individual nor on the importance of the policy involved to the state. In civil law systems, it follows from the fundamental dichotomy between private law, the law governing the rights of individuals *inter se*, and public law, the law regulating the activities of the state. This division closely (although not perfectly) tracks a division of

---

[49] 521 U.S. 346 (1997).
[50] *Id.* at 363.
[51] 512 U.S. 821 (1994).
[52] *Id.* at 837.

jurisdiction between the ordinary courts, which determine questions of private and criminal law, and the administrative courts, which adjudicate matters of public law. Although, eventually, the administrative courts developed their own, formidable bodies of law, the segregation of matters of public administration was premised originally on an implicit assumption that the ordinary courts and judicial procedure were unsuited to regulate the proper exercise of public authority.[53]

Commentators on the English common law, on the other hand, have traditionally regarded the distinction between ordinary, private law and public law as incompatible with the basic assumptions of the common law. Albert Venn Dicey in his classic *Introduction to the Study of the Law of the Constitution* made a sharp contrast between British constitutional law and the French 'droit administratif': 'Any official who exceeds the authority given him by the law', wrote Dicey, 'incurs the common law responsibility for his wrongful act; he is amenable to the authority of the ordinary courts; and the ordinary courts have themselves jurisdiction to determine what is the extent of his legal power, and whether the orders under which he has acted were legal and valid'.[54]

Dicey's remarks, however, may overstate the amenability of public officials to judicial control in British law, and there are certain categories of public decisionmaking which might still be characterized as outside the jurisdiction of the ordinary courts. The British Crown, represented for practically all purposes by the government of the day, has always been understood to possess certain 'prerogative' powers beyond the reach of the common law. While the constitutional revolution of the seventeenth century established the principle that such power could be limited and controlled by Parliamentary act, some residual prerogative power has survived. These powers relate largely to matters of appointments and foreign and military affairs, but have also been held to extend to some matters affecting regulation of the civil service and the maintenance of public order. Although there are some recent indications that the courts may be more willing to require that something like the standards of 'natural justice' be followed, the government was traditionally thought to be immune from judicial regulation of the procedure which it employed while acting pursuant to prerogative power.[55] Even apart from the royal prerogative, British law evidences certain occasions where something like the distinction between public rights and civil rights is utilized. The courts have held that, in certain circumstances, Parliament, having committed certain decisions to ministers or agencies, must be taken to have also entrusted such bodies with the power to decide on the proper procedure for making those decisions.[56] For example, when the Department of the Environment held a public inquiry as to the proper route for a motorway, the House of Lords held that natural justice did not

---

[53] *See* J. H. Merryman, *The Civil Law Tradition* 87–8, 92–3, 97 (2nd ed. 1985); A. T. von Mehren & J. R. Gordley, *The Civil Law System*, 343–4 (1977).

[54] A. V. Dicey, *Introduction to the Study of the Law of the Constitution*, 256 (8th ed. 1915) (Liberty Classics Reprint 1987). For a more recent comparative treatment of the public – private law distinction *see* J. Allison, *A Continental Distinction in the Common Law: A Historical and Comparative Perspective on English Public Law* (1996).

[55] *See* A. W. Bradley & K. D. Ewing, *Constitutional and Administrative Law* 280–85 (12th ed. 1999).

[56] *See id.* at 733–47.

require that even though they stood to be adversely affected by the outcome, persons objecting to the proposed route be given an opportunity to cross-examine witnesses. In terms not dissimilar to the civil law-public law distinction, some of the judgments emphasized the difference between the character of such an inquiry and that of the ordinary judicial trial. Viscount Dilhorne, in his judgment noted:

A trial ends with a decision in favour of one party. An inquiry does not. There is no lis between a minister and his department on the one hand and the objectors on the other . . . The minister then has to decide and in reaching his decision he may have regard to the policy considerations not discussed at the inquiry. If there was a lis between the minister putting forward a scheme or proposal and the objectors, then indeed the minister would be judge in his own cause.[57]

Indeed, in such cases, Lord Diplock insisted that it was more suitable to require that the proceedings be 'fair' than that they follow the requirements of natural justice, as the latter term suggested a judicial procedure which was inappropriate in this kind of proceeding.[58]

This idea of 'public rights' also has some distinct analogues in North American law, especially in connection with determining the proper forum for resolving disputes. As in the civil law system, it is founded on the idea that there is some inevitable discretion inherent in the operation of government. Some decisions could quite reasonably be taken by officials without any formal procedure. No one acquires a right to a particular decision or process just because the government sets up a more formal judicial-style mechanism. In the United States the concept is employed in identifying the questions which must be committed to federal courts staffed by judges with life tenure and salaries which may not be reduced under Article III of the Constitution. That Article exclusively vests the 'judicial power of the United States' in such courts. The Supreme Court, however, has decided that matters of 'public rights' may be decided by non-Article III tribunals created by the Congress. The permissible jurisdiction of such 'legislative' courts was discussed in *Northern Pipeline Const. Co. v. Marathon Pipeline Co.*:[59]

. . . The doctrine extends only to matters arising 'between the Government and persons subject to its authority in connection with the performance of the constitutional functions of the executive or legislative departments', *Crowell v. Benson* 285 U.S. 22, 50 (1932), and only to matters that historically could have been determined exclusively by those departments. . . . The understanding of these cases is that the Framers expected that Congress would be free to commit such matters completely to non-judicial executive determination, and that as a result there can be no constitutional objection to Congress' employing the less drastic expedient of committing their determination to a legislative court or an administrative agency.

The public-rights doctrine is grounded in a historically recognized distinction between matters that could be conclusively determined by the Executive and Legislative Branches and matters that are 'inherently . . . judicial'. . . .

---

[57] *Bushell v. Secretary of State for the Environment* [1981] A.C. 75, 107.
[58] *Id.* at 95.
[59] 458 U.S. 50 (1982).

The distinction between public rights and private rights has not been definitively explained in our precedents. Nor is it necessary to do so in the present case, for it suffices to observe that a matter of public rights must at a minimum arise 'between the government and others'. In contrast, 'the liability of one individual to another under the law as defined', is a matter of private rights. Our precedents clearly establish that *only* controversies in the former category may be removed from Article III courts and delegated to legislative courts or administrative agencies for their determination. . . . Private-rights disputes on the other hand, lie at the core of the historically recognized judicial power.[60]

Similarly, under the Canadian Constitution Act, 1867 it has become necessary to decide which matters may be decided by provincially created tribunals and which must be heard in 's. 96' Superior Courts in which the judges are appointed and salaries set by the federal government. The Supreme Court of Canada addressed the question in *Re Residential Tenancies Act*[61] in which it considered a provincial scheme for resolving disputes between residential tenants and landlords. It formulated a three-part test for deciding whether the power of a provincial tribunal conflicted with the exclusive jurisdiction of the Superior Courts. First, a court had to decide if the decision at issue was one within the jurisdiction of superior, district or county courts in 1867, the time of confederation. If so, it would have to be considered whether, in light of the institutional setting of the challenged action, it could still reasonably be regarded as stating a 'judicial question':

. . . The primary issue is the nature of the question which the tribunal is called upon to decide. Where the tribunal is faced with a private dispute between parties, and is called upon to adjudicate through the application of a recognized body of rules in a manner consistent with fairness and impartiality, then, normally, it is acting in a 'judicial capacity'. To borrow the terminology of Professor Ronald Dworkin, the judicial task involves questions of 'principle', that is, consideration of the competing rights of individuals or groups. This can be contrasted with questions of 'policy' involving competing views of the collective good of the community as a whole. (See Dworkin, *Taking Rights Seriously* (Duckworth, 1977) pp. 82–90). . . .

. . . [I]f the power or jurisdiction is exercised in a judicial manner, then it becomes necessary to proceed to the third and final step in the analysis and review the tribunal's function as a whole in order to appraise the impugned function in its entire institutional context. . . . It will all depend on the context of the exercise of the power. It may be that the impugned 'judicial powers' are merely subsidiary or ancillary to general administrative functions assigned to the tribunal . . . or the powers may be necessarily incidental to the achievement of a broader policy goal of the legislature. . . . In such a situation, the grant of judicial power to provincial appointees is valid. The scheme is only invalid when the adjudicative function is a sole or central function of the tribunal . . . so that the tribunal can be said to be operating 'like a s. 96 court'. . . .[62]

---

[60] *Id.* at 67–70.
[61] [1981] 1 S.C.R. 714.
[62] [1981] 1 S.C.R. at 734–6.

4. FELDBRUGGE *V.* THE NETHERLANDS

Judgment of 29 May 1986
(No. 99), 8 E.H.R.R. 425

11. Mrs. Geziena Hendrika Maria Feldbrugge was born in 1945 and is resident at Anna Paulowna. She is of Dutch nationality.

In or about 1978, although she had been unemployed for some time, Mrs. Feldbrugge ceased to register at the Regional Employment Exchange. This was because she had fallen ill and did not consider herself sufficiently recovered to be fit to work.

On 11 April 1978, the Governing Board of the Occupational Association of the Banking and Insurance Wholesale Trade and Self-Employment Sector in Amsterdam decided that as from 24 March 1978 she was no longer entitled to the sickness allowances she had been receiving until then, as the Association's consulting doctor had judged her fit to resume work on that date.

12. She appealed to the Appeals Board in Haarlem.

The President of the Appeals Board sought the opinion of one of the permanent medical experts attached to the Board, a gynaecologist. . . . After consulting three other doctors (a gynaecologist and two general practitioners, including Mrs. Feldbrugge's), the expert concluded on 1 June 1978 that, gynaecologically speaking, she had been fit for work since 24 March; however, he felt it necessary also to consult an orthopaedic specialist.

On 18 August 1978, another permanent medical expert, an orthopaedic surgeon, examined the applicant and offered her the opportunity to comment. He also sought the views of the three practitioners mentioned above. In his report of 22 August 1978, he too found that Mrs. Feldbrugge had been fit to resume employment as from 24 March of that year.

On the basis of these two reports, the President of the Appeals Board ruled against the applicant.

[Further appeals by the applicant were unsuccessful.]

15. As far as health insurance is concerned, social security in the Netherlands is managed jointly by the State—which in general confines itself to establishing the legal framework of the scheme and to seeing to co-ordination—by employers and by employees.

The branches of the economy, including the liberal professions, are divided into sectors, each with an occupational association responsible for implementation of the social security legislation. . . .

16. . . . In case of unfitness for work through sickness, an employed person receives an allowance of 80 percent of his daily pay. He or she applies directly to the occupational association to which his or her employer belongs.

The entitlement to an allowance flows directly from the Act.

17. The scheme is administered by the occupational associations, and the funding is provided entirely by employers and employees. . . .

18. . . . On the lodging of an appeal of this kind, the President of the Appeals Board (there are twelve in the Netherlands) may immediately instruct its permanent medical expert to carry out an enquiry into the matter.

Within three days of notification of the appeal, the authority that delivered the decision which is challenged must submit all relevant files on the case.

The permanent medical expert consults the private practitioner of the person concerned and the relevant occupational association doctor, except where the file shows that they share his opinion. He summons and examines the appellant; he may consult another practitioner. Finally, he makes a written report to the President of the Appeals Board.

The President—who is a judge appointed for life—gives a reasoned decision which refers to the conclusions of the medical expert. . . .

26. According to the case law of the Court, 'the notion of "civil rights and obligations" cannot be interpreted solely by reference to the domestic law of the respondent State' . . .

29. There exists great diversity in the legislation and case law of the member states of the Council of Europe as regards the juridical nature of the entitlement to health insurance benefits under social security schemes, that is to say as regards the category of law to which such entitlement belongs. Some States—including the Netherlands—treat it as a public-law right, whereas others, on the contrary, treat it as a private-law right; others still would appear to operate a mixed system. What is more, even within the same legal order differences of approach can be found in the case law. Thus, in some States where the public-law aspect is predominant, some court decisions have nonetheless held Article 6(1) to be applicable to claims similar to the one in issue in the present case. Accordingly, there exists no common standard pointing to a uniform European notion in this regard. . . .

31. A number of factors might tend to suggest that the dispute in question should be considered as one falling within the sphere of public law. . . .

32. The first such factor is the character of the legislation. The legal rules governing social security benefits in the context of health insurance differ in many respects from the rules which apply to insurance in general and which are part of civil law. The Netherlands State has assumed the responsibility of regulating the framework of the health insurance scheme and of overseeing the operation of that scheme. To this end, it specifies the categories of beneficiaries, defines the limits of the protection afforded, lays down the rates of the contributions and the allowances, etc.

In several cases, State intervention by means of a statute or delegated legislation has nonetheless not prevented the Court from finding the right in issue to have a private, and hence civil, character. In the present case likewise, such intervention cannot suffice to bring within the sphere of public law the right asserted by the applicant. . . .

33. A second factor of relevance is the obligation to be insured against illness or, more precisely, the fact of being covered by insurance in the event of fulfilling the conditions laid down by the legislation. In other words, those concerned can neither opt out of the benefits nor avoid having to pay the relevant contributions.

Comparable obligations can be found in other fields. Examples are provided by the rules making insurance cover compulsory for the performance of certain activities—such as driving a motor vehicle—or for householders. Yet the entitlement to benefits to which this kind of insurance contract gives rise cannot be qualified as a public-law right. The Court does not therefore discern why the obligation to belong to a health insurance scheme should change the nature of the corresponding right . . .

34. One final aspect to be considered is the assumption, by the State or by public or semi-public institutions, of full or partial responsibility for ensuring social protection. This was what happened in the present case by virtue of the health insurance scheme operated by the Occupational Association of the Banking and Insurance, Wholesale Trade and Self-Employment Sector in

Amsterdam. Whether viewed as the culmination of or a stage in the development of the role of the State, such a factor implies, *prima facie*, an extension of the public-law domain.

On the other hand—and the Court will revert to the point later—the present case concerns a matter having affinities with insurance under the ordinary law, which insurance is traditionally governed by private law. It thus seems difficult to draw from the consequences of the extent of State intervention any firm conclusion as to the nature of the right in issue.

35. In sum, even taken together the three foregoing factors, on analysis, do not suffice to establish that Article 6 is inapplicable. . . .

36. In contrast, various considerations argue in favour of the opposite conclusion. . . .

37. To begin with, Mrs. Feldbrugge was not affected in her relations with the public authorities as such, acting in the exercise of discretionary powers, but in her personal capacity as a private individual. She suffered an interference with her means of subsistence and was claiming a right flowing from specific rules laid down by the legislation in force.

For the individual asserting it, such a right is often of crucial importance; this is especially so in the case of health insurance benefits when the employee who is unable to work by reason of illness enjoys no other source of income. In short, the right in question was a personal, economic and individual right, a factor that brought it close to the civil sphere. . . .

38. Secondly, the position of Mrs. Feldbrugge was closely linked with the fact of her being a member of the working population, having been a salaried employee. The applicant was admittedly unemployed at the relevant time, but the availability of the health benefits was determined by reference to the terms of her former contract of employment and the legislation applicable to that contract.

The legal basis of the work that she had performed was a contract of employment governed by private law. Whilst it is true that the insurance provisions derived directly from statute and not from an express clause in the contract, these provisions were in a way grafted onto the contract. They thus formed one of the constituents of the relationship between employer and employee.

In addition, the sickness allowance claimed by Mrs. Feldbrugge was a substitute for the salary payable under the contract, the civil character of this salary being beyond doubt. This allowance shared the same nature as the contract and hence was also invested with a civil character for the purposes of the Convention. . . .

39. Finally, the Dutch health insurance is similar in several respects to insurance under the ordinary law. Thus, under the Dutch health insurance scheme recourse is had to techniques of risk covering and to management methods which are inspired by those current in the private insurance sphere. In the Netherlands, the occupational associations conduct their dealings, notably with those insured, in the same way as a company providing insurance under the ordinary law, for example as regards collection of contributions, calculation of risks, verification of fulfilment of the conditions for receipt of benefits, and payment of allowances.

There exists a further feature of relevance. Complementary insurance policies, taken out with friendly societies or private insurance companies, allow employees to improve their social protection at the price of an increased or fresh financial outlay; such policies constitute in sum an optional extension of compulsory insurance cover. Proceedings instituted in their connection are incontestably civil proceedings. Yet in both cases the risk insured against (for example, ill-health) is the same and, whilst the extent of the cover increases, the nature of the cover does not change.

Such differences as may exist between private sector insurance and social security insurance do not affect the essential character of the link between the insured and the insurer.

Finally, the Court would draw attention to the fact that in the Netherlands, as in some other countries, the insured themselves participate in the financing of all or some of the social security schemes. Deductions at source are made from their salaries, which deductions establish a close connection between the contributions called for and the allowances granted. Thus, when Mrs. Feldbrugge was working, her employer withheld from her pay a sum paid over to the Occupational Association. In addition, her employer also bore a portion of the insurance contributions, which were included in the firm's accounts under the head of social insurance expenses. The Netherlands State, for its part, was not involved in the financing of the scheme. . . .

40. Having thus evaluated the relative cogency of the features of public and private law present in the instant case, the Court finds the latter to be predominant. None of these various features of private law is decisive on its own, but taken together and cumulatively they confer on the asserted entitlement the character of a civil right within the meaning of Article 6(1) of the Convention, which was thus applicable. . . .

41. The Court must therefore inquire whether the proceedings before the bodies responsible for determining Mrs. Feldbrugge's asserted right satisfied the conditions laid down in Article 6(1). . . .

42. . . . [The applicant] submitted that she had been denied a 'fair hearing' before the President of the Appeals Board. In this connection, she alleged a twofold violation of the principle of equality of arms with the Occupational Association. In the first place, she had not had the opportunity of appearing—either in person or represented by a lawyer—to argue her case. Secondly, the reports of the two permanent medical experts had not been made available to her, with the result that she had not been able either to comment on them or, if thought necessary, to call for further reports; yet in practice these documents provided the President of the Appeals Board with the sole basis for his decision.

43. The Government replied that the President is not able himself to enter into the merits of a medical dispute and is thus bound to confine himself to verifying that the permanent medical expert has observed the procedure prescribed by the Appeals Act, notably the obligation to consult the doctors of both parties and to examine the person concerned. . . .

44. It is not within the province of the Court to review in isolation the Dutch institution of the permanent medical expert. The Court confines itself to nothing that the permanent medical expert cannot himself determine a dispute over a civil right. The sole responsibility for taking the decision falls to the President of the Appeals Board, even when—as in the instant case—he does no more than ratify the opinion of the expert. . . .

. . . [T]he procedure followed before the President of the Appeals Board by virtue of the Dutch legislation was clearly not such as to allow proper participation of the contending parties, at any rate during the final and decisive stage of that procedure. To begin with, the President neither heard the applicant nor asked her to file written pleadings. Secondly, he did not afford her or her representative the opportunity to consult the evidence in the case file, in particular the two reports—which were the basis of the decision—drawn up by the permanent experts, and to formulate her objections thereto. Whilst the experts admittedly examined Mrs. Feldbrugge and gave her the opportunity to formulate any comments she might have had, the resultant failing was not thereby cured. In short, the proceedings conducted before the President of the Appeals Board were not attended, to a sufficient degree, by one of the principle guarantees of a judicial procedure. . . .

[The Court held by ten votes to seven that there was a violation of Art. 6(1).]

[A declaration by Judge Pinheiro Farinha is omitted.]

Joint Dissenting Opinion of Judges Ryssdal, Bindschedler-Robert, Lagergren, Matscher, Sir Vincent Evans, Bernhardt and Gersing:

1. We agree with the view of the majority of the Court as to the existence in the present case of a *'contestation'* (dispute) over a right claimed by the applicant, Mrs. Feldbrugge. In our opinion, however, the dispute did not involve the determination of her 'civil rights and obligations', within the meaning of Article 6(1) of the Convention. Our conclusion, therefore, is that Article 6(1) is not applicable in the present case. . . .

13. The right to a sickness allowance claimed by Mrs. Feldbrugge was an economic right deriving, not from the private contract between herself and her former employer, but from a collective scheme of protection of the working population set up by the legislature. An allocation of society's resources as generated within the employment context has been decided upon by the domestic legislature; and the applicant, as a member of the section of society concerned, was compelled to participate in that scheme. Such schemes represent performance of society's duty to protect the health and welfare of its members; they are not merely examples of the State taking on or regulating an insurance activity equally capable of being carried on by the private sector. . . .

15. . . . The judicialisation of dispute procedures, as guaranteed by Article 6(1), is eminently appropriate in the realm of relations between individuals but not necessarily so in the administrative sphere, where organisational, social and economic considerations may legitimately warrant dispute procedures of a less judicial and formal kind. The present case is concerned with the operation of a collective statutory scheme for the allocation of public welfare. As examples of the special characteristics of such schemes, material to the issue of procedural safeguards, one might cite the large numbers of decisions to be taken, the medical aspects, the lack of resources or expertise of the persons affected, the need to balance the public interest for efficient administration against the private interest. Judicialisation of procedures for allocation of public welfare benefits would in many cases necessitate recourse by claimants to lawyers and medical experts and hence lead to an increase in expense and the length of the proceedings. . . .

16. We have not overlooked the fact that the overall object of the Convention is the humanitarian one of the protection of the individual and that, for the man or woman in the street, entitlement to social security benefits is of extreme importance for his or her daily life. However, as the Delegate of the Commission submitted, the economic importance for Mrs. Feldbrugge's livelihood of the allowance claimed is insufficient, on its own, to bring into play the applicability of Article 6(1) and its specific judicial guarantees. Of course, it is equally essential that in the administrative field justice should be done and the individual's claims should be investigated in a responsible and objective manner in accordance with the rules laid down, but that is not to say that all the various requirements of Article 6(1) of the Convention are therefore applicable. Indeed, as pointed out above, in the present opinion, there exist underlying considerations justifying special procedures in social welfare cases. . . .

19. The foregoing analysis is corroborated by the fact that the relevant legislation predates the elaboration of the Convention by some decades, and there existed similar legislation predating the Convention in many other of the Contracting States. It is therefore reasonable to assume that the intention of the drafters of Article 6(1) was not to include such statutory schemes of collective social protection within its ambit. On examination, the drafting history confirms this reading of the text.

20. The adjective 'civil' was added to the English version of Article 6(1) in November 1950 on the day before the Convention was opened for signature, when a committee of experts examined the text of the Convention for the last time and 'made a certain number of formal corrections and corrections of translations'. Whilst no specific explanation was given for the last-minute change to Article 6(1), it is a fair inference that the reason was merely to align the English text more closely with the language of the French text: prior to the change, although the French version had spoken, as now, of '*droits et obligations de caractère civil*', the English version had read 'rights and obligations in a suit of law'.

These two expressions had first been introduced at a meeting (March 1950) of the Committee of Experts on Human Rights of the Council of Europe and were evidently taken directly from the equivalent Article of the then existing draft of the International Covenant on Civil and Political Rights of the United Nations. It is therefore relevant to trace their history in the *travaux préparatoires* of the International Covenant.

21. The crucial discussion on the draft International Covenant took place on 1 June 1949 during the fifth session of the United Nations Commission on Human Rights. The French and Egyptian delegations had presented an amendment that referred to '*droits et obligations*' 'rights and obligations', without qualification. The reaction of the Danish representative (Mr. Sørensen) to this amendment was reported as follows:

> The representatives of France and Egypt proposed that everyone should have the right to have a tribunal determine his rights and obligations. Mr. Sørensen considered that that provision was much too broad in scope; it would tend to submit to a judicial decision any action taken by administrative organs exercising discretionary power conferred on them by law. He appreciated that the individual should be ensured protection against any abuse of power by administrative organs but the question was extremely delicate and it was doubtful whether the Commission would settle it there and then. The study of the division of power between administrative and judicial organs could be undertaken later. . . . Mr. Sørensen asked the representatives of France and Egypt whether the scope of the provision in question might be limited to indicate that only cases between individuals and not those between individuals and the State were intended.

The French representative (Mr. Cassin), speaking in French, replied that 'the Danish representative's statement had convinced him that it was very difficult to settle in that Article all questions concerning the exercise of justice in the relationships between individuals and governments'. He was therefore prepared to let the words '*soit de ses droits et obligations*' in the first sentence of the Franco-Egyptian amendment be replaced by the expression '*soit des contestations sur ses droits et obligations de caractère civil*' (rendered in the English version of the summary record as 'or of his rights and obligations in a suit of law'). He agreed that the problem 'had not been fully thrashed out and should be examined more thoroughly'.

Later the same day, a drafting committee produced a text which contained the expression 'in a suit of law' in English and '*de caractère civil*' in French. The formula employed in this text is the one that was ultimately adopted for Article 14 of the International Covenant in 1966.

22. It thus seems reasonably clear that the intended effect of the insertion of the qualifying term '*de caractère civil*' in the French text of the draft International Covenant was to exclude from the scope of the provision certain categories of disputes in the field of administration 'concerning the exercise of justice in the relationships between individuals and governments'. . . .

5. THE ENLARGEMENT OF 'CIVIL RIGHTS AND OBLIGATIONS'

Article 6 provides the right to certain procedures 'in the determination of . . . civil rights and obligations'. On its face this provision might be understood to apply only to situations where a person finds him- or herself facing a formal legal procedure in which his or her rights have been placed in jeopardy. That is, it might be read as a 'defendant's' right. In *Golder v. United Kingdom*,[63] an important early case, the European Court held that Article 6 also includes a right to invoke legal procedures consistent with the article when a person faces a loss of rights or an imposition of obligations. That is, it recognized a 'plaintiff's' right as well. The Court reached this conclusion partly by a close examination of the French and English texts but also for the more general reason that 'one can scarcely conceive of the rule of law without there being a possibility of having access to the Courts'.[64]

It would be inconceivable, in the opinion of the Court, that Article 6§1 should describe in detail the procedural guarantees afforded to parties in a pending lawsuit and should not first protect that which alone makes it in fact possible to benefit from such guarantees, that is, access to a Court.[65]

The right of access to a Court has been construed as including the right to effective enforcement of judgments. In a decision in which it held that article was violated when an eviction order went unenforced for 13 years the Strasbourg Court repeated dicta it had applied in prior cases:

the right to a court would be illusory if a Contracting State's domestic legal system allowed a final, binding judicial decision to remain inoperative to the detriment of one party. It would be inconceivable that Article 6 §1 should describe in detail procedural guarantees afforded to the litigants—proceedings that are fair, public and expeditious—without protecting the implementation of judicial decisions; to construe Article 6 as being concerned exclusively with access to a court and the conduct of proceedings would be likely to lead to situations incompatible with the principle of the rule of law which the Contracting State undertook to respect when they ratified the Convention. Execution of a judgment given by any Court must therefore be regarded as an integral part of the 'trial' for the purposes of Article 6.[66]

In the *Feldbrugge* case it was not contested that the applicant was entitled by law to the benefits she sought on a showing of certain facts. The only issue was the character of such a right. In some cases, however, a prior question is whether or not the applicant's claim involves a procedure for the determination of something properly called a 'right' at all. Unlike the question whether a right is public or civil, the

---

[63] 7 May 1974 (No. 18), 1 E.H.R.R. 524.
[64] *Id.* at para. 34.
[65] *Id.* at para. 35.
[66] *Immobiliare Saffi v. Italy*, 26 July 1999 (not yet reported) para. 63 citing *Hornsby v. Greece*, 19 Mar. 1997, Reports, 1997–II 510, 24 E.H.R.R. 250, para. 40.

existence of a right is determined solely by reference to the law of the state involved. It must be shown that the dispute was over 'a "right" which can be said, at least on arguable grounds, to be recognized under domestic law'.[67] This requires a close examination of the municipal law sources with an aim to seeing if they define a set of conditions and procedure which trigger an entitlement to the benefit claimed.[68] In *Masson & Van Zon v. The Netherlands*[69] the applicants complained about the procedure for determining whether they were entitled to compensation for their detention in connection with criminal charges on which they were later acquitted. The Netherlands law on which they relied provided that a court 'may' order such compensation if it was 'of the opinion that [there are] reasons in equity' to do so. The Strasbourg Court held that '[t]he grant to a public authority of such a measure of discretion indicates that no actual right is recognized'.[70] This holding may be compared with *Werner v. Austria*[71] where Austrian procedures for similar compensation claims were considered. In the latter case the Court held that Article 6 was applicable. Compensation under Austrian law was to be awarded if 'the suspicion that he committed the offence has been dispelled'. The Court held that unlike *Masson & Van Zon* in which the decision 'was left entirely to the discretion of the Court', in this case there was a 'right to be compensated . . . provided the statutory requirements were satisfied'.[72]

Compare the Court's approach to deciding whether a 'right' is in issue in these cases with the view of Judge de Meyer in a concurring opinion:

> Any right which a citizen (civis) may feel entitled to assert, either under national law or under supranational or international law has indeed to be considered a 'civil' right within the meaning of Article 6, para. 1 of the Convention, which enshrines a right which is so prominent that 'there can be no justification for interpreting [it] restrictively'.[73]

The sources of domestic law which may support rights are extensive. The Court has, for example, held that individuals obtained a right to compensation from an international protocol between France and Morocco establishing a lump sum payment for French-owned property expropriated by Morocco. The protocol stated (without further specification) that the apportionment of this payment was to be the responsibility of the French government.[74]

The Strasbourg Court's formulation of the issue is similar to that developed under

---

67 *Masson & Van Zon v. The Netherlands*, 28 Sept. 1995 (No 327A), 22 E.H.R.R. 491, para. 44.

68 *See, e.g., Rolf Gustafson v. Sweden*, 1 July 1997, Reports, 1997–IV 1149, 25 E.H.R.R. 623, para. 40.

69 28 Sept. 1995 (No. 327A), 22 E.H.R.R. 491.

70 *Id.* at para. 51. *See also Andersson v. Sweden*, 27 Aug. 1997, Reports, 1997–IV 1407, 25 E.H.R.R. 722; *M.S. v. Sweden*, 27 Aug. 1997, Reports, 1997–IV 1437, 28 E.H.R.R. 313.

71 24 Nov. 1997, Reports, 1997–VII 2496, 26 E.H.R.R. 310.

72 *Id.* at paras. 33–5. *See also Szucs v. Austria*, 24 Nov. 1997, Reports, 1997–VII 2468, 26 E.H.R.R. 310.

73 *Rolf Gustafson v. Sweden*, 1 July 1997, Reports, 1997–IV 1149, 25 E.H.R.R. 623 (concurring opinion) (quoting *Moreira de Azevedo v. Portugal*, 23 Oct. 1990 (No. 189), 13 E.H.R.R. 721, at para. 66).

74 *Beaumartin v. France*, 24 Nov. 1994 (No. 296B), 19 E.H.R.R. 485.

the United States Constitution to decide whether a person is complaining of a deprivation of 'liberty' or 'property', so as to bring into play a state's obligation to provide
'due process of law' under the Fourteenth Amendment. The gist of the Supreme
Courts's modern jurisprudence on this matter is that such a deprivation occurs whenever someone has lost a benefit to which he is entitled by law, be it the common law of
property or contract or a positive enactment by the state. In such cases an individual is
entitled to a fair procedure for determining whether the state's action was in accordance with the governing law. This reasoning has been applied to the termination of
such state benefits as drivers' licences,[75] public education,[76] and non-probationary government employment.[77] Similarly, public welfare benefits may not be terminated in the
absence of a fair hearing, since to do so would be a deprivation of 'property' without
due process of law.[78]

A cognizable claim under Article 6 requires more than just showing a dispute over a
'right'. The applicant must also show that the procedure about which he or she is
complaining was decisive for the determination of that right. In *Fayed v. United
Kingdom*[79] the applicant was the target of an investigation by the Department of Trade
and Industry concerning possible fraudulent statements made in connection with his
acquisition of a public company. The applicant believed the publication of the report
of the investigation injured his reputation. The European Court agreed that under
English law, the applicant had a right against unjustified attacks on his reputation. But
the investigation did not, as a matter of law, determine liability in connection with
that right:

However, the Court is satisfied that the functions performed by the Inspector were, in practice as
well as in theory, essentially investigative (see the similar analysis by the Supreme Court of the
United States of America of the functions of the Federal Civil Rights Commission in the case of
Hannah v. Larche (363 U.S. 420 (1960))). The inspectors did not adjudicate, either in form or in
substance. They themselves said in their report that their findings would not be dispositive of
anything. They did not make a legal determination as to criminal or civil liability concerning the
Fayed brothers, and in particular concerning the latter's civil right to honour and reputation.
The purpose of their inquiry was to ascertain and record facts which might subsequently be used
as the basis for action by other competent authorities—prosecuting, regulatory, disciplinary or
even legislative.[80]

The Court has also held that parties objecting to the licensing procedure for nuclear
plants in Switzerland stated no Article 6 claim because they had not established that
the operation of the plant posed a risk to their physical health. Since they were relying

---

[75] *Bell v. Burson*, 402 U.S. 535 (1971).

[76] *Goss v. Lopez*, 419 U.S. 565 (1975).

[77] *Perry v. Sindermann*, 408 U.S. 593 (1972).

[78] *Goldberg v. Kelly*, 397 U.S. 254 (1970).

[79] 21 Sept. 1994 (No 294B), 18 E.H.R.R. 393.

[80] *Id.* at para. 61. *See also Bushell v. Secretary of State for the Environment* [1980] 2 All E.R. 608, discussed at
section B. 3 *supra* concerning procedures in public inquiries in the United Kingdom; *Canada (Attorney-
General) v. Canada (Commission of Inquiry on the Blood System)* [1997] 3 S.C.R. 440 (same in Canada).

on a right to physical integrity conceded to be part of Swiss law, this lack of proof was fatal to any conclusion that the procedure complained of was decisive for the determination of that right.[81] On the other hand, the European Court has held that, not withstanding their special character, Constitutional Courts are subject to Article 6 where their decisions have a decisive effect on the outcome of litigation in which civil rights are at stake in ordinary courts.[82]

Cases subsequent to *Feldbrugge* have cast doubt on the character of the inquiry appropriate for deciding whether the provision of social services gives rise to 'civil rights' triggering the provisions of Article 6. In *Salesi v. Italy*[83] the applicant complained of the length of the proceedings associated with her appeal of a decision to deny her a disability pension. The disability benefits scheme at issue in *Salesi* differed significantly from that involved in *Feldbrugge*. The benefits were not associated with a private employment contract and they were entirely funded by the state, involving no private contributions. Notwithstanding the consequent absence of many of the private law aspects of the prior case, the Court found Article 6 applicable. It held that the differences 'cannot be regarded as fundamental'. The Court found decisive the fact that 'the applicant was claiming an individual economic right flowing from specific rules laid down in a statute. . .'.[84] The Court has also found disputes over employers' contributions to social welfare plans to involve 'civil rights and obligations' and thus to be subject to Article 6.[85]

Other cases decided after *Feldbrugge* also de-emphasized the importance of the relative balance of the public and private law elements of the right claimed. The Court has held, for example, that Article 6 applies to proceedings to revoke transport licences[86] or to reinstate disbarred attorneys.[87] This inclination was particularly pronounced in *Tre Traktörer Aktiebolag v. Sweden*.[88] The Court held the applicant was entitled to a determination by an impartial tribunal on the revocation of its licence to sell liquor in its restaurant. This notwithstanding that the sale of liquor was a state monopoly, the state exercised wide discretion in its choice of licensees, and the licences were not transferable. The Court found private law attributes in the fact that the licences were entrusted to private persons and that those persons then utilized the licences to make private contracts with third parties, namely their customers. The effect of this line of cases may have been to redirect the legal inquiry from the particular character of the right claimed to the mere presence of a substantial injury to an individual caused by an action of the state argued to be in violation of state law.

---

[81] *Balmer-Schafroth & Others v. Switzerland*, 26 Aug. 1997, Reports, 1997–IV 1346, 25 E.H.R.R. 598, para. 40.

[82] *See, e.g., Sussman v. Germany*, 16 Sept. 1996, Reports, 1996–IV 1158, 25 E.H.R.R. 64, para. 40.

[83] 6 Feb. 1993 (No. 257E), 26 E.H.R.R. 250.

[84] *Id.* at para. 19. See also *Schuler-Zgraggen v. Switzerland*, 24 June 1993 (No. 263), 16 E.H.R.R. 405.

[85] *Schouten & Meldrum v. The Netherlands*, 9 Dec. 1994 (No 304), 19 E.H.R.R. 432.

[86] *Pudas v. Sweden*, 27 Oct. 1987 (No. 125), 10 E.H.R.R. 380.

[87] *H v. Belgium*, 30 Nov. 1987 (No. 127), 10 E.H.R.R. 339.

[88] 7 July 1989 (No. 159), 13 E.H.R.R. 309.

In a potentially substantial extension of the range of proceedings governed by Article 6, the Court held it applicable to complaints of individuals who claim an interest in disputes between the state and third parties. For example, it has held that a claim by adjacent landowners that a permit to dispose of hazardous waste should not have been granted to a third party without more stringent conditions protecting the water supply on their property was covered. The Strasbourg Court held that since the applicant had the right under national law to request that the issuing board impose the conditions, as well as a right to appeal the decisions to the government, they had an arguable entitlement in municipal law to the requested protection. Since, moreover, their claim concerned the ability to use the well on their property for drinking purposes, it was essentially based on a property right which was a 'civil right' under Article 6.[89] Likewise it has found that Article 6 applied to the procedure for dealing with a neighbouring landowner's objection to a development plan for the construction of housing. The government had argued that the issues turned on legal provisions implementing public environmental policy. The Court, however, was more impressed with the fact that the applicant 'wished to avoid any infringement of her pecuniary rights because she considered that the works on the land adjoining her property would jeopardise her enjoyment of it and would reduce its market value'.[90]

The Court's judgments in these cases seem to embody a general rule that any legal issue, the determination of which entails financial consequences for a person involves his or her 'civil rights and obligations'. In an often repeated formula the Court has stated that Article 6(1) 'applies where the subject matter of an action is "pecuniary" in nature and is founded on an alleged infringement of rights which are likewise pecuniary'.[91] Thus a claim under anti-discrimination law has been adjudicated a civil right and not a public right because the decision might result in a financial benefit to the applicant.[92] The right to initiate a criminal prosecution as a civil party complainant was held to come under Article 6 because of the prospect of possible compensation.[93] In a subsequent case, however, the Court declined to find that the state's refusal to initiate criminal proceedings which the applicant might have joined as a civil party raised Article 6 issues. It noted that it was open to the applicant to seek compensation in a civil action.[94] The Court has not, therefore, made the presence of a financial interest sufficient to a make out a claim of a civil right. In *Schouten & Meldrum v. The Netherlands*[95] it held that Article 6 did apply to a dispute concerning the obligation of an employer to contribute to social insurance plans, but it voiced this caution:

---

[89] *Zander v. Sweden*, 25 Nov. 1993 (No. 279B), 18 E.H.R.R. 175.

[90] *Ortenberg v. Austria*, 25 Nov. 1994 (No. 295B), 19 E.H.R.R. 524, para. 28.

[91] *Id.*

[92] *Tinnelly & Sons Ltd. & Others and McElduff & Others v. United Kingdom*, 10 July 1998, Reports, 1998–IV 1663, 27 E.H.R.R. 249.

[93] *Ait-Mouhous v. France*, 28 Oct. 1998, Reports, 1998–III 3214.

[94] *Assenov and Others v Bulgaria*, 28 Oct. 1998, Reports, 1998–VIII 3264, 28 E.H.R.R. 652, paras. 107–13.

[95] 9 Dec. 1994 (No. 304), 19 E.H.R.R. 432.

Nor is it in itself sufficient to show that a dispute is 'pecuniary' in nature. There may exist 'pecuniary' obligations *vis-à-vis* the State or its subordinate authorities which, for the purpose of Article 6 §1, are to be considered as belonging exclusively to the realm of public law and are accordingly not covered by the notion of 'civil rights and obligations.' Apart from fines imposed by way of 'criminal sanction', this will be the case, in particular, when an obligation which is pecuniary in nature derives from tax legislation or is otherwise part of normal civic duties in a democratic society.[96]

The Court applied this limitation in *Pierre-Bloch v. France*.[97] In this case the applicant complained of the procedure of the Constitutional Council in deciding that he had exceeded limits on spending in his campaign to be elected to Parliament. He was barred from seeking election for one year and ordered to pay to the state an amount equal to his excessive expenditure. Despite the obvious financial impact of this decision, the Strasbourg Court held that Article 6 did not apply. The obligation to pay was a corollary of the obligation to limit election spending. As such, it was a component of the right to stand for election—'a political one and not a civil one'.[98] 'Besides, proceedings do not become "civil" merely because they also raise an economic issue'.[99]

One question that has occupied much of the Court's attention with respect to the extent of 'civil rights and obligations' involves disputes associated with civil service employment.[100] The relationship between a state and its employees presents numerous features of classic public law concerns. The Strasbourg Court's jurisprudence shows a tension between its recognition of this fact and its desire to subject financial disputes to the strictures of Article 6. In *Massa v. Italy*[101] dealing with the pension rights of the widower of a public employee, it endorsed a formula which it has continued to cite: '[d]isputes relating to the recruitment, careers and termination of service of public servants are as a general rule outside the scope of Article 6 §1. . . '.[102] The issues in the *Massa* case were not within this exclusion since they involved a simple legal obligation to pay money in accordance with controlling law, as would have been the case with a private employer and employee. Article 6 was therefore applicable.[103] In its next consideration of this question, in *Neigel v. France*,[104] the dispute involved the right of an employee who had taken an unpaid leave to be reinstated. The Court distinguished *Massa* by noting that here the dispute related to the applicant's 'recruitment, career and termination of service'. Therefore it was outside the reach of Article 6. The claim to back pay did not alter the nature of the case as it was a mere incident of the principal complaint demanding reinstatement.[105]

---

[96] *Id.* at para. 50.

[97] 21 Oct. 1997, Reports, 1997–VI 202, 26 E.H.R.R. 202.

[98] *Id.* at para. 50.

[99] *Id.* at para. 51.

[100] For a discussion of the applicability of the Convention's right of free expression to civil servants see Chapter 5, section D, *supra*.

[101] 24 Aug. 1993 (No 265B), 18 E.H.R.R. 266.

[102] *Id.* at para. 26.

[103] *Id.*

[104] 17 Mar. 1997, Reports, 1997–II 399.

[105] *Id.* at para. 44.

The Court applied this distinction in deciding a group of 18 cases on 2 September 1997. In 14 of these cases the applicants complained about various public decisions regarding their positions such as promotion, job assignments or reinstatements. Consistently with *Neigel*, the Court held Article 6 inapplicable.[106] In four cases the complaints focused on non-payment of salary due under statute or agreement. In these cases the Court, following *Massa*, held that Article 6 applied.[107] In his dissenting opinion in the cases finding Article 6 applicable Judge Bernhardt noted that all of these claims had 'financial' implications:

> As I see it, the phrase 'recruitment, careers, and termination of service' is to be read as a whole, covering the employment relationship between a civil servant and the State from its inception to its termination. It would be artificial to hold, for example, that pecuniary claims dependent on 'career' moves in the narrow sense, such as promotion, transfer, and reinstatement, should be outside the scope of Article 6§1, whereas those dependent on other aspects of the rules governing remuneration under the employment relationship should not. I fail to perceive how in the latter category the features of private law are predominant if they are not in the former category. In my view, in both categories the features of public law are predominant precisely because of 'the basic distinction between civil servants and employees governed by private law'.[108]

The Court has, however, continued to apply the distinction used in the Italian cases and it continues to mark an unusually fine line. In *Huber v. France*[109] a teacher who contested a decision to place him on compulsory sick leave was held not to have stated a case under Article 6. In *Couez v. France*[110] a police officer who suffered a heart attack in a police-sponsored cross-country race was denied extended sick leave on the ground that his disability was not work related. When he refused a transfer to administrative duty he was put on leave without pay and then retired because of unfitness to serve. The Court distinguished *Huber*, noting that in that case the principal claim was for reinstatement. Agreeing that 'at first sight' Couez's claim 'concerned his "career" and the "termination of (his) service"', it emphasized that the resolution of this dispute 'was bound to have a decisive effect on his economic rights'. If the authority had recognized his disability as work-related he could have collected his salary for one year and half of his salary for another two years. Having made this observation, the Court concluded that 'therefore . . . the dispute . . . did not put in issue the authorities' special rights; if Mr. Couez had succeeded in his claim, the state would have been obliged to apply those arrangements to him in accordance with the legislation in force'.[111] In his dissenting opinion, Judge Petitti doubted the Court's attempted distinction of *Neigel* and *Huber*. '[W]hat was in issue in all three [cases]

---

[106] *Argento, Fusco, Gallo, DiLuca & Saluzzi, Orlandini, Laghi, Pizzi, Scarfo, Ryllo, Soldani, Spurio, Trombetta, Viero, Zilaghe v. Italy,* 2 Sept. 1997, Reports, 1997–V 1576, 1787, 28 E.H.R.R. 719.

[107] *Abenavol, DeSanta, Lapalorcia, Nicodemo v. Italy,* 2 Sept. 1997, Reports, 1997–V 1686, 1659, 1672, 1699.

[108] *Id.* (dissenting opinion of Judge Bernhardt joined by Judge Baka).

[109] 19 Feb 1998, Reports, 1998–V 105, 26 E.H.R.R. 457.

[110] 24 Aug. 1998, Reports, 1998–V 2256.

[111] *Id.* at para. 25. *See also Benkessiouer v. France,* 24 Aug. 1998, Reports, 1998–V 2278.

was the application of the rules and their effects on career and career misfortunes.' He went on to make clear that he regarded the judgment as a sharp departure from the prior law but, as the case was not decided by a Grand Chamber, the holding of the prior cases must 'be considered as still representing the prevailing trend of the European Court of Human Rights'.[112]

C. THE IMPARTIAL TRIBUNAL

1. PIERSACK *V.* BELGIUM

Judgment of 1 Oct. 1982
(No. 53), 5 E.H.R.R. 169

7. The applicant, a Belgian national born in 1948, is a gunsmith. He is in the process of serving in Mons prison a sentence of 18 years hard labour imposed on him on 10 November 1978 by the Brabant Assize Court for murder.

8. During the night of 22–23 April 1976, two Frenchmen, Mr. Gilles Gros and Mr. Michel Dulon, were killed by revolver shots in Brussels whilst they were in a motor-car with Mr. Piersack, Mr. Constantions Kavadias (against whom proceedings were subsequently discontinued) and a Portuguese national, Mr. Joao Tadeo Santos de Sousa Gravo. . . .

9. On 9 July 1976, Mr. Preuveneers, an investigating judge at the Brussels Court of First Instance, issued a warrant for the arrest of the applicant, who was suspected of having caused both deaths. He was in France at the time, but was arrested by the French authorities who, after agreeing to grant his extradition, handed him over to the Belgian police on 13 January 1977. The Coutrai *procureur du Roi* (public prosecutor) so informed his colleague in Brussels by a letter of the same date. Mr. Pierre Van de Walle, a senior deputy *procureur*, initialled the letter and forwarded it to the official in the public prosecutor's department who was dealing with the case, Mrs. del Carril. She transmitted it to Mr. Preuveneers with a covering note dated 17 January.

10. On 4 February 1977, the investigating judge wrote to the Brussels *procureur du Roi* to enquire whether, as regards the co-accused Santos de Sousa, the public prosecutor's department intended to report the facts to the Portuguese authorities, those authorities apparently being no longer willing to grant his extradition. On his covering note, the judge added in manuscript, between brackets, the words 'for the attention of Mr. P. Van de Walle'. Mrs. del Carril replied to Mr. Preuveneers on 9 February 1977.

11. On 20 June, the *procureur général* (State prosecutor) attached to the Brussels Court of Appeal sent to the *procureur du Roi* the results of letters rogatory executed in Portugal concerning Mr. Santos de Sousa. After initialling the covering note, Mr. Van de Walle forwarded it to Mr. De Nauw, the deputy who had taken over from Mrs. del Carril in dealing with the case; Mr. De Nauw transmitted the note to the investigating judge on 22 June.

---

[112] *Couez*, n. 110 *supra* (dissenting opinion of Judge Petiti joined by Judge Golcuklu).

12. On 13 December 1977, Mr. Van de Walle took his oath as a judge of the Brussels Court of Appeal, to which office he had been appointed on 18 November. Most of the investigations had been completed by that time, although some further formal steps were taken at a later date. . . .

14. The trial took place from 6 to 10 November 1978 before the Assize Court which was presided over by Mr. Van de Walle. After the Court had heard, amongst others, numerous prosecution and defence witnesses, the 12 members of the jury withdrew to consider their verdict. Mr. Piersack had maintained throughout that he was innocent. On the third question put to them, concerning the 'principal count', they arrived at a verdict of guilty, but only by seven votes to five. After deliberating on that question in private, the President and the two other judges declared that they agreed with the majority.

In the final event, the Assize Court convicted the applicant of the murder of Mr. Dulon and acquitted him as regards the other charges; it accepted that there were mitigating circumstances and sentenced him on 10 November 1978 to 18 years' hard labour. It also recorded that on account of his nationality it had not been possible to obtain the extradition to Belgium of Mr. Santos de Sousa, who had been arrested in Portugal.

15. The applicant then appealed on points of law to the Court of Cassation. His sixth ground of appeal, the only ground that is relevant in the present case, was that there had been a violation of Article 127 of the Judicial Code, which provides that 'proceedings before an assize court shall be null and void if they have been presided over by a judicial officer who has acted in the case as public prosecutor . . . '. [The Court of Cassation dismissed the appeal.] . . .

29. . . . According to the Government, at the relevant time it was the *procureur du Roi* himself, and not the senior deputy, Mr. Van de Walle, who handled cases involving an indictable offence; they maintained that each of the deputies—on this occasion, Mrs. del Carril and then Mr. De Nauw—reported to the *procureur* on such cases directly and not through Mr. Van de Walle, the latter's role being principally an administrative one that was unconnected with the conduct of the prosecution and consisted, *inter alia*, of initialling numerous documents, such as the covering notes of 13 January and 20 June 1977. As regards the covering note of 4 February 1977, the investigating judge, Mr. Preuveneers, was said to have written thereon the words 'for the attention of Mr. P. Van de Walle' solely because he knew that Mrs. del Carril was frequently on sick-leave. In addition, so the Government stated, there was no evidence to show that Mr. Van de Walle had received that note and, in any event, it was not he but Mrs. del Carril who had replied to Mr. Preuveneers.

30. Whilst impartiality normally denotes absence of prejudice or bias, its existence or otherwise can, notably under Article 6(1) of the Convention, be tested in various ways. A distinction can be drawn in this context between a subjective approach, that is endeavouring to ascertain the personal conviction of a given judge in a given case, and an objective approach, that is determining whether he offered guarantees sufficient to exclude any legitimate doubt in this respect.

(a) As regards the first approach, the Court notes that the applicant is pleased to pay tribute to Mr. Van de Walle's personal impartiality; it does not itself have any cause for doubt on this score and indeed personal impartiality is to be presumed until there is proof to the contrary.

However, it is not possible to confine oneself to a purely subjective test. In this area, even appearances may be of a certain importance. As the Belgian Court of Cassation observed in its judgment of 21 February 1979, any judge in respect of whom there is a legitimate reason to fear a lack of impartiality must withdraw. What is at stake is the confidence which the courts must inspire in the public in a democratic society.

(b) It would be going too far to the opposite extreme to maintain that former judicial officers in the public prosecutor's department were unable to sit on the bench in every case that had been examined initially by that department, even though they had never had to deal with the case themselves. So radical a solution, based on an inflexible and formalistic conception of the unity and indivisibility of the public prosecutor's department, would erect a virtually impenetrable barrier between that department and the bench. It would lead to an upheaval in the judicial system of several Contracting States where transfers from one of those offices to the other are a frequent occurrence. Above all, the mere fact that a judge was once a member of the public prosecutor's department is not a reason for fearing that he lacks impartiality; the Court concurs with the Government on this point.

(c) The Belgian Court of Cassation, which took Article 6(1) into consideration of its own motion, adopted in this case a criterion based on the functions exercised, namely whether the judge had previously intervened 'in the case in or on the occasion of the exercise of . . . functions as a judicial officer in the public prosecutor's department'. It dismissed Mr. Piersack's appeal on points of law because the documents before it did not, in its view, show that there had been any such intervention on the part of Mr. Van de Walle in the capacity of senior deputy to the Brussels *procureur du Roi*, even in some form other than the adoption of a personal standpoint or the taking of a specific step in the process of prosecution or investigation.

(d) Even when clarified in the manner just mentioned, a criterion of this kind does not fully meet the requirements of Article 6(1). In order that the courts may inspire in the public the confidence which is indispensable, account must also be taken of questions of internal organisation. If an individual, after holding in the public prosecutor's department an office whose nature is such that he may have to deal with a given matter in the course of his duties, subsequently sits in the same case as a judge, the public are entitled to fear that he does not offer sufficient guarantees of impartiality.

31. This was what occurred in the present case. In November 1978, Mr. Van de Walle presided over the Brabant Assize Court before which the Indictments Chamber of the Brussels Court of Appeal had remitted the applicant for trial. In that capacity, he enjoyed during the hearings and the deliberations extensive powers to which, moreover, he was led to have recourse, for example the discretionary power of deciding, with the other judges, on the guilt of the accused should the jury arrive at a verdict of guilty by no more than a simple majority.

Yet previously and until November 1977, Mr. Van de Walle had been the head of section B of the Brussels public prosecutor's department, which was responsible for the prosecution instituted against Mr. Piersack. As the hierarchical superior of the deputies in charge of the file, Mrs. del Carril and then Mr. De Nauw, he had been entitled to revise any written submissions by them to the courts, to discuss with them the approach to be adopted in the case and to give them advice on points of law. Besides, the information obtained by the Commission and the Court tends to confirm that Mr. Van de Walle did in fact play a certain part in the proceedings.

Whether or not Mr. Piersack was, as the Government believe, unaware of all these facts at the relevant time is of little moment. Neither is it necessary to endeavour to gauge the precise extent of the role played by Mr. Van de Walle, by undertaking further enquiries in order to ascertain, for example, whether or not he received the covering note of 4 February 1977 himself and whether or not he discussed this particular case with Mrs. del Carril and Mr. De Nauw. It is sufficient to find that the impartiality of the 'tribunal' which had to determine the merits (in the French text: `bien-fondé') of the charge was capable of appearing open to doubt.

[The Court held unanimously that there had been a violation of Article 6(1).]

2. DEFINITIONS OF AN IMPARTIAL TRIBUNAL

The idea that a fair tribunal must exclude persons who have had a previous part in the legal proceedings is based on an assumption that human beings are predisposed to maintain positions they have formed, even if in a different role. In that sense they will be evaluating themselves in the relevant case, violating the principle expressed in the common law axiom that no person may be a judge in his own case.[113] The European Court has, for example, ruled that the Luxembourg Council of State which reviewed the legality of administrative decisions was not acting consistently with Article 6 when four of its five members sat on a panel that had previously given an advisory opinion concerning the matter in question. In such a case the applicant 'had legitimate grounds for fearing that the members of the Judicial Committee [of the Council] had felt bound by the opinion previously given'.[114]

In judgments subsequent to the Piersack case the European Court has considered how much prior involvement of a judge is consistent with the maintenance of impartiality under Article 6(1). In each case, the Court has reviewed the precise actions of the judge in the earlier stages of the proceeding to determine whether or not such involvement could reasonably be perceived as creating a likelihood that the judge had formed an adverse opinion as to the guilt of the applicant.

In *DeCubber v. Belgium*,[115] one of three judges at the applicant's trial for forgery had previously served as an 'investigating judge' in the case and, as such, had been in charge of the preliminary investigation. The investigating judge was authorized by Belgian law to 'summon the accused to appear or issue a warrant for his detention, production before a court or arrest; question the accused, hear witnesses, confront witnesses with each other, visit the scene of the crime, visit and search premises, take possession of evidence, and so on. . . . ' The government argued that these functions did not impair the objectivity of the judge:

They pointed out that in Belgium an investigating judge is fully independent in the performance of his duties; that unlike the judicial officers in the public prosecutor's department, whose submissions are not binding on him, he does not have the status of party to criminal proceedings and is not 'an instrument of the prosecution'; that 'the object of his activity' is not, despite Mr. DeCubber's allegations, 'to establish the guilt of the person he believes to be guilty', but to 'assemble in an impartial manner evidence in favour of as well as against the accused', whilst

---

[113] *Dr. Bonham's Case* (1610) 8 Co. Rep. 114a.

[114] *Procola v. Luxembourg*, 28 Sept. 1995 (No. 326), 22 E.H.R.R. 193, para. 45.

[115] 26 Oct. 1984 (No 86), 7 E.H.R.R. 236.

maintaining, 'a just balance between prosecution and defence', since he 'never ceases to be a judge'; . . .[116]

The European Court, however, held these factors not to be decisive. The Court noted that an investigating judge had many of the same duties as a prosecutor and was, at least formally, under the supervision of the *procureur général*. In this case, the measures taken by the challenged judge in conducting the investigation were likely to have been extensive. They were, moreover, conducted in secret. In light of the fact that the judge would become quite familiar with the details of the case, an accused might well fear that he had already formed an opinion on guilt or innocence, as well as that he would have inordinate influence in the decisions of the trial court, including possibly a review of his own decisions as investigating judge. On this basis, the Court found that the applicant had been denied his right to trial before an independent and impartial tribunal.

The holding in *DeCubber* raised problems for judicial systems with limited personnel where it is not uncommon for a judge to deal with the same matter at different stages and in different capacities. The rule of the case was later applied to a situation where an appeal court had decided adversely to a criminal defendant on a preliminary question whether an essential element of the crime had been alleged. The European Court held that some judges could not, consistently with Article 6, hear the appeal of the subsequent conviction.[117] In *Thomann v. Switzerland*,[118] however, no violation was found where the same panel of judges who had convicted an applicant in absentia sat on the later trial in his presence. The Court observed 'that the instant case does not concern the successive exercise of different judicial functions, but judges who sat twice in the same capacity'.[119]

In later cases, the Court has further developed a framework for dealing with these questions. In *Hauschildt v. Denmark*[120] it held that the mere fact that a Danish judge had made preliminary decisions in a criminal case, including decisions on the custody of the accused, did not, under Article 6, prevent such a judge from presiding at the trial. In Denmark, unlike Belgium, there is no investigating judge. Investigation and prosecution are conducted entirely by police and prosecutors. The pre-trial judge merely decides if sufficient evidence has been produced to justify detention. Ordinarily this would not give rise to the same apprehension as those held by the applicant in *DeCubber*. Under the actual facts of *Hauschildt*, however, the challenged judge had made repeated rulings under a particular section of the Administration of Justice Act which required proof of a 'particularly confirmed suspicion'. The Court held that the

---

[116] *Id.* at para. 28.

[117] *Oberschlick v. Austria*, 23 May 1991 (No. 204), 19 E.H.R.R. 389. *See also De Haan v. The Netherlands*, 26 Aug. 1997, Reports, 1997–IV 1379, 26 E.H.R.R. 417, finding a violation of Art. 6 where the presiding judge on an employment benefits appeals tribunal sat in the Chamber considering the applicant's objection to his prior decision.

[118] 10 June 1996, Reports, 1996–III 806, 24 E.H.R.R. 553.

[119] *Id.* at para. 32.

[120] 24 May 1989 (No. 154), 12 E.H.R.R. 226.

difference between this finding and the one a judge would have to make at trial was 'tenuous' and, in these circumstances, there was a violation of Article 6. The same result was reached when a judge in the Court convicting the applicants had presided over another trial in which the other participants in the same criminal incident had been convicted. In that case the Court noted that the judge in question had made repeated reference to the applicants as 'co-perpetrators'.[121]

In other cases the Court has evaluated critically claims that the judge was disqualified by virtue of some prior involvement. 'The mere fact that [a judge] made pre-trial decisions . . . cannot be taken as in itself justifying fears as to his impartiality; what matters is the scope and nature of these decisions.'[122] Thus, it has found no violation where, at earlier hearings, the trial judge had been entitled to act for an absent prosecutor. Under the actual facts of the case, the Court found that the judge had taken no actions of any significance.[123] Nor, in another case, did the fact that two of three trial judges had participated previously in review of a decision refusing to release the applicant from detention pending trial, lead to the finding of a violation. The previous decision had been 'confined to making a brief assessment of the available facts in order to establish whether, *prima facie*, the police suspicions had some substance and gave grounds for fearing that there was a risk of the accused's absconding'. Given this limited action, any fears of bias were not 'objectively justified'.[124] In *Fey v. Austria*,[125] the trial judge in the Austrian District Court had interviewed a witness and had written to parties with relevant information. She had also made the decision to set the case down for trial. Under Austrian law a District Court judge could carry out 'preliminary inquiries' and in so doing was bound to observe the same rules as those that were applicable to an investigating judge of the regional court. The European Court found the case distinguishable from *DeCubber* in that the measures taken were limited and formal, whereas in *DeCubber* the judge had 'carried out extensive investigations in the case, including numerous interrogations of the accused'.[126] The fact that a member of the Court had previously questioned two witnesses was similarly held not to taint the impartiality of the tribunal in *Bulut v. Austria*.[127] The judge's prior actions 'did not entail any assessment of the evidence by him nor did it require him to reach any kind of conclusion as to the applicant's involvement'.[128]

---

[121] *Ferrantelli & Santangelo v. Italy*, 7 Aug. 1996, Reports, 1996–III 937, 23 E.H.R.R. 288, paras. 54–60. *See also Castillo Algar v. Spain*, 28 Oct. 1998, Reports 1998–VIII 3103.

[122] *Nortier v. The Netherlands*, 24 Aug. 1993 (No. 267), 17 E.H.R.R. 273.

[123] *Thorgeir Thorgeirson v. Iceland*, 25 June 1992 (No. 239), 14 E.H.R.R. 843.

[124] *Sainte-Marie v. France*, 16 Dec. 1992 (No. 253A), 16 E.H.R.R. 116. To the same effect see *Nortier v. The Netherlands, supra* n. 122; *Saravia de Carvahlo v. Portugal*, 22 April 1994, (No. 286B), 18 E.H.R.R. 543.

[125] 24 Feb. 1993 (No. 255), 16 E.H.R.R. 387.

[126] *Id.* at para. 35. See also *Padovani v. Italy*, 26 Feb. 1993 (No. 257B).

[127] 22 Feb. 1996, Reports, 1996–II 346, 24 E.H.R.R. 84.

[128] *Id.* at para. 34. Compare *2747–3174 Quebec Inc. v. Quebec (Régie des Permis d'Alcohol)* [1996] 3 S.C.R. 919, in which the Supreme Court of Canada found that there could be a reasonable apprehension of bias in an administrative agency in which the same person who decides to initiate a proceeding and convene a hearing participated in the decision. *Id.* at paras. 59–60.

The idea that a judge cannot be considered impartial from an objective point of view when he or she has previously taken actions of substance in a case was challenged by Judge van Dijk's dissent in *De Haan v. The Netherlands*,[129] in which the Court found a violation of Article 6 in the Dutch procedure for dealing with disputes over entitlement to sick pay. The Court held that a judge who had issued a preliminary ruling on the applicant's claim could not, consistently with the Convention, sit on the panel reviewing the applicant's objection to that ruling. Judge van Dijk pointed out that in this case, unlike others in which a violation had been found, 'the judge . . . sat twice in the same capacity at the same instance'.[130] But his objection went much further, questioning the psychological premise on which much of the Court's jurisprudence rests. Since, to use the language of the Belgian government in *DeCubber*, a judge 'never ceases to be a judge', on what grounds can we conclude that he or she will be unable to take a fresh and unbiased view of a case in which he or she had previously participated? 'Of course', he wrote, 'Judge S had formed an opinion about the case before the hearing and made it known to the applicant. This does not imply that he no longer offered sufficient guarantees that in participating in the Chamber, he based his opinion solely on the law and the facts; foreknowledge is not the same as bias.[131] He went on to quote the Court's judgment in an earlier case that judges' 'professional training and experience' ensure that a subsequent action would not be 'predetermined' by a previous decision.[132]

In *Delcourt v. Belgium*,[133] decided in 1970, the applicant complained about the participation of the *avocat général*, a member of the department of the *Procureur Général*, in the decision of appeals in criminal cases to the Belgian Court of Cassation. The *avocat général* submitted his views of the case to the Court after the parties had been heard and participated in the court's deliberations. The European Court found that such an arrangement did not render the Court of Cassation less than independent and impartial. The section of the *Procureur Général's* department attached to the court was found to be independent of that part of the department that had been involved in the prosecution of the applicant. As such, it served as an impartial adviser to the court. In 1991, however, the same Belgian procedure was challenged successfully before the European Court in *Borgers v. Belgium*.[134] The Court had been invited by the report of the Commission to reconsider its decision in *Delcourt*, but it held instead that the prior case's findings on the Court of Cassation's independence and impartiality 'remain entirely valid'. But it went on to question whether the participation of the *avocat général*, nonetheless, violated Article 6's requirements, as interpreted in case law following *Delcourt*, that criminal defendants be given a fair opportunity to present

---

[129] 26 Aug. 1997, Reports, 1997–IV 1379, 26 E.H.R.R. 417.

[130] *Id.* (dissenting opinion of Judge van Dijk joined by Judge Matscher). For American law on this point *see infra*.

[131] *Id.*

[132] *Id.* quoting *Thomann v. Switzerland*, 10 June 1996, Reports, 1996–II 806, 24 E.H.R.R. 553, para. 71.

[133] 17 Jan. 1970 (No. 11), 1 E.H.R.R. 355.

[134] 30 Oct. 1991 (No. 214B), 15 E.H.R.R. 92.

their defence and be accorded an 'equality of arms' with the prosecution.[135] The Court found these principles were infringed in the Belgian appellate procedure in that the applicant had no right to respond to the *avocat général's* submission and was put at a further disadvantage by that officer's participation in the deliberations. As to the observation that the *avocat général* could not be considered a party to the proceedings, the judgment stated:

No one questions the objectivity with which the *procureur général's* department at the Court of Cassation discharges its functions. . . . Nevertheless the opinion of the *procureur général's* department cannot be regarded as neutral from the point of view of the parties to the cassation proceedings. By recommending that an accused's appeal be allowed or dismissed, the official of the *procureur général's* department becomes objectively speaking his ally or opponent. In the latter event, Article 6, s. 1 requires that the rights of defence and the principle of equality of arms be respected.[136]

A number of the separate opinions in *Borgers* proceeded on the assumption that the judgment had overruled *Delcourt*.[137] The holding in *Borgers* was extended to civil cases in *Lobo Machado v. Portugal*.[138] In that case a Deputy Attorney-General made a preliminary recommendation on an appeal to the Supreme Court and was present during the Court's deliberations. The case was an employment complaint brought against a state controlled company. The European Court received a submission from the government of Belgium as amicus curiae in support of the Portuguese procedure which was also followed in Belgian Civil appeals.[139]

In its various cases examining the impartiality of a tribunal, the Court has not been entirely consistent in its formulation of the proper standard for deciding whether or not a decisionmaker met the required level of 'objective impartiality'. In *DeCubber*, the Court found a violation because the judge 'might in the eyes of the accused' appear to be predisposed against him.[140] In *Borgers*, the neutrality of the *avocat général* was to be regarded from 'the point of view of the parties'.[140A] These formulations, it will be observed, are versions of the maxim that not only justice but the appearance of justice is required. But they take the, at least contestable, position that the critical

---

[135] *Id.* at para. 24. On the concepts of rights of defence and equality of arms see generally Stephanos Stavros, *The Guarantees for Accused Persons Under Article 6 of the European Convention on Human Rights*, 52–4, 175–86 (1993).

[136] *Borgers, supra* n. 134.

[137] See also the cases on the impartiality of British court-martial tribunals discussed *infra; Bulut v. Austria*, 22 Feb. 1996, Reports, 1996–II 346, 24 E.H.R.R. 84. The Court has applied a similar analysis to that employed under Article 6(1) in deciding whether a detained person has been 'brought promptly before a judge or other officer authorized by law to exercise judicial power' as required by Article 5(4). It has held that such an officer must be 'independent of the parties'. Therefore it is, in principle, impermissible for the detention decision to be made by a prosecutor who might at a later point take part in the criminal prosecution since the 'impartiality' of such a person is 'capable of appearing open to doubt'. *See*, e.g. *Huber v. Switzerland*, 23 Oct. 1990 (No. 188), (337 above) overruling *Schiesser v. Switzerland*, 4 Dec. 1979 (No. 34), 2 E.H.R.R. 417; *Brincat v. Italy*, 26 Nov. 1992 (No. 249A), 16 E.H.R.R. 591.

[138] 20 Feb. 1996, Reports, 1996–I 195, 23 E.H.R.R. 79.

[139] *Id.* at para. 27.

[140] 26 Oct. 1984 (No. 86), 7 E.H.R.R., para. 29.

[140A] *Borgers, supra* n. 134 at para. 26.

appearance is that perceived *by the accused*. In *Hauschildt v. Denmark*, discussed above, however, the Court offered a somewhat different test that has been repeated verbatim in several later judgments:

[A]ny judge in respect of whom there is a legitimate reason to fear a lack of impartiality must withdraw . . . This implies that . . . the standpoint of the accused is important but not decisive. What is decisive is whether the fear can be held objectively justified.[141]

The European Court's formulation of the standard of objective impartiality may be compared with that made by the House of Lords in *R. v. Gough*.[142] The Law Lords had in that case been confronted with two potential tests for situations in which a judge or juror should be disqualified. It rejected that which held disqualification proper whenever 'a reasonable person might reasonably suspect bias'. Rather it held (as stated in the judgment of Lord Goff of Chieveley) the proper test to be:

whether, having regard to [the relevant] circumstances; there was a real danger of bias on the part of the relevant member of the tribunal in question, in the sense that he might unfairly regard (or have unfairly regarded) with favour or disfavour, the case of a party to the issue under consideration before him.[143]

This 'real danger' test was, according to Lord Goff, superior to the suspicion of the reasonable person, because 'the court has first to ascertain the relevant circumstances from the available evidence, knowledge of which would not necessarily be available to an observer in court at the relevant time'. Similarly, the Supreme Court of Canada has stated the test as being 'whether a well-informed and reasonable observer would perceive that judicial independence has been compromised.'[144] The term 'real danger' was also preferable to 'real likelihood' because it would better 'ensure that the court is thinking in terms of possibility rather than probability of bias'.[145] This formulation, he stated, was fully capable of enforcing the principle 'that justice must manifestly be seen to be done'.[146] Even if there are no reasonable grounds for inferring a 'real danger' of bias, an English judge is automatically disqualified if he or she has a personal interest in the outcome of a case The much noted decision of the House of Lords in *R. v. Bow Street Metropolitan Stipendiary Magistrate ex parte Pinochet Ugarte* (No. 2)[147] made clear that the character of such interests extends beyond the pecuniary or proprietary. In that case Lord Hoffmann, who had sat on the House's original decision on the extradition of Pinochet to Spain for human rights violations was found to have substantial links to Amnesty International which had intervened in the case. In his speech Lord Browne-Wilkinson noted that if the controversy 'does not relate to money or economic advantage but is concerned with the promotion of the cause, the

---

[141] [1993] A.C. 646.

[142] 24 May 1989 (No. 154), 12 E.H.R.R. 266, para 48.

[143] *Id.* at 670.

[144] *Canada (Minister of Citizenship and Immigration) v. Tobiass*, [1997] 3 S.C.R. 391, at para. 70.

[145] *R. v. Gough*, [1993] A.C. 646 at 670.

[146] *Id.* at 661.

[147] [1999] 1 All E.R. 577.

rationale disqualifying a judge applies just as much if the judge's decision will lead to the promotion of a cause in which the judge is involved together with one of the parties'.[148]

The problem exemplified by *Piersack*, given common career patterns, is a necessarily frequent occurrence. In the United States, the various jurisdictions differ with respect to the standards which have been developed to deal with this problem. But, as in the European cases, courts tend to examine the particular involvement which a judge had in previous aspects of a pending case. The code of Judicial Conduct, promulgated by the American Bar Association and widely adopted by state judiciaries, specifies in Canon 3.c(1)(b) that a judge should disqualify himself when 'he served as lawyer in the matter in controversy, or a lawyer with whom he previously practised law served during such association as a lawyer concerning the matter'. The Commentary to the section states that '[a] lawyer in a governmental agency does not necessarily have an association with other lawyers employed by that agency within the meaning of this subsection; a judge formerly employed by a governmental agency, however, should disqualify himself in a proceeding if his impartiality might reasonably be questioned because of such association'.

Federal statutes governing disqualification of federal judges are not much more specific, insisting judges recuse themselves when they have been of counsel in a case before them.[149] Case law has generally developed an approach in which the more personal responsibility and specific work a prosecutor had in a case, the more likely he is to be disqualified from sitting on it as a judge. Thus, the mere fact that a judge had once held a position as a prosecutor has been held insufficient grounds for recusal in criminal cases. It is necessary to show that the judge was actually involved enough in the particular case at issue as to have developed a substantial interest.[150] Conducting the particular prosecution clearly meets this test and participating in the investigation of a case has been held to require the same conclusion.[151] Other courts have held that prosecuting attorneys involved in drafting pleadings or who received a conviction or guilty plea are also disqualified. But merely drafting an indictment has been held insufficient involvement to call for recusal.[152]

In contrast to some of the European judgments,[153] the federal law in the United States on judicial disqualification has been interpreted quite strictly with respect to claims of bias based on previous statements or actions by the judge in his or her

[148] *Id.* at 588. Given its decision on the basis of Lord Hoffmann's personal interest in the outcome, the House did not apply the test of *Gough*. It therefore, declined to consider suggestions that the rule in *Gough* be modified. *See id.* at 589.

[149] 28 U.S.C.A. §455.

[150] *See Edelstein v. Wilentz*, 812 F. 2d 128, 131 (3rd Cir. 1987); *United States v. Wilson*, 426 F.2d 268, 269 (6th Cir. 1970).

[151] *See Barry v. United States*, 528 F.2d 1094 (7th Cir. 1976) *cert. denied* 429 U.S. 820 (1977); *Adams v. United States*, 302 F.2d 307 (5th Cir. 1962).

[152] Compare *United States v. Vasilick*, 160 F.2d 631, 632 (3rd Cir. 1947) with *General Tire and Rubber Co. v. Watkins*, 363 F.2d 87, 89 (4th Cir. 1966) *cert. denied* 385 U.S. 899 (1966).

[153] *See, e.g. De Haan v. The Netherlands*, 26 Aug. 1997, Reports, 1997–IV 1379, 26 E.H.R.R. 417.

judicial capacity. The Supreme Court has held that 'judicial rulings alone almost never constitute valid basis for a bias or partiality motion'. Moreover:

opinions formed by the judge on the basis of facts introduced or events occurring in the course of the current proceedings, or of prior proceedings, do not constitute a basis for a bias or partiality motion unless they display a deep-seated favoritism or antagonism that would make fair judgment impossible. Thus, judicial remarks, during the course of a trial that are critical or disapproving of, or even hostile to counsel, the parties, or their cases ordinarily do not support a bias or partiality challenge.[154]

A distinction between a judge's conduct 'as judge' in the course of litigation and his or her conduct outside that role may not always be simple to draw. For example, the Supreme Court of Canada held that a judge had engaged in unacceptable behaviour when, during a trial, he called a high official in the Attorney-General's office to complain about the way a crown attorney was behaving, asking that the attorney be removed, and suggesting that he (the judge) would 'secure that end' if no action were taken. The Supreme Court had little difficulty concluding that the action gave rise to a 'reasonable apprehension of bias'.[155] The English Court of Appeal in *National Bank v. Haue*,[156] also considered the extent to which the involvement of a judge at a prior stage of civil proceedings might disqualify him from serving on a panel hearing an appeal in the same case. The judge in question had made provisional *ex parte* orders extending the time in which a writ could be served and allowing substitute service. After full argument a second judge had refused to discharge those orders, and it was the second decision which was the subject of the appeal on which the first judge (now a judge of the Court of Appeal) was to sit. The Court held that the judge could hear this appeal without violating a statute barring judges from hearing appeals of judgments or orders 'made in any case by himself'. Nor was there any impropriety merely because the judge had some involvement with the question on appeal. In her judgment, Butler-Sloss, L.J. said 'it stands out a mile . . . that Evans J's part has been throughout peripheral'. Indeed, the judge in question might well have reversed his own decision after full hearing:

He has formed no concluded view about the rightness of the order which he made *ex parte*. He is equally able to think he might have been wrong as he might have thought had he heard the evidence that Creswell, J. heard . . .

There is no sharp dividing line between Article 6's requirements that a tribunal be 'impartial' and 'independent'. The latter quality, however, seems to point more to the institutional aspects of the decision-making body than to the personal experiences and attitudes of the human beings comprising it. Much of the Court's doctrine on the content of independence has developed in cases dealing with administrative agencies

---

154 *Liteky v. United States*, 510 U.S. 540 (1994).

155 *R. v. Curragh* [1997] 1 S.C.R. 537, at para. 3. Two judges dissented arguing, *inter alia*, that the telephone call did not demonstrate bias towards the defendant. One might conclude, they said, that the trial judge was partial to the crown 'since he seemed concerned that the Crown case be conducted effectively'. *Id.* at para. 104 (McLachlin and Major J.J. dissenting).

156 [1994] [Transcript: John Larking, 21 Jan., 1994 in LEXIS, Enggen Library, Cases File].

and disciplinary bodies which will be treated in the next section. It has also considered such factors in cases where ordinary judicial duties have been conferred on officers and bodies who might be thought dependent on or too closely associated with the executive department.

In *Belilos v. Switzerland*[157] the European Court decided that adjudication of minor criminal offences by a Police Board, whose findings of fact could not be reviewed, violated Article 6(1). In the Swiss canton involved, such a Board could consist of a single police official. This official was not under police supervision and could not be removed during his or her four-year term. But the Court decided that the fact that such an official might ultimately return to other police functions might feel subordinate to other police officials and might have a sense of loyalty to his or her colleagues could undermine the perception of impartiality. Since a defendant could 'legitimately have doubts as to the independence and organizational impartiality of the Police Board'.[158] Article 6 (1) had not been satisfied.

In two recent cases from Slovakia, the Court found a violation of Article 6 in the state's decision to commit the adjudication of 'minor offences' to local and district officials. There was no general definition of such offences. Rather, they were identified in various laws. On conviction a person was subject to reprimand, prohibition of certain activities, or fines or confiscation. If the last two sanctions were of a value of 2,000 Slovakian Koruna (at the time about US$57 or £35) the penalty could be reviewed by a court. The European Court noted that '[i]n order to determine whether a body can be considered to be "independent" of the executive it is necessary to have regard to the manner of its appointment of its members and the duration of their term of office, the existence of guarantees against outside pressures and the question whether the body presents an appearance of independence'. The appointment of these officials was in the hands of the Executive and their status was that of salaried employees. As such there were insufficient 'guarantees against outside pressure' and these bodies could not be judged 'independent' in the absence of further judicial review.[159]

These considerations have also led the Court to examine critically the composition of courts martial which traditionally have been integrated into the military command structure. The Court found the courts martial in the United Kingdom, prior to reforms implemented in 1996, were inconsistent with Article 6's requirements of impartiality and independence. It noted that all members of a court were appointed by a 'convening officer', an officer superior in rank to and often holding direct or indirect command over the appointed members. The convening officer was also a key figure in the prosecution, making the decision to proceed with the trial, holding supervisory authority over decisions of the prosecuting officers, and confirming the judgment of the Court. In these circumstances a defendant might well

---

[157] 29 Apr. 1988 (No. 132), 10 E.H.R.R. 466.

[158] *Id.* at para. 67.

[159] *Lauko v. Slovakia*, 2 Sept 1998, Reports, 1998–IV 2492, paras. 63–4; *Kadubec v. Slovakia*, 2 Sept. 1998, Reports, 1998–VI 2518, paras. 56–7.

have objectively justified misgivings about the Court's independence and impartiality.[160]

The European Court's doctrine with regard to military judges was taken a step further in *Incal v. Turkey*,[161] In which the Court held that the composition of Turkey's National Security Courts violated Article 6. These courts were provided for in the Turkish Constitution. They had jurisdiction to try crimes 'against the Republic— whose constituent qualities are enunciated in the Constitution—against the indivisible unity of the State—meaning both the national territory and its people—or against the free democratic system of government and offences directly affecting the State's internal or external security'. They consisted of two civilian judges and one military judge.[162] The courts were constituted this way, as the government noted in a later case, because of the 'experience of the armed forces in the anti-terrorism campaign. [To] strengthen these courts [they] includ[ed] a military judge in order to provide them with the necessary expertise and knowledge to deal with threats to the security and integrity of the State.'[163] Unlike in the United Kingdom, Turkish military judges were not appointed by or under the command of any authorities involved in the prosecution of the case.[164] The Strasbourg Court's objection to their participation was stated in the following terms:

Other aspects of these judges' status make it questionable. Firstly they are servicemen who still belong to the army, which in turn takes its orders from the executive. Secondly, they remain subject to military discipline and assessment reports are compiled on them by the army for that purpose. Decisions pertaining to their appointment are to a great extent taken by the administrative authorities and the army. Lastly, their term of office as National Security Court judges is only four years and can be renewed. ... In addition, the Court attaches great importance to the fact that a civilian had to appear before a Court composed, even if only in part, of members of the armed forces. ... It follows that the applicant could legitimately fear that because one of the judges of the Izmir National Security Court was a military judge it might allow itself to be unduly influenced by considerations which had nothing to do with the nature of the case.[165]

The Supreme Court of Canada made an extensive review of the attributes of the independence of courts guaranteed by section 11(d) of the Canadian Charter of Rights and Freedoms in a reference concerning various aspects of the terms, appointment and compensation of provincial court judges. Provincial courts comprise the lowest tier of the Canadian judiciary and, unlike in superior courts, the judges are appointed and paid by the provincial governments. The Supreme Court

---

[160] *Findlay v. United Kingdom*, 25 Feb. 1997, Reports, 1997–I 263, 24 E.H.R.R. 221, paras. 74–80. *See also Coyne v United Kingdom*, 24 Sept. 1997, Reports, 1997–V 1848; *Hood v. United Kingdom*, 18 Feb. 1999; *Moore & Gordon v United Kingdom*, 29 Sept 1999; *Smith & Ford v United Kingdom*, 29 Sept. 1999 (not yet reported).

[161] 9 June 1998, Reports, 1998–IV 1547.

[162] *Id.* at para. 28.

[163] *Okçuoglu v. Turkey*, 8 July 1999, (not yet reported) para. 55.

[164] *Incal, supra* n. 161, paras. 28–9; *Okçuoglu, supra* n. 163, para. 55.

[165] *Incal, supra* n. 161, paras. 68, 72.

listed three 'core characteristics' of judicial independence—security of tenure, financial security and administrative independence. Each of these characteristics was important with respect to its impact on both individual judges and on courts as institutions.[166] These factors dictated that any freeze or reduction in judicial salaries be preceded by a non-binding consultation with an independent and apolitical commission. The Court suggested further that any pay reduction singling judges out from other public employees would entail a heavy burden of justification. The Court also stated that it was inconsistent with judicial independence for there to be any judicial negotiation with the executive or legislative authorities over judicial remuneration. Finally, any salary reduction could not take compensation to a level where judges could be perceived as susceptible to political pressure through economic manipulation.[167]

The requirement of an impartial tribunal has been held by the Strasbourg Court to extend to members of juries. In *Holm v. Sweden*[168] it was held that a private prosecutor in a criminal libel case was deprived of an impartial jury. A majority of the jurors were members of a political party that owned the company which had published the alleged libel. The relevant writing, moreover, concerned the political activities of the applicant, partly in opposition to that party.[169] But in *Pullar v. United Kingdom*[170] the Court refused to find a violation where a juror was an employee of one of the main prosecution witnesses in a solicitation of bribery case. The Court noted that the juror in question had not been shown to have had personal knowledge of the events at issue. It also relied on the fact that the juror was one of 15 (the verdict in this Scottish court was by majority vote) and that he had taken an oath to judge the facts dispassionately.[171]

In two cases the Court has dealt with claims that racist attitudes in a jury prevented a court from being impartial. In the first the Court held that Article 6 required a judge to take action, or at least to make further inquiry, when it was alleged that one of the jurors selected in a homicide trial against an Algerian defendant had been overheard declaring himself a racist.[172] But in the second case the Court held that an English judge acted consistently with Article 6 when he responded to an ambiguous note from the jury suggesting some racial aspects to its deliberations by a strongly worded instruction to act solely on the evidence.[173] The judge's responses in this situation were limited by the English rule against any inquiry into the content of a jury's deliberations, a rule

---

[166] *Re. Remuneration of Judges* [1997] 3 S.C.R. 3, paras. 115–20. Compare these factors to those listed by the European Court in, for example, *Lauko v. Slovakia*, 2 Sept 1998, Reports, 1998–VI 2492, para. 56.

[167] [1997] 3 S.C.R. 3, at paras. 133–5.

[168] 25 Nov. 1993 (No. 279A), 18 E.H.R.R. 79.

[169] The House of Lords has also held that the same test of bias is applicable to judges and jurors. *R. v. Gough* [1993] A.C. 646, 2 All E.R. 724.

[170] 10 June 1996, Reports, 1996–III 783, 22 E.H.R.R. 391.

[171] *Id.* at paras. 39–40.

[172] *Remli v. France*, 23 Apr. 1996, Reports, 1996–II 559, 22 E.H.R.R. 253.

[173] *Gregory v. United Kingdom*, 25 Feb. 1997, Reports, 1997–I 296, 25 E.H.R.R. 577.

the Strasbourg Court accepted as a 'crucial and legitimate feature of English trial law which serves to reinforce the jury's role as the ultimate arbiter of fact and to guarantee open and frank deliberation'.[174]

The Supreme Court of Canada has held that before trial a criminal defendant is entitled to examine potential jurors for possible racial prejudice even in the absence of any *prima facie* indication of such an attitude. The Court in *R. v. Williams*[175] noted that potential jurors in Canada are 'presumed to be indifferent or impartial' and that before they may be questioned to establish the contrary some basis for suspecting bias must be brought forward. This could be supplied by evidence of widespread racial prejudice on either a national or a provincial scale. Once this was shown potential jurors could be examined to determine whether they shared such attitudes and whether they were able, nonetheless, to act impartially.[176] The Court expressed its view that this liberalized approach to jury challenges need not 'evolve into the approach in the United States of routine and sometimes lengthy challenges for cause of every juror in every case with attendant cost, delay and invasion of juror privacy'.[177]

As indicated by this quotation, examination of potential jurors for partiality in the United States is both common and extensive. Such examination, even to discover racial bias, however, has not been held to be constitutionally required in the guilt determination phase of criminal trials absent the presence of some racial element in the crime charged.[178] A majority of the United States Supreme Court has held, however, that such an inquiry *must* be permitted in capital cases arising from interracial crimes. Given the unusual discretion accorded juries in deciding the appropriateness of capital punishment, there is a 'unique opportunity for racial prejudice to operate but remain undetected'.[179]

3. IMPARTIAL ADJUDICATION IN ADMINISTRATIVE AGENCIES AND DISCIPLINARY BODIES

Article 6's requirement of an independent and impartial tribunal has been applied to actions outside the familiar context of judicial proceedings. In *Demicoli v. Malta* the European Court decided that the Maltese House of Representatives was not an impartial tribunal for the purpose of deciding whether an applicant was guilty of breaching the privileges of the House by publishing a satirical article allegedly defaming that body. The Court noted particularly the fact that certain members who had been especially ridiculed in the article participated in the proceedings.[180]

But by far the most important extra-judicial application of Article 6 is with respect

---

[174] *Id.* at para. 44.
[175] [1998] 1 S.C.R. 1128.
[176] *Id.* at paras. 30, 33.
[177] *Id.* at paras. 51–7.
[178] *Ristaino v. Ross*, 424 U.S. 589 (1976).
[179] *Turner v. Murray*, 476 U.S. 28, 35 (1986).
[180] 27 Aug. 1991 (No. 210), 14 E.H.R.R. 47.

to the activities of administrative agencies and other regulatory bodies—as illustrated by the *Feldbrugge* case reported above.[181] The requirement of impartiality in this context has at least two important aspects. First, such agencies tend to become identified with certain policies and interests in the fields they regulate. Second, the agencies often play multiple roles in the legal process of regulation—making rules, overseeing their enforcement and adjudicating disputes concerning them.[182] Naturally, these arrangements raise the concerns which are evident in the principal cases.

The character of the first difficulty noted is also evident in bodies regulating particular professions or trades: The Court dealt with such a situation in *Albert and LeCompte v. Belgium*,[183] where the Court held that the Belgian procedure for discipline of physicians did not violate Article 6(1). First, the Court found that, since the right to practise their profession was in issue, the applicants had presented a case involving the determination of a civil right and not a mere 'public right'.[184]

It is not for the Court to go beyond the facts submitted for its consideration and determine whether, for the medical profession as a whole, this right is a civil right, within the meaning of Article 6(1). It is sufficient to note that it is by means of private relationships with their clients and patients that doctors in private practice, such as the applicants, avail themselves of the right to continue to practise; in Belgium, these relationships are usually contractual and, in any event, are directly established between individuals on a personal basis. Accordingly, the right to continue to practise constituted, in the case of the applicants, a private right and thus a civil right within the meaning of Article 6(1) notwithstanding the specific character of the medical profession—a profession which is exercised in the general interest—and the special duties incumbent on its members.[185]

It then held that the fact that the adjudicatory body was in part, staffed with physicians did not prevent it from being an impartial tribunal in the absence of a showing of individual bias. The physician-members sat not as representatives of the profession but in a 'personal capacity'.[186]

In *H v. Belgium*,[187] the Court expressly declined to consider the structural impartiality of the Council of the *Orders des avocats*, in light of its finding that the procedure followed by the Council was otherwise defective in ways that violated Article 6(1). The Council, which decided applications for the re-admission of disbarred attorneys, was composed entirely of lawyers. In separate statements, judges expressed doubts as to the impartiality of such a tribunal.

It has been held that the procedure for investigating and adjudicating charges of professional misconduct against barristers in England did not violate the principle of

---

[181] *See* Section (B)(4) *supra*.

[182] *See* A. W. Bradley & K. D. Ewing, *Constitutional and Administrative Law* 697–715 (12th ed. 1999).

[183] 10 Feb. 1983 (No. 58), 5 E.H.R.R. 533.

[184] On 'public rights' *see* Section (B)(4) *supra*.

[185] *Albert & LeCompte v. Belgium, supra* n. 183, para. 28.

[186] *Id.* at para. 32. *See also, Debled v. Belgium*, 22 Sept. 1994 (No. 292B), 19 E.H.R.R. 506 (Procedure for dealing with challenges to members of physician disciplinary bodies compatible with Article 6(1)).

[187] 30 Nov. 1987 (No. 127), 10 E.H.R.R. 339.

impartiality merely because members of the tribunal and members of the Professional Conduct Committee charged with investigation and prosecution were drawn from the same governing body. The relevant rules provided that no one who had served on the Committee while the charges were being considered could serve on the tribunal. Nor was the tribunal held to be biased merely because a majority of its members were barristers: '[I]t has always been accepted that professional men are peculiarly well fitted ... to determine whether there has been a breach of the code of conduct governing the profession and to judge the gravity of it if it is proven'.[188]

The same type of issue was presented to the United States Supreme Court in *Gibson v. Berryhill*.[189] The appellees challenged the constitutionality of professional discipline proceedings brought against them by the Alabama Optometry Association before the Alabama Board of Optometry. The unprofessional conduct alleged consisted of the appellees' employment by a corporation. This, the Association claimed, facilitated the unlicensed practice of optometry by the corporation. By statute the membership of the Board was restricted to members of the Association and expressly excluded any optometrists employed by another person or entity. The Supreme Court affirmed the District Court's judgment that this arrangement involved sufficient risk of bias to make the proceedings inconsistent with the Fourteenth Amendment's prohibition against deprivations without due process of law. Note that the facts in *Gibson* present a far stronger case for finding potential unfairness than those before the Court in the *Albert and LeCompte* case.

The European Court did, however, find a violation on the grounds of lack of impartiality outside the context of disciplinary bodies in *Lanborger v. Sweden*.[190] The applicant, a tenant in an apartment building, initiated proceedings to delete from his lease a 'rent negotiation clause', whereby he and the landlord were bound by rent agreements negotiated by the National Tenants' Union and the Landlords' Union. Two of the four judges who sat on the Housing and Tenancy Court, which ruled on his request, were 'lay assessors', one nominated by the Tenants' Union, the other by the Landlords' Union. While each assessor acted in a personal capacity, each had a long-standing association with the nominating union. Those unions, the Court noted, each 'had an interest in the negotiation clause. As the applicant sought the deletion from the lease of this clause, he could legitimately fear that the lay assessors had a common interest contrary to his own . . .'.[191] In their dissenting opinion, Judges Valticos and Pettiti noted that tribunals in which interested parties were represented were deemed useful in the resolution of industrial and social conflicts. In the case at issue, moreover, no decision could be made without the assent of the two professional judges. To find these kinds of panels unacceptable, they argued, would place the legitimacy of many of these specialized courts in doubt.

---

[188] *In Re S (A Barrister)* [1981] Q.B. 683. This judgment was given by a panel of three High Court judges sitting as visitors to the Inns of Court.

[189] 411 U.S. 564 (1973).

[190] 22 June 1989 (No. 155), 12 E.H.R.R. 416.

[191] *Id.* at para. 35.

The Strasbourg Court has also upheld the procedure for challenging land reform orders issued by local authorities in Austria. Affected landowners could bring suit and appeal to a provincial Land Reform Board and from there to a National Supreme Land Reform Board. The majority of those boards were, in each case, composed of civil servants with expertise in agricultural specialties. This fact alone was held insufficient to bring the Boards' impartiality into question. The expert members, moreover, were practically irremovable during their five year term and did not act pursuant to any instructions from their superiors.[192]

The second issue, the mixing of adjudicatory and administrative and rule making functions, was raised in *Campbell and Fells v. United Kingdom*,[193] involving the determination of breaches of prison disciplinary rules by a Board of Visitors:

32. A Board of Visitors is a body that had to be appointed, by the Home Secretary, for each prison in England and Wales; its members . . . hold office for three years or such less period as the Home Secretary may appoint. They may be re-appointed.

There are 115 Boards in all and each has between 8 and 24 members, who are unpaid but are reimbursed their expenses . . . [T]here is no express statutory provision enabling the Home Secretary to dismiss a member and resignation before expiry of a term of office would, according to the Government, be required only in the most exceptional circumstances.

33. A Board's duties include, in addition to inquiring into charges of disciplinary offences, satisfying itself as to the state of the premises, the administration of the prison and the treatment of inmates, hearing a prisoner's complaints or requests, directing the governor's attention to matters calling for his attention and making reports to the Home Secretary . . . Its members are required to visit the prison frequently, have a right of access to every part of the prison and to prison records and may interview any prisoner out of the sight and hearing of officers. A Board's adjudicatory functions generally account for a small proportion of its overall duties and, of the small percentage of prison disciplinary proceedings which are conducted before Boards, few concern 'especially grave offences'. . . .

81. . . . [A] Board is, as the Government pointed out, intended to exercise an independent oversight of the administration of the prison. In the nature of things, supervision must involve a Board in frequent contacts with the prison officials and just as much with the inmates themselves; yet this in no way alters the fact that its function, even when discharging its administrative duties, is to 'hold the ring' between the parties concerned, independently of both of them. The impression which prisoners may have that Boards are closely associated with the executive and the prison administration is a factor of greater weight, particularly bearing in mind the importance in the context of Article 6 of the maxim 'justice must not only be done: it must also be seen to be done'. However, the existence of such sentiments on the part of inmates, which is probably unavoidable in a custodial setting, is not sufficient to establish a lack of 'independence'. This requirement of Article 6 would not be satisfied if prisoners were reasonably entitled, on account of the frequent contacts between a Board and the authorities, to think that the former was dependent on the latter (see, the abovementioned *Piersack* judgment); however, the Court does not consider that the mere

---

[192] *Ettl v. Austria*, 23 Apr. 1987 (No. 117), 10 E.H.R.R. 255.
[193] 28 June 1984 (No. 80), 7 E.H.R.R. 165.

fact of these contacts, which exist also with the prisoners themselves, could justify such an impression.

82. In the light of the foregoing, the Court sees no reason to conclude that the Board in question was not 'independent', within the meaning of Article 6.

In *Withrow v. Larkin*,[194] the United States Supreme Court considered whether the fact that a professional disciplinary board investigated, presented charges and adjudicated, constituted a violation of the requirement of due process:

The contention that the combination of investigative and adjudicative functions necessarily creates an unconstitutional risk of bias in administrative adjudication has a much more difficult burden of persuasion to carry. It must overcome a presumption of honesty and integrity in those serving as adjudicators; and it must convince that, under a realistic appraisal of psychological tendencies and human weakness, conferring investigative and adjudicative powers on the same individuals poses such a risk of actual bias or prejudgment that the practice must be forbidden if the guarantee of due process is to be adequately implemented.[195]

> [The Court quoted from *FTC v. Cement Institute*,[196] in which the fairness of the Federal Trade Commission's adjudication of the legality of a cement pricing method was challenged in light of some of the Commissioners' previous investigation of and public statements about the pricing system.]

'[T]he fact that the Commission had entertained such views as the result of its prior *ex parte* investigations did not necessarily mean that the minds of its members were irrevocably closed on the subject of the respondents' basing point practices. Here, in contrast to the Commission's investigations, members of the cement industry were legally authorized participants in the hearings. They produced evidence—volumes of it. They were free to point out to the Commission by testimony, by cross-examination of witnesses, and by arguments, conditions of the trade practices under attack which they thought kept these practices within the range of legally permissible business activities.' . . .

That is not to say that there is nothing to the argument that those who have investigated should not then adjudicate. The issue is substantial, it is not new, and legislators and others concerned with the operations of administrative agencies have given much attention to whether and to what extent distinctive administrative functions should be performed by the same persons. No single answer has been reached. Indeed, the growth, variety, and complexity of the administrative processes have made any one solution highly unlikely. Within the Federal Government itself, Congress has addressed the issue in several different ways, providing for varying degrees of separation from complete separation of functions to virtually none at all . . .

That the combination of investigative and adjudicative functions does not, without more, constitute a due process violation, does not, of course, preclude a court from determining from the special facts and circumstances present in the case before it that the risk of unfairness is intolerably high.[197] Compare the judgment of the Supreme Court of Canada in *2747–3174 Quebec Inc. v. Quebec (Régie des Permis d'Alcool)*.[198] In

---

[194] 421 U.S. 35 (1975).
[195] *Id.* at 47.
[196] 333 U.S. 683 (1948).
[197] *Id.* at 48, 51–2, 58.
[198] [1996] 3 S.C.R.R. 919.

that case the Court held that the Quebec procedure for cancellation of liquor permits was inconsistent with section 23 of the Quebec Charter of Human Rights and Freedoms because the Régie did not operate in the context of an 'independent and impartial tribunal'. The Court noted that the governing statute allowed 'employees of the Régie to participate in the investigation, the filing of complaints, the presentation of the case to the directors and the decision'.[199] It agreed that a combination of such functions in the same agency did not, by itself, create a constitutional problem.[200] In this case, however, there was no assurance by rule or statute that a single individual might not exercise several of these functions successively in the same case. 'The possibility that a jurist who has made submissions to the directors might advise them in respect of the same matter is disturbing, especially since some of the directors have no legal training'.[201]

D. THE REQUIREMENTS OF PROMPT ADJUDICATION

Delays in the resolution of legal disputes have been the single most litigated issue before the European Court of Human Rights. The principle of prompt adjudication is almost universal in western democracies. The European Convention, the Constitution of the United States, and the Canadian Charter of Rights and Freedoms, all make provision for the right to prompt adjudication. However, the manner in which this right is recognized and the scope it is given varies in each of the relevant judicial systems.

Some of the issues relating to the timing of judicial proceedings have already been canvassed in connection with Article 5's protection against restraint of personal liberty. Article 6's concerns are more general. The Article states: 'In the determination of his civil rights and obligations or of any criminal charge . . . everyone is entitled to a . . . hearing within a reasonable time by a . . . tribunal . . . ' Article 6(1) guarantees expeditious resolution of judicial proceedings and also lays down the more general principle of prompt administration of justice.[202] The purpose of the Article is to 'ensure that the accused person does not have to be under a charge too long and that the charge is determined'.[203] It is important to note, however, that the right covers civil as well as criminal litigation.

The length of time governed by Article 6(1) has been defined as the time between the 'charge' or 'judicial notification'[204] and the day of judgment, even if reached on appeal.[205] In civil proceedings, the 'reasonable time' referred to in Article 6(1) normally

---

[199] *Id.* at para. 46.
[200] *Id.* at para. 47.
[201] *Id.* at para. 54.
[202] *See Boddaert v. Belgium*, 12 Oct. 1992 (No. 235D), 16 E.H.R.R. 242, para. 39.
[203] *Wemhoff v. Germany*, 27 June 1968 (No. 7), 1 E.H.R.R. 55, para. 18.
[204] *Corrigliano v. Italy*, 10 Dec. 1982 (No. 57), 5 E.H.R.R. 334, paras. 34–35.
[205] *Wemhoff v. Germany*, *supra* n. 203 at para. 18.

begins to run from the moment the action was instituted before the 'tribunal'.[206] It is deemed to continue, moreover, until the conclusion of enforcement proceedings in which the amount of any damages owing is calculated.[207] In criminal matters, 'reasonable time' begins to run as soon as a person is 'charged', which may occur on a date prior to the case coming before the trial court, such as the date of arrest, the date preliminary investigations were opened, or the date a person was officially notified that he would be prosecuted or that there has been an allegation that he has committed a criminal offence.[208] To determine whether or not proceedings before the state's constitutional court are to be included in the reckoning of the relevant period, '[i]t has to be considered whether the Constitutional Court's decision was capable of affecting the outcome of the case which has been litigated before the ordinary courts'.[209]

In determining what constitutes a 'reasonable time', the European Court has held that the individual circumstances of the case control:

The court has to have regard, inter alia, to the complexity of the factual or legal issues raised by the case, to the conduct of the applicants and the competent authorities and to what was at stake for the former; in addition, only delays attributable to the State may justify a finding of a failure to comply with the 'reasonable time' requirement.[210]

The same factors may not be examined in the same way in every case. Sometimes the circumstances 'call for a global assessment so that the Court does not consider it necessary to consider these questions in detail'.[211]

---

[206] *Poiss v. Austria*, 23 Apr. 1987 (No. 117), 10 E.H.R.R. 231, para. 50.

[207] *Silva Pontes v. Portugal*, 23 Mar. 1994 (No. 286A), 18 E.H.R.R. 156; *Torri v. Italy*, 1 July 1997, Reports, 1997–IV 1199, para. 19. In *Hornsby v. Greece*, 19 Mar. 1997, Reports, 1997–II 495, 24 E.H.R.R. 250. A violation of Art. 6(1) was found where administrative authorities refrained for over five years from complying with two judgments of the Supreme Administrative Court, refusing to grant applicants authorization to open a language school: '[w]here administrative authorities refuse or fail to comply, or even delay doing so, the guarantees under Article 6 enjoyed by a litigant during the judicial phase of the proceedings are rendered devoid of purpose.' *Id.* at para. 41. *See also Estima Jorge v. Portugal*, 21 Apr. 1998, Reports, 1998–II 762, applying Art. 6(1) to enforcement proceedings concerning not a judgment, but a notarial deed providing security for a specific debt, enforceable through the courts in the same manner. Though the proceedings presupposed that the applicant's right had already been established, and hence did not concern a 'dispute', the Court noted that 'the word "contestation" (dispute) should not be construed too technically . . . and should be given a substantive rather than a formal meaning', *Id.* at para. 37.

[208] *Eckle v. Germany*, 15 July 1982 (No. 51), 5 E.H.R.R. 1, at para. 73; *Hozee v. The Netherlands*, 22 May 1998, Reports, 1998–III 1091, para. 43. Essentially the time begins to run when the situation of the suspect has been substantially affected: *Eckle* at para. 73. In *Hozee*, the Court did not consider the applicant substantially affected until he himself was first questioned as a suspect in a tax fraud investigation, though his companies had been investigated and assessed penalties for some time. *Hozee* at paras. 44–6.

[209] *Bock v. Germany*, 29 Mar. 1989 (No. 150), 12 E.H.R.R. 247, para. 37. This is also the test where the proceedings at issue consist only of those in a constitutional court, i.e. they are not an 'extension' of proceedings in the ordinary courts, *Sussmann v. Germany*, 16 Sept. 1996, Reports, 1996–IV 1158, 25 E.H.R.R. 64, paras. 40–6.

[210] *Zimmerman and Steiner v. Switzerland*, 13 July 1983 (No. 66), 6 E.H.R.R. 17, para. 24.

[211] *Obermeier v. Austria*, 28 June 1990 (No. 179), 13 E.H.R.R. 290, para. 72. *See also Paskhalidis v. Greece*, 19 Mar. 1997, Reports, 1997–II 473, concerning the claims of 93 applicants.

Once the Court has declared a time period to be unreasonable on its face, the state is required to offer justification for the delay. In the *König v. Germany*[212] a delay of over ten years offered a clear example of such an unreasonable delay. Delays of slightly over three years at a single jurisdictional level also have been held to be presumptively unreasonable.[213] But even a longer time period, that may have appeared unreasonable on its face has been allowed if the case dealt with complex legal issue, arose in a sensitive political climate, involved several jurisdictional levels or required many witnesses or sources of information.[214] On the other hand, the Court has stressed the need for more expeditious decisions in certain types of disputes such as those involving pensions and other employment issues, thus finding, for instance, a delay of more than nine years in reaching a final decision excessive even when the case was very complex.[215]

As the quoted language indicates, the Court is reluctant to find a violation if the delay is attributable mainly to the applicant's conduct. The Court clarified the duty of the applicant in this regard in a case where national law provided that the responsibility for the progress of proceedings rested with the parties. This did not, the Court held:

absolve the courts from ensuring compliance with the requirements of Article 6 concerning reasonable time. . . . [T]he Court considers that the person concerned is required only to show diligence in carrying out the procedural steps relating to him, to refrain from using delaying tactics and to avail himself of the scope afforded by domestic law for shortening the proceedings. He is under no duty to take action which is not apt for the purpose.[216]

However, the Court has held that, in a criminal case, although the applicant was not required to co-operate with the prosecutors, he was responsible for any delays caused

---

[212] 28 June 1978 (No. 27), 2 E.H.R.R. 170.

[213] *Zimmerman and Steiner v. Switzerland, supra* n. 210 para. 23. *But see Katikaridis v. Greece,* 15 Nov. 1996, Reports, 1996–V 1673, finding no violation where proceedings lasted over three years in the Court of Cassation as a result of the matter coming before three different benches of that Court. Two Divisions' rulings on a complex matter were in conflict, and needed to be resolved by the full Court. *Id.* at para. 42. And in *Sussmann v. Germany,* note 209 *supra,* proceedings in the Federal Constitutional Court lasting over three years, four months were held not to violate Article 6(1). The Court noted that while the 'obligation [to hear cases within a reasonable time] also applies to a Constitutional Court . . . [Article 6(1)] cannot be construed in the same way as for an ordinary court. Its role as a guardian of the Constitution makes it particularly necessary for a Constitutional Court sometimes to take into account other considerations than the mere chronological order in which cases are entered on the list, such as the nature of the case and its importance in political and social terms.' *Id.* at para. 56.

[214] *See, e.g. Wemhoff v. Germany, supra* n. 203; *Acquaviva v. France,* 21 Nov. 1995 (No. 333A); (at the end) *Hozee v. The Netherlands, supra* n. 208. *Matznetter v. Austria,* 10 Nov. 1969 (No. 10), 1 E.H.R.R. 198; *Buchholz v. Germany,* 5 May 1981 (No. 42), 3 E.H.R.R. 597.

[215] *Obermeier v. Austria, supra* n. 211 para. 72. *See also,* most recently, *Steffano v. Italy,* 27 Feb. 1992 (No. 230C), paras. 16–17; *Trevisan v. Italy,* 26 Feb. 1993 (No. 257F), para. 18. *Doustaly v. France,* 23 Apr. 1998, Reports, 1998–II 850, at paras. 48–49; *Stryanowski v. Poland,* 30 Oct. 1998, Reports, 1997–VIII 3367, at paras. 56–57.

[216] *Union Alimentaria Sandars, S.A. v. Spain,* 7 July 1989 (No. 157), 12 E.H.R.R. 24, para. 35, citing, *Martins Moreira v. Portugal,* 26 Oct. 1988 (No. 143), 13 E.H.R.R. 517, para. 46; *Guincho v. Portugal,* 28 June 1984 (No. 81), 7 E.H.R.R. 223, para. 34.

by his behaviour.[217] If it is shown in a civil case that 'the applicant did not display the diligence to be expected of a party to litigation of this kind' and, therefore, 'contributed to prolonging the proceedings', a violation will not be found.[218] Although 'applicants cannot be blamed for making full use of the remedies available to them under domestic law' their 'behaviour ... constitutes an objective fact which cannot be attributed to the respondent State and which must be taken into account for the purpose of determining whether or not the reasonable time referred to in Article 6(1) has been exceeded'.[219] Thus, in *Vernillo v. France*,[220] where the civil action began in December 1977 and ended on 5 June 1985, the proceedings were not found to be excessive where only a year of that time was caused by 'abnormal' court delays while the defendants were responsible for one year and eight and a half months' worth of delays and the plaintiffs were responsible for about two and a half years of delay time.

In contrast, an unreasonable delay will be a violation if it is due mainly to the actions of the state.[221] Sometimes such delays are the result of individual decisions in particular cases.[222] But often such a delay is caused by the backlog of cases in the judicial system.[223] The Court has divided these backlogs into two types. The first type involves

---

[217] *See, Buchholz v. Germany, supra* n. 214 para. 63. The principle that a person charged with a criminal offence is not required by Article 6(1) to co-operate actively with the judicial authorities was reiterated in *Corrigliano v. Italy, supra* n. 204 para. 42, and, *I.A. v. France*, 23 Sept. 1998, Reports, 1998–VII 2951 para. 121. Moreover, 'People charged with criminal offences cannot . . . be criticised for sending to the judicial officers handling the investigation of their case evidence that they consider establishes their innocence or for asking them to investigate particular matters'. *Reinhardt & Slimane-Kaid v. France*, 31 Mar. 1998, Reports, 1998–II 640 para. 99. *See also Portington v. Greece*, 23 Sept. 1998, Reports, 1998–VI 2623 para. 29, rejecting the Government's submission that the applicant's requesting of adjournments, without availing himself of the possibility under the Code of Criminal Procedure to ask for brief ones, made him primarily responsible for delays in criminal appeal proceedings lasting nearly eight years. *Dobbertin v. France*, 25 Feb. 1993 (No. 256D), 16 E.H.R.R. 558, para. 43.

[218] *Deumeland v. Germany, supra* n. 206 para. 80. *See also, Pretto and Others v. Italy*, 8 Dec. 1983 (No. 71), 6 E.H.R.R. 182, paras. 33–34; *H. v. France*, 24 Oct. 1989 (No. 162), 12 E.H.R.R. 74, para. 55. *See also Proszak v. Poland*, 16 Dec. 1997, Reports, 1997–VIII 2765, paras. 40–5.

[219] *Poiss v. Austria, supra* n. 206 at para. 57.

[220] 20 Feb. 1991 (No. 198), 13 E.H.R.R. 880. *See also Ciricosta & Viola v. Italy*, 4 Dec. 1995 (No. 337A), in which delays in civil proceedings lasting 15 years and still pending were found to be mainly attributable to the applicants, who had requested or acceded to some 23 adjournments.

[221] *See H. v. United Kingdom*, 8 July 1987 (No. 120B), 10 E.H.R.R. 958; *H. v. France, supra* n. 218 para. 55.

[222] Some examples include failure of the state to separate the applicant's case from that of a co-accused, where the co-accused had to be extradited and the extradition proceedings caused the delay: *Kemmache v. France*, 27 Nov. 1991 (No. 218), 14 E.H.R.R. 520, paras. 68–71; where a national court spent too much time trying to determine petitioner's mental state before according him his divorce; *Bock v. Germany, supra* n. 209 paras. 47–49; where the time spent by parties in negotiations to reach friendly settlement was excessive; *Wiesinger v. Austria*, 24 Sept. 1991 (No. 213), 16 E.H.R.R. 258, paras. 63–64, where the national authorities refused to grant an applicant's requests for production of a vital piece of evidence.

[223] The basic principle that contracting states have the obligation to organize their legal systems so as to allow the national courts to comply with Article 6(1) has been repeated again and again by the Court. *See, e.g. Massa v. Italy*, 24 Aug. 1993 (No. 265B), 18 E.H.R.R. 266, para. 31. *Podbielski v. Poland*, 30 Oct. 1998, Reports, 1998–VIII 3387, at para. 38.

an emergency situation, such as a recession,[224] where the state has no prior warning of a massive increase in litigation and, once aware of the problem, takes fast and effective steps to eliminate it:

The Convention places the Contracting States under a duty to organise their legal systems so as to enable the courts to comply with the requirements of Article 6(1), including that of trial within a 'reasonable time'; nonetheless, a temporary backlog of business does not involve liability on the part of the Contracting States provided that they take, with the requisite promptness, remedial action to deal with an exceptional situation of this kind.[225]

The second type of backlog is a structural one, where more cases exist than can be handled by the judicial system. 'Less important' cases are continually put on hold to accommodate more critical ones, or the state has reacted to a critical situation in an ineffective or inefficient manner. In such circumstances the Court will find it improper for the state to extend the time period beyond what would be presumptively reasonable. Thus, the Court has held violations to occur when the texts of judgments are inordinately late[226] or hearings are delayed[227] due to the excessive workload of the judge or when judgments are not registered in a timely manner.[228] The European Court of Human Rights' lack of sympathy for structural delays was particularly evident in *Guincho v. Portugal.*[229] In that case, the Court held that since the flood of litigation resulting from a return to democracy in Portugal was not totally unforeseen, efforts taken by Portugal which proved ineffective were not sufficient to avoid liability.[230] Thus,

---

[224] *See Buchholz v. Germany, supra* n. 214.

[225] *Milasi v. Italy,* 25 June 1987 (No. 119), 10 E.H.R.R. 333, para. 18.

[226] e.g., *B. v. Austria,* 28 Mar. 1990 (No. 175), 13 E.H.R.R. 20, paras. 53–54.

[227] e.g., *Caleffi v. Italy,* 24 May 1991 (No. 206B), paras. 16–17; *Portington v. Greece, supra* n. 217, at para. 33.

[228] e.g., *Monaco v. Italy,* 26 Feb. 1992 (No. 228D), para. 17. A similar result was obtained when the delay was due to the actions of extra-judicial state agencies. *See Martins Moreira v. Portugal, supra* n. 216 para. 60 where the State was held responsible for delays by the Lisbon Institute of Forensic Medicine; *Wiesinger v. Austria, supra* n. 222 paras. 62–4 where the State was held responsible for delays caused by a lack of coordination between the municipal and agricultural authorities in carrying out a consolidation and rezoning plan; *Tomasi v. France,* 27 Aug. 1992 (No. 241A), 15 E.H.R.R. 1, para. 125, where delays caused by the public prosecutor were laid to the State. Moreover, violations of Article 6(1) have been found when the delay is caused by expert witnesses, because they are 'acting in the context of judicial proceedings supervised by the judge; [therefore] the latter remained responsible for preparation of the case and for the speedy conduct of the trial': *Capuano v. Italy,* 25 June 1987 (No. 119), 13 E.H.R.R. 271, paras. 30–32. *See also, Ridi v. Italy,* 27 Feb. 1992 (No. 229B), paras. 16–18; *Billi v. Italy,* 26 Feb. 1993 (No. 257G), paras. 19–20; *Zappia v. Italy,* 26 Sept. 1996, Reports, 1996–IV 1403, para. 25. But *see Pafitis v. Greece,* 26 Feb. 1998, Reports, 1998–I 436, 27 E.H.R.R. 566, where the Court refused to impute to the state time which elapsed during a strike by the Athens Bar ('notwithstanding the Bar's legal personality under public law . . . in calling on its members to withdraw their services it was taking action designed to defend their professional interests, not exercising one of the functions of a public authority'), and during an adjournment called by the Athens District Court to refer a question to the European Court of Justice, which lasted over 2 years, 7 months ('to take it into account would adversely affect the system instituted by Article 177 of the EEC treaty and work against the aim pursued in substance in that Article'). *Id.* at paras. 95–6.

[229] *Supra* n. 216.

[230] *Id.* para. 40. See also, the similar holding relating to the restoration of democracy in Spain, *Case of Union Alimentaria Sandars, S.A., supra* n. 216.

while the Court is willing to assess a particular case in light of recently instituted structural reforms, they will not necessarily be found to justify the delay.[231]

The Court has held that what is at stake for the applicant has to be taken into account in assessing the reasonableness of the length of proceedings. When certain issues are involved the courts must act even more expeditiously. In cases of special importance to the applicant and which have a 'particular quality of irreversibility', the authorities 'are under a duty to exercise exceptional diligence since . . . there is always the danger that any procedural delay will result in the de facto determination of the issue submitted to the court before it has held its hearing'.[232] This has been found to be true in cases involving familial relationships,[233] employment,[234] the contracting of AIDS through contaminated blood supplies,[235] and where the applicant is held in detention pending determination of a criminal charge against him.[236]

Provisions concerning the right to prompt adjudication also appear in Article 5 of the Convention. The materials in the previous chapter have dealt with this question insofar as Article 5 demands that every arrested person be brought promptly before a judge and that every detained person has a right to challenge speedily the legality of his or her detention. Article 5(3)[237] seems to offer the judicial authorities a choice between conducting the trial within a reasonable time or releasing the suspect until the trial date. 'Reasonable time' as used in Article 5(3) applies only to the length of the detention, not the length of the proceedings. (The latter question is determined, as discussed above, in relation to Article 6.) This period runs from the time of detention until the person is released with a guarantee or until the day of judgment: 'Obviously, the "time", the reasonable character of which must be assessed, ceases when the person in question is released if he is released before judgment is given in the first instance.'[238] Note that as the inquiry under Article 5 relates only to the applicant's

---

[231] See *Fisanotti v. Italy*, 23 Apr. 1998, Reports, 1998–II 840, para. 22, and *S.R. v. Italy*, 23 Apr. 1998, Reports, 1998–II 830, para. 21, where the Court considered delays in pension litigation exceeding five and seven years, respectively, to be unaffected by reforms designed to speed up the examination of cases in the Court of Audit.

[232] *H. v. United Kingdom, supra* n. 221 para. 85.

[233] *Id.* para. 71; *Bock v. Germany, supra* n. 209. *Paulsen-Medalen v. Sweden*, 19 Feb. 1998, Reports, 1998–I 131, 26 E.H.R.R. 260. *But see Hokkanen v. Finland*, 23 Sept. 1994 (No. 299A), 19 E.H.R.R. 139.

[234] *See* cases noted *supra* at n. 215.

[235] *X. v. France* 23 Mar. 1991 (No. 2349C), 14 E.H.R.R. 483. *See also A & Others v. Denmark*, 8 Feb. 1996, Reports, 1996–I 85, 22 E.H.R.R. 458; *F.E. v. France*, 30 Oct. 1998, Reports, 1998–VIII 3332; *Leterme v. France*, 29 Apr. 1998, Reports, 1998–III 987; *Henra v. France*, 29 Apr. 1998, Reports, 1998–II 965; *Richard v. France*, 22 Apr. 1998, Reports, 1998–II 809; *Railot v. France*, 22 Apr. 1998, Reports, 1998–II 787.

[236] *Tomasi v. France, supra* n. 228 para. 84; *Herczegfalvy v. Austria*, 24 Sept. 1992 (No. 242B), 15 E.H.R.R. 437, paras. 71–72; *Abdoella v. the Netherlands*, 25 Nov. 1992 (No. 248A), para. 24.

[237] See Chapter 7, section (F)(2) *supra*.

[238] *Neumeister v. Austria*, 27 June 1968 (No. 8), 1 E.H.R.R. 91, para. 6. When the amount of security for bail is fixed at a very high sum which requires some time to collect and there is no negligence by the applicant with respect to the deposit of his security, the end of the period of detention is not the date on which the conditional order for bail is made, but that on which the security is paid and the applicant is actually released. *Van der Tang v. Spain*, 13 July 1995 (No. 321), 22 E.H.R.R. 363, para. 59.

deprivation of liberty, a proceeding which complies with that Article may still contravene Article 6(1) if the final resolution of the charge is inordinately delayed.[239]

As in the case law under Article 6(1), the Court has declined to set rigid standards for deciding the reasonableness of a period of detention.[240] Rather, the matter 'must be assessed in each case according to its special features'.[241] However, the Court has held that, given the connotation of immediacy in the use of the word '*aussitôt*' in the French text, its flexibility in determining promptness:

> is limited even if the attendant circumstances can never be ignored for the purposes of the assessment under [Section 5(3)]. Whereas promptness is to be assessed in each case according to its special features . . . , the significance to be attached to those features can never be taken to the point of impairing the very essence of the right guaranteed by Article 5 § 3, that is to the point of effectively negativing the State's obligation to ensure a prompt release or a prompt appearance before a judicial authority.[242]

The reasons given by national authorities to justify pre-trial detention must be weighed against the reasons the suspect asserts for his release. As the Court put it in *Letellier v. France*:

> It falls in the first place to the national judicial authorities to ensure that, in a given case, the pre-trial detention of an accused person does not exceed a reasonable time. To this end they must examine all the facts arguing for and against the existence of a genuine requirement of public interest justifying, with due regard to the principle of the presumption of innocence, a departure from the rule of respect for individual liberty and set them out in their decisions on the applications for release. It is essentially on the basis of the reasons given in these decisions and of the true facts mentioned by the applicant in his appeals, that the Court is called upon to decide whether or not there has been a violation of Article 5 §3.[243]

Among the factors justifying detention, persistence of the reasonable suspicion, which led to the arrest, is a *sine qua non*,[244] although such suspicion itself has been held to be insufficient after the lapse of some period of time.[245] The Court also accepts that certain

---

[239] *See, Wemhoff v. Germany, supra* n. 203 para. 4 (a violation of Article 6(1) may be still be found when the applicant has been released.) *See also Abdoella v. the Netherlands, supra* n. 236 para. 24 (the time a person is kept in detention pending the determination of criminal charges can be a factor in assessing whether the requirement under Article 6(1) that there be a decision on the merits in a reasonable time has been met). *Cf. I.A. v. France, supra* n. 217, at paras. 112, 122, finding a violation of Art. 5(3) but not Art. 6(1).

[240] *See,* for instance, *W. v. Switzerland,* 26 Jan. 1993 (No. 254A), 17 E.H.R.R. 60, para. 30: ('The Commission's opinion was based on the idea that Article 5 §3 implies a maximum length of pre-trial detention: The Court cannot subscribe to this opinion, which moreover finds no support in its case-law.')

[241] *Wemhoff v. Germany, supra* n. 203 para. 10.

[242] *Koster v. the Netherlands,* 28 Nov. 1991 (No. 221), 14 E.H.R.R. 396, para. 24. *See also, Brogan and Others v. United Kingdom,* 29 Nov. 1988 (No. 145B), 11 E.H.R.R. 117, paras. 59, 62 and dissents.

[243] 26 June 1991 (No. 207), 14 E.H.R.R. 83, para. 35. Repeated orders justifying detention that use identical, generalized language without providing specific explanations will not suffice under Art. 5(3). *Yagci & Sargin v. Turkey,* 8 June 1995 (No. 319A), paras. 52–3. *See also I.A. v. France, supra* n. 217 para. 103: ('[A]lthough the decisions set out the "legal" grounds on which they are based, many of them contain very few details about the "factual" considerations underpinning them').

[244] *Id.*

[245] *Id. See also Kemmache v. France, supra* n. 222 para. 50.

offences, because of their gravity and public reaction to them, may give rise to social disturbance capable of justifying pretrial detention. 'However, this ground can be regarded as relevant and sufficient only provided that it is based on facts capable of showing that the accused's release would actually disturb public order. In addition, detention will continue to be legitimate only if public order remains actually threatened'.[246] Moreover, even when such reasons are 'relevant' and 'sufficient', the authorities must display 'special diligence' in the conduct of the proceedings.[247]

Other reasons for detention include: the complexity of the investigation,[248] the safety of the accused,[249] fear that the accused will suppress evidence, fear that the accused will repeat the offence, and the danger the accused will abscond.[250] The possibility that the accused may abscond, however, is not sufficient to justify detention if it is possible to obtain 'guarantees' of his appearance for trial.[251] Furthermore, the Court has held:

. . . the danger of an accused absconding does not result just because it is possible or easy for him to cross the frontier; there must be a whole set of circumstances, particularly, the heavy sentence to be expected or the accused's particular distaste for detention, or the lack of well established ties in the country, which give reason to suppose that the consequences and hazards of flight will seem to him to be the lesser evil than continued imprisonment.[252]

Moreover, in making the assessment whether or not the accused may abscond, 'regard must be had in particular to the character of the person involved, his morals, his assets, his links with the State in which he is being prosecuted and his international contacts'.[253]

While risk of flight might sometimes justify continuing detention, other characteristics of the accused might indicate the propriety of release. These include the inability to commit further offences of a similar kind, poor health and the improbability of

---

[246] *Id.* para. 52. *See also I.A. v. France, supra* n. 217, para. 104.

[247] *Letellier v. France supra* n. 243 at para. 35. Where an applicant's case on its own is not complex and could have been dealt with more speedily, but forms part of an extremely complicated investigation, the diligence that the competent authorities must show is diligence in relation to the whole investigation. *Van der Tang v. Spain, supra* n. 238, at paras. 68–75. The fact that the accused has already admitted the offences of which he is accused can be relevant in assessing the complexity of the case, and thus the needs of the ongoing investigation.

[248] *Van der Tang, supra* n. 238 at para. 55.

[249] *I.A. v. France, supra* n. 217, at para. 108. ('However, this can be so only in exceptional circumstances having to do with the nature of the offences concerned, the conditions in which they were committed and the context in which they took place.') *Id.*

[250] *See id.* paras. 13, 14–15; *Stögmüller v. Austria,* 10 Nov. 1969 (No. 9), 1 E.H.R.R. 155, paras. 14–15; *Matznetter v. Austria, supra* n. 214 at paras. 8–9; *Ringeisen v. Austria,* 16 July 1971 (No. 13), 1 E.H.R.R. 455, paras. 106–8; and most recently, *W. v. Switzerland, supra* n. 240, para. 31.

[251] *Wemhoff v. Germany, supra* n. 203 para. 15.

[252] *Stögmüller v. Austria, supra* n. 250 para. 33. However, 'the danger of an accused's absconding cannot be gauged solely on the basis of the severity of the sentence risked'. *Mansur v. Turkey,* 8 June 1995 (No. 319B), 20 E.H.R.R. 535, at para. 55.

[253] *W. v. Switzerland, supra* n. 240 para. 33. *See also Quinn v. France,* 22 Mar. 1995 (No. 311), 21 E.H.R.R. 529, where a one year detention of an applicant charged in an international fraudulent investment scheme was found justified in light of the danger of his absconding, where he was a foreign national who had been arrested in possession of false passports, had several residences outside France, and a large number of accomplices.

flight.[254] In assessing whether or not there has been a violation of Article 5(3), the Court also recognizes that the right of an accused in detention to have his case examined with 'particular expedition' must not unduly hinder the efforts of the judicial authorities to carry out their tasks with proper care.[255] While the Court accepts that the investigation of terrorist offences presents the authorities with special problems, 'this does not mean . . . that the investigating authorities have carte blanche under Article 5 to arrest suspects for questioning, free from effective control by the domestic courts . . . whenever they choose to assert that terrorism is involved'.[256] The Court also balances the delay caused by the accused's actions with those caused by the authorities to determine whether or not the accused's rights under Article 5(3) have been violated by continued detention.[257]

In the United States, a speedy trial is a 'fundamental right' guaranteed to an accused by the Sixth Amendment to the Constitution[258] and imposed on the states by the due process clause of the Fourteenth Amendment. 'The speedy trial guarantee is designed to minimize the possibility of lengthy incarceration prior to trial, to reduce the lesser, but nevertheless substantial, impairment of liberty imposed on an accused while released on bail, and to shorten the disruption of life caused by arrest and the presence of unresolved criminal charges.'[259] The Sixth Amendment right to speedy trial combines characteristics of both Articles 5 and 6 of the European Convention. Limiting pre-trial incarceration is an element of Article 5, while seeking to minimize the time a person is under a charge is found in Article 6. The Sixth Amendment (like Article 5) applies only in criminal prosecutions not, in civil cases, as does the 'speedy trial' right granted by the Convention under Article 6(1).

The scope of the American right to a speedy trial also differs from the 'reasonable time' requirements of the European Convention. Article 6 of the Convention mandates that a judicial *determination* be made within a reasonable time, while the Sixth Amendment guarantees only that the accused be brought to trial speedily. While most American courts have based their decisions on the assumption that the Sixth Amendment right extends through the initial sentencing, the Supreme Court has never explicitly so held.[260] The European Court also considers the time spent on inter-

---

[254] *Id.* at para. 16; *Matznetter v. Austria, supra* n. 214 para. 76.

[255] *Wemhoff v. Germany, supra* n. 203 para. 17.

[256] *Sakik v. Turkey*, 26 Nov. 1997, Reports, 1997–VII 2609, 27 E.H.R.R. 662, at para. 44. The applicants' detention in police custody of 12 to 14 days without judicial intervention was held to violate Art. 5(3), even supposing that the activities of which they stood accused were linked to a terrorist threat. *Id.* at paras. 45–6. A violation may still be found where the state attempts to derogate from its Art. 5 obligations under Art. 15. *Demir v. Turkey*, 23 Sept. 1998, Reports, 1998–VI 2640, at paras. 52–8. *See also* Chapter 8(G) *infra*.

[257] *See*, for instance, *Toth v. Austria*, 12 Dec. 1991 (No. 224), 14 E.H.R.R. 551, paras. 74–77; *Clooth v. Belgium*, 12 Dec. 1991 (No. 225), 14 E.H.R.R. 717, para. 43.

[258] The Sixth Amendment reads in pertinent part: 'In all criminal prosecutions, the accused shall enjoy the right to a speedy . . . trial, by an impartial jury of the State and district wherein the crime shall have been committed'.

[259] *United States v. MacDonald*, 456 U.S. 1, 8 (1982).

[260] *See Tinghitella v. California*, 718 F.2d 308, 312 (9th Cir. 1983).

locutory appeals which the American courts generally exclude from the time consideration.[261]

The time period prescribed by the Sixth Amendment is not expressly defined. It has been held that 'a violation of the right to a speedy trial [does not exist] unless the circumstances of the case are such that further delay would endanger the values the right protects'.[262] Like the European Court, the Supreme Court has held that the reasonable time for trial under the Sixth Amendment depends on the particular circumstances of the case.

The Supreme Court has identified factors to be used in determining if the accused has been deprived of his right to a speedy trial. Four factors were established in *Barker v. Wingo* in 1972: 'length of delay, the reason for delay, the defendant's assertion of his right, and prejudice to the defendant'.[263]

The length of delay must be prejudicial on its face to compel examination of the other factors. What makes a delay 'presumptively prejudicial' is dependent on the circumstances of the case. Both the European Court and the Supreme Court consider the complexity of the case in evaluating whether or not a violation has occurred. The Supreme Court has noted that 'the delay that can be tolerated for an ordinary street crime is considerably less than for a serious, complex conspiracy charge'.[264]

Once a delay is deemed 'presumptively prejudicial', the courts will examine the reasons for delay. Different weights are attributed to different reasons and the culpability of the state for any delay is considered. *Barker v. Wingo* offered examples of the weighing system:

— A deliberate attempt to delay the trial in order to hamper the defense should be weighed heavily against the government.

— A more neutral reason such as negligence or overcrowded courts should be weighed less heavily but nevertheless should be considered since the ultimate responsibility for such circumstances must rest with the government rather than the defendant.

— Finally, a valid reason, such as a missing witness, should serve to justify appropriate delay.[265]

The American system of weighing differently the reasons for delay has no counterpart in the European Court. The European Court weighs all delays attributable to the domestic state identically, no concessions are made for those which are 'neutral' or merely negligent in nature. The practical effect of this is that a delay due to ordinary judicial backlog in the courts may be excused to a certain extent, under the American system, but not under the European Convention, unless substantial and effective steps have been taken to remedy the situation.[266]

---

[261] *See United States v. Loud Hawk*, 474 U.S. 302 (1986).

[262] *Barker v. Wingo*, 407 U.S. 514, 522 (1972).

[263] *Id.* at 530.

[264] *Id.* at 531.

[265] *Id.*

[266] *Compare Strunk v. United States*, 412 U.S. 434, 435 (1973) with *Guincho v. Portugal, supra* n. 216 paras. 37–40.

Prejudice due to delay is not assumed automatically under the Speedy Trial Clause of the Sixth Amendment. 'Prejudice . . . should be assessed in light of the interests of defendants which the speedy trial was designed to protect: (i) to prevent oppressive pre-trial incarcerations; (ii) to minimize anxiety and concerns of the accused; and (iii) to limit the possibility that the defense will be impaired.[267] The courts, therefore, review the damage that delay may have done to the defendant's case. If no damage is found or it appears that the delay was to the defendant's advantage, it is likely that no prejudice will be found.[268] However, if the delay is substantial enough, and the government is responsible for that delay, a plurality of the Court has held that:

consideration of prejudice is not limited to the specifically demonstrable. . . . And though time can tilt the case against either side . . . one cannot generally be sure which of them it has prejudiced more severely. Thus, we generally have to recognize that excessive delay presumptively compromises the reliability of a trial in ways that neither party can prove or, for that matter, identify.[269]

The mere presence of one or more of the factors, including 'presumptive prejudice', does not necessarily constitute a deprivation of the right to a speedy trial without regard to the other *Barker* factors.[270] The Supreme Court stated in *Barker v. Wingo* that 'these factors have no talismanic qualities; courts must still engage in a difficult and sensitive balancing process'.[271] 'Presumptive prejudice' is, moreover, 'a part of the mix of relevant facts, and its importance increases with the length of delay'.[272]

The Canadian Charter of Rights and Freedoms also contains provisions concerning the right to prompt adjudication. Section 11(b) states: 'Any person charged with an offence has the right . . . to be tried within a reasonable time. . . .' The purpose of the Canadian right is essentially the same as that of Articles 5 and 6 of the European Convention and the Sixth Amendment to the United States Constitution: 'to secure within a specific framework, the more extensive right to liberty and security of person of which no one may be deprived except in accordance with the principles of fundamental justice'.[273] Like the Sixth Amendment and Article 5 of the Convention, but unlike Article 6, this right is limited to criminal defendants.

The time period under consideration in determining what is a 'reasonable time' is 'the period between the laying of the charge and the conclusion of the trial'.[274] The Canadian courts have expressly held that pre-charge (i.e., before an information is sworn or an indictment preferred) delays are not to be counted in determining the

---

[267] *Barker supra* n. 262 at 537 (1972).
[268] *Id.* at 534.
[269] *Doggett v. United States*, 505 U.S. 647, 655 (1992) (opinion of Souter J.). In this case, the criminal defendant had been indicted eight and a half years before his arrest for conspiracy to import cocaine. It was found that he did not know of his indictment before his arrest and that the government was negligent in not tracking him down before during the six years he was living openly under his own name.
[270] *Id.*
[271] *Barker supra* n. 262 at 531.
[272] *Dogget v. United States, supra* n. 269 at 655.
[273] *R. v. Rahey* [1987] 1 S.C.R. 588.
[274] *R. v. Kalanj* [1989] 1 S.C.R. 1594.

length of the delay when reviewing possible Section 11(b) violations[275] and that Section 11(b) does not apply to delay in respect to an appeal from conviction by the accused nor an appeal from an acquittal by the Crown.[276] The Art. 11(b) right does, however, extend through the post-conviction sentencing phase.[277] The time period considered, thus, is most similar to that which has been explicitly recognized by the United States courts as covered by the Sixth Amendment and by Article 5(3) of the European Convention.[278]

The scope of the Canadian right more closely resembles the American version than that of the European Convention insofar as it also covers impairments of liberty incurred by restrictions while released on bail. Furthermore, both the Canadian and the United States Supreme Courts have explicitly recognized that the interests protected by the right to a speedy trial are both individual and community or societal interests.[279] Thus, in *R. v. Morin*[280] Sopinka, J. writing for the majority of the Court stated:

The individual rights which the section seeks to protect are: (1) the right to security of the person, (2) the right to liberty, and (3) the right to a fair trial. . . . The secondary societal interest is most obvious when it parallels that of the accused. Society as a whole has an interest in seeing that the least fortunate of its citizens who are accused of crimes are treated humanely and fairly. In this respect trials held promptly enjoy the confidence of the public. . . . In some cases, however, the accused has no interest in an early trial and society's interest will not parallel that of the accused.[281]

Although, like both the European Court and the Supreme Court of the United States, the Canadian Court is sensitive to the individual aspects of a particular case, it has, like American courts, adopted an explicit list of factors to determine violations. In deciding whether a delay is too long, the Court considers the following factors:

1. the length of the delay;

2. waiver of time periods;

3. the reasons for the delay, including

   (a) inherent time requirements of the case,

   (b) actions of the accused,

   (c) actions of the Crown,

   (d) limits on institutional resources, and

   (e) other reasons for delay; and

---

[275] *Id.* at 1608–10.

[276] *R. v. Potvin* [1993] 2 S.C.R. 880.

[277] *R. v. MacDougall* [1998] 3 S.C.R. 45, paras. 9–39. The Court noted that the values that Art. 11(b) were intended to protect are directly implicated during sentencing, though they should have a more limited scope at this stage. *Id.* at para. 32.

[278] *See, R. v. Potvin, supra* n. 276 (discussing the distinction between the language in Section 11(b) of the Charter and Articles 5(3) and 6(1) of the Convention, as discussed in the *Wemhoff Case, supra* n. 203, and American jurisprudence on the Sixth Amendment's Speedy Trial Clause).

[279] *See R. v. Askov* [1990] 2 S.C.R. 1199, 1208–9, 1219–20; *Barker supra* n. 262 at 520–1.

[280] [1992] 1 S.C.R. 771.

[281] *Id.* at 786.

4. prejudice to the accused.[282]

Unlike the United States Court, however, particular weights have not been given by the Canadian Court to different reasons for delay. Nor is the burden of proof on the State once it has been determined that there has been an unreasonable delay, as in the European Court.[283] The preferred method of determining when there has been a violation of Section 11(b) of the Canadian Charter is 'balancing' all of these factors insofar as they are relevant in a given case.[284]

The method for determining a violation of Section 11(b) of the Canadian Charter, then, is more closely aligned to the method used by the United States courts in connection with the Speedy Trial Clause of the Sixth Amendment than it is to that of the European Court of Human Rights under Article 6 or Articles 5(3) or 5(4). Given the closer overall resemblance between the rights secured by Section 11(b) of the Canadian Charter to those secured by the Sixth Amendment than to those secured by the Convention, this similarity is unsurprising.

---

[282] *Id.* at 787–8. These factors were discussed in the earlier cases, *R. v. Smith* [1989] 2 S.C.R. 1120 at 1131 and *R. v. Askov supra* n. 279 at 1231–2. This test replaces the balancing articulated in *R v. Mills* [1986] 1 S.C.R. 863, para. 219 of the 'growing impairment of the interests of the accused by the passage of time' against: 'the waiver of time periods; the time requirements inherent in the nature of the case; and the limited nature of institutional resources'.

[283] *R. v. Smith, supra* n. 282.

[284] *See R. v. Morin,* [1992] 1 S.C.R. 771, 788. 'The analysis must not proceed in a mechanical manner. The factors and framework set out in *Askov* and *Morin* are not immutable or inflexible. . . . [T]he list of factors can never be exhaustive. Nor is an unyielding focus on only certain periods of the delay appropriate. In every case it must be borne in mind that the ultimate question for determination is the reasonableness of the overall delay'. *R. v. MacDougall, supra* n. 277 at para. 41.

PART III
THE IMPACT OF THE STRASBOURG SYSTEM

9

THE EFFECT IN NATIONAL LAW OF THE EUROPEAN CONVENTION ON HUMAN RIGHTS

A. THE DIVERSE LEGAL SYSTEMS IN EUROPE

We have seen in earlier chapters how the Convention enables the European Court of Human Rights to exercise a form of quasi-constitutional supervision over the exercise of state power. This control may be exercised whether the action complained of results directly from primary legislation, from judicial decisions made by the courts, or from executive measures taken by government departments or other public authorities.

Each of the 40 states which are party to the Convention has its own constitutional and political history and legal system. Wide variations exist between these different constitutions and legal systems. Some constitutions are well over 100 years old. Others have been created in recent years[1], as central and eastern Europe has shaken off the effects of Communism. In nearly all states, the national constitution provides in some measure for the liberties and rights of the individual. But the constitutions differ widely—both in how they define the rights and freedoms which are protected (the 'catalogue' of rights), and also in the procedure provided for enforcing those rights.

In Germany, for instance, the Federal Constitutional Court is the ultimate guardian of the very full catalogue of fundamental rights contained in Part I of the Basic Law: the Court exercises the function of constitutional review over federal legislation or executive action which infringes those rights. There are also administrative courts whose primary function is to control the acts of public authorities on grounds of legality. Another form of review is found in the Constitution of the Fifth French Republic, by which the conformity to the Constitution of a proposed law may be considered by the Conseil Constitutionnel. But the ordinary courts in France have no power to review the constitutionality of enacted laws. The Conseil d'Etat and the

---

[1] In this chapter, any reference to a state or to a European state will, unless the context dictates a different meaning, refer to a state that is a party to the Convention.

tribunaux administratifs exercise a controlling jurisdiction over the acts and decisions of the government and public authorities. This jurisdiction extends to disputes over the contractual and non-contractual liability of public authorities, disputes which in most other European legal systems are entrusted to the ordinary civil courts. By contrast with both France and Germany, the position of the United Kingdom has been notable for the lack of both a written constitution and of a catalogue of fundamental rights; the doctrine of the legislative supremacy, or sovereignty, of Parliament has prevented the courts from having power to review the contents of legislation enacted by Parliament. However, the ordinary courts have long exercised an important function of review and supervision, on grounds of legality, over the acts of government departments and other authorities; this control extends to such matters as secondary legislation, departmental policies and guidelines, and decisions made in the exercise of statutory and common law powers. The evolution of this public law jurisdiction has moved into an important new phase with the enactment at Westminster of the Human Rights Act 1998, which made far-reaching changes in the British system for protecting rights under the European Convention.[2]

Differing as they do from Germany, France and the United Kingdom, each of the European states that adheres to the Convention has its own legal system and its own historical experience of protecting human rights. It must be emphasized that, notwithstanding the existence of the Convention, it is on these diverse national court systems that the primary burden of protecting the individual's rights and freedoms must fall. The role of the Convention is to complement those systems, and provide redress at an international level where shortcomings in them exist.

B. THE DUTY OF STATES TO GIVE EFFECT TO THE CONVENTION IN NATIONAL LAW

Even if decisions of the Strasbourg Court may have a quasi-constitutional effect, the formal status of the Convention remains that of a treaty at international law. The existence, content, interpretation and binding effect of a treaty as between the parties to it are matters governed by international law. By contrast, the question whether a treaty has any effect within national law is a matter governed essentially by the constitutional law of the state in question.[3] If a treaty *requires* effect to be given to it in national law (as did the treaties which set up the European Communities), such an obligation prevails over any supposed obstacles that exist in national law (and see Section E below). The reason for this is that at international law, the national law of a state (which includes its constitutional law) may not be relied on by that state as a

---

[2] See section D *infra*.
[3] *See* F. G. Jacobs and S. Roberts (eds.) *The Effect of Treaties in Domestic Law* (1987), xxiv.

justification for failure to perform its obligations under a treaty (and see the Vienna Convention on Treaties, Article 27).

Against this background, several related questions arise:

(1) does the Convention *require* states (a) to give direct effect in national law to the substantive rights and freedoms protected by the Convention? and (b) to provide a procedure in national law for enabling individuals to remedy breaches of their Convention rights? and

(2) is it the *duty* of a state to comply with remedial measures required following a breach of the Convention?

While the answers to these questions depend on interpretation of the Convention, and the extent of the obligations imposed on states is a matter of international law, provisions of the Convention may in some states have direct effect in national law; moreover, a state may well give greater protection to human rights in its own legal system than is required by the Convention.

1. DOES THE CONVENTION REQUIRE STATES (A) TO GIVE DIRECT EFFECT IN NATIONAL LAW TO THE SUBSTANTIVE RIGHTS AND FREEDOMS PROTECTED BY THE CONVENTION? AND (B) TO PROVIDE A PROCEDURE IN NATIONAL LAW FOR ENABLING INDIVIDUALS TO REMEDY BREACHES OF THEIR CONVENTION RIGHTS?

Article 1 imposes on each state the fundamental duty of securing to everyone within their jurisdiction the rights and freedoms defined in the Convention. By Article 13, everyone whose rights and freedoms so defined are violated:

shall have an effective remedy before a national authority notwithstanding that the violation has been committed by persons acting in an official capacity.

In *Swedish Engine Drivers' Union v. Sweden*[4] a trade union, representing a minority of employees of the Swedish State railways, complained of a breach of their rights under Article 11 (freedom of association). The complaint was that the union was excluded from taking part in the collective bargaining procedures for the railways, which were confined to the union representing the majority of railway employees. The Court held that Article 11 did not extend to giving any union the right to take part in collective bargaining. The union also complained of a breach of Article 13 in that, under Swedish law, it had no effective remedy for redressing its grievance, other than complaining to the Swedish Labour Court. On this aspect of the case, the Court said:

50. The Court notes that Swedish legislation offered the applicant union a remedy of which,

---

[4] 6 Feb. 1976 (No. 20), 1 E.H.R.R. 617.

moreover, the union had availed itself, namely the institution of proceedings before the Labour Court. The claim of the applicant union was no doubt rejected, but this fact alone cannot establish that the remedy was ineffective. On the contrary, a reading of the judgment of 18 February 1972 reveals that the Labour Court carefully examined the complaints brought before it in the light of the legislation in force and . . . taking into account Sweden's international undertakings. In addition, neither Article 13 nor the Convention in general lays down for the Contracting States any given manner for ensuring within their internal law the effective implementation of any of the provisions of the Convention.

The Court thus reaches a conclusion in line with the secondary argument advanced by the Government on the issue under consideration. In these circumstances, the Court is not called upon to rule whether, as the Government contended in its main submission and the Commission affirmed at paragraph 98 of its report, Article 13 is applicable only when a right guaranteed by another Article of the Convention has been violated.

In *Republic of Ireland v. United Kingdom*[5] the Irish government claimed that Article 1 of the Convention had been breached because the law in Northern Ireland did not expressly prohibit infringement of the relevant Convention rights:

236. The Irish Government's submission is as follows: the laws in force in [Northern Ireland] did not in terms prohibit violations of the rights and freedoms protected by Articles 3, 5, 6 and 14; several of those laws, as well as certain administrative practices, even authorized or permitted such violations; the United Kingdom was thereby in breach, in respect of each of those Articles, of an inter-State obligation separate from its obligations towards individuals and arising from Article 1, which provides:

> The High Contracting Parties shall secure to everyone within their jurisdiction the rights and freedoms defined in Section 1 of [the] Convention.

Neither the British Government nor the Commission in its report concur with this argument. They consider, briefly, that Article 1 cannot be the subject of a separate breach since it grants no rights in addition to those mentioned in Section I. . . .

238. Article 1, together with Articles 14, 2 to 13 and 63, demarcates the scope of the Convention *ratione personae, materiae* and *loci*; it is also one of the many Articles that attest the binding character of the Convention. Article 1 is drafted by reference to the provisions contained in Section I and thus comes into operation only when taken in conjunction with them; a violation of Article 1 follows automatically from, but adds nothing to, a breach of those provisions; hitherto, when the Court has found such a breach, it has never held that Article 1 has been violated.

239. However, the Irish Government's argument prompts the Court to clarify the nature of the engagements placed under its supervision. Unlike international treaties of the classic kind, the Convention comprises more than mere reciprocal engagements between contracting States. It creates, over and above a network of mutual, bilateral undertakings, objective obligations which, in the words of the Preamble, benefit from a 'collective enforcement'. By virtue of Article 24, the Convention allows Contracting States to require the observance of those obligations without having to justify an interest deriving, for example, from the fact that a measure they complain of has prejudiced one of their own nationals. By substituting the words 'shall secure' for the words

---

[5] 18 Jan. 1978 (No. 25), 2 E.H.R.R. 25 reprinted in part at Chapter 4 (A)(1) *supra*.

'undertake to secure' in the text of Article 1, the drafters of the Convention also intended to make it clear that the rights and freedoms set out in Section I would be directly secured to anyone within the jurisdiction of the Contracting States.[6] That intention finds a particularly faithful reflection in those instances where the Convention has been incorporated into domestic law.[7]

The Convention does not merely oblige the higher authorities of the Contracting States to respect for their own part the rights and freedoms it embodies; as is shown by Article 14 and the English text of Article 1 ('shall secure'), the Convention also has the consequence that, in order to secure the enjoyment of those rights and freedoms, those authorities must prevent or remedy any breach at subordinate levels.

240. The problem in the present case is essentially whether a Contracting State is entitled to challenge under the Convention a law *in abstracto*.

The answer to this problem is to be found much less in Article 1 than in Article 24 [now 33]. Whereas, in order to be able to lodge a valid petition, a 'person, non-governmental organization or group of individuals' must, under Article 25 [now 34], claim 'to be the victim of a violation . . . of the rights set forth', Article 24 enables each Contracting State to refer to the Commission 'any alleged breach of [any of] the provisions of the Convention by another [State]'.

Such a 'breach' results from the mere existence of a law which introduces, directs or authorizes measures incompatible with the rights and freedoms safeguarded; this is confirmed unequivocally by the *travaux préparatoires*.[8]

Nevertheless, the institutions established by the Convention may find a breach of this kind only if the law challenged pursuant to Article 24 [now 33] is couched in terms sufficiently clear and precise to make the breach immediately apparent; otherwise, the decision of the Convention institutions must be arrived at by reference to the manner in which the respondent State interprets and applies *in concreto* the impugned text or texts.

The absence of a law expressly prohibiting this or that violation does not suffice to establish a breach since such a prohibition does not represent the sole method of securing the enjoyment of the rights and freedoms guaranteed.

241. In the present case, the Court has found two practices in breach of Article 3 . . . Those practices automatically infringed Article 1 as well, but this is a finding which adds nothing to the previous finding and which there is no reason to include in the operative provisions of this judgment.

Examination *in abstracto* of the legislation in force at the relevant time in Northern Ireland reveals that it never introduced, directed or authorized recourse to torture or to inhuman or degrading treatment. On the contrary, it forbade any such ill-treatment in increasingly clear terms. . . . More generally, as from the end of August 1971, the higher authorities in the United Kingdom took a number of appropriate steps to prevent or remedy the individual violations of Article 3 . . .

The Court considered other aspects of the legislation authorizing detention without trial in Northern Ireland, outlined the pattern of events, and held that in the public emergency threatening the life of the nation, the British government enjoyed a margin of appreciation which had not been exceeded.

---

[6] Document H (61) 4, pp. 664, 703 and 927.

[7] *De Wilde, Ooms and Versyp v. Belgium*, 18 June 1971 (No. 12), 1 E.H.R.R. 438, para. 82; and *Swedish Engine Drivers' Union v. Sweden*, *supra* n. 4, para. 50.

[8] Document H (61) 4, pp. 384, 502, 703 and 706.

The Court has consistently held that a state is not obliged to adopt a particular method of ensuring the observance of rights guaranteed by the Convention—in particular, that a state is not required to incorporate the terms of the Convention in national law. What matters is that the substance of the guaranteed rights should in fact be enjoyed by the individuals affected by state action.

This approach has influenced the Court's interpretation of Article 13. Many applicants have argued (often without success) that Article 13 requires there to be an effective remedy in national law for apparent breaches of the Convention. In 1984, two judges (Matscher and Pinheiro Farina) said in a dissenting opinion:

We recognize that Article 13 constitutes one of the most obscure clauses in the Convention and that its application raises extremely difficult and complicated problems of interpretation. This is probably the reason why, for approximately two decades, the Convention institutions avoided analysing this provision, for the most part advancing barely convincing reasons.[9]

They also commented that, in several recent decisions, in particular *Klass v. Germany* and *Silver v. United Kingdom*, the Court had laid the foundation for a coherent meaning to be given to Article 13.

(A) KLASS V. GERMANY

Judgment of 6 Sept. 1978
(No. 28), 2 E.H.R.R. 214

[Five German lawyers claimed that their Convention rights (under Articles 6, 8 and 13) had been infringed by a federal law of 1968 (called for convenience 'the G10') which authorized the opening of letters and the tapping of telephones. The applicants relied, *inter alia*, on the fact that their rights might be infringed by secret surveillance. The Court examined the purposes, conditions and procedural safeguards stated in law for the exercise of these powers and found that Articles 6 and 8 had not been breached.]

62. In the applicants' view, the Contracting States are obliged under Article 13 to provide an effective remedy for any *alleged* breach of the Convention; any other interpretation of this provision would render it meaningless. On the other hand, both the Government and the Commission consider that there is no basis for the application of Article 13 unless a right guaranteed by another Article of the Convention has been violated.

63. In *Swedish Engine Drivers' Union v. Sweden*[10] the Court, having found there to be in fact an effective remedy before a national authority, considered that it was not called upon to rule whether Article 13 was applicable only when a right guaranteed by another Article of the Convention has been violated. The Court proposes in the present case to decide on the applicability of Article 13, before examining, if necessary, the effectiveness of any relevant remedy under German law.

---

[9] *Malone v. United Kingdom*, 2 Aug. 1984 (No. 82), 7 E.H.R.R. 14, para. 48. The Court in *Malone* had held (by 16–2) that because of its finding that a breach of Art. 8 had occurred, it was not necessary to consider the alleged breach of Art. 13.

[10] *Supra* n. 4. *See also De Wilde, Ooms and Versyp v. Belgium*, *supra* n. 7.

64. Article 13 states that any individual whose Convention rights and freedoms 'are violated' is to have an effective remedy before a national authority even where 'the violation has been committed' by persons in an official capacity. This provision, read literally, seems to say that a person is entitled to a national remedy only if a 'violation' has occurred. However, a person cannot establish a 'violation' before a national authority unless he is first able to lodge with such an authority a complaint to that effect. Consequently, . . . it cannot be a prerequisite for the application of Article 13 that the Convention be in fact violated. In the Court's view, Article 13 requires that where an individual considers himself to have been prejudiced by a measure allegedly in breach of the Convention, he should have a remedy before a national authority in order both to have his claim decided and, if appropriate, to obtain redress. Thus, Article 13 must be interpreted as guaranteeing an 'effective remedy before a national authority' to everyone who *claims* that his rights and freedoms under the Convention have been violated.

65. Accordingly, although the Court has found no breach of the right guaranteed to the applicants by Article 8, it falls to be ascertained whether German law afforded the applicants 'an effective remedy before a national authority' within the meaning of Article 13.

The applicants are not claiming that, in relation to particular surveillance measures actually applied to them, they lacked an effective remedy for alleged violation of their rights under the Convention. Rather, their complaint is directed against what they consider to be a shortcoming in the content of the contested legislation. While conceding that some forms of recourse exist in certain circumstances, they contend that the legislation itself, since it prevents them from even knowing whether their rights under the Convention have been interfered with by a concrete measure of surveillance, thereby denies them in principle an effective remedy under national law. Neither the Commission nor the Government agree with this contention. Consequently, although the applicants are challenging the terms of the legislation itself, the Court must examine, *inter alia*, what remedies are in fact available under German law and whether these remedies are effective in the circumstances.

66. The Court observes firstly that the applicants themselves enjoyed 'an effective remedy', within the meaning of Article 13, in so far as they challenged before the Federal Constitutional Court the conformity of the relevant legislation with their right to respect for correspondence and with their right of access to the courts. Admittedly, that Court examined the applicants' complaints with reference not to the Convention but solely to the Basic Law. It should be noted, however, that the rights invoked by the applicants before the Constitutional Court are substantially the same as those whose violation was alleged before the Convention institutions,[11] reading of the judgment of 15 December 1970 reveals that the Constitutional Court carefully examined the complaints brought before it in the light, *inter alia*, of the fundamental principles and democratic values embodied in the Basic Law.

67. As regards the issue whether there is 'an effective remedy' in relation to the implementation of concrete surveillance measures under the G10, the applicants argued in the first place that to qualify as a 'national authority', within the meaning of Article 13, a body should at least be composed of members who are impartial and who enjoy the safeguards of judicial independence. The Government in reply submitted that, in contrast to Article 6, Article 13 does not require a legal remedy through the courts.

In the Court's opinion, the authority referred to in Article 13 may not necessarily in all

[11] *Cf. mutatis mutandis Swedish Engine Drivers' Union v. Sweden, supra* n. 4.

instances be a judicial authority in the strict sense.[12] Nevertheless, the powers and procedural guarantees an authority possesses are relevant in determining whether the remedy before it is effective.

68. The concept of an 'effective remedy', in the applicants' submission, presupposes that the person concerned should be placed in a position, by means of subsequent information, to defend himself against any inadmissible encroachment upon his guaranteed rights. Both the Government and the Commission were agreed that no unrestricted right to notification of surveillance measures can be deduced from Article 13 once the contested legislation, including the lack of information, has been held to be 'necessary in a democratic society' for any one of the purposes mentioned in Article 8.

The Court has already pointed out that it is the secrecy of the measures which renders it difficult, if not impossible, for the person concerned to seek any remedy of his own accord, particularly while surveillance is in progress . . . Secret surveillance and its implications are facts that the Court, albeit to its regret, has held to be necessary, in modern-day conditions in a democratic society, in the interests of national security and for the prevention of disorder or crime . . . The Convention is to be read as a whole and therefore, as the Commission indicated in its report, any interpretation of Article 13 must be in harmony with the logic of the Convention. The Court cannot interpret or apply Article 13 so as to arrive at a result tantamount in fact to nullifying its conclusion that the absence of notification to the persons concerned is compatible with Article 8 in order to ensure the efficacy of surveillance measures . . . Consequently, the Court, consistently with its conclusions concerning Article 8, holds that the lack of notification does not, in the circumstances of the case, entail a breach of Article 13.

69. For the purposes of the present proceedings, an 'effective remedy' under Article 13 must mean a remedy that is as effective as can be having regard to the restricted scope for recourse inherent in any system of secret surveillance. It therefore remains to examine the various remedies available to the applicants under German law in order to see whether they are 'effective' in this limited sense.

70. Although, according to the G10, there can be no recourse to the courts in respect of the ordering and implementation of restrictive measures, certain other remedies are nevertheless open to the individual believing himself to be under surveillance: he has the opportunity of complaining to the G10 Commission and to the Constitutional Court. . . . Admittedly, the effectiveness of these remedies is limited and they will in principle apply only in exceptional cases. However, in the circumstances of the present proceedings, it is hard to conceive of more effective remedies being possible.

71. On the other hand, in pursuance of the Federal Constitutional Court's judgment of 15 December 1970, the competent authority is bound to inform the person concerned as soon as the surveillance measures are discontinued and notification can be made without jeopardizing the purpose of the restriction . . . From the moment of such notification, various legal remedies— before the courts—become available to the individual. According to the information supplied by the Government, the individual may have reviewed by an administrative court, in an action for a declaration, the lawfulness of the application to him of the G10 and the conformity with the law of the surveillance measures ordered; bring an action for damages in a civil court if he has been prejudiced; bring an action for the destruction or, if appropriate, restitution of documents; finally,

---

[12] See *Golder v. United Kingdom*, 21 Feb. 1975 (No. 18), 1 E.H.R.R. 524.

if none of these remedies is successful, apply to the Federal Constitutional Court for a ruling as to whether there has been a breach of the Basic Law. . . .

72. Accordingly, the Court considers that, in the particular circumstances of this case, the aggregate of remedies provided for under German law satisfies the requirements of Article 13 . . .

(C) SILVER V. UNITED KINGDOM

Judgment of 25 March 1983
(No. 61), 5 E.H.R.R. 347

[Here the Court had reviewed in detail the manner in which prison authorities censored the correspondence of convicted prisoners and held that both Articles 6(1) and 8 had been breached. In relation to the breach of Article 6(1), the Court held it to be unnecessary to examine the complaint under Article 13 since the requirements of Article 6(1) had 'absorbed' the requirements of Article 13. The Court examined the alleged breach of Article 13 taken together with Article 8.]

113. The principles that emerge from the Court's *jurisprudence* on the interpretation of Article 13 include the following:

(a) where an individual has an arguable claim to be the victim of a violation of the rights set forth in the Convention, he should have a remedy before a national authority in order both to have his claim decided and, if appropriate, to obtain redress;

(b) the authority referred to in Article 13 may not necessarily be a judicial authority but, if it is not, its powers and the guarantees which it affords are relevant in determining whether the remedy before it is effective;

(c) although no single remedy may itself entirely satisfy the requirements of Article 13, the aggregate of remedies provided for under domestic law may do so;

(d) neither Article 13 nor the Convention in general lays down for the Contracting States any given manner for ensuring within their internal law the effective implementation of any of the provisions of the Convention—for example, by incorporating the Convention into domestic law.

It follows from the last-mentioned principle that the application of Article 13 in a given case will depend upon the manner in which the Contracting State concerned has chosen to discharge its obligation under Article 1 directly to secure to anyone within its jurisdiction the rights and freedoms set out in section 1.[13]

114. In the present case, it was not suggested that any remedies were available to the applicants other than the four channels of complaint examined by the Commission, namely an application to the Board of Visitors, an application to the Parliamentary [Ombudsman], a petition to the Home secretary and the institution of proceedings before the English courts.

115. As regards the first two channels, the Court, like the Commission, considers that they do not constitute an 'effective remedy' for the present purposes.

The Board of Visitors cannot enforce its conclusions . . . nor can it entertain applications from individuals like Mrs. Colne who are not in prison.

---

[13] *See Ireland v. United Kingdom, supra* n. 5 at para. 239.

As regards the Parliamentary [Ombudsman], it suffices to note that he has himself no power to render a binding decision granting redress. . . .

116. As for the Home Secretary, if there were a complaint to him as to the validity of an Order or Instruction under which a measure of control over correspondence had been carried out, he could not be considered to have a sufficiently independent standpoint to satisfy the requirements of Article 13 [since] as the author of the directives in question, he would in reality be judge in his own cause. The position, however, would be otherwise if the complainant alleged that a measure of control resulted from a misapplication of one of those directives. The Court is satisfied that in such cases a petition to the Home Secretary would in general be effective to secure compliance with the directive, if the complaint was well-founded. The Court notes, however, that even in these cases . . . , the conditions for the submission of such petitions imposed limitations on the availability of this remedy in some circumstances. . . .

117. The English courts, for their part, are endowed with a certain supervisory jurisdiction over the exercise of the powers conferred on the Home Secretary and the prison authorities by the Prison Act and the Rules . . . However, their jurisdiction is limited to determining whether or not those powers have been exercised arbitrarily, in bad faith, for an improper motive or in an *ultra vires* manner. . . .

118. The applicants made no allegation that the interferences with their correspondence were contrary to English law . . . Like the Commission, the Court has found that the majority of the measures complained of in the present proceedings were incompatible with the Convention . . . In most of the cases, the Government did not contest the Commission's findings. Neither did they maintain that the English courts could have found the measures to have been taken arbitrarily, in bad faith, for an improper motive or in an *ultra vires* manner.

In the Court's view, to the extent that the applicable norms, whether contained in the Rules or in the relevant Orders of Instructions, were incompatible with the Convention there could be no effective remedy as required by Article 13 and consequently there has been a violation of that Article.

To the extent, however, that the said norms were compatible with Article 8, the aggregate of the remedies available satisfied the requirements of Article 13, at least in those cases in which it was possible for a petition to be submitted to the Home Secretary (see paragraph 116 above): a petition to the Home Secretary was available to secure compliance with the directives issued by him and as regards compliance with the Rules, the English courts had the supervisory jurisdiction described in paragraph 117 above.

119. To sum up, in those instances where the norms in question were incompatible with the Convention and where the Court has found a violation of Article 8 to have occurred there was no effective remedy and Article 13 has therefore also been violated. In the remaining cases, there is no reason to assume that the applicants' complaints could not have been duly examined by the Home Secretary and/or the English courts and Article 13 has therefore not been violated; . . .

In *Lithgow v. United Kingdom*[14] the owners of a shipbuilding company which had been nationalized by Act of Parliament challenged the basis of the compensation laid down in the legislation, arguing that it fell below the level guaranteed by Article 1 of the First

---

[14] 8 July 1986 (No. 102), 8 E.H.R.R. 329.

Protocol to the Convention and alleging as regards Article 13 that no 'effective remedy' was available to them in the British courts. Rejecting this complaint, the Court said:

206. The Convention is not part of the domestic law of the United Kingdom, nor does there exist any constitutional procedure permitting the validity of laws to be challenged for non-observance of fundamental rights. There thus was, and could be, no domestic remedy in respect of a complaint by Sir William Lithgow that the nationalization legislation itself did not measure up to the standards of the Convention and Protocol No. 1. The Court, however, concurs with the Commission that Article 13 does not go so far as to guarantee a remedy allowing a Contracting State's laws as such to be challenged before a national authority on the ground of being contrary to the Convention or to equivalent domestic legal norms.[15] The Court is therefore unable to uphold the applicant's allegation in so far as it may relate to the 1977 Act as such.

207. In so far as the allegation relates to the application of the legislation, the Court notes that it was open to the Stockholders' representative in any case to refer the question of compensation to the Arbitration Tribunal or to test in the ordinary courts whether the Secretary of State had erred in law by misinterpreting or misapplying the 1977 Act. Even if these remedies were not directly available to Sir William Lithgow himself, he did have the benefit of the collective system established by the Act. The Court has found this system not to be in breach of the requirements of Article 6(1), an Article whose requirements are stricter than those of Article 13. In addition, the applicant would have had a remedy in the domestic courts against the Kincaid Stockholders' Representative for failure to comply with his obligations under the 1977 Act or with his common law obligations as agent.

In these circumstances, the Court concludes that the aggregate of remedies available to Sir William Lithgow did constitute domestic machinery whereby he could, to a sufficient degree, secure compliance with the relevant legislation.

By a majority of 15 to three, the Court held that there had been no breach of Article 13.

In *Boyle and Rice v. United Kingdom*,[16] convicted prisoners in Scotland complained of interferences with their correspondence and family life, and of discriminatory prison regimes; they also complained of the lack of effective remedies in respect of these matters. The European Court said:

52. The stopping of one of Mr. Boyle's letters has been found by the Court to constitute a breach of Article 8. All the remaining claims of violation forming the basis of the applicants' complaints under Article 13 were rejected by the Commission at the admissibility stage on the ground of being manifestly ill-founded. . . .

Notwithstanding the terms of Article 13 read literally, the existence of an actual breach of another provision of the Convention (a 'substantive' provision) is not a prerequisite for the application of the Article.[17] Article 13 guarantees the availability of a remedy at national level to

---

[15] This interpretation of Art. 13 has also been applied in cases such as *James v. United Kingdom*, 21 Feb. 1986 (No. 98), 8 E.H.R.R. 123, para. 85 and *Leander v. Sweden* 25 Mar. 1987 (No. 116), 9 E.H.R.R. 443, para. 77.

[16] 27 April 1988 (No. 131), 10 E.H.R.R. 425.

[17] *See Klass v. Germany*, 6 Sept. 1978 (No. 28), 2 E.H.R.R. 214, para. 64 reprinted at Section (B)(1)(A) *supra*.

enforce—and hence to allege non-compliance with—the substance of the Convention rights and freedoms in whatever form they may happen to be secured in the domestic legal order.[18]

However, Article 13 cannot reasonably be interpreted so as to require a remedy in domestic law in respect of any supposed grievance under the Convention that an individual may have, no matter how unmeritorious his complaint may be: the grievance must be an arguable one in terms of the Convention.[19]

53. The Government maintained that a claim of violation of one of the substantive Articles of the Convention which has been declared by the Commission to be 'manifestly ill-founded' cannot be regarded as 'arguable' for the purposes of Article 13.

The Commission did not agree with this contention. According to the Delegate, in deciding whether a complaint is 'manifestly ill-founded' under Article 27(2) [now 35(3)] the Commission applied a spectrum of standards that encompassed but ranged beyond absence of arguability. In his submission, to be arguable a claim 'only needs to raise a Convention issue which merits further examination', whereas a conclusion that a complaint is manifestly ill-founded may be reached after considerable written and oral argument.

54. As the Court pointed out in its *Airey* judgment of 9 October 1979, rejection of a complaint as 'manifestly ill-founded' amounts to a decision that 'there is not even a *prima facie* case against the respondent state'.[20] On the ordinary meaning of the words, it is difficult to conceive how a claim that is 'manifestly ill-founded' can nevertheless be 'arguable', and *vice versa*.

This does not mean, however, that the Court must hold a claim to be excluded from the operation of Article 13 if the Commission has previously declared it manifestly ill-founded under the substantive Article. The Commission's decision declaring an application admissible determines the scope of the case brought before the Court.[21] The Court is precluded from reviewing on their merits under the relevant Article the complaints rejected as manifestly ill-founded, but empowered to entertain those complaints which the Commission had declared admissible and which have been duly referred to it. The Court is thus competent to take cognizance of all questions of fact and of law arising in the context of the complaints before it under Article 13, including the arguability or not of the claims of violation of the substantive provisions. In this connection, the Commission's decision on the admissibility of the underlying claims and the reasoning therein, whilst not being decisive, provide significant pointers as to the arguable character of the claims for the purposes of Article 13.

55. The Court does not think that it should give an abstract definition of the notion of arguability. Rather it must be determined, in the light of the particular facts and the nature of the legal issue or issues raised, whether each individual claim of violation forming the basis of a complaint under Article 13 was arguable and, if so, whether the requirements of Article 13 were met in relation thereto.

Having examined the complaints of the applicants in detail, the Court found that in most of the complaints there was no arguable claim of violation of the Convention and thus no breach of Article 13. In the case of some complaints, the Court found that there might have been an arguable breach of a Convention right, but that there was a

---

[18] *See Lithgow v. United Kingdom*, 8 July 1986 (No. 102), 8 E.H.R.R., para. 205 and the authorities cited there.

[19] *See Leander v. Sweden* 26 Mar. 1987 (No. 116), 9 E.H.R.R. 443, para. 79(a).

[20] *Airey v. Ireland*, 9 Oct. 1979 (No. 32), 2 E.H.R.R., para. 18.

[21] *See Ireland v. United Kingdom, supra* n. 5 at para 157.

sufficient remedy available to the applicants in the form of a petition to the Secretary of State for Scotland, backed up by a possible application for judicial review should an adverse decision on the petition be made by the Secretary of State.

As *Lithgow* and *Boyle and Rice* demonstrate, while the Convention's status in the United Kingdom was that of an unincorporated treaty, it was difficult to know whether the remedy of judicial review was sufficiently effective to satisfy Article 13. The same difficulty is evident in the next two cases, *Vilvarajah* and *Chahal*, when the Court had to decide whether the available remedy enabled the national court to deal with the substance of the human rights dispute.

(C) VILVARAJAH V. UNITED KINGDOM

Judgment of 30 Oct. 1991
(No. 215), 14 E.H.R.R. 248

[Five Tamils from Sri Lanka, whose request for political asylum in the United Kingdom had been rejected, challenged the procedure by which the Home Secretary's decision had been made. The Commission had decided by 13 to one that the remedy of judicial review which the Tamils had resorted to without success was not an 'effective remedy' within Article 13, since the scope of the remedy was too narrow in view of what was at stake for the Tamils facing a forced return to conditions of persecution. Before the Court, the applicants argued that they had no effective remedy in national law in respect of their Article 3 complaint as required by Article 13.]

118. In their submission, in judicial review proceedings the courts do not control the merits of the Secretary of State's refusal of asylum but only the manner in which the decision on the merits was taken. In particular, they do not ascertain whether the Secretary of State was correct in his assessment of the risks to which those concerned would be subjected. Moreover, the courts have constantly stated that in reviewing the exercise of discretion in such cases they will not substitute their views on the merits of the case for that of the Secretary of State.

The applicants accepted that judicial review might be an effective remedy where, as in the *Soering* case[22] the facts were not in dispute between the parties and the issue was whether the decision was such that no reasonable Secretary of State could have made it. However, this was not so in their case where the question of the risks to which they would be exposed if sent back to Sri Lanka was the very substance of the dispute with the Secretary of State. . . .

120. The Government considered that judicial review proceedings provided an effective remedy in respect of a complaint under Article 3 as the Court had found in its *Soering* judgment,[23] there being no material difference in that respect between that case and the present one. It was not accepted that the evidential issues in the *Soering* case were less complex or that there was no dispute between the parties as to the risk of the applicant facing inhuman and degrading treatment. In both cases the issues were the same, namely, whether there existed a real and substantial risk that the applicants would be exposed to inhuman and degrading treatment. It was open to the applicants on the basis of objections now advanced to the Secretary of State's decision to challenge those decisions, on the ground of '*Wednesbury* unreasonableness' but they did not do so.

---

[22] *Soering v. United Kingdom*, 7 July 1989 (No. 161), 11 E.H.R.R. 439.
[23] *Id.* at paras. 116–24.

Judicial review on this ground does have the effect of controlling the merits of the Secretary of State's decision, as illustrated by the *Bugdaycay, Jeyakumaran* and *Yemoh* cases,[24] and is, in the circumstances, a sufficient means of doing so.

121. It is not disputed before the court that the applicants' claim under Article 3 was an 'arguable' one on its merits.[25]

122. Article 13 guarantees the availability of a remedy at national level to enforce the sub-stance of the Convention rights and freedoms in whatever form they may happen to be secured in the domestic legal order (*ibid.*). Its effect is thus to require the provision of a domestic remedy allowing the competent 'national authority' both to deal with the substance of the relevant Convention complaint and to grant appropriate relief.[26] However, Article 13 does not go so far as to require any particular form of remedy. . . .

123. In its *Soering* judgment of 7 July 1989[27] the Court considered judicial review proceedings to be an effective remedy in relation to Mr. Soering's complaint. It was satisfied that the English courts could review the 'reasonableness' of an extradition decision in the light of the kind of factors relied on by the applicant before the Convention institutions in the context of Article 3. In particular it noted, that in judicial review proceedings a court may rule the exercise of executive discretion unlawful on the ground that it is tainted with illegality, irrationality or procedural impropriety and that the test of 'irrationality' on the basis of the '*Wednesbury* principles' would be that no reasonable Secretary of State could have made an order for surrender in the circum-stances. Further, according to the U.K. Government, a court would have jurisdiction to quash a challenged decision to send a fugitive to a country where it was established that there was a serious risk of inhuman or degrading treatment, on the ground that in all the circumstances of the case the decision was one that no reasonable Secretary of State could take.

124. The Court does not consider that there are any material differences between the present case and the *Soering* case which should lead it to reach a different conclusion in this respect.

125. It is not in dispute that the English courts are able in asylum cases to review the Sec-retary of State's refusal to grant asylum with reference to the same principles of judicial review as considered in the *Soering* case and to quash a decision in similar circumstances and that they have done so in decided cases. Indeed the courts have stressed their special responsibility to subject administrative decisions in this area to the most anxious scrutiny where an applicant's life or liberty may be at risk. Moreover, the practice is that an asylum seeker will not be removed from the U.K. until proceedings are complete once he has obtained leave to apply for judicial review.

126. While it is true that there are limitations on the powers of the courts in judicial review proceedings the Court is of the opinion that these powers, exercisable as they are by the highest tribunals in the land, do provide an effective degree of control over the decisions of the administra-tive authorities in asylum cases and are sufficient to satisfy the requirements of Article 13.

127. The applicants thus had available to them an effective remedy in relation to their com-plaint under Article 3. There is accordingly no breach of Article 13.

The Court held accordingly (by seven to two) that the applicants had available to

---

[24] Respectively *R. v. Secretary of State for the Home Department, ex p. Bugdaycay* [1987] AC 415; (the same) *ex p. Jeyakumaran* (High Court, 28 June 1985); (the same) *ex p. Yemoh* (High Court, 14 July 1988).

[25] See, inter alia, *Boyle and Rice v. United Kingdom supra* n. 16 at para. 50.

[26] See, inter alia, *Soering v. United Kingdom, supra* n. 22, at para. 120.

[27] *Id.* at paras. 121 and 124.

them an effective remedy for the purposes of Article 13. Judges Walsh and Russo, dissenting, pointed to the limitations in English law on the remedy of judicial review, which was not equipped to deal with the disputes of fact which arose in the case. They considered that the power of the English courts to set aside an executive decision as 'unreasonable' in the *Wednesbury* sense[28] did not enable the courts to decide whether or not the facts disclosed a breach of the Convention.

(D) CHAHAL V. UNITED KINGDOM

Judgment of 15 November 1996
(1996), 23 E.H.R.R. 413

[In this case, Article 3 and 5 were held to have been breached.[29] Had there also been a breach of Article 13 in relation to Article 3? The applicants sought to distinguish *Vilvarajah*, arguing that the remedy of judicial review did not provide an evaluation of considerations relating to Article 3, but could determine only whether the proposed deportation of Mr Chahal was reasonable as a matter of English administrative law.]

148. The Court recalls that in its *Vilvarajah* judgment, it found judicial review proceedings to be an effective remedy in relation to the applicants' complaints under Article 3. It was satisfied that the English courts could review a decision by the Secretary of State to refuse asylum and could rule it unlawful on the grounds that it was tainted with illegality, irrationality or procedural impropriety. In particular, it was accepted that a court would have jurisdiction to quash a challenged decision to send a fugitive to a country where it was established that there was a serious risk of inhuman or degrading treatment, on the ground that in all the circumstances of the case the decision was one that no reasonable Secretary of State could take.

149. The Court further recalls that in assessing whether there exists a real risk of treatment in breach of Article 3 in expulsion cases such as the present, the fact that the person is perceived as a danger to the national security of the respondent State is not a material consideration.

150. It is true, as the Government have pointed out, that in the cases of *Klass and Others v. Germany* and *Leander v. Sweden*[30] the Court held that Article 13 only required a remedy that was 'as effective as can be' in circumstances where national security considerations did not permit the divulging of certain sensitive information. However, it must be borne in mind that these cases concerned complaints under Articles 8 and 10 of the Convention and that their examination required the Court to have regard to the national security claims which had been advanced by the Government. The requirement of a remedy which is 'as effective as can be' is not appropriate in respect of a complaint that a person's deportation will expose him or her to a real risk of treatment in breach of Article 3, where the issues concerning national security are immaterial.

151. In such cases, given the irreversible nature of the harm that might occur if the risk of ill-treatment materialized and the importance the Court attaches to Article 3, the notion of an effective remedy under Article 13 requires independent scrutiny of the claim that there exist

---

[28] In *Associated Provincial Picture Houses Ltd v. Wednesbury Corporation* [1948] 1 K.B. 223, the English Court of Appeal held that the courts could review a decision taken by the competent authority if it was 'so unreasonable that no reasonable authority could ever have come to it'.

[29] See section (B)(1)(c) *supra*.

[30] See *Klass v. Germany supra* n. 17 and *Leander v. Sweden supra* n. 19.

substantial grounds for fearing a real risk of treatment contrary to Article 3. This scrutiny must be carried out without regard to what the person may have done to warrant expulsion or to any perceived threat to the national security of the expelling State.

152. Such scrutiny need not be provided by a judicial authority but, if it is not, the powers and guarantees which it affords are relevant in determining whether the remedy before it is effective.

153. In the present case, neither the advisory panel nor the courts could review the decision of the Home Secretary to deport Mr Chahal to India with reference solely to the question of risk, leaving aside national security considerations. On the contrary, the courts' approach was one of satisfying themselves that the Home Secretary had balanced the risk to Mr Chahal against the danger to national security. It follows from the above considerations that these cannot be considered effective remedies in respect of Mr Chahal's Article 3 complaint for the purposes of Article 13 of the Convention.

154. Moreover, the Court notes that in the proceedings before the advisory panel the applicant was not entitled, *inter alia*, to legal representation, that he was only given an outline of the grounds for the notice of intention to deport, that the panel had no power of decision and that its advice to the Home Secretary was not binding and was not disclosed. In these circumstances, the advisory panel could not be considered to offer sufficient procedural safeguards for the purposes of Article 13.

155. Having regard to the extent of the deficiencies of both judicial review proceedings and the advisory panel, the Court cannot consider that the remedies taken together satisfy the requirements of Article 13 in conjunction with Article 3.

Accordingly, there has been a violation of Article 13.

In *D v. United Kingdom*[31] the Court held, following *Vilvarajah*, that there was no breach of Article 13 where the national court in judicial review proceedings had expressly considered, but rejected, the submissions of an applicant who was seriously ill with AIDS against removal to a small Caribbean island with inferior medical facilities.

Article 13 requires that national remedies must be effective, not theoretical. In many cases involving serious breaches of human rights, the Turkish legal system has failed to provide an effective remedy even though the action of the authorities may have been unlawful in national law. In *Aksoy v. Turkey*,[32] allegations were made that the applicant had been tortured while in police custody; the Court took judicial notice of the fact that such allegations are extremely difficult for the victim to substantiate if he is held in isolation, without access to doctors, lawyers, family or friends.

98. The nature of the right safeguarded under Article 3 of the Convention has implications for Article 13. Given the fundamental importance of the prohibition of torture and the especially vulnerable position of torture victims, Article 13 imposes, without prejudice to any other remedy available under the domestic system, an obligation on States to carry out a thorough and effective investigation of incidents of torture.

Accordingly, as regards Article 13, where an individual has an arguable claim that he has been tortured by agents of the State, the notion of an 'effective remedy' entails, in addition to the

---

[31] 2 May 1997, Reports, 1997–III 778, 24 E.H.R.R. 423.
[32] 18 Dec. 1996, Reports, 1996–IV 2260, 23 E.H.R.R. 553 discussed at Chapter 4 (A)(2) *supra*.

payment of compensation where appropriate, a thorough and effective investigation capable of leading to the identification and punishment of those responsible and including effective access for the complainant to the investigatory procedure. It is true that no express provision exists in the Convention such as can be found in Article 12 of the 1984 United Nations Convention against Torture and Other Cruel, Inhuman or Degrading Treatment or Punishment, which imposes a duty to proceed to a 'prompt and impartial' investigation whenever there is a reasonable ground to believe that an act of torture has been committed. However, in the Court's view, such a requirement is implicit in the notion of an 'effective remedy' under Article 13.

99. Indeed, under Turkish law the Prosecutor was under a duty to carry out an investigation. However, and whether or not Mr Aksoy made an explicit complaint to him, he ignored the visible evidence before him that the latter had been tortured and no investigation took place. No evidence has been adduced before the Court to show that any other action was taken, despite the Prosecutor's awareness of the applicant's injuries.

Moreover, in the Court's view, in the circumstances of Mr Aksoy's case, such an attitude from a State official under a duty to investigate criminal offences was tantamount to undermining the effectiveness of any other remedies that may have existed.

100. Accordingly, in view in particular of the lack of any investigation, the Court finds that the applicant was denied an effective remedy in respect of his allegation of torture.

Similarly, in *Aydin v. Turkey*,[33] where a female detainee alleged that she had been tortured, raped and denied access to a court, she and her family had made specific complaints to the public prosecutor. Although he was required by Turkish law to investigate the allegations, the prosecutor made an incomplete inquiry, failing to visit the scene of events and failing to question officers who were implicated.

His failure to look for corroborating evidence at the headquarters and his deferential attitude to the members of the security forces must be considered to be a particularly serious shortcoming in the investigation [paragraph 106].

He had ordered three medical examinations to be made of the applicant with the aim of discovering whether she had lost her virginity, rather than whether she had been a rape victim.

107. . . . The Court notes that the requirement of a thorough and effective investigation into an allegation of rape in custody at the hands of a state official also implies that the victim be examined, with all appropriate sensitivity, by medical professionals with particular competence in this area and whose independence is not circumscribed by instructions given by the prosecuting authority as to the scope of the examination . . .

The Court by 16 votes to five found that no effective investigation had been made into the allegations and that this failure undermined the effectiveness of other remedies which may have existed in Turkish law. The minority of five judges viewed the facts differently, finding that the conduct of the applicant and her representatives in relation to her complaint made it impossible to find a violation of her rights under Articles 6(1) and 13. Breaches of Article 13 also occurred when the applicant's son

---

[33] 25 Sept. 1997 Reports, 1997–VI 1866, 25 E.H.R.R. 251.

had disappeared, last seen in custody of Turkish security forces[34] and when those forces were alleged to have deliberately destroyed applicants' homes and possessions.[35] The nature and gravity of such complaints have implications for Article 13, which requires thorough investigation to be made, capable of leading to the identification and punishment of those responsible.

Article 13 was breached in a different setting when the owner of a house that was searched unlawfully in Switzerland was denied a remedy in national law for the reason that the search had been completed;[36] and when a prisoner had no redress against a judge's decision that correspondence with his lawyer be censored.[37] But there was no breach of Article 13 where a civil remedy for assault existed relating to the corporal punishment of a schoolboy by his head-teacher, even if it was uncertain whether such proceedings would have succeeded.[38]

Where other Convention provisions (particularly Articles 5(4) and 6(1) confer on an individual the right to a judicial decision on a matter, the Court will not consider the Article 13 claim, since duties under Article 13 are absorbed by the stricter requirements of Article 5(4) or 6(1).[39]

As well as emphasizing that the state must not connive at the breach of an individual's rights by officials, Article 13 encourages states to deal with complaints by domestic procedure, thus reducing the need for recourse to Strasbourg. It reinforces the rule under Article 35(1) that for an application to be admissible, an applicant to Strasbourg must first have exhausted the domestic remedies available.[40]

2. IS IT THE DUTY OF A STATE TO COMPLY WITH REMEDIAL MEASURES REQUIRED FOLLOWING A BREACH OF THE CONVENTION?

While a state may well contend that there has been no breach of human rights in a particular case, this stance is untenable once the Court has held that Convention rights have been breached. So far as a remedy for the applicant is concerned, by Article 41, if national law allows only partial reparation to be made, 'the Court shall, if necessary, afford just satisfaction to the injured party'.[41] Under Article 46(1), states

---

[34] *Kurt v. Turkey*, 25 May 1998 Reports, 1998–III 1152, 27 E.H.R.R. 373.

[35] *Mentes v. Turkey*, 28 Nov. 1997, Reports, 1997–VIII 2689, 26 E.H.R.R. 595. *See also Yasa v. Turkey* (allegations of murder and attempted murder) 2 Sept. 1998, Reports, 1998–VI 2411, 28 E.H.R.R. 408.

[36] *Camenzind v. Switzerland*, 16 Dec. 1997, Reports, 1997–VIII 2880, 28 E.H.R.R. 458.

[37] *Domenichini v. Italy*, 15 Nov. 1996 Reports, 1996–V 1789. And *see Halford v. United Kingdom* (1997) Reports, 1997–III 1004, 24 E.H.R.R. 523 (no remedy where senior police officer's personal calls intercepted by other police).

[38] *Costello-Roberts v. United Kingdom*, 25 Mar. 1993 (No. 247C) 19 E.H.R.R. 112.

[39] *Hentrich v. France*, 18 E.H.R.R. 440, *Murray v. United Kingdom*, 28 Oct. 1994 (No. 300A), 19 E.H.R.R. 193, *Balmer-Schafroth v. Switzerland*, 26 Aug. 1997, Reports 1997–IV 1346 25 E.H.R.R. 398 and *Vasilescu v. Romania*, 22 May 1998, Reports, 1998–III 1064 28 E.H.R.R. 241.

[40] *See* e.g. *Beis v. Greece*, 20 Mar. 1997, Reports, 1997–II 555 25 E.H.R.R. 335.

[41] *See* A. R. Mowbray, 'The European Court of Human Rights' Approach to Just Satisfaction', [1997] *Public Law* 647.

'undertake to abide by the final judgment of the Court in any case to which they are parties'. By Article 46(2), the final judgment of the Court is transmitted to the Committee of Ministers (of the Council of Europe), which body 'shall supervise its execution'.

The duty to comply with Court decisions is an essential part of the Convention scheme. If a state paid no regard to them and allowed rights to be abused on a wide scale, its place in the Council of Europe could be at risk, since membership is open only to a state that 'accepts the principles of the rule of law and of the enjoyment by all persons within its jurisdiction of human rights and fundamental freedoms'. If a state were to be in serious breach of this obligation, it could be suspended from membership or forced to withdraw from the Council.[42]

In practice, narrower questions of compliance often arise. If, for instance, the Court decides that a breach of a Convention right was caused by national legislation, similar breaches will occur unless the legislation is amended or unless a way is found of applying the legislation differently. A failure to amend the legislation might come before the Committee of Ministers under Article 46(2) as a failure in execution of the judgment. If further violations of rights occur because the same legislation is still applied, the victims may make their own applications to the Court. One question that has arisen is whether, if the law must be changed, a state has a reasonable time for the legislative process to operate, even though further violations may occur until the new legislation takes effect—or must the decision of the Court be given effect without delay?

(A) VERMEIRE V. BELGIUM

Judgment of 29 Nov. 1991
(No. 214), 15 E.H.R.R. 488

[This decision is a sequel to the Court's decision in *Marckx v. Belgium*[43] which held that Belgian legislation on family succession was in breach of the Convention because of its failure to make provision for children born outside marriage.]

19. The applicant complained of having been excluded from inheritance rights in her paternal grandparents' estates. She relied on Article 8 in conjunction with Article 14 of the Convention. . . .

She pointed out that in the *Marckx* judgment of 13 June 1979 the European Court had held that the total lack of inheritance rights on intestacy by reason solely of the 'illegitimate' nature of the affiliation between one of the applicants and her near relatives on her mother's side was discriminatory and hence incompatible with these Articles. Mrs. Vermeire maintained that the domestic courts should have applied Article 8 and 14, so interpreted, directly to the estates in which she was interested; at the very least the Belgian legislature should have given the Act of 31 March 1987, amending the legislation complained of, retrospective effect as from the date of that judgment.

---

[42] Arts. 3 and 8, Statute of the Council of Europe. For comparable procedure in relation to the European Union, see Art. 6 TEU (old F. 1) and Art. 309 (old Art. 236) of TEC.

[43] 13 June 1979 (No. 31), 2 E.H.R.R. 330 discussed at Chapter 6 (A)(3) *supra*.

20. The Court stated in the *Marckx* case that the principle of legal certainty absolved the Belgian State from reopening legal acts or situations that antedated the delivery of the judgment.

The present case concerns the estates of a grandmother who died before and a grandfather who died after that date.

A. The grandmother's estate

21. The applicant maintained that the succession to her grandmother's estate could not be regarded as having taken place before 13 June 1979. The date of death was indeed 16 January 1975, but the distribution, which alone determined the nature and extent of the heirs' claims, had not been carried out until after that judgment, jointly with that of the grandfather's estate.

22. The succession to Irma Vermeire née Van den Berghe took place on her death and the estate devolved on her 'legitimate' heirs as of that date.

The estate was undoubtedly not wound up until after 13 June 1979, but by reason of its declaratory nature the distribution had effect as from the date of death, that is to say, 16 January 1975.

What is at issue here is therefore a legal situation antedating the delivery of the *Marckx* judgment. There is no reason to reopen it.

B. The grandfather's estate

23. With reference to her grandfather's estate, the applicant alleged that it was for the Belgian authorities to ensure that it was distributed in a manner consistent with Articles 8 and 14 as interpreted by the European Court in the *Marckx* judgment. In her opinion they could have performed their obligation either by direct application of those Articles or by amending the legislation, retrospectively if need be.

24. The Government stated that it did not dispute the principles which followed from the *Marckx* judgment; it considered, however, that these principles compelled the Belgian State to carry out a thorough revision of the legal status of children born out of wedlock. Responsibility for this fell exclusively on the legislative power as the only body in a position to make full use of the freedom left to the State to choose the means to be utilised in its domestic legal system for fulfilling its undertaking under Article 53 [now Article 46(1)]. Articles 8 and 14 were not sufficiently precise and comprehensive on the points at issue in this case, and were thus not suitable for direct application by the domestic courts.

The Government further maintained that the legislature could not be criticised for any want of diligence. A first draft reform had been introduced on 15 February 1978. That it had taken over nine years to complete the task could be explained both by the acknowledged complexity of the issue and by Parliament's foresight. Rather than partial, fragmentary alterations, Parliament had preferred an overall and systematic revision, extending, *inter alia*, to the delicate question of the status of children born in adultery. It had also pondered long over the temporal extent to be given to the new provisions; in the end concern for the legal certainty to be preserved in the interests of families, third parties and the state, together with the fear that a large number of lawsuits would follow, had induced it not to give the Act of 31 March 1987 any retrospective effect.

25. The *Marckx* judgment held that the total lack of inheritance rights on intestacy, based only on the 'illegitimate' nature of the affiliation, was discriminatory.

This finding related to facts which were so close to those of the instant case that it applies equally to the succession in issue, which took place after its delivery.

It cannot be seen what could have prevented the Brussels Court of Appeal and the Court of Cassation from complying with the findings of the *Marckx* judgment, as the Court of First Instance had done. There was nothing imprecise or incomplete about the rule which prohibited discrimination against Astrid Vermeire compared with her cousins Francine and Michel, on the grounds of the 'illegitimate' nature of the kinship between her and the deceased.

26. An overall revision of the legislation, with the aim of carrying out a thoroughgoing and consistent amendment of the whole of the law on affiliation and inheritance on intestacy, was not necessary at all as an essential preliminary to compliance with the Convention as interpreted by the Court in the *Marckx* case.

The freedom of choice allowed to a State as to the means of fulfilling its obligation under Article 53 [now Article 46(1)] cannot allow it to suspend the application of the Convention while waiting for such a reform to be completed, to the extent of compelling the Court to reject in 1991, with respect to a succession which took effect on 22 July 1980, complaints identical to those which it upheld on 13 June 1979.

27. In a case similar to the present one, from the point of view of Articles 6 and 6*bis* of the Belgian Constitution according to which all Belgians are equal before the law and must be able to enjoy their rights and freedoms without discrimination, the Belgian Court of Arbitration, relying in particular on the *Marckx* judgment, held that 'the old Article 756 of the Civil Code, preserved in force by virtue of section 107 of the Act of 31 March 1987, breach[ed] Articles 6 and 6*bis* [aforesaid] in so far as it appli[ed] to successions taking place from 13 June 1979 on'.[44]

28. Similarly, it should be found that the applicant's exclusion from the estate of her grandfather Camiel Vermeire violated Article 14 in conjunction with Article 8 of the Convention. . . .

It will be evident from *Vermeire* that, in general, no retrospective remedial action is required, but a state which has been found by the Court to have breached its Convention obligations as a result of national legislation is at risk of committing similar breaches of the Convention until remedial legislation has been enacted. As can be seen from the next Section, this risk is reduced in states in which direct effect is given to the Convention rights, since the national courts may then be able to provide adequate protection for those rights.

Nonetheless, there are innumerable instances in which a decision by the Court that a breach of rights has occurred leads directly to remedial action being taken, often in the form of legislation to change the law so that a similar breach does not recur. To give but one example, the Court's decision in *Benthem v. The Netherlands*[45] that the Dutch system of administrative appeals to the Crown was in breach of Article 6(1) led

---

[44] 18/91 of 4 July 1991, *Verryt v. Van Calster* [1991] M.B. 18144, 18149 and 18153.

[45] 23 Oct. 1985 (No. 97), 8 E.H.R.R. 1. *See* note by N. Verheij, [1990] *Public Law* 23. *Benthem* was 'one of the most disturbing decisions of the European Court for the Dutch legal order': Y. Klerk and E.J. de Jonge, 'The Netherlands' C. Gearty (ed.) *European Civil Liberties and the ECHR* (1997), 105, 131. This informative work assesses the impact of Strasbourg decisions on the laws of France, Germany, Ireland, Italy, Netherlands, Sweden, and the United Kingdom.

to significant structural changes in the system. Similarly, decisions of the Court have been the cause of very many legislative changes in the United Kingdom.[46]

C. INCORPORATION OF THE CONVENTION—
THE PRACTICE OF STATES

As we have seen from decisions such as *Ireland v. United Kingdom*,[47] the Court does not require states to give direct effect to the Convention within national law: it is not a breach of the Convention that national courts may not directly enforce the Convention rights. In fact, in some states the Convention may, as a treaty that has been concluded in accordance with national law, be capable of having domestic effect and may be applied by national courts. In other states, the Convention may have no direct effect in national law in the absence of legislation that expressly 'incorporates' it in the national legal system.

In this respect, the Convention is in a weaker position than the European Community treaties, which require the courts in *all* member states to be able uniformly to protect the individual's Community rights, even if this means overriding or disapplying provisions of national law.[48]

Because the Convention does not call for a particular solution to this question, there is wide variation in the extent to which states have given effect to the Convention within national law.[49] This variation largely reflects different provisions and traditions in national law relating to the power of the executive to enter into treaties and to the relationship between international and national law. In some countries, the legal tradition is inclined towards 'monism', which seeks to minimise the divergence between international and national law. In others, the tradition favours 'dualism', which maintains a strict distinction between national and international law. It is not necessary to summarize those different traditions here,[50] but some examples of differing national practice may be given.

In *Austria*, which has gone furthest in incorporating the Convention, it has been

---

[46] *See* R. R. Churchill and J. R. Young, 'Compliance with Judgments of the European Court of Human Rights and Decisions of the Committee of Ministers: the Experience of the United Kingdom 1975–1987' [1991] B.Y.I.L. 283, and Gearty, n. 45 *supra*.

[47] *See supra* n. 5.

[48] *See e.g. R. v. Secretary of State for Transport, ex parte Factortame Ltd. (No. 2)* Case C-213/89, [1991] 1 A.C. 603.

[49] *See* A. Drzemczewski, *European Human Rights Convention in Domestic Law* (1983): G. Ress, 'The Effects of Judgments and Decisions in Domestic Law', in R. St. J. Macdonald, F. Matscher and H. Petzold. (ed.) *The European System for the Protection of Human Rights* (1993), pp. 801–51; and Gearty, *supra* n. 45. The material which appears in this Section is largely drawn from these sources.

[50] *See* F. G. Jacobs and S. Roberts (eds.), *The Effect of Treaties in Domestic Law* (1987) examining the position in (inter alia) Belgium, Denmark, France, Germany, Italy, the Netherlands and the United Kingdom. Jacobs emphasizes (p. xxiv) that the reality is always more complex than a simple contrast between the extreme models of monism and dualism.

given the status of a provision of the national constitution; as such, it prevails over conflicting rules of national law of whatever date; and the Austrian Constitutional Court has been prepared to apply decisions by the Strasbourg Court interpreting the Convention.

In *Belgium, France, the Netherlands* and *Switzerland*, the directly applicable provisions of the Convention (without being incorporated in the national constitution) have direct effect in national law and may prevail over inconsistent provisions in national legislation of whatever date; to this extent the Convention has a greater effect than ordinary legislation, since the general rule is that in the event of conflict between two provisions of the same rank in the hierarchy of norms, the later in time prevails (*lex posterior derogat lege priori*).

In Belgium, the Convention has benefited from an influential decision of the Cour de Cassation in 1971 holding, in a case involving European Community law, that the directly applicable provisions of *all* treaties prevail over conflicting provisions of national legislation, regardless of whether that legislation was enacted before or after the ratification of the treaty.[51] In France, decisions of similar significance were made by the Cour de Cassation in 1975 and by the Conseil d'Etat in 1989,[52] applying Article 55 of the French Constitution of 1958 whereby treaties that have been signed, ratified and published take precedence over French statutes of whatever date. In the Netherlands, a similar constitutional provision has led to an increasing tendency on the part of national judges to give direct effect to the Convention, since national legislation may be reviewed for incompatibility with fundamental rights guaranteed by treaties such as the Convention, although judicial review of legislation on constitutional grounds is excluded by the Dutch constitution.[53] The Swiss courts have frequently given effect to the Strasbourg Court's case law since Swiss ratification of the Convention in 1974.

In *Germany* and *Italy*, the directly applicable provisions of the Convention have broadly the force of ordinary legislation, i.e. in principle they prevail over legislation enacted earlier than the date on which the Convention came into effect in national law, but legislation enacted after that date may prevail over provisions of the Convention. In Germany, the courts attribute greater weight to the authority of the Convention than this statement of the formal position would suggest,[54] although the impact of the Convention is reduced by the high level of human rights protection afforded by

---

51   *SA fromagerie franco-suisse 'Le Ski'*, Pas. Bel. (27 May 1971) 1. 886; in English translation at [1972] CMLR 330.

52   *See* respectively *Administration des Douanes c. Sociéié J. Vabre*, (24 May 1975) D. 1975 497, concl. Touffait; and *Nicolo* (20 October 1989), Rec., p. 190. For the application of the Convention by the Conseil d'Etat, see R. Errera in [1991] *Public Law* 134 and 458; and [1992] *Public Law* 343 and 653. And see E. Steiner, 'France' in C. Gearty, *supra* n., chap. 7.

53   Y. Klerk and E.J. de Jonge, in Gearty, *supra* n. 45, chap 3. The authors conclude that the Convention is now 'part and parcel of the Dutch legal order, not only in theory, but also in practice' (at 139).

54   In 1987 the Federal Constitutional Court in Germany held that in principle the Convention prevails over subsequent legislation unless the contrary will of the legislature is clearly established; and that the Basic Law is to be interpreted in the light of the Convention: Ress, *supra* n. 49, 831–6.

the German constitution.[55] In Italy, while it has been commented that the courts seldom enforce Convention rights directly,[56] the Convention has a significant influence in the interpretation of all legislation whenever enacted; it has been held to have what is termed a 'special legal force' (*forza di resistenza*) that enables it to prevail by process of interpretation over both earlier and later statutes that are inconsistent with it.[57]

In *Ireland* and the *United Kingdom*, where the legal systems share a common law background that favours a dualist approach to treaties, the Convention can have direct effect within national law only so far as this is brought about by legislation. In the next section, we examine the United Kingdom's Human Rights Act 1998. In Ireland, where the Constitution provides for the judicial protection of fundamental rights, no legislation to incorporate the Convention has been enacted; in deciding constitutional issues that involve fundamental rights, the Irish courts may consider Strasbourg decisions alongside decisions of national courts.[58] It was formerly the position in the Scandinavian countries that the Convention did not have effect in national law, but incorporating legislation has now been enacted in Denmark (taking effect on 1 July 1992), Iceland (30 May 1994), Sweden (1 January 1995)[59] and Norway (21 May 1999).

The effect of a dualist approach is that a national court may reject an individual's claim against a public authority as unfounded, even though Convention rights may well have been breached,[60] Such a failure in national courts may be a strong indicator of a different outcome once it is possible, as it always will be in the Strasbourg Court, for the Convention arguments to be in the forefront of the case. The awkwardness of this position was particularly acute in the United Kingdom, where the unwritten constitution gave no formal protection for fundamental rights, nor permitted judicial review of primary legislation.

D. THE EFFECT OF THE CONVENTION IN THE LAW OF THE UNITED KINGDOM

The United Kingdom government has full power under the royal prerogative to enter into international treaties and exercised this power in ratifying the Convention. However, without the authority of an Act of Parliament, a treaty may not alter the law of the United Kingdom. Except to the extent that a treaty is incorporated into national

---

[55] E. Voss, 'Germany' in Gearty, *supra* n. 45, chap 4, at 158.

[56] Ress, *supra* n. 49, 845–6.

[57] D.A. Leonardi, 'Italy' in Gearty, *supra* n. 45 chap 8, at 320–3, citing the decision in *re Medrano*, 12 May 1993 [1994] *Cassazione penale* 439.

[58] *See* L. Flynn, 'Ireland' in Gearty, *supra* n. 45, chap. 5.

[59] *See* I. Cameron, 'Protection of Constitutional Rights in Sweden' [1997] *Public Law* 488; and 'Sweden' in Gearty, *supra* n. 45, chap. 6.

[60] *See* e.g. the cases cited in n. 65 *infra* relating to the exclusion of homosexuals from the United Kingdom armed forces.

law by statute, the courts have no power to enforce treaty rights and obligations.[61] Although the United Kingdom was the first state to ratify the Convention in 1951, it was the policy of successive governments until 1997 that it was unnecessary to incorporate the Convention into national law. This policy was based on two assumptions: (a) that although the United Kingdom lacked formal machinery for protecting human rights, in substance the Convention rights were observed in national law and practice; (b) that if the Strasbourg Court should hold that Convention rights had been violated in the United Kingdom, the government would comply with the judgment and, if necessary, ensure that legislation was enacted to achieve specific compliance.

Although national courts did not give direct effect to the Convention, they could in some circumstances take it into account. Thus the courts observed a principle of interpretation that, if legislation was ambiguous, the court should adopt the meaning that was consistent with the Convention, rather than a meaning that was not. This principle, at its strongest where the legislation had been enacted to give effect to a Convention obligation, was summarized in these words:

it is a principle of construction of United Kingdom statutes, now too well established to call for citation of authority, that the words of a statute passed after the treaty has been signed and dealing with the subject matter of the international obligation of the United Kingdom, are to be construed, if they are reasonably capable of bearing such a meaning, as intended to carry out the obligation and not to be inconsistent with it.[62]

Further, if a point of the common law was not settled, the courts could take the Convention into account as an aid to the process of developing the law and resolving uncertainties.[63] Although it was argued that all officials ought to be aware of the state's international obligations in taking discretionary decisions which affected individuals, the courts did not accept that this was the case in the absence of legislation to give domestic effect to the Convention; nor that an executive power was limited by the need to ensure that Convention rights were not breached.[64] However, by development in administrative law, the courts came to accept that where an executive power directly affected a person's fundamental rights, such as the right to life or the right not to be tortured, the court must take that into account in deciding whether a challenge to a discretionary decision should succeed. The new position was summarized in this way:

The court may not interfere with the exercise of an administrative discretion on substantive grounds save where the court is satisfied that the decision is unreasonable in the sense that it is beyond the range of responses open to a reasonable decision-maker. But in judging whether the

[61] *Rayner (Mincing Lane) Ltd v. Department of Trade* [1990] 2 A.C. 418, 577.

[62] *Garland v. British Rail Engineering Ltd.* [1983] A.C. 751, 771 (Lord Diplock). In various forms, this approach is found in other legal systems—see Jacobs and Roberts, *supra* n., 50 at 33 (Denmark), 60 (France), 69 (Germany), 100 (Italy) and 160 (U.S.A.).

[63] For analysis of the circumstances in which English courts could apply the Convention before it was incorporated into national law, see M. Hunt, *Using Human Rights Law in English Courts* (1997).

[64] On both these points, see *R. v. Secretary of State for the Home Department, ex parte Brind*, Section D. 2 *infra.*

decision-maker has exceeded this margin of appreciation the human rights context is important. The more substantial the interference with human rights, the more the court will require by way of justification before it is satisfied that the decision is reasonable in the sense outlined above.[65]

Initially, Scottish courts took an outright dualist view that, absent incorporating legislation, the Convention could not be relied on for any purpose in Scots law, but in 1996 the Court of Session abandoned this position and held that Scottish judges should adopt the same approach as the English courts.[66]

In this section, two cases, *Malone* and *ex parte Brind*, illustrate the position before the Convention had effect within United Kingdom law. There follows material outlining the government's reasons for its decision in 1997 to introduce legislation giving effect to the Convention in national law, and the section concludes with brief comment on the Human Rights Act 1998.[67]

1. MALONE V. METROPOLITAN POLICE COMMISSIONER

[1979] Ch. 344

[In 1978 a London antique dealer, Malone, who had been tried and acquitted on charges of dishonesty, sought a declaration from the High Court that the police had no lawful authority to tap his phone. As part of his case, Malone relied on the decision of the European Court in *Klass v. Germany*.[68] He claimed that in the absence of legislation to authorize and control the tapping of telephones, tapping his phone had infringed his right to privacy under Article 8 of the Convention. The judge (Megarry V.C.) gave a full account of the decision in *Klass v. Germany*, emphasizing the safeguards in the system of surveillance then operating in West Germany:]

I have devoted some space to setting out a summary of the *Klass* decision because counsel for the plaintiff placed so much weight on it, and because of the background that it provides for the present case. The main thrust of his argument . . . was that although a treaty forms no part of the law of this country, it might nevertheless have some effect in English law. In this case, he said, the Convention, as construed in the *Klass* case, could and should have a significant effect in determining what the law was on a point which, like this, was devoid of any direct authority. On this he put before me a number of recent authorities in the Court of Appeal.

[The judge reviewed those authorities and continued:]

It is not for me, sitting at first instance, to resolve the variant shades of meaning in the dicta, and I do not attempt to do so. For the present, all that I say is that I take note of the Convention, as construed in the *Klass* case, and I shall give it due consideration in discussing English law on the

---

[65] This was approved in *R. v. Ministry of Defence, ex parte Smith* [1996] Q.B. 517; although the Court of Appeal upheld the policy of excluding homosexuals from the armed forces, the policy was held at Strasbourg to breach Art. 8: *Lustig-Prean and Beckett v. United Kingdom* Judgment of 27 Sept. 1999 (not yet reported).

[66] See *Kaur v. Lord Advocate* [1980] 3 C.M.L.R. 79 and *Moore v. Secretary of State for Scotland* 1985 S.L.T. 38 (discussed by J.L. Murdoch 'The European Convention on Human Rights in Scots Law' [1991] *Public Law* 40) and *T Petitioner* (1996) S.C.L.R. 897.

[67] For which, see Appendix C.

[68] See supra n. 17.

point. As for the direct right which the Convention confers, it seems to me to be plain that this is a direct right in relation to the European Commission of Human Rights and the European Court of Human Rights, the bodies established by the Convention, but not in relation to the courts of this country. The Convention is plainly not of itself law in this country, however much it may fall to be considered as indicating what the law of this country should be, or should be construed as being.

> [Citing Article 1 of the Convention, the judge said that the obligation which this created was not justiciable in British courts: the Convention 'does not, as a matter of English law, confer any direct rights on the plaintiff that he can enforce in the English courts'.[69] He compared the position in England where telephone tapping was unregulated by law with the Court's decision in *Klass v. Germany* and concluded that 'adequate and effective safeguards against abuse' were lacking.]

I therefore find it impossible to see how English law could be said to satisfy the requirements of the Convention, as interpreted in the *Klass* case, unless that law not only prohibited all telephone tapping save in suitably limited classes of case, but also laid down detailed restrictions on the exercise of the power in those limited classes. It may perhaps be that the common law is sufficiently fertile to achieve what is required by the first limb of this; possible ways of expressing such a rule may be seen in what I have already said. But I see the greatest difficulty in the common law framing the safeguards required by the second limb. Various institutions or offices would have to be brought into being to exercise various defined functions. The more complex and indefinite the subject-matter, the greater the difficulty in the court doing what it is really appropriate, and only appropriate, for the legislature to do. . . .

It appears to me that to decide this case in the way that counsel for the plaintiff seeks would carry me far beyond any possible function of the Convention as influencing English law that has ever been suggested; and it would be most undesirable. Any regulation of so complex a matter as telephone tapping is essentially a matter for Parliament, not the courts; and neither the Convention nor the *Klass* case can, I think, play any proper part in deciding the issue before me. Accordingly, the second limb of counsel's second main contention for the plaintiff also fails.

I would only add that, even if it was not clear before, this case seems to me to make it plain that telephone tapping is a subject which cries out for legislation. . . .

Notwithstanding this decision, the British government refused to introduce legislation on telephone-tapping. Malone took the matter to Strasbourg and the Court upheld Malone's claim that his rights under Article 8 had been breached.[70] It was only after this that the Interception of Communications Act 1985 gave telephone-tapping a firm basis in United Kingdom law and laid down certain restrictions and remedies in respect of allegations of unlawful tapping. Even so, it is not certain that the system of control set up by the 1985 Act meets all the requirements of the Convention.[71] The scope of the 1985 Act was confined to regulating telephone-tapping, and the Act did not create a right to privacy in national law. Legislation on a specific topic such as telephone-tapping did not, of course, affect the legal status of the Convention in national law. There continued to be pressure from litigants upon British courts to go

---

[69] [1979] Ch. 344, 378.
[70] *Malone v. United Kingdom*, 2 Aug. 1984 (No 82), 7 E.H.R.R. 14.
[71] *See* R. R. Churchill and J. R. Young, *supra* n. 46 at 321–6.

further in protecting the rights guaranteed by the Convention, especially by extending the grounds on which executive decisions were subject to judicial review.

2. R. *V.* SECRETARY OF STATE FOR THE HOME DEPARTMENT
ex parte BRIND

[1991] 1 A.C. 696

[The Home Secretary, responsible for regulating broadcasting, issued directives to the broadcasting authorities in Britain under the Broadcasting Act 1981 imposing a ban on the direct transmission of the spoken words of representatives or supporters of proscribed terrorist organizations in Northern Ireland. A news reporter challenged the ban, claiming, *inter alia*, that the directives violated Article 10 of the Convention and that the Home Secretary's powers under the 1981 Act were limited by his duty to observe Article 10:]

Lord Bridge of Harwich My Lords, this appeal has been argued primarily on the basis that the power of the Secretary of State . . . to impose restrictions on the matters which the Independent Broadcasting Authority (the IBA) and the BBC respectively may broadcast may only be lawfully exercised in accordance with Art. 10 of the European Convention on Human Rights. Any exercise by the Secretary of State of the power in question necessarily imposes some restriction on freedom of expression. The obligations of the United Kingdom, as a party to the Convention, are to secure to every one within its jurisdiction the rights which the Convention defines, including both the right to freedom of expression under art. 10 and the right under art. 13 to 'an effective remedy before a national authority' for any violation of the other rights secured by the Convention. It is accepted, of course, by the appellants that, like any other treaty obligations which have not been embodied in the law by statute, the Convention is not part of the domestic law, that the courts accordingly have no power to enforce Convention rights directly and that, if domestic legislation conflicts with the Convention, the courts must nevertheless enforce it. But it is already well settled that, in construing any provision in domestic legislation which is ambiguous in the sense that it is capable of a meaning which either conforms to or conflicts with the Convention, the courts will presume that Parliament intended to legislate in conformity with the Convention, not in conflict with it. Hence, it is submitted, when a statute confers upon an administrative authority a discretion capable of being exercised in a way which infringes any basic human right protected by the Convention, it may similarly be presumed that the legislative intention was that the discretion should be exercised within the limitations which the Convention imposes. I confess that I found considerable persuasive force in this submission. But in the end I have been convinced that the logic of it is flawed. When confronted with a simple choice between two possible interpretations of some specific statutory provision, the presumption whereby the courts prefer that which avoids conflict between our domestic legislation and our international treaty obligations is a mere canon of construction which involves no importation of international law into the domestic field. But where Parliament has conferred on the executive an administrative discretion without indicating the precise limits within which it must be exercised, to presume that it must be exercised within Convention limits would be to go far beyond the resolution of an ambiguity. It would be to impute to Parliament an intention not only that the executive should exercise the discretion in conformity with the Convention, but also that the domestic courts should enforce that conformity by the importation into domestic administrative law of the text of the Convention and the jurisprudence of the European Court of Human Rights in the interpretation and application of it. If such a presumption is to apply to the statutory discretion exercised by the Secretary of State under s. 29(3) of the 1981 Act in the instant case, it must also apply to any other statutory discretion exercised by the executive which is capable of involving an infringement of Convention rights. When Parliament has been content for so long to leave those who complain that their Convention rights have been infringed to seek their remedy in Strasbourg, it would be surprising suddenly to find that the judiciary had, without Parliament's aid, the means to incorporate the Convention into such an important area of domestic law and I cannot escape the conclusion that this would be a judicial usurpation of the legislative function.

But I do not accept that this conclusion means that the courts are powerless to prevent the exercise by the executive of administrative discretions, even when conferred, as in the instant case, in terms which are on their face unlimited, in a way which infringes fundamental human rights. Most of the rights spelled out in terms in the Convention, including the right to freedom of expression, are less than absolute and must in some cases yield to the claims of competing public interests.

[In deciding whether the Secretary of State, in the exercise of his discretion, could reasonably impose the restriction he has imposed on the broadcasting organizations, the judges are entitled]

. . . [T]o start from the premise that any restriction of the right to freedom of expression requires to be justified and that nothing less than an important competing public interest will be sufficient to justify it. The primary judgment as to whether the particular competing public interest justifies the particular restriction imposed falls to be made by the Secretary of State to whom Parliament has entrusted the discretion. But we are entitled to exercise a secondary judgment by asking whether a reasonable Secretary of State, on the material before him, could reasonably make that primary judgment.

Applying these principles to the circumstances of the case, . . . I find it impossible to say that the Secretary of State exceeded the limits of his discretion. In any civilized and law-abiding society the defeat of the terrorist is a public interest of the first importance. That some restriction on the freedom of the terrorist and his supporters to propagate his cause may well be justified in support of that public interest is a proposition which I apprehend the appellants hardly dispute . . . . The Secretary of State, for the reasons he made so clear in Parliament, decided that it was necessary to deny to the terrorist and his supporters the opportunity to speak directly to the public through the most influential of all the media of communication and that this justified some interference with editorial freedom. I do not see how this judgment can be categorized as unreasonable. . . .

Lord Ackner [having summarized the provisions of the Broadcasting Act under which the Home Secretary had imposed the restrictions on the broadcasting authorities, dealt with the argument that the Home Secretary had failed to have proper regard for Article 10 of the Convention:]

[Counsel for the appellant] claims that the Secretary of State before issuing his directives should have considered not only the Convention (it is accepted that he in fact did so) but that he should have properly construed it and correctly taken it into consideration. It was therefore a relevant, indeed a vital, factor to which he was obliged to have proper regard pursuant to the *Wednesbury* doctrine[72] with the result that his failure to do so rendered his decision unlawful. The fallacy of this submission is however plain. If the Secretary of State was obliged to have proper regard to the Convention, i.e. to conform with art. 10, this inevitably would result in incorporating the

---

[72] For what is meant by this, see the introductory material to this section (D) *supra*.

Convention into English domestic law by the back door. It would oblige the courts to police the operation of the Convention and to ask itself in each case, where there was a challenge, whether the restrictions were 'necessary in a democratic society . . . ' applying the principles enunciated in the decisions of the European Court of Human Rights. The treaty, not having been incorporated in English law, cannot be a source of rights and obligations and the question—did the Secretary of State act in breach of art. 10?—does not therefore arise. . . .

Lords Roskill, Templeman and Lowry gave concurring judgments. As well as rejecting the challenge based on the *Wednesbury* doctrine of unreasonableness, the judges rejected the appellant's argument that, because freedom of expression under Article 10(1) was limited by the decision, the Home Secretary ought to have applied the test of proportionality that would be applied by the Strasbourg Court in considering whether a restriction on that freedom was justifiable under Article 10(2)[73]

In *Derbyshire County Council v. Times Newspapers Ltd*,[74] a local authority sued a Sunday newspaper claiming damages in defamation in respect of articles which alleged that the authority had managed investments for its superannuation fund improperly. The action raised an important issue in the common law of defamation, namely whether a local council had the right to sue a newspaper for defamation of character. The Court of Appeal held that, as the common law on the issue was uncertain, it was appropriate to take into account Article 10 of the Convention and decisions such as *Lingens v. Austria*;[75] the court applied the 'balancing exercise' required by Article 10, and concluded that there was no pressing social need for a public authority to have the right to sue in defamation to protect its reputation. On appeal to the House of Lords, giving the sole reasoned speech, Lord Keith dealt with the issue primarily as a matter of common law:

> The conclusion must be, in my opinion, that under the common law of England a local author-ity does not have the right to maintain an action of damages for defamation. That was the conclusion reached by the Court of Appeal, which did so principally by reference to art. 10 of the European Convention on Human Rights . . . to which the United Kingdom has adhered but which has not been enacted into domestic law.

[Having summarized the manner in which the Court of Appeal had applied the case law of the Strasbourg Court, Lord Keith concluded his speech in this way:]

> My Lords, I have reached my conclusion upon the common law of England without finding any need to rely upon the European Convention. Lord Goff of Chieveley in *AG v. Guardian Newspapers Ltd (No. 2)*[76] expressed the opinion that in the field of freedom of speech there was no difference in principle between English law on the subject and art. 10 of the Conven-tion. I agree, and can only add that I find it satisfactory to be able to conclude that the common law of England is consistent with the obligations assumed by the Crown under the treaty in this particular field.
>   For these reasons I would dismiss the appeal. . . .

---

[73] Brind's subsequent challenge at Strasbourg to the restriction on live broadcasting by terrorist representa-tives was rejected by the Commission: *Brind v. United Kingdom*, Application No 18714/91 (1994) 77–A DR 42.
[74] [1993] A.C. 534.
[75] 8 July 1986 (No. 103), 8 E.H.R.R. 407 reprinted at Chapter 5 (C)(1)(A) *supra*.
[76] [1990] 1 A.C. 109 at 283–84.

Although the outcome of the substantive dispute in this case was consistent with the Convention, the stance of the House of Lords in developing the common law on an important issue of freedom of expression without acknowledging the relevance of decisions by the Strasbourg Court under Article 10 was unsatisfactory. It is difficult to accept that the judges were not influenced by the Strasbourg decisions, even if they denied this. Certainly the fact that they could not give direct effect to Convention rights in national law imposed a serious restriction on their decision-making, that continued to be felt even while senior British judges were developing a greater awareness of the Convention.[77]

The legislative sovereignty of the British Parliament has been considered by some to present a serious and possibly insuperable obstacle to incorporation of the Convention,[78] at least in the sense of 'entrenching' the Convention as a text that would bind the future power of Parliament. But as we have seen, the Convention does not require that states give it this status in national law.

During the 1980s and early 1990s, several Bills seeking to give effect to the Convention in domestic law succeeded in the House of Lords, but all such attempts failed to become law.[79] At the general election in May 1997, the joint constitutional programme of the Labour and Liberal Democrat parties included a commitment to incorporating the Convention in national law. In October 1997, the United Kingdom government published a White Paper outlining from a British perspective the reasons for giving legal effect to the Convention and explaining the proposed Human Rights Bill. Some of these reasons are more persuasive than others.

3. LEGAL EFFECT FOR THE CONVENTION IN UNITED KINGDOM LAW

A. RIGHTS BROUGHT HOME: THE HUMAN RIGHTS BILL

(Cm 3782, 1997)

Relationship to current law in the United Kingdom

1.11 When the United Kingdom ratified the Convention the view was taken that the rights and freedoms which the Convention guarantees were already, in substance, fully protected in British law. It was not considered necessary to write the Convention itself into British law, or to introduce

---

[77] For the views of two judges on the influence of the Convention, *see* Lord Browne-Wilkinson 'The Infiltration of a Bill of Rights' [1992] *Public Law* 397 and Sir John Laws 'Is the High Court the Guardian of Fundamental Constitutional Rights?' [1993] *Public Law* 59.

[78] *See e.g.* the Report of a Committee of the House of Lords on a Bill of Rights (H.L. 176, 1977–8). For the Committee's summary of the arguments for and against incorporation of the Convention in the form of a Bill of Rights, see the 1st edn. of this work at 460–5.

[79] The last of this line of Bills was approved by the House of Lords in 1995. For the government's opposition, see H. L. Debs., vol. 560, cols. 1163–70 (25 Jan. 1995). And *see* Lord Lester 'The Mouse that Roared: The Human Rights Bill 1995' [1995] *Public Law* 198.

any new laws in the United Kingdom in order to be sure of being able to comply with the Convention.

1.12 From the point of view of the *international* obligation which the United Kingdom was undertaking when it signed and ratified the Convention, this was understandable. Moreover, the European Court of Human Rights explicitly confirmed that it was not a necessary part of proper observance of the Convention that it should be incorporated into the laws of the States concerned.

1.13 However, since its drafting nearly 50 years ago, almost all the States which are party to the European Convention on Human Rights have gradually incorporated it into their domestic law in one way or another. . . .

The case for incorporation

1.14 The effect of non-incorporation on the British people is a very practical one. The rights, originally developed with major help from the United Kingdom Government, are no longer actually seen as British rights. And enforcing them takes too long and costs too much. It takes on average five years to get an action into the European Court of Human Rights once all domestic remedies have been exhausted; and it costs an average of £30,000. Bringing these rights home will mean that the British people will be able to argue for their rights in the British courts—without this inordinate delay and cost. It will also mean that the rights will be brought much more fully into the jurisprudence of the courts throughout the United Kingdom, and their interpretation will thus be far more subtly and powerfully woven into our law. And there will be another distinct benefit. British judges will be enabled to make a distinctively British contribution to the development of the jurisprudence of human rights in Europe.

1.15 Moreover, in the Government's view, the approach which the United Kingdom has so far adopted towards the Convention does not sufficiently reflect its importance and has not stood the test of time.

1.16 The most obvious proof of this lies in the number of cases in which the European Commission and Court have found that there have been violations of the Convention rights in the United Kingdom. The causes vary. The Government recognizes that interpretations of the rights guaranteed under the Convention have developed over the years, reflecting changes in society and attitudes. Sometimes United Kingdom laws have proved to be inherently at odds with the Convention rights. On other occasions, although the law has been satisfactory, something has been done which our courts have held to be lawful by United Kingdom standards but which breaches the Convention. In other cases again, there has simply been no framework within which the compatibility with the Convention rights of an executive act or decision can be tested in the British courts:. . . . It is plainly unsatisfactory that someone should be the victim of a breach of the Convention standards by the State yet cannot bring any case at all in the British courts, simply because British law does not recognise the right in the same terms as one contained in the Convention.

1.17 For individuals, and for those advising them, the road to Strasbourg is long and hard. Even when they get there, the Convention enforcement machinery is subject to long delays. . . .

Bringing rights home

1.18 We therefore believe that the time has come to enable people to enforce their Convention rights against the State in the British courts, rather than having to incur the delays and expense which are involved in taking a case to the European Human Rights Commission and Court in

Strasbourg and which may altogether deter some people from pursuing their rights. Enabling courts in the United Kingdom to rule on the application of the Convention will also help to influence the development of case law on the Convention by the European Court of Human Rights on the basis of familiarity with our laws and customs and of sensitivity to practices and procedures in the United Kingdom. . . . Enabling the Convention rights to be judged by British courts will also lead to closer scrutiny of the human rights implications of new legislation and new policies. If legislation is enacted which is incompatible with the Convention, a ruling by the domestic courts to that effect will be much more direct and immediate than a ruling from the European Court of Human Rights. The Government of the day, and Parliament, will want to minimise the risk of that happening.

1.19 Our aim is a straightforward one. It is to make more directly accessible the rights which the British people already enjoy under the Convention. In other words, to bring those rights home.

[The document proceeds to explain the choices made by the government in structuring the Bill.]

A new requirement on public authorities

2.2 Although the United Kingdom has an international obligation to comply with the Convention, there at present is no requirement in our domestic law on central and local government, or others exercising similar executive powers, to exercise those powers in a way which is compatible with the Convention. This Bill will change that by making it unlawful for public authorities to act in a way which is incompatible with the Convention rights. The definition of what constitutes a public authority is in wide terms. Examples of persons or organizations whose acts or omissions it is intended should be able to be challenged include central government (including executive agencies); local government; the police; immigration officers; prisons; courts and tribunals themselves; and, to the extent that they are exercising public functions, companies responsible for areas of activity which were previously within the public sector, such as the privatized utilities. The actions of Parliament, however, are excluded.

2.3 A person who is aggrieved by an act or omission on the part of a public authority which is incompatible with the Convention rights will be able to challenge the act or omission in the courts. The effects will be wide-ranging. They will extend both to legal actions which a public authority pursues against individuals (for example, where a criminal prosecution is brought or where an administrative decision is being enforced through legal proceedings) and to cases which individuals pursue against a public authority (for example, for judicial review of an executive decision). Convention points will normally be taken in the context of proceedings instituted against individuals or already open to them, but, if none is available, it will be possible for people to bring cases on Convention grounds alone. Individuals or organizations seeking judicial review of decisions by public authorities on Convention grounds will need to show that they have been directly affected, as they must if they take a case to Strasbourg.

2.4 It is our intention that people or organisations should be able to argue that their Convention rights have been infringed by a public authority in our courts at any level. This will enable the Convention rights to be applied from the outset against the facts and background of a particular case, and the people concerned to obtain their remedy at the earliest possible moment. . . . In considering Convention points, our courts will be required to take account of relevant decisions of the European Commission and Court of Human Rights (although these will not be binding).

2.5 The Convention is often described as a 'living instrument' because it is interpreted by the

European Court in the light of present day conditions and therefore reflects changing social attitudes and the changes in the circumstances of society. In future our judges will be able to contribute to this dynamic and evolving interpretation of the Convention. . . .

Remedies for a failure to comply with the Convention

2.6 A public authority which is found to have acted unlawfully by failing to comply with the Convention will not be exposed to criminal penalties. But the court or tribunal will be able to grant the injured person any remedy which is within its normal powers to grant and which it considers appropriate and just in the circumstances. . . . In some cases, the right course may be for the decision of the public authority in the particular case to be quashed. In other cases, the only appropriate remedy may be an award of damages. The Bill provides that, in considering an award of damages on Convention grounds, the courts are to take into account the principles applied by the European Court of Human Rights in awarding compensation. . . .

Interpretation of legislation

2.7 The Bill provides for legislation—both Acts of Parliament and secondary legislation—to be interpreted so far as possible so as to be compatible with the Convention. This goes far beyond the present rule which enables the courts to take the Convention into account in resolving any ambiguity in a legislative provision. The courts will be required to interpret legislation so as to uphold the Convention rights unless the legislation itself is so clearly incompatible with the Convention that it is impossible to do so.

2.8 This 'rule of construction' is to apply to past as well as to future legislation. To the extent that it affects the meaning of a legislative provision, the courts will not be bound by previous interpretations. They will be able to build a new body of case law, taking into account the Convention rights.

A declaration of incompatibility with the convention rights

2.9 If the courts decide in any case that it is impossible to interpret an Act of Parliament in a way which is compatible with the Convention, the Bill enables a formal declaration to be made that its provisions are incompatible with the Convention. A declaration of incompatibility will be an important statement to make, and the power to make it will be reserved to the higher courts. . . . The Government will have the right to intervene in any proceedings where such a declaration is a possible outcome. A decision by the High Court or Court of Appeal, determining whether or not such a declaration should be made, will itself be appealable.

Effect of court decisions on legislation

2.10 A declaration that legislation is incompatible with the Convention rights will not of itself have the effect of changing the law, which will continue to apply. But it will almost certainly prompt the Government and Parliament to change the law.

2.11 The Government has considered very carefully whether it would be right for the Bill to go further, and give to courts in the United Kingdom the power to set aside an Act of Parliament which they believe is incompatible with the Convention rights. In considering this question, we have looked at a number of models. The Canadian Charter of Rights and Freedoms 1982 enables the courts to strike down any legislation which is inconsistent with the Charter, unless the legislation contains an explicit statement that it is to apply 'notwithstanding' the provisions of the Charter. But legislation which has been struck down may be re-enacted with a 'notwithstanding' clause. In New Zealand, on the other hand . . . [the] New Zealand Bill of Rights Act 1990 is an 'interpretative' statute which requires past and future legislation to be interpreted consistently with the rights contained in the Act as far as possible but provides that legislation stands if that is impossible. In Hong Kong, a middle course was adopted. The Hong Kong Bill of Rights Ordinance 1991 distinguishes between legislation enacted before and after the Ordinance took effect: previous legislation is subordinated to the provisions of the Ordinance, but subsequent legislation takes precedence over it. . . .

2.13 The Government has reached the conclusion that courts should not have the power to set aside primary legislation, past or future, on the ground of incompatibility with the Convention. This conclusion arises from the importance which the Government attaches to Parliamentary sovereignty. In this context, Parliamentary sovereignty means that Parliament is competent to make any law on any matter of its choosing and no court may question the validity of any Act that it passes. In enacting legislation, Parliament is making decisions about important matters of public policy. The authority to make those decisions derives from a democratic mandate. Members of Parliament in the House of Commons possess such a mandate because they are elected, accountable and representative. To make provision in the Bill for the courts to set aside Acts of Parliament would confer on the judiciary a general power over the decisions of Parliament which under our present constitutional arrangements they do not possess, and would be likely on occasions to draw the judiciary into serious conflict with Parliament. There is no evidence to suggest that they desire this power, nor that the public wish them to have it. Certainly, this Government has no mandate for any such change.

2.14 It has been suggested that the courts should be able to uphold the rights in the Human Rights Bill in preference to any provisions of earlier legislation which are incompatible with those rights. This is on the basis that a later Act of Parliament takes precedence over an earlier Act if there is a conflict. But the Human Rights Bill is intended to provide a new basis for judicial interpretation of all legislation, not a basis for striking down any part of it.

2.15 The courts will, however, be able to strike down or set aside secondary legislation which is incompatible with the Convention, unless the terms of the parent statute make this impossible. The courts can already strike down or set aside secondary legislation when they consider it to be outside the powers conferred by the statute under which it is made, and it is right that they should be able to do so when it is incompatible with the Convention rights and could have been framed differently.

Entrenchment

2.16 On one view, human rights legislation is so important that it should be given added protection from subsequent amendment or repeal. . . . But an arrangement of this kind could not be reconciled with our own constitutional traditions, which allow any Act of Parliament to be amended or repealed by a subsequent Act of Parliament. We do not believe that it is necessary or would be desirable to attempt to devise such a special arrangement for this Bill.

Amending legislation

2.17 Although the Bill does not allow the courts to set aside Acts of Parliament, it will nevertheless have a profound impact on the way that legislation is interpreted and applied, and it will have the effect of putting the issues squarely to the Government and Parliament for further consideration. It is important to ensure that the Government and Parliament, for their part, can respond quickly . . .

2.18 The Bill provides for a fast-track procedure for changing legislation in response either to a declaration of incompatibility by our own higher courts or to a finding of a violation of the Convention in Strasbourg. The appropriate Government Minister will be able to amend the legislation by Order so as to make it compatible with the Convention. The Order will be subject to approval by both Houses of Parliament before taking effect, except where the need to amend the legislation is particularly urgent, when the Order will take effect immediately but will expire after a short period if not approved by Parliament. . . .

Scotland

2.20 In Scotland, the position with regard to Acts of the Westminster Parliament will be the same as in England and Wales. All courts will be required to interpret the legislation in a way which is compatible with the Convention so far as possible. If a provision is found to be incompatible with the Convention, the Court of Session or the High Court will be able to make a declarator to that effect, but this will not affect the validity or continuing operation of the provision.

2.21 The position will be different, however, in relation to Acts of the Scottish Parliament when it is established. The Government has decided that the Scottish Parliament will have no power to legislate in a way which is incompatible with the Convention; and similarly that the Scottish Executive will have no power to make subordinate legislation or to take executive action which is incompatible with the Convention. It will accordingly be possible to challenge such legislation and actions in the Scottish courts on the ground that the Scottish Parliament or Executive has incorrectly applied its powers. If the challenge is successful then the legislation or action would be held to be unlawful. . . .

The Human Rights Act 1998, which is based upon the reasoning set out above, received the Royal Assent on 9 November 1998. Extracts from the Act are in Appendix C. As we have already seen in section C, states may exercise a wide discretion in deciding how the Convention should have effect within national law and there is no prescribed method of 'incorporation' that must apply. The 1998 Act provides that the substantive Convention rights are 'to have effect for the purposes of this Act' (section 1(2)), not that they are to have full effect in national law so that they prevail in all legal circumstances.[80] The Act proceeds to set out the purposes for which Convention rights are to have effect, how they must be recognized and enforced by courts, tribunals and public authorities, and the methods by which those who may be victims of a breach of those rights can have the issue decided by national courts and secure relief. Specific aspects of the scheme have been criticized,[81] but the criticisms are of minor signifi-

---

[80] Thus the Human Rights Act does not go so far as the European Communities Act 1972 did in giving direct affect to rights under European Community law.

[81] See e.g. (1) the rule in s. 7(3) that only whose who may at Strasbourg claim to be victims of a breach of Convention right can rely on Convention rights in applying for judicial review; (2) the omission of Art 13 from the Convention rights directly protected by the Act; (3) the doubts raised by the Act as to the so-called 'horizontal effect' of Convention rights in relations between private persons; and (4) the government's decision against creating a Human Rights Commission with enforcement and educational tasks.

cance compared with the main features established by the Act. These are: (a) the duty of all those entrusted with public powers or exercising public functions to have regard to Convention rights in the interpretation and application of statutory powers (section 3); (b) the duty of courts and tribunals to take account of Strasbourg jurisprudence where this is relevant to issues raised in national courts (section 2); (c) the power of courts and tribunals to set aside delegated legislation, administrative policies and individual decisions for non-compliance with the Convention (implied by sections 3, 4 and 6); (d) the power of superior courts to declare provisions of primary legislation to be incompatible with the Convention (section 5); (e) the power of the government, where a declaration of incompatibility is made under (d), to amend the offending legislation by exercising new delegated powers (section 10); and (f) the provision of appropriate remedies, including a right to compensation, where Convention rights have been infringed (sections 7–9).

From the viewpoint of bringing national law into conformity with Convention rights, the Act indeed goes a long way, even though the policy that underlies it stresses the need to maintain the 'sovereignty' of the national legislature.[82] If the United Kingdom judges make energetic use of the new approach to statutory interpretation, it should rarely be necessary for the superior courts to issue a 'declaration of incompatibility'. In this and other respects, much depends on the response of the national judiciary.[83] Thus, one matter not expressly dealt with by the Act is the extent to which the courts may re-visit and if necessary re-state rules of common law where these are inconsistent with Convention rights. One possibility that the Act leaves open is that British courts, while taking into account Strasbourg case law, may set higher standards for national authorities in fulfilling Convention rights than those set at Strasbourg; for example, on the issue of whether Article 6(1) has been breached by unreasonable delays in justice, a delay that might not be excessive in comparison with many European states might yet be unacceptable when it is compared with good practice in the United Kingdom. So too, the reasoning by which the Strasbourg Court allows leeway to states by permitting a 'margin of appreciation'[84] seems inappropriate when a national court is reviewing executive conduct within its own legal system.

Whatever will result from the Act on such questions, the Act resolves the primary difficulties that arose from the situation in which the Convention had been ratified as a treaty by the state but not incorporated in national law.[85] However, similar difficulties will continue to arise with regard to other human rights treaties in the same situation, and these are outside the scope of the Human Rights Act.[86]

---

[82] See section 2.13 of 16 excerpted material supra.

[83] See as auguries of future decisions R. v. Director of Public Prosecutions, ex p Kebeline [1999] 4 All E.R. 801 and Starrs v. Procurator Fiscal, Linlithgow, (1999) 8 B.H.R.C. 1.

[84] See for a critique of the 'margin of appreciation' doctrine, T. H. Jones, 'The Devaluation of Human Rights under the European Convention' [1995] Public Law 430.

[85] Cf Minister for Immigration and Ethnic Affairs v. Teoh (1995) 128 A.L.R. 353, Aust High Ct.

[86] See e.g. R. v. Uxbridge Magistrates' Court, ex parte Adimi [1999] 4 All E.R. 520.

E. THE RELATION BETWEEN THE
CONVENTION AND COMMUNITY LAW

In this book, we have examined the significance of the Convention in international law, how the Convention is applied by the Strasbourg Court, how the Convention has developed as legal process since it came into effect in 1953, and also the relationship between the Convention and national legal systems in Europe. Over the same period of time, the countries of western Europe have co-operated in the scheme for economic integration that was initiated in 1957 when the European Economic Community with six members was created by the Treaty of Rome. Its subsequent development, expansion into other spheres and geographical enlargement have led to the present European Union of 15 states. This complex structure is founded on a system of law interpreted and applied by courts sitting in Luxembourg (the European Court of Justice and the Court of First Instance), that are quite separate from the European Court of Human Rights at Strasbourg.

Although it derives from a series of treaties, Community law depends for its efficacy on the fundamental rule that it has direct effect within the national laws of the member states. As the European Court of Justice has repeatedly held:

every national court must, in a case within its jurisdiction, apply Community law in its entirety and protect rights which the latter confers on individuals and must accordingly set aside any provision of national law which may conflict with it, whether prior or subsequent to the Community rule.[87]

Although the Treaty of Rome of 1957 sought to establish specific freedoms of an economic nature, such as the free movement of workers, no general reference to human or fundamental rights of the individual was made in the Treaty. It was formerly a matter of controversy whether such rights could be taken into account by the European Court of Justice in developing the general principles of Community law, or by national courts when they were applying Community law. One difficulty was that, as we have seen, the definition of fundamental rights in national constitutions differs from state to state; the primacy of Community law excluded the possibility of a differential application of Community rules according to national constitutions. Nor could the European Court of Justice choose one or two national constitutions as the model for a Community scheme of fundamental rights. There was, therefore, an advantage in taking the definition of human rights for Community purposes from a common, international source. And by 1974, the European Convention on Human Rights had been ratified by all Community states.

One factor that helped to propel growth within Community law of protection for fundamental rights was the opposition to development of Community law that came from states such as Germany and Italy in which such rights received a high degree of

---

[87] Case 106/77, *Amministrazione delle Finanze dello Stato v. Simmenthal* [1978] E.C.R. 629.

formal constitutional protection. Unless a way could be found of assuring protection for fundamental rights in Community law, the legitimacy of the exercise of powers by Community organs at Brussels was called into question, since the transfer of functions from national governments to the Community would mean that the exercise of those powers would no longer be limited by the need to protect fundamental rights.[88]

After initial hesitation, the European Court of Justice declared in 1969 that it would ensure respect for fundamental human rights in the context of the European Community.[89] Thereafter, in an important series of decisions, the Court went progressively further by declaring that in considering the fundamental rights to be protected, it would have regard not merely to common principles that emerged from the constitutional traditions of member states but also to human rights treaties, in particular the European Convention.[90] Without giving up the primacy and autonomy of Community law, the Court is now prepared if necessary to take into account the extent to which national constitutions protect particular rights and the effect of the Convention itself.[91] The duty to respect fundamental rights has been declared to apply not only to measures adopted by organs of the Community,[92] but also to action taken by national authorities whether in implementing Community law[93] or in derogating from freedoms protected by Community law.[94] But the Luxembourg Court has refused to intervene to protect fundamental rights in the case of national legislation that lies outside the scope of Community law.[95]

The European Court of Justice has thus created an unwritten charter of rights for the Community, by means of a series of judicial decisions and without waiting for a written charter of rights to emerge from the political process. The Court has been criticized for expanding its jurisdiction into areas that should be reserved for national courts. One risk that this dimension of Community law creates is the possibility of

[88] The German Constitutional Court at first refused to accept that Community law should prevail over national protection for human rights (the *Internationale Handelsgesellschaft Case* [1974] 2 C.M.L.R. 540), changing its position only when it had become clear that the European Court of Justice would protect human rights in ensuring the observance of general principles of law in interpretation and application of the European Treaties (the *Wilnsche Handelsgesellschaft Case* [1987] 3 C.M.L.R. 225).

[89] Case 29/69. *Stauder v. City of Ulm* [1969] E.C.R. 419.

[90] The cases are reviewed in T.C. Hartley, *The Foundations of European Community Law* (4th edn, 1998), chap. 5; and P. Craig and G. de Burca, *EU Law: Text, Cases and Materials* (2nd edn, 1998), chap. 7. *See also* M. Hunt, *Using Human Rights Law in English Courts* (1997), chap. 7; N. Grief, 'The Domestic Impact of the E.C.H.R. as mediated through Community Law' [1991] *Public Law* 555; and Ress, *supra* n. 49 at 849–51.

[91] Case 44/79, *Hauer v. Land Rheinland-Pfalz*, [1979] E.C.R. 3727 (review of restrictions on right of property under the Convention, First Protocol, Art. 1 and the German, Italian and Irish constitutions).

[92] As in the *Stauder, Internationale Handelsgesellschaft* and *Hauer* cases *supra*. *See* e.g. Case C–331/88, *R. v. Ministry of Agriculture, ex parte Fédération Europénne de la Santé Animale* [1991] 1 C.M.L.R. 507; Council Dir. 88/146/EEC could not authorize retrospective criminal proceedings in breach of Art 7, E.C.H.R.

[93] *See* e.g. *Johnston v. Chief Constable, Royal Constabulary* Case No. 222/84, [1986] E.C.R. 1651; para. 18 of the judgment notes that Arts. 6 and 13 E.C.H.R. embody a requirement of judicial control which is a 'general principle of law which underlies the constitutional traditions common to the member states'. *See also* Case 63/83, *R. v. Kent Kirk* [1984] E.C.R. 2689 and Case 5/88, *Wachauf v. Germany* [1989] E.C.R. 2609.

[94] Case C–260/89, *ERT case* [1991] E.C.R. 1–2925.

[95] *See* e.g. Case 12/86, *Demirel v. Stadt Schwäbisch Gmünd* [1987] E.C.R. 3719 (Turkish woman ordered to leave Germany).

divergent decisions being made by the Luxembourg and Strasbourg Courts. The danger is not merely that the two Courts take a different view of the same fundamental rights, although this has occurred,[96] but also that conflicts may develop between the two jurisdictions. In fact, so far as the acts of Community organs are concerned, an actual conflict is unlikely for the reason that the Community and its organs are not parties to the Convention and are thus outside Strasbourg's jurisdiction.[97] The position is different in respect of action by national authorities that may fall within the province of Community law, since action by those authorities is in principle subject to the Convention. Thus a national decision may be challenged for breach of fundamental rights before the Luxembourg Court and for breach of Convention rights before the Strasbourg Court, and may succeed in one and not in the other.[98] No way yet exists of preventing such conflicts, which scarcely make for legal certainty.

The development of this evolving relationship has not been solely the work of the European Court of Justice. On 5 April 1977, the European Parliament, Council and Commission adopted a joint declaration which stressed the importance that they attached to the protection of fundamental rights, derived in particular from national constitutions and the Convention. In 1989, the European Parliament issued a Declaration of Fundamental Rights and Freedoms, although this lacked the force of law.[99]

In 1992, by Article F(2) of the Treaty of Maastricht, which created the European Union, the 12 Community states resolved that the Union would respect fundamental rights, guaranteed by the Convention and by constitutional traditions common to the member states, as general principles of Community law. The Community's commitment to protecting fundamental rights was taken further by the Amsterdam Treaty of 1 October 1997, which confirmed the Maastricht provision by declaring that the European Union:

is founded on the principles of liberty, democracy, respect for human rights and fundamental freedoms, and the rule of law, principles which are common to the Member States.

Respect for human rights was stated to be a precondition for accession to the Community. The 1997 Treaty also extended the power of the European Court of Justice to supervise co-operative measures in the fields of justice and home affairs, and author-

---

[96] Thus in 1989 the E.C.J. held that Art. 8 E.C.H.R. did not protect business premises against an intrusive search in enforcement of competition law: Cases 46/87 & 227/88 *Hoechst v. Commission* [1989] E.C.R. 2859. The Strasbourg Court has held that Art. 8 is capable of protecting business premises: *Niemietz v. Germany*, 16 Dec. 1992 (No. 251B), 16 E.H.R.R. 97. For different approaches to the right not to incriminate oneself, see Case 374/87 *Orkem v. Commission* [1989] E.C.R. 3283 and *Funke v. France*, 25 Feb. 1993 (No. 256A), 16 E.H.R.R. 297.

[97] On 28 Mar. 1996, the European Court of Justice in *Opinion 2/94* [1996] E.C.R. I–1759 held that the Treaty of Rome would need to be amended by the Member States to enable the Community to accede to the Convention.

[98] See e.g. Case C–159/90, *Society for Protection of Unborn Children (Ireland) Ltd v. Grogan* [1991] E.C.R. I–4685 (E.C.J.) and *Open Door Counselling and Dublin Woman v. Ireland*, 29 Oct. 1992 (No. 246), 15 E.H.R.R. 244.

[99] [1989] OJ C120/51; EC Bull. 4/1989.

ized the imposition of sanctions upon states that seriously and persistently violate fundamental rights. These new provisions did not, however, settle comprehensively the position of fundamental rights within the European Union. In June 1999, the meeting of the European Council at Cologne initiated a process designed to lead to the adoption of a European Union Charter to consolidate fundamental rights at the level of the Union. This Charter was to contain a statement of fundamental rights and freedoms as well as the rights guaranteed by the European Convention on Human Rights and derived from the constitutional traditions common to Member States and already enjoyed as general principles of Community law. While account would be taken of economic and social rights, it had not been decided whether the Charter would serve a declaratory purpose in making a political statement, or would be a justiciable instrument capable of being judicially enforced. Nor had its formal relationship to the European Court and Convention on Human Rights been settled. In October 1999, the European Council authorized the appointment of a 'Convention' to prepare such a Charter, it being intended that a final draft would be ready for approval by the Council in December 2000.[100]

Thus at the start of the twenty-first century, large questions about the relationship between the European Union and the European Convention on Human Rights are yet to be resolved. They are not merely questions as to technicalities, involving as they do far-reaching issues about the future integration of European law and government.[101]

---

[100] And see 8th Report of the Select Committee of the House of Lords on European Union, H.L. 67, May 2000.

[101] See P. Alston (ed.), *The EU and Human Rights* (1999). The vast literature on the subject includes 1. Persaud, 'The Reconstruction of Human Rights in the European Legal Order', in Gearty, *supra* n. 45, chap. 9; A.G. Toth, 'The European Union and Human Rights: The Way Forward' (1997) 34 C.M.L. Rev. 491; and C. Turner, 'Human Rights Protection in the European Community' (1999) 5 *European Public Law* 453. Turner rightly rejects an unattractive and implausible proposal by Toth that once the European Union has put its own house in order in respect of human rights, EU Member States should withdraw *en bloc* from the E.C.H.R.

APPENDIX A

CONVENTION FOR THE PROTECTION OF HUMAN RIGHTS AND FUNDAMENTAL FREEDOMS

Rome, 4.XI.1950

'The text of the Convention had been amended according to the provisions of *Protocol No. 3* (ETS No. 45), which entered into force on 21 September 1970, of *Protocol No. 5* (ETS No. 55), which entered into force on 20 December 1971 and of *Protocol No. 8* (ETS No. 118), which entered into force on 1 January 1990, and comprised also the text of *Protocol No. 2* (ETS No. 44) which, in accordance with Article 5, paragraph 3 thereof, had been an integral part of the Convention since its entry into force on 21 September 1970. All provisions which had been amended or added by these Protocols are replaced by *Protocol No. 11* (ETS No. 155), as from the date of its entry into force on 1 November 1998. As from that date, *Protocol No. 9* (ETS No. 140), which entered into force on 1 October 1994, is repealed and *Protocol No. 10* (ETS No. 146), which has not entered into force, has lost its purpose.'

The governments signatory hereto, being members of the Council of Europe,

Considering the Universal Declaration of Human Rights proclaimed by the General Assembly of the United Nations on 10th December 1948;

Considering that this Declaration aims at securing the universal and effective recognition and observance of the Rights therein declared;

Considering that the aim of the Council of Europe is the achievement of greater unity between its members and that one of the methods by which that aim is to be pursued is the maintenance and further realization of human rights and fundamental freedoms;

Reaffirming their profound belief in those fundamental freedoms which are the foundation of justice and peace in the world and are best maintained on the one hand by an effective political democracy and on the other by a common understanding and observance of the human rights upon which they depend;

Being resolved, as the governments of European countries which are like-minded and have a common heritage of political traditions, ideals, freedom and the rule of law, to take the first steps for the collective enforcement of certain of the rights stated in the Universal Declaration,

Have agreed as follows:

Article 1—Obligation to respect human rights

The High Contracting Parties shall secure to everyone within their jurisdiction the rights and freedoms defined in Section I of this Convention.

Section I—Rights and freedoms

Article 2—Right to life

1 Everyone's right to life shall be protected by law. No one shall be deprived of his life intentionally save in the execution of a sentence of a court following his conviction of a crime for which this penalty is provided by law.

2 Deprivation of life shall not be regarded as inflicted in contravention of this article when it results from the use of force which is no more than absolutely necessary:

  a in defence of any person from unlawful violence;

  b in order to effect a lawful arrest or to prevent the escape of a person lawfully detained;

  c in action lawfully taken for the purpose of quelling a riot or insurrection.

Article 3—Prohibition of torture

No one shall be subjected to torture or to inhuman or degrading treatment or punishment.

Article 4—Prohibition of slavery and forced labour

1 No one shall be held in slavery or servitude.

2 No one shall be required to perform forced or compulsory labour.

3 For the purpose of this article the term 'forced or compulsory labour' shall not include:

  a any work required to be done in the ordinary course of detention imposed according to the provisions of Article 5 of this Convention or during conditional release from such detention;

  b any service of a military character or, in case of conscientious objectors in countries where they are recognized, service exacted instead of compulsory military service;

  c any service exacted in case of an emergency or calamity threatening the life or well-being of the community;

  d any work or service which forms part of normal civic obligations.

Article 5—Right to liberty and security

1 Everyone has the right to liberty and security of person. No one shall be deprived of

his liberty save in the following cases and in accordance with a procedure prescribed by law:

a the lawful detention of a person after conviction by a competent court;

b the lawful arrest or detention of a person for non-compliance with the lawful order of a court or in order to secure the fulfilment of any obligation prescribed by law;

c the lawful arrest or detention of a person effected for the purpose of bringing him before the competent legal authority on reasonable suspicion of having committed an offense or when it is reasonably considered necessary to prevent his committing an offense or fleeing after having done so;

d the detention of a minor by lawful order for the purpose of educational supervision or his lawful detention for the purpose of bringing him before the competent legal authority;

e the lawful detention of persons for the prevention of the spreading of infectious diseases, of persons of unsound mind, alcoholics or drug addicts or vagrants;

f the lawful arrest or detention of a person to prevent his effecting an unauthorized entry into the country or of a person against whom action is being taken with a view to deportation or extradition.

2 Everyone who is arrested shall be informed promptly, in a language which he understands, of the reasons for his arrest and of any charge against him.

3 Everyone arrested or detained in accordance with the provisions of paragraph 1.c of this article shall be brought promptly before a judge or other officer authorized by law to exercise judicial power and shall be entitled to trial within a reasonable time or to release pending trial. Release may be conditioned by guarantees to appear for trial.

4 Everyone who is deprived of his liberty by arrest or detention shall be entitled to take proceedings by which the lawfulness of his detention shall be decided speedily by a court and his release ordered if the detention is not lawful.

5 Everyone who has been the victim of arrest or detention in contravention of the provisions of this article shall have an enforceable right to compensation.

Article 6—Right to a fair trial

1 In the determination of his civil rights and obligations or of any criminal charge against him, everyone is entitled to a fair and public hearing within a reasonable time by an independent and impartial tribunal established by law. Judgment shall be pronounced publicly but the press and public may be excluded from all or part of the trial in the interests of morals, public order or national security in a democratic society, where the interests of juveniles or the protection of the private life of the parties so require, or to the extent strictly necessary in the opinion of the court in special circumstances where publicity would prejudice the interests of justice.

2 Everyone charged with a criminal offense shall be presumed innocent until proved guilty according to law.

3 Everyone charged with a criminal offense has the following minimum rights:

  a to be informed promptly, in a language which he understands and in detail, of the nature and cause of the accusation against him;

  b to have adequate time and facilities for the preparation of his defence;

  c to defend himself in person or through legal assistance of his own choosing or, if he has not sufficient means to pay for legal assistance, to be given it free when the interests of justice so require;

  d to examine or have examined witnesses against him and to obtain the attendance and examination of witnesses on his behalf under the same conditions as witnesses against him;

  e to have the free assistance of an interpreter if he cannot understand or speak the language used in court.

Article 7—No punishment without law

1 No one shall be held guilty of any criminal offence on account of any act or omission which did not constitute a criminal offence under national or international law at the time when it was committed. Nor shall a heavier penalty be imposed than the one that was applicable at the time the criminal offence was committed.

2 This article shall not prejudice the trial and punishment of any person for any act or omission which, at the time when it was committed, was criminal according to the general principles of law recognized by civilized nations.

Article 8—Right to respect for private and family life

1 Everyone has the right to respect for his private and family life, his home and his correspondence.

2 There shall be no interference by a public authority with the exercise of this right except such as is in accordance with the law and is necessary in a democratic society in the interests of national security, public safety or the economic well-being of the country, for the prevention of disorder or crime, for the protection of health or morals, or for the protection of the rights and freedoms of others.

Article 9—Freedom of thought, conscience and religion

1 Everyone has the right to freedom of thought, conscience and religion; this right includes freedom to change his religion or belief and freedom, either alone or in community with others and in public or private, to manifest his religion or belief, in worship, teaching, practice and observance.

2 Freedom to manifest one's religion or beliefs shall be subject only to such limitations as are prescribed by law and are necessary in a democratic society in the interests of public safety, for the protection of public order, health or morals, or for the protection of the rights and freedoms of others.

Article 10—Freedom of expression

1 Everyone has the right to freedom of expression. This right shall include freedom to hold opinions and to receive and impart information and ideas without interference by public authority and regardless of frontiers. This article shall not prevent States from requiring the licensing of broadcasting, television or cinema enterprises.

2 The exercise of these freedoms, since it carries with it duties and responsibilities, may be subject to such formalities, conditions, restrictions or penalties as are prescribed by law and are necessary in a democratic society, in the interests of national security, territorial integrity or public safety, for the prevention of disorder or crime, for the protection of health or morals, for the protection of the reputation or rights of others, for preventing the disclosure of information received in confidence, or for maintaining the authority and impartiality of the judiciary.

Article 11—Freedom of assembly and association

1 Everyone has the right to freedom of peaceful assembly and to freedom of association with others, including the right to form and to join trade unions for the protection of his interests.

2 No restrictions shall be placed on the exercise of these rights other than such as are prescribed by law and are necessary in a democratic society in the interests of national security or public safety, for the prevention of disorder or crime, for the protection of health or morals or for the protection of the rights and freedoms of others. This article shall not prevent the imposition of lawful restrictions on the exercise of these rights by members of the armed forces, of the police or of the administration of the State.

Article 12—Right to marry

Men and women of marriageable age have the right to marry and to found a family, according to the national laws governing the exercise of this right.

Article 13—Right to an effective remedy

Everyone whose rights and freedoms as set forth in this Convention are violated shall have an effective remedy before a national authority notwithstanding that the violation has been committed by persons acting in an official capacity.

Article 14—Prohibition of discrimination

The enjoyment of the rights and freedoms set forth in this Convention shall be secured without discrimination on any ground such as sex, race, colour, language, religion, political or other opinion, national or social origin, association with a national minority, property, birth or other status.

Article 15—Derogation in time of emergency

1 In time of war or other public emergency threatening the life of the nation any High Contracting Party may take measures derogating from its obligations under this Convention to the extent strictly required by the exigencies of the situation, provided that such measures are not inconsistent with its other obligations under international law.

2 No derogation from Article 2, except in respect of deaths resulting from lawful acts of war, or from Articles 3, 4 (paragraph 1) and 7 shall be made under this provision.

3 Any High Contracting Party availing itself of this right of derogation shall keep the Secretary General of the Council of Europe fully informed of the measures which it has taken and the reasons therefor. It shall also inform the Secretary General of the Council of Europe when such measures have ceased to operate and the provisions of the Convention are again being fully executed.

Article 16—Restrictions on political activity of aliens

Nothing in Articles 10, 11 and 14 shall be regarded as preventing the High Contracting Parties from imposing restrictions on the political activity of aliens.

Article 17—Prohibition of abuse of rights

Nothing in this Convention may be interpreted as implying for any State, group or person any right to engage in any activity or perform any act aimed at the destruction of any of the rights and freedoms set forth herein or at their limitation to a greater extent than is provided for in the Convention.

Article 18—Limitation on use of restrictions on rights

The restrictions permitted under this Convention to the said rights and freedoms shall not be applied for any purpose other than those for which they have been prescribed.

Section II—European Court of Human Rights

Article 19—Establishment of the Court

To ensure the observance of the engagements undertaken by the High Contracting Parties in the Convention and the Protocols thereto, there shall be set up a European Court of Human Rights, hereinafter referred to as 'the Court'. It shall function on a permanent basis.

Article 20—Number of judges

The Court shall consist of a number of judges equal to that of the High Contracting Parties.

Article 21—Criteria for office

1 The judges shall be of high moral character and must either possess the qualifications required for appointment to high judicial office or be jurisconsults of recognized competence.

2 The judges shall sit on the Court in their individual capacity.

3 During their term of office the judges shall not engage in any activity which is incompatible with their independence, impartiality or with the demands of a full-time office; all questions arising from the application of this paragraph shall be decided by the Court.

Article 22—Election of judges

1 The judges shall be elected by the Parliamentary Assembly with respect to each High Contracting Party by a majority of votes cast from a list of three candidates nominated by the High Contracting Party.

2 The same procedure shall be followed to complete the Court in the event of the accession of new High Contracting Parties and in filling casual vacancies.

Article 23—Terms of office

1 The judges shall be elected for a period of six years. They may be re-elected. However, the terms of office of one-half of the judges elected at the first election shall expire at the end of three years.

2 The judges whose terms of office are to expire at the end of the initial period of three years shall be chosen by lot by the Secretary General of the Council of Europe immediately after their election.

3 In order to ensure that, as far as possible, the terms of office of one-half of the judges are renewed every three years, the Parliamentary Assembly may decide, before proceeding to any subsequent election, that the term or terms of office of one or more judges to be elected shall be for a period other than six years but not more than nine and not less than three years.

4 In cases where more than one term of office is involved and where the Parliamentary Assembly applies the preceding paragraph, the allocation of the terms of office shall be effected by a drawing of lots by the Secretary General of the Council of Europe immediately after the election.

5 A judge elected to replace a judge whose term of office has not expired shall hold office for the remainder of his predecessor's term.

6 The terms of office of judges shall expire when they reach the age of 70.

7 The judges shall hold office until replaced. They shall, however, continue to deal with such cases as they already have under consideration.

Article 24—Dismissal

No judge may be dismissed from his office unless the other judges decide by a majority of two-thirds that he has ceased to fulfill the required conditions.

Article 25—Registry and legal secretaries

The Court shall have a registry, the functions and organization of which shall be laid down in the rules of the Court. The Court shall be assisted by legal secretaries.

Article 26—Plenary Court

The plenary Court shall

  a elect its President and one or two Vice-Presidents for a period of three years; they may be re-elected;

  b set up Chambers, constituted for a fixed period of time;

  c elect the Presidents of the Chambers of the Court; they may be re-elected;

  d adopt the rules of the Court, and

  e elect the Registrar and one or more Deputy Registrars.

Article 27—Committees, Chambers and Grand Chamber

1 To consider cases brought before it, the Court shall sit in committees of three judges, in Chambers of seven judges and in a Grand Chamber of seventeen judges. The Court's Chambers shall set up committees for a fixed period of time.

2 There shall sit as an *ex officio* member of the Chamber and the Grand Chamber the judge elected in respect of the State Party concerned or, if there is none or if he is unable to sit, a person of its choice who shall sit in the capacity of judge.

3 The Grand Chamber shall also include the President of the Court, the Vice-Presidents, the Presidents of the Chambers and other judges chosen in accordance with the rules of the Court. When a case is referred to the Grand Chamber under Article 43, no judge from the Chamber which rendered the judgment shall sit in the Grand Chamber, with the exception of the President of the Chamber and the judge who sat in respect of the State Party concerned.

Article 28—Declarations of inadmissibility by committees

A committee may, by a unanimous vote, declare inadmissible or strike out of its list of cases an application submitted under Article 34 where such a decision can be taken without further examination. The decision shall be final.

Article 29—Decisions by Chambers on admissibility and merits

1 If no decision is taken under Article 28, a Chamber shall decide on the admissibility and merits of individual applications submitted under Article 34.

2 A Chamber shall decide on the admissibility and merits of inter-State applications submitted under Article 33.

3 The decision on admissibility shall be taken separately unless the Court, in exceptional cases, decides otherwise.

Article 30—Relinquishment of jurisdiction to the Grand Chamber

Where a case pending before a Chamber raises a serious question affecting the interpretation of the Convention or the protocols thereto, or where the resolution of a question before the Chamber might have a result inconsistent with a judgment previously delivered by the Court, the Chamber may, at any time before it has rendered its judgment, relinquish jurisdiction in favour of the Grand Chamber, unless one of the parties to the case objects.

Article 31—Powers of the Grand Chamber

The Grand Chamber shall

a determine applications submitted either under Article 33 or Article 34 when a Chamber has relinquished jurisdiction under Article 30 or when the case has been referred to it under Article 43; and

b consider requests for advisory opinions submitted under Article 47.

Article 32—Jurisdiction of the Court

1 The jurisdiction of the Court shall extend to all matters concerning the interpretation and application of the Convention and the protocols thereto which are referred to it as provided in Articles 33, 34 and 47.

2 In the event of dispute as to whether the Court has jurisdiction, the Court shall decide.

Article 33—Inter-State cases

Any High Contracting Party may refer to the Court any alleged breach of the provisions of the Convention and the protocols thereto by another High Contracting Party.

Article 34—Individual applications

The Court may receive applications from any person, non-governmental organization or group of individuals claiming to be the victim of a violation by one of the High Contracting Parties of the rights set forth in the Convention or the protocols thereto. The High Contracting Parties undertake not to hinder in any way the effective exercise of this right.

Article 35—Admissibility criteria

1 The Court may only deal with the matter after all domestic remedies have been

exhausted, according to the generally recognized rules of international law, and within a period of six months from the date on which the final decision was taken.

2 The Court shall not deal with any application submitted under Article 34 that

  a is anonymous; or

  b is substantially the same as a matter that has already been examined by the Court or has already been submitted to another procedure of international investigation or settlement and contains no relevant new information.

3 The Court shall declare inadmissible any individual application submitted under Article 34 which it considers incompatible with the provisions of the Convention or the protocols thereto, manifestly ill-founded, or an abuse of the right of application.

4 The Court shall reject any application which it considers inadmissible under this Article. It may do so at any stage of the proceedings.

Article 36—Third party intervention

1 In all cases before a Chamber of the Grand Chamber, a High Contracting Party one of whose nationals is an applicant shall have the right to submit written comments and to take part in hearings.

2 The President of the Court may, in the interest of the proper administration of justice, invite any High Contracting Party which is not a party to the proceedings or any person concerned who is not the applicant to submit written comments or take part in hearings.

Article 37—Striking out applications

1 The Court may at any stage of the proceedings decide to strike an application out of its list of cases where the circumstances lead to the conclusion that

  a the applicant does not intend to pursue his application; or

  b the matter has been resolved; or

  c for any other reason established by the Court, it is no longer justified to continue the examination of the application.

However, the Court shall continue the examination of the application if respect for human rights as defined in the Convention and the protocols thereto so requires.

2 The Court may decide to restore an application to its list of cases if it considers that the circumstances justify such a course.

Article 38—Examination of the case and friendly settlement proceedings

1 If the Court declares the application admissible, it shall

  a pursue the examination of the case, together with the representatives of the parties, and if need be, undertake an investigation, for the effective conduct of which the States concerned shall furnish all necessary facilities;

b place itself at the disposal of the parties concerned with a view to securing a friendly settlement of the matter on the basis of respect for human rights as defined in the Convention and the protocols thereto.

2 Proceedings conducted under paragraph 1.b shall be confidential.

Article 39—Finding of a friendly settlement
If a friendly settlement is effected, the Court shall strike the case out of its list by means of a decision which shall be confined to a brief statement of the facts and of the solution reached.

Article 40—Public hearings and access to documents
1 Hearings shall be in public unless the Court in exceptional circumstances decides otherwise.

2 Documents deposited with the Registrar shall be accessible to the public unless the President of the Court decides otherwise.

Article 41—Just satisfaction
If the Court finds that there has been a violation of the Convention or the protocols thereto, and if the internal law of the High Contracting Party concerned allows only partial reparation to be made, the Court shall, if necessary, afford just satisfaction to the injured party.

Article 42—Judgments of Chambers
Judgments of Chambers shall become final in accordance with the provisions of Article 44, paragraph 2.

Article 43—Referral to the Grand Chamber
1 Within a period of three months from the date of the judgment of the Chamber, any party to the case may, in exceptional cases, request that the case be referred to the Grand Chamber.

2 A panel of five judges of the Grand Chamber shall accept the request if the case raises a serious question affecting the interpretation or application of the Convention or the protocols thereto, or a serious issue of general importance.

3 If the panel accepts the request, the Grand Chamber shall decide the case by means of a judgment.

Article 44—Final judgments
1 The judgment of the Grand Chamber shall be final.

2 The judgment of a Chamber shall become final

a when the parties declare that they will not request that the case be referred to the Grand Chamber; or

b three months after the date of the judgment, if reference of the case to the Grand Chamber has not been requested; or

c when the panel of the Grand Chamber rejects the request to refer under Article 43.

3 The final judgment shall be published.

Article 45—Reasons for judgments and decisions

1 Reasons shall be given for judgments as well as for decisions declaring applications admissible or inadmissible.

2 If a judgment does not represent, in whole or in part, the unanimous opinion of the judges, any judge shall be entitled to deliver a separate opinion.

Article 46—Binding force and execution of judgments

1 The High Contracting Parties undertake to abide by the final judgment of the Court in any case to which they are parties.

2 The final judgment of the Court shall be transmitted to the Committee of Ministers, which shall supervise its execution.

Article 47—Advisory opinions

1 The Court may, at the request of the Committee of Ministers, give advisory opinions on legal questions concerning the interpretation of the Convention and the protocols thereto.

2 Such opinions shall not deal with any question relating to the content or scope of the rights or freedoms defined in Section I of the Convention and the protocols thereto, or with any other question which the Court or the Committee of Ministers might have to consider in consequence of any such proceedings as could be instituted in accordance with the Convention.

3 Decisions of the Committee of Ministers to request an advisory opinion of the Court shall require a majority vote of the representatives entitled to sit on the Committee.

Article 48—Advisory jurisdiction of the Court

The Court shall decide whether a request for an advisory opinion submitted by the Committee of Ministers is within its competence as defined in Article 47.

Article 49—Reasons for advisory opinions

1 Reasons shall be given for advisory opinions of the Court.

2 If the advisory opinion does not represent, in whole or in part, the unanimous opinion of the judges, any judge shall be entitled to deliver a separate opinion.

3 Advisory opinions of the Court shall be communicated to the Committee of Ministers.

Article 50—Expenditure on the Court
The expenditure on the Court shall be borne by the Council of Europe.

Article 51—Privileges and immunities of judges
The judges shall be entitled, during the exercise of their functions, to the privileges and immunities provided for in Article 40 of the Statute of the Council of Europe and in the agreements made thereunder.

Section III—Miscellaneous provisions

Article 52—Inquiries by the Secretary General
On receipt of a request from the Secretary General of the Council of Europe any High Contracting Party shall furnish an explanation of the manner in which its internal law ensures the effective implementation of any of the provisions of the Convention.

Article 53—Safeguard for existing human rights
Nothing in this Convention shall be construed as limiting or derogating from any of the human rights and fundamental freedoms which may be ensured under the laws of any High Contracting Party or under any other agreement to which it is a Party.

Article 54—Powers of the Committee of Ministers
Nothing in this Convention shall prejudice the powers conferred on the Committee of Ministers by the Statute of the Council of Europe.

Article 55—Exclusion of other means of dispute settlement
The High Contracting Parties agree that, except by special agreement, they will not avail themselves of treaties, conventions or declarations in force between them for the purpose of submitting, by way of petition, a dispute arising out of the interpretation or application of this Convention to a means of settlement other than those provided for in this Convention.

Article 56—Territorial application
1 Any State may at the time of its ratification or at any time thereafter declare by notification addressed to the Secretary General of the Council of Europe that the present Convention shall, subject to paragraph 4 of this Article, extend to all or any of the territories for whose international relations it is responsible.

2 The Convention shall extend to the territory or territories named in the

notification as from the thirtieth day after the receipt of this notification by the Secretary General of the Council of Europe.

3 The provisions of this Convention shall be applied in such territories with due regard, however, to local requirements.

4 Any State which has made a declaration in accordance with paragraph 1 of this article may at any time thereafter declare on behalf of one or more of the territories to which the declaration relates that it accepts the competence of the Court to receive applications from individuals, non-governmental organizations or groups of individuals as provided by Article 34 of the Convention.

Article 57—Reservations
1 Any State may, when signing this Convention or when depositing its instrument of ratification, make a reservation in respect of any particular provision of the Convention to the extent that any law then in force in its territory is not in conformity with the provision. Reservations of a general character shall not be permitted under this article.

2 Any reservation made under this article shall contain a brief statement of the law concerned.

Article 58—Denunciation
1 A High Contracting Party may denounce the present Convention only after the expiry of five years from the date on which it became a party to it and after six months' notice contained in a notification addressed to the Secretary General of the Council of Europe, who shall inform the other High Contracting Parties.

2 Such a denunciation shall not have the effect of releasing the High Contracting Party concerned from its obligations under this Convention in respect of any act which, being capable of constituting a violation of such obligations, may have been performed by it before the date at which the denunciation became effective.

3 Any High Contracting Party which shall cease to be a member of the Council of Europe shall cease to be a Party to this Convention under the same conditions.

4 The Convention may be denounced in accordance with the provisions of the preceding paragraphs in respect of any territory to which it has been declared to extend under the terms of Article 56.

Article 59—Signature and ratification
1 This Convention shall be open to the signature of the members of the Council of Europe. It shall be ratified. Ratifications shall be deposited with the Secretary General of the Council of Europe.

2 The present Convention shall come into force after the deposit of ten instruments of ratification.

3 As regards any signatory ratifying subsequently, the Convention shall come into force at the date of the deposit of its instrument of ratification.

4 The Secretary General of the Council of Europe shall notify all the members of the Council of Európe of the entry into force of the Convention, the names of the High Contracting Parties who have ratified it, and the deposit of all instruments of ratification which may be effected subsequently.

Done at Rome this 4th day of November 1950, in English and French, both texts being equally authentic, in a single copy which shall remain deposited in the archives of the Council of Europe. The Secretary General shall transmit certified copies to each of the signatories.

APPENDIX B

THE SUBSTANTIVE PROTOCOLS TO THE CONVENTION

1. PROTOCOL NO. 1, 20 MARCH 1952

The governments signatory hereto, being members of the Council of Europe,

Being resolved to take steps to ensure the collective enforcement of certain rights and freedoms other than those already included in Section I of the Convention for the Protection of Human Rights and Fundamental Freedoms signed at Rome on 4 November 1950 (hereinafter referred to as 'the Convention'),

Have agreed as follows:

Article 1—Protection of property
Every natural or legal person is entitled to the peaceful enjoyment of his possessions. No one shall be deprived of his possessions except in the public interest and subject to the conditions provided for by law and by the general principles of international law.

The preceding provisions shall not, however, in any way impair the right of a State to enforce such laws as it deems necessary to control the use of property in accordance with the general interest or to secure the payment of taxes or other contributions or penalties.

Article 2—Right to education
No person shall be denied the right to education. In the exercise of any functions which it assumes in relation to education and to teaching, the State shall respect the right of parents to ensure such education and teaching in conformity with their own religious and philosophical convictions.

Article 3—Right to free elections
The High Contracting Parties undertake to hold free elections at reasonable intervals by secret ballot, under conditions which will ensure the free expression of the opinion of the people in the choice of the legislature.

Article 4[1]—Territorial application
Any High Contracting Party may at the time of signature or ratification or at any time thereafter communicate to the Secretary General of the Council of Europe a declaration stating the extent to which it undertakes that the provisions of the present

Protocol shall apply to such of the territories for the international relations of which it is responsible as are named therein.

Any High Contracting Party which has communicated a declaration in virtue of the preceding paragraph may from time to time communicate a further declaration modifying the terms of any former declaration or terminating the application of the provisions of this Protocol in respect of any territory.

A declaration made in accordance with this article shall be deemed to have been made in accordance with paragraph 1 of Article 56 of the Convention.

Article 5—Relationship to the Convention
As between the High Contracting Parties the provisions of Articles 1, 2, 3 and 4 of this Protocol shall be regarded as additional articles to the Convention and all the provisions of the Convention shall apply accordingly.

Article 6—Signature and ratification
This Protocol shall be open for signature by the members of the Council of Europe, who are the signatories of the Convention; it shall be ratified at the same time as or after the ratification of the Convention. It shall enter into force after the deposit of ten instruments of ratification. As regards any signatory ratifying subsequently, the Protocol shall enter into force at the date of the deposit of its instrument of ratification.

The instruments of ratification shall be deposited with the Secretary General of the Council of Europe, who will notify all members of the names of those who have ratified.

Done at Paris on the 20th day of March 1952, in English and French, both texts being equally authentic, in a single copy which shall remain deposited in the archives of the Council of Europe. The Secretary General shall transmit certified copies to each of the signatory governments.

[1] Text amended according to the provisions of Protocol No. 11 (ETS No. 155).

2. PROTOCOL NO. 4, 16 SEPTEMBER 1963

The governments signatory hereto, being members of the Council of Europe,

Being resolved to take steps to ensure the collective enforcement of certain rights and freedoms other than those already included in Section 1 of the Convention for the Protection of Human Rights and Fundamental Freedoms signed at Rome on 4th November 1950 (hereinafter referred to as the 'Convention') and in Articles 1 to 3 of the First Protocol to the Convention, signed at Paris on 20th March 1952,

Have agreed as follows:

Article 1—Prohibition of imprisonment for debt
No one shall be deprived of his liberty merely on the ground of inability to fulfill a contractual obligation.

Article 2—Freedom of movement
1 Everyone lawfully within the territory of a State shall, within that territory, have the right to liberty of movement and freedom to choose his residence.

2 Everyone shall be free to leave any country, including his own.

3 No restrictions shall be placed on the exercise of these rights other than such as are in accordance with law and are necessary in a democratic society in the interests of national security or public safety, for the maintenance of *ordre public*, for the prevention of crime, for the protection of health or morals, or for the protection of the rights and freedoms of others.

4 The rights set forth in paragraph 1 may also be subject, in particular areas, to restrictions imposed in accordance with law and justified by the public interest in a democratic society.

Article 3—Prohibition of expulsion of nationals
1 No one shall be expelled, by means either of an individual or of a collective measure, from the territory of the State of which he is a national.

2 No one shall be deprived of the right to enter the territory of the state of which he is a national.

Article 4—Prohibition of collective expulsion of aliens
Collective expulsion of aliens is prohibited.

Article 5—Territorial application
1 Any High Contracting Party may, at the time of signature or ratification of this Protocol, or at any time thereafter, communicate to the Secretary General of the

Council of Europe a declaration stating the extent to which it undertakes that the provisions of this Protocol shall apply to such of the territories for the international relations of which it is responsible as are named therein.

2 Any High Contracting Party which has communicated a declaration in virtue of the preceding paragraph may, from time to time, communicate a further declaration modifying the terms of any former declaration or terminating the application of the provisions of this Protocol in respect of any territory.

3 A declaration made in accordance with this article shall be deemed to have been made in accordance with paragraph 1 of Article 56 of the Convention.

4 The territory of any State to which this Protocol applies by virtue of ratification or acceptance by that State, and each territory to which this Protocol is applied by virtue of a declaration by that State under this article, shall be treated as separate territories for the purpose of the references in Articles 2 and 3 to the territory of a State.

5 Any State which has made a declaration in accordance with paragraph 1 or 2 of this Article may at any time thereafter declare on behalf of one or more of the territories to which the declaration relates that it accepts the competence of the Court to receive applications from individuals, non-governmental organizations or groups of individuals as provided in Article 34 of the Convention in respect of all or any of Articles 1 to 4 of this Protocol.

Article 6—Relationship to the Convention
As between the High Contracting Parties the provisions of Articles 1 to 5 of this Protocol shall be regarded as additional Articles to the Convention, and all the provisions of the Convention shall apply accordingly.

Article 7—Signature and ratification
1 This Protocol shall be open for signature by the members of the Council of Europe who are the signatories of the Convention; it shall be ratified at the same time as or after the ratification of the Convention. It shall enter into force after the deposit of five instruments of ratification. As regards any signatory ratifying subsequently, the Protocol shall enter into force at the date of the deposit of its instrument of ratification.

2 The instruments of ratification shall be deposited with the Secretary General of the Council of Europe, who will notify all members of the names of those who have ratified.

In witness whereof the undersigned, being duly authorized thereto, have signed this Protocol.

Done at Strasbourg, this 16th day of September 1963, in English and in French both texts being equally authoritative, in a single copy which shall remain deposited in the archives of the Council of Europe. The Secretary General shall transmit certified copies to each of the signatory states.

3. PROTOCOL NO. 6, 28 APRIL 1983

The member States of the Council of Europe, signatory to this Protocol to the Convention for the Protection of Human Rights and Fundamental Freedoms, signed at Rome on 4 November 1950 (hereinafter referred to as 'the Convention'),

Considering that the evolution that has occurred in several member States of the Council of Europe expresses a general tendency in favour of abolition of the death penalty;

Have agreed as follows:

Article 1—Abolition of the death penalty

The death penalty shall be abolished. No-one shall be condemned to such penalty or executed.

Article 2—Death penalty in time of war

A State may make provision in its law for the death penalty in respect of acts committed in time of war or of imminent threat of war; such penalty shall be applied only in the instances laid down in the law and in accordance with its provisions. The State shall communicate to the Secretary General of the Council of Europe the relevant provisions of that law.

Article 3—Prohibition of derogations

No derogation from the provisions of this Protocol shall be made under Article 15 of the Convention.

Article 4—Prohibition of reservations

No reservation may be made under Article 57 of the Convention in respect of the provisions of this Protocol.

Article 5—Territorial application

1 Any State may at the time of signature or when depositing its instrument of ratification, acceptance or approval, specify the territory or territories to which this Protocol shall apply.

2 Any State may at any later date, by a declaration addressed to the Secretary General of the Council of Europe, extend the application of this Protocol to any other territory specified in the declaration. In respect of such territory the Protocol shall enter into force on the first day of the month following the date of receipt of such declaration by the Secretary General.

3 Any declaration made under the two preceding paragraphs may, in respect of any territory specified in such declaration, be withdrawn by a notification addressed to

the Secretary General. The withdrawal shall become effective on the first day of the month following the date of receipt of such notification by the Secretary General.

Article 6—Relationship to the Convention

As between the States Parties the provisions of Articles 1 to 5 of this Protocol shall be regarded as additional articles to the Convention and all the provisions of the Convention shall apply accordingly.

Article 7—Signature and ratification

The Protocol shall be open for signature by the member States of the Council of Europe, signatories to the Convention. It shall be subject to ratification, acceptance or approval. A member State of the Council of Europe may not ratify, accept or approve this Protocol unless it has, simultaneously or previously, ratified the Convention. Instruments of ratification, acceptance or approval shall be deposited with the Secretary General of the Council of Europe.

Article 8—Entry into force

1 This Protocol shall enter into force on the first day of the month following the date on which five member States of the Council of Europe have expressed their consent to be bound by the Protocol in accordance with the provisions of Article 7.

2 In respect of any member State which subsequently expresses its consent to be bound by it, the Protocol shall enter into force on the first day of the month following the date of the deposit of the instrument of ratification, acceptance or approval.

Article 9—Depositary functions

The Secretary General of the Council of Europe shall notify the member States of the Council of:

a any signature;
b the deposit of any instrument of ratification, acceptance or approval;
c any date of entry into force of this Protocol in accordance with Articles 5 and 8;
d any other act, notification or communication relating to this Protocol.

In witness whereof the undersigned, being duly authorised thereto, have signed this Protocol.

Done at Strasbourg, this 28th day of April 1983, in English and in French both texts being equally authentic, in a single copy which shall be deposited in the archives of the Council of Europe. The Secretary General of the Council of Europe shall transmit certified copies to each member State of the Council of Europe.

4. PROTOCOL NO. 7, 22 NOVEMBER 1984

The member States of the Council of Europe signatory hereto,

Being resolved to take further steps to ensure the collective enforcement of certain rights and freedoms by means of the Convention for the Protection of Human Rights and Fundamental Freedoms signed at Rome on 4 November 1950 (hereinafter referred to as 'the Convention'),

Have agreed as follows:

Article 1—Procedural safeguards relating to expulsion of aliens

1 An alien lawfully resident in the territory of a State shall not be expelled therefrom except in pursuance of a decision reached in accordance with law and shall be allowed:

a to submit reasons against his expulsion,
b to have his case reviewed, and
c to be represented for these purposes before the competent authority or a person or persons designated by that authority.

2 An alien may be expelled before the exercise of his rights under paragraph 1.a, b and c of this Article, when such expulsion is necessary in the interests of public order or is grounded on reasons of national security.

Article 2—Right of appeal in criminal matters

1 Everyone convicted of a criminal offence by a tribunal shall have the right to have his conviction or sentence reviewed by a higher tribunal. The exercise of this right, including the grounds on which it may be exercised, shall be governed by law.

2 This right may be subject to exceptions in regard to offences of a minor character, as prescribed by law, or in cases in which the person concerned was tried in the first instance by the highest tribunal or was convicted following an appeal against acquittal.

Article 3—Compensation for wrongful conviction

When a person has by a final decision been convicted of a criminal offense and when subsequently his conviction has been reversed, or he has been pardoned, on the ground that a new or newly discovered fact shows conclusively that there has been a miscarriage of justice, the person who has suffered punishment as a result of such conviction shall be compensated according to the law or the practice of the State concerned, unless it is proved that the non-disclosure of the unknown fact in time is wholly or partly attributable to him.

Article 4—Right not to be tried or punished twice

1 No one shall be liable to be tried or punished again in criminal proceedings under the jurisdiction of the same State for an offence for which he has already been finally acquitted or convicted in accordance with the law and penal procedure of that State.

2 The provisions of the preceding paragraph shall not prevent the reopening of the case in accordance with the law and penal procedure of the State concerned, if there is evidence of new or newly discovered facts, or if there has been a fundamental defect in the previous proceedings, which could affect the outcome of the case.

3 No derogation from this Article shall be made under Article 15 of the Convention.

Article 5—Equality between spouses

Spouses shall enjoy equality of rights and responsibilities of a private law character between them, and in their relations with their children, as to marriage, during marriage and in the event of its dissolution. This Article shall not prevent States from taking such measures as are necessary in the interests of the children.

Article 6—Territorial application

1 Any State may at the time of signature or when depositing its instrument of ratification, acceptance or approval, specify the territory or territories to which the Protocol shall apply and state the extent to which it undertakes that the provisions of this Protocol shall apply to such territory or territories.

2 Any State may at any later date, by a declaration addressed to the Secretary General of the Council of Europe, extend the application of this Protocol to any other territory specified in the declaration. In respect of such territory the Protocol shall enter into force on the first day of the month following the expiration of a period of two months after the date of receipt by the Secretary General of such declaration.

3 Any declaration made under the two preceding paragraphs may, in respect of any territory specified in such declaration, be withdrawn or modified by a notification addressed to the Secretary General. The withdrawal or modification shall become effective on the first day of the month following the expiration of a period of two months after the date of receipt of such notification by the Secretary General.

4 A declaration made in accordance with this Article shall be deemed to have been made in accordance with paragraph 1 of Article 56 of the Convention.

5 The territory of any State to which this Protocol applies by virtue of ratification, acceptance or approval by that State, and each territory to which this Protocol is applied by virtue of a declaration by that State under this Article, may be treated as of the reference in Article 1 to the territory of a State.

6 Any State which has made a declaration in accordance with paragraph 1 or 2 of this Article may at any time thereafter declare on behalf of one or more of the territories

to which the declaration relates that it accepts the competence of the Court to receive applications from individuals, non-governmental organizations or groups of individuals as provided in Article 34 of the Convention in respect of Articles 1 to 5 of this Protocol.

Article 7—Relationship to the Convention

As between the States Parties, the provisions of Article 1 to 6 of this Protocol shall be regarded as additional Articles to the Convention, and all the provisions of the Convention shall apply accordingly.

Article 8—Signature and ratification

This Protocol shall be open for signature by member States of the Council of Europe which have signed the Convention. It is subject to ratification, acceptance or approval. A member State of the Council of Europe may not ratify, accept or approve this Protocol without previously or simultaneously ratifying the Convention. Instruments of ratification, acceptance or approval shall be deposited with the Secretary General of the Council of Europe.

Article 9—Entry into force

1 This Protocol shall enter into force on the first day of the month following the expiration of a period of two months after the date on which seven member States of the Council of Europe have expressed their consent to be bound by the Protocol in accordance with the provisions of Article 8.

2 In respect of any member State which subsequently expresses its consent to be bound by it, the Protocol shall enter into force on the first day of the month following the expiration of a period of two months after the date of the deposit of the instrument of ratification, acceptance or approval.

Article 10—Depositary functions

The Secretary General of the Council of Europe shall notify all the member States of the Council of Europe of:

a any signature;
b the deposit of any instrument of ratification, acceptance or approval;
c any date of entry into force of this Protocol in accordance with Articles 6 and 9;
d any other act, notification or declaration relating to this Protocol.

In witness whereof, the undersigned, being duly authorized thereto, have signed this Protocol.

Done at Strasbourg, this 22nd day of November 1984, in English and French both texts being equally authentic, in a single copy which shall be deposited in the archives of the Council of Europe. The Secretary General of the Council of Europe shall transmit certified copies to each member State of the Council of Europe.

APPENDIX C

THE HUMAN RIGHTS ACT 1998 (UNITED KINGDOM)

The effect of the European Convention on Human Rights in the law of the United Kingdom was examined in Chapter 9, Section D. The Human Rights Act 1998 was enacted on 9 November 1998, but it comes fully into effect only on 2 October 2000. The following text omits Schedule 1, which sets out Articles 2–12, 14 and 16–18 of the Convention, together with Articles 1–3 of the First Protocol to the Convention and Articles 1 and 2 of the Sixth Protocol. These Articles are all found in Appendices A and B above. Also omitted from this Appendix are (1) Section 18, subsections (4) to (7) (provisions consequential upon the appointment to the Strasbourg Court of a person who holds judicial office in the United Kingdom); (2) Schedule 3 (which sets out in full (a) the United Kingdom derogation under Article 15(1) of the Convention, relating to the detention of suspected terrorists under legislation, as to which see *Brogan v United Kingdom* (Chapter 1 (F)(2)) and *Branigan v United Kingdom* (Chapter 7 (G)(3)); and (b) the United Kingdom reservation made in ratifying the First Protocol. Article 2 (right to education)); and (3) Schedule 4 (judical pensions).

HUMAN RIGHTS ACT 1998

1998 chapter 42

An Act to give further effect to rights and freedoms guaranteed under the European Convention on Human Rights; to make provision with respect to holders of certain judicial offices who become judges of the European Court of Human Rights; and for connected purposes.

[9th November 1998]

Introduction

1. The Convention Rights

(1) In this Act 'the Convention rights' means the rights and fundamental freedoms set out in—

(a) Articles 2 to 12 and 14 of the Convention,

(b) Articles 1 to 3 of the First Protocol, and

(c) Articles 1 and 2 of the Sixth Protocol,

as read with Articles 16 to 18 of the Convention.

(2) Those Articles are to have effect for the purposes of this Act subject to any designated derogation or reservation (as to which see sections 14 and 15).

(3) The Articles are set out in Schedule 1.

(4) The Secretary of State may by order make such amendments to this Act as he considers appropriate to reflect the effect, in relation to the United Kingdom, of a protocol.

(5) In subsection (4) 'protocol' means a protocol to the Convention—

    (a) which the United Kingdom has ratified; or

    (b) which the United Kingdom has signed with a view to ratification.

(6) No amendment may be made by an order under subsection (4) so as to come into force before the protocol concerned is in force in relation to the United Kingdom.

2. Interpretation of Convention rights

(1) A court of tribunal determining a question which has arisen in connection with a Convention right must take into account any—

    (a) judgment, decision, declaration or advisory opinion of the European Court of Human Rights,

    (b) opinion of the Commission given in a report adopted under Article 31 of the Convention,

    (c) decision of the Commission in connection with Article 26 or 27(2) of the Convention, or

    (d) decision of the Committee of Ministers taken under Article 46 of the Convention,

whenever made or given, so far as, in the opinion of the court or tribunal, it is relevant to the proceedings in which that question has arisen.

(2) Evidence of any judgment, decision, declaration or opinion of which account may have to be taken under this section is to be given in proceedings before any court or tribunal in such manner as may be provided by rules.

(3) In this section 'rules' means rules of court or, in the case of proceedings before a tribunal, rules made for the purposes of this section—

    (a) by the Lord Chancellor or the Secretary of State, in relation to any proceedings outside Scotland;

    (b) by the Secretary of State, in relation to proceedings in Scotland; or

    (c) by a Northern Ireland department, in relation to proceedings before a tribunal in Northern Ireland—

        (i)   which deals with transferred matters; and

        (ii) for which no rules made under paragraph (a) are in force.

Legislation

3. Interpretation of legislation

(1) So far as it is possible to do so, primary legislation and subordinate legislation must be read and given effect in a way which is compatible with the Convention rights.

(2) This section—

    (a) applies to primary legislation and subordinate legislation whenever enacted;

    (b) does not affect the validity, continuing operation or enforcement of any incompatible primary legislation; and

    (c) does not affect the validity, continuing operation or enforcement of any incompatible subordinate legislation if (disregarding any possibility of revocation) primary legislation prevents removal of the incompatibility.

4. Declaration of incompatibility

(1) Subsection (2) applies in any proceedings in which a court determines whether a provision of primary legislation is compatible with a Convention right.

(2) If the court is satisfied that the provision is incompatible with a Convention right, it may make a declaration of that incompatibility.

(3) Subsection (4) applies in any proceedings in which a court determines whether a provision of subordinate legislation, made in the exercise of a power conferred by primary legislation, is compatible with a Convention right.

(4) If the court is satisfied—

    (a) that the provision is incompatible with a Convention right, and

    (b) that (disregarding any possibility of revocation) the primary legislation concerned prevents removal of that incompatibility, it may make a declaration of that incompatibility.

(5) In this section 'court' means—

    (a) the House of Lords;

    (b) the Judicial Committee of the Privy Council;

    (c) the Courts-Martial Appeal Court;

    (d) in Scotland, the High Court of Justiciary sitting otherwise than as a trial court or the Court of Session;

    (e) in England and Wales or Northern Ireland, the High Court or the Court of Appeal.

(6) A declaration under this section ('a declaration of incompatibility')—

    (a) does not affect the validity, continuing operation or enforcement of the provision in respect of which it is given; and

    (b) is not binding on the parties to the proceedings in which it is made.

5. Right of Crown to intervene

(1) Where a court is considering whether to make a declaration of incompatibility, the Crown is entitled to notice in accordance with rules of court.

(2) In any case to which subsection (1) applies—

    (a) a Minister of the Crown (or a person nominated by him),

    (b) a member of the Scottish Executive,

    (c) a Northern Ireland Minister,

    (d) a Northern Ireland department,

is entitled, on giving notice in accordance with rules of court, to be joined as a party to the proceedings.

(3) Notice under subsection (2) may be given at any time during the proceedings.

(4) A person who has been made a party to criminal proceedings (other than in Scotland) as the result of a notice under subsection (2) may, with leave, appeal to the House of Lords against any declaration of incompatibility made in the proceedings.

(5) In subsection (4)—

'criminal proceedings' includes all proceedings before the Courts-Martial Appeal Court; and

'leave' means leave granted by the court making the declaration of incompatibility or by the House of Lords.

Public authorities

6. Acts of public authorities

(1) It is unlawful for a public authority to act in a way which is incompatible with a Convention right.

(2) Subsection (1) does not apply to an act if—

    (a) as the result of one or more provisions of primary legislation, the authority could not have acted differently; or

    (b) in the case of one or more provisions of, or made under, primary legislation which cannot be read or given effect in a way which is compatible with the Convention rights, the authority was acting so as to give effect to or enforce those provisions.

(3) In this section 'public authority' includes—

    (a) a court or tribunal, and

    (b) any person certain of whose functions are functions of a public nature,

    but does not include either House of Parliament or a person exercising functions in connection with proceedings in Parliament.

(4) In subsection (3) 'Parliament' does not include the House of Lords in its judicial capacity.

(5) In relation to a particular act, a person is not a public authority by virtue only of subsection (3)(b) if the nature of the act is private.

(6) 'An act' includes a failure to act but does not include a failure to—

    (a) introduce in, or lay before, Parliament a proposal for legislation; or

    (b) make any primary legislation or remedial order.

7. Proceedings

(1) A person who claims that a public authority has acted (or proposes to act) in a way which is made unlawful by section 6(1) may—

    (a) bring proceedings against the authority under this Act in the appropriate court or tribunal, or

(b) rely on the Convention right or rights concerned in any legal proceedings, but only if he is (or would be) a victim of the unlawful act.

(2) In subsection (1)(a) 'appropriate court or tribunal' means such court or tribunal as may be determined in accordance with rules; and proceedings against an authority include a counterclaim or similar proceeding.

(3) If the proceedings are brought on an application for judicial review, the applicant is to be taken to have a sufficient interest in relation to the unlawful act only if he is, or would be, a victim of that act.

(4) If the proceedings are made by way of a petition for judicial review in Scotland, the applicant shall be taken to have title and interest to sue in relation to the unlawful act only if he is, or would be, a victim of that act.

(5) Proceedings under subsection (1)(a) must be brought before the end of—

(a) the period of one year beginning with the date on which the act complained of took place; or

(b) such longer period as the court or tribunal considers equitable having regard to all the circumstances,

but that is subject to any rule imposing a stricter time limit in relation to the procedure in question.

(6) In subsection (1)(b) 'legal proceedings' includes—

(a) proceedings brought by or at the instigation of a public authority; and

(b) an appeal against the decision of a court or tribunal.

(7) For the purposes of this section, a person is a victim of an unlawful act only if he would be a victim for the purposes of Article 34 of the Convention if proceedings were brought in the European Court of Human Rights in respect of that act.

(8) Nothing in this Act creates a criminal offence.

(9) In this section 'rules' means—

(a) in relation to proceedings before a court or tribunal outside Scotland, rules made by the Lord Chancellor or the Secretary of State for the purposes of this section or rules of court,

(b) in relation to proceedings before a court or tribunal in Scotland, rules made by the Secretary of State for those purposes,

(c) in relation to proceedings before a tribunal in Northern Ireland—

(i)   which deals with transferred matters; and

(ii) for which no rules made under paragraph (a) are in force,

rules made by a Northern Ireland department for those purposes,

and includes provision made by order under section 1 of the Courts and Legal. Services Act 1990.

(10) In making rules, regard must be had to section 9.

(11) The Minister who has power to make rules in relation to a particular tribunal may, to the extent he considers it necessary to ensure that the tribunal can provide an appropriate remedy in relation to an act (or proposed act) of a public authority which is (or would be) unlawful as a result of section 6(1), by order add to—

(a) the relief or remedies which the tribunal may grant; or

(b) the grounds on which it may grant any of them.

(12) An order made under subsection (11) may contain such incidental, supplemental, consequential or transitional provision as the Minister making it considers appropriate.

(13) 'The Minister' includes the Northern Ireland department concerned.

8. Judicial remedies

(1) In relation to any act (or proposed act) of a public authority which the court finds is (or would be) unlawful, it may grant such relief or remedy, or make such order, within its powers as it considers just and appropriate.

(2) But damages may be awarded only by a court which has power to award damages, or to order the payment of compensation, in civil proceedings.

(3) No award of damages is to be made unless, taking account of all the circumstances of the case, including—

(a) any other relief or remedy granted, or order made, in relation to the act in question (by that or any other court), and

(b) the consequences of any decision (of that or any other court) in respect of that act,

the court is satisfied that the award is necessary to afford just satisfaction to the person in whose favour it is made.

(4) In determining—

(a) whether to award damages, or

(b) the amount of an award,

the court must take into account the principles applied by the European Court of Human Rights in relation to the award of compensation under Article 41 of the Convention.

(5) A public authority against which damages are awarded is to be treated—

(a) in Scotland, for the purposes of section 3 of the Law Reform (Miscellaneous Provisions) (Scotland) Act 1940 as if the award were made in an action of damages in which the authority has been found liable in respect of loss or damage to the person to whom the award is made;

(b) for the purposes of the Civil Liability (Contribution) Act 1978 as liable in respect of damage suffered by the person to whom the award is made.

(6) In this section—

'court' includes a tribunal;

'damages' means damages for an unlawful act of a public authority; and

'unlawful' means unlawful under section 6(1).

9. Judicial acts

(1) Proceedings under section 7(1)(a) in respect of a judicial act may be brought only—

(a) by exercising a right of appeal;

(b) on an application (in Scotland a petition) for judicial review; or

(c) in such other forum as may be prescribed by rules.

(2) That does not affect any rule of law which prevents a court from being the subject of judicial review.

(3) In proceedings under this Act in respect of a judicial act done in good faith, damages may not be awarded otherwise than to compensate a person to the extent required by Article 5(5) of the Convention.

(4) An award of damages permitted by subsection (3) is to be made against the Crown; but no award may be made unless the appropriate person, if not a party to the proceedings, is joined.

(5) In this section—

'appropriate person' means the Minister responsible for the court concerned, or a person or government department nominated by him;

'court' includes a tribunal;

'judge' includes a member of a tribunal, a justice of the peace and a clerk or other officer entitled to exercise the jurisdiction of a court;

'judicial act' means a judicial act of a court and includes an act done on the instructions, or on behalf, of a judge; and

'rules' has the same meaning as in section 7(9).

Remedial action

10. Power to take remedial action

(1) This section applies if—

(a) a provision of legislation has been declared under section 4 to be incompat-ible with a Convention right and, if an appeal lies—

(i) all persons who may appeal have stated in writing that they do not intend to do so;

(ii) the time for bringing an appeal has expired and no appeal has been brought within that time; or

(iii) an appeal brought within that time has been determined or abandoned; or

(b) it appears to a Minister of the Crown or Her Majesty in Council that, having regard to a finding of the European Court of Human Rights made after the coming into force of this section in proceedings against the United King-dom, a provision of legislation is incompatible with an obligation of the United Kingdom arising from the Convention.

(2) If a Minister of the Crown considers that there are compelling reasons for proceeding under this section, he may by order make such amendments to the legisla-tion as he considers necessary to remove the incompatibility.

(3) If, in the case of subordinate legislation, a Minister of the Crown considers—

(a) that it is necessary to amend the primary legislation under which the sub-ordinate legislation in question was made, in order to enable the incompatibility to be removed, and

(b) that there are compelling reasons for proceeding under this section, he may by order make such amendments to the primary legislation as he considers necessary.

(4) This section also applies where the provision in question is in subordinate legislation and has been quashed, or declared invalid, by reason of incompatibility with a Convention right and the Minister proposes to proceed under paragraph 2(b) of Schedule 2.

(5) If the legislation is an Order in Council, the power conferred by subsection (2) or (3) is exercisable by Her Majesty in Council.

(6) In this section 'legislation' does not include a Measure of the Church Assembly or of the General Synod of the Church of England.

(7) Schedule 2 makes further provision about remedial orders.

Other rights and proceedings

11. Safeguard for existing human rights
A person's reliance on a Convention right does not restrict—
(a) any other right or freedom conferred on him by or under any law having effect in any part of the United Kingdom; or
(b) his right to make any claim or bring any proceedings which he could make or bring apart from sections 7 to 9.

12. Freedom of expression
(1) This section applies if a court is considering whether to grant any relief which, if granted, might affect the exercise of the Convention right to freedom of expression.

(2) If the person against whom the application for relief is made ('the respondent') is neither present nor represented, no such relief is to be granted unless the court is satisfied—
(a) that the applicant has taken all practicable steps to notify the respondent; or
(b) that there are compelling reasons why the respondent should not be notified.

(3) No such relief is to be granted so as to restrain publication before trial unless the court is satisfied that the applicant is likely to establish that publication should not be allowed.

(4) The court must have particular regard to the importance of the Convention right to freedom of expression and, where the proceedings relate to material which the respondent claims, or which appears to the court, to be journalistic, literary or artistic material (or to conduct connected with such material), to—
(a) the extent to which—
(i) the material has, or is about to, become available to the public; or

(ii) it is, or would be, in the public interest for the material to be published;

(b) any relevant privacy code.

(5) In this section—

'court' includes a tribunal; and

'relief' includes any remedy or order (other than in criminal proceedings).

13. Freedom of thought, conscience and religion

(1) If a court's determination of any question arising under this Act might affect the exercise by a religious organization (itself or its members collectively) of the Convention right to freedom of thought, conscience and religion, it must have particular regard to the importance of that right.

(2) In this section 'court' includes a tribunal.

Derogations and reservations

14. Derogations

(1) In this Act 'designated derogation' means—

(a) the United Kingdom's derogation from Article 5(3) of the Convention; and

(b) any derogation by the United Kingdom from an Article of the Convention, or of any protocol to the Convention, which is designated for the purposes of this Act in an order made by the Secretary of State.

(2) The derogation referred to in subsection (1)(a) is set out in Part I of Schedule 3. [*Not reproduced*]

(3) If a designated derogation is amended or replaced it ceases to be a designated derogation.

(4) But subsection (3) does not prevent the Secretary of State from exercising his power under subsection (1)(b) to make a fresh designation order in respect of the Article concerned.

(5) The Secretary of State must by order make such amendments to Schedule 3 as he considers appropriate to reflect—

(a) any designation order; or

(b) the effect of subsection (3).

(6) A designation order may be made in anticipation of the making by the United Kingdom of a proposed derogation.

15. Reservations

(1) In this Act 'designated reservation' means—

(a) the United Kingdom's reservation to Article 2 of the First Protocol to the Convention; and

(b) any other reservation by the United Kingdom to an Article of the Convention, or of any protocol to the Convention, which is designated for the purposes of this Act in an order made by the Secretary of State.

(2) The text of the reservation referred to in subsection (1)(a) is set out in Part II of Schedule 3. [*Not reproduced*]

(3) If a designated reservation is withdrawn wholly or in part it ceases to be a designated reservation.

(4) But subsection (3) does not prevent the Secretary of State from exercising his power under subsection (1)(b) to make a fresh designation order in respect of the Article concerned.

(5) The Secretary of State must by order make such amendments to this Act as he considers appropriate to reflect—

   (a) any designation order; or
   (b) the effect of subsection (3).

16. Period for which designated derogations have effect

(1) If it has not already been withdrawn by the United Kingdom, a designated derogation ceases to have effect for the purposes of this Act—

   (a) in the case of the derogation referred to in section 14(1)(a), at the end of the period of five years beginning with the date on which section 1(2) came into force;
   (b) in the case of any other derogation, at the end of the period of five years beginning with the date on which the order designating it was made.

(2) At any time before the period—

   (a) fixed by subsection (1)(a) or (b), or
   (b) extended by an order under this subsection,

comes to an end, the Secretary of State may by order extend it by a further period of five years.

(3) An order under section 14(1)(b) ceases to have effect at the end of the period for consideration, unless a resolution has been passed by each House approving the order.

(4) Subsection (3) does not affect—

   (a) anything done in reliance on the order; or
   (b) the power to make a fresh order under section 14(1)(b).

(5) In subsection (3) 'period for consideration' means the period of forty days beginning with the day on which the order was made.

(6) In calculating the period for consideration, no account is to be taken of any time during which—

   (a) Parliament is dissolved or prorogued; or
   (b) both Houses are adjourned for more than four days.

(7) If a designated derogation is withdrawn by the United Kingdom, the Secretary of State must by order make such amendments to this Act as he considers are required to reflect that withdrawal.

17. Periodic review of designated reservations

(1) The appropriate Minister must review the designated reservation referred to in section 15(1)(a)—

    (a) before the end of the period of five years beginning with the date on which section 1(2) came into force; and

    (b) if that designation is still in force, before the end of the period of five years beginning with the date on which the last report relating to it was laid under subsection (3).

(2) The appropriate Minister must review each of the other designated reservations (if any)—

    (a) before the end of the period of five years beginning with the date on which the order designating the reservation first came into force; and

    (b) if the designation is still in force, before the end of the period of five years beginning with the date on which the last report relating to it was laid under subsection (3).

(3) The Minister conducting a review under this section must prepare a report on the result of the review and lay a copy of it before each House of Parliament.

Judges of the European Court of Human Rights

18. Appointment to European Court of Human Rights

(1) In this section 'judicial office' means the office of—

    (a) Lord Justice of Appeal, Justice of the High Court or Circuit judge, in England and Wales;

    (b) judge of the Court of Session or sheriff, in Scotland;

    (c) Lord Justice of Appeal, judge of the High Court or county court judge, in Northern Ireland.

(2) The holder of a judicial office may become a judge of the European Court of Human Rights ('the Court') without being required to relinquish his office.

(3) But he is not required to perform the duties of his judicial office while he is a judge of the Court.

[Subsections (4)–(7) not reproduced]
Parliamentary procedure

19. Statements of compatibility

(1) A Minister of the Crown in charge of a Bill in either House of Parliament must, before Second Reading of the Bill—

    (a) make a statement to the effect that in his view the provisions of the Bill are compatible with the Convention rights ('a statement of compatibility'); or

    (b) make a statement to the effect that although he is unable to make a statement of compatibility the government nevertheless wishes the House to proceed with the Bill.

(2) The statement must be in writing and be published in such manner as the Minister making it considers appropriate.

Supplemental

20. Orders etc. under this Act

(1) Any power of a Minister of the Crown to make an order under this Act is exercisable by statutory instrument.

(2) The power of the Lord Chancellor or the Secretary of State to make rules (other than rules of court) under section 2(3) or 7(9) is exercisable by statutory instrument.

(3) Any statutory instrument made under section 14, 15 or 16(7) must be laid before Parliament.

(4) No order may be made by the Lord Chancellor or the Secretary of State under section 1(4), 7(11) or 16(2) unless a draft of the order has been laid before, and approved by, each House of Parliament.

(5) Any statutory instrument made under section 18(7) or Schedule 4, or to which subsection (2) applies, shall be subject to annulment in pursuance of a resolution of either House of Parliament.

(6) The power of a Northern Ireland department to make—

(a) rules under section 2(3)(c) or 7(9)(c), or

(b) an order under section 7(11),

is exercisable by statutory rule for the purposes of the Statutory Rules (Northern Ireland) Order 1979.

(7) Any rules made under section 2(3)(c) or 7(9)(c) shall be subject to negative resolution; and section 41(6) of the Interpretation Act (Northern Ireland) 1954 (meaning of 'subject to negative resolution') shall apply as if the power to make the rules were conferred by an Act of the Northern Ireland Assembly.

(8) No order may be made by a Northern Ireland department under section 7(11) unless a draft of the order has been laid before, and approved by, the Northern Ireland Assembly.

21. Interpretation etc.

(1) In this Act—

'amend' includes repeal and apply (with or without modifications);

'the appropriate Minister' means the Minister of the Crown having charge of the appropriate authorized government department (within the meaning of the Crown Proceedings Act 1947);

'the Commission' means the European Commission of Human Rights;

'the Convention' means the Convention for the Protection of Human Rights and Fundamental Freedoms, agreed by the Council of Europe at Rome on 4th November 1950 as it has effect for the time being in relation to the United Kingdom;

'declaration of incompatibility' means a declaration under section 4;

'Minister of the Crown' has the same meaning as in the Ministers of the Crown Act 1975;

'Northern Ireland Minister' includes the First Minister and the deputy First Minister in Northern Ireland;

'primary legislation' means any—

(a) public general Act;

(b) local and personal Act;

(c) private Act;

(d) Measure of the Church Assembly;

(e) Measure of the General Synod of the Church of England;

(f) Order in Council—

    (i) made in exercise of Her Majesty's Royal Prerogative;

    (ii) made under section 38(1)(a) of the Northern Ireland Constitution Act 1973 or the corresponding provision of the Northern Ireland Act 1998; or

    (iii) amending an Act of a kind mentioned in paragraph (a), (b) or (c);

and includes an order or other instrument made under primary legislation (otherwise than by the National Assembly for Wales, a member of the Scottish Executive, a Northern Ireland Minister or a Northern Ireland department) to the extent to which it operates to bring one or more provisions of that legislation into force or amends any primary legislation;

'the First Protocol' means the protocol to the Convention agreed at Paris on 20th March 1952;

'the Sixth Protocol' means the protocol to the Convention agreed at Strasbourg on 28th April 1983;

'the Eleventh Protocol' means the protocol to the Convention (restructuring the control machinery established by the Convention) agreed at Strasbourg on 11th May 1994;

'remedial order' means an order under section 10;

'subordinate legislation' means any—

(a) Order in Council other than one—

    (i) made in exercise of Her Majesty's Royal Prerogative;

    (ii) made under section 38(1)(a) of the Northern Ireland Constitution Act 1973 or the corresponding provision of the Northern Ireland Act 1998; or

    (iii) amending an Act of a kind mentioned in the definition of primary legislation;

(b) Act of the Scottish Parliament;

(c) Act of the Parliament of Northern Ireland;

(d) Measure of the Assembly established under section 1 of the Northern Ireland Assembly Act 1973;

(e) Act of the Northern Ireland Assembly;

(f) order, rules, regulations, scheme, warrant, byelaw or other instrument made under primary legislation (except to the extent to which it operates to bring one or more provisions of that legislation into force or amends any primary legislation);

(g) order, rules, regulations, scheme, warrant, byelaw or other instrument made under legislation mentioned in paragraph (b), (c), (d) or (e) or made under an Order in Council applying only to Northern Ireland;

(h) order, rules, regulations, scheme, warrant, byelaw or other instrument made by a member of the Scottish Executive, a Northern Ireland Minister or a Northern Ireland department in exercise of prerogative or other executive functions of Her Majesty which are exercisable by such a person on behalf of Her Majesty;

'transferred matters' has the same meaning as in the Northern Ireland Act 1998; and

'tribunal' means any tribunal in which legal proceedings may be brought.

(2) The references in paragraphs (b) and (c) of section 2(1) to Articles are to Articles of the Convention as they had effect immediately before the coming into force of the Eleventh Protocol.

(3) The reference in paragraph (d) of section 2(1) to Article 46 includes a reference to Articles 32 and 54 of the Convention as they had effect immediately before the coming into force of the Eleventh Protocol.

(4) The references in section 2(1) to a report or decision of the Commission or a decision of the Committee of Ministers include references to a report or decision made as provided by paragraphs 3, 4 and 6 of Article 5 of the Eleventh Protocol (transitional provisions).

(5) Any liability under the Army Act 1955, the Air Force Act 1955 or the Naval Discipline Act 1957 to suffer death for an offence is replaced by a liability to imprisonment for life or any less punishment authorised by those Acts; and those Acts shall accordingly have effect with the necessary modifications.

22. Short title, commencement, application and extent

(1) This Act may be cited as the Human Rights Act 1998.

(2) Sections 18, 20 and 21(5) and this section come into force on the passing of this Act.

(3) The other provisions of this Act come into force on such day as the Secretary of State may by order appoint; and different days may be appointed for different purposes.

(4) Paragraph (b) of subsection (1) of section 7 applies to proceedings brought by or at the instigation of a public authority whenever the act in question took place; but otherwise that subsection does not apply to an act taking place before the coming into force of that section.

(5) This Act binds the Crown.

(6) This Act extends to Northern Ireland.

(7) Section 21(5), so far as it relates to any provision contained in the Army Act

1955, the Air Force Act 1955 or the Naval Discipline Act 1957, extends to any place to which that provision extends.

[SCHEDULE 1 NOT REPRODUCED]

Schedule 2

REMEDIAL ORDERS

Orders

1.—(1) A remedial order may—
   (a) contain such incidental, supplemental, consequential or transitional provision as the person making it considers appropriate;
   (b) be made so as to have effect from a date earlier than that on which it is made;
   (c) make provision for the delegation of specific functions;
   (d) make different provision for different cases.

(2) The power conferred by sub-paragraph (1)(a) includes—
   (a) power to amend primary legislation (including primary legislation other than that which contains the incompatible provision); and
   (b) power to amend or revoke subordinate legislation (including subordinate legislation other than that which contains the incompatible provision).

(3) A remedial order may be made so as to have the same extent as the legislation which it affects.

(4) No person is to be guilty of an offence solely as a result of the retrospective effect of a remedial order.

Procedure

2. No remedial order may be made unless—
   (a) a draft of the order has been approved by a resolution of each House of Parliament made after the end of the period of 60 days beginning with the day on which the draft was laid; or
   (b) it is declared in the order that it appears to the person making it that, because of the urgency of the matter, it is necessary to make the order without a draft being so approved.

Orders laid in draft

3.—(1) No draft may be laid under paragraph 2(a) unless—
   (a) the person proposing to make the order has laid before Parliament a document which contains a draft of the proposed order and the required information; and

(b) the period of 60 days, beginning with the day on which the document required by this sub-paragraph was laid, has ended.

(2) If representations have been made during that period, the draft laid under paragraph 2(a) must be accompanied by a statement containing—
    (a) a summary of the representations; and
    (b) if, as a result of the representations, the proposed order has been changed, details of the changes.

Urgent cases

4.—(1) If a remedial order ('the original order') is made without being approved in draft, the person making it must lay it before Parliament, accompanied by the required information, after it is made.

(2) If representations have been made during the period of 60 days beginning with the day on which the original order was made, the person making it must (after the end of that period) lay before Parliament a statement containing—
    (a) a summary of the representations; and
    (b) if, as a result of the representations, he considers it appropriate to make changes to the original order, details of the changes.

(3) If sub-paragraph (2)(b) applies, the person making the statement must—
    (a) make a further remedial order replacing the original order; and
    (b) lay the replacement order before Parliament.

(4) If, at the end of the period of 120 days beginning with the day on which the original order was made, a resolution has not been passed by each House approving the original or replacement order, the order ceases to have effect (but without that affecting anything previously done under either order or the power to make a fresh remedial order).

Definitions

5. In this Schedule—
'representations' means representations about a remedial order (or proposed remedial order) made to the person making (or proposing to make) it and includes any relevant Parliamentary report or resolution; and
'required information' means—
    (a) an explanation of the incompatibility which the order (or proposed order) seeks to remove, including particulars of the relevant declaration, finding or order; and
    (b) a statement of the reasons for proceeding under section 10 and for making an order in those terms.

Calculating periods

6. In calculating any period for the purposes of this Schedule, no account is to be taken of any time during which—

(a) Parliament is dissolved or prorogued; or
(b) both Houses are adjourned for more than four days.

[SCHEDULE 3 (DEROGATION AND RESERVATION) AND
SCHEDULE 4 (JUDICAL PENSIONS) NOT REPRODUCED]

INDEX